WEATHER

BASICS

by

Joseph J. Balsama

and

Peter R. Chaston

To: Father Carmichael
with best wishes!
Joe Balsama

Chaston Scientific, Inc.
P.O. Box 758
Kearney, MO 64060
phone: 816-628-4770
fax: 816-628-9975

Second Printing: 2001

COPYRIGHT © 1997 by CHASTON SCIENTIFIC, INC.

Library of Congress Catalog Card Number: 97-94460

ISBN 0-9645172-5-6

cover photo: Lightning over the harbor at Swampscott, Massachusetts; photo courtesy of Mark Garfinkel.

Dedications

Joseph J. (JOE) Balsama:

I dedicate this book to my wife, Barbara, who has been a source of inspiration and encouragement; to my grandmother, Maria Bucci, who first introduced me to weather; to Oscar Tenenbaum, former Meteorologist-in-Charge of the National Weather Service Forecast Office at Boston's Logan Airport and my teacher at Boston University; to Robert E. Lautzenheiser, retired Massachusetts State Climatologist, with whom I have enjoyed many years of friendship; and to all my former students.

Peter R. (PETE) Chaston:

I dedicate this book to my wife, Mary, and to my daughter, Valerie, who are the joys of my life, and to my second joy: the love of weather. Therefore, I also dedicate this book to everyone who enjoys and is enthralled by the vagaries of weather.

ACKNOWLEDGEMENTS

NOAA = National Oceanic and Atmospheric Administration

NWS = National Weather Service

NOS = National Ocean Survey

FAA = Federal Aviation Administration

DOC = Department of Commerce

DOA = Department of Agriculture

DOD = Department of Defense

DOE = Department of Energy

DOT = Department of Transportation

USAF = United States Air Force

USN = United States Navy

NHC = National Hurricane Center

The authors also wish to thank and acknowledge the following:
United States Library of Congress
Forest Service of the U.S. Department of Agriculture
Environment Canada
World Meteorological Organization
Missouri Department of Conservation
Massachusetts Emergency Management Agency
Virginia Department of Highways
Hans Neuberger & George Nicholas
Robert E. White Instruments, Inc. of Boston, Massachusetts
Christopher Ratley
Meredith Porro
Vincent Schaefer
Robert E. Lautzenheiser
Mark Garfinkel
Lawrence O. Power
Productive Alternatives, Inc.

WEATHER BASICS

TABLE OF CONTENTS

(continued)

(continued)

(continued)

INTRODUCTION

Consider the following weather facts:

- When you are walking in a fog, you are walking through a cloud.
- It is probable that in a major snowstorm, no two snowflakes would look exactly alike under the microscope.
- The highest winds ever reported in a hurricane or typhoon were 230 miles per hour, and the highest ever on the surface of the earth was at Mt. Washington, New Hampshire where the winds howled at 231 mph! Such a wind would pick up and carry a typical adult through the air.
- A rare type of lightning called "ball lightning", which is about the size of a basketball and looks like a ball of sparks, falls out of a thunderstorm and is attracted to any animate object. Thus, ball lightning will chase a person or an animal, even squeezing itself into a house, then resuming its ball shape and chasing a person around the room!
- In the incredible Buffalo, New York blizzard of January 1977, snow was blown by the winds to cover entire two-story homes, and some residents had to dig tunnels through the snow from their front doors to the streets which were later plowed, just to get out of their houses.
- Tornadoes that have passed over swampy areas have scooped up small animals such as frogs, carried them into the clouds, and after the tornado ended, the clouds then dropped the frogs on the next town, causing it to rain frogs.
- In 1995, hailstones as big as basketballs pounded a province in China, killing people and animals.
- In 1815, an East Indies volcano known as Tambora exploded, ejecting an enormous volume of volcanic ash into the stratosphere. The ash soon encircled the globe, effectively blocking out some of the sun's radiation. This resulted in the following year, 1816, being "The Year Without a Summer". In parts of the northern United States, it snowed every month of the year, with ice forming on lakes in Upstate New York in June, July and August.
- Yet, even with extremes of weather and with violent storms, the human race could not exist on Earth without our basically-agreeable climate.

Thus, we are all fascinated by the weather, and sometimes are left awestruck at its immense beauty and also at its horrifying fury.

The purpose of this book is to make weather information available to you in a concise understandable manner. Each chapter deals with one popular weather topic and most are written so that you will get all the necessary information on that topic without having to read the previous chapters for background information. This book can used as a textbook for basic courses in weather and climate, and also as a reference for units of weather and climate that are included in earth and environmental science courses. Some students may want to use it as a supplement to their class notes. The book has also been written for the weather enthusiast, since observing, studying and forecasting the weather is one of life's most enjoyable avocations!

However you use this book, we hope that you find it informative, easy-to-understand and fun to read.

As a side-note, you can truly enjoy following the weather and even make your own weather forecasts if you have a computer and subscibe to a computer on-line service. Weather maps, weather radar images and weather satellite pictures are available for free via the internet! For help in learning how to read and use all the main weather maps, we suggest you get a copy of the book, "WEATHER MAPS - How to Read and Interpret all the Basic Weather Charts". The book costs $29 and is available from Chaston Scientific, Inc.; P.O. Box 758; Kearney, MO 64060. Having weather for a hobby or avocation is one of life's most enjoyable activities, and now that the weather data is available for free via the internet, we can all participate and enjoy the science!

---Joe Balsama & Pete Chaston   PAGE 9

ABOUT THE AUTHORS

JOSEPH J. ("Joe") BALSAMA and PETER R. ("Pete") CHASTON are an ideal pair for writing this book. Joe is a science educator and Pete is a meteorologist.

JOSEPH J. ("Joe") BALSAMA was born in Belmont, Massachusetts. His grandmother, Maria Bucci, sparked his interest in weather when he was about six years old. Whenever there was a thunderstorm, he would leave his home and walk to his grandmother's house to observe the storm from her upstairs porch, which ran the length of the house.

After graduating from Belmont High School, Joe earned his Bachelor of Arts degree in biology from Boston University, and then his Masters degree in Science Education. He retired in June 1995 as head of the Science Department at Swampscott High School where he taught the following subjects over a 36-year period: climatology, marine science, biology, chemistry, physics, physical science and earth science. Joe worked for the National Weather Service during the summers of 1961, 1962, 1963 and 1966. He was director of the Swampscott Summer School program during the summers of 1972 through 1985. During the summer of 1980 he served as the Assistant Director of the Marine Science Institute at Salem State College in Salem, Massachusetts. During the summers of 1989 to 1991 he taught weather workshops to middle and elementary school teachers at the University of Missouri at Columbia, Missouri.

Joe served as president of the Greater Boston Chapter of the American Meteorological Society for two terms, as president of the Swampscott Historical Society for two terms, as president of the Massachusetts Association of Science Supervisors for one term, and as president of the Lynn Mineral Club for seven terms. He also was hospitality chairperson during the National Science Teachers Association convention in Boston in 1992.

On May 5, 1993, Joe Balsama was inducted into the Massachusetts Hall of Fame for Science Educators, and in March 1992 he was presented the Massachusetts Association of Science Supervisors' Outstanding Science Educators Award. He was nominated Teacher of the Year in 1971, 1974 and 1987 by the Swampscott School System. In 1982, Joe was named Outstanding Teacher of Essex County by the Massachusetts Association of Science Teachers. In March 1984, he received an award from the Massachusetts Marine Educators for dedicated service and outstanding contributions to the field of marine education. The same organization also presented Joe the Massachusetts Marine Educators Service Award in 1995 for many years of outstanding assistance and contributions to teachers, students and colleagues in marine science.

Joe lives with his wife, Barbara Cammarano, in Swampscott, Massachusetts. He remains very active in the community, serving as a Town Meeting member, a member of the Swampscott Conservation Commission, and as chairperson of the Swampscott War Memorial Scholarship Fund. At St. John the Evangelist Church in Swampscott, Joe is a member of the Parish Council, sings in the adult choir and serves as a Eucharistic Minister. He is a cooperative weather observer and local TV weatherperson for WCTV in Lynn. He also writes a monthly weather feature for the newspaper, the Swampscott Reporter.

PETER R. ("Pete") CHASTON's biography is on the next page.

PETER R. ("Pete") CHASTON became fascinated with weather as a young boy. His personal affinity for the science of meteorology began when he experienced a few hurricanes while growing up along the East Coast. He was fascinated by having the eye of a tropical storm named Brenda go right over his home weather station, followed some two months later by Hurricane Donna's 100 + mph winds and driving sheets of horizontal rain. Winter snowstorms and blizzards also thrilled him, and weather grew to be Pete Chaston's main interest.

Having weather as an intense hobby eventually led to a career in meteorology. Pete started reading college texts and everything else he could find on weather through secondary school, and then served as a weather observer in the Air Force for four years, saving money for college.

Pete Chaston received his Bachelor of Science degree in Meteorology and Oceanography from New York University, and later, while a National Weather Service (weather bureau) forecaster, was selected for the weather service Fellowship to graduate school, underwhich he earned his Master of Science degree in Meteorology from the University of Wisconsin. It was at Wisconsin where he met Mary Gabrielski and they married almost two years later.

Pete Chaston served as a National Weather Service meteorologist from 1971 through 1995, afterwhich he took advantage of an early retirement option to found Chaston Scientific, Inc., under whose auspices this book is written.

In the weather service, Pete served at Binghamton, New York and at Hartford, Connecticut before transferring to the forecast office at Pittsburgh, Pennsylvania. He then was the Meteorologist-in-Charge of the National Weather Service Office at Rochester, New York and later became Technical Project Leader for the National Weather Service Training Center in Kansas City, Missouri.

Pete has written several books on meteorology, had a weekly newspaper column on weather, did television and radio weather and numerous talk shows, and is a regular lecturer and speechgiver. He played the role of a meteorologist in the movie, "Water", filmed for the PBS TV network and...for something different... even appeared in a Stephen King movie, "Sometimes They Come Back", and has a popular Kansas City radio program called "The Pete Chaston Doowop Show". He has taught at the State University of New York, the University of Missouri at Kansas City, the University of Kansas at Lawrence, Kansas and lectured at other colleges. Pete Chaston has also worked with several grants involving training the nation's earth science teachers in meteorology, and has presented seminars to the National Science Teachers Association and various Academies of Science. He also gives training seminars on weather.

Pete was President of the Kansas City Chapter of the American Meteorological Society for two terms.

Pete Chaston has published scientific research articles in magazines and journals, including the National Weather Digest and Weatherwise. He developed a technique for forecasting heavy snow amounts that is widely used by forecasters nationwide. The technique is called "The Magic Chart" because it is straightforward and easy to use. He also pioneered new operational forecasting procedures now commonplace in contemporary meteorology. Some of the books Pete has writtten include "WEATHER MAPS - How to Read and Interpret all the Basic Weather Charts", "TERROR FROM THE SKIES!", "HURRICANES!" and "THUNDERSTORMS, TORNADOES AND HAIL!". With fellow meteorologist Dr. James Moore he co-authored a humorous book entitled, "JOKES AND PUNS FOR GROAN-UPS". Thus, Pete Chaston has varied interests and derives great fun and enjoyment from all of them.

Chapter 1. THE HISTORY OF METEOROLOGY

Figure 1-1. The best weather forecasts first require the best weather observations. The sketch above shows an avid weather enthusiast going to the instrument shelter to read weather instruments, and, with a measuring stick in hand, to determine the snow depth.

Early writings and art works demonstrate that our earliest ancestors were fascinated by the weather. They had to cope with its extremes, and marvelled at its varieties, and so do we. As the human race became wiser, we started to measure and then tried to predict the weather elements.

There are evidences of rain gauges in ancient Greece and ancient China. The earliest Native American Indians, from the Arctic to South America, followed and tried to understand the vagaries of weather; indeed, their lives and food supplies depended upon it.

The English word "weather" comes from the Indo-European words "we" for wind and "vydra" for storm. These words are from the Sanskrit language, which our linguistic scientists believe was first codified about the year 3000 B.C. Later, in the Anglo-Saxon and Middle-English language development, the word became "weder" and later evolved into "weather".

The first documented routine weather observations were done in ancient Greece around 500 B.C. The Greeks were recording rainfall with rain gauge networks, and were keeping records of the wind direction after they invented the wind vane. These observations were written down and displayed publicly in the cities and for farmers. Then, about 350 B.C., genuine research of weather was underway in Greece.

Around 450 B.C., the Greek philosopher Socrates promoted education about everything, including Nature. One of his pupils, Plato, founded a school called The Academy in the year 386 B.C. He lectured and wrote, continuing the legacy of Socrates. One of Plato's pupils, Aristotle, who became the personal tutor of Alexander the Great, authored books and treatises in areas such as ethics and morals, politics, the scientific research method, and the natural sciences. Around 350 B.C., Aristotle wrote a book which he entitled, **"METEOROLOGICA"**, from the Greek word, "meteoron", and its plural, "meteora", meaning "things in the air". The word meteor (and meteorite when it hits a planet's or moon's surface), comes from this root. Also, the word METEOROLOGY comes from the same root. Aristotle's book was the first major treatise about weather.

Through the next 19 to 20 centuries, people followed the weather, recorded the precipitation and wind direction, and learned to tell from the clouds in the sky what was likely to follow. Agricultural interests became adept at watching the signs in the sky and the wind, for their survival depended upon the weather.

Eventually, a series of weather instruments was invented to focus better on the observing and predicting of the weather.

In 1593, Galileo Galilei of Italy invented the thermometer. Then in 1643, a pupil of Galileo's, Evangelista Torricelli, invented the mercury barometer to measure air pressure, which is the weight of a column of air from the top of the atmosphere to the surface where the pressure is being measured. Thus, the air pressure is simply the weight of the air column per unit area.

In 1714, Gabriel Daniel Fahrenheit of Germany created his Fahrenheit temperature scale, setting 32 degrees for the freezing of water, and 100 degrees for near the average human body temperature, and 212 degrees for the boiling point of water. Then in 1742, Anders Celsius of Sweden created his Centigrade, now called Celsius, temperature scale, in which he set 0 degrees for water's freezing point and 100 degrees for its boiling (originally he set 0 for boiling and 100 for freezing, but later reversed his designation). In 1848, Lord Kelvin invented his "Absolute temperature scale", which we now refer to as the Kelvin temperature scale, which uses Celsius intervals but sets zero degrees at the point of no molecular or atomic motion (the coldest it can be), which makes approximately 273 degrees the freezing point of water and approximately 373 degrees its boiling point.

At least three of the Founding Fathers of the United States were avid weather fans. George Washington, Thomas Jefferson and Benjamin Franklin kept meticulous weather records and diaries. Benjamin Franklin became so enmeshed with weather that he had friends and acquaintances up and down the East Coast record simultaneous weather observations to support his hypothesis that sometimes storms will move up the East Coast, dumping heavy rain and snow. From his set of weather observations, Benjamin Franklin concluded in 1743 that there exist organized weather systems and that these systems form, mature and die, and that these systems move. He did not realize it at the time, but Franklin was documenting the development and movement of a type of low pressure system now known as the Nor'easter. (High and low pressure systems were not "discovered" until the 1800's.) Franklin is also famous for discovering that lightning is electricity. He flew a kite into a thunderstorm and attached a key to the end of the wire where he held it. When lightning struck the kite, Franklin was jolted by the electric charge he received by touching the key.

Figure 1-2. Benjamin Franklin,
the first American Meteorologist.
This sketch illustrates Franklin sending
a kite into a thunderstorm to determine
if lightning is electricity. Franklin's kite
was likely more box-like.

Thomas Jefferson tried to determine
the nation's climate. He collected
weather records from as far west as the
Mississippi River. Jefferson purchased a
thermometer while writing the Declaration
of Independence, and then bought his first
barometer a few days after the Declaration
was signed. Thomas Jefferson recorded
routine weather observations at his home
in Monticello, Virginia from 1772 through
1778. For much of 1776 through 1778,
Jefferson and the President of William and
Mary College in Williamsburg, VA recorded
the first known simultaneous weather observations in America.

In 1803, Luke Howard of England named the clouds, using Latin names. Also in the early 1800s,
Emperor Napoleon Bonaparte of France issued a decree mandating that the Centigrade (now known
as Celsius) temperature scale would replace the Fahrenheit scale throughout the empire. The
Celsius scale still remains the standard in most of the world.

Then came the development of weather maps, drawn from simultaneously-taken weather
observations. In the United States, during the War of 1812, the U.S. Army hospital surgeons
started taking and recording weather observations. The first weather maps, however, were drawn
by H. W. Brandes at the University of Breslau in Europe. Observations taken at the same time
across much of Europe were mailed to Brandes, who then plotted the data and located areas of
high and low pressure and areas of warm and cold air.

However, the big break-through in using simultaneously-taken weather observations to analyze and
forecast the weather occurred after Samuel Finley Breese Morse invented the telegraph in 1837.
Now these weather observations could be transmitted anywhere that telegraph lines connected
various locations. In 1849, the U.S. Department of War's Army Signal Corps started taking
weather observations and also transmitted them via telegraph. In 1850, the Smithsonian Institution
in Washington, D.C. started using telegraphed weather observations to produce the first DAILY
weather maps.

The next obvious step was to organize weather bureaus or weather services in as many countries
of the world as possible. The first officially sanctioned national weather service was begun by
France in 1855. Back in the United States, a weather scientist had an audience with President
Abraham Lincoln in the early-to-mid 1860s, proposing the establishment of a U.S. national weather
service. So Lincoln challenged the scientist to make a forecast to prove his point. The scientist
predicted fair weather and it rained, so Lincoln refused to see him again. However, Lincoln's
successor, President Ulysses Grant, was convinced that the establishment of a weather bureau
would be good for this country. In 1870, the weather bureau of the United States was created
with 20 original weather offices, in the Army Signal Corps, and in 1890 was transferred as the
United States Weather Bureau to the Department of Agriculture. In 1940, the weather bureau was
then transferred to the Department of Commerce. In 1970, under President Richard Nixon, the
United States Weather Bureau had its name changed to the National Weather Service.   PAGE 14

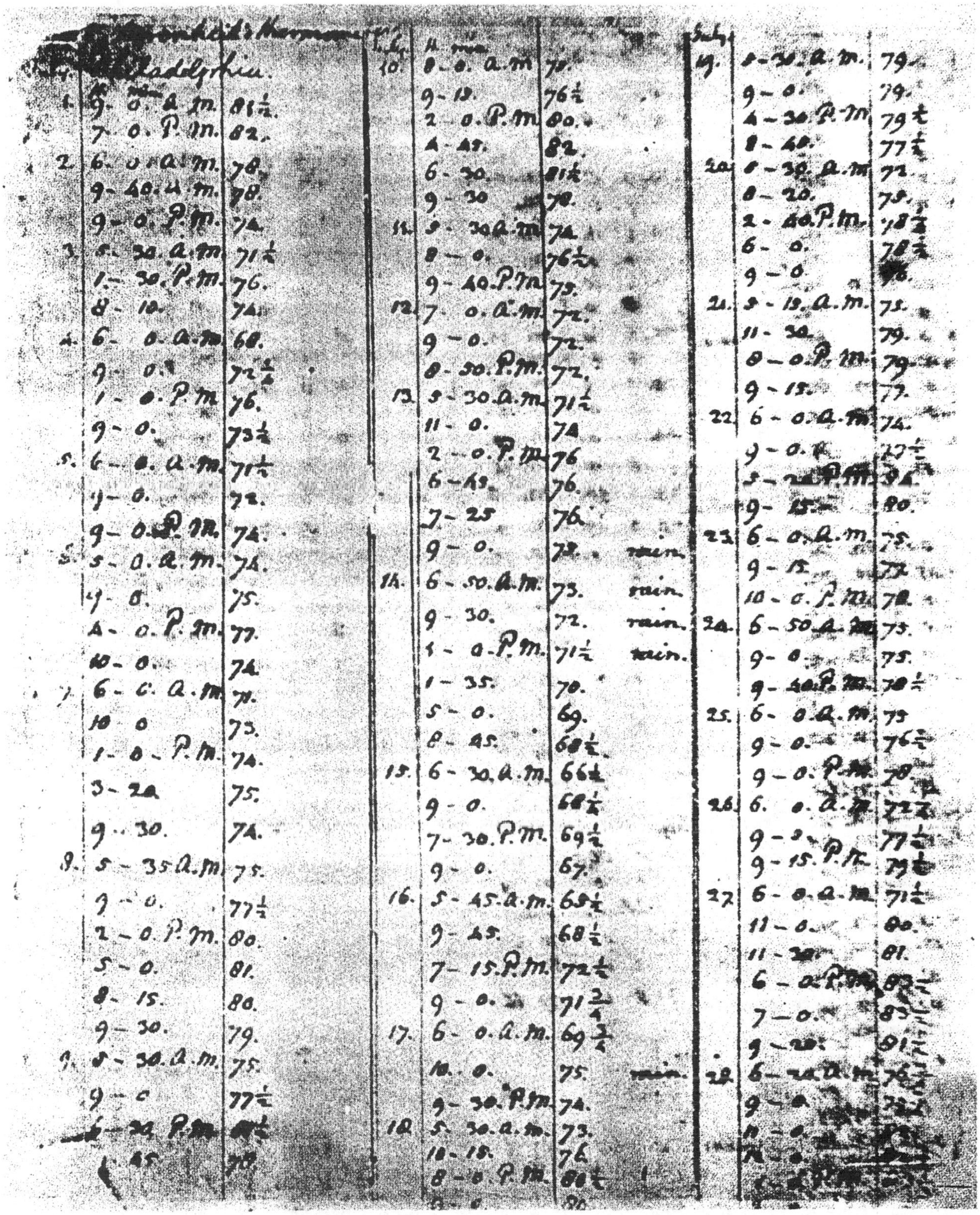

Figure 1-3. An actual page from Thomas Jefferson's weather diary, written in ink. These are Thomas Jefferson's weather observations that he recorded in Philadelphia in July 1776. (source: Library of Congress)

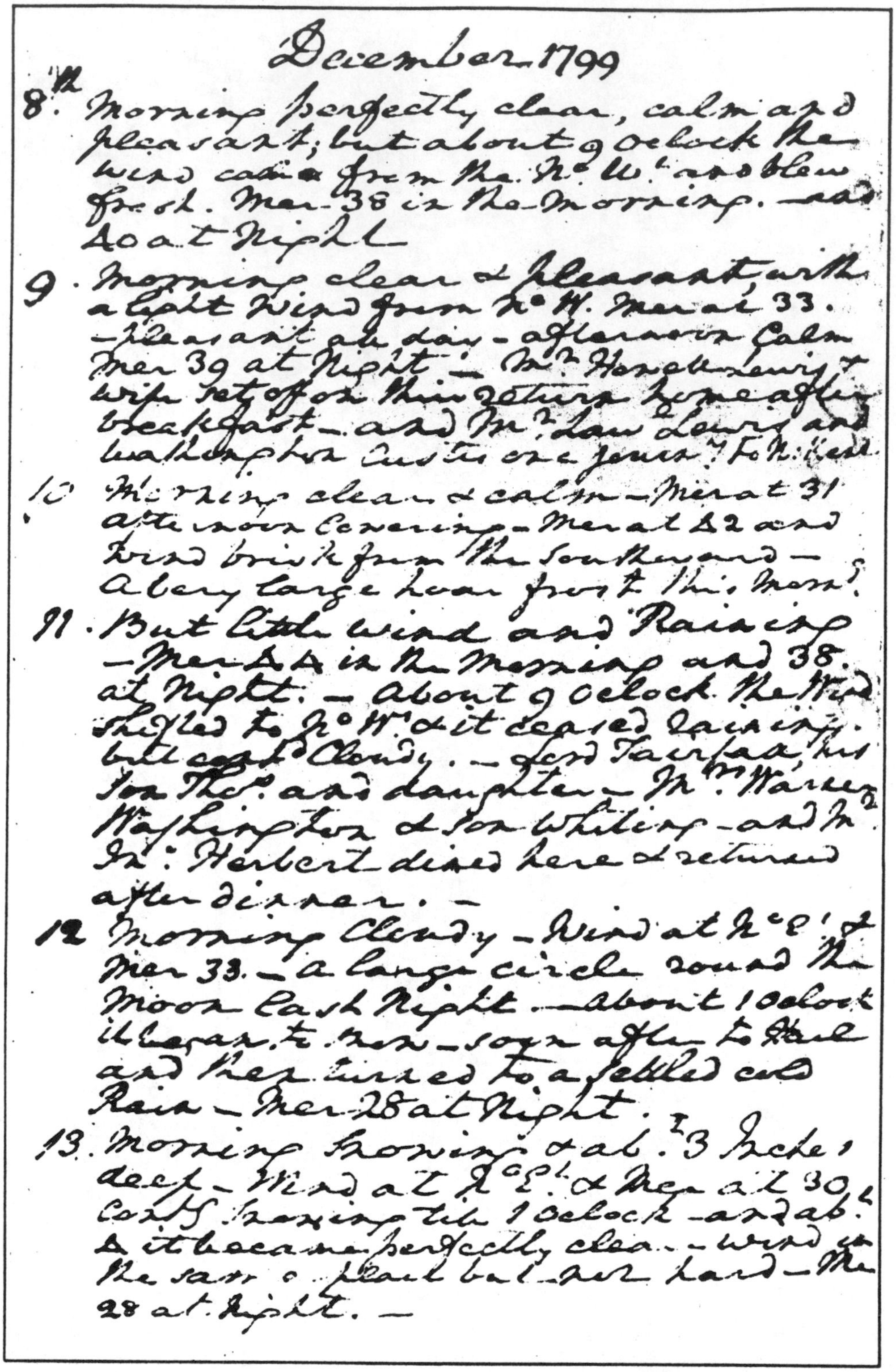
December 1799
8th. Morning perfectly clear, calm and
pleasant; but about 9 oclock the
wind came from the No. Wt. and blew
fresh. Mer. 38 in the Morning — and
40 at Night
9. Morning clear & pleasant with
a light wind from No. W. Mer at 33.
— Pleasant all day — afternoon Calm
Mer 39 at Night — Mr. Howell Lewis &
wife set off on their return home after
breakfast — and Mr. Law Lewis and
Washington Custis on a journey to N. Kent.
10 Morning clear & calm — Mer at 31
afternoon lowering — Mer at 42 and
wind brisk from the Southward —
A very large hoar frost this morng.
11. But little wind and Raining
— Mer 44 in the Morning and 38.
at Night. — About 9 oclock the Wind
shifted to No. Wt. & it ceased raining
but contd. Cloudy. — Lord Fairfax, his
Son Thos. and daughter — Mrs. Warner
Washington & Son Whiting — and Mr.
Jno. Herbert dined here & returned
after dinner. —
12 Morning Cloudy — Wind at No. E. &
Mer 33. — A large circle round the
Moon last Night — About 1 oclock
it began to snow — soon after to Hail
and then turned to a settled cold
Rain — Mer 28 at Night.
13. Morning Snowing & abt. 3 Inches
deep — Wind at No. Et. & Mer at 30
Contg. Snowing till 1 oclock — and abt.
4 it became perfectly clear — Wind in
the same place but not hard — Mer
28 at Night. —

Figure 1-4. Here is a rare historical treasure: a page in George Washington's handwriting, of his weather diary entries for six days in December 1799. His last entry was on December 13th; Washington died the next day. (source: Library of Congress)

In 1876, the word "cyclone" was coined by Henry Piddington of England, meaning "coil of a snake", to be used to describe the air circulation in a storm. Piddington was President of the Marine Courts at Calcutta, India.

From 1899 through 1902, Teisserence deBort sent up kites and balloons with maximum and minimum temperature thermometers attached to profile the temperature changes in the vertical in the lower atmosphere. Based on his findings, he named the first layer "the troposphere", meaning "sphere of mixing", and the next higher layer "the stratosphere", for "sphere of stratification".

By the early 1900s, air masses and areas of high and low pressure were known to exist. Fronts, which separate air masses, were discovered during World War I, 1914-1918, by Norwegian meteorologists. Since the war was raging across Europe, the leading edge of a cold mass of air was called a cold "battlefront" or "front", and the leading edge of advancing warm air on the surface was termed a warm "battlefront" or "front". The terminology, front", stays with us today.

Also during World War I, Lewis F. Richardson of England, while on war duty in France as a medical corpsman, wrote a manuscript describing how data of current weather parameters at the surface and aloft could be used with the equations of motion of the atmosphere to make a forecast "by the numbers". In other words, Richardson showed that we could forecast the state of the atmosphere say 12 to 24 hours later by taking the current conditions of the atmosphere and using them in the governing equations of the atmosphere, solving these equations to predict the state of the atmosphere hours later. This scheme is known as "numerical forecasting" and requires a mathematical "model" of the atmosphere to work with.

Richardson's manuscript was lost in a coal bin but recovered several months later, refined, and published in 1922 as "Weather Prediction by Numerical Process". (Earlier, in 1900, Vilhelm Bjerknes postulated that the state of the atmosphere could be forecasted using numerical computations.) These basic equations defining atmospheric motions and processes became known as the "primitive equations" of the atmosphere.

Richardson determined that by using hand calculators, it would require some 6000 persons, all working simultaneously, to perform the necessary computations to generate a 12- to 24-hour forecast. Computers were not even a viable concept at that time.

Finally, in 1948, John von Neumann, a Hungarian mathematician working at Princeton University in New Jersey, used one of the very first vacuum-tube computers to successfully make a numerical forecast. Today, most of the prognostic (called "prog") charts or forecast weather maps are created by computer models. Many countries run these "numerical forecast models". In the United States, a branch of the National Centers for Environmental Prediction, a part of the National Weather Service, outside Washington, D.C., runs several numerical models to generate forecast weather maps for the surface, for aloft, and for layers of the atmosphere.

Thus, the history of weather or meteorology is still evolving. Studies of weather include the larger scale, called the synoptic scale, such as about high and low pressure systems, the medium scale, called the mesoscale, such as about thunderstorms, tornadoes and lake-effect snowstorms, and the microscale, such as about dew, frost and cloud droplets. Thus, the study, and the history, of weather or meteorology is exciting and is still evolving.

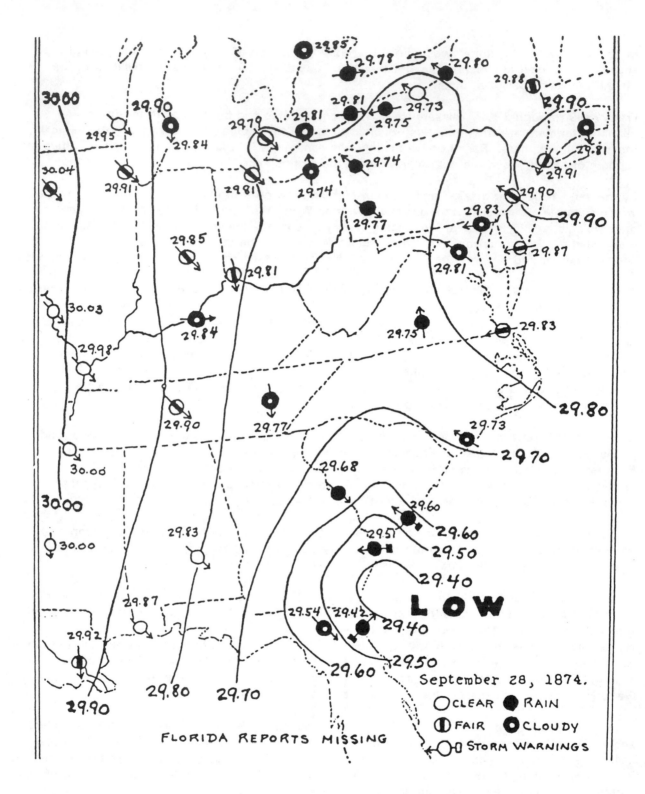

Figure 1-5. One of the first "Daily Weather Maps". This surface weather map was plotted and analyzed by hand from the weather observations sent via telegraph to the United States Weather Bureau. Local weather offices printed forecasts on post cards and then took them to the post office, which was sometimes co-located with the weather bureau office, in the morning for delivery the same day to local subscribers.

Chapter 2. WEATHER AND CLIMATE

WEATHER is the state of atmospheric conditions existing at the present time. These conditions include sky condition, visibility, air temperature and dewpoint (moisture content), precipitation, obscuring phenomena, wind and atmospheric pressure. These are also referred to as weather elements. Meteorology is the study of weather.

As soon as a snapshot of the weather is taken, this snapshot is obsolete at the next moment because the weather is always changing.

The predicted future weather is the weather forecast. A trained scientist in weather who predicts the weather and issues warnings of impending severe and dangerous weather is known as a meteorologist. Although the word "meteorology" has been around since the days of ancient Greece, the term "meteorologist" for a weather scientist was not created until the 20th century. As you shall see in reading this book, the fascinating science of meteorology requires a knowledge of physics, chemistry, mathematics, geology, geography, oceanography, astronomy and hydrology. The science can be quite complex; however, when it is studied through the individual components that comprise meteorology, this science is readily understandable by all of us who are interested in weather.

Figure 2-1. Weather on earth depends on air, heat and water vapor. (source: DOA)

According to our definition, if one of these items is missing, we cannot have any weather. Since the moon has no atmosphere, it has no weather. Because the upper layers of the atmosphere contain very little air, there is no weather occurring there. Most of the volume of the atmosphere is within the first ten miles up form the surface. If the sun were to stop shining, we would receive no heat and therefore after we reached very low temperatures, we would have no weather. If our planet contained no water vapor, we would have no clouds and no precipitation, so we would have no weather. Other planets throughout the universe, such as Venus and Jupiter in our own solar system, may have clouds comprised of gasses other than water vapor; therefore, their weather is bizarre by our standards, with perhaps precipitation of acids. But by our definition on earth, our clouds are based on water vapor being present.

CLIMATE is the average long-term weather, including the range of extremes. Weather observations from across the planet for many decades have been analyzed using statistical techniques to tell us what the average conditions are like for all areas of the world for all months and seasons. The systematic widespread recording of the weather conditions did not begin until the latter half of the 19th century. The study of climate is called <u>climatology</u>. Climatology therefore is the study of past weather.

Each country usually keeps climatological records. For example, in the United States, the climate for the country is determined by records kept at the National Climatic Data Center in Asheville, North Carolina. For example, the daily high and low temperatures and the daily precipitation and other weather elements for the past thirty years can be averaged to yield the recent climate for each major metropolitan area or for any small region in the country. The climatology can be updated every ten or twenty years, using the past 30 years of records, to indicate whether the climate has changed significantly. One who studies climate is a <u>climatologist</u>. A climatologist examines the climatological records to look for possible climatic trends or changes, and tries to determine what internal and external influences may be causing and changing our climate. Internal influences involve anything occurring within the earth-atmosphere system, and external influences involve anything from outside the earth-atmosphere system. Chapter 43 discusses the causes of climatic change. The science of climatology requires a knowledge of geography, biology, mathematics (especially statistics), oceanography, hydrology and geology.

Climatology can tell us for our area such items as the average date of the last frost, the average daily wind speed, the "normal" or average daily high and low temperatures, and many other useful data sets. Thus, climatology is essential for civilization, since we use the information to determine where to live, where and how to grow food, and how to cope with the weather.

SECTION II: SUNSHINE

Chapter 3. DAY AND NIGHT AND THE SEASONS

Day and Night:

Day and night are caused by the earth **rotating** on its **axis**. This axis is an imaginary line beginning at the North Pole, going through the center of the earth, and ending at the South Pole. An easy way to understand this is to pretend that the sun does not move and that the earth spins rapidly. The part of the earth that faces the sun has daylight, and the part that does not has nighttime. The speed of rotation is about 1000 miles per hour at the equator. As we approach the poles, the speed gets less and less. It takes 23 hours 56 minutes 4.09 seconds (nearly 24 hours) for the earth to make one complete turn. Another way of saying this is that the period of rotation of the earth on its axis is about 24 hours.

The Seasons:

There are two reasons why we have seasons. The first is that the earth revolves (moves around) the sun. The second is that the earth's axis is tilted 23½ degrees instead of being vertical.

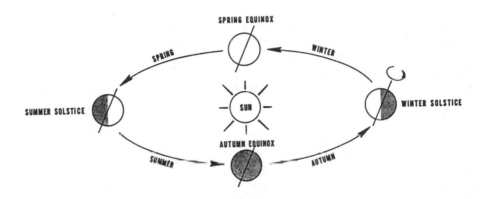

Figure 3-1. The earth revolving around the sun, showing the earth's position in relation to the sun at the beginning of each of the four Northern Hemisphere seasons. In the Southern Hemisphere, the seasons are reversed; that is, when the northern half of the planet has summer, the southern half has winter; when it is spring in the Northern Hemisphere, it is autumn (fall) in the Southern Hemisphere. (source: NOAA)

Note also that in the Northern Hemisphere, far northern locations such as just north of Fairbanks, Alaska, in northern Scandinavia and in far north Russia, there are up to 24 hours of daylight in late spring and early summer. Even as the earth rotates, those regions remain in sunlight. In the far southern parts of the Southern Hemisphere, there are up to 24 hours of darkness at this time. Note also from the figure above that in late fall and early winter, the far northern parts of the Northern Hemisphere have up to 24 hours of darkness. During the transitions during spring and autumn, the amount of daylight changes by up to several minutes each day, with increasingly more daylight as we head towards summer, and decreasingly less daylight as we head towards winter.

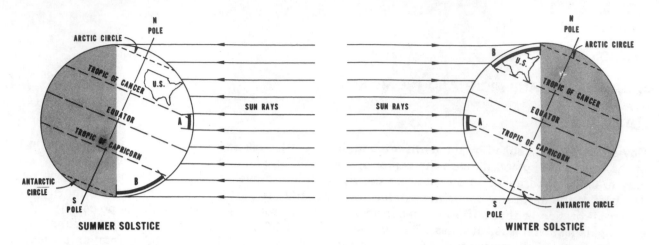

SUMMER SOLSTICE   WINTER SOLSTICE

Figure 3-2. The earth and sunlight impinging on it on the day of the Northern Hemisphere summer solstice (the first day of summer), and on the day of the Northern Hemisphere winter solstice (the first day of winter). The straight line from pole to pole represents the earth's axis, about which our planet rotates. Note how even with a full day's rotation, the far north stays in sunlight for 24 hours in the left figure, and stays in darkness for 24 hours in the right figure. (source: NOAA)

Now let us explore further these two reasons for the seasons: the earth's revolution around the sun, and the earth's axis, about which it rotates, being tilted about 23½ degrees instead of being straight up and down.

● It takes 365 days 5 hours 48 minutes 46 seconds (or about 365¼ days) for the earth to make one complete trip around the sun. Thus, this time, which is called the <u>period of revolution</u> of the earth around the sun, is approximately 365¼ days. To account for the one-quarter day, one day is added to February every four years (e.g, the years 2000 and 2004), and such a year is called a _ <u>leap</u> <u>year</u>. The year's number must be divisible by 4 (no fraction left over) to be a leap year, and if it is a century number, such as the year 2000, it must be divisible by 200.

●Because the earth's axis is tilted about 23½ degrees from the vertical instead of being straight up and down, this causes the Northern and Southern Hemispheres to tilt toward the sun when each has its respective summer, and to tilt away from the sun when it has its respective winter. Thus, the seasons in the Southern Hemisphere are opposite those of the Northern Hemisphere. For examples, when it is spring in the United States, it is autumn in Australia, and when it is winter in South Africa, it is summer in Poland.

Before discussing the seasons further, consider the significant latitude lines, called parallels, in the figure below.

Figure 3-3. The important latitude parallels that essentially divide the earth into its general climatic zones.

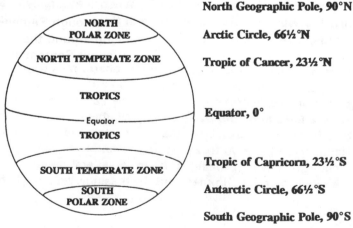

North Geographic Pole, 90°N

Arctic Circle, 66½°N

Tropic of Cancer, 23½°N

Equator, 0°

Tropic of Capricorn, 23½°S

Antarctic Circle, 66½°S

South Geographic Pole, 90°S

PAGE 22

When you look at a globe, you can see that most of the land masses are found north of the equator, that is, in the Northern Hemisphere; there is more ocean in the Southern Hemisphere. In the Northern Hemisphere are all of North America, part of South America, all of Europe, all of Asia and most of Africa; in the Southern Hemisphere are all of Australia, all of Antarctica, part of Africa and most of South America.

Climatologically, the planet can be divided into three general climatic regimes: tropical, temperate and polar. In these zones, the temperature ranges are greatest over large land masses than over oceanic areas, because the land heats up and cools off faster than do the oceans. Water has a high heat capacity compared to land, which means that it takes water longer to warm up than land, but also the water retains its heat longer than does land. Thus, water also cools off more slowly than land.

THE TROPICS:
The tropical zone is located between the latitude parallel known as the Tropic of Cancer, which is 23½ degrees North latitude, and the Tropic of Capricorn, which is 23½ degrees South latitude. In the tropics, summertime weather exists throughout the year, except on high mountains. There is always around 12 hours of daylight and 12 hours of nighttime. (The farther in latitude we travel away from the equator towards the poles, the greater the seasonal variations in amounts of daylight and nighttime.)

THE TEMPERATE ZONES:
Most of the world's population lives in the temperate zones. The North Temperate Zone lies between the Tropic of Cancer (23½°N) and the Arctic Circle (66½°N); the South Temperate Zone lies between the Tropic of Capricorn (23½°S) and the Antarctic Circle (66½°S). The temperate zones have the variety of mid-latitude weather that occurs with the four seasons of spring, summer, autumn and winter. The non-tropical low pressure systems are most frequent and intense in the temperate zones, because these zones are where the clashes occur between warm and cold air masses, some being moist and some being fairly dry. During the spring and summer, there are more than 12 hours of daylight and less than 12 hours of nighttime, and during the autumn and winter there are less than 12 hours of daylight and more than 12 hours of nighttime.

THE POLAR ZONES:
The North Polar Zone is between the Arctic Circle (66½°N) and the geographic North Pole (90°N); the South Polar Zone is between the Antarctic Circle (66½°S) and the geographic South Pole (90°S). The polar zones are characterized by having winter-like conditions virtually all year; for example, it can snow every month of the year. No months are freeze-free.

The closer to the poles we get, the longer is the length of daylight during the summer. Right at the North Pole itself, from about March 21st through September 23rd, the sun stays above the horizon. To the observer, it appears to make a loop around the horizon. At the South Pole, there are at this time 24 hours of darkness. Then from about September 23rd through March 21st, the South Pole is in continuous sunlight with the North Pole is in darkness.

Note: **the astronomical start of a season is about three weeks after the meteorological start of a season.** For record-keeping weather purposes, the spring months are March, April, May, summer is June, July, August, autumn is September, October, November, and winter is December, January, February. This is because the hottest months are typically June, July and August, and the coldest are typically December, January and February.

The table on the next page shows the time from sunrise to sunset at different latitudes on the planet at different times throughout the year.

Figure 3-4. The time from sunrise to sunset at different latitudes at different times of the year. Note how at the equator the length of daylight and nighttime are always 12 hours each, and note when continuous daylight or continuous darkness occurs at the poles.

LATITUDE	MARCH 21st	JUNE 21st	SEPT. 21st	DEC. 21st
0° (equator)	12 hrs	12 hrs	12 hrs	12 hrs
NORTHERN HEMISPHERE:				
30°N	12 hrs	13 hrs 54 mins	12 hrs	10 hrs 06 mins
60°N	12 hrs	18 hrs 24 mins	12 hrs	5 hrs 30 mins
90°N (N. Pole)	12 hrs	24 hours	12 hrs	0 hrs
SOUTHERN HEMISPHERE:				
30°S	12 hrs	10 hrs 06 mins	12 hrs	13 hrs 54 mins
60°S	12 hrs	5 hrs 30 mins	12 hrs	18 hrs 24 mins
90°S (S. Pole)	12 hrs	0 hrs	12 hrs	24 hours

We can also look at the times of longest sunlight as follows:

Figure 3-5. Longest Possible Duration of Sunlight (Insolation):

LATITUDE	LONGEST POSSIBLE AMOUNT OF CONTINUOUS DAYLIGHT
0° (equator)	12 hours
17°	13 hours
41°	15 hours
49°	16 hours
63°	20 hours
66½°	24 hours
67°91'	1 month
90° (North & South Poles)	6 months

Thus, at latitudes around 41 to 43 degrees, which would include New York City, Chicago and the California-Oregon border, the first day of summer and days surrounding it would have from 15 to 15½ hours of sunlight, plus at least an hour of twilight before sunrise and at least an hour of twilight after sunset. On a clear or mostly clear day, that is a considerable amount of light. The closer to the poles we get, the longer is the sunlight during the warmer part of the year, although the sun's rays are more oblique there.

Just the opposite is true in the colder part of the year: the farther poleward we go, the less amount of sunlight is received.

Thus, people in Minnesota, Canada, Alaska, Great Britain and Scandinavia have more usable time of sunlight in the summertime than do people in Southern California, Texas, Florida, Saudi Arabia and the Philippines, but in the wintertime, people in these northern areas have fewer hours of sunlight than do the southern locations.

With all of the summertime sunlight in the polar regions, why don't the ice-caps experience significant melting? The reason is that the sun's rays there are coming in at an angle (obliquely), and are therefore weaker than if they were more direct.

VERTICAL (DIRECT) RAYS   **SLANTED (OBLIQUE) RAYS**

Figure 3-6. The more vertical (direct) the sun's rays upon the earth's surface, the stronger they are for heating the earth's surface; the solar rays are not as strong when they impinge the surface obliquely. Note that when the rays are vertical, more of them fit between the two dots, which represent a given area.

The First Day of Each Season:

●SPRING: In the Northern Hemisphere, the first day of spring is typically March 20th, 21st or 22nd. In the Southern Hemisphere, the first day of spring is typically around September 20th, 21st or 22nd. When spring officially begins is called the **VERNAL EQUINOX**. "Vernal" is from the Latin referring to the "green" arriving in spring, and "equinox" also derives from the Latin, meaning "equal night", because on the first day of spring the sun is out about 12 hours and the nighttime is about 12 hours ("equal daytime" and "equal nighttime") all over the world. At 12 o'clock solar noon, the sun is directly over the equator. For the Northern Hemisphere spring, the sun is "heading" northward.

●SUMMER: In the Northern Hemisphere, the first day of summer is typically June 20th or 21st or 22nd. In the Southern Hemisphere, the first day of summer is typically December 20th, 21st or 22nd. When summer officially begins is called the **SUMMER SOLSTICE**. "Solstice" is derived from the Latin, referring to the sun, "sol". The sun is over the Tropic of Cancer, 23½°N, on the Northern Hemisphere summer solstice, and is over the Tropic of Capricorn, 23½°S, on the Southern Hemisphere summer solstice. The solstices represent the farthest north and south the sun will be during the year. After a solstice, the sun begins "moving" towards the equator and continues to the other hemisphere up to the next solstice. The local time for the actual solstice, as for an equinox time, depends on where you are and where the sun is directly overhead at noon. Thus, e.g., on the Northern Hemisphere summer solstice, the sun is directly over the Tropic of Cancer at some longitude at noon, but for you, if you are not at that spot, this same moment will be occurring at whatever time it is then where you are.

●FALL: In the Northern Hemisphere, the first day of autumn is typically about September 20th, 21st, 22nd or 23rd. In the Southern Hemisphere, the first day of autumn is typically March 20th, 21st or 22nd. When fall (autumn) officially begins is called the **AUTUMNAL EQUINOX**.

"Autumnal" is derived from the Latin "autumnus" for "autumn". Again, as with the vernal equinox, the days and nights are each about 12 hours long, and the sun is directly over the equator.

●WINTER: In the Northern Hemisphere, the first day of winter is typically December 20th, 21st or 22nd. In the Southern Hemisphere, the first day of winter is typically June 20th, 21st or 22nd. When winter officially begins is called the **WINTER SOLSTICE**. For the Northern Hemisphere winter solstice, the sun at noon is directly over a point on the Tropic of Capricorn, 23½°S, and in the Southern Hemisphere winter solstice, the sun at noon is directly over a point on the Tropic of Cancer, 23½°N.

Meteorologically, the hottest days occur from one to two months after the first day of astronomical summer, and the coldest days occur from one to two months after the first day of astronomical winter. There is a temperature lag in the atmosphere. In the summertime, there is more heat coming in from the sun than the earth is losing, even one to two months after the first day of summer, so the effect is a net heat build-up. In the wintertime, there is more heat being lost into space than is being received by the sun, even one to two months after the first day of winter, so the effect is a net cooling.

The <u>heat equator</u> is the place on earth where the sun's rays are the strongest. It shifts daily. On or around June 21st, the heat equator is on the Tropic of Cancer (23½°N); on or around September 21st and March 21st, the strongest rays of the sun are at the equator (0° latitude); on or around December 21st, the heat equator is at the Tropic of Capricorn (23½°S).

Figure 3-7. Table comparing the strength of the sun's rays for the Northern Hemisphere from the Tropic of Cancer (23½°N) to the North Pole (90°N). For example, the sun's rays on February 21st are just about as strong as they are on October 21st. In the higher latitudes, it is typically warmer on October 21st than on February 21st because, in October, the ground has not had a chance to cool off. Although the sun's rays are just about as strong on May 21st as they are on July 21st, we find that July 21st is typically warmer than May 21st because, on July 21st, the earth's surface in the higher latitudes has had all of May and June and most of July to warm up. However, if you go to the beach on May 21st, you will burn about as fast as you would on July 21st, because (in the Northern Hemisphere), the sun's rays as about as strong on July 21st as on May 21st on a sunny day. In the Southern Hemisphere, add six months to the months in the figure. In the Southern Hemisphere, the sun's rays are strongest around Dec. 21st and weakest around June 21st.

June 21 (strongest)		
May 21	=	July 21
April 21	=	August 21
March 21	=	September 21
February 21	=	October 21
January 21	=	November 21
December 21 (weakest)		

Earth's orbit around the sun:

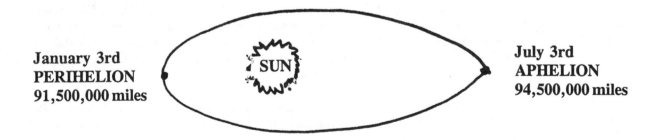

January 3rd
PERIHELION
91,500,000 miles

July 3rd
APHELION
94,500,000 miles

(elliptical orbit exaggerated; not drawn to scale)

Figure 3-8. The earth's orbit around the sun is not exactly circular: it is somewhat elliptical. The average distance of the earth from the sun is about 93,000,000 miles or 150,000,000 kilometers, but around January 3rd, the earth is the closest to the sun, about 91,500,000 miles away, whereas about July 3rd, the earth is the farthest from the sun, about 94,500,000 miles away. The Greek word "helios", for sun, is used in the word, **PERIHELION,** is the name used for the closest distance the earth is from the sun, and the word, **APHELION,** is the name used for the farthest distance the earth is from the sun.   PAGE 26

Thus, since the sun and earth are farthest apart in the Southern Hemisphere winter and closest in the Southern Hemisphere summer, we might suspect that the winters are colder and summers warmer in that hemisphere compared with the Northern Hemisphere. However, because the Southern Hemisphere is mostly covered by ocean, the thermal effects are significantly moderated. Fortunately for the Northern Hemisphere, the sun isn't the closest in July and farthest in January, because, with our much larger land masses to heat up and cool down, our summers would be hotter and our winters would be colder!

Latitude, Longitude and Time Zones:

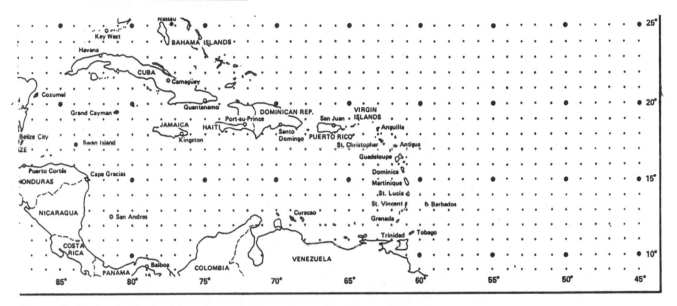

Figure 3-9. **Latitude and longitude lines across the globe.** The latitude lines are called **parallels** and give locations north and south of the equator. Latitude lines run west-to-east. 0° latitude is the equator, 90° North latitude is the North Pole, and 90° South latitude is the South Pole. The longitude lines are called **meridians** and give locations east and west of Greenwich, England. Longitude lines run south-to-north. The meridian going through Greenwich, England is 0° longitude and is called the Prime Meridian, and half-way around the word from there is the International Date Line, at 180° longitude. Going west from zero degrees longitude is West longitude until the dateline is reached, and going east from zero degrees longitude is East longitude, until the dateline (180 degrees longitude) is reached.

Notice that longitude lines come closer together as they approach the Poles. This is called the **convergence of meridians.** Thus, the distance between longitude lines is not the same throughout the globe. However, the distance between latitude lines is the same. One degree of latitude is 60 nautical miles (which is approximately 69 statute miles).

One degree of latitude or longitude is subdivided into units of distance called minutes. This is not the time unit, minute, but a distance unit that uses the same word. **One degree of latitude or longitude equals 60 minutes.**

Each minute is subdivided into units of distance called seconds. Each minute of latitude or longitude equals 60 seconds.

Thus, if you are at a location in central Florida, your "coordinates" might be 28°54'23"N and 81°30'03" W, which means you are located at latitude 28 degrees 54 minutes and 23 second North, and longitude 81 degrees, 30 minutes and 3 seconds West.

If you are visiting a location in eastern Australia, your coordinates might be 27°10'44" S, 152°10'34" E, which means you are located at latitude 27 degrees 10 minutes 44 seconds South, and longitude 152 degrees 10 minutes 34 seconds East.

Because the sun cannot be in the same position in the sky everywhere on earth, the world is divided into **time zones**. Generally, every 15 degrees of longitude is the width of a time zone. Thus, there are 24 time zones (24 times 15 = 360 degrees around the globe). The center of the first time zone is 0° longitude, which goes through Greenwich, England and is sometimes referred to as Greenwich Mean Time and is labelled on weather maps as "Z", from the old U.S. military phonetic alphabet, "zulu" for "z". Thus, if a surface weather map is labelled 12Z today, then it is the weather map for noon at 0 degrees longitude. The world standard now calls z-time **UTC, for Universale Temps Coordinee**, or Universal Coordinated Time.

The first reference time zone extends about 7½ degrees longitude either side of the 0° (Greenwich, England) meridian, and then for every 15 degrees east and west of that meridian is the center of another time zone. For example, consider the four time zones of the contiguous 48 states of the United States. The Eastern Time Zone extends from 7½° west through 7½° east of the 75th meridian (from about 82½°W through 67½°W longitude). The time zone is not exactly on these borders, since these boundaries zig and zag just a little so that one city or county does not find itself split with part of it in one time zone and another part in another. Thus, a whole county would be in either the Eastern Time Zone or the next time zone

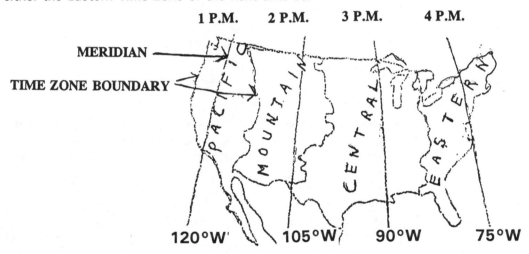

Figure 3-10. Time zones in the connected 48 states:

Eastern Standard Time: centered on 75°W

Central Standard Time: centered on 90°W

Mountain Standard Time: centered on 105°W

Pacific Standard Time: centered on 120°W.

Most of Alaska is in the Alaskan time zone, which is 9 hours earlier than the time in Greenwich, England; however, the Aleutian Islands that are west of 169.30°W, and the Hawaiian Islands, are in the Hawaii-Aleutian time zone, which is 10 hours earlier than Greenwich mean time. Thus, when it is noon in England, it is 7 a.m. in New York, 4 a.m. in California, and 2 a.m. in Honolulu, Hawaii, all local standard time.

PAGE 28

For **Daylight Savings Time**, make the time one hour later. This 20th century invention, done initially during World War I, was done during the warmer months to add one or two hours of "usable daylight"; that is, by temporarily setting the clock ahead one or two hours, the sun rises one or two hours later, but it sets one or two hours later, thus it may not get dark at 8 p.m. but at 9 or 10 p.m., so that you could stay outside longer with daylight. Nowadays, in the U.S.A., most states go on daylight savings time. The first Sunday morning (at 1 a.m.) in April, the clocks are turned ahead one hour to make it 2 a.m., and the last Sunday in October (at 2 a.m. daylight time), the clocks are turned back to make it 1 a.m. The slogan is "SPRING AHEAD, FALL BACK". As of this writing, Arizona, Hawaii and parts of Indiana do not observe Daylight Savings Time.

As you head westward from one time zone to another, you have to set your watch one hour earlier. Thus, if you travel out of the Eastern Time Zone into the Central Time Zone, and your watch said 2:30 p.m., it must now be set to 1:30 p.m. if you are staying in the Central Time Zone on a visit. Conversely, as you head eastward into the next time zone, it is one hour later.

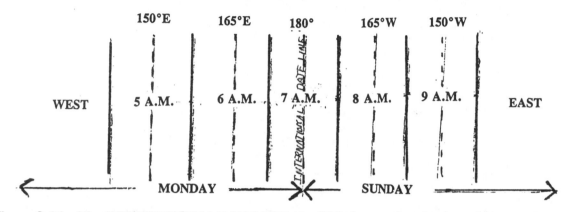

Figure 3-11. The **INTERNATIONAL DATELINE is at 180 degrees longitude, where east meets west on the longitude scale.** When you cross the dateline heading westward, you make it the next day. Thus, if it is Sunday and you cross the International Dateline, it is now Monday. It keeps getting earlier as you head westward, but once you cross that dateline, it automatically becomes the next day. Conversely, if you cross the dateline heading eastward, say travelling from Asia to North America, it becomes one day earlier. Your Tuesday is suddenly Monday.

Although the International Dateline in the figure is shown as a straight line, it is an irregular line along the 180th meridian in the Pacific Ocean so that an island or small nation will remain in the same day! The dateline is half-way around the world from Greenwich, England. Therefore, when it is noon in England it is midnight, the beginning of a new day, on the International Dateline.

Note the following:

• Because you lose an hour (it becomes an hour later) when travelling eastward across each time zone boundary, you gain a day when you travel eastward across the International Dateline. This makes up for all the hours that you lost, if you travelled eastward across all the time zones.

• In like manner, because you gain an hour (it becomes an hour earlier) when travelling westward across each time zone boundary, you lose a day when you travel west across the International Dateline. This makes up for all the hours that you gained, if you travelled westward across all the time zones.

• When you cross the International Dateline (the 180th meridian, i.e., 180° longitude), the time does not change, only the day does. You need to cross a time-zone boundary for the time to change.

• In the figure on the previous page, the meridians to the west of the International Dateline are labelled 165°E and 150°E, respectively. These are east of Greenwich, England, the reference location for longitude. If you travel east from Greenwich, and go half-way around the world, then you will end up approaching the International Dateline from the west. In like manner, the meridians to the east of the International Dateline are labelled 165°W and 150°W, respectively. These are west of Greenwich. If you travel west from Greenwich, England and go half-way around the world, then you will end up approaching the International Dateline from the east.

The 24-hour clock system:

Figure 3-12. In a 24-hour clock system, a.m. and p.m. are not referred. When a 24-hour clock is used rather than a.m. and p.m., 12:05 a.m. is 0005, e.g., 8 a.m. is 0800, e.g., and 3:35 p.m. is 1535 hours, for another example. The start of the day, midnight, is 0000 hours. "a.m." for morning means "ante meridiem", which is Latin, meaning "before noon", and "p.m." for the second half of the day means "post meridiem", Latin for "after noon". The use of a 24-hour clock avoids using the terms "a.m." and "p.m.".

A.M. And P.M. System	24-Hour System	A.M. and P.M. System	24-Hour System
12:00 midnight	0000	12:30 P.M.	1230
12:16 A.M.	0016	1:00 P.M.	1300
12:52 A.M.	0052	1:30 P.M.	1330
1:00 A.M.	0100	2:21 P.M.	1421
1:32 A.M.	0132	3:35 P.M.	1535
2:00 A.M.	0200	4:45 P.M.	1645
2:45 A.M.	0245	5:33 P.M.	1733
3:27 A.M.	0327	6:42 P.M.	1842
4:22 A.M.	0422	7:19 P.M.	1919
5:01 A.M.	0501	8:20 P.M.	2020
6:30 A.M.	0630	9:37 P.M.	2137
7:15 A.M.	0715	10:40 P.M.	2240
8:55 A.M.	0855	11:36 P.M.	2336
9:32 A.M.	0932	11:59 P.M.	2359
10:01 A.M.	1001	12:01 A.M.	0001
11:30 A.M.	1130	12:59 A.M.	0059
12:00 noon	1200		

Figure 3-13. An example of the usefulness of latitude and longitude. Note how the tracks of two hurricanes were plotted, showing the locations of the eye (center) of each storm at 7 a.m. Eastern Daylight Time each day.

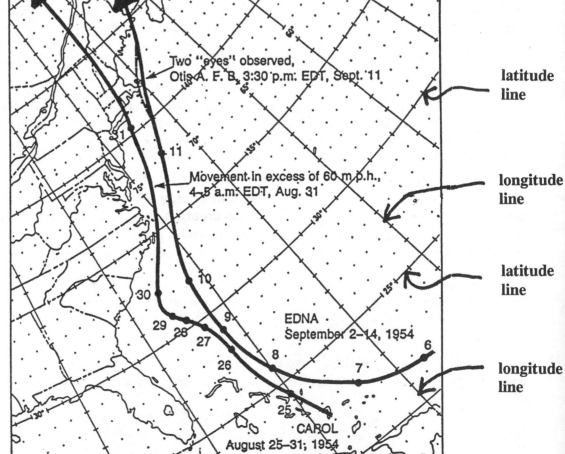

PAGE 30

Chapter 4. SOLAR ENERGY

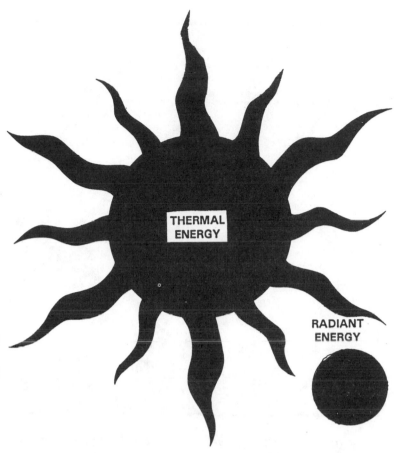

Figure 4-1. Solar energy is the energy emitted by our solar system's star, the sun. It consists of energy we can see (light) and other forms, including ultraviolet radiation (which causes sunburn), infra-red radiation (which transfers heat), x-rays and other wavelengths of radiation.

Our sun is an average star in size and brightness. It appears bigger and brighter than the other stars because of its closeness to us...averaging about 93,000,000 miles (150,000,000 kilometers) from earth (our closest distance to the sun is about 91,500,000 miles and our farthest is about 94,500,000 miles). If we could place all the known stars including our sun at the same distance from the earth, we would find that there are about as many that are larger and about as many that are smaller than our sun, and just about as many that are brighter and about as many as are dimmer than our sun. Unlike a planet, which typically depends on a star (sun) for light and heat, a star produces its own energy by a process known as <u>nuclear fusion</u>. In fusion, a star combines four hydrogen atoms to produce one helium atom, and whatever material is left over becomes energy.

Where fusion is occurring, below the sun's surface, the temperature is about 30,000,000°F, as compared to its surface temperature of about 10,000°F.

During every second, our sun converts some 564 million tons of hydrogen to some 560 million tons of helium. The remaining 4 million tons is converted into energy.

$$E = mc^2$$

is Albert Einstein's equation which states that energy and matter can be converted into one another. A small amount of matter can create a relatively enormous amount of energy. E is energy, m is the amount of mass and c is the speed of light. c^2 means that the speed of light is multiplied by itself (is squared), which gives an enormously large number. The speed of light is about 186,000 miles (300,000 kilometers) per <u>second</u>. You can see that you are going to get a large amount of energy even from only one gram of matter.

The sun is just the right distance from the earth to allow life as we know it. Since the intensity of the sun's radiation decreases the farther out it goes, and since we face only one part of the sun at a time, we receive only about one two--billionth of its energy output! The figure on the next page shows the disposition of the one two-billionth of the sun's energy that the earth receives.

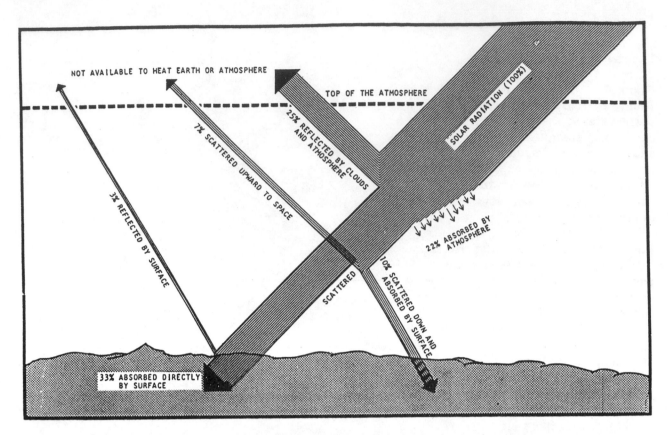

Figure 4-2. Average values for what happens to solar radiation entering earth's atmosphere. The atmosphere directly absorbs about 22%, which heats the air. 35% is reflected back to space (25% reflected by clouds, 7% lost by being scattered and 3% reflected by the earth's surface). 43% heats the earth's surface (much of which in turn heats the lower atmosphere) (of this 43%, 33% heats the earth by direct rays, and 10% heats the earth by scattering). (source: NOAA)

We refer to the amount of energy that we receive from the sun as <u>incoming solar radiation</u>, which led to the invention of the shorter word for it, <u>insolation</u>. (The word "insolation" is not to be confused with the word "insulation" which is material such as fibreglass used to insulate your home.)

Figure 4-3. We know that on the average, the earth must be radiating out into space the same amount of energy as it is receiving from the sun. Otherwise, our overall climate would either be getting hotter or colder! (source: NOAA)

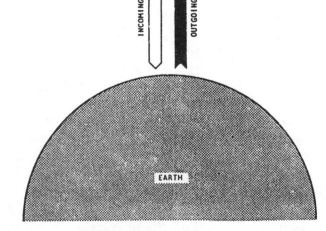

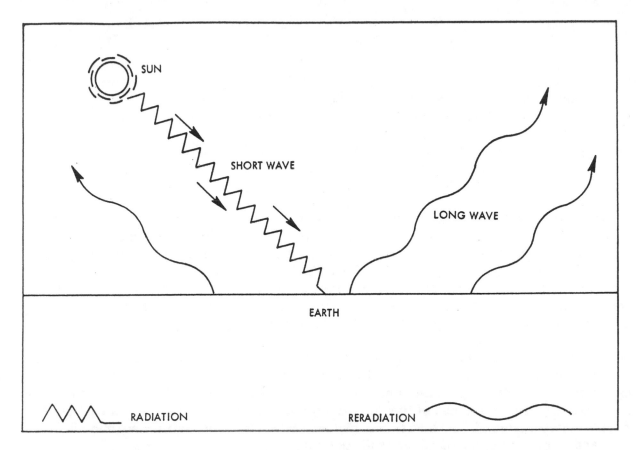

Figure 4-4. Most of the insolation reaching the earth is in the form of short-wave radiation, such as visible light, ultra-violet radiation and x-rays. However, the earth radiates back mostly long-wave radiation, mostly being infra-red radiation. (source: NOAA)

The amount of insolation we receive in our local area depends on many factors, including:

• the energy output of the sun;

• the distance between the sun and the earth;

• the local atmosphere's cloud cover, moisture content and particulate matter content;

• the local latitude;

• the season;

• the length of the daily sunlight period; and

• the surface configuration of the land.

If the sun's output were to noticeably vary, great climatic changes would occur on the earth.

As discussed in chapter 3, the tilt of the earth's axis and its varying distance from the sun account for the season's and the amount of energy we receive locally.

When the sky is overcast, we do not receive as much of the insolation compared with when the sky is clear. Although much radiation reaches the earth's surface through the clouds, the clouds themselves scatter and reflect radiation away from the surface.

Water vapor in the air absorbs some of the insolation, which results in warming the air. Various pollutants help scatter and reflect some of the insolation, with some being scattered towards the earth and some away.

The closer your local area is to the equator, the more of the sun's energy will be absorbed, because the rays of the sun in the tropics are more vertical than in higher latitudes. The more vertical the rays are, the more can be absorbed in a given area, and the warmer it gets. The more slanted the rays are, the fewer fit in a given area, and as a result it does not warm up as much. Whenever the sun's rays are coming in slantedly, they have to travel through a thicker layer of air, which reflects, scatters and absorbs some of the energy, before the remainder reaches the earth's surface.

When the Northern Hemisphere is having summer, it is tilted towards the sun, resulting in more direct rays of sun, which warm a given area more. At this time, the Southern Hemisphere is experiencing winter, and is tilted more away from the sun, resulting in more slanted rays and therefore less of the sun's energy being received in a given area, resulting in cooler temperatures. Then the reverse happens when the Northern Hemisphere is in winter and the Southern Hemisphere is in summer.

Outside the tropics, the daily daylight periods are longer in spring and summer than they are in fall and winter, so these higher latitudes receive more insolation in spring and summer.

Figure 4-5. A beam of insolation of the same width, impinging on the surface slantedly, must cover a larger surface area than a beam striking perpendicularly. Thus, the summer energy warms the earth more. (source: DOA)

Figure 4-6. **Top figure:** surfaces that are more nearly perpendicular to incoming solar radiation receive more heat per unit area, and thus become warmer, than do surfaces that are more nearly parallel to the incoming sun's rays.

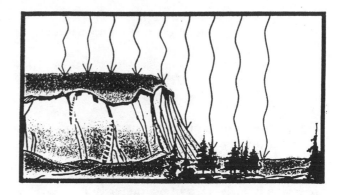

Bottom figure: as the sun arcs across the sky, its rays are more nearly perpendicular to different slopes and aspects as various hours. In the Northern Hemisphere, outside of the tropics, the south-facing slopes receive more nearly direct rays than do the north-facing slopes, and in the Southern Hemisphere, the reverse is true. (source: DOA)

In the Northern Hemisphere, outside of the tropics, southern slopes of hills and mountains receive more direct rays of the sun than do the northern slopes, which are partially or entirely in shade. We have a similar situation around our homes. The south side of houses receive more sunlight than the north side. If you were to build a greenhouse, you would place it on the south side. Winter snows take longer to melt on the north side. In the Southern Hemisphere, outside the tropics, it is the north side of hills, mountains and buildings that receives more sunlight; the south side receives less.

Some other terms you may hear and read in scientific discussions involving the sun are the following.

SOLAR CONSTANT: The amount of energy from the sun being received at the top of the earth's atmosphere perpendicular to the sun's rays. This amount is virtually the same at all times, about 1.97 grams per square centimeter per minute or about 1372 watts per square meter. Throughout the year, however, there is a slight fluctuation of the solar constant from about 1330 w/m² at aphelion to about to 1421 w/m² at perihelion. Although there may be some fluctuation due to changes in the thermonuclear processes on the sun, we known there are annual changes based on the varying distance from earth to sun. If there were greater fluctuations in the sun's energy output were to occur, the earth would experience a drastic change in climate.

SOLAR WIND: This is the flow of energy being emitted by the sun. All nine planets and their natural satellites in our solar system are within the flow of mass and energy particles emitting from the sun. The aurora, for example, is caused by some of the solar particles being electrified by the magnetic field of the earth.

SUN SPOTS: These are cooler areas that form, migrate and die on the surface of the sun.

PROMINENCES: These are sudden ejections of mass and energy from the sun; the prominences can shoot out for millions of miles.

How sunlight received on earth is measured:

Figure 4-7. The amount of energy per unit area per unit time is measured by any of a variety of devices used to measure the intensity of the insolation received; such a device is called a **pyrheliometer** (from the Latin and Greek roots for fire).

Weather records also keep track of the actual minutes of sunshine compared with the actual minutes of possible sunshine. As long as the full disk of the sun is essentially shining through thin clouds, it is still considered as sunshine. For example, if the daytime is 600 minutes long and we receive 300 minutes of sunshine, then we have received 50% of he possible sunshine for that day; if the daytime is 900 minutes long and we have received 300 minutes of sunshine, we have received 33% of the possible sunshine for that day. However, on the longer day, which would be in summer in higher latitudes, the intensity of the sunshine energy received would be greater than in the winter, even though in both examples we received 300 minutes of sunshine for the day.

Ultraviolet radiation (uv)

Ultraviolet radiation ("uv" for short) has a wavelength shorter than visible light. Too much uv reaching the earth can be harmful, and fortunately much is blocked from reaching us by stratospheric ozone.

Harmful effects of receiving too much ultraviolet radiation:

●If the sun is high enough in the sky and you stay out in the sun too much, especially for fair-skinned people, sunburn will occur. Excessive exposure to the sun may lead to skin cancer.

●An excess of uv has been linked to cataract and other eye problems, premature aging and possibly some suppression of the immune system.

UV levels are highest when the sun is high in the sky (late spring through early autumn), and from about 9 a.m. to 3 p.m. standard time. Sunny days of course provide the most sunshine, but much uv penetrates even through an overcast of high, cirrostratus clouds. The uv intensity is strongest in low latitudes where the sun is more overhead, than in high latitudes where the sun is closer to the horizon. UV increases with altitude, as we move into thinner air on mountains. Some uv is reflected by surfaces, especially by freshly fallen heavy snow, after the sun comes out. Thus, when out in the warmer-season sun during the peak uv hours, caps, hats, sunscreen (sunblocker lotion), sunglasses that block uv and trying to avoid prolonged exposure when unprotected, are advised actions.

Chapter 5. RADIATIONAL COOLING

<u>Radiational cooling</u> is the earth giving off a type of long-wave radiation known as infra-red radiation, or, simply, heat. The most heat is lost towards space on clear, calm, dry nights. High humidity and cloud cover prevent most of the heat from escaping. Therefore, all else being equal, clear nights are colder than cloudy nights. Just the opposite is usually true during the daylight: clear daytime hours are usually warmer than cloudy daytimes.

During clear days, your area receives all the sunlight it possibly could, but on a cloudy day, much of the sunlight never reaches the surface because it is reflected back into space by the cloudiness.

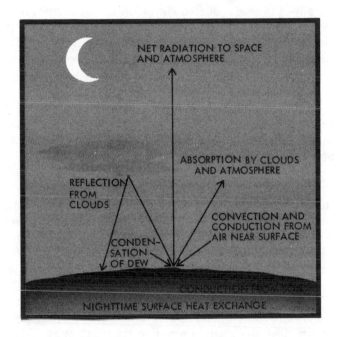

Figure 5-1. At night, there is net cooling of the earth's surface as heat is radiated out, although there is some heat returned. (source: DOA)

The earth is actually radiating heat out into space both day and night, but during the day more heat is coming in from the sun than is leaving the earth. During the Arctic winter and during the Antarctic winter, when there is virtually no sunlight, there is almost continuous loss of heat, which is why the frigid air masses build up and move into lower latitudes giving them winter's cold waves. In the tropics, the opposite happens: there is a net build-up of heat, which then moves into higher latitudes. Hurricanes move and disperse some of this heat energy as well.

At night, the earth radiates long-wave radiation known as **infra-red radiation**, which is a way for transferring out heat energy. Notice from the figure above that even though the net effect is typically cooling, there is some heat added to the lower atmosphere through a variety of processes. The soil surface cools, so the temporarily somewhat warmer layer just below the surface will heat the soil above it through the process known as conduction. **Conduction** is the transfer of heat by two objects in contact with each other, or between parts of the same object (i.e., between molecules of an object). When dew or frost form, some heat is released as the water vapor changes directly to dew, which is liquid water, or directly to frost, which is ice.

When there are clouds at night, especially lower and thicker clouds, then some of the outgoing heat will be reflected back to the surface. Cloudiness acts like a blanket, trapping some of the outgoing **terrestrial** (earth) radiation and reflecting some of it back to the ground. The clouds actually reflect, absorb and re-radiate the terrestrial radiation.

If you were in a space vehicle above the earth's atmosphere, then during the daylight the parts of the earth covered by clouds would appear brighter than the land or ocean, because much of the sunlight is being reflected away from the earth. The cloudless areas appear darker, because much of the sunlight is being absorbed (and converted into heat).

Let us make the following comparison: You are on a beach during a sunny, hot day and beside you is a large tent. If you go into the tent you will feel cooler, because the tent prevents some of the sunlight from entering. The tent is analogous to clouds in the daytime. If you step outside the tent, then you will feel hotter. On the other hand, if you were on the beach at night, you would feel warmer inside the tent, because the tent, like clouds, prevents some of the heat which has accumulated inside of it from escaping. If you step outside the tent, then you would feel much cooler.

Thought question:
If the sun is at its highest point in the sky at noon, which means we are receiving the greatest amount of incoming solar radiation (insolation) at noon, why is the maximum temperature for the day usually around mid-afternoon?

Answer:
Recall that the earth emits heat out into space both day and night, but during much of the daytime, it receives from the sun more heat than it loses, so our local temperature warms up. At noon, your area is receiving its most solar energy, but even for the next few hours after noon, more heat is coming in than the earth is radiating out, so the temperature keeps increasing. This net "build-up" of heat results in the daytime high temperature usually being in the mid-afternoon.

The rate at which the earth is emitting heat is a function of the earth's surface temperature. Thus, the higher the temperature, the more heat is being sent towards space. Even at the time of the maximum temperature for the day, the earth is emitting its most heat. At the time of the minimum temperature, which is usually just after dawn, the earth is emitting its least amount of heat, after having cooled off to its lowest temperature.

Other factors can supersede the above effects, such as having a strong cold front and very cold air moving in during the daytime, or having a surge of much warmer air moving in overnight as a warm front approaches. However, these factors are not caused by solar or terrestrial radiation; rather, the cold or warm air moving in was already a product of previous radiational effects, although that air too will be modified by ongoing radiational affects.

The coldest night of the year typically occurs on a calm, clear night, especially if there is a layer of fresh, heavy snow. Radiational cooling is then maximized. **Any wind over about 7 mph would cause too much mixing to allow for the maximum cooling.** The coldest air will drain into the lowest areas, such as valleys and hollows. If the temperature of the air next to the ground cools to its dewpoint, then dew forms. If the layer of air a few feet deep in contact with the ground cools to its dewpoint, then ground fog will form. This radiational fog will grow until just after sunrise. If the temperature of the air next to the ground cools to its dewpoint and the dewpoint is freezing or below, then frost forms. Radiational cooling typically is best when the center of a dry high pressure system is over the area at night, and is characterized by clear skies and calm conditions.

SECTION III: THE ATMOSPHERE

Chapter 6. THE COMPOSITION OF THE ATMOSPHERE

Air is a mixture of gasses, the most important of which
are nitrogen, oxygen, carbon dioxide and water vapor.

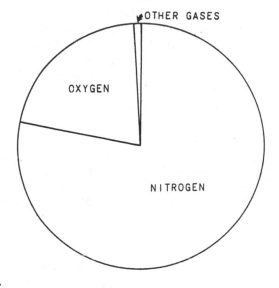

**Figure 6-1. By volume, the atmosphere is
comprised as follows:**
  NITROGEN: about 78%
  OXYGEN   :   about 21%
  ARGON   :   about 0.9%
  Other gasses: about 0.1%

**Water vapor in the atmosphere varies
locally by volume from zero to about 4%.**

Let's look at these components of our planet's atmosphere.

Nitrogen:

Nitrogen is the major component of the earth's atmosphere, making up about 78% of it by volume.
If you are reading this inside a room right now, then about 78% of the room is filled with nitrogen.
We exhale about the same amount of nitrogen that we inhale. Nitrogen has no color and no smell,
although when combined with some other elements, for example hydrogen to form ammonia, the
compound produced could have a pungent odor.

One of the most important cycles in nature is the nitrogen cycle. The nitrogen cycle illustrates how
nature recycles materials. Decay bacteria break down dead plants, animals and other organisms
into ammonia. Other helpful bacteria convert the ammonia to nitrates and nitrites. Plants use the
nitrates to make plant protein, and when animals eat plants, they produce animal protein. When
we humans eat plants and animals, we produce human protein. When plants and animals die, the
cycle repeats itself.

Included in the nitrogen cycle is the effect of lightning from thunderstorms. The lightning causes
free nitrogen in the air to combine with oxygen to make nitrates, which dissolve in rainwater and
fall to the ground as an additional source of nitrates for plants to use (to make plant protein).

Another source of nitrates are leguminous plants (i.e., peas, beans, clover, alfalfa, etc.). Living in
the nodules of their roots is another group of beneficial bacteria called nitrogen-fixing bacteria.
These are capable of combining gaseous nitrogen and oxygen into nitrates, which are soluble solids.
The only threat to the nitrate stockpile is from a bacteria group called denitrifying bacteria, that
break down nitrates into gaseous nitrogen and oxygen. These bacteria are found in areas that have
poor drainage. Thus, if your property is well-drained, then you should not be bothered by these
robbers of one of our most valuable natural fertilizers, nitrates.

Oxygen:

As far as humans and many other species are concerned, oxygen is the most important component
gas of earth's atmosphere, comprising about 21% of it by volume. Thus, if you are in a room right
now, slightly over one-fifth of the room's air is made up of oxygen.

In most **vertebrates** (animals with backbones), oxygen is absorbed by the blood and transported with digested food to every cell in the body. Inside each cell, digested food combines with oxygen for the release of energy and carbon dioxide. This process is called **respiration**. It might surprise you to know that your exhaled breath may still contain up to about 18% oxygen. It might be less during strenuous exercise and other activities. The relatively high percentage of oxygen makes it possible for you to administer mouth-to-mouth artificial respiration, if ever necessary.

Oxygen readily combines with many other elements (e.g., it combines with hydrogen to form water), and is vital to animal (including human) and plant respiration. Oxygen is also needed for most burning to occur.

Rotting organic matter takes oxygen out of the air, and we humans take in oxygen as we breathe, exhaling carbon dioxide and some oxygen, as stated above. Plants produce oxygen, adding it to the atmosphere, and they absorb carbon dioxide.

Argon:

Argon is a gas that comprises about nine-tenths of a percent of the volume of the atmosphere. It has no color and no odor. Argon is also an **inert** gas, meaning it really does not do much except take up space; i.e., it does not readily react with other elements or with compounds, and thus form few if any compounds. The word "argon" is derived from the Greek, meaning "without work", thus, "idle".

Argon does have its uses, however. It is used in electric light bulbs, especially incandescent bulbs, and is used as an inert gas shield in arc welding.

Water vapor:

Without water and water vapor, life on this planet as we know it would not exist. The warmer the air is, the more water vapor it can hold, when a source or sources of the moisture are available. Thus, the amount of water vapor that exists locally is a variable, ranging from near zero to about 4% of the local environment's atmosphere. In most places most of the time, the water vapor content of the air varies from a fraction of a percent to about 3%.

One means for water vapor entering the atmosphere is through evaporation of water from the oceans, lakes, rivers and other bodies of water. Another major method of adding water vapor into the air is by plants emitting surplus moisture through the pores of their leaves. This process is called **transpiration**. A term that is used which accounts for both evaporative and transpirative methods of adding water vapor into the atmosphere is called **evapo-transpiration**.

When moisture is transpiring from plants, your body can sense it...actually feel it...occurring when you are in a very warm and moist greenhouse or in a tropical jungle. Even in mid-latitudes, if you are in a heavily vegetated area in the summer and the sun comes blazing out after a heavy thunderstorm, you can feel the moisture rising back into the air, as well as see condensation rising from wet blacktop surfaces that are being heated by the sun. When you are among a stand of white pine trees in such a situation, the refreshing scent of pine is enhanced, which you might find exhilarating.

Mature trees in the summertime can evapo-transpirate an enormous amount of water. For example, a mature pine or oak tree on a sunny day in the mid-latitudes, emits about 50 gallons of water into the lowest layer of the atmosphere! Imagine how much water vapor an entire pine forest can produce. You may notice on a summer day when the air is unstable, that the first puffy cumulus clouds will likely form over a wooded region first, thanks to the availability of sufficient water vapor to make the clouds.

One single apple tree may not give off as much moisture, but in a single growing season, it typically emits enough moisture to equal about 1800 gallons of liquid water when condensed into liquid water.

When you think about it, you can readily conclude how important trees are to our survival:

• trees absorb a lot of precipitation, inhibiting erosion;
• trees act as windbreaks;
• trees take in carbon dioxide and produce oxygen which we need to breathe;
• trees provide shelter and food for various animal and bird species; and
• trees are aesthetically pleasing, which enhances our sense of well-being.

When a large forest burns, it is possible that the region just downwind will experience a somewhat drier climate, at least temporarily.

Thus, the role of water vapor in our atmosphere is essential to our survival on this planet.

Other constituent gasses of earth's atmosphere:

Although the rest of the gasses that comprise our air are each only a small fraction of a percent of the total volume of the atmosphere, and although all of them combined total under one percent of the atmosphere, some of them are also important to human life. The following is an overview of these constituent gasses.

The greenhouse effect and greenhouse gasses:
The greenhouse effect is good for life on this planet; a runaway greenhouse effect would be disastrous for life. This effect is analogizing the "thermostat" of the earth's climate with that of a greenhouse. Certain gasses in our atmosphere are necessary to trap some of the heat, similar to how a greenhouse traps heat and moisture to keep its interior always warm and moist so that the plants and other vegetation in it will prosper. The glass or plastic-like walls and roof of the greenhouse trap much of the radiation and water vapor that try to escape, as well as allowing incoming solar radiation to pass through the glass to warm the greenhouse interior.

For the earth, the presence of water vapor in the atmosphere results in some absorption of terrestrial radiation, which therefore causes the air to warm. This warmth is reradiated in all directions, including back to the ground. Thus, the natural greenhouse effect moderates our climate and keeps us warmer than we would otherwise be. (The runaway greenhouse effect is discussed in chapter 43 in the discussion on climatic change.)

Water vapor is not the only greenhouse effect gas that keeps our planet warmer. The following gasses also contribute to adding warmth to the planet: carbon dioxide, methane, nitrous oxide and chlorofluorocarbons. Even though these gasses represent a tiny part of the total volume of the atmosphere, and even though most of them are concentrated in the lowest parts of the atmosphere, they can have a significant effect on climate if they were to increase significantly in amount.

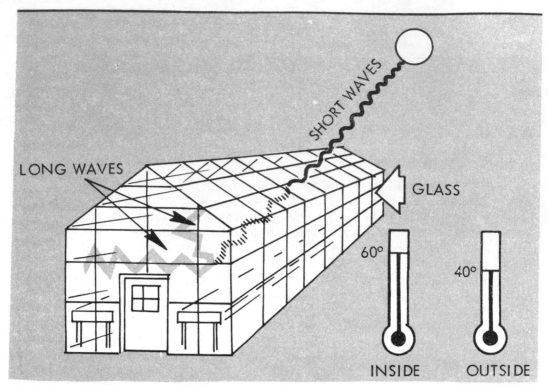

Figure 6-2. The greenhouse effect. The glass allows the short-wave energy from the sun to enter the greenhouse to heat the interior, but after this energy is converted into heat (long-wave radiation), the glass does not allow this heat to leave since this long-wave radiation cannot readily go through the glass. Thus, the interior of the greenhouse warms up. The earth's atmosphere has a natural greenhouse effect, due primarily to water vapor and carbon dioxide, which absorb some of the outgoing long-wave radiation and then reradiate it, with some of this re-radiation going back towards the earth's surface. Thus, the natural greenhouse effect keeps earth's climate warmer than it otherwise would be. (source: NOAA)

<u>Carbon dioxide</u>:

Carbon dioxide, CO_2, absorbs heat and acts as a greenhouse effect gas also. Thus, if the burning of fossil fuels such as coal, gas and wood, and the emissions from automobiles, were to significantly increase the amount of carbon dioxide in the atmosphere, we could undergo "global warming" which would change our climate significantly. This topic is discussed in chapter 43, section e. The oceans absorb a tremendous amount of excess carbon dioxide, so that the effect of CO_2 is a topic for interesting discussion and debate.

Carbon dioxide makes up a little under 0.04% of the atmosphere, by volume. Thus, not quite 4 out of every 10,000 (or 1 out of every 2500) volumetric units of the atmosphere is comprised of carbon dioxide. This proportion is higher (about 3%) when you exhale, but almost as fast as it leaves your body, it is utilized by green plants, and certain one-celled organisms that contain chlorophyll, in photosynthesis. <u>Photosynthesis</u> is the process by which organisms with chlorophyll, with the help of sunlight, combine carbon dioxide from the air, with water, to make glucose, which is a sugar. The by-product of photosynthesis is oxygen. (By definition, a plant is a multicellular organism with chlorophyll. There are also some one-celled organisms such as one-celled algae, some protozoans plus some bacteria that also contain chlorophyll, and like plants are able to make their own food by photosynthesis.)

You can therefore see that an organism with chlorophyll depends upon all other organisms, which, by the way, do not possess chlorophyll for their supply of carbon dioxide. All other organisms depend upon plants and other organisms with chlorophyll to replenish their supply of oxygen.

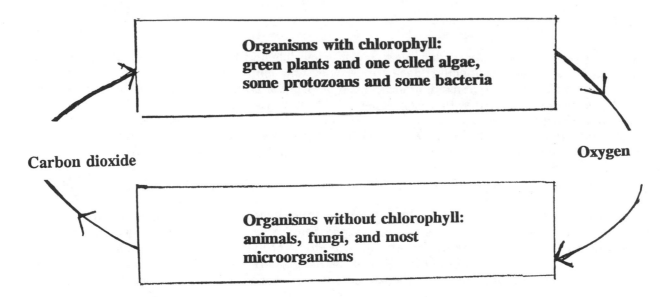

Figure 6-3. The interdependence of organisms through the carbon dioxide-oxygen cycle.

Fortunately for us humans, about 90% of all photosynthesis occurs every day of the year in the ocean by one-celled organisms called <u>diatoms</u>, which are a special group of algae. Their by-product, oxygen, bubbles up from the ocean and diffuses (mixes thoroughly) with the air over the land, helping to provide us with sufficient oxygen even in the wintertime when most of our plants are dead or dormant (inactive).

As stated earlier, another major source for carbon dioxide is the burning of fossil fuels, which are organic compounds. <u>Organic compounds</u> are either alive or come from something that was alive. All organic compounds contain carbon. Paper is organic, because it comes from wood, which in turn comes from trees. On the other hand, table salt (sodium chloride) is <u>inorganic</u>, because it is not alive and never came from anything that was alive. Whenever an organic compound is burnt, some of the carbon that makes it up combines with oxygen to produce carbon dioxide. <u>Burning</u> means combining with oxygen.

<u>Methane</u>:

Methane, CH_4, is removed from the air by certain molecules and by some microbes in the soil, but it is added to the air by cattle and humans passing gas. As the human and cattle populations increase, more methane is being generated. Since methane is a greenhouse effect gas, any significant increase could increase the greenhouse effect.

<u>Ozone</u>:

Ozone, O_3, is a form of oxygen which is considered to be a pollutant in the troposphere, but is beneficial higher up where it alone is responsible for the existence of the stratosphere. Ozone in the stratosphere absorbs a considerable amount of the ultraviolet radiation coming at us from the sun. Too much ultra-violet radiation reaching the earth's surface would heat the earth more and have other adverse effects such as increasing the risk of skin cancer and eyesight problems. This topic is so important that ozone is given its own section in chapter 43, later in this book.

Radon:

Radon is a radioactive gas occurring in nature. It is invisible and has no smell. Radon comes from the natural breakdown (radioactive) decay of uranium, and can be found in high concentrations in soils and rocks containing uranium, granite, shale, phosphate and pitchblende. Radon may also be found in soils contaminated with certain types of industrial wastes, such as the by-products from uranium or phosphate mining. In outdoor air, radon is diluted to such low concentrations that it is usually nothing to worry about. However, once inside an enclosed space, radon can accumulate. The topic of radon and radon build-up is covered in chapter 8, Atmospheric Pollutants.

Gas distribution in the atmosphere:

The gasses are not evenly mixed up throughout the entire depth of the atmosphere. Because of the earth's gravity, the heaviest gasses are found closest to the earth, and as we go higher, the atmosphere eventually ends as molecules and then atoms of hydrogen at its top, which is about 600 miles (some 1000 kilometers) out. Half of the atmosphere's mass is in the first 3½ miles from the earth's surface on up, and the other half is from 3½ miles to about 1000 miles!

Demonstration illustrating how gasses diffuse:

1. Place several drops of perfume at one end of a large room.

2. The perfume will evaporate (change to a gas) and quickly mix thoroughly with the air in the room.

3. You can now smell the perfume at the opposite end of the room.

Other atmospheric constituents:

Besides the nitrogen, oxygen, argon, water vapor, carbon dioxide, methane and ozone, there are traces of many other gasses in the mixture we call the atmosphere. Each gas has its own weight and its own pressure. Therefore, the total atmospheric pressure (air pressure) is the sum of the partial pressures of its constituent gasses. The pressure of the variable water vapor, for example, is called the vapor pressure.

Microscopic particles of dust, ash, pollen, sea-spray salt and other tiny objects are also in our atmosphere, and are essential to our survival because they are the condensation nuclei about which cloud droplets that eventually become precipitation, grow.

Other particles in our atmosphere include pollutants, meteoritic dust from meteorites that burn up as they enter our atmosphere and tiny living organisms (germs) such as bacteria, fungi and viruses.

Also, radiation is moving through our atmosphere.

Thus, our atmosphere is indeed a vibrant domain!

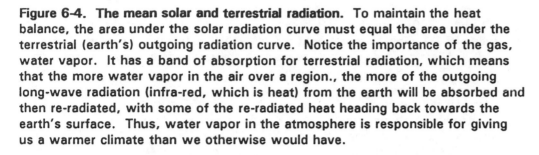

Figure 6-4. The mean solar and terrestrial radiation. To maintain the heat balance, the area under the solar radiation curve must equal the area under the terrestrial (earth's) outgoing radiation curve. Notice the importance of the gas, water vapor. It has a band of absorption for terrestrial radiation, which means that the more water vapor in the air over a region., the more of the outgoing long-wave radiation (infra-red, which is heat) from the earth will be absorbed and then re-radiated, with some of the re-radiated heat heading back towards the earth's surface. Thus, water vapor in the atmosphere is responsible for giving us a warmer climate than we otherwise would have.

In a dry area, such as over a desert, the diurnal temperature range is greater than over a moister region, because the desert will cool off more at night since there are fewer molecules of water vapor to absorb some of the heat heading out to space. (source: NOAA)

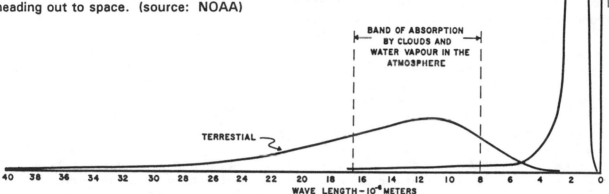

The following outline summarizes the composition of the atmosphere:

Major components by volume:
Nitrogen............................78.08%
Oxygen.............................20.95%
Argon.................................00.93%
Carbon Dioxide...................00.04%
Water vapor......................varies from 0 to 4%, sometimes somewhat more

Rare gasses:
Neon...Helium...Xenon...Krypton...Methane...Nitrous oxide...Nitrogen dioxide...
Iodine...Sulfur dioxide...Nitric oxide...Hydrogen...Ozone...Ammonia...
Carbon monoxide...Radon...Sulfur trioxide...Hydrogen sulfide...Chlorofluorocarbons

Dust and Ash particles:
Smoke from burning, fires and industry...Volcanic ash...Meteoritic burnt particles (meteoritic dust)

Tiny living organisms ("germs"):
Bacteria...Fungi...Viruses

Miscellaneous:
Pollen...Salt from ocean spray...Radiation

Chapter 7. THE VERTICAL STRUCTURE OF THE ATMOSPHERE

The earth's atmosphere is about 600 miles thick. Half of the volume of the atmosphere is from the surface to about 3 1/2 miles (5 1/2 kilometers) up, and the other half is from 3 1/2 miles up to about 600 miles (nearly 1000 kilometers) out. That means that the heaviest gasses that comprise our atmosphere are closest to the earth.

The atmosphere can be defined by five layers:
TROPOSPHERE - from the ground to about 7 miles up;
STRATOSPHERE - from about 7 to 28 miles up;
MESOSPHERE - from about 28 to 47 miles up;
THERMOSPHERE - from about 47 to 200 miles up;
NEAR OUTER SPACE - (sometimes referred to as the exosphere) from about 200 to 600
            miles up.

Beyond about 600 miles up is outer space.

The tops of the first four layers have identifying names. The top of the troposphere is the tropopause, the top of the stratosphere is the stratopause, etc.

The following is a discussion of the different layers.

The troposphere:

The troposphere extends from the surface to about 7 miles up. Almost all weather occurs here, because most of the air that makes up the atmosphere is found in the troposphere. Above this layer, the air is so thin that it cannot really produce weather. The temperature usually decreases with height.

The reasons the temperature usually decreases with height in the troposphere are:
1. As we ascend, there are fewer air molecules. The fewer the molecules, the less likely are there chances for collisions. The fewer the air parcel collisions, the lower the amount of heat produced by friction as a result of collisions. At the surface where the air is thicker, the collision chances are much greater, which therefore produces more heat.

2. As the sun shines on the earth, its rays are absorbed by the earth's surface and changed to heat. This heat warms the surface, but as we rise, the heat becomes less, just as it does when we move away from a heat source such as a fire in a fireplace. The earth is the chief source of this heat because it changes the sunlight's short-wave radiation into long-wave (infra-red) radiation which is heat. Thus, the sun heats the earth which in turn heats the air just above it. There is also some heating directly of the air in the troposphere by the sun, but that heating is significantly less than the indirect heating by the earth as the sun heats the earth.

The boundary between the troposphere and the next layer up is called the tropopause. The height of the tropopause varies. It is higher over the tropics and gradually decreases in height as we move towards the poles. Also, the tropopause is higher in the summer than in the winter. During World War II, when jet pilots flew at the top of the troposphere, they came in contact with very strong winds blowing in a general west-to-east direction. These areas of powerful upper-level winds are parts of a jet-stream.

<u>The stratosphere</u>:

The stratosphere extends from about 7 to 28 miles above the earth's mean sea-level. It is usually very calm with any clouds being rare, except for the tops of thunderstorms that often grow into the bottom of the stratosphere. Although the air temperature in the stratosphere typically increases with height, it is still very cold. The ozone layer is found here and is the reason for the warming (see chapter 43). The boundary between the stratosphere and the next layer up is called the <u>stratopause</u>.

<u>The mesosphere</u>:

The mesosphere extends from about 28 to about 47 miles up. The atmosphere here is extremely thin, so the air pressure is extremely low. The temperature decrease with increasing height through the mesosphere. The temperature decreases with height because through this layer, there is a lack of such gasses as ozone that absorb ultraviolet radiation from the sun and warm up. The heavier gasses are closest to the earth because of the gravitational force. As we ascend through the atmosphere, the gas types that comprise earth's atmosphere become the lighter and lighter ones. The boundary between the mesosphere and the next layer up is called the <u>mesopause</u>.

<u>The thermosphere</u>:

The thermosphere extends from about 47 to 200 miles up. Because the air is so thin at this height, it is not easy to determine the temperature in the usual way. Closer to the earth's surface, we can use the correlation between the speed and other motions (such as vibration, rotation, etc.) of molecules and their temperature. The higher the temperature, the faster the molecules move. In the thermosphere, however, there are so few molecules and atoms that they move very fast. If molecules that were very numerous moved so fast, the temperature would be quite high. We do know that monatomic oxygen (O rather than O_2) in the thermosphere absorbs some ultraviolet and other short-wave radiation from the sun and warms up, so the temperature does rise with height in the thermosphere. The boundary between the thermosphere and the next layer up is called the <u>thermopause</u>.

<u>Near outer space (the exosphere)</u>:

"Near outer space" or the exosphere is the top layer of the atmosphere, extending from about 200 miles up to anywhere from 600 to 1000 miles out. Beyond that is outer space. Thus, the very top layer of earth's atmosphere gradually thins out into outer space as we find the last hydrogen atoms at the atmosphere's top.

Since each of the atmospheric gasses has weight, each has a partial pressure it exerts on the surface of the earth. Thus, the total air pressure we measure on the barometer is the sum of the partial pressure of each of the constituent gasses of the atmosphere.

At or near sea-level, the atmosphere has a pressure of about 14.7 pounds per square inch, which is about 29.92" on the barometer, or about 1013.2 millibars of pressure. But at about 18,000 feet up, the air pressure from the air above that level is only about 7.35 pounds per square inch or about 15" (500 millibars or hectoPascals) on the barometer. Thus, at about 18,000 feet or some 3 1/2 miles up, half the weight of the atmosphere is below you and the other half is above you. (Note: the term "millibar", which is also referred to as "hectoPascal", is another term for a unit of pressure.)

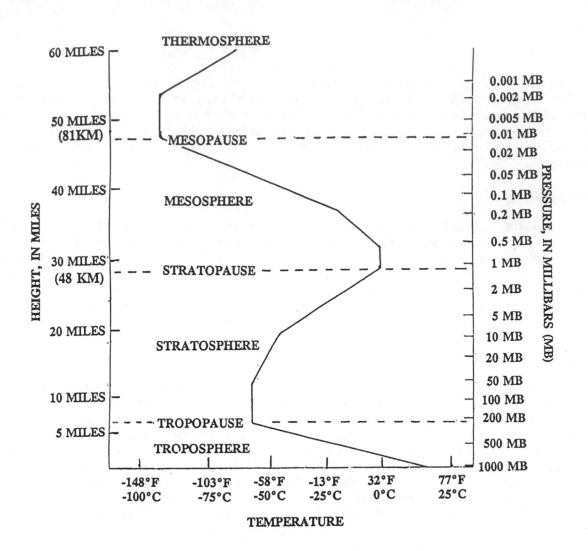

Figure 7-1. **The vertical structure of the atmosphere.** The figure is not drawn to scale, because half of the atmosphere is in the lower 18,000 feet above the earth's surface, and the other half is from about 18,000 feet (about 3 1/2 miles) to about 600 miles up. The higher we go, the lighter are the gasses that comprise the atmosphere, until at the top of the atmosphere we find the atoms of the lightest gas, hydrogen.

The ionosphere

The ionosphere is not a separate layer of the earth's atmosphere. It includes parts of the mesosphere, thermosphere and near outer space (which is also called the exosphere). The ionosphere starts at about 35 miles up and extends to about 600 miles. The ionosphere is the region of the atmosphere through which we find concentrations of electrically-charged particles called ions, as well as finding free electrons, which also have electrical charge. This helps to produce interesting electrical phenomena and effects, such as the aurora.

Here is what we know about the ionosphere at this time.

Particles from the sun, cosmic rays, and particles from supernova explosions bombard air atoms, causing them to lose electrons and become positively charged (the charged particles are the ions). Thus, the ionosphere is an electrified depth of the atmosphere. It is responsible for the reflection of AM and short-wave radio waves.

There are four main regions of the ionosphere, which have been given identifying letters rather than names:

<u>The ionospheric layers</u>:

D region: from about 35 to 70 miles up;

E region: from about 70 to 100 miles up;

F1 region: from about 100 to 135 miles up;

F2 region: from about 135 to 600 miles up (maybe up to the top of the atmosphere).

The F1 and F2 regions are subsets of the F region, which is from about 100 miles up and up to the top of the atmosphere.

AM radio signals are normally absorbed, weakened and reflected back to earth by the D region and to a lesser extent by the E region. However, the radio and television signals of shorter wavelengths travel farther out into space. Short-wave radio signals reflect back from a higher level (in the F level) and therefore can be picked up at greater distances from their source. Therefore, short-wave radio communications travel all around the world.

AM radio waves are normally reflected by the D region during the day and the F region at night. Short waves are reflected by the F layer. FM radio signals and television must be reflected back to earth by satellites if they are to be heard for long distances; otherwise, FM and TV signals are "line-of-sight", which means that they travel essentially in a straight line from the transmission tower, and cannot be picked up past the curve of the earth, Increasing the FM and TV power helps, but cannot improve beyond a certain range. Even a powerful one million watt FM station would have trouble being heard beyond about 125 miles.

During the day, the D region is well-developed, because the atoms at this height are being bombarded by particles from the sun, making many of them become ions. The AM radio waves being transmitted are reflected back to earth by the D region, and are picked up by your radio antennae. Because the D region absorbs much of the AM signal, the power supplied by the radio station transmitter is increased at sunrise. After sunset, the positive ions combine with free electrons and the D region gradually breaks down, resulting in the AM radio waves now being able to penetrate into the higher F region. The F region does not break down as easily because the air therein is so thin that the positive ions and electrons are farther apart and therefore do not recombine as easily. Because the F region does not absorb the AM radio waves as much as does the D region, these waves bounce back and forth between the earth and the F layer, resulting in your being able to pick up at night AM radio stations at farther distances.

If more than one AM station share the same frequency and are close enough in distance, then at night they will interfere with each other and you may hear two radio stations broadcasting at the same time. Thus, AM radio stations can broadcast over a far greater distance at night than during the daytime, and they usually reduce their power after sunset to avoid interference.

Radio signals can be adversely affected by solar storms, which occur when solar flares erupt on the sun's surface and the sun ejects streams of particles into space. When the earth is in the path of these streams, these particles interact with our magnetic field, air molecules and air atoms and can disrupt radio communications, sometimes for days.

Another ionospheric phenomenon is the aurora. The <u>aurora</u> is the visible glowing of atmospheric atoms due to their being impacted upon by charged particles from the sun. The flow of charged solar particles (protons and electrons) from the sun is the <u>solar wind</u>. In the Northern Hemisphere, the aurora is called the <u>aurora borealis</u>, and in the Southern Hemisphere it is the <u>aurora australis</u>.

When the aurora is occurring in the Northern Hemisphere, it is also occurring at the same latitudes south in the Southern Hemisphere, and appears there as a "mirror image" of what it looks like in the Northern Hemisphere. This is because the solar wind is also interacting with the earth's magnetic field (the earth is a big magnet, or acts as if it has a big magnet within it, stretching from the magnetic pole located in the Northern Hemisphere to the one located in the Southern Hemisphere.) The magnetic lines of force extend over and around the globe from one magnetic pole to the other.

The aurora appears as shimmering curtains, ribbons or areas of light in the sky, typically in shades of white, green, red, purple and sometimes other colors. It occurs most often in the highest (polar) latitudes, but can occur even in mid and low latitudes. It occurs during the daylight also, but cannot be seen then; thus, it is visible to us at night. The sky must obviously be clear and you need to be away from the lights of the city. Most auroras occur between about 50 to 150 miles up.

The different colors of the aurora are due to the different gasses with which the solar particles collide. Moreover, even the same gas can produce different colors, depending upon the speed with which the particles hit the gas. In general, the higher the altitude, the faster the speed of the particles, since there are fewer air molecules and atoms to slow these solar particles down. For example, when atomic oxygen is hit by a solar particle at 60 miles up, it emits a green light, but at 150 miles up, the atomic oxygen when hit produces a red light.

Figure 7-2. An episode of the aurora borealis. The aurora borealis is also called the Northern Lights. (The aurora australis is also known as the Southern Lights.) The aurora is one of the most beautiful of Nature's displays. (source: USAF)

DEMONSTRATION: MAKING LINES OF FORCE VISIBLE

A <u>field</u> is an area in space where a force has an effect on an object. The forces in a field travel along paths called <u>lines of force</u>. In general, objects that are affected by the forces within a field tend to move along the lines of force. For example, if we place a steel paper clip on a string and suspend it from an object so that it can move freely, then as we approach the paper clip with a magnet, the paper clip will move towards the magnet once it is within the magnet's magnetic field. The path that it takes is along the magnetic lines of force. Since magnetic lines of force are invisible, it might be interesting to make them visible.

Materials needed: two bar magnets whose poles are labeled (N for north and S for south); a container of iron filings; and a piece of cardboard.

1. Sprinkle a thin layer of iron filings over the middle section of the cardboard.

2. Place two bar magnets on a table so that two like poles face each other and are about one inch (about 2.5 centimeters) apart.

3. Now carefully place the cardboard with the iron filings on top of the magnets.

4. Gently tap the cardboard. The iron filings should arrange themselves along the magnetic lines of force, thus making these lines visible.

5. Remove the cardboard and gently rub the iron filings so that they are once again evenly distributed over the middle section of the cardboard.

6. Place the bar magnets so that two unlike poles face each other and are about one inch (about 2.5 centimeters) apart.

7. Now carefully place the cardboard with the iron filings on top of the magnets.

8. Gently tap the cardboard. How do the magnetic lines of force compare with the ones produced when two like poles were facing each other?

DEMONSTRATION: MAKING YOUR OWN COMPASS

As you probably know, a magnetic compass is a magnet that is allowed to swing freely. If we think of the earth as having a large magnet within it, then magnetic lines of force extend over the entire globe from one magnetic pole to the other. A magnetic compass is forced to point to the magnetic pole(s) and will point to it in the same direction as the magnetic lines of force that are close to it.

Since the geographic poles and the magnetic poles are not in the same location, a magnetic compass points to the magnetic pole, not to the geographic pole unless it is on a line whereby pointing to the magnetic pole also points to the geographic pole. In most cases, this does not happen, resulting in the magnetic compass pointing not to true north in the Northern Hemisphere, or not to true south in the Southern Hemisphere. The number of degrees the magnetic compass is off from pointing to the geographic pole is referred to as <u>declination</u>.

(continued)

Figure 7-3. Declinations at four different locations in the Northern Hemisphere. At point A, the compass is pointing to the geographic pole at the same time that it is pointing to the magnetic pole. The declination is 0 because the compass is pointing to true north. At point B, the compass is pointing east. Its declination is therefore 90° or 90° east. At point C, the compass is pointing south; therefore its declination is 180°. At point D the compass is pointing west, giving it a declination of 270° or 90° west.

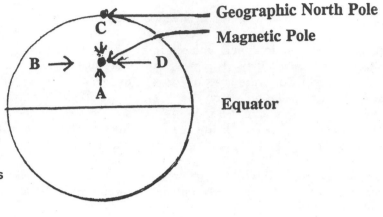

Materials needed:
a ring stand with a clamp in which a 12-inch (30-centimeter) rod has been placed;
string;
2 bar magnets on which the poles are labeled;
2 steel common pins or needles;
2 small corks that are shorter than the lengths of the common pins or needles; and
1 large container such as a casserole dish.

Procedure:
1. Tie a piece of string to the center of a bar magnet and tie it to the rod on the ring stand. Adjust the string so that the magnet is balanced: that is, so that it is horizontally suspended and moves freely.
2. Wait until it stops moving. The North Pole of the magnet will be pointing towards the magnetic pole.
3. Is the North Pole of the magnet pointing to the magnetic pole? (In the Northern Hemisphere, what is the polarity of the earth's magnetic pole that is located in this hemisphere? Recall that in magnetism, unlike poles attract and like poles repel.)
4. Why should we not refer to the magnetic pole that is located in the Northern Hemisphere as the North Magnetic Pole?
5. How should we refer to the magnetic pole that is located in the Southern Hemisphere?
6. Fill a casserole dish nearly full with water.
7. Magnetize two steel pins or needles by stroking them in one direction with a bar magnet near the vicinity of the poles.
8. Place each pin or needle through a cork so that they protrude on both sides of the cork.
9. Place the pins or needles, with the corks, on the surface of the water in the casserole dish. Ensure that the pins or needles are parallel to the water surface. If they touch the side of the container, then move them towards the center. Ensure that you do not record any observations during any times the needles are touching the sides of the container.
10. How does the orientation of each pin or needle compare with the orientation of the bar magnet, which is attached to the ring stand?

Chapter 8. Atmospheric Pollutants

A pollutant is an unwanted substance that contaminates the environment. Too much pollution of air, food and water is harmful to life.

Examples of air pollutants include cigarette smoke, which is extremely dangerous to human health, waste gasses from industrial and some burning activities, exhaust materials from automotive vehicles and pollutants created by Nature (e.g., volcanic ash, radon gas).

Thus, air pollution consists of unwanted build-ups of certain gasses and of tiny, suspended solid particles.

Because there are more people, more cars and more industry in urban areas, these regions have more pollution than rural areas. When winds are very light, pollution builds up; when it is breezy or windy, the pollutants are dispersed, and eventually most of them settle to the ground and sea or combine with other agents in the air and eventually are dispersed.

Meteorological factors that affect air pollution:

1. Wind speed

When winds are strong, pollutants disperse more readily. Moreover, strong winds make the air more turbulent, thus mixing the pollutants with cleaner air from above. Therefore, you can see that air pollution problems are associated with periods of light wind, especially prolonged periods of calm or light wind.

2. Stable air masses and temperature inversions

Temperature inversions occur when a layer of warmer air is on top of a layer of relatively cooler air. This is called a stable to very stable condition, because the cold air, which is heavier than the warm air, tends to remain close to the surface, and the lighter warmer air tends to remain above. As a result, the pollutants are trapped below in the colder air hugging the earth's surface, and we have a pollution build-up as more automotive emissions and the products of burning are released into the lowest layer of the atmosphere. Temperature inversions are most likely on clear, calm or nearly calm nights, when heat from the surface is lost due to radiational cooling.

When the air is stable, with little if any upward vertical motion, there may be a pollution build-up. Fog occurs under stable conditions. A prolonged period of fog can also lead to fog plus pollutants hanging over the area.

When air is unstable, we find rising air currents. This condition may lead to showers and thunderstorms. Locally, where this is occurring, pollutants are unlikely to build up.

Temperature inversions are most likely in valleys. During a clear, calm night, the radiational cooling and the sinking of the denser cool air towards the valley bottom results in the temperature near the ground being colder than the temperature several hundred feet above.

Even in a local countryside area, you may walk late on a summer's evening down a hill into a low area and feel on a skin a sudden drop in temperature from what it was at the higher elevation.

In Donora, Pennsylvania in October 1948, several days of stable air and nearly calm winds led to a few days of persistent dense fog. Fumes from a steel mill, a smelter and other polluting sources "hung" in the fog and was breathed in by people there. Twenty-two people died from this extreme case of air pollution, and about 7000 became ill. Most of the victims were people with cardiac and respiratory problems, such as people who smoked cigarettes. This was one of the worst air pollution disasters in the United States.

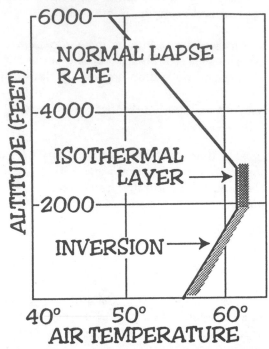

Figure 8-1. A figure showing temperature lapse rates. A <u>lapse rate</u> is the change of temperature with height. Normally, the air temperature gets colder as we rise in elevation until we reach the stratosphere. In this example, note that the temperature gets warmer from the surface to 2000 feet up. This is called a temperature inversion. "Isothermal" means the temperature remains the same with height. (source: USN)

Figure 8-2. Smoke that is released into an inversion layer rises until its temperature equals that of the surrounding air, at which point the smoke flattens out and spreads horizontally. Eventually, much of it may also work its way back downwards. (source: DOA)

Figure 8-3. A temperature inversion in a valley, showing the temperature at different elevations. The zone of warm nighttime temperatures near the top of the inversion is called "the thermal belt". (source: DOA)

Temperature inversions require clear or nearly clear skies so that the earth and air in contact with it in that region can radiate out into space the maximum amount of heat, to cool off the most possible. Clouds trap some of that outgoing radiation and reradiate it back to the surface; in other words, cloud cover keeps the area warmer than it otherwise would be at night. Moreover, if the winds are above about 6 miles per hour, then there will be some mixing of the nighttime air, and it will not cool as much. Thus, to have a nocturnal temperature inversion, we need very precise conditions: clear skies and near-calm or calm winds. If the air cools early enough to its dewpoint, dew will form and then fog. If the fog is very deep and becomes fairly widespread, then these stable conditions can remain for days, until a strong weather system comes in to disperse it. Under prolonged inversions, pollutants build up because they are trapped in that inversion air layer.

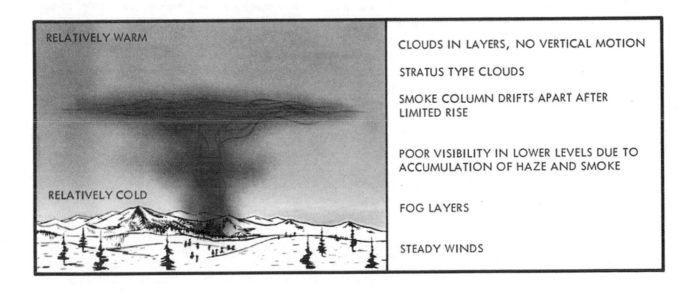

Figure 8-4. Visible indicators of a stable atmosphere, (source: DOA)

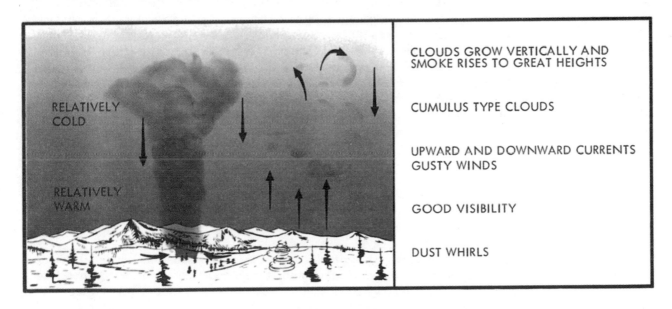

Figure 8-5. Visible indicators of an unstable atmosphere. (source: DOA)

3. When the center of a large high pressure area remains over the same region

Light winds, clear skies and excellent nocturnal radiational cooling are usually associated with the center of a large high pressure system. In most cases, this set of conditions allows the build-up of pollutants. A large region, sometimes several states across, can have pollution episodes that persist for days when the large high pressure system remains over the area. This event is known as an <u>air stagnation</u> episode. A notable exception is when the center of the high pressure system is over oceanic coastal regions with sunny days, especially during the spring and summer, because a sea-breeze usually develops and disperses some of the pollutants in the region within several miles of the shore.

Our air is never perfectly clean. Thus, the definition of air includes some particles we call pollution. Even without human influence, there are natural causes of air pollution. For example, volcanic ash from the eruption of ash volcanoes, will add particles to the atmosphere. Other natural causes are salt particles which evaporate from breaking waves, smoke from forest and brush fires, wind-blown dust and sand, pollen grains, mold spores, bacteria, viruses and other microorganisms. Some of these particles function as   condensation nuclei about which cloud droplets and precipitation form. We could not have rain, for example, were it not for these particles in the air.

Some human causes of air pollution include the burning of fossil fuels, automotive emissions, waste products from nuclear reactions, roasting, refining, mining, quarrying and farming.

<u>Primary pollutants</u> are emitted into the atmosphere from an identifiable source. The chief sources include industries and motor vehicles. These pollutants include particulates, sulfur oxides, nitrogen oxides, volatile organic compounds, carbon monoxide and lead.

<u>Secondary pollutants</u> are produced when chemical reactions between primary pollutants occur within the atmosphere. For example, sulfuric acid is produced when sulfur dioxide combines with oxygen to form sulfur trioxide. When the latter combines with water, it produces sulfuric acid. Many reactions that produce secondary pollutants are caused when primary pollutants react with sunlight. These reactions are called <u>photochemical reactions</u>. One of the most irritating products that results is ozone. Recall that in the stratosphere, ozone is produced by natural processes and is considered "good ozone" because it prevents too much ultraviolet radiation from reaching the earth's surface. However, when ozone is <u>produced at the surface</u>, it is a pollutant. It is typically found in high concentrations in urban areas during episodes of hot, hazy, humid weather. It is harmful to plants, including many tree species, and, when in high concentrations, this ozone can be harmful us humans. Some symptoms of ozone sickness include a developing cough, chest pain, headache, eye irritation and asthma. People with heart and lung problems need to stay indoors in an air-conditioned environment because ozone pollutants aggravate their illness. Vigorous exercise for all people is discouraged during high pollution days. Because ozone levels typically peak in the afternoon on these hot, hazy and humid days, exercising should be done in the morning or late in the evening.

<u>Ozone</u> itself is a form of oxygen. A molecule of oxygen differs from a molecule of ozone in that the oxygen molecule contains two atoms of oxygen whereas the ozone molecule contains three atoms of oxygen. This seemingly small difference is all that it takes to make ozone have very different properties from those of oxygen.

Ozone is an extremely unstable gas; that is, it breaks down easily and becomes oxygen. The third oxygen atom from the molecule combines with other substances, thus oxidizing them; therefore, ozone is a powerful oxidizing agent and its usefulness is to bleach starch, flour, oils and waxes. Sometimes it is used for bleaching wood pulp and textile fibers. In some areas it is used to purify water. Its uses are limited, however, because it is expensive to manufacture commercially, and it is difficult to store.

Ozone has a pale blue color and a pungent odor. It is about ten times as soluble in water as is oxygen. You probably have produced ozone if you ever produced sparks when pulling an electric cord from a wall socket. In the physics lab, ozone is produced by sparks from almost any electrical equipment such as a static electricity generator, radio transformer, dynamos, Geissler tubes, and by various types of Crookes ray tubes.

In the troposphere near the surface, ozone is formed when pollutants, especially oxides of nitrogen (which form as a result of automotive gasoline combustion) react with sunlight. This is one of the components of photochemical smog. At concentrations as low as 0.1 part per million, ozone can over time crack rubber, corrode metals, and damage plant and animal tissues. As it continues to react with hydrocarbons that escape from gasoline tanks or are emitted during incomplete combustion of gasoline, compounds are produced which cause burning eyes and are harmful to individuals with heart or respiratory disease. As you can see, ozone is not a desirable substance to have around on or near the surface of the earth. Thus, whereas stratospheric ozone is the "good ozone", tropospheric ozone is the "bad ozone".

The stratospheric ozone protects the earth's surface from receiving too much ultraviolet radiation. Most of the ozone is produced about 15 to 30 miles up by sunlight hitting oxygen molecules that are in the presence of a catalyst, causing many of the oxygen (O_2) molecules, that are comprised of two oxygen atoms, to be split into atoms of oxygen, O and O. Some of the Os combine with the O_2s that have not broken up, to form O_3, a tri-atomic molecule of oxygen known as ozone. If enough stratospheric ozone were to be depleted, some possible effects, based on recent research, are the following.

There would be an increase in the amount of ultraviolet radiation (UV) reaching the earth's surface. This can be damaging in the following ways.

1. Too much UV causes damage to the ocean's phytoplankton, which are tiny plant-like organisms that are capable of making their own food through the process of photosynthesis, and giving off oxygen as a by-product. They are considered to be the base of the ocean's food chain, because they serve as food to zooplankton, which are tiny animal-like organisms that swim or float near the surface of the water, which are, in turn, food for small animals which, in turn, are food for larger animals. We depend upon the phytoplankton (which are responsible for about 90% of world's photosynthesis) to replace much of the oxygen that we use up through the processes of breathing and combustion. In mid-latitudes, this latter point is crucial in the wintertime when most of the green plants are dead or dormant.

2. Too much UV can diminish the yield of certain agricultural crops. Particularly vulnerable appear to be peas, beans, melons and cabbage.

3. Too much UV generates photochemical smog, which can increase the greenhouse effect.

4. Too much UV causes sunburn, premature wrinkling and aging of the skin.

5. Too much UV produces an increased number of cancer cases, especially skin cancer.

6. Too much UV can increase the frequency of cataracts, which an lead to blindness if not properly treated. It can also damage the retina of the eye and lead to blindness.

7. Too much UV can decrease the effectiveness of a person's immune system, which would make us more susceptible to diseases.

8. Too much UV can destroy DNA (deoxyribonucleic acid), which is a substance that produces

genes, which are individual units of heredity. Thus, the theory is that organisms which have reproductive cycles only during the time of year when the sun's rays are the strongest, could become extinct. Thus, species diversity is reduced.

At issue have been the chemicals known as chlorofluorocarbons (CFCs) working their way upward into the stratosphere and reacting with some of the stratospheric ozone to possibly destroy it. The CFCs (and other ozone-destroying agents) get into the stratosphere through atmospheric dispersion and transporting processes, including the air thrust into the lower stratosphere by well-developed thunderstorms, thunderstorm complexes, tropical cyclones and large extratropical low-pressure systems. The ozone is broken down into regular oxygen plus heat.

"Freon 11" and "freon 12" were two CFCs that were used widely in the latter half of the 20th century. Their uses include air conditioners, refrigerators, aerosol propellants, plastic foams, in various solvents, insulation in buildings, and in the cleaning of computer chips and circuit boards. These two freon types are nontoxic, nonflammable and inexpensive to manufacture. Thus, they greatly improve out standard of living.

Unfortunately, it was discovered in the 1970s that when CFCs work their way into the ozone layer of the stratosphere, they are capable of destroying some of the ozone, and measurements of ozone in the 1970s, 1980s and 1990s showed depletions and "ozone holes" that would appear from time to time. What was not known is whether the CFCs had anything to do with this. Keep in mind that we have absolutely no record of previous ozone readings in the stratosphere, so we cannot compare the stratospheric ozone flux and variability that we now observe, with any record from the past. Thus, you can see how the debate began. Essentially, the big question is, "Is human activity in producing CFCs harming the ozone layer, or is the variability of the stratospheric ozone a normal aspect of Nature?"

If we stop producing CFCs, we take a giant leap backward in our standard of living (no air conditioning, for example). However, if we substitute other agents for CFCs, and these agents do not harm stratospheric ozone (assuming they reach the stratosphere), then even the threat of an ozone-depletion problem would be eliminated. However, suppose these replacement substances are harmful or more harmful than what they replaced? Thus, an interesting debate is underway on the broad scope of this issue.

Suppose that the CFCs do reach the stratosphere and do indeed destroy ozone. The high concentration of UV and very cold temperatures, especially over polar regions, cause these CFCs to release chlorine, and it is the chlorine that has been blamed for breaking down the ozone molecule.

Initial research indicated that surprisingly small quantities of chlorine could break down large quantities of ozone. One estimate suggests that one molecule of chlorine can destroy 100,000 molecules of ozone!

Ozone data has been collected via satellite sensors and from what are called Dobson spectrophotometers which are based on the earth's surface. A spectrophotometer is an instrument that measures the intensity of various wavelengths in a spectrum of light. It allows scientists to estimate the amount of ozone and other gasses. Measurements showed that from the 1970s through the 1990s, stratospheric ozone was diminishing and even holes in the ozone layer were observed. Thus you can see how concern arose about CFCs and stratospheric ozone depletion and the threat of increased UV reaching the earth's surface to cause harm. There are also climatic change concerns which are addressed in chapter 43.

Some other aspects of CFCs are the following.

It takes about ten years for freon to break down, releasing chlorine that damages ozone. Also, chlorine itself is widely used in killing germs by chlorinating drinking water and swimming pools, and to treat sewage. The oceans and volcanoes also give us chlorine. Freon also is found in the oceans, especially in the coldest waters.

Another gas that breaks down the ozone gas in the stratosphere is nitric oxide. Nitric oxide is produced by jet aircraft while burning fuel at high temperatures. Denitrifying bacteria, which are able to live by energy released when they break down nitrates in the soil, release free nitrogen, which is harmless, but also release nitrogen dioxide, which breaks down to nitric oxide.

Yet a third oxide of nitrogen, nitrous oxide, which is sometimes called "laughing gas", may also play a role in this issue. It is an anesthetic for minor operations such as removal of a tooth. It is supplied to dentists and surgeons in liquid form in small tanks. Nitrous oxide breaks down into pure nitrogen and nitric oxide when released into the atmosphere. As stated above, it is the nitric oxide which also destroys ozone in the stratosphere.

Brominated compounds release bromine into the atmosphere. Bromine breaks down the stratospheric ozone in much the same way as does chlorine. Methyl bromide, which is used as a fumigant by many commercial farmers, is mixed with the soil, thus ridding it of most insects. Seeds are then planted and become well-established before the insects return. It has been estimated that at least 20% of the bromine in this compound gets into the atmosphere. Dibromomethane, which is a gasoline additive, also ultimately emits bromine. Halon 1301, a substance used to extinguish fires, releases bromine as well.

Thus, we have a dilemma. These substances are quite useful to us here in the troposphere, but may be having an adverse effect on the stratospheric ozone. So what should be our response? The consensus at the present time seems to be to play it safe and replace some of these substances with others, hoping that the replacements are safe.

Not all UV is potentially harmful. Some UV is needed to allow photosynthesis, for example, and we need the proper amount of it to help warm the earth.

Radon:

Radon is a radioactive gas occurring in nature. You cannot see, smell or taste it. Radon comes from the natural breakdown (radioactive decay) of uranium, and can be found in high concentrations in soils and rocks containing uranium, granite, shale, phosphate and pitchblende. Radon may also be found in soils contaminated with certain types of industrial wastes, such as the by-products from uranium or phosphate mining. In outdoor air, radon is diluted to such low concentrations that it is usually nothing to worry about. However, once inside an enclosed space (such as in a home), radon can accumulate. Indoor levels depend upon both a building's construction and the radon concentration in the underlying soil and/or rock.

A known health effect caused by exposure to elevated levels of radon is an increased risk of developing lung cancer. Not everyone exposed to elevated levels of radon will develop lung cancer, and the time between exposure and the onset of the disease may be many years. In general, the risk increases as the level of radon and the length of exposure increase.

Radon itself breaks down naturally, forming radioactive decay products, which as known as radon daughters. They are solids, not gasses, and stick to surfaces such as dust particles in the air. As one breathes, the radon decay products become trapped in the lungs. As these decay products further break down, they release small bursts of energy which can damage lung tissue and lead to lung cancer.

Most homes, schools and businesses contain a low concentration of radon; however, some buildings do have highly elevated levels. In the zeal to "seal up" buildings to conserve heat in winter and cool air in summer, we also seal in contaminants in the air. Ventilation, therefore, or exchanging inside and outside air, reduces the build-up of indoor radon.

Radon is a gas which can move through small spaces in the soil and rock under a building. It can seep into a home through dirt floors, cracks in concrete, through floors and walls, through floor drains,sumps, joints, tiny cracks and trough pores in hollow-block walls. It can also enter water within private wells and be released into a home when the water is used. Usually it is not a problem with large community water supplies, where it is typically released into the outside air before the water reaches the homes and other buildings. In some unusual situations, radon may be released from materials used in the construction of a home; e.g., it may be a problem if a house has a large stone fireplace or has a solar heating system in which heat is stored in large beds of stone.

Fortunately, there are radon detectors for use in buildings, especially in basements.

Radioactivity is measured in a unit called the curie. A curie is a unit of radioactivity giving 37 billion (3.7×10^{10}) disintegrations per second; a picocurie is one one-trillionth (10^{-12}) of a curie.

If the radon level is about 200 picocuries per liter, or higher, then immediate action is necessary to reduce this level. If the level is between 20 and 200 picocuries per liter, then action should be taken within a few months. If the level is between 4 and 20 picocuries per liter, then exposures in this range are considered above average and action should be taken to lower the levels to about 4 picocuries per liter. If the results are about 4 picocuries per liter or lower, then this is considered average or slightly above for residential structures.

Some corrective measures to reduce the potential health risk from radon in the home, school or business:

●No cigarette smoking, since having more than one cancer-causing factor will more-readily trigger the cancer.

●If your basement has a high concentration of radon, then spend less time there.

●When practical, allow outside air into the house and inside air to go out, especially in the basement. Simply opening windows from time to time will help greatly.

●Home that have crawl spaces should have these spaces ventilated.

●In buildings with high radon concentrations, air-exchange systems might help reduce the concentration of radon to an acceptable level.

For advice, it is probably best to consult your local and state health officials.

Methane:

Methane, CH_4, (also called natural gas and marsh gas) is found in oil wells, mines and marshes, and is produced by animals (e.g., by cattle) when they belch or pass gas. It is removed from the air by certain molecules and by some microbes in the soil, but is added to the air by cattle and humans passing gas. As the human and cattle populations increase, more methane is being generated. Since methane is a greenhouse-effect gas, any significant increases could increase the greenhouse effect.

Carbon monoxide:

Carbon monoxide is a colorless, odorless and tasteless gas and therefore is difficult to detect. It is slightly lighter than air, and is practically insoluble in water. Carbon monoxide is flammable, burning with a blue flame. With hydrogen, it made "water gas", which used to be used for cooking. Water gas is poisonous, because of its containing carbon monoxide, and so it has been replaced by "natural gas", which is methane, which is piped into buildings from oil wells.

Because carbon monoxide prevents hemoglobin, which is the red pigment in red blood cells, from combining with oxygen, the blood is unable to deliver oxygen to all the cells of the body, including the brain cells. The carbon monoxide combines with the hemoglobin to form carboxyhemoglobin, which slows down the blood's ability to carry oxygen.

When the concentration of carboxyhemoglobin approaches 15%, some of the following symptoms, which are similar to influenza symptoms, may occur:

- dizziness
- fatigue
- headache
- nausea
- irregular breathing (shortness of breath)
- unclear thinking
- vision problems
- loss of muscle control
- weakness

If a person experiences any of the above symptoms in the house, and they disappear when outside the house, but reoccur after reentering the house, then there may be a build-up of carbon monoxide inside.

Persons with a heart condition can be harmed by even lower doses. In fact, higher levels of carbon monoxide pollution increase the risk of congestive heart failure. When the concentration of carboxyhemoglobin approaches 50%, death may result in minutes to hours.

Large amounts of carbon monoxide are produced by incomplete combustion of coal, charcoal, oil, natural gas, propane, gasoline (in automotive engines), etc. The last one is why it is dangerous to leave an automobile running in a closed garage.

In nature, carbon monoxide is found in the atmosphere in trace amounts. It is also found in volcanic gasses along with hydrogen, sulfur dioxide, water vapor and carbon dioxide. Carbon monoxide is also formed in mine explosions.

When fuel-burning appliances such as furnaces, ranges, stoves (including wood-burning stoves), fireplaces, hot water heaters, space heaters, etc. are not working properly, carbon monoxide, which normally is vented to outside the house, may stay indoors, leading to a dangerous carbon monoxide build-up. Signs of carbon monoxide build-up inside include stuffy, stale or smelly air, high humidity or soot coming from a fireplace or heating system. Another cause of carbon monoxide build-up would be if someone brought a barbeque grill indoors to cook inside the house or closed garage; this must never be done.

It is an excellent idea to have a qualified technician check the furnace periodically. Carbon monoxide detectors are available.

SECTION IV: TEMPERATURE

Chapter 9. Temperature Scales and Thermometers

Three temperature scales are used in the United States, the Fahrenheit scale, which is from the English system of measurement, and the Celsius and Kelvin scales, which are from the metric system of measurement. For most of the rest of the world, the metric system is used. In the United States, we use the Fahrenheit temperature scale for most requirements (most research in the U.S. uses Celsius or Kelvin). The Celsius scale was originally called the Centigrade scale, but was changed in 1954 to Celsius in honor of its inventor. See chapter 1, the History of Meteorology, for more information on Messrs. Fahrenheit and Celsius.

The Fahrenheit scale (degrees Fahrenheit or °F.):

1. The freezing point of water (melting point of ice) at standard sea-level pressure is 32°F.

2. The boiling point of water at standard sea-level pressure is 212°F.

3. There are 180° between the freezing point of water and its boiling point.

4. <u>Absolute zero</u>, the temperature at which all molecular motion stops, is -459.67°F.

The Celsius scale (degrees Celsius or °C):

1. The freezing point of water (melting point of ice) at standard sea-level pressure is 0°C.

2. The boiling point of water at standard sea-level pressure is 100°C.

3. There are 100° between the freezing point of water and its boiling point.

4. Absolute zero, the temperature at which all molecular motion stops (there is no vibration, rotation or translation of even the smallest particles of matter within a mass) is -273.15°C.

General information about both Fahrenheit and Celsius scales:

1. Because there are 180 degrees between the freezing point of water and its boiling point in the Fahrenheit scale, and only 100 degrees between the freezing point of water and its boiling point in the Celsius scale, a change or difference of one Celsius degree is larger than a change or difference of one Fahrenheit degree. One Celsius degree is 9/5 or 1.8 Fahrenheit degrees. One Fahrenheit degree is 5/9 or .5555 Celsius degree.

2. Where the two scales read the same is at -40°; that is, forty degrees below zero Celsius equals forty degrees below zero Fahrenheit.

Figure 9-1. The Fahrenheit and Celsius temperature scales.
On the Celsius (C) scale, the freezing point of water at sea-level is set at zero degrees, and the boiling point at 100°C. On the Fahrenheit scale, freezing is 32°F and boiling is 212°F. Notice on the scale in the left of the figure, that one full Celsius degree equals 1.8 (or 9/5 ths) Fahrenheit degrees. (source: DOA)

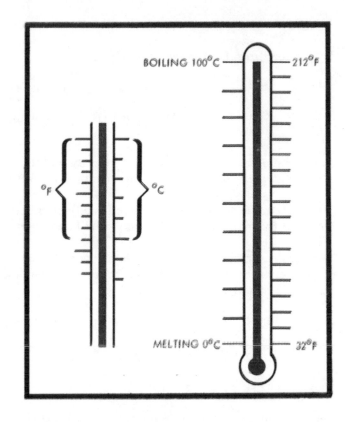

Three methods of converting from Fahrenheit to Celsius and vice versa are:

1. Use a thermometer that has both scales on it, such as in figure 9-1.

2. Use a table that gives the Fahrenheit reading in one column and its Celsius equivalent in the corresponding column.

By remembering a few conversions, it is easily to relate Celsius to Fahrenheit:

0 °C = 32°F	Notice that for every 5 degree change in Celsius
5° C = 41°F	degrees we have a 9 degree change in Fahrenheit
10°C = 50°F	degrees. For every 10 degree Celsius change,
15°C = 59°F	we have an 18 degree Fahrenheit change.
20°C = 68°F	
25°C = 77°F	
30°C = 86°F	
35°C = 95°F	
40°C = 104°F	

3. Use mathematics to convert between the Fahrenheit and Celsius temperature scales.

To convert from Celsius to Fahrenheit:

$$F = (9/5) C + 32$$

Example: Convert 30°C into degrees F: F = (9/5) 30 + 32 = 54 + 32 = 86°F

Another method is to multiply the Celsius temperature by 1.8 and then add 32:
Example: 30 x 1.8 = 54, then add 32 = 86°F

To convert from Fahrenheit to Celsius:

$$C = (F - 32) \times 5/9$$

Example: Convert minus 4 degrees (-4°F) into degrees C: C = (-4 -32) x 5/9 = -36 x 5/9 = -20°F

Another method is to subtract 32 from the Fahrenheit temperature and then multiply the result by 5/9: Example: -4 -32 = -36, then multiply by 5/9 which gives -20°C

Although many temperature scales have been invented and most discarded, three scales have emerged to be our favorites of use: the Fahrenheit scale, the Celsius scale and the Kelvin scale.

The Kelvin scale sets zero degrees as "absolute zero", the temperature at which there is absolutely no molecular or atomic or even subatomic movement...everything stops moving. A substance has no thermal energy at absolute zero.

0°K = -273.15°C = -459.67°F (to the nearest whole degree, absolute zero is -273°C)

To convert from Celsius to Kelvin:

K = C + 273

Thus, there are no negative numbers in the Kelvin scale, since the lowest the temperature of anything can ever be is absolute zero, which is set at zero degrees Kelvin (0°K).

Note that a change of one Kelvin degree is the same as a change of one Celsius degree.

We should note that some American engineers still use a temperature scale called the Rankine scale, where absolute zero is 0°R, and the degrees are the same as Fahrenheit degrees. Thus, since absolute zero is -460°F, then 0°F = 460°R. To convert from F to R, add 460 to the F temperature, and to convert from R to F, subtract 460 from the R temperature.

Thermometers:

There are several types of thermometers. The first type we will discuss is the liquid-in-glass thermometer. Refer to figure 9-1. A liquid, which expands when heated and contracts when cooled, is in a sealed glass tube upon which the degrees are marked.

The two major types of liquid-in-glass thermometers are the mercury thermometer and the colored alcohol thermometer.

The mercury thermometer uses mercury, which is a liquid metal until it is cooled to -38°F, which is when it becomes solid. Mercury is silver in color. Mercury thermometers are used in places that are not expected to even approach such a cold reading.

The colored alcohol thermometer uses alcohol, which is colored with a dye to make the liquid visible. Since the alcohol would freeze at about -174°F, and the coldest temperature reported in the world in the 20th century was -128.6°F in Antarctica, alcohol thermometers are widely used.

Figure 9-2. A special type of liquid-in-glass thermometer known as the U-tube thermometer. It records maximum, minimum and current temperatures. As the temperature rises, the mercury moves the metal index on the right to its highest reading; as the temperature falls, it moves the metal index on the left to its lowest reading. The current temperature is found by reading the top of the mercury column on the right side. (source: courtesy of Robert E. White Instruments, Inc.; Boston, MA)

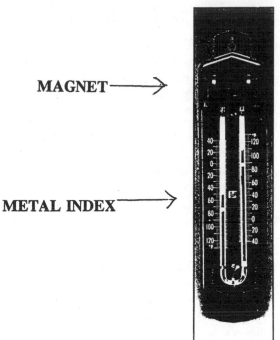

MAGNET——→

METAL INDEX——→

Figure 9-3. An instrument shelter. Weather instruments such as thermometers to measure temperature and hygrometers to measure relative humidity are mounted inside instrument shelters such as this one. Keep in mind that all temperatures for weather records purposes are temperatures taken in the SHADE, with the thermometers also protected from any falling and blowing precipitation, yet adequately ventilated by the air flowing through the louvered sides.

There are also special liquid-in-glass thermometers known as maximum thermometers and minimum thermometers. Both of these thermometers are mounted on a support such that the maximum thermometer can be whirled around, and the minimum thermometer can be turned upside down. The maximum thermometer has mercury in it but has a slight narrowing or constriction just above the thermometer bulb. The result is that as the temperature rises, the mercury in the glass tube rises, but when the temperature then falls, the mercury column then stays at the height it reached when the high temperature was hit. Thus, you can see how high the temperature got since the last time the thermometer was reset. To rest the maximum thermometer, the entire thermometer is whirled around for a minute or more, until the mercury is forced back through the constriction so that the thermometer then reads the current temperature. The minimum thermometer has colored alcohol in it, as well as a little (about an inch or so long) piece of dumbbell-shaped bamboo within the liquid column. The bamboo's weight is so light, that it moves down with the column as the temperature falls. The top of the bamboo piece would give the lowest temperature reading since the last time the thermometer was reset. The bamboo does not rise when warming causes the temperature to rise. To reset the minimum thermometer, turn it upside down so that the bamboo piece moves to the top of the alcohol column. Thus, the minimum thermometer also gives the current temperature.

Figure 9-4. A <u>dial-type thermometer</u>. Two dissimilar metals are welded together, forming what is called a compound bar. Both metals expand when heated and contract when cooled, but each metal at a different rate. Thus, the bar bends. The metal that expands and contracts the most is on the bend's outside. The thermometer dial is attached to the compound bar in a way to cause the dial to move to the right as the temperature rises, and left as it falls. These thermometers are slightly less accurate than liquid-in-glass thermometers, but are more rugged. (courtesy of Robert E. White Instruments, Inc.; Boston, MA)

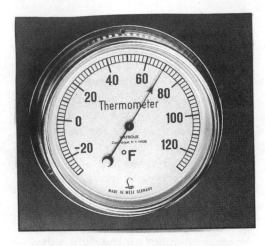

A light-weight and very narrow dial can be added to either side of the main dial, so that as the temperature rises, the maximum temperature can be read where the rightmost dial is pointing to on the scale, and the minimum temperature can be read where the leftmost dial is pointing to on the scale. As the main dial, the current temperature dial, moves to the right or left, it pushes the right or left dial along. These dials then stay at the high or low readings until reset by turning a little knob that moves yet another dial that lies outside all the others. That dial pushes the high and low dials back to the current temperature.

Figure 9-5. A <u>thermograph</u>. This is a recording thermometer, so that we have a continuous record of the temperature. It can be run by a clock-driven wind-up drum, or by electricity, as shown by the electric thermograph at right. However, should power fail and there is no back-up electric generator, then part of a record will be lost in an electrically-powered recorder. The object on the lower right is the sensing element, which is placed outdoors. (courtesy: Robert E. White Instruments, Inc.; Boston, MA)

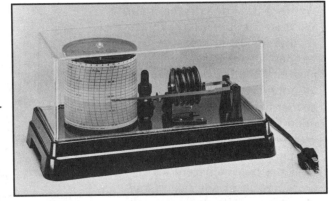

Both wind-up-type and electric-powered models have the temperature-recording paper, known as the thermogram, mounted on the drum, so that a week's worth of temperature recordings can be recorded on this special graph paper. Thus, a new thermogram is attached to the drum after removing the old one, only once a week. Clock-driven models require winding at this time, only once weekly. Periodically, ink must be added to the inkwell from which the recording dial gets its ink. (See figure 9-8.)

Another type of thermometer is the chemically-driven type. A <u>chemical thermometer</u> uses liquid crystals which activate by reflecting light and color at that temperature. For example, when the temperature is 80°F, the crystals in the paint seem to glow, because they are reflecting light and color. Then when the temperature rises to 81°, the chemical in the 80-degree digit becomes less active and no longer glows, but the chemical in the 81-degree paint does.

76

Figure 9-6. Display of a chemical thermometer. (photo by Joseph Balsama)

Figure 9-7. A digital thermometer. A <u>digital thermometer</u> can also be an <u>indoor-outdoor</u> <u>thermometer</u>, with a wire running to the outdoor sensor, as well as having an indoor sensor. Some indoor/outdoor thermometers are two liquid-in-tube thermometers mounted together. One thermometer records the indoor temperature and the other records the outdoor temperature. The outdoor thermometer has a sensing element attached to it, which is placed outdoors through a window or hole through an outside wall. Typical "bank thermometers" that you read as you drive by, are digital-type systems. They are typically electronically-powered. Electronic impulses from the outdoor sensing element are transmitted to the display sign, appearing as a lit-up digital output that gives the temperature, and can be programmed to give in series the time as well as the temperature in degrees F and C. Note the outdoor sensing element on the lower right.
(courtesy: Robert E. White Instruments, Inc.; Boston, MA)

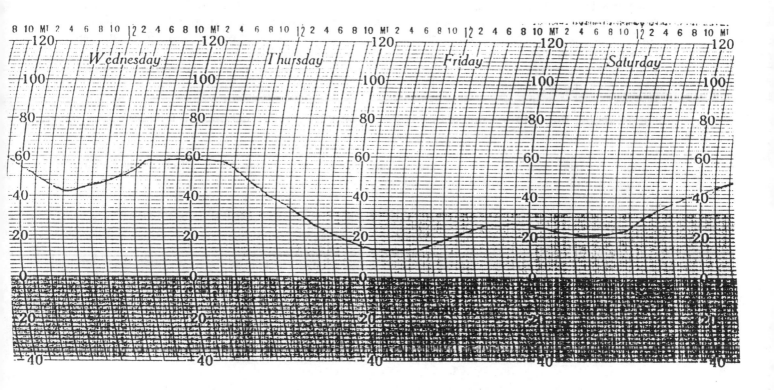

Figure 9-8. Part of a thermogram record.

Chapter 10. MAXIMUM, MINIMUM AND MEAN TEMPERATURES; HEATING, COOLING AND GROWING DEGREE DAYS; TEMPERATURE NORMALS AND EXTREMES

The daily <u>maximum temperature</u> is the highest that the temperature rises in a given day which begins at midnight and ends just before the next midnight. Records are kept with respect to standard time, so that even when we are on daylight savings time, the weather records remain on standard time. When there is no front or different air mass moving in, the highest temperature reading for the day typically occurs about 3 p.m. to 6 p.m. during daylight savings time, and about 2 p.m. to 5 p.m. during standard time.

The daily <u>minimum temperature</u> is the lowest that the temperature falls in a given day. When no weather system is coming in to change the air mass, or to change between clear and cloudy conditions (cloudy skies at night keep the air warmer), the lowest temperature reading for the day then typically occurs just after sunrise.

The daily <u>mean temperature</u> is the average for the day of the maximum and minimum temperatures.

Example: Yesterday's high temperature was 96°F, and yesterday's low was 72°F. What was the mean temperature for yesterday?

96° + 72° = 168°, then divide the sum by 2 to get 84°F for the mean temperature for yesterday.

<u>Heating degree days and cooling degree days:</u>

During the 1950s, heating engineers from the coal, gas, oil and electric industries, agreed that when the mean temperature for the day is below 65°F, then heating is required in buildings for people to be comfortable, and when the mean temperature for the day is above 65°F, then air conditioning is required. This is an average guideline and is used to help keep track of fuel consumption for heating and cooling. In the following discussion, **heating degree days can be thought of as heat deficiency units, and cooling degree days as heat surplus units.**

<u>Heating degree days</u> are the number of degrees that the mean temperature falls below (the base of) 65°F.

Example: Yesterday's high temperature was 45°F and the low was 15°F. How many heating degree days did we accumulate for the day?

First, compute the mean temperature: ½(45 + 15) = 30. Then subtract the mean from 65: 65 - 30 = 35. Thus, we had 35 heating degree days yesterday.

Records can be kept of monthly and seasonal totals of heating degree days, and can be compared with monthly and seasonal totals of fuel units used for heating, as well as with the cost of heating the building.

The heating degree day year begins on July 1st and ends on June 30th the following year.

<u>Cooling degree days</u> are the number of degrees that the mean temperature rises above 65°F.

Example: Yesterday's high temperature was 100°F and the low was 76°F. How many cooling degree days accumulated yesterday?

First, compute the mean temperature: ½(100 + 76) = 88. Then subtract 65 form the mean: 88 - 65 = 23. Thus, we had 23 cooling degree days yesterday.

As with the heating degree days, records are kept of the monthly and seasonal totals of cooling degree days, and can be compared with monthly and seasonal totals of fuel units used for cooling and dehumidifying, as well as with the cost of cooling the building. Unlike heating degree days, the cooling degree days year begins on January 1st and ends on December 31st.

Here is an example of keeping track of heating and cooling degree days for a community in North Dakota during a stretch of days in mid-September:

Day	Maximum Temperature	Minimum Temperature	Mean Temperature	Heating Degree Days	Cooling Degree Days
12th	85°F	65°F	75°F	0	10
13th	80°F	58°F	69°F	0	4
14th	74°F	56°F	65°F	0	0
15th	68°F	42°F	55°F	10	0
16th	45°F	25°F	35°F	30	0

Growing degree days: These are used in agricultural, in similar fashion to how the other degree days are computed, with the base temperature varying with the type of crop.

Example: A certain variety of corn was planted at a local farm on April 15th. If the corn is to be picked at its peak flavor, it must accumulate 890 growing degree days based on an average temperature of 55°F or higher. This particular strain of corn germinates, grows and matures only when the average temperature is 55 degrees or higher. After the crop has accumulated 890 growing degree days, the farmer picks the corn so that it can be sold, canned or frozen at its peak flavor.

The growing degree day scheme cannot be used if the area undergoes an prolonged period of unusually hot weather during the particular crop's growing season. In the example above, if an unusual month-long heat wave occurred and the 890 growing degree days were reached and surpassed well before the crop is ready for picking, then obviously this method for picking would be discarded for that season.

Normals are 30-year averages of each of the various weather elements such as temperature, barometric pressure, rainfall, snowfall, wind speed, etc. Records are also kept for the highest and lowest values ever reported of each of these variables, and are referred to as the extremes.

Normals are also calculated for such items as number of days with thunderstorms, the heating and cooling degree days, days with fog, daily percent of possible sunshine, and other items of climatological interest. Before moving to a new area, it is a good idea to check out the climatological record to know the normals and the extremes what has occurred and likely can be expected!

Current policy in the United States is to generate a new set of "normals" or averages every ten years, using the past 30 years of records. Changes in climate can be found by comparing the latest normals with previous sets.

Copies of records are stored at the National Climatic Data Center (NCDC) in Asheville, North Carolina, which also serves as a repository for the weather records of the United States. You can obtain copies of meteorological as well as climatological data from the NCDC.

Figure 10-1. Normal daily maximum and minimum temperatures for some American cities during selected months.

Keep in mind that these are AVERAGE readings, and also include all the extreme high and low readings during the 30-year period. Thus, for example, the average July daily high temperature for New York City is 84 degrees Fahrenheit, but the all-time highest temperature ever recorded in July may be 106 degrees. But the normals are useful to show the typical range of temperatures, which is also the range within which the temperatures are likely to be most of the time.

Thus, if someone is going to visit or stay or move to one of these regions, he or she can get an excellent idea of that climate by looking at the normals and the extremes of such weather elements as temperature, snowfall and rainfall, wind speed and cloud cover.

City	Jan	Mar	May	Jul	Sep	Nov
Boston, MA	36/22	45/32	67/50	81/65	72/57	52/39
Chicago, IL	31/15	45/27	70/47	83/61	75/52	48/31
Gulfport, MS	61/42	70/51	84/66	91/73	88/69	70/49
Honolulu, HI	79/65	80/66	84/70	87/73	87/73	83/70
Jacksonville, FL	65/44	72/50	85/64	90/72	86/70	71/51
Key West, FL	76/66	79/70	85/76	89/80	88/79	80/71
Memphis, TN	49/32	61/41	81/61	92/72	84/63	62/40
Minneapolis, MN	21/03	37/20	68/46	82/61	71/49	41/24
New Orleans, LA	62/44	70/51	85/65	90/73	87/70	70/50
New York, NY	38/26	47/34	70/54	84/69	75/61	53/41
Norfolk, VA	49/32	57/39	76/57	87/70	80/64	60/43
Pensacola, FL	61/43	70/51	84/66	90/74	86/70	70/49
Portland, ME	31/12	41/23	64/42	79/57	70/47	47/30
San Diego, CA	65/46	66/50	69/57	75/64	77/63	70/52
San Francisco, CA	55/41	61/45	67/50	71/54	74/54	63/47
Seattle, WN	43/33	52/37	64/46	75/54	69/50	50/39
Washington, DC	41/23	53/31	74/51	86/64	79/55	56/34

DEMONSTRATION: SOME EXAMPLES OF USING CLIMATOLOGICAL DATA

The purpose of this activity is to carefully guide you through a series of steps in using climatological data. All necessary tables of data are provided by the National Weather Service.

The following table gives the latest thirty-year set of normals for the maximum, minimum, mean (average) temperatures, heating degree days, cooling degree days and precipitation for a location of interest for the first five days of September.

Date	Maximum Temp. (°F)	Minimum Temp. (°F)	Mean (average) Temp. (°F)	Heating Degree Days	Cooling Degree Days	Precipitation
1	76	61	68	1	4	.11
2	76	61	68	1	4	.11
3	76	61	68	1	4	.11
4	76	60	68	1	4	.11
5	76	60	68	1	4	.11

The table below gives what was actually recorded at this same location during the first five days of September. Start with the second table and go to the first one to answer the questions.

Day	Maximum Temp. (°F)	Minimum Temp. (°F)	Mean (average) Temp. (°F)	Heating Degree Days	Cooling Degree Days	Precipitation
1	90	82	86	0	21	1.42
2	82	48	65	0	0	.62
3	60	38	49	16	0	0.00
4	65	45	55	10	0	0.00
5	82	68	75	0	10	1.53

Question #1: What was the departure from normal of the maximum temperature for Sept. 1st?

Solution: 90°F (actual maximum temperature for Sept. 1st for this location)
 - 76°F (normal maximum temperature for Sept. 1st for this location)
    14°F above normal or a +14°F departure from normal

Question #2: What was the departure from normal of the minimum temperature for this date?

Solution: 82°F (actual minimum temperature for Sept. 1st for this location)
 - 61°F (normal minimum temperature for Sept. 1st for this location)
    21°F above normal or a +21°F departure from normal

Question #3: Do the same for the departure from normal for the mean temperature for Sept. 1st and you will find the answer to be a +18°F departure from normal.

The same procedure is done to determine if there are any departures for degree days. Precipitation "normals" are simply distributing the average monthly rainfall throughout the month on a daily basis.

Day	Max.	Year	Min.	Year
1	90	1881	36	1992
2	88	1954	34	1889
3	85	1922	35	1889
4	85	1983*	34	1888
5	87	1922	28	1881
6	86	1990*	31	1883
7	90	1963	30	1883
8	88	1879	35	1964
9	82	1935	32	1873
10	87	1939	32	1979
11	82	1955	32	1979*
12	90	1954	31	1876
13	87	1930	30	1875
14	81	1923	31	1875
15	86	1897	30	1883
16	88	1897	30	1883
17	89	1947	27	1886
18	82	1947	31	1939*
19	84	1945	28	1922
20	79	1969	32	1974*
21	82	1920	30	1974
22	83	1979	28	1940
23	84	1947	29	1883
24	80	1900	30	1969
25	80	1963	26	1879
26	84	1963	25	1879
27	85	1963	25	1936
28	81	1927	28	1936
29	79	1918	26	1876
30	78	1918	28	1928
31	81	1946	27	1904

Let us take a look at a table, at right, of the all-time daily record temperatures recorded at Boston, Massachusetts.

These official records are for the month of October, and are continous since the year 1870. Suppose a new record high occurs this year on the 1st, with a reading of 94 degrees F. Then you would obviously cross out the old record of 90 degrees and the old year of 1881 and replace these with 94 degrees and this year, respectively.

You can record and keep your own records at home, and after several years begin to have your own developing climatological records. It is useful as well as enjoyable to keep your own records of the various weather parameters, as well as having a set of the daily, monthly and yearly records, including the normals, of such parameters as temperature, precipitation, windspeed and barometric pressure. In areas that receive snow, the snowfall records, including the normals, are particularly fascinating. If there is no continuously reporting weather station reasonably close to you (or even if there is), you might want to start your own weather observation station and keep your own records, if you are not already doing so. Weather is indeed one of the most enjoyable pasttimes!

* Also occurred in earlier years.

(prepared by Robert E. Lautzenheiser, former Massachusetts State Climatologist)

An important note about climatological averages or normals:

So-called normals are not really "normals" at all, except in the sense that they give us the averages of observed weather parameters for the most recent thirty year period of record that was used to compute them. If the climate is changing, then the next computation of "normals" will be different. Assuming that if there is any climatic change, that it is very gradual, then the value of using climatological normals is that we can indeed see the departures from these normals of weather parameters such as the daily and monthly high, low and mean temperatures, and the monthly rainfall, snowfall and percent of possible sunshine, for examples. Keep in mind that the complete data base also includes the extremes of values of weather parameters ever recorded for each location. It is important to know what the daily, monthly and all-time record high and low temperatures are, as well as the extremes of the most and least rain and snow, the strongest winds, the most days with thunderstorms, etc. These weather factors affect our lifestyles. Before we move to a location, we would want to check out the climatological information to determine how we will accommodate to the climate in that location.

Chapter 11. HEAT INDEX; WIND CHILL

The temperature alone may not account for the stress put on humans and animals during very hot and very cold conditions. For example, during heat waves, physical exertion needs to be tempered to avoid heat stress or heat stroke, especially when the heat is combined with high humidity.

Over the years, scientists have developed various indices to describe what the temperature feels like, compared with what it really is. During high temperatures, the increase in humidity, that is, of moisture in the air, makes it seem hotter than it actually is, and during very cold weather, any increase in wind speed makes it feel colder than it actually is.

High humidity with hot temperatures prevent a good amount of perspiration from evaporating and cooling us. Strong winds with very cold weather take heat away from the body faster than without the wind.

HEAT INDEX CHART

Temperature (°F) and % of Relative Humidity versus Heat Index (apparent temperature)

	0%	5%	10%	15%	20%	25%	30%	35%	40%	45%	50%	55%	60%	65%	70%	75%	80%	85%	90%	95%	100%
140°F	125																				
135°F	120	128																			
130°F	117	122	131																		
125°F	111	116	123	131	141																
120°F	107	111	116	123	130	139	148														
115°F	103	107	111	115	120	127	135	143	151												
110°F	99	102	105	108	112	117	123	130	137	143	150										
105°F	95	97	100	102	105	109	113	118	123	129	135	142	149								
100°F	91	93	95	97	99	101	104	107	110	115	120	126	132	138	144						
95°F	87	88	90	91	93	94	96	98	101	104	107	110	114	119	124	130	136				
90°F	83	84	85	86	87	88	90	91	93	95	96	98	100	102	106	109	113	117	122		
85°F	78	79	80	81	82	83	84	85	86	87	88	89	90	91	93	95	97	99	102	105	108
80°F	73	74	75	76	77	77	78	79	79	80	81	81	82	83	85	86	86	87	88	89	91

Figure 11-1. Heat Index Table. Combine the current air temperature (left column) with the current relative humidity (top column) to find what the temperature actually feels like (the heat index), found in a box in the table. For example, a temperature of 95 degrees F. with a relative humidity of 55% gives an apparent temperature (heat index) of 110 degrees. (source: NWS)

Most people feel uncomfortable when high temperatures are combined with high humidities. When the relative humidity is low with high temperatures, our body can more readily evaporate perspiration to give some cooling effect. However, the higher the humidity, the less perspiration is evaporated.

Over the years, various attempts to describe the apparent temperature by combining the temperature and humidity (or dewpoint) have been done. In the 1960s, a "discomfort index" (later called a "comfort index") was developed, which was soon replaced by the "temperature-humidity index" or "THI". The THI could still be used today, if we wanted to utilize it. Its formula is:

THI = 15 + 0.4 (dry-bulb temperature + wet-bulb temperature).
[Note: temperatures are in degrees F.]

The dry-bulb temperature is simply the current air temperature using a liquid-in-glass thermometer whose bulb is not wet, and the wet-bulb temperature is the temperature of a thermometer which has a wick around its bulb which is dipped in water and then whirled around or fanned until the temperature reading is lowered and cannot be lowered any more. Thus, maximum cooling by evaporation is done on the wet bulb. The closer the dry and wet bulb temperatures are to each other, the moister is the air. The wet bulb temperature is not the dewpoint temperature, but the dewpoint can be computed by knowing the dry and wet bulb temperatures.

We can interpret the THI values as follows:

a THI of 70 suggests that most everyone is comfortable;
each THI increase of 1 means about 10% more of the population is uncomfortable;
thus, a THI of 76 e.g. means that about 60% of us are uncomfortable;
a THI of 80 means just about everyone is uncomfortable due to the combination of heat and humidity;
any THI of 80 or above is dangerous for strenuous work, especially outside under a blazing sun.

The heat index has replaced the THI although both measurement systems of comfort/discomfort may be used.

The following table shows the estimated relationship of heat indices to potential health dangers:

Heat Index	Condition	Heat Effect on Humans
85° to 94° F.	caution	fatigue with prolonged exposure and physical activities
95° to 105°F.	extreme	sunstroke, heat cramps, or heat exhaustion possible with prolonged exposure and physical activities
above 105°F.	danger	heatstroke, sunstroke or heat exhaustion a good possibility with prolonged exposure and physical activity

The heat effects or heat syndromes on humans and animals can be fatal. The heat syndromes caused by the reduction of the body's ability to lose sufficient heat in sufficient time include heat cramps, heat exhaustion and heat stroke.

Heat exhaustion is accompanied by profuse perspiring (colloquially called "sweating"). Light-skinned people turn pale. The skins of us humans of all our various colors will become cool and clammy. The pulse rate may become weak with breathing becoming rapid. The blood pressure is unusually low. A person may feel dizzy and faint. Headache and muscular cramps may develop. Ironically, with heat exhaustion, the body temperature is usually normal or lower than normal. A person suffering heat exhaustion should be laid down in a cool quiet place with his/her feet slightly raised. Clothing should be loosened and liquids should be given.

Heat stroke has no perspiring of "sweating", but the body temperature rises to about 104°F or higher. The skin of lighter people becomes flushed and pink initially, and later appears ashen or purplish. For all people suffering heat stroke, no matter what color our skin, there will be a rapid pulse and an elevation in blood pressure. The victim may become confused and slip into a coma. Medical attention or hospitalization is required immediately. To delay can be fatal. While awaiting medical attention, remove as much clothing as possible and wrap the victim in a cold wet sheet or sponge the person with cold water. Fan him/her by hand or use a hair dryer set to cold.

Here are recommendations that are common knowledge in dealing with hot and humid weather:

- Slow down. Do only what is absolutely necessary. Put off outdoor activities until the weather cools down.
- Drink plenty of liquids, but not caffeinated or alcoholic beverages.
- Wear a cap or hat and sunglasses, and use sunscreen protection. Sunburn can slow down the skin's ability to shed excess heat.
- Wear light-colored and lightweight clothing outdoors. Lighter colors repel more of the sunlight.
- Never leave anyone, including children, and pets, waiting in a closed automobile. The sun beating down on the vehicle can raise the inside temperature to well in excess of 100°F.

Consider one example of a prolonged heat wave in just one metropolitan area. In July 1995, many daily and some all-time high temperature records were set across much of the United States. In Chicago, the heat index exceeded 120 degrees. At least 550 people died in Chicago alone from this one heat wave.

Life-threatening situations also occur with very cold weather, if we are not protected against this cold. The U.S. military developed the wind chill temperature based on experiments about how fast heat is removed from the body as the wind increases. The combination of cold and wind makes us feel even colder than if there were no wind. Thus, heat is removed from the unprotected body faster when it is windy compared to when it is calm, and we feel colder. The table below gives the wind chill temperature based on this combination of actual temperature and wind speed.

AIR TEMPERATURE (°F)

Wind Speed (miles per hour)	35	30	25	20	15	10	5	0	-5	-10	-15	-20	-25	-30	-35	-40	-45
4	35	30	25	20	15	10	5	0	-5	-10	-15	-20	-25	-30	-35	-40	-45
5	32	27	22	16	11	6	0	-5	-10	-15	-21	-26	-31	-36	-42	-47	-52
10	22	16	10	3	-3	-9	-15	-22	-27	-34	-40	-46	-52	-58	-64	-71	-77
15	16	9	2	-5	-11	-18	-25	-31	-38	-45	-51	-58	-65	-72	-78	-85	-92
20	12	4	-3	-10	-17	-24	-31	-39	-46	-53	-60	-67	-74	-81	-88	-95	-103
25	8	1	-7	-15	-22	-29	-36	-44	-51	-59	-66	-74	-81	-88	-96	-103	-110
30	6	-2	-10	-18	-25	-33	-41	-49	-56	-64	-71	-79	-86	-93	-101	-109	-116
35	4	-4	-12	-20	-27	-35	-43	-52	-58	-67	-74	-82	-89	-97	-105	-113	-120
40	3	-5	-13	-21	-29	-37	-45	-53	-60	-69	-76	-84	-92	-100	-107	-115	-123
45	2	-6	-14	-22	-30	-38	-46	-54	-62	-70	-78	-85	-93	-102	-109	-117	-125

WIND SPEEDS GREATER THAN 40 MPH HAVE LITTLE ADDITIONAL CHILLING EFFECT

Figure 11-2. The wind chill chart. This is used only for cold temperatures. As the temperature gets lower and the wind speed increases, we feel colder since heat is removed from the uncovered body faster. For example, from the chart, a temperature of zero degrees Fahrenheit with a wind of 30 miles per hour feels like 49 degrees below zero Fahrenheit. This would be extremely dangerous for exposed flesh, which would freeze in a very short time. PAGE 75

Figure 11-3. We can enjoy the great outdoors, but we must be properly protected from harsh winter weather conditions. Wearing layers of warm clothing is essential, as well as covering exposed parts of the body. Much heat is lost through the head, which is why a warm hat is necessary during cold and windy weather. Consider this: with a wind chill temperature of 25 below zero F., exposed human flesh will freeze within one minute!

Two very serious conditions can occur with dangerous wind chill temperatures: frostbite and hypothermia.

Frostbite occurs when very cold temperatures stop the flow of blood. In severe cases, the skin may be permanently damaged and gangrene may result, necessitating the amputation of the affected area. (Gangrene is the death and decay of body tissue due to an insufficient flow of blood.) Body tips such as toes, fingers, hands, feet, nose, ears, face, etc. are the most vulnerable and must be protected against low wind chill temperatures.

If a frostbitten area is treated quickly, the skin may be saved. Initially, the skin of a light-colored person turns pale, since the blood and tissue fluids freeze. When thawing out, the skin becomes red and painful, and blisters may form. The frostbite victim needs immediate medical attention.

Fingers and toes can be placed in lukewarm water, and as they thaw out, the victim should move them to encourage blood circulation. If outdoors, frostbitten areas must be covered up and warmed. Never rub the skin, as damage may result.

Hypothermia is abnormally low body temperature. Average body temperature is 98.6°F. Exposure to cold temperatures of the air or in water for a long-enough time will cause the body's temperature to drop. Death can result if hypothermia persists for a few hours, especially if the body temperature drops below 90 degrees Fahrenheit.

A victim suffering hypothermia requires immediate medical attention. Pale and cold skin and loss of consciousness occurs. Cardio-pulmonary resuscitation (CPR) must be applied to an unconscious victim, who must also be taken out of cold and wet clothing and covered with warm blankets and similar material. If the person is conscious, give him/her warm drinks. **Gradual warming** is required, since too rapid a warming may cause blood vessels to dilate, filling with blood so rapidly that vital organs may be deprived of their supply of blood.

When travelling, working or playing outdoors in cold weather, especially in very cold and windy weather, we must:
● Wear several layers of clothing. This is better than one heavy coat since the layers of air between the clothing act as insulators.
● Wear gloves, a hat, wool-type stockings and insulated boots. Cover your face with a scarf or pull-down cap. The body loses a large amount of heat through the head, which is why wearing a warm hat that covers the ears is vital.
● Eat a well-balanced diet, since your body uses up digested food to generate internal heat.

Figure 11-4. Human comfort and safety often require that we take common-sense actions when the weather is excessively hot or excessively cold. (source: USN)

SECTION V: ATMOSPHERIC PRESSURE

Chapter 12. AIR PRESSURE; BAROMETERS

Before we can discuss atmospheric pressure (also called barometric pressure), we must recall that cold air weighs more than warm air, and that dry air weighs more than moist air. Here is the explanation.

Cold air is heavier than warm air: The colder the air, the slower its molecules move, and the less space they take; therefore, more of them can be placed in a given area. For example, if we have a six-passenger elevator, we can easily fit six adults into it, especially if they do not move about. If they decided to dance, we would have to open the door to allow most of them to dance on the platform. By analogy, the reason cold air weighs more than warm is that there are more air molecules in a mass of cold air than in a mass of warm air.

Dry air is heavier than moist air: Moist air contains more water vapor (water in the form of a gas) than does dry air. We know that (liquid) water weighs more than air; however, here we are concerned with water vapor. Let us assume that dry air is comprised of about 99% by volume of oxygen and nitrogen, and ignore the other gasses. To determine the molecular weight of dry air, we make the following calculations in the table below.

GASES THAT MAKE UP DRY AIR	FORMULA OF GASES	ATOMIC MASS (SUM OF THE PROTONS AND NEUTRONS IN A SINGLE ATOM)	NUMBER OF ATOMS THAT MAKE UP A SINGLE MOLECULE	MOLECULAR WEIGHT (THE SUM OF THE ATOMIC MASSES OF ALL ITS ATOMS)	PERCENT OF ATM. BY VOLUME	CORRECTED VALUE
Oxygen	O_2	16 x	2 =	32 x	21 =	7
Nitrogen	N_2	14 x	2 =	28 x	78 =	22

Note that from the table above we can conclude that the molecular weight of dry air is about 29 (i.e., 7 + 22).

Now let us determine the molecular weight of water vapor in the table below.

GASES THAT MAKE UP WATER VAPOR	FORMULA OF EACH GAS IN THE MOLECULE	ATOMIC MASS (SUM OF THE PROTONS AND NEUTRONS IN A SINGLE ATOM)	NUMBER OF ATOMS THAT MAKE UP A SINGLE MOLECULE	MOLECULAR WEIGHT (THE SUM OF THE ATOMIC MASSES OF ALL ITS ATOMS)
Hydrogen	H_2	1 x	2 =	2
Oxygen	O	16 x	1 =	16

Note that from the table above we can conclude that the molecular weight of water vapor is about 18 (i.e., 2 for 2 atoms of hydrogen, each weighing 1 atomic unit, and 1 atom of oxygen, weighing 16 atomic units).

Most of the time, the percentage by volume of water vapor in the lower atmosphere over any local area varies from near zero to about 4%. Thus, wherever and whenever the percentage of water vapor increases, we are replacing some dry air, which has a molecular weight of 29, with water vapor, which has a molecular weight of 18. Because the total number of molecules in a column of both dry or moist air remains the same, the moist air, which is comprised of dry air plus water vapor, weighs less than does all dry air, which is comprised mostly of nitrogen and oxygen.

Another way of looking at this is to think of a mass of dry air as a pile of heavy bricks (nitrogen and oxygen molecules with a molecular weight of 29), and a mass of moist air as a pile of bricks from which several have been replaced by lighter brick-shaped sponges (water vapor molecules with a molecular weight of 18).

At the bottom of the atmosphere we find that almost 99% of our air, if it were completely dry, is comprised of nitrogen and oxygen, with the other about 1% being argon, with traces of other gasses. However, when the air is moist, as stated earlier, water vapor can comprise up to about 4 percent of the volume.

The atmospheric pressure, therefore, is the sum total of the individual or partial pressure exerted by each component gas of the atmosphere.

Now we are ready to define pressure precisely: **pressure is force per unit area.** It is measured in metric units of dynes per square centimeter, joules per meter, hectoPascals (which are also called millibars), bars (there are 1000 millibars in a bar), or in English units of pounds per square inch or atmospheres. One bar of pressure is one million dynes per square centimeter, so one millibar (which is one one-thousandth of a bar) of pressure is 1000 dynes per square centimeter.

The atmospheric pressure you feel is the weight of the atmosphere above you pushing down on every square inch of you. At sea-level, the average atmospheric pressure is about 14.7 pounds per square inch or about 1013.25 millibars (hectoPascals) [which reads 29.925" on the barometer]. Using the English units for our explanation, this means that on every square inch of the outside of your body, if you were at sea-level, you would have 14.7 pounds per square inch pushing in. You might ask, why doesn't the human body get crushed or pushed in by the air pressure weighing on every square inch of us? The reason the air does not start to crush us is that we also have air inside of us, which helps to push out at 14.7 pounds per square inch also, so that the net pressure effect on our body is zero. However, we still notice rapid pressure changes when the body has not quite had enough time to adapt, such as when you take a rapid elevator ride to the top of a tall skyscraper. You are going higher in altitude so there is somewhat less air from you to the top of the atmosphere (the air pressure is then less on you because the total weight of the column of air from you on up is less). You might have 14.5 pounds of pressure per square inch on you, but the pressure from inside your body is still 14.7 and needs up to few seconds to decrease to 14.5. The result is that your ears "pop". Air is pushing out and it is easily sensed in your ear channels.

As long as the pressure on the outside of an object (if underwater the pressure would come from the water, not the air) is equal the pressure on the inside, the object is in a state of pressure equilibrium. When a balloon is not inflated, the pressure on its inside pushing outward is equal to the pressure on its outside pushing inward. When we inflate the balloon, the pressure on the inside pushing out is greater than the outside pressure pushing in. If we untie the opening of the balloon, the air will flow from the inside to the outside, creating WIND. A wind blows from a region where the pressure is relatively high to adjoining regions where the pressure is lower. The greater the difference in pressure over the same distance, the stronger is the wind (the faster the air moves). Thus, in our balloon example, the more air you place into the balloon without bursting it, the faster the air will come out during deflation.

When an air mass is cold and dry, its highest air pressure is likely higher than 14.7 pounds per square inch, since cold air weighs more than warm air, and dry air weighs more than the same volume of air with some moisture in it. Likewise, when the air is warm and moist, its lowest air pressure is likely lower than 14.7 pounds per square inch.

Now let us consider a day when the barometric pressure (the barometer measures the atmospheric pressure) is 14.7 pounds per square inch. We can take a three foot (just under a meter) long glass tube that is closed at one end, and fill it with mercury, which is a liquid metal that readily responds to changes in atmospheric pressure. We then invert the mercury-filled tube into a container of mercury. The 14.7 pounds per square inch of air pressure will force the mercury to rise to a level of about 29.92" (about 760 millimeters) upward in the tube.

When the air pressure is less, i.e., when it falls, it can no longer support (force) the mercury to remain at 29.92", so the mercury level drops to a lower height. When the air pressure is higher, i.e., when it rises, above 14.7 lbs/sq. in., it forces the mercury to rise higher in the tube.

What we have just described is a mercury barometer, first invented by one of Galileo's students, Evangelista Torricelli.

Sometimes a reference is made to "whole atmospheres", where a 29.925" reading is "one whole atmosphere", and values above one and below one are proportional to how the pressure readings rise or fall below one atmosphere.

Figure 12-1. Units of atmospheric pressure measured by a barometer, showing and comparing the different measurement scales. The average <u>sea-level</u> pressure is underlined.

Millibars (hectoPascals)	Inches of Mercury	Centimeters of Mercury	Millimeters of Mercury	Atmospheres
940	27.76	70.49	704.9	0.926
950	28.05	71.25	712.5	0.937
960	28.35	72.01	720.1	0.947
970	28.65	72.77	727.7	0.957
980	28.94	73.51	735.1	0.967
990	29.24	74.27	742.7	0.977
1000	29.53	75.01	750.1	0.987
1010	29.83	75.77	757.7	0.997
<u>1013.2</u>	<u>29.92</u>	<u>76.00</u>	<u>760.0</u>	<u>1.000</u>
1020	30.12	76.50	765.0	1.006
1030	30.42	77.27	772.7	1.016
1040	30.71	78.00	780.0	1.026
1050	31.01	78.77	787.7	1.035

Figure 12-2. Atmospheric pressure is analyzed on surface weather maps. Lines that connect locations with equal pressure are drawn, called <u>isobars</u>). The units used to measure atmospheric pressure on this map are in millibars, also called hectoPascals (e.g., 1016 millibars, 1020 millibars of pressure). H designates the centers of highest pressure, and L the centers of lowest pressure. We shall study these weather features later in this book. (source: USN)

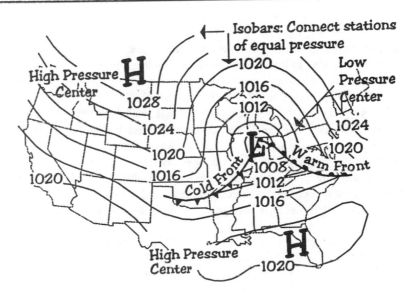

<u>DEMONSTRATION</u>: HOW STRONG CAN AIR PRESSURE BE?

<u>Materials needed</u>: an empty metal can; a solid rubber stopper that fits the can's opening; a heat source such as a stove or Bunsen burner; and a measuring cup or graduated cylinder.

<u>Procedure</u>:
1. Before starting the demonstration, ensure that the metal can is clean on both inside and outside, especially if it was used to hold a flammable liquid.
2. Replace any screw-on metal cap with the solid rubber stopper of the right size. Do not use a cork because of its porosity.
3. Using a measuring cup or graduated cylinder, pour about 200 milliliters (about 8 ounces) of water into the can.
4. Place the can without the stopper on the heat source and allow the water to boil vigorously for about two minutes.
5. Remove the can from the heat source and immediately place the rubber stopper on its opening, making sure that the seal is tight. Do NOT place the rubber stopper on the can while it is on the heat source.
6. Now wait a few minutes. What do you observe?
7. Explain why what you observed happened.

BAROMETERS

A <u>barometer</u> is an instrument which measures atmospheric pressure. The original barometers used colored water, but the glass tube required was well over 30 feet high, which is why Torricelli invented the mercurial barometer, which requires a tube of no more than about three feet.

<u>DEMONSTRATION</u>: MAKING A MERCURY BAROMETER

<u>WARNING</u>: Mercury is a toxic element. This demonstration must be done by an appropriate science teacher or other person experienced in this matter. The demonstration must also be done in a fume hood. The fumes of mercury (mercury vapor) are poisonous, and the mercury liquid itself can be absorbed by the skin, so that latex gloves must be used during this demonstration.

<u>Materials needed</u>: mercury; a 50 to 100 milliliter beaker; a medicine dropper; an electric vacuum pump; some petroleum jelly; a three-foot (or nearly one meter) tube that is open on one end and closed on the other end; a tall bell jar that will fit over the glass tube; a meter stick.

<u>Procedure</u>:

1. Everyone using the mercury must put on latex gloves.
2. Fill the 50 milliliter beaker about one-quarter with mercury.
3. Using the medicine dropper, carefully fill the tube with mercury. It might take two people to do this: one to hold the tube and the other to fill it with mercury.
4. Block the opening of the tube with a finger that is protected by a latex glove, and invert the tube into the beaker of mercury. Remove the finger from the opening when the opening is below the surface of the mercury.
5. The air pressure in the room will force the mercury in the beaker to rise into the tube. The higher the air pressure, the higher is the height of the mercury in the tube. The space above the mercury column is a vacuum, since all the air was forced out of the tube when it was initially filled with mercury.
6. Place the beaker and tube of mercury on the vacuum pump.
7. Coat the base of the bell jar with petroleum jelly and carefully place it over the tube, making sure that its base makes a tight seal.
8. Using your meter stick measure the height of the mercury in the tube, in centimeters, and to the nearest quarter-inch. (Recall you can convert centimeters to millimeters by multiplying the number of centimeters by ten). What you have just measured is the barometric pressure of the air.
(continued)

9. Now turn on the vacuum pump and watch the mercury level in the tube fall, since the air pressure inside the bell jar is being reduced.
10. When the mercury level stops falling, measure its height in centimeters and to the nearest quarter inch.
11. Turn off the vacuum pump and notice how the pressure begins to rise.
12. Why are you not able to move or remove the bell jar before the barometric pressure returns to what it was before you turned on the vacuum pump?

Mercury barometers can be purchased through many suppliers of scientific instrumentation. Because they are the most accurate of all types of barometers, they are used in weather stations and in many science (such as physics) laboratories where many of the lab activities require the correct barometric pressure.

Note: Mercury also expands some when heated and contracts some when cooled, so there is a temperature effect on this metal, not just a pressure effect. In weather stations, there is a slight correction to the mercurial level reading, based on the average temperature for the past twelve hours.

Figure 12-3 is a generalized diagram of a mercurial barometer.

Figure 12-3. A generalized illustration of how a mercury barometer works.

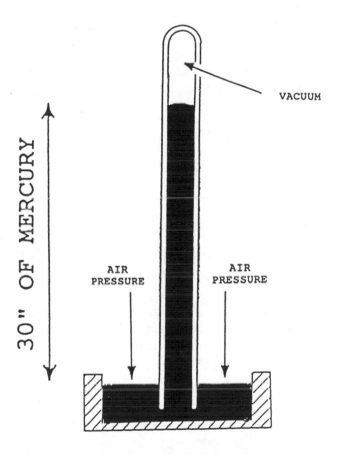

Nowadays, most barometers do not use mercury at all. Instead, they use a small metal container such as a cylinder, which has all the air taken from it. Thus, there is a vacuum inside the cylinder, and if the metal is soft enough, this cylinder will slightly compress inward as the air pressure rises, and slightly expand when the air pressure falls. A spring and dial are attached to this cylinder so that the dial moves in one direction when the pressure rises, and the opposite direction when it falls. The other end of the dial moves across a calibrated scale which uses the same units as does the mercurial barometer, e.g., 30.10", 29.45", 30.74", etc. This type of barometer is called an **aneroid barometer** (see next figure).

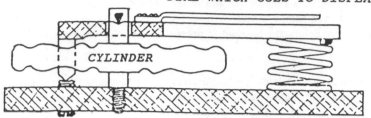

DIAL WHICH GOES TO DISPLAY

CYLINDER

DISPLAY

Figure 12-4. An Aneroid Barometer. As the air pressure changes, the vacated cylinder expands or contracts, causing the dial to move.

In 1648, Blaise Pascal of France carried a barometer up a mountain to show that atmospheric pressure decreases with increasing altitude. If you are at sea-level, you have all the air parcels from you to the top of the atmosphere weighing down on you at about 14.7 pounds per square inch. But if you are on top of a 10,000-foot high mountain, then you have only the atmosphere from 10,000 feet up to the top weighing down at you, and at that elevation you'd have a force of about 10.3 pounds per square inch.

If the air pressure at sea-level happens to be 30.00", then:

ELEVATION:	PRESSURE WOULD BE:
sea-level	30.00"
5,000 feet	about 25.50"
10,000 feet	about 21.00"
18,000 feet	about 15.00"
29,000 feet	about 9.00"
39,000 feet	about 6.00"

Thus, there is not a linear relationship between the altitude and the pressure except for the first few thousand feet. That is, the pressure does not decrease at the same rate for the same increase in altitude. Only in the first few thousand feet can we say that the air pressure decreases about one inch on the barometer for every 900 feet increase in elevation.

As we go above 5000 feet, then the pressure decreases more and more slowly as we keep going up. This is because most of the heavier molecules of gasses that comprise the mixture of gasses we call the atmosphere are found in the lowest parts of the atmosphere, and as we go up we find the lighter gasses such as hydrogen and helium which gradually thin out until there are no more molecules and atoms of the lightest gas, hydrogen. The top of the atmosphere is about 600 miles out.

Figure 12-5. Temperature has an affect on pressure. At right are representations of three columns of air. One column is cold, one (the middle one) is average or moderate, and the last column is warm or hot. The pressure at the bottom of each column of air is the same. Also,

THE EFFECT OF TEMPERATURE ON PRESSURE

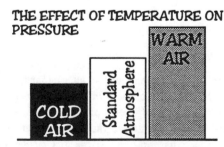

the pressure at the top of each column of air is the same. Notice that the cold air is denser: the column is not as tall as the warmer columns. The warm or hot column is the tallest. Therefore, the rate of decrease of the air pressure as we go up, also depends on the temperature of the air. (source: USN)

PAGE 82

Figure 12-6. A record of the atmospheric
pressure at your house can be kept by a
recording barograph. The chart of a clock-
driven drum will slowly rotate, as the
recording pen attached to the aneroid
barometer makes its trace on the chart.
An entire week of barometric pressure
record can be taken this way. The
barograph can be powered by the winding
of a spring every week, or, as in this picture,
by electricity. (source: Robert E. White
Instruments, Inc.; Boston, MA)

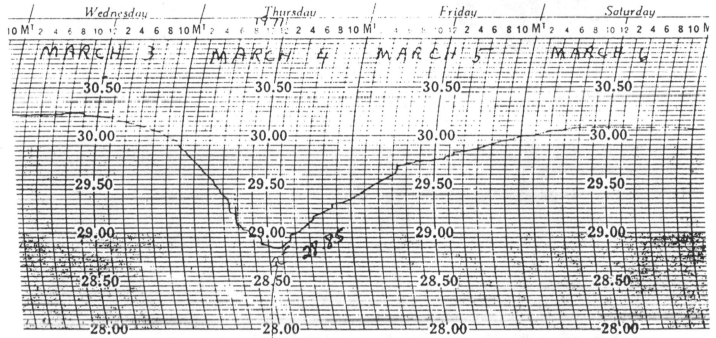

Figure 12-7. A part of a weekly barograph record, a barogram, showing how the pressure went
down during a major storm (low pressure system)
and then rose as high pressure moved in when the
storm left. Time goes from left to right on this chart.
(source: Joseph J. Balsama)

Figure 12-8. A rapid fall of
air pressure during the
passage of a hurricane at
Sandy Hook, New Jersey.
    Notice how the pressure
fell from 29.60" at 10 a.m.
to 28.70" at 2 p.m. When
the air pressure changes
so rapidly, very high winds
are occurring. We shall
study this later in this book.
(source: NWS)

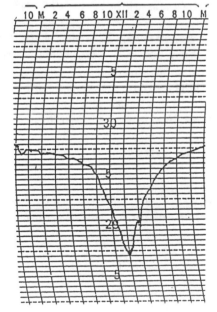

An aneroid barometer that is graduated to read in feet above the ground rather than in inches of mercury is called an altimeter. Pilots use altimeters which are adjusted as the pressure readings change at the surface locations over which they are flying.

Figure 12-9. An altimeter dial showing altitude, and its interior mechanism, which is an aneroid barometer. (source: USAF)

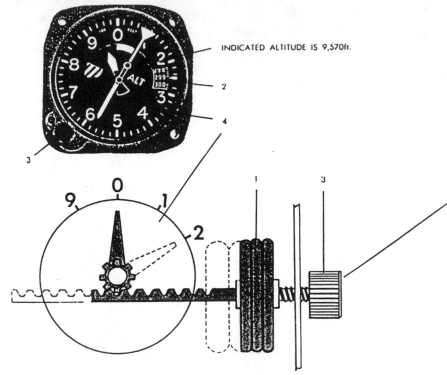

INDICATED ALTITUDE IS 9,570ft.

1. Aneroid cell expands in low pressure to indicate altitude in feet above MSL in standard atmosphere with reported station pressure set into Kollsman window.

2. Barometric scale.

3. Barometric pressure set knob

4. Altitude indication scale.

• Because surface pressures are always changing, a means of changing the altimeter reference is necessary. A barometric set knob is provided to change the reference shown on the barometric scale and is designed to change the altimeter indication approximately 10 feet for each .01" Hg change on the scale. This approximates the rate of pressure change found in the first 10,000 feet of atmosphere; i.e., 1" Hg for each 1,000 feet.

• Increasing the barometric setting will cause the altitude indication to increase, while decreasing the value on the barometric scale will cause the altitude indication to decrease. The majority of altimeters have mechanical stops at or just beyond the barometric scale limits (28.10 to 31.00)

Some all-time barometric pressure records up through when this book was published:

Highest sea-level pressure: 32.01" at Agata, Siberia on December 31, 1968.

Highest sea-level pressure in the United States: 31.85" at Barrow, Alaska on January 31, 1989.

Lowest sea-level pressure: 25.71" in the eye of Typhoon Tip over the western Pacific Ocean on October 12, 1979. The pressure probably was lower between reconnaissance aircraft observations.

Lowest sea-level pressure in or around North America: 26.13" in the eye of Hurricane Gilbert in the southwest Caribbean Sea on September 1988; however, Gilbert was rapidly intensifying when this reading was taken by reconnaissance aircraft, so the lowest pressure may have dipped below 26".

Lowest sea-level pressure in the United States: 26.36" in the eye of the Florida Keys Hurricane on September 2 and 3, 1935.

The lowest sea-level pressures anywhere are inside the most intense tornadoes, which probably have pressures below 20" and may be considerably lower than that.

PRESSURE	HEIGHT
beyond 600 to 1000 miles is outer space	
0 mb	600 to 1000 miles
0.0000000001 mb $(1 \times 10^{-10}$ mb)	445 miles
0.01 mb	53 miles
0.1 mb	45 miles
1 mb	30 miles
10 mb	100,000 feet (19 miles)
50 mb	67,000 feet (13 miles)
100 mb	53,000 feet
200 mb	39,000 feet
300 mb	29,000 feet
500 mb	18,000 feet
700 mb	10,000 feet
850 mb	5,000 feet
1000 mb	near sea-level

Figure 12-10. How the air pressure decreases with increasing height. Pressure is force per unit area, so air pressure is the weight of the air above you pushing down on you. At the 500 millibar level, which averages about 10,000 feet above sea-level, half the weight of the atmosphere is below you and half is above you. Notice that as we get higher and higher, the rate of thinning of the atmosphere greatly stretches out. We need rise only 18,000 feet (about 3½ miles) to go through half the atmosphere, but we have to go from 3½ miles to at least 600 miles up to go through the top half of the atmosphere!

SECTION VI: MOISTURE IN THE ATMOSPHERE

Chapter 13. WATER IN THE ATMOSPHERE

Over 70 percent of the earth's surface is covered by water. As discussed in chapter 20 on the hydrologic cycle, all the water in the earth-atmosphere-cryosphere (ice-covered areas) system is essentially a constant. It is being recycled through evaporation, precipitation and condensation.

We speak of **PHASES OF WATER**: the solid phase is ice, the liquid phase is water and the gaseous phase is water vapor.

Ice is a solid form of water. Like all other solids, it has a definite shape and size (volume). The molecules in a solid are very close together. In order for ice to melt (go from a solid to a liquid), heat is required. This heat is absorbed from the environment.

We measure heat in units called calories. A small calorie (gram calorie, calorie with a small "c") is the amount of heat necessary to raise the temperature of one gram of water one Celsius degree. In dieting, we use the large calorie (kilocalorie or Calorie with a capital "C"). We can define a large calorie as the amount of heat necessary to raise the temperature of 1000 grams of water 1 Celsius degree, or the amount of heat necessary to raise the temperature of 1 gram of water 1000 Celsius degrees.

For every gram of ice that melts into water, 80 small calories (gram calories) (calories) are required. This is called the **LATENT HEAT OF FUSION**. The word **LATENT** is used to define the amount of heat required but not yet used, and is dropped when the process is actually being done. Thus, the latent heat of fusion to melt one gram of ice is 80 calories, and when one gram of ice is in the process of melting, the heat of fusion is being taken from the environment. Latent heat is the amount of heat energy either absorbed or released during a change of phase (solid to liquid, liquid to gas, solid to gas, gas to solid, gas to liquid, liquid to solid). When going from solid to liquid, solid to gas, or liquid to gas, heat is absorbed or taken from the environment, and when going from gas to liquid, gas to solid or liquid to solid, heat is given off to the environment.

When a gram of ice absorbs this 80 small calories (gram calories) (calories), the temperature of the area from which this heat is absorbed goes down, but the temperature of the ice, which becomes water, does not change. The energy (heat energy in this case) is used to break down the crystalline structure of ice.

If you were along the shore of a lake during an ice-melt, you would experience some drop in temperature because heat is being taken from the environment.

Water is a liquid. Like all other liquids, it has a definite volume but no definite shape. Its shape depends upon the containing system it is in. As in all other liquids, the molecules are farther apart than they would be in the solid form of that substance. When water freezes, going from a liquid to a solid, it gives off heat to the environment. For every gram of water that freezes, 80 small calories (gram calories) (calories) of heat are released to the environment. This heat energy, once again, is known as the **(LATENT) HEAT OF FUSION**. If you were along the shore of a lake as the water freezes, you would experience some rise in temperature because heat is being given off to the environment.

When a liquid changes into a gas or vapor, heat is required, and is absorbed from the environment. For every gram of water that becomes a vapor, 600 small calories (gram calories) (calories) are absorbed from the environment. This is called the **LATENT HEAT OF VAPORIZATION**. The process of going from a liquid to a gas is called vaporization. If it occurs slowly, it is called evaporation, and the gas formed is water vapor.

Water vapor is invisible. The room you are in now may contain a lot of water vapor, but you cannot see it. If the vaporization process occurs rapidly, it is called boiling, and the gas formed is steam. Steam is hot water vapor, and it is also invisible.

The molecules in a gas are very far apart. You could take all the air in your bedroom and compress it into a relatively small cylinder; however, if your bedroom were the only room in the house with air, and someone then opened the door, then the air from your bedroom would distribute itself equally throughout the house.

When a gas changes into a liquid, the process is called condensation, and heat is released to the environment. For every gram of water vapor or steam that changes back to water, 600 small calories (gram calories) (calories) are given off, which is referred to as the (LATENT) HEAT OF VAPORIZATION. The term "heat of vaporization" is used for both the liquid changing into a gas, and for the gas changing into a liquid.

Since steam is invisible, what most of us commonly refer to as "steam" is not steam at all, but steam that has condensed into tiny droplets of water. We see this whenever we boil water on the stove. Some of the steam is condensing back to water as it enters the cooler air. When we exhale outside on a cold day, the water vapor coming out of our mouth and nose condenses into tiny droplets of water and we "see" our breath. Clouds and fog form in a similar way: that is, water vapor, which is a gas, condenses into tiny droplets of water that float in the air.

When a solid changes directly into a gas, or a gas changes directly into a solid, without ever being a liquid, the process is called sublimation. Sometimes the term deposition is used to define the process of a gas changing into a solid.

For every gram of ice that changes to water vapor, 680 small calories (gram calories) (calories) of heat must be absorbed. This is called the (LATENT) HEAT OF SUBLIMATION. This number is the sum of the latent heat of fusion (80 calories) and the latent heat of vaporization (600 calories).

For every gram of water vapor that sublimes directly into ice, 680 small calories (gram calories) (calories) of heat are given off. This is, again, the heat of sublimation, which is the sum of the heats of vaporization and fusion.

Frost forms when water vapor next to the ground sublimes into ice crystals. Snow occurs when water vapor in the clouds sublimes into ice crystals. Although snow melts into water, some of it can sublime directly into water vapor, especially with temperatures below freezing.

Another example of sublimation is the formation of solid carbon dioxide, commonly known as "dry ice". When carbon dioxide gas is cooled to about 110°F below zero while being subjected to a considerable amount of pressure, "dry ice", a solid, forms. When a piece of "dry ice" is left in a room at your typical room temperature of about 72°F, it seems to disappear, because it changes to carbon dioxide gas, which is invisible.

DEMONSTRATION: SUBLIMATION

This demonstration must be done in a fume hood (safety glasses must be worn):

1. Place a small amount of iodine crystals in an evaporating dish which is then placed on a tripod with a wire gauze on top of it.

2. Place a Bunsen burner under the tripod and light it.

3. When purple vapor forms, turn off the Bunsen burner and cover the evaporating dish with a glass square.

4. After about 15 to 20 minutes, lift the glass plate off the evaporating dish and you will see crystals of iodine that have sublimed on the glass plate when the purple vapor cooled.

This demonstration shows sublimation twice: first, when the solid iodine crystals change to a purple vapor, and second, when the purple vapor forms crystals on the glass plate.

If you leave both the evaporating dish and the glass square in a running fume hood overnight, then all the solid iodine will sublime, and no cleaning or washing will be necessary.

Types of ice:

There are two types of ice that form in Nature. One type is when water freezes and the other type is when water vapor sublimes into ice (e.g., frost and snow).

Ice That Forms When Water Freezes	Ice That Forms When Water Vapor Sublimes
1. It is hard.	1. It is soft.
2. It is difficult to scrape off of a surface	2. It is easy to scrape off of a surface.
3. It is smooth	3. It is rough.
4. It appears colorless*	4. It appears white.

*Sometimes ice that forms when water freezes can appear whitish, especially if air is trapped when the water freezes. This may occur during the formation of sleet and hail.

Figure 13-1. Comparing the two types of ice that form in Nature.

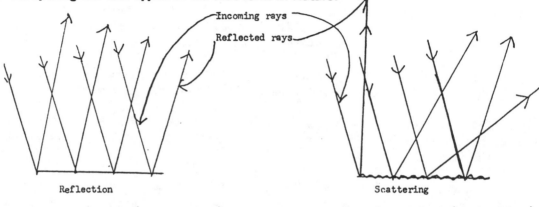

Incoming rays

Reflected rays

Reflection

Scattering

Ice cube (smooth surface)

Snow or frost (rough surface)

Figure 13-2. Why some ice is clear and some ice appears white or slightly bluish. If snow and frost were truly white (contained a white pigment), then when they melted they would result in a white liquid, looking like milk. We know, however, that when we melt snow, or frost or an ice cube, we get water which is colorless. The figure at the left represents light rays hitting an ice cube, and the figure at the right represents light rays hitting snow or frost. In both figures, the incoming rays, which are called INCIDENT RAYS, are parallel because the sun is so far away. The ice cube is smooth, which results in all the reflected rays also being parallel. This also occurs with glass and mirrors where an image can be seen. However, the surface of frost or snow is rough. The rays are therefore reflected back in different directions; this is called SCATTERING. All the colors of the rainbow combine to show white. Sometimes, with a high water-content snow, the shorter visible wavelengths, the blues, are also scattered out, so that the snow surface of a freshly-fallen heavy "wet" snow, or a glacial iceberg, might appear not only white but slightly blue.

Consider a rough surface such as a cinder-block wall. When you paint it with several coatings of white paint, some of the rough areas become smoother as the paint fills in the crevices. As a result, you begin to see your reflection on the wall. When you polish furniture, it shines, enabling you to see your reflection, because the polish smoothes out some of the scratches, cracks and nicks.

DEMONSTRATION: TRANSFORMING SMOOTH COLORLESS ICE INTO ROUGH WHITE ICE
1. Wrap 4 or 5 ice cubes in a piece of cloth
2. Smash the ice cubes with a hammer.
3. Unwrap the cloth and notice that the crushed ice appears white.
By smashing the ice cubes, you have made them rough and thus they scatter light.

Chapter 14. DEWPOINT AND RELATIVE HUMIDITY; DEW AND FROST

Before discussing dewpoint, it is important to consider that warm air can hold more water vapor than can cold air. This is because in warm air, the air molecules are farther apart than in cold air. Where there is significant space between the air molecules, then the molecules of water, in vapor form, can fit in between the air molecules more easily. When the air cools, the molecules get closer together, expelling the water molecules. An analogy is a sponge soaking up water. Squeeze the sponge and the water is released.

DEWPOINT: Now let us consider the dewpoint, also referred to as the "dewpoint temperature". The dewpoint is the temperature to which the air must be cooled in order for moisture to come out of it.

On an essentially clear night with light or no wind, if the dewpoint is 52°F and the air cools to 52°, then dew forms on the grass and on other surfaces. If, on a nearly-calm and clear night the dewpoint is at or below freezing and the temperature drops to that value, then frost will form.

The higher the dewpoint temperature, the more moisture the air is holding. Consider a parcel of air with a temperature of 70°F and a dewpoint of 50°F. If the air pressure remains the same and their is no additional moisture going into the parcel and no moisture being taken out, then that 50° dewpoint is the temperature to which the air must be cooled for the parcel to be saturated, that is, to have 100% relative humidity.

In the summer months, the moisture content of the air, i.e., the dewpoint, has an effect on how comfortable we feel. The more moisture there is in the air around us, the more difficult it is to cool off. Our body cools when microscopically small droplets of perspiration evaporate from our pores. Most of the time, the perspiration evaporates before it accumulates on our skin. As it evaporates, it absorbs heat from our body. You probably have experienced water evaporating from your body and swim suit when you come out of the water after swimming. Even though the air temperature may be in the 90s F., you feel cool until your skin is dry.

Substances that evaporate faster than water make you feel cooler. For example, if you place a drop of alcohol on your skin, it will evaporate so fast that your skin where you placed the alcohol feels even colder.

As the dewpoint goes up (the moisture or water vapor in the air increases), it becomes increasingly more difficult to evaporate the perspiration. The perspiration (commonly called "sweat"), will accumulate and subsequently roll down your forehead, face and other parts of the body. You say, "I am sweating." When you are doing strenuous exercise, more heat is generated and your body requires more cooling; consequently, more perspiration is secreted.

You are perspiring every moment you are alive, but you notice it when it does not evaporate as fast as it forms because the air has a lot of moisture in it and/or you are doing a lot of physical activity, thus generating more perspiration.

Figure 14-1. The table relates dewpoint temperatures to comfort level, for the summertime.

DEWPOINT TEMPERATURE	COMFORT LEVEL
Under 55° F	Comfortable
56 to 60° F	Slightly uncomfortable
61 to 65° F	Uncomfortable
66 to 70° F	Very uncomfortable
Above 70° F	Oppresive

Dewpoint products:

DEW occurs when the temperature of the air next to the ground cools to its dewpoint. Example: if the dewpoint is 50°F (10°C) and the temperature of the air next to the ground is 50°F, then dew will form. You will notice that the grass, pavement, roof of your car, street, etc. will be wet.

FOG occurs when the temperature of the air above the ground cools to the dewpoint and stays at it for hours. Fog is comprised of tiny droplets of water floating in the air. It is actually a low cloud (a stratus cloud). Example: if the dewpoint is 59°F (15°C) and the temperature of the air above the ground on a clear, nearly calm night drops to 59°F early in the night, fog is likely to form. Fog and dew typically occur at the same time. If only the first few feet (one to two meters) of air above the ground are at the dewpoint, then shallow fog known as GROUND FOG forms. You probably have noticed that during ground fog, when you look up, you can see the sky, stars, moon or sun. As soon as the temperature of the air above the ground goes above the dewpoint, the water droplets that make up the ground fog evaporate. Thicker and deeper FOG, which has had more time to develop, can be hundreds of feet deep, obscuring the sky and reducing the visibility to below a few hundred feet...even to zero. This fog takes longer to "burn off" than does ground fog. All fog "burns away" faster when the sky is sunny to mostly sunny above the fog once the sun rises.

CLOUDS form when the temperature of the air well above the ground cools to its dewpoint. Clouds, like fog, are comprised of tiny droplets of water floating in the air. Thus, fog is a cloud whose base is on the surface. Example: if the dewpoint is 41°F (5°C) around 3300 feet (1000 meters) up, and the air temperature at that elevation is the same, then clouds are likely to form. When the temperature and dewpoint are the same through a depth of the lower atmosphere, and the air is rising and cooling, clouds will form. Like fog, clouds will evaporate when the air temperature in them rises above the dewpoint. It is possible to have clouds, fog and dew occurring simultaneously.

FROST occurs when the temperature of the air next to the ground cools to its dewpoint which is at freezing or below. Frost is not frozen dew, although at times dew that has already formed can freeze, but the new deposition after that would be frost. Example: if the late afternoon temperature is 35 degrees F and the dewpoint is 25 degrees F, but clear skies and light winds allow the air to cool at night to its dewpoint, then frost will likely form. Thus, frost occurs when the gaseous water vapor in the air changes directly into ice crystals, without ever having been water. This process is called SUBLIMATION. The ice crystals formed by sublimation are white, soft, rough and can easily be scraped off a surface such as a windshield. In the case of frozen dew, or any water that freezes, the ice that forms, unlike the ice of frost, is smooth, hard, colorless and difficult to scrape off a surface. A thin layer of such ice, as in frozen dew, freezing precipitation (freezing rain or freezing drizzle), or totally- or partially-melted snow that refreezes, can be hard to see, and is sometimes referred to as BLACK ICE.

ICE FOG, especially common in the winter in far northern climates including inland Alaska, forms on clear, calm and very cold nights, when the temperature is typically below zero Fahrenheit (-18 Celsius) and has cooled to its dewpoint. It can be analogized to frost forming above the ground. The crystals of ice are so light that they float. They can coat the top of a car or the ground with a thin layer of what looks like snow.

ICE CLOUDS are clouds that form when the temperature aloft cools to the dewpoint which is at or below freezing. The feathery-looking cirrus clouds, which in mid-latitudes are from about 20,000 to 40,000 feet up, are comprised of ice crystals. Cirroform clouds (cirrus, cirrostratus, cirrocumulus) are typically comprised of ice crystals. For example, when warm moist air overrides a large mass of cold air, the rising air is cooled to its dewpoint, and clouds form. If this dewpoint is at or below freezing, the clouds are comprised of ice crystals rather than of water droplets. These clouds are like ice fog, but at a much higher elevation.

The dewpoint can often be used as a forecast tool in predicting tonight's low temperature. If we are remaining in the same air mass, with no moving-in of more cold or warm air, then, if the sky is expected to be clear or mostly clear overnight with light winds, then the late afternoon dewpoint temperature reading is going to be about what the temperature will drop to by around daybreak for the morning low. Dew or frost may form under these conditions. Whenever water vapor, which is a gas, changes into water droplets in the case of dew, and into ice crystals in the case of frost, heat is given off to the environment, which slow down somewhat the cooling process. Any significant cloudiness will prevent the earth from radiating enough heat out into space to cool the air to its dewpoint. The clouds will reflect back to the ground some of the heat that the ground and air are trying to send out. Moreover, if it is sufficiently windy (above 10 mph), then some stirring and mixing of the air will usually prevent the temperature from cooling overnight to its dewpoint. Of course, if a strong cold front or warm front will be passing overnight, then the air temperature and dewpoint will be changing due to the new air mass moving in. Try your skill at forecasting the overnight low temperatures by using the late afternoon dewpoint when the nights are expected to be clear or mostly clear with light winds and no fronts moving through.

<u>How the dewpoint is measured:</u>
Figure 14-2. At most major weather observing sites, a HYGROTHERMOMETER, such as the one shown to the right, measures the dewpoint.
Hygrothermometers have a sensor typically coated with a hygroscopic (water or moisture absorbing) chemical such as lithium chloride. The sensor works via electroconductivity. What happens is that when the air is moist, this weather instrument conducts more electricity, registering a higher number than when the air is drier. Instead of registering in amperes, the reading is calibrated in degrees of dewpoint temperature.

A little later in this chapter, we'll explain how you can compute the dewpoint and the relative humidity.

RELATIVE HUMIDITY: The relative humidity is the amount of water vapor a parcel of air is actually holding, compared with the amount that it is capable of holding at that air temperature and atmospheric pressure. It is expressed as a percent.

What is measured are GRAMS of water vapor. For example, suppose a parcel of 1000 grams of air at a certain temperature and pressure can hold as much as 40 grams of water vapor. However, it contains only 20 grams of water vapor. Thus, the relative humidity is (20 grams divided by 40 grams) which is 0.50. To express the result as a percentage, multiply that 0.50 times 100% to get 50%, which is our relative humidity.

If the relative humidity is under 40%, the air is fairly dry, and evaporation is relatively fast. As the humidity exceeds 60% and approaches 100%, the air is relatively moist, and evaporation is slow and little.

<u>How you can determine the dewpoint and the relative humidity:</u>
By using two thermometers, a cotton-type or muslin wick, water, a fan and a calculation table, you can compute the relative humidity, and by using a calculation graphic, you can compute the dewpoint temperature.

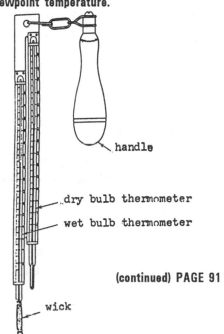

Figure 14-3. To compute the dewpoint and the relative humidity, you need to make or obtain a SLING PSYCHROMETER, such as the one shown at the right, or else have a fan blow on the thermometer with the wick, which is wet by water, to cause evaporation and a cooling of the "wet bulb" thermometer.

handle

dry bulb thermometer

wet bulb thermometer

All temperature readings are taken in the shade, in a sheltered area not in precipitation. Dip the bulb of the thermometer that has the wick around it into a small container of water to completely saturate the wick. Now fan or whirl around (sling) the sling psychrometer to evaporate water from the wet bulb and wick. Evaporation uses (takes away) heat from the thermometer bulb, so the wet-bulb temperature drops. Keep slinging or fanning the wet bulb until its temperature reading drops no more. Read the dry bulb (outside air) temperature and the wet-bulb temperature.

(continued) PAGE 91

wick

Now use the table below to compute the relative humidity from the dry- and wet-bulb temperature readings, and then use the following graph to determine the dewpoint from the air temperature (dry-bulb reading) and the relative humidity.

Figure 14-4. Table to compute the relative humidity from the dry- and wet-bulb temperature readings.

DIFFERENCE BETWEEN DRY AND WET BULB THERMOMETERS

Degrees.....	1	2	3	4	5	6	7	8	9	10	11	12	13	14	15
Reading of dry-bulb thermometer					Relative humidity in per cent										
63	95	89	84	79	74	69	64	60	55	51	46	42	38	33	29
64	95	89	84	79	74	70	65	60	56	51	47	43	38	34	30
65	95	90	85	80	75	70	65	61	56	52	48	44	39	35	31
66	95	90	85	80	75	71	66	61	57	53	49	45	40	36	32
67	95	90	85	80	76	71	66	62	58	53	49	45	41	37	33
68	95	90	85	81	76	71	67	63	58	54	50	46	42	38	34
69	95	90	86	81	76	72	67	63	59	55	51	47	43	39	35
70	95	90	86	81	77	72	68	64	60	55	52	48	44	40	36
71	95	91	86	81	77	72	68	64	60	56	52	48	45	41	37
72	95	91	86	82	77	73	69	65	61	57	53	49	45	42	38
73	95	91	86	82	78	73	69	65	61	57	53	50	46	42	39
74	95	91	86	82	78	74	70	66	62	58	54	50	47	43	40
75	95	91	87	82	78	74	70	66	62	58	55	51	47	44	40

Figure 14-5. Graph to compute the dewpoint from the temperature and relative humidity values.

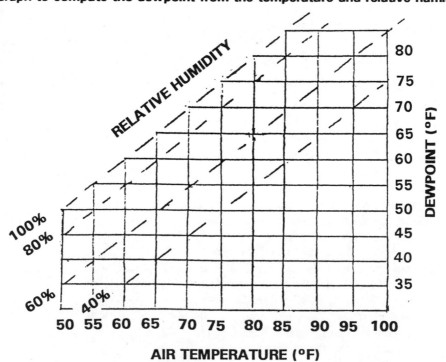

Let's do an example. Suppose the dry-bulb temperature is 70 degrees F. and the wet-bulb temperature is 61 degrees Fahrenheit. Determine the relative humidity and the dewpoint.

Solution:

1. Go to the table and place your left index finger under the dry-bulb reading, which in this case is 70°F.
2. Subtract the wet-bulb reading from the dry-bulb reading. The difference is 9.
3. Now look at the top of the table for the column that has a difference of 9.
4. With your right index finger, go down that column until it is opposite the left index finger.
5. Your right index finger should be on the number 60. This means that the relative humidity is 60%.
6. Now go to the graph. From a temperature reading of 70°F on the bottom line, we go up until we intersect the diagonal line that represents a relative humidity of 60%.
7. Then from that intersection, we go to the right to obtain our dewpoint reading, which is 55°.

DEMONSTRATION: DETERMINING THE DEWPOINT
1. Fill a metal can about three-quarters with room-temperature water.
2. Place a thermometer into the water and gradually add ice cubes. Gently stir the water constantly with the thermometer.
3. As soon as you see moisture condensing on the outside of the metal can, read the thermometer. This is your dewpoint temperature!
The principle is that the temperature of the can has been cooled to the dewpoint temperature of the air, so that moisture (dew) forms on the outside of the can!

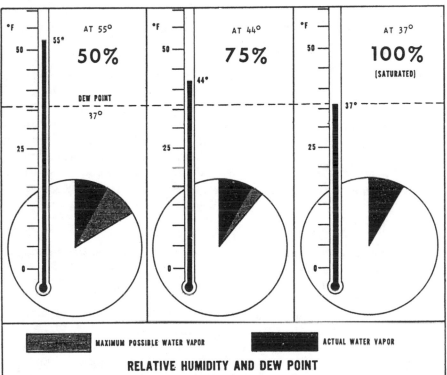

Figure 14-6. An illustrative depiction of how dewpoint, temperature and relative humidity relate. The dewpoint temperature is the same in all three examples above. That means that the moisture content is the same. Typically, near the earth's surface, for every 1000 grams of air, a few to a few dozen grams are comprised of water vapor. In the three examples above, therefore, the amount of grams of water vapor in each case is the same, so the dewpoint is the same (37°F.). The relative humidity is a function of both the temperature and the water vapor content, with the water vapor content expressed as the dewpoint. In the left example, the temperature is 55° and the dewpoint is 37°, but the relative humidity is only 50%, because the air at 55° is holding only 50% of the water vapor that it could hold. The warmer the air, the more moisture it can hold. In the middle example, the temperature is cooler, 44°F., with the same 37°F. dewpoint. Now the relative humidity is 75%, meaning that the air at 44°F. is holding 75% of the moisture that it is capable of holding. In the right example, the air temperature is the same as the dewpoint temperature, 37°F., so it is holding all the water vapor it could; when the temperature and the dewpoint are the same, the relative humidity is 100%; the air is then said to be **saturated**. Saturated air cannot hold any more moisture; if Nature tries to inject more moisture, then the excess will precipitate out as a liquid (water) or a solid (ice). Thus, when air cools to its dewpoint, it becomes saturated. (source: NOAA)

Chapter 15. CLOUDS AND CEILING

Clouds, like fog which is a stratus cloud whose base is on the ground, are comprised of tiny droplets of water floating in the air. The higher clouds are made of ice crystals. Clouds with great vertical extent, cumulonimbus clouds, have water droplets in their lower levels and ice crystals aloft, and a mixture in-between.

Clouds form when air that has moisture in it, is cooled to its dewpoint. When this happens along the ground, fog, which is a stratus clouds whose base is on the ground, forms. When this process happens off the surface, clouds form and have different appearances depending upon the ambient conditions.

Most often, clouds form when air is cooled by rising. This rising can be caused by dynamic forcing such as "warm air advection", or warmer air moving in. Since the air is warmer and lighter than the air it is trying to replace, it rises. Thus, for example, ahead of an advancing warm front is one region where we would expect cloudiness, as long as there is ample moisture to lift and cool to form clouds. Thus, we need a lifting mechanism plus adequate moisture.

Another type of lifting mechanism is related to an aspect of vorticity or spinning of air parcels caused by curvature of the flow and/or vertical wind shear (change of wind direction and/or speed with height). [See chapter 29 on vorticity for an explanation on how this process works.]

There are also mechanical causes of lift, such as air flowing up an upsloping terrain or rising over mountains.

Any process that causes parcels of air to converge in low levels results in air being forced to rise, which expends parcel energy so that the parcels cool. Rising air keeps most of its original moisture content with it (it keeps most of its dewpoint temperature). There is actually a slight lowering of the dewpoint as a parcel rises. Thus, eventually, if the air is cooled to its dewpoint we have 100% relative humidity, i.e., the air parcels are now saturated. If the atmosphere is then still lifting and therefore cooling the now-saturated air parcels, moisture is wrung out of them as precipitation. Even without additional lift, cloud droplets can coalesce to form moisture droplets or particles heavy enough to fall out of the clouds as precipitation. You cannot naturally cause the air temperature to be lower than its dewpoint. When nature tries, by lifting already saturated parcels of air, precipitation results.

However, cloud droplets will not form unless there are microscopic particles suspended in the air, about which the moisture can coalesce and condense. These dust, ash, salt, etc. particles are called condensation nuclei, as explained later in chapter 18.

Clouds associated with the steady rain or snow from a well-developed winter storm are caused chiefly by slow, steady lifting over a broad area, called synoptic-scale lifting. Clouds caused by localized convection, such as on a hot and humid summer afternoon, or by convective processes imbedded within a synoptic-scale lift area, are caused by convective-scale lifting. Whereas the clouds from a winter snowstorm may not be much over 20,000 to 25,000 feet high, the clouds from individual thunderstorms may be over 45,000 feet high, even over 60,000 feet in some of the most severe thunderstorms.

The following graphics illustrate common cloud-forming processes.

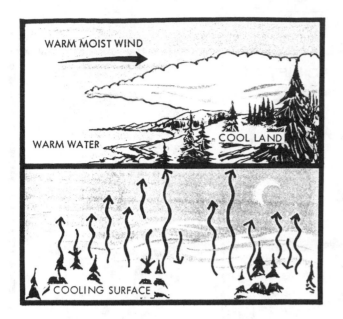
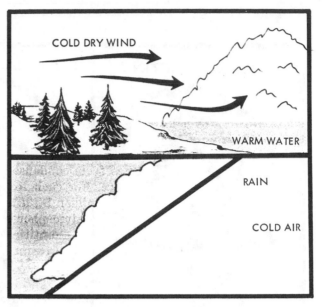

Figures 15-1 and 15-2. At left, moist air is being cooled to its dewpoint, becoming saturated as it passes over cool land or water surfaces. Radiational nocturnal cooling of the ground and the subsequent cooling of adjacent moist air can produce saturation and fog. At right, air is becoming saturated by the addition of moisture. This can happen by evaporation as cold, dry air passes over warm water, or as warm rain from above a front falls through cold air beneath the front. (source: DOA)

Figure 15-3. Examples of <u>orographic lifting</u>. Moist air from the ocean is being forced to rise up and over mountain ranges. The air is cooled to its dewpoint, forming clouds and subsequent precipitation, mostly on the windward side of the mountains (the side of the mountains facing the incoming wind). Lower lands to the east of the mountain ranges are considerably drier. The process that forces air to rise up and over mountains is called orographic lifting. (source: DOA)

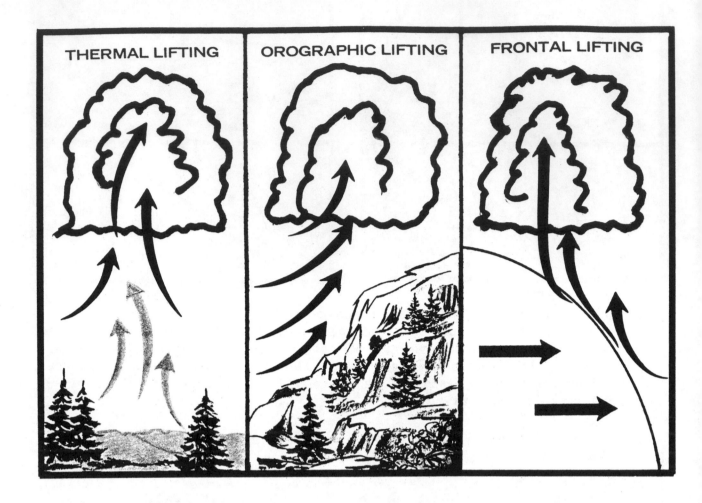

Figure 15-4. The most significant method of cloud formation is the adiabatic cooling of air to saturation because of lifting. Adiabatic means that essentially no heat is given to or taken away from the parcels in the short-term, by their environment. Above are three examples of adiabatic cooling because of lifting. Thus, the cooling of the parcels is simply because they are rising and giving up heat. These parcels do work as they rise...they expend energy, giving it off as heat; thus, the parcels are cooling as they rise. Above are examples of lifting. Thermal lifting is due to the sun heating the ground which in turn heats the air parcels above it, causing them to rise. Orographic lifting occurs when the air flow forces the parcels to ascend mountains. Frontal lifting is air being forced up due to a front moving through.
(source: DOA)

The following essay on cloud formation and precipitation is taken from the excellent work done by the Forest Service of the U.S. Department of Agriculture.

Cloud formation and precipitation:

We are all familiar with condensation and sublimation. We have noticed the condensation of our breath on cold days, and of steam rising from boiling water. We have seen dew formed on grass at night, or on cold water pipes and cold glasses, and have noticed the sublimation of water vapor into frost on cold window panes in winter.

For condensation or sublimation to occur in the free air, a particle or nucleus must be present for water-vapor molecules to cling to. These fine particles are of two types: **condensation nuclei** and **sublimation nuclei**. Condensation nuclei, on which liquid cloud droplets form, consist of salt particles, droplets of sulfuric acid, and combustion products. They are usually abundant in the atmosphere so that cloud droplets form when saturation is reached. Sublimation nuclei, on which ice crystals form, consist of dust, volcanic ash, and other crystalline materials. Because of differences in composition and structure, different nuclei are effective at different below-freezing temperatures. As the temperature decreases, additional nuclei become active in the sublimation process. These nuclei are not as plentiful as condensation nuclei. Even at temperatures well below freezing, there frequently are too few effective nuclei to initiate more than a scattering of ice crystals.

The small particles that act as condensation nuclei are usually **hygroscopic**; that is, they have a chemical affinity for water. They may absorb water well before the humidity reaches saturation, sometimes at humidities as low as 80 percent. Condensation forms first on the larger nuclei, and a haze develops which reduces visibility. As the relative humidity increases, these particles take on more water and grow in size while condensation also begins on smaller nuclei. Near saturation, the particles have become large enough to be classed as fog or cloud droplets, averaging 1/2500-inch in diameter, and dense enough so that the mass becomes visible. Rapid cooling of the air, such as in strong upward currents, can produce humidities of over 100 percent—super-saturation—temporarily. Under such conditions droplets grow rapidly, very small nuclei become active and start to grow, and many thousands of droplets per cubic inch will form. With supersaturation even nonhygroscopic particles will serve as condensation nuclei, but usually there are sufficient hygroscopic nuclei so that the others do not have a chance.

As condensation proceeds, droplets continue to grow until they reach a maximum size of about 1/100 inch in diameter, the size of small drizzle drops. The condensation process is unable to produce larger droplets for several reasons. As vapor is used up in droplet formation, supersaturation decreases and the cloud approaches an equilibrium state at saturation. Also, as droplets grow, the mass of water vapor changing to liquid becomes large and the resultant latent heat released in the condensation process warms the droplet and decreases the vapor pressure difference between it and the surrounding vapor. **Thus the vast majority of clouds do not produce rain.** If growth to raindrop size is to take place, one or more of the precipitation processes must come into play. We will discuss these later.

An important phenomenon in the physics of condensation and precipitation is that liquid cloud droplets form and persist at temperatures well below freezing. Although ice melts at 32°F., water can be cooled much below this before it changes to ice. Liquid cloud droplets can exist at temperatures as low as —40°F. More commonly in the atmosphere though, cloud droplets remain liquid down to about 15°F. Liquid droplets below 32°F. are said to be **supercooled**. At temperatures above 32°F., clouds are composed only of liquid droplets. At temperatures much below 15°F. they are usually composed mostly of ice crystals, while at intermediate temperatures they may be made up of supercooled droplets, ice crystals, or both.

Why don't ice crystals form more readily? First, the formation of ice crystals at temperatures higher than —40°F. requires sublimation nuclei. As was mentioned above, these usually are scarce in the atmosphere, especially at higher elevations. Also, many types of nuclei are effective only at temperatures considerably below freezing. But another reason why vapor condenses into liquid droplets, rather than sublimes into ice crystals, is that condensation can begin at relative humidities well under 100 percent while sublimation requires at least saturation conditions and usually supersaturation.

Given the necessary conditions of below-freezing temperature, effective sublimation nuclei, and supersaturation, sublimation starts by direct transfer of water vapor to the solid phase on a sublimation nucleus. There is no haze phase as in the case of condensation. Once sublimation starts, ice crystals will grow freely under conditions of supersaturation. Since there are fewer sublimation than condensation nuclei available, the ice crystals that form grow to a greater size than water droplets and can fall from the base of the cloud.

Only very light snow, or rain if the crystals melt, can be produced by sublimation alone. Moderate or heavy precipitation requires one of the precipitation processes in addition to sublimation.

After condensation or sublimation processes have gone as far as they can, some additional process is necessary for droplets or crystals to grow to a size large enough to fall freely from the cloud and reach the ground as snow or rain. Cloud droplets, because of their small size and consequent slight pull of gravity, have a negligible rate of fall, and for all practical purposes are suspended in the air. Even drizzle droplets seem to float in the air. Raindrops range in size from about 1/50 inch to 1/5 inch in diameter. Drops larger than 1/5 inch tend to break up when they fall. It takes about 30 million cloud droplets of average size to make one raindrop about 1/8 inch in diameter.

There seem to be two processes which act together or separately to cause millions of cloud droplets to grow into a raindrop. One is the **ice-crystal** process and the other is the **coalescence** process.

The Ice-Crystal Process

We have seen that ice crystals and cloud droplets can coexist in clouds with subfreezing temperatures. For the ice-crystal process of precipitation to take place, clouds must be composed of both ice crystals and supercooled liquid cloud droplets.

Water-vapor molecules which escape to the air displace air molecules and contribute their proportionate share to the total atmospheric pressure. This portion is called the partial pressure due to water vapor, or for simplicity, the **vapor pressure.**

Vapor pressure depends on the actual water vapor in the air, and it may vary from near zero in cold, dry air to about 2 inches of mercury in warm, moist air. High values can occur only in the warm, lower layers of the troposphere.

When the vapor pressure in the atmosphere is in equilibrium with the vapor pressure of a water or ice surface, there is no net exchange of water molecules in either direction, and the atmosphere is said to be saturated. A saturated volume of air contains all the vapor that it can hold. The vapor pressure at saturation is called the **saturation vapor pressure.** The saturation vapor pressure varies with the temperature of the air and is identical to the vapor pressure of water at that temperature. The higher the temperature, the more water vapor a volume of air can hold, and the higher the saturation vapor pressure. Conversely, the lower the temperature, the lower the saturation vapor pressure. The saturation vapor pressure with respect to ice is somewhat less than that with respect to supercooled water at the same temperature, as shown in the following table:

Comparative Saturation Vapor Pressures over Water and Ice

Temperature (°F.)	Saturation vapor pressure Over water	Over ice	Relative humidity over ice (Percent)
	(Inches of mercury)		
0	0.045	0.038	119
10	.071	.063	112
20	.110	.104	106
30	.166	.164	101

If a cloud containing supercooled water droplets is saturated with respect to water, then it is supersaturated with respect to ice, and the relative humidity with respect to ice is greater than 100 percent. The force resulting from the difference between vapor pressure over water and over ice causes vapor molecules to be attracted to ice crystals, and the ice crystals will grow rapidly. As the ice crystals gather up vapor molecules in the cloud, the relative humidity with respect to water drops below 100 percent, and liquid cloud droplets begin to evaporate. Vapor molecules move to the ice crystals and crystallize there. Thus, the ice crystals grow at the expense of the water droplets and may attain a size large enough to fall out of the cloud as snowflakes. If the snowflakes reach warmer levels, they melt and become raindrops. This is the ice-crystal precipitation process.

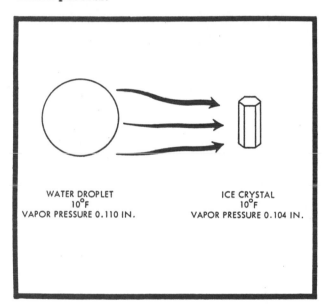

Figure 15-5.

In the ice-crystal precipitation process, ice crystals grow at the expense of water droplets. Because of the difference in vapor pressure over ice and over water at the same temperature, a vapor-pressure gradient exists between supercooled water droplets and ice crystals in mixed clouds. Vapor molecules leave the water droplets and sublime on the ice crystals.   (source: DOA)

Artificial Nucleation

The knowledge that frequently there is a scarcity of sublimation nuclei and ice crystals in supercooled clouds has led to the discovery that precipitation can be initiated artificially. It has been found that silver-iodide crystals, which have a structure similar to ice crystals, can be effective sublimation nuclei in supercooled clouds at temperatures below about 20°F. Silver-iodide crystals can be released in the cloud by aircraft or rockets, or carried to the cloud by convection from ground generators.

Ice crystals can be created in a supercooled cloud by dropping pellets of dry ice, solid carbon dioxide, into the cloud from above. The dry ice, which has a sublimation temperature of —108°F., cools droplets along its path to temperatures lower than —40°F. so that they can freeze into ice crystals without the presence of sublimation nuclei. Once crystals are produced, they act as nucleating particles themselves and affect other parts of the cloud.

Once formed in a supercooled water cloud, ice crystals may grow by the ice-crystal process and coalescence processes until they are large enough to precipitate. Studies have provided evidence that the artificial nucleation of supercooled clouds can, under the proper conditions, increase local precipitation significantly.

Coalescence

Since rain also falls from clouds which are entirely above freezing, there must be a second precipitation process. This is a simple process in which cloud droplets collide and fuse together, or coalesce. Clouds which produce precipitation are composed of cloud droplets of varying sizes. Because of the different sizes, cloud droplets move about at different speeds. As they collide, some of them stick together to form larger drops. The larger cloud droplets grow at the expense of smaller ones, and actually become more effective in the collecting process as they become larger. As larger drops begin to fall, they tend to sweep out the smaller drops ahead of them.

The coalescence process takes place in clouds of both above-freezing and below-freezing temperatures. Snowflakes coalesce with other snowflakes as they fall to form the large clumps which we sometimes observe. They may also coalesce with supercooled water droplets to form snow pellets.

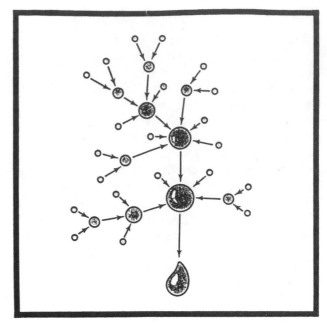

Figure 15-6.

In the coalescence process of precipitation, small droplets collide and fuse together to become larger droplets. The process continues until enough droplets are accumulated into large drops so that the large drops fall because of gravity. Snowflakes coalesce into snowflake masses in a similar manner.   (source: DOA)

<u>Sky cover</u>:

The term, "sky cover" is used to describe how much of the sky is covered by clouds and/or is obscured. Obscuring phenomena include fog, haze, smog, smoke from fires, and heavy-enough precipitation to block the viewing of part or all of the sky or any cloud decks.

The sky condition or sky cover is reported in octals (eighths) of coverage. The description of the sky is as follows:

CLEAR = no clouds or obscuring phenomena

FEW CLOUDS = clouds covering 1/8 th to 2/8 ths of the sky

SCATTERED = clouds covering 3/8 ths through 4/8 ths of the sky

BROKEN = clouds covering 5/8 ths through 7/8 ths of the sky

OVERCAST = clouds covering 8/8 ths of the sky.

There can be BINOVC, which is "breaks in the overcast".

PARTIAL OBSCURATION = part of the sky cover is obscured from being seen because of obscuring phenomena (such as fog, haze, smog, smoke and heavy-enough precipitation)

OBSCURATION = the entire sky cover is obscured

Ceiling:

The term, ceiling, is an aviation term, meaning the height above the ground of the <u>bases</u> of the lowest layer of clouds that gives a cumulative total of a broken or more sky condition (5/8 ths sky cover or more).

Sky cover is cumulative, adding from the lowest cloud layer up. Example: suppose right now, outside, we have the following:

1/8 th sky cover with cloud bases at 1000 feet above the ground, and
2/8 ths sky cover above that, with that second cloud deck having its bases at 4500 feet, and
3/8 ths sky cover above the second layer, with the third layer having its bases at 20,000 feet.

The sky condition would be reported as: 1000 scattered, 4500 scattered, 20,000 broken.

The sum of the coverage of the lowest two decks is 3/8 ths, so this is still a scattered condition, but when we add in the third deck, we now have a sum of 6/8 ths for the sky cover, which makes that deck give us a broken sky condition.

If you can see the sky through some or all of the clouds, then these clouds are reported as "thin". If half or more of the cloud deck is thin, even if broken, then the cloud deck is not a ceiling. Thus, the opaqueness of cloud is taken into consideration.

A sky cover with clouds may or may not be a ceiling. To be termed a "ceiling", the sum of the clouds and any obscuring phenomena must give at least a broken condition.

Sky cover is one of the crucial weather elements for aviators. Pilots have either VFR or IFR licenses. VFR means they can fly under "Visual Flight Rules", and IFR stands for "Instrument Flight Rules". When the ceiling and/or visibility are too low for visual flying (for small, general aviation aircraft), then only those pilots who have qualified for IFR flying, that is, flying by instruments so that they can fly in clouds, etc., can fly.

●IFR conditions are ceiling below 1000 feet and/or horizontal surface visibility below 3 miles;

●MVFR (Marginal VFR) conditions are ceiling from 1000 to 3000 feet and horizontal surface visibility from 3 to 5 miles;

●VFR conditions are ceiling above 3000 feet AND visibility over 5 miles.

Accurate and timely weather information is therefore critical to the aviation community. (The next chapter discusses the naming and identification of clouds.)

How is ceiling measured?

Estimated ceiling:
A well-trained and experienced weather observer can look up at the sky and across the horizon and estimate both the amount of sky cover and the height of the bases of any cloud decks. He or she can also estimate how much of the sky may be obscured by any phenomena.

The best scenario is to have instruments measure the height of lower cloud decks, and to have the observer record the eights of sky cover. No instrument has yet been developed that can replace the human observer for accuracy of cloud and obscuring amounts.

A trained observer knows, for example, that stratocumulus clouds have bases no higher than about 6500 feet. If cumuloform clouds have bases between about 6500 feet and 20,000 feet, then they are called altocumulus, a "middle-layer" cloud ("alto" means "middle"). The bases of cirroform clouds (cirrus, cirrostratus and cirrocumulus) are at least 20,000 feet high, and can be as high as about 35,000 feet (although cirroform clouds can be much higher when they extend out from the tops of well-developed thunderstorms).

Here is how the bases are measured using ceiling balloons or instruments.

Ceiling balloons:
A ceiling balloon is not the same as the big weather balloon that carries up a radiosonde to measure some of the weather variables in the vertical. A ceiling balloon is a small balloon that is inflated with helium, and has a little weight at its mouth. The balloon rises at a known rate. Thus, for a "10 gram balloon". for example, all the observer needs to do is time the number of seconds until half the balloon disappears into the first cloud deck it encounters. These balloons are launched only when there is a ceiling (broken or overcast sky cover). During an obscuration, such as when in a dense fog, a balloon may also be lauched so that when at least half of it disappears, then the maxium height that one can see vertically through the obscuration can be determined. For example, a 500-foot obscuration means that you can see objects as far as 500 feet up. Again, this is of crucial importance to aviation.

Since the ceiling balloon rises vertically (as well as laterally if any wind), and its rate of rise is known, we can determine the height of the clouds since speed equals distance times the time.

Sample problem:
Find the ceiling when a ceiling balloon that rises at 10 feet per second disappears into the clouds in 50 seconds.

speed = distance divided by time ($v = d/t$); therefore, since we are solving for the distance, d, :
d = v X t = 10 feet per second TIMES 50 seconds = 500 feet.

In the first few thousand feet, which are the most critical for aviation concerns, the ceiling balloons rise at a fairly constant rate. A balloon of a different weight would rise at a different rate, but as long as the rate is known, the height of the ceiling base can be determined. If it is precipitating very hard as the brightly colored balloon is launched, then it is possible for the precipitation to cause a slight drag effect on the balloon's ascent, and the observer may need to slightly modify by lowereing the balloon ceiling.

At night, a small battery-powered light is attached to the balloon so that it can be visually followed.

Clinometer and light projector:

An observer stands a known distance (say 500 to 1000 feet) from a powerful searchlight (light projector) that projects a vertical beam of light onto the cloud base. The observer uses an angle measuring tube with protractor called a <u>clinometer</u>, aiming it at the point where the light beam hits the cloud base. Then, using the clinometer, he or she determines the angle between the horizontal ground where the observer is standing, and the line of sight to the cloud base.

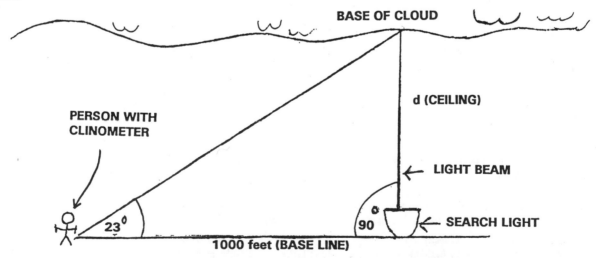

Figure 15-7. Using trigonometry to measure the ceiling using a clinometer and ceiling light.
PAGE 102

The lower the clouds, the smaller the angle; the higher the clouds, the larger the angle. We are using the tangent of the clinometer angle, since the angle between the ceiling light and the baseline is a right angle.

Sample problem:

• Our baseline (distance from the observer to the ceiling light) is 1000 feet;

• the clinometer angle is 23°;

What is the height of the clouds?

Solution:

Let d be the distance of the light beam from the ceiling light to the cloud base (i.e., d is the height of the clouds).

From simple trigonometry, use the tangent formula:

tangent = opposite side divided by adjacent side.

Thus, the tangent of 23° = d / 1000 feet.

You look up in the trigonometric tables the value of the tangent of 23 degrees, which is 0.42.

Thus, 0.42 = d / 1000 feet, and now solve for d.

d = (0.42) (1000 feet) = 420 feet.

Thus, the height of the cloud base is 420 feet, or, since cloud bases are reported to the nearest 100 feet for low values, the cloud base would be given as 400 feet. If the sky is overcast, e.g., then we have a 400 foot overcast ceiling.

Rotating-beam ceilometer:

Figure 15-8. A rotating-beam ceilometer is a device that uses the same trigonometric principle of tangent of the angle to determine the ceiling. The ceilometer beam scans up and down until it hits the cloud base, at which point the light is reflected and scattered by the cloud, with some of the light reaching the detector directly below. We have a baseline which is a known distance, and a known ceilometer angle, and a 90° angle between the distance d and the baseline, so again we have a right triangle, as explained in the clinometer

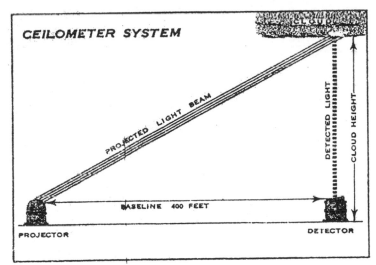

example. The information is electronically returned to the weather office, giving the ceiling.

Laser ceilometer:
A laser ceilometer sends up a narrow, focused light beam which hits the cloud base and then some of the light returns to a detector below which is part of the laser ceilometer. Since the speed of the light is known, and the time it takes for the beam to hit the clouds and return is known, the distance from the ground to the cloud base can be determined. Refraction of the light radiation needs to be built into the formulation.

Chapter 16. NAMING AND IDENTIFYING CLOUDS

In 1803 Luke Howard of England named all the clouds, using Latin names. Thus, puffy clouds caused by convection (rising air currents of 20 to 40 mph or more) were called cumulus clouds. The more straight-looking clouds were named stratus clouds. The high thin wispy clouds comprised of ice crystals, and often looking feathery, were called cirrus clouds. Thus, cumulus, stratus and cirrus are the three main cloud families. Combinations of types led to cirrostratus, stratocumulus and cirrocumulus.

Clouds are also categorized by the height of their bases above the ground. In middle latitudes, cloud bases from zero to about 6500 feet high are called low clouds, from about 6500 to about 20,000 feet high are called middle clouds, and clouds bases from about 20,000 feet high and higher are called high clouds. The middle clouds are given the Latin prefix, alto; thus, if cumulus or stratus clouds have their bases between about 6500 and 20,000 feet, we call them, respectively, altocumulus and altostratus clouds. Thunderstorm clouds are cumulonimbus. These names cover most of the clouds. The prefix "nimbo" for nimbus (Latin for "cloud") is sometimes used for clouds of steady precipitation. Fog is a stratus cloud whose cloud base is on the ground. Thus, when you are in fog, you are in a stratus cloud.

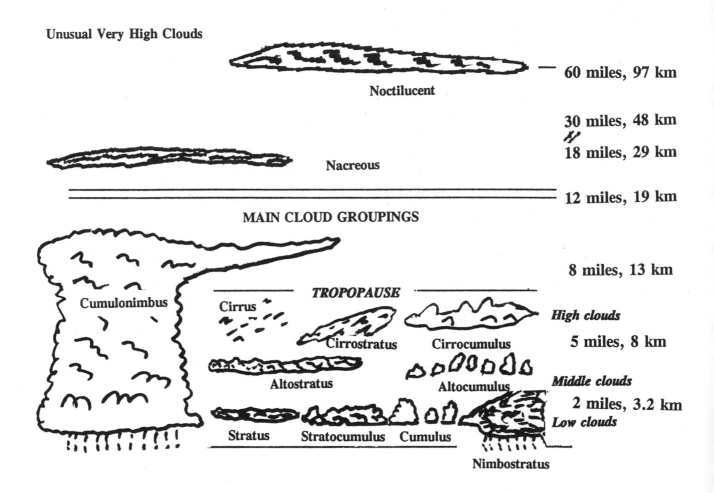

Figure 16-1. A diagram showing cloud types. (Nacreous and noctilucent clouds are high altitude clouds made up partially or totally of solid particles such as meteoritic dust or volcanic ash. They may, especially the nacreous clouds, contain moisture.)

Now we will describe the clouds. Pictures of these cloud types follow the physical descriptions.

Classification of clouds by heights of their bases:

The following descriptions are for the middle latitudes. Clouds often occur at higher levels, and grow to higher heights, in the tropics, and their bases and tops are lower in the polar regions. This is primarily because the tropopause is higher in the tropics and lower in the polar regions, compared with the middle latitudes, and since the air is stable in the stratosphere, with only trace amounts of resident water vapor, it is difficult to get moist enough air to rise and form clouds in the stratosphere. However, cumulonimbus clouds of thunderstorms often shoot up into the lower stratosphere, but their rapid upward vertical motion starts in the troposphere.

In the middle latitudes, low clouds have their bases from the ground up to about 6500 feet, middle clouds are between about 6500 and 20,000 feet, and high clouds are above about 20,000 feet.

The main cloud classifications according to base heights are:

low clouds: stratus, stratocumulus, cumulus, cumulonimbus, nimbostratus;

middle clouds: altostratus, altocumulus;

high clouds: cirrus, cirrostratus, cirrocumulus.

Sometimes, higher-based thunderstorms will occur in an unstable layer aloft, which happens occasionally in the western plains of the U.S.   Then, cumulonimbus clouds would have their bases in the middle cloud category.

Cumuloform clouds have great vertical extent. These clouds, such as towering cumulus and cumulonimbus can be classified as a special family, clouds with significant vertical development. When cumulus clouds keep growing, they become towering cumulus, with their tops reaching over 10,000 feet high. If towering cumulus grow to about 25,000 feet tops and higher, they become cumulonimbus, which are thunderstorm clouds. For example, a cumulonimbus cloud of a well-developed thunderstorm may have its base at 2000 feet and its top at over 50,000 feet! A thunderstorm cloud is dark because it can be ten miles or more deep, loaded with water vapor and precipitation, and during the daytime, reflecting back to space most of the sunlight hitting it.

When moist air is rising in middle latitudes, it can form stratus or cumulus clouds with bases between about 6500 and 20,000 feet. Then, these clouds are called, respectively, altostratus and altocumulus, from the Latin "alto" for "middle" (e.g., altosaxophone).

When stratus and cumulus clouds occur at high cloud level, they are called cirrostratus and cirrocumulus, respectively, using "cirro" as a prefix. At this level, the clouds are comprised of ice crystals.

Strange, mysterious very high clouds:

Clouds are formed by condensing water vapor in the air. We know that only trace amounts of water vapor exist at high altitudes, such as 20 miles (32 kilometers) and 60 miles (97 kilometers). Yet beautiful and rare clouds do occur at these altitudes. Are they comprised of moisture or dust or both? Since these clouds are so high, they can be seen even after the sun has set or a little before it rises, since although the sun is below the horizon, its rays will reach these clouds to make them visible to us observers below, on an otherwise clear or mostly clear night.

Nacreous clouds can be seen at around 18 to 20 miles up, and noctilucent at about 50 to 60 miles. Noctilucent clouds often appear with neon-like, translucent colors; thus, they can be quite beautiful. Otherwise, they look like extremely high cirrus-type clouds.

If these clouds are comprised of moisture around condensation nuclei, how do pockets of moisture get that high? Is there enough injection of moisture into the stratosphere from rapidly-growing big thunderstorms, and the moisture advects around in the stratosphere? Is some moisture coming into our atmosphere from space, associated with meteoritic, comet or asteroid debris as they burn up entering our atmosphere? What about the injection of gasses from high altitude aircraft, rockets, etc.? If these clouds are comprised of dust and/or ash particles, did these particles get so high due to eruptions from ash volcanoes? What about meteoritic dust left over from meteor showers, for example? They are questions begging for answers. We do see beautiful sunrises and sunsets for months after the eruption of an ash volcano, as the sunlight scatters out in different colors after hitting the particles. The colors depend in part on the sizes (the wavelengths) of the particles. Can these clouds be clouds of dust or moisture or dust and moisture? Thus, nacreous and especially noctilucent clouds are still a mystery. (An intriguing book on this and other unusual and extreme weather is "Terror From the Skies!", available from the address on the back cover. Its cost is $29.)

Now let us describe the main weather clouds in the low, middle and high clouds families. (Their pictures follow this description section.)

LOW CLOUDS:

<u>Stratus clouds</u>:   Stratus clouds are called fog when their bases are on the ground. Above the surface, they still look like fog, but aloft. As you travel towards a city, you might not see the tops of buildings because of the tops being obscured by these low clouds. When they do produce precipitation, it is drizzle.

<u>Stratocumulus clouds</u>: Stratocumulus clouds have an irregular shape. They are thin and often appear grayish on the bottom and white on top. They can spread out in a rolling to puffy layer. They can even resemble a package of bacon. These low clouds can produce precipitation, but when the precipitation becomes significant, these clouds have formed into nimbostratus.

<u>Nimbostratus clouds</u>: Nimbostratus clouds produce rain, snow, sleet and freezing rain. They make the sky appear uniformly gray and are sufficiently thick to prevent sunshine and moonshine from coming through then.

<u>Cumulus clouds</u>: Cumulus clouds appear white and puffy, but become darker when they grow into the taller towering cumulus and higher-still cumulonimbus. Since they are formed by rising bubbles of air, their shapes keep changing.

<u>Cumulonimbus clouds</u>: Cumulonimbus clouds are puffy clouds of great vertical extent, becoming darker since they can grow to be over 50,000 feet thick and will block out considerable sunlight plus contain huge amounts of moisture. These are the thunderstorm clouds and sometimes also produce Nature's most violent storm, the tornado. A large part of a hurricane/typhoon is comprised of cumulonimbus clouds. They often contain a cirrus/cirrostratus anvil top, especially when they grow to great heights. They stop growing soon after they reach into the stable lower stratosphere.

MIDDLE CLOUDS:

<u>Altostratus clouds</u>: Altostratus clouds make the sky appear uniformly gray, although when they cause an overcast, it can be just thin enough so that you can barely see the sun or moon. The sun appears as though seen through frosted glass. These middle clouds sometimes appear fibrous. When dense enough, they may produce precipitation, but since their bases are so high, all or some of the precipitation may initially evaporate as it falls through drier air before reaching the ground. When these clouds lower and become stratocumulus, the precipitation chances increase.

<u>Altocumulus clouds</u>: Altocumulus clouds appear as patches or layers of puffy or roll-like clouds, which vary in color from whitish to gray. They look like balls of cotton, and during the daytime if the sky is blue (no thick clouds) above them, they resemble cotton pasted on blue construction paper. Sunlight shining through them can produce a corona that is usually pale blue or yellow in the inside and reddish on the outside. These middle clouds sometimes appear in rows, which are caused by waves of air rising and sinking like a snapped rope as the air waves move along; where the air is rising (with enough moisture), the clouds form, and where it is sinking, the air dries out and has no clouds.

HIGH CLOUDS:

Cirrus clouds: Cirrus clouds are comprised of ice crystals and appear thin and feathery. They are often blown by the upper winds into feathery strands called "mare's tails". Cirrus clouds do not usually cover the entire sky.

Cirrostratus clouds: Cirrostratus clouds look like thin sheets of fine veils. When wind-blown, they can resemble torn patches of gauze. Most of the time they are thin enough to allow the sun or moon to shine through them, forming a halo around the sun or moon. The halo is usually white or whitish, but sometimes the ice crystals that comprise these high clouds will act as prisms to spread out some or all the colors of the rainbow in the halo. As a well-developed low pressure system or warm front approach, cirrus and cirrostratus clouds appear in the sky first, and then lower into altostratus and eventually stratocumulus and nimbostratus with precipitation. Any imbedded convection will also yield cumuloform clouds with their showery/thunderstorm precipitation as well.

Cirrocumulus clouds: Cirrocumulus clouds are thin patchy high clouds with a puffy appearance. They do not occur often, because they are very high-based cumulus clouds, indicating convective currents due to instability in the high levels of the troposphere.

Contrails: A "contrail" is a "condensation trail" caused by high-flying aircraft exhaust in a moist environment aloft. These are the white streaks in the sky that we sometimes observe behind aircraft flying at from 20,000 to about 35,000 feet. Contrails often spread out and temporarily form cirrus or cirrostratus clouds before dispersing.

DEMONSTRATION: OBSERVING CLOUDS
The best method for observing and identifying clouds is have a cloud chart posted on some stiff hardboard, hanging on a wall. With pictures of each cloud type, you can then identify the clouds you observe from your windows. You can also do this outside, bringing the cloud chart with you. You will be amazed at how fast you can learn the cloud types. If you do not have a cloud chart, use the following photographs. Often, there are more than one type of cloud in the sky.

Figure 16-2. STRATUS CLOUDS. These are low, grayish clouds that appear fairly straight and uniform. They can cause drizzle or snow drizzle (called snow grains). Dense fog can lift and form stratus clouds. (source: DOA)

Figure 16-3. STRATOCUMULUS CLOUDS. These are somewhat puffy, but are a mixture of straight and puffy, and range from white to grayish to partially dark. When a solid shield, they can produce more steady precipitation. (source: DOA)

Figure 16-4. NIMBOSTRATUS CLOUDS. Nimbostratus clouds are a type of stratocumulus cloud that is producing steady non-convective and non-drizzle precipitation, i.e., steady rain, snow, sleet or freezing rain, or combinations of these four precipitation types. Nimbostratus clouds are now classified as a type of stratocumulus, but are associated with a weather feature producing widespread steady precipitation. Thus, you will find them associated with, for example, a well-developed winter low pressure system. They make the sky appear more-or-less uniformly gray and are sufficiently thick to prevent much sunshine from coming through them, and no moonshine will come through. (photo by Joseph Balsama).

Figure 16-5. CUMULUS CLOUDS. These are puffy clouds caused by convection, and resemble cauliflower or popcorn. (source: DOA)

Figure 16-6. TOWERING CUMULUS CLOUDS. If cumulus clouds keep growing vertically, they become towers of cumulus called towering cumulus. In mid-latitudes, when their tops reach or exceed about 25,000 feet above the ground, they typically produce the first lightning and thunder and become cumulonimbus clouds, the thunderstorm (next picture). (source: DOT)

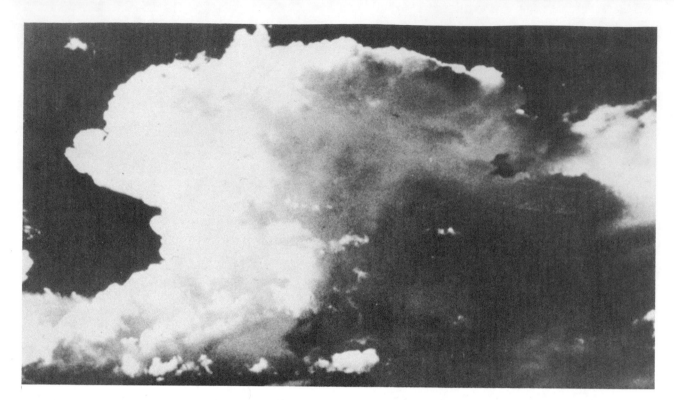

Figure 16-7. CUMULONIMBUS CLOUDS. These bubbly-looking clouds often have very dark regions because they are loaded with moisture and can be over ten miles deep, vertically. These are thunderstorm clouds. They typically have a spreading anvil on top as their tops stop growing when they rise into more stable air aloft, such as when they reach the lower stratosphere. Much cirrus and cirrostratus may also spread out from their tops. (source: DOA)

Figure 16-8. ALTOSTRATUS CLOUDS. These are fairly straight, grayish mid-level clouds, often occurring simultaneously with altocumulus. (source: DOA)

Figure 16-9. ALTOCUMULUS CLOUDS. These are puffy mid-level clouds, which are actually high-based cumulus clouds. (source: DOC)

Figure 16-10. CIRRUS CLOUDS. These are high clouds (from about 20,000 feet off the ground to about 45,000 up) which are comprised of ice crystals and have a feathery appearance. (source: DOT)

Figure 16-11. CIRROSTRATUS CLOUDS. These are fairly straight high clouds that may be thin or can partially block out the moon, sun and sky or can be dense enough to block out the sun, moon and sky. Typically, when these clouds become that dense, they have lowered into altostratus as an approaching warm front and or low pressure system approaches. A ring (halo) around the sun or moon is caused typically by cirrostratus clouds that are thin. (source: DOA)

Figure 16-12. CIRROCUMULUS CLOUDS. These are very high based cumulus clouds, caused by convective currents in unstable air above about 20,000 feet. They appear puffy. (source: DOC)

SOME SPECIAL CLOUD FORMS:

Figure 16-13. CONTRAILS. "Contrails" is an acronym for "condensation trails" caused by aircraft flying between about 20,000 and 45,000 feet (the cirroform clouds layer) with moisture at the aircraft level that has not been lifted to condense into cirrus clouds. A contrail appears initially as a streak in the sky, showing the path of the airplane that caused it. It is in fact a man-made cirrus cloud, comprised of ice crystals. In time, the contrail spreads laterally and eventually disperses. (source: DOC)

Figure 16-14. MAMMATOCUMULUS CLOUDS. Also called cumulonimbus mammatus, these clouds are named for the pendulous "breasts" that they look like. These pouches are mid-level clouds and do not extend downward to produce a tornado, although they are associated with severe thunderstorms that can be tornadic, and indicate extreme turbulence aloft. (source: DOT)   PAGE 113

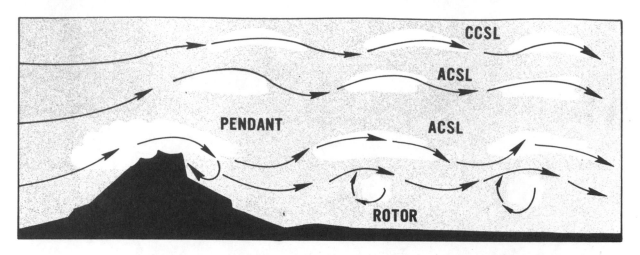

Figure 16-15. MOUNTAIN WAVE CLOUDS. A strong air flow with enough moisture coming over high mountains can sometimes cause a variety of interesting-looking clouds. Some examples are altocumulus standing lenticular (ACSL), cirrocumulus standing lenticular (CCSL), pendant and rotor clouds. (source: DOT)

Figure 16-16. STANDING LENTICULAR CLOUDS caused by a mountain wave. (source: DOT)

Figure 16-17. ROTOR CLOUDS which indicate a rotary circulation beneath a mountain wave. (source: DOT)

Note: when a tornado, waterspout or cold air funnel is extending downward from the cloud base but is not reaching the ground, it is called a **"FUNNEL CLOUD"**, since you are seeing clouds in the circulation.

Figure 16-18. WIND SHEAR BLOWING CLOUD TOPS DOWNSTREAM. When the winds aloft are quite strong, they can shear off the tops of developing clouds and/or can blow these tops downwind. (source: DOT) PAGE 115

VIRGA:

Figure 16-19. VIRGA. Virga is precipitation falling from the clouds but evaporating before reaching the ground. The word "virga" is Latin for "twigs", since sometimes the precipitation appears as streaks. If virga persists, then eventually the drier environment below the clouds moistens enough so that the falling drops or flakes make it to the ground as precipitation. (source: DOT)

Figure 16-20. NOCTILUCENT CLOUDS. These very-high altitude (from about 40 to 60 miles up) clouds may be comprised of dust/ash and may also contain water vapor. They often appear fluorescent with neon colors before sunrise and after sunset. Their beauty can be spectacular. (source: NOAA)

Chapter 17. FOG, HAZE AND VISIBILITY

Figure 17-1. A shallow layer of fog, known as ground fog. When the fog is deeper than 6 feet, it is termed "fog", rather than "ground fog". (source: DOD)

Fog forms when the air temperature cools to its dewpoint early enough in the night so that the surface layer of air remains saturated, and if the winds are light so as to not mix the air with some drier air aloft and inhibit fog development. Fog can also form when water vapor is being added to the air, raising the dewpoint to the air temperature.

Dew typically accompanies fog.

<u>Fog</u> is comprised of tiny droplets of water floating in the air. These droplets, which are actually cloud droplets, are so light that they do not fall to the ground. When enough of these droplets merge within the fog, becoming heavier as they grow, they form drizzle, also known as mist, and fall to the ground. These drizzle drops are smaller than raindrops, smaller than one-half millimeter in diameter. The fog itself is actually a STRATUS CLOUD, whose base is at the surface rather than being aloft.

When you look through fog in the vicinity of a street light, you can see the tiny droplets floating in the air. When you are in an airplane flying through a cloud, you can also see tiny droplets of water floating in the air, and you get the same effect as though you were walking in fog.

Fog classification is based on visibility and depth. <u>Ground fog</u>, as indicated above, is fog whose depth is no more than about six feet; if deeper, it is fog. <u>Visibility</u> is the average distance of how far you can see looking horizontally.

On the New England, Washington, Oregon or British Columbia coasts, for example, on a clear day when you look out over the ocean, you can see the ocean surface for out to only 18 miles, because the curvature of the earth causes the surface to gently curve away from your vision; in the sky, however, you may see high clouds over 100 miles away. If you want to see the ocean surface farther than 18 miles out, you would have to climb a tower or hill, or go to the top of a building. You could be on an ocean beach, watching an ocean liner moving out to sea, and notice that its bottom seems to disappear first, then the top levels, then the smoke stack(s) and finally then the smoke.

The visibility criterion for fog is:
- light fog: visibility of 5/8 of a mile to 6 miles;
- moderate fog: visibility between 5/16 mile to just under 5/8 mile;
- dense fog: visibility under 5/16 mile, down to zero.

The more water droplets floating in the air, the more the light is scattered and the lower the visibility.

Here is a list of weather phenomena that restrict visibility:
fog...haze...smoke...smog...smaze...other pollutants...precipitation...wind-whipped particles: blowing snow, blowing dust, blowing sand, blowing spray (from water surfaces), etc.

Before we consider the various types of fog, let's look at some of the other phenomena that reduce visibility.

Haze comes in two forms: dry haze and moist haze. Dry haze is comprised of fine particles of dust and/or salt suspended in the air. They scatter light from distant objects, making them difficult to see. Moist haze forms in the same way as fog, but the visibility is better, typically no worse than a mile, and usually between 1 and 6 miles. In fact, both types of haze rarely reduce by themselves the visibility to below one mile. Moist haze has tiny water droplets around the suspended particles, and appears dull gray or white. It also scatters light from distant objects, making them difficult to see. Because the moist haze has water droplets and dust and salt particles, the moist haze particles are larger than those of dry haze. Vegetation is apparently also a source of other particles can help form haze. Thus, although dust and salt are main contributors, there are other fine suspended particles that contribute to haze formation. Dark objects viewed through haze tend to have a bluish tinge, while bright objects such as the sun or distant lights tend to have a dirty yellow or reddish hue.

Smaze is a word coined in the 1950s and used by some people to describe a mixture of smoke and haze.

Smog is a term more commonly used, and is a mixture of smoke and fog, although nowadays the term smog is used generically for any combination of fog and pollutants or fog and particulate matter.

Smog and smaze are apt to occur during a relatively calm day and within a stable air mass. In a stable air mass, there is little up and down movement of the air because the colder air has settled on the bottom or the temperature drop in the vertical is not as great as at other times.

Other pollutants can also reduce visibility, as can volcanic ash.

Obviously, if it rains, snows, sleets, etc. hard enough, the precipitation will also reduce the visibility. A common cause of reduced visibility is the combination of precipitation and fog.

Wind-whipped snow, dust and sand are examples of visibility-reducing phenomena in which the wind is a factor. Water spray from off the ocean, a lake or other large water body can also reduce visibility.

HOW VISIBILITY IS MEASURED IN A WEATHER OBSERVATION:

"VISIBILITY", as used in weather observations, is the prevailing visibility: it is the greatest distance you can see in at least 180 degrees around you, or, if the visibility is changing so rapidly that it is difficult to determine, then it is the average distance you can see around you.

You can devise your own visibility chart for visual visibility observations. (An example is shown below.) Visibility is given in statute miles looking for known prominent permanent objects in all directions, or is estimated using a machine known as a <u>transmissometer</u>, which is described a little later.

If, for example, you have a structure, say a tower, which is ten miles to your north, and you can see it today, then your visibility in that direction is at least ten miles. The prevailing visibility is what is reported. It is possible to not have a uniform visibility in all directions; i.e., one sector may have a higher or lower value. Moreover, you can also devise a second visibility chart for one mile and under, with more specific visibility markers at every 1/16th of a mile, e.g. Now let's look at an example of a visibility chart for use for day and for nighttime visibility markers.

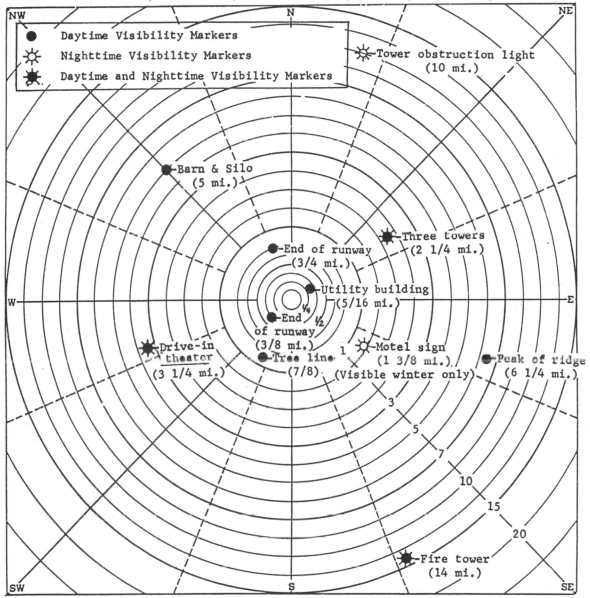

Figure 17-2. An example of a visibility chart for use at an airport weather observatory. Note that some visibility markers can be seen only during the daytime, so it is necessary to locate daytime and nighttime visibility markers. Obscuring elements such as precipitation, fog, haze, blowing snow, etc. reduce the visibility. For example, snow occurring alone (i.e., there is nothing else, such as fog, lowering the visibility) can be defined as light, moderate or heavy in terms of snowfall intensity, based on the visibility it produces. If snow reduces the visibility to no less than 5/8ths mile, it is light snow; if the visbility is less than 5/8ths mile but no less than 5/16ths mile, it is moderate snow; and if the snow reduces the visibility of less than 5/16ths mile, it is heavy snow (typically falling at one to two inches per hour or at even a greater rate). (source: NWS)

Figure 17-3. If you do not know the direct distance from your observation site to each visibility marker, go to each marker and get the height of the object. Then stand at your observing site and with a simple protractor that measure angles, take the angle from you to the top of each object. Since you know the angle and the object's height, use simple trigonometry...the tangent of the angle, to find the horizontal distance to each visibility marker! You can devise one visibility chart for from one to fifteen miles out (or farther), and a low-visibility chart for from one mile down to zero.

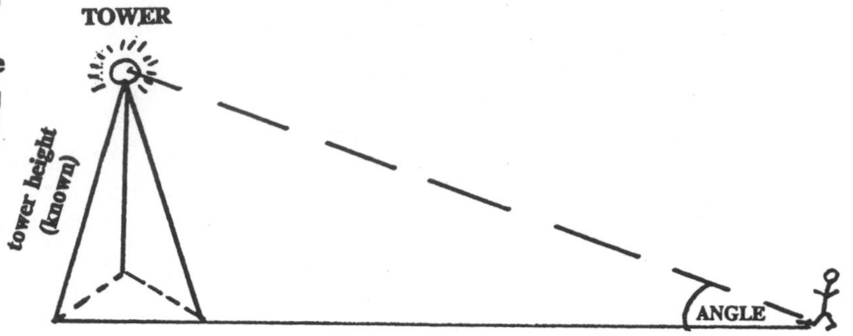

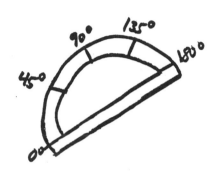

Figure 17-4. With this device, a protractor, you can measure the angle from your observation site to the top of each visibility marker whose height you obtained.

Estimating the horizontal visibility using a transmissometer:

A clever instrument called the transmissometer was invented for use at airports and other observation sites where visibility measurements are needed. Thus, at airports, a transmissometer may be located along or near a runway.

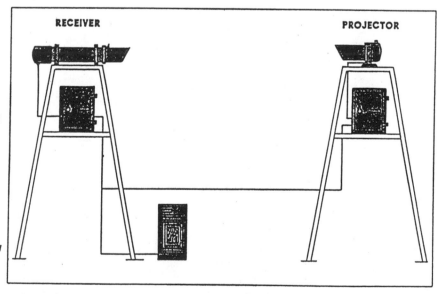

Figure 17-5. A transmissometer for measuring horizontal visibility. The projector sends out a beam of light (similar to a car's headlight) to a target receiver a known distance away (e.g., 750 feet or 1500 feet). Whenever any obscuring phenomenon or phenomena would occur, it would reduce the amount of light making it to the target. The amount of light received is proportional to the visibility, and a readout at the weather office or airport tower, e.g., would show the visibility value. Thus, even though the receiver is only about a few hundred feet from the light source projector, when so much fog and/or snow or other obscuring phenomenon or phenomena come between the projector and receiver, the transmissometer is calibrated so that it can tell you if this means that the visibility due to the obscuring particles is say, 1 mile or 3/4 miles, for example. The receiver uses a photoelectric cell to measure the amount of light penetrating through the obscuring phenomenon/phenomena. (source: NOAA)

Now that we have looked at methods of observing the visibility, of which fog is most often the obscuring factor, we conclude this chapter by looking at how fog is classified based on the conditions under which it forms.

The four types of fog are:

●RADIATION FOG,

●ADVECTION FOG.

●UPSLOPE FOG and

●EVAPORATION FOG.

RADIATION FOG:
At night, the earth is radiating more heat out into space than it is receiving. This is known as net RADIATIONAL COOLING. When skies are essentially clear, the wind is light and no strong fronts are expected to move through that night, then the temperature will fall, and if it falls to its dewpoint, then dew forms. If the dewpoint temperature is reached well before dawn, then besides dew deposition, fog is likely to form. Fog which forms in this way is called radiation fog. At first it will be a shallow layer, which is called ground fog, but if it grows to be more than six feet deep, then it is called fog rather than ground fog.

ADVECTION FOG:
When the winds bring warm and moist air over a cooler surface, advection fog may form. The dewpoint of the warm air is higher than that of the cooler air it is replacing, and the cool ground easily cools the warm air to its dewpoint, leading to fog formation.

Some examples of advection fog are the following. Winter sea fog along and off the New England coast forms when a warm humid air mass moves northward over the cooler waters. The warm air is cooled to its dewpoint, leading to fog formation. Another example is along the Gulf of Mexico coastline and in the southeast U.S. during the cooler months. When southerly winds bring the warm and moist Gulf air over the cooler land, the cold ground cools the temperature of the Gulf air to the dewpoint, resulting in fog formation over the coastal areas.

Advection fog that forms over the ocean and then moves inland is also called **sea fog**.

Advection fog can also form when warm moist air passes over a snow-covered terrain.

UPSLOPE FOG:
Figure 17-6. Cirrostratus clouds above a layer of stratocumulus clouds which are above upslope fog. When air with sufficient moisture content is forced up a mountainside and cools to its dewpoint temperature, fog can result. This type of fog is called upslope fog. If you were at the bottom of the mountain and saw the fog
starting half-way up the mountain, you would call it a cloud; however, if you were half-way up the mountain in this cloud, you would call it fog. (source: DOD)

EVAPORATION FOG:
When rain falls through the air into drier air below and initially evaporates, this is adding moisture to the air below the clouds, thereby raising the air's dewpoint. If the dewpoint temperature is raised to the temperature of the air and surface, fog will form. Evaporation fog occurs often in the vicinity of warm fronts.

A special type of evaporation fog is called <u>sea smoke</u>, which some people refer to as "steam fog". The later name is not good, since steam in invisible. Sea smoke occurs when very cold air moves over relatively warm water. The warmer water heats a very thin layer of air above it and evaporates into the air as water vapor. As the warmed air moves just a few inches above the water surface, it is rapidly cooled to its dewpoint, at which
time the water vapor condenses into tiny droplets of water which look like streamers above the water surface. Sea smoke can occur over lakes, rivers, ponds or streams, giving them an eerie appearance. It typically occurs when the air temperature (F.) is in the teens , single numbers or below zero (below about minus 7 C.).

Figure 17-7. "Sea smoke" over the water in Salem Harbor, Massachusetts. (photo by Joseph Balsama)

Figure 17-8. Valley fog below, and cirrostratus clouds above.
(photo by Meredith Porro)

Quick quiz: suppose on a hot summer day, a thunderstorm then occurs, which covers the ground with a layer of hailstones. Shallow ground fog then forms. Why?

Answer: The fog forms because the cold hailstones lower the temperature of the air at the surface to its dewpoint, which was much higher than the temperature of the hailstones of ice. In a way, this is a form of advection fog, with warm and moist air over a cold surface.

Figure 17-9. Advection fog blowing onshore along the coast of Swampscott. Massachusetts. (photo by Joseph Balsama)

Chapter 18. TYPES OF PRECIPITATION (HYDROMETEORS)

The types of precipitation are: RAIN, DRIZZLE, SNOW (including snow pellets and snow grains), SLEET (ice pellets), FREEZING RAIN and FREEZING DRIZZLE, HAIL, and ICE CRYSTALS (also called ice needles).

Except for ice crystals which can form in clear and very cold air, all precipitation forms in clouds. Clouds form when the air rises and cools to its dewpoint, saturating the air. Where the temperature is above freezing, the cloud droplets are comprised of water, and where the temperature is freezing or below, the cloud droplets are comprised of ice. Cloud droplets are extremely small, being about one five-hundredth of a centimeter across (about one two-hundredth of an inch in diameter). Each cloud droplet, however, is not comprised of pure water. It needs a substance about which to condense. This center of the cloud droplet is called a CONDENSATION NUCLEI, which is a microscopic and hygroscopic (attracts/absorbs moisture) particle. Examples of condensation nuclei include pieces of dust, ash, salt from ocean spray, or similar substances. A condensation nuclei is about one one-hundredth the size of the cloud droplet. In this chapter we are using the term "condensation nuclei" to include sublimation nuclei; page 97 describes the subtle difference between them.

a. rain

When cloud droplets combine through accreting or coalescing and grow to be about 2 millimeters in diameter, they are typically large enough to fall out of the cloud as a raindrop. Gravity helps to cause the raindrop to fall, although strong winds can suspend the rain in the clouds a little longer. If the air below the cloud and towards the surface is very dry, then the raindrops may evaporate before reaching the ground. This evaporating rainfall is called VIRGA.

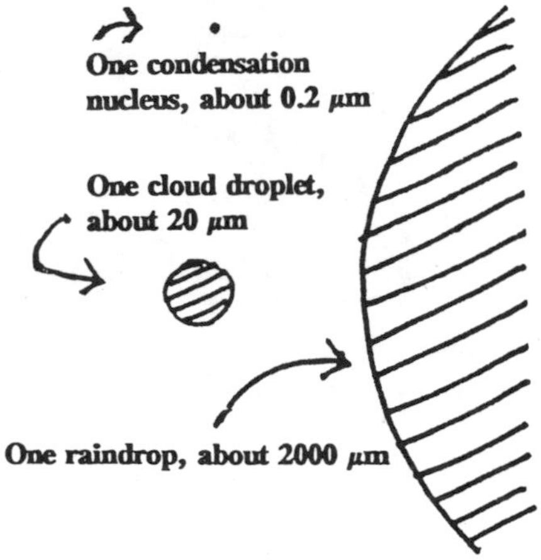

Figure 18-1. Comparing the relative sizes of condensation nuclei, cloud droplets and a raindrop. This figure depicts them much larger than actual size, but in their relative proportions to each other. Raindrops can grow from about 2 millimeters (less than 1/10th inch) diameter, to several times that. Very large raindrops may break apart into smaller ones as they fall. When raindrops start as snowflakes because they form in subfreezing air in the clouds, they may have a wide variety of sizes. Rain is not drizzle, which is explained next.
(1μm = one one/millionth of a meter; there are 39.37" in 1 meter)

One condensation nucleus, about 0.2 μm

One cloud droplet, about 20 μm

One raindrop, about 2000 μm

1 inch of rain is about 2.3 million cubic feet of water per square mile, which is about 18.1 million gallons of water per square mile, which would weigh about 145 million pounds per square mile or about 225,000 pounds of water weight per acre. Thus, water is quite heavy, which you would know if you ever carried a bucket of water in each hand for any distance!

b. drizzle

Very light rain is not drizzle. Drizzle is very fine water drops, smaller than one-half millimeter in diameter, that form in stratus clouds such as fog. In fact, when drizzle is occurring, there is typically fairly dense to very dense fog. Drizzle is created when sufficient fog particles (stratus cloud particles) combine to form these drops which then fall through the cloud to the surface. Because drizzle drops are so fine, it may drizzle all day long yet deliver no more than a few hundredths of an inch of precipitation.

c. snow, snow pellets and snow grains

The traditional Eskimos have some 40 words to describe snow. Snowflakes come in different sizes and shapes, and have varying amounts of water content. A heavy snowstorm or a raging blizzard is one of the most fascinating weather events to observe.

Snow forms directly in the clouds which are at or below freezing, subliming from supercooled water vapor into snowflakes. As with rain, each snowflake also requires a condensation nuclei. The difference between rain and snow formation is that for rain, the cloud temperature is above freezing.

Because of the tremendous amount of snowflake shapes that form in a snowstorm, it is fascinating to take a microscope outside during the storm, and look at the variety of appearances of individual snowflakes. In fact, it has been argued by some meteorologists that in a typical snowstorm, it is unlikely that any two snowflakes will look exactly alike under the microscope!

On the ground, accumulated snow makes a sound when the air temperature is around or below zero Fahrenheit. When the snow is so cold, the air spaces within and between the flakes will make a crunching sound as you walk upon the snow. The snow itself also affects the air temperature. Freshly-fallen heavy snow (six inches or more) will reflect back into space about 85% to 90% of the sunlight striking it, so that the air, which is warmed by the ground that is warmed by the sunlight, warms very little, even if the day is sunny, unless a new air mass is bringing in much warmer air. This reflectivity is also called ALBEDO. Thus, fresh snow has an albedo of about .87 or .88 (87% to 88%), meaning that about 87% to 88% of the sunlight is reflected. Snow that is a few days old has a much lower albedo, approaching .55 (about 55% of the sunlight is reflected back into space). Thus, on a clear night under a cold high pressure system just after a snowstorm has passed through, the overnight low temperature may be 10 or more F. degrees colder than it would be if there were no heavy snow on the ground. This is especially true with light winds, so that the air is allow to radiate some of its heat into space rather than having some of it mixing around in the wind. This cooling is called RADIATIONAL COOLING.

A blanket of snow covering the landscape is not only beautiful but serves as a good insulator. It prevents the ground from getting too cold. Gardeners may lose some of their perennials during winters that have extremely cold temperatures and little snow cover. Frozen ground very often prevents spring rains from penetrating into the soil. The result is rapid runoff and flooding. A heavy snowcover absorbs rain like a sponge, thus slowing down or delaying runoff.

Freshly-fallen snow can absorb sound just like acoustic tiles. Therefore, after a snowfall it seems quieter than usual if there is no major increase in the wind speed. Because snow is white, it scatters light that falls upon it, making the night appear lighter. At night, you can see people and objects better when there is a snow cover. The light comes from the moon, street lights, buildings, etc. During the daytime, freshly-fallen snow reflects so much light that it forces us to wear sunglasses to cut down the glare.

In the following chapter is a section explaining how to accurately measure snow.

Figure 18-2. Some of the shapes of snowflakes, as seen under a microscope. Notice that ALL SNOWFLAKES ARE SIX-SIDED.

Figure 18-3. When snowfall well in excess of 18 inches falls, the weight of the snow might be a problem for some roofs, especially for flat roofs. The warmer the temperature when snow is falling, the more water content (and therefore weight) it is likely to have. Recall that warmer air can hold more moisture than colder air. In areas prone to very heavy snowfalls, such as the Upper Peninsula of Michigan and the "lake-effect snow" areas of Upstate New York, many residents and businesses have snow-rakes, on long, extendable handles, that are used to push off and pull off much of the snow from the roofs, to avoid roof collapse. (source: NOAA)

With temperatures in the 20s Fahrenheit, a foot of freshly fallen snow, when you melt it, yields about one inch of water. With temperatures around zero F., a foot of freshly fallen snow would yield about one-half inch of water to as little as about two-tenths of an inch.

Snow falling at around freezing, because of its high water content, is commonly referred to as "WET SNOW"; its weight is relatively heavy. Snow falling at temperatures from the low 20s F. and colder is commonly referred to as "DRY SNOW", which is more powdery and fluffy because of its relatively low weight due to a lower water content. The snow is not dry...it contains moisture; the term is a relative term, comparing this snow with "wet snow".

DEMONSTRATION:
A METHOD OF PRESERVING SNOW CRYSTALS
This is a fun project that produces replicas of
the snow crystals easily and cheaply.

Materials needed:
- Clean glass - a small piece of glass at least 2" x 2" (at least 5 cm x 5 cm)
- Holder - use any insulating material; e.g., use a piece of wood with a low edge to prevent the glass from slipping
- Spray - Use any 5% transparent spray in a push-button can, such as Krylon Crystal clear #1301 (sprays are available from hardware stores)

Procedure:
1. Place all the above materials in the freezer of a refrigerator for several minutes so that they become below freezing.
2. Place the glass on the (wood) holder. (Careful!: if the glass is held in the hand, the heat from the fingers could melt the snowflakes.)
3. Spray an even coating of Krylon (or similar) spray on the glass, tilting the glass so that any excess runs to one edge.
4. Let several falling snowflakes land on the glass.
5. Place the glass and its holder in a cold, ventilated place for about 15 minutes or until the solvent has evaporated.

Results:
Each snowflake is replaced by the plastic spray; moreover, the result will be white, just like the snowflake! These are delicate snowflake replicas and should not be touched or handled roughly. This is how you can examine closely the shapes of snowflakes under a magnifying glass or microscope.

Snowflake replicas can also be mounted in a slide and projected for short periods of time.:

Slide prepared for projection

2" x 2" GLASS

PLASTIC SNOW
CRYSTAL REPLICAS

CARDBOARD SPACER
AROUND 4 SIDES

BIND WITH TAPE AROUND 4 SIDES

Slides may be labelled with the date, name of collector and types of crystals.
(source: modified from Vincent Schaefer)

Differently-colored snow:

Snow as it falls and accumulates is almost always white. On very rare occasion, snow will occur in other colors. In Saskatchewan, an early-season snow included flakes which formed around certain pollen grains which had been kicked up just previously by high winds. This pollen served as condensation nuclei about which the snowflakes formed. To the astonishment of the sparse population in that area, the snowfall was YELLOW, and accumulated on the ground as several inches of yellow snow.

Sometimes, fine sand particles from the Sahara-Libyan Desert are transported into Europe and serve as some of the condensation nuclei for rain or snow. A dramatic such event occurred over a large part of Germany in December 1859 when that area received a heavy snowstorm of RED SNOW! Red rains and snows have occurred over parts of Asia, although they are rare.

Purple, orange and red snow was experienced by American troops during war duty in northern Italy in 1944. The causes were ash and dust particles from an erupting (explosive) ash volcano, which served as the host condensation nuclei for the multi-colored snow.

Snow pellets and snow grains:

Sometimes snowflakes may also accrete some rime icing in the clouds, and sometimes snowflakes may partially melt and then refreeze. When they hit the ground, they are little white balls. If the flakes melt and then refreeze, we have one form of sleet, rather than pellets of partially-melted and refrozen snow. Snow pellets will bounce and may break apart when they strike the surface. Snow pellets are accreting supercooled water onto them as they pass through the cloud, causing this water to freeze (rime-ing). (In the past, some people referred to these small masses of ice with small air bubbles in them as "graupel".) It is possible for some water to exist in the clouds as a liquid when the cloud temperature is below freezing. Some updrafting and downdrafting of air creates the paths of these precipitation particles; thus, they typically fall from cumuloform clouds that may occur alone or imbedded within a larger storm, and thus snow pellets are showery in nature.

Snow grains are snow drizzle, occurring in fog (stratus clouds based on the ground) or in the stratus clouds just off the surface. If the clouds are too cold for rain but he temperature is freezing or below from the ground on up through these clouds, then snow drizzle, known as snow grains occurs. They are very fine snow, typically under 1 millimeter across (25.4 millimeters equals one inch), and yield very light accumulations.

d. sleet
e. freezing rain and freezing drizzle

Sometimes very shallow cold air hugs the surface, and several hundred feet to say about 1500 feet above the surface, the temperature is above freezing. Much higher up, the precipitation may start as snow, but then fall into the warmer air and partially or totally melt, subsequently falling into the shallow sub-freezing air layer hugging the surface, causing either freezing rain or sleet. Thus, the thermal profile of the lower atmosphere determines the type of precipitation.

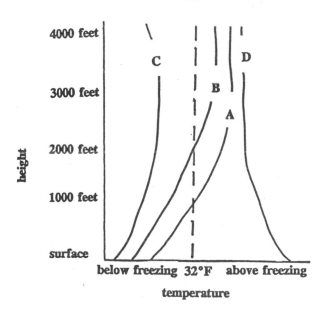

Figure 18-4. The vertical temperature profiles for rain, snow, sleet and freezing rain. Note that when the surface-based sub-freezing layer is under about 1000 feet deep, freezing rain occurs. This is because the rain has not been falling long enough through sub-freezing air to freeze into ice, so it freezes on contact with any surface that is at or below the freezing temperature. As the surface-based sub-freezing layer approaches about 2000 feet, the rain will have fallen through a sufficiently thick sub-freezing layer to become little pellets of ice (sleet) by the time they reach the surface. When the sub-freezing air is between about 1000 and 2000 feet of thickness, combinations of sleet and freezing rain may occur. Thus, depending upon the changing vertical thermal profiles, it is possible to have combinations of rain, snow and sleet, and of snow, sleet and freezing rain.

 A = freezing rain, B = sleet, C = snow, D = rain

Freezing rain and freezing drizzle are perhaps the worst types of precipitation, because it is just about impossible to drive, even with chains on the tires, on a surface coated with ice. More traffic accidents occur during ice storms (glaze) than during any other weather-caused driving problem.

Sometimes, with low-level temperatures around freezing, some of the snowflakes partially melt and then fuse with other snowflakes, resulting in blobs of snow falling from the sky. In exteme cases, these supersnowflakes have been observed to be two to three inches in diameter...snowballs from the clouds!

Freezing drizzle occurs in surface-based fog, falling when forming within the first few hundred feet of the surface, when the air is just below freezing. Snow grains or freezing drizzle can occur under these conditions.

Figure 18-5. Although an ice-storm is physically beautiful, especially when it is over and the sunlight is glistening through the ice, it is a dangerous storm and creates widespread damage. Trees and powerlines will break due to the heavy weight of ice, especially if the ice accumulates to an inch to two inches or more. The worst case scenario is such a heavy ice storm of freezing rain, followed by very cold temperatures which inhibit melting, accompanied by strong winds. The strong winds acting on the brittle wood will cause tree limbs to snap and fall, and will fell power lines and poles. (source: NOAA)

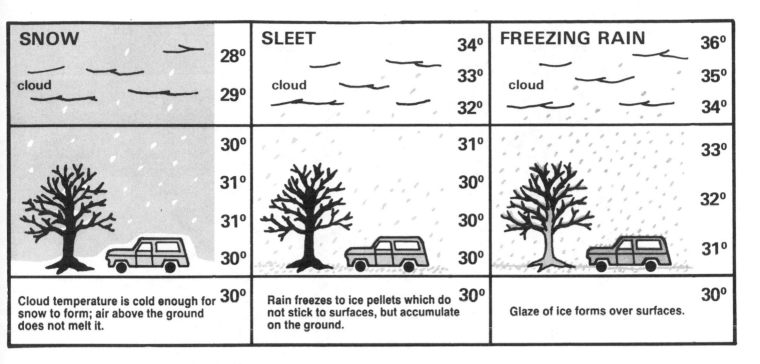

SNOW		SLEET		FREEZING RAIN	
cloud	28° 29°	cloud	34° 33° 32°	cloud	36° 35° 34°
	30° 31° 31° 30°		31° 30° 30° 30°		33° 32° 31°
Cloud temperature is cold enough for snow to form; air above the ground does not melt it.	30°	Rain freezes to ice pellets which do not stick to surfaces, but accumulate on the ground.	30°	Glaze of ice forms over surfaces.	30°

Figure 18-6. Snow vs. sleet vs. freezing rain. (source: NOAA)

Figure 18-7. Sunlight glistening through the accumulated ice is ironically beautiful. (photo by Joseph Balsama)

f. hail

Figure 18-8. A violent hailstorm with large hailstones covering the surface during a severe thunderstorm.

Hail is not sleet. Whereas sleet occurs typically in stratiform clouds such as stratocumulus, hail forms in the cumulonimbus clouds of thunderstorms, whose cloud tops can grow into the lower stratosphere. Meteorological research has still not proven conclusively how hail forms. We do know that when large hailstones are cut in half, we observe layers of ice, similar in appearance to layers of an onion. This implies that hail formation involves an ice accretion process.

Early theories speculated that the hailstone must be undergoing successive rides up and down through the thunderstorm, going above and below the freezing level, propelled by updrafts acting perhaps in a gusty fashion. Each time a hailstone would fall below the freezing level, it would pick up another coating of water, and if carried by gusty updrafts to above the freezing level, that water would subsequently freeze, adding another layer of ice to the hailstone. The hail would then perhaps undergo the process again and again. Ultimately, the hailstone would fall to earth only when it became too heavy to be supported by updrafts or the updrafts weaken.

This theory also assumed that the hailstones formed around the freezing level in thunderstorms, which on a summer day in mid-latitudes could be 12,000 feet or higher above the ground, and in spring, often from 6,000 to 9,000 feet elevation. What vertical depth the hailstones travel in their creation process is unknown. Some researchers proposed that the stones may not travel up and down too far, but would keep accreting layers of ice around the freezing level in the thunderstorm cloud.

Figure 18-9. In the United States, the worst hailstorms occur in the central plains of the U.S. Compare the size of these hailstones with the doorknob in the left of the picture.

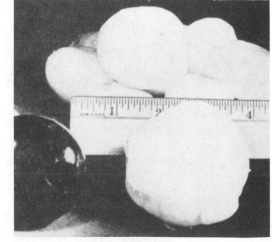

A later theory of hailstone formation proposed that the hail forms as a frozen raindrop or partially-melted or totally-melted snowflake that refreezes, being held up in the cloud by an updraft, during which time the hailstone has supercooled drops of water adhering to it and freezing, forming new ice layers. (Supercooled water is water existing in the liquid phase even though the temperature is somewhat below freezing. We know that this can occur in clouds.)

The popular theory now is that some small object needs to serve as the nucleus for hail. This object could be a large, frozen raindrop or, because small objects such as insects have been found inside the middle of hailstones, even insects could serve as hailstone nuclei. The nucleus then accumulates supercooled liquid droplets (cloud droplets) through accretion. Updrafts carry the hailstone through some portions of the cloud, and through varying liquid concentrations. When the layers of ice that form around the nucleus cause the hailstone to be too large to be held aloft by updrafts, or if the hailstone is flung out of an updraft, then, thanks to gravity, and maybe also to a downdraft, it heads for earth.

The actual cause of hail probably embodies at least part of all these theories.

Many small hailstones melt into rain before reaching the surface. Also, hailstones can have layers of clear and opaque ice.

The largest hailstones have been over five inches (13 centimeters) in diameter. In 1995, Chinese weather bureau meteorologists reported basketball-size hail in one of China's provinces. Such enormous hail killed people and demolished homes and crops. Sometimes hail falls for over ten minutes and accumulates, even forming hail drifts when pushed by flash-flood flowing water. These hail drifts, which can be several feet deep, can persist for a few days, even in summer, before totally melting. Grapefruit-size hailstones require updrafts on the order of 60 to 70 meters per second (about 125 to 150 miles per hour). Imagine being in an aircraft flying through such an updraft!

<u>How to preserve large hailstones:</u>

Figure 18-10. A large hailstone, cut in half to show the layers of ice.

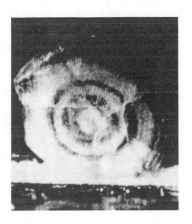

If you experience large hail such as the hailstone in this picture, and you want to temporarily save some of the largest hailstones to show them to others and to take pictures and video of them, do not simply place them in a freezer, especially a frost-free freezer, since the ice will eventually pass into the vapor phase, causing your 3-inch hailstones to become pea-size and then disappear. Instead, place the hailstones in a plastic-like bag or container and seal the bag or container tightly, and then put them in the freezer. This prevents the sublimation from ice to vapor, and will therefore preserve your hailstones.

g. ice crystals

Ice crystals, sometimes called ice needles, are the only type of precipitation that does not require clouds. Cirrus and cirrostratus clouds, at 20,000 feet up and higher, are also comprised of ice crystals, which may be the same or similar to these precipitating ice crystals.

Ice crystals are tiny needles of ice that form only in air that is very cold, typically around and below zero Fahrenheit. The air must be clear or nearly so, and the wind must be calm or nearly so. They occur mostly at night. When the sun is out, the ice crystals sublime and disappear. When the sun is just rising, the sunlight shining through ice crystals will create rainbowish columns or areas of scattered colored light.

<u>Cloud Seeding</u>:

Cloud seeding is sometimes used in an attempt to enhance precipitation during droughts. In order for cloud seeding to be successful, there must exist clouds. The condensation nuclei (seeding agents) are added to the cloud, typically via aircraft. The two most common substances used are "dry ice" (solid carbon dioxide) and silver iodide.

There is still much to be learned about cloud seeding. In some cases it can lead to more precipitation, but in others, less. There is always a question of how much rain would have fallen in spite of the fact that the clouds were seeded.

According to some researchers, another method of causing cloud droplets to come together to make raindrops (or causing small raindrops to join, producing larger raindrops) that occurs in Nature is lightning. Surrounding a lightning bolt is an <u>electric field</u>, which exerts a force on water droplets, causing them to come together. Perhaps we should take time out and give a practical definition of a field. A <u>field</u> is an area in space where a force has an influence on an object. You are familiar with a <u>magnetic field</u>. The following experiment is an illustration.

<u>DEMONSTRATION</u>: ILLUSTRATING A MAGNETIC FIELD

1. Suspend a paper clip or any other small metallic object from a picture hook that is mounted on the wall. Use a piece of string for this.

2. Approach, but do not touch, the paper clip with a magnet. The instant that you notice the paper clip moving, you can conclude that the clip is being acted upon by a magnetic force and is within the magnet's magnetic field.

In like manner, if you jump off a table, you are pulled down by the earth's gravitational force; therefore, you are within the earth's <u>gravitational field</u>.

A lightning bolt produces electrical forces that cause cloud droplets and small raindrops to come together to produce larger drops. The raindrops are being forced together by the electrical forces within the lightning bolt's electrical field. How often have you noticed that in a shower that is growing into a thunderstorm, the heavy rain does not begin until there has been at least one bolt of lightning with its accompanying thunder? The following demonstration shows this very nicely.

<u>DEMONSTRATION</u>: DEMONSTRATING COALESCENCE OF DROPLETS IN AN ELECTRIC FIELD

1. Using a Bunsen burner with a wing tip, heat a piece of small glass tubing by rotating it in the flame until it gives off a yellow glow and feels as if it is about to collapse.
2. At this point, pull it apart while it is still in the flame, until you form a thread-like fiber.
3. Remove the tubing from the flame and allow it to cool.
4. Using a triangular file, cut the fine thread-like fiber until you have a very small opening.
5. Place a 12-inch piece of rubber or plastic tubing on the end of the glass tubing that was not stretched. Make sure that the rubber or plastic tubing fits tightly on the glass tubing.
6. Now attach the rubber tubing to a faucet that has a narrow opening, such as you would find in a sink in a science room.
7. With a clamp, attach the rubber tubing where it meets the glass tubing to a ring stand. This will allow the small opening to be vertical. Place this set-up in a sink.
8. Very slowly and carefully turn on the water until you have created a fountain with a very fine spray.
9. Rub a hard rubber rod (or comb) with a piece of wool for about 15 seconds.
10. Slowly approach the fountain. Try not to get the wool or rod wet. As you approach, you will notice that the small drops will come together and form larger drops. You can make this appear more dramatic if you bring the charged rod close to the bottom of the water column at the point where it comes out of the glass tubing.
11. As you walk away from the fountain with the rubber rod, you will notice that the droplets become smaller; that is, you end up with a finer spray.
12. Repeat steps 10 and 11 as many times as you wish.

Chapter 19. MEASURING PRECIPITATION

All precipitation is recorded in liquid form, with a separate category for snow (which also includes sleet). By liquid form is meant that even snow and sleet are melted so that its water content is recorded as precipitation.

Rainfall is measured by a RAIN GAUGE, which is simply a bucket placed securely on a post in an open area, away from buildings and trees that could block precipitation from reaching the gauge. A bucket by itself leads to errors, since a ruler or measuring stick would have to be placed in the bucket and taken out, being read where the water level rose to. A narrow tube is inserted inside the larger bucket or container, so that one inch of precipitation in the larger container would completely fill the inner tube. A magnified scale is printed on the side of the inner tube. In the United States, this scale is for every 0.01". Elsewhere, the scale is for every millimeter or half-millimeter. (Approximately 25.4 millimeters equals one inch.) See **Figure 19-1 below**. This is **a typical plastic rain gauge, capable of holding up to twelve inches of water, with the inner tube such that the first one inch would fill the inner tube before overflowing into the larger container.** When over one inch of rain falls, the inner tube is read and then emptied, and what is left in the larger container is then emptied into the inner tube so that the rainfall can be read to the nearest one-hundredth of an inch. If over two inches of rain falls, the inner tube is filled as many times as necessary to obtain the total rainfall.

During the time of the year when the air temperature is expected to fall below freezing, the inner tube is taken indoors or else it might crack if water freezes and therefore expands inside the tube. When solid precipitation such as snow and sleet fall, only the larger container is used to catch it. The container is brought inside to melt the snow, and its water equivalent is then recorded. Another method is to fill the inner tube with hot water, and then pour it into the larger tube which contains the snow, sleet or freezing rain. After that all melts, measure the total water content and subtract the hot water amount that was added. (Figure 19-2 on the next page shows the parts of this rain gauge.)

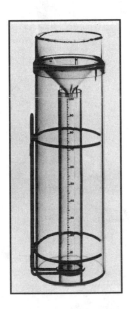

Figure 19-1. Exterior view of a typical plastic rain gauge.

(source: Robert E. White Instruments, Inc.; Boston, Massachusetts)

This type is rain gauge is recommended over a smaller "wedge-type" rain gauge, because it has a wider opening to representatively catch the rain. In other words, a good rain gauge will give you an accurate rainfall record, whereas a small gauge will only give you an approximation, which will be too low. Recommended is a rain gauge in which the larger container has an opening of at least four inches (ten centimeters).

Daily rainfall should be recorded at the end of the day, always staying in standard time, not daylight time.

If you are home at the end of a thunderstorm during a summer afternoon, for example, it is good to measure the rain then, to which any additional rain events for that day can be added later for the total for the day. The reason is that if the sun comes blazing out on a hot day after a shower or thunderstorm, it will evaporate some of the rainfall from the gauge, leading to a somewhat lower reading if you read it many hours later.

There are other, more expensive, rain gauges used by agencies such as the National Weather Service in the U.S. and other weather services worldwide. These gauges are discussed later in this chapter.

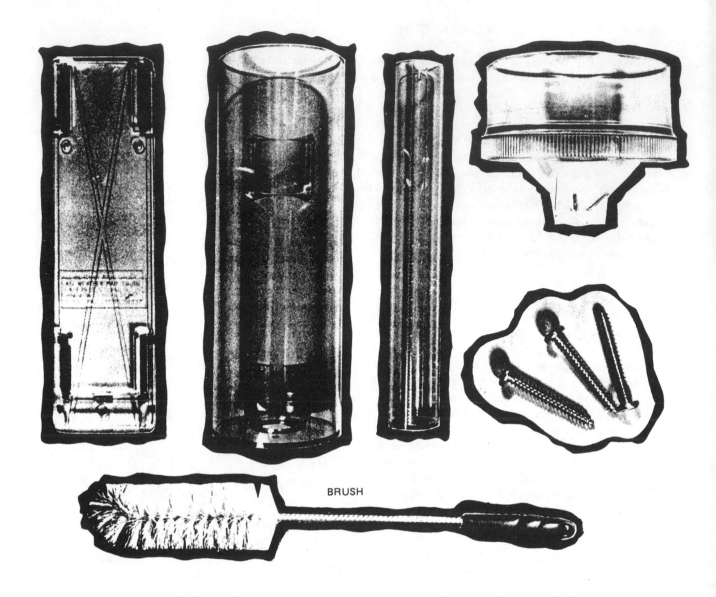

BRUSH

Figure 19-2. Parts of a rain gauge. From left to right: backplate for attaching to a post, outer (larger) container, inner tube, top funnel and screws for backplate, and on bottom, cleaning brush. (source: Productive Alternatives, Inc.; Fergus Falls, MN)

Another type of rain gauge is the <u>standard eight-inch rain gauge</u>. (See figure 19-3 on next page.) "Eight-inch" refers to the opening at the top (the diameter of the gauge). The gauge is used with a measuring stick, and consists of a metal stand, a funnel, an outer can and an inner tube. The principle is the same as for the plastic rain gauge detailed in the two previous pages. The funnel top collects the rain or drizzle which falls into the inner tube. Since the entrance area of the inner tube is one-tenth that of the larger can, an inch of rain will be ten inches deep in the inner tube. This makes measuring the rain easier, because it is much easier to measure larger quantities of rain than smaller amounts. The rain measuring stick is calibrated for this so that one inch of rain (on the measuring stick) equals 10 inches on a regular ruler. One tenth of an inch of rain equals one inch on a regular ruler, and, in like manner, one hundredth of an inch equals one tenth of an inch on a ruler. The measuring stick, which is calibrated in hundredths of an inch, is stuck into the inner tube and then withdrawn. The stick is wet up to a certain point, which shows how much liquid precipitation fell. If the inner tube fills with rainwater, the rest overflows into the larger container.

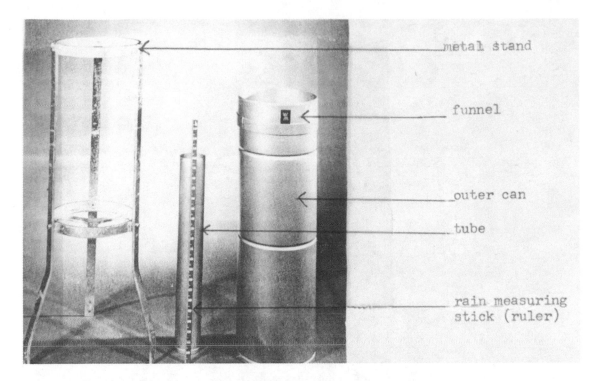

metal stand

funnel

outer can

tube

rain measuring
stick (ruler)

Figure 19-3. The standard eight-inch (eight-inch diameter opening on top of the larger outer can) rain gauge. (photo courtesy of Robert E. White Instruments, Inc.; Boston, MA)

To measure the rainfall, the observer places the measuring stick into the inner tube until it hits bottom. The top of the wet portion of the stick shows the rainfall amount. The tube is emptied after the reading is taken. Since the tube is 20 inches tall, it can hold only two inches of water. When it rains over 2 inches, the excess overflows into the outer container, in which case the first two inches are already in the inner tube, which is emptied when the rainfall measurement is being done, and the rest is then measured by pouring it into the inner tube and adding it to the two inches. For example, if 4.66" falls, the inner tube would be filled, and the rest (2.66") is in the outer can. The observer would carefully pour the water from the outer can to fill up the inner tube again, recording the two more inches and then emptying the tube. Then he/she would pour the remaining water into the inner tube and measure the remaining 0.66" with the stick. The total rainfall of 4.66" would thusly be read.

During the time of year when the air temperature is expected to fall below freezing, the funnel and tube are brought inside, so that the frozen or freezing precipitation falls directly into the larger container. When it rains, the water from the outer container is poured into the inner tube and measured as before, and when frozen or freezing precipitation occurs, such as snow, sleet and freezing rain, the can is brought inside to melt the ice in it and a spare can replaces it outside. After the ice melts, its water equivalent is measured the same way rain is measured. Snowfall is therefore measured as well as its water equivalent.

Another type of rain gauge is the weighing rain gauge. (See figure 19-4 on the next page.) The rain falls into a bucket (pail) that sits on a scale which relates the weight of the rain to its amount (in inches and fractions of an inch). Thus, the scale is calibrated in inches and hundredths. A pen from the scale writes on a chart that is on a drum that is driven by a wind-up clock mechanism. Thus, a clock-driven drum has a graphpaper-like recording sheet attached to it and it slowly rotates. By reading the chart, you can tell when rain began and ended, since the recording trace keeps going up the graph as it rains. When the bucket is emptied, the recording pen is set back to zero at the bottom of the recording chart. Weighing rain gauges can record up to one week's worth of precipitation records on one chart.

In freezing and colder air, some antifreeze is placed in the bucket to melt frozen and freezing precipitation as it falls. Some rain gauges have heaters which melt frozen and freezing precipitation.

The recording chart is always set back to zero after the rainfall is read and bucket emptied.

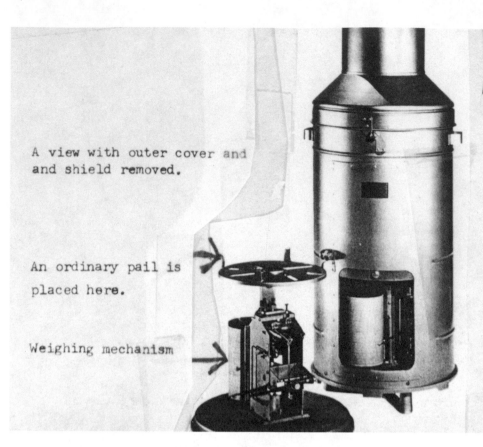

A view with outer cover and
and shield removed.

An ordinary pail is
placed here.

Weighing mechanism

View with outer cover
and shield. Sliding door is
opened to show recording pen
and chart.

Figure 19-4. A weighing rain gauge. (photo courtesy of Robert E. White Instruments, Inc.; Boston, MA)

It is important to note that a rain gauge must be placed in an open area away from buildings and trees that would block some of the precipitation from entering the gauge. In areas with a lot of snow, a snow fence is placed around the gauge so that blowing snow that has already fallen does not enter the gauge to given erroneous extra precipitation to the record.

Yet another type of rain gauge is the <u>tipping-bucket rain gauge</u>. (See figure 19-5 on the next page.)

The tipping bucket rain gauge has two little buckets inside, such that when one side fills with one one-hundredth of an inch of water, it tips and empties, which records 0.01" on a counter. Then when the other side fills up, it empties 0.01" and records it.

Note on the most commonly-used rain gauges for all of us who enjoy keeping our own precipitation records: If you have a plastic-type rain gauge, or plan to acquire one, remember to take the inner tube inside when the temperature is expected to go below freezing. If water in the inner tube freezes, it will expand and may crack the tube. The thicker, outer cylinder remains outside to catch frozen and freezing precipitation whose water equivalent will be found later. We prefer to have spare rain gauges, so that on the rare occasion of excessive rainfall, you can run outside and rapidly replace the gauge or the inner tube and take inside the rain-filled one for reading. In Holt, Missouri (in northwest Missouri), it once rained 12 inches in 42 minutes; thus, if the rain gauge could not hold twelve inches, one gauge alone would not have documented this record rain event. Moreover, we have found that having two rain gauges allows you to take one in at the end of the day during a raging snow, sleet or ice-storm, so that you can replace it with the other gauge and then melt the snow, sleet or ice for recording it for the day's precipitation.

   Your precipitation record includes a daily column for rain and water equivalent, and a daily column for snow, which also includes sleet. Freezing rain and freezing drizzle are recorded as rainfall, with a note that all or part of it was freezing precipitation. Hailstones are not recorded in the snow column, but notes about the size of the largest stones and whether they covered the ground should be noted. The melted hail becomes part of the rainfall measurement.

Figure 19-5. A tipping-bucket rain gauge (left) and a standard eight-inch rain gauge (right).
(photo source: Joseph Balsama)

How to measure snow:

1. Take your yardstick or snow measuring stick outside to an open area away from trees and buildings.
2. Find an area where the snowdepth looks fairly representative of the average depth; do not go into an area with large drifts and/or where the snow has been drifted/blown away from to a great extent. Some drifts and drifted-away areas are acceptable.
3. If measuring the depth of newly-fallen snow, stick your measuring stick all the way through the new snow and read its depth, in about eight to ten or so locations in which the depth looks fairly representative. In a windy storm, some drifting is to be expected.
4. Take the average of all snow readings to determine your snowfall. For a snowdepth reading which may include old snow also, push your measuring stick all the way through both new and old snow. New snow is measured to the nearest tenth of an inch. A half of a tenth inch would be rounded up to 0.1". Below this amount is recorded as a "TRACE" of snowfall. SNOW-DEPTH, which is the total of old and new snow, is measured to the nearest inch. One-half inch is rounded up to 1". Anything below a half-inch is recorded as a "TRACE" of snow-depth. "Snowfall" and "snow-depth" also include sleet.
5. During a snowstorm, the new snowfall should be measured every one to three hours. This is because as snow accumulates, it compacts (settles). Thus, a 24-hour storm may dump 20.4 inches of snow, but if it is measured at only the end of the storm, the depth may be 15.3 inches. Thus, the snowfall must be reported as 20.4", not 15.3".
6. When snow falls with the temperature around freezing, or the sun is coming in and out of clouds, there will be melting. Sometimes estimating the snow as it falls is necessary.
7. A large piece of plywood or some similar surface can be used to measure snow every one to three hours if the wind is not so strong as to cause significant drifting. This SNOWBOARD can be wiped clean after each measurement, so that your next measurement would include the snowfall since the board was cleaned off, and this new amount would then be added to the previous total snowfall amount to give your current total snowfall from this storm.

SNOWFALL IS MEASURED TO THE NEAREST 0.1"; SNOW-DEPTH IS MEASURED TO THE NEAREST INCH. Snow-depth is the amount of snow on the ground.

How to determine the water equivalent of snow and sleet:

There are two sets of precipitation records. One is simply "precipitation", which means all liquid precipitation and the melted water content of frozen precipitation. The second set is that for snow and sleet (frozen precipitation). For record purposes, freezing precipitation (freezing rain and freezing drizzle) are recorded as liquid, since melting one inch of freezing rain would yield one inch of water. Thus, liquid, freezing and frozen are combined for the total precipitation, with the water amount of the melted snow and melted sleet (called the water equivalent of the snow and sleet) added to the amount of liquid precipitation (rain and drizzle).

Another way of looking at the water equivalent is: how much rain would have fallen if the snow that just fell were rain instead? For example, since warmer air can hold more moisture than very cold air, then when we have a snowstorm with the temperature near freezing, every eight inches of snow might melt to yield one inch of water equivalent, but when we have a snowstorm with the temperature below about 10 degrees F., then it may take twenty-five inches of snow to yield one inch of water equivalent.

The following example illustrates a water equivalent from a snowstorm:

1. During a particular snowstorm, 13.4" of snow was measured using a snow measuring stick.
2. When the snow from the outer tube of the rain gauge was brought inside and melted, it gave 2.00 inches of water equivalent.
3. Dividing the 13.4" by 2.00" yields 6.7. Therefore, the snow-to-water ratio from this snow event was 6.7 (that is, every 6.7" of snow melts to give one inch of water).

What is a trace of precipitation?

For rain and water equivalents of melted snow/sleet, a trace is under one one-hundredth of an inch (under 0.01"), since rain is measured to the nearest 0.01";

For falling snow and sleet, a trace is under one-tenth of an inch (under 0.1"), since snow and sleet are measured to the nearest one-tenth of an inch;

For snowdepth on the ground, a trace is under a half-inch, since snowdepth is measured to the nearest inch (a half-inch would be rounded up to be one inch).

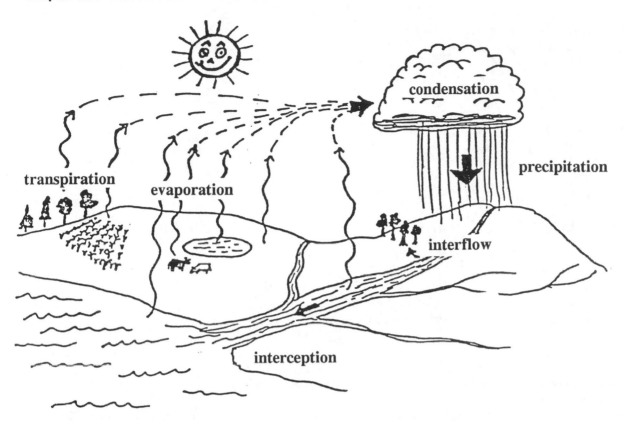

Figure 20-1. The Hydrologic Cycle. The sum total of all the moisture in solid, liquid and gaseous form in the earth-atmosphere system is a constant; thus, the moisture keeps recycling. The water that you used to take your last shower or bath is part of the same water used by Adam and Eve as well as by the dinosaurs!

The hydrologic cycle (water cycle) demonstrates how Nature reuses water. Moisture enters the atmosphere through the <u>evaporation</u> of water from land, bodies of water, vegetation, etc. into water vapor, a gas. Some water enters the atmosphere through <u>transpiration</u>, which is the process of plants and trees giving off excess water chiefly through the pores (stomata) of their leaves. The two processes of emitting moisture into the atmosphere are also referred to in one combined term called <u>evapo-transpiration</u>.

Water returns to the earth chiefly through precipitation. Most of the precipitation and snowmelt moves along the surface as <u>runoff</u>, eventually emptying into rivers and streams and their tributaries, as well as being impounded by bodies of water such as ponds and lakes. <u>Interception</u> is the term used to describe runoff that ends up in such a water body. Some water flows beneath the surface as <u>interflow</u> or rests in a region of the soil that is always saturated: this water is called <u>groundwater</u>. The top of the groundwater is called the <u>water table</u>. When we have a prolonged and heavy rainy period, the amount of ground water under a house's foundation increases and can lead to water in the basement. Areas of land that are normally below the water table are bodies of water such as lakes, ponds, rivers and streams. Groundwater moves under the ground similar to rivers on the surface. The areas where groundwater is stored are called <u>aquifers</u>. In low areas. groundwater can move into open areas to again become part of the runoff.

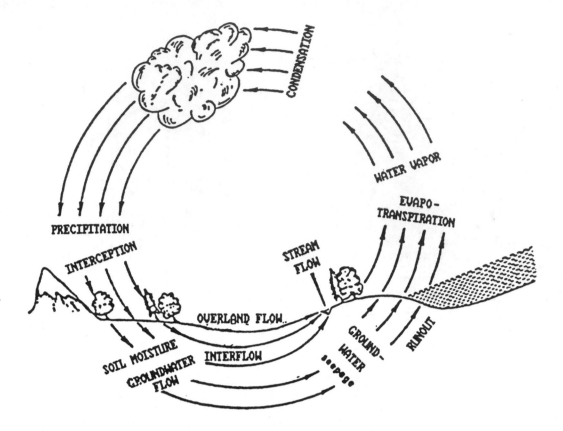

Figure 20-2. The aspects of the hydrologic cycle. (source: NWS)

The planet is divided into drainage basins, which can be analogized to bathtubs, with water flowing from the surrounding highest borders inward towards the lowest elevation, which is where we would find a stream or river flowing when there is sufficient water. Drainage basins are also called watersheds. The rain and melted snow in a watershed drains into streams, rivers, lakes, ponds and some of it eventually drains into the ocean.

The amount of rainfall and/or snowmelt that becomes runoff determines what the streamflow is in a channel of flowing water (a stream [creek] or river). The streamflow is the volume of water passing by you per unit time as you watch the river or stream flowing. It is measured in either hundreds of cubic feet per second (hundreds of CFS) or in cubic meters per second. The river or stream stage is the height of the top of the water.

Whereas the science of meteorology includes forecasting precipitation, the science of hydrology is about what happens to the water when it reaches the earth's surface.

SECTION VII: WIND

Chapter 21. What Causes the Wind?

Wind is air in motion. Air flows from areas where there is a build-up of a lot of air (high pressure areas) to where there is less air (low pressure areas). Consider the example of a balloon filled with air which is then released. The air flows from inside the balloon, where the pressure is higher, to the outside, where the pressure is lower. The more you inflate the balloon, the faster will the air flow out of it, since the greater the difference in pressure, the stronger the wind. Another way of saying this is the greater the difference in pressure over the same distance, the stronger the wind speed.

Thus, it is easy to picture why air blows from high to low pressure. In a high pressure system, the air weighs more -- it is heavier. In a low pressure system, the air weighs less because there is less of it to weigh. Wind is created because of these pressure differences. Higher pressure forces the air to move into regions of lower pressure. The difference in pressure from one place to another nearby is called the **pressure gradient**. We can define the horizontal **pressure gradient force** as the difference in pressure between points A and B where the pressure at A is higher than at B, and also consider the distance between A and B.

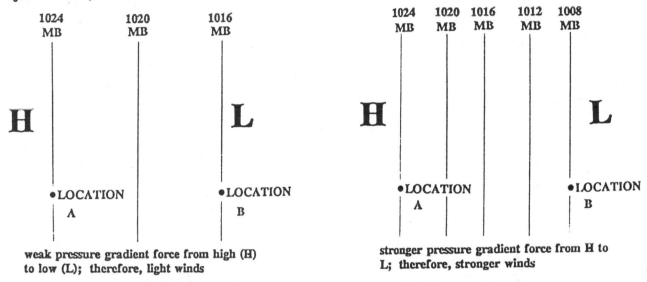

weak pressure gradient force from high (H) to low (L); therefore, light winds

stronger pressure gradient force from H to L; therefore, stronger winds

Figure 21-1. The pressure gradient force changes as the pressure difference between points varies and the distance between these points varies. This diagram would be true for a nonrotating, frictionless earth.

Later, we will look at the real, rotating earth, with friction between the wind and the earth's surface. But for now, consider just the pressure gradient force by itself. We know that air blows from high to low pressure. This is the wind. Where the pressure difference is greater over the same distance, the pressure gradient force is greater and therefore the wind speed is stronger. Moreover, when the lines on the surface weather map that give the air pressure, the **isobars**, are closer together, the pressure gradient is stronger and therefore the winds in that region are stronger. Thus, in a major low pressure system such as a strong winter storm or a hurricane, the isobars are very close around the low center: these close isobars therefore indicate strong winds. A pressure difference of 4 mb every 60 miles would give winds of about 50 mph, whereas a pressure difference of 4 mb every 300 miles would give winds of about 10 mph.

However, the earth rotates. As we look down on the earth from over the North Pole, we would see the planet rotating from west to east. Since the circumference of the earth around the equator is about 25,000 miles, and we know that a day is about 24 hours long, then at the equator the earth must rotate at a little over 1,000 miles per hour. Why then don't we feel one thousand mile per hour winds? The reason is because the earth **and the atmosphere** are all rotating at that same speed. We are also in that frame of reference; therefore, at the equator we are moving at 1,000 mph along with the earth, its atmosphere and everything within the earth-atmosphere system.

So we know that pressure differences cause air to move. However, because the earth rotates from west to east, this moving air, the wind, is deflected to the right in the Northern Hemisphere, and to the left in the Southern Hemisphere. This deflecting force due to the earth's rotation is called the **Coriolis force**, named for the scientist who discovered the effect. It is analogous to placing a tiny ball in the middle of an old phonograph record on a turntable, and then pushing the ball towards the edge of the record. When the turntable is not moving, the ball will continue straight towards the record's edge, but when you repeat the experiment with the turntable rotating, the ball will head towards the edge and systematically turn 90 degrees. On the earth, the pressure gradient force pushes the air from high to low pressure and it turns to the right in the Northern Hemisphere due to the Coriolis force. (Chapter 22 has more information on the Coriolis force, along with a demonstration.)

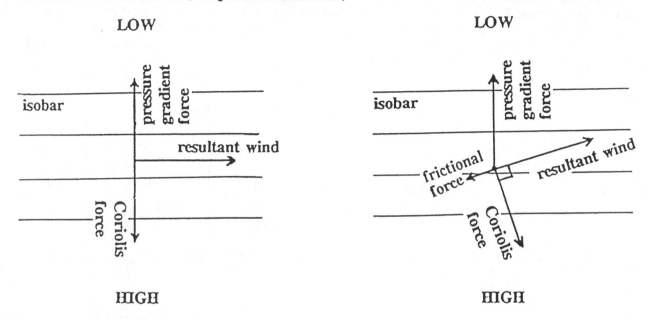

Figure 21-2. The movement of air due to the pressure gradient and Coriolis forces if there were no friction with the ground and objects on it, and the same air movement with the effect of friction between the air and the earth's surface and objects on the surface.

However, friction between the air and the surface it is flowing over will slow down the air flow and also change its direction. This frictional effect is significant in the first 1500 to 2000 feet from the surface up. This "frictional layer" of atmosphere is called the **planetary boundary layer**. Above the planetary boundary layer, the wind is steered by the net result of the pressure gradient and Coriolis forces, although a curved flow also introduces a centrifugal force ("fleeing" from the center of curvature) which will be discussed with the upper-level charts later.

Within the planetary boundary layer, the wind is the result of the effects of:
        a. the pressure gradient force,
        b. the Coriolis force, and
        c. the frictional force.

There are vertical motions too, and these are essential to the weather we get. However, we look at other causes of motion in the vertical, because the vertical pressure gradient force is suppressed by the weight of the atmosphere, so that upward and downward moving air needs to be instigated by other dynamical or mechanical forcing mechanisms.

Wind direction

The wind direction is from where the wind is coming. Thus, when we speak of, for example, a northerly wind, we are saying that the wind is coming _from_ the north.

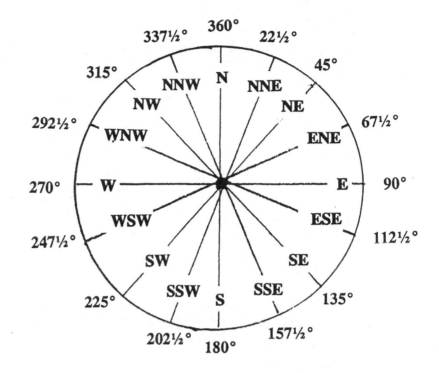

Figure 21-3. The wind directions and their points on the compass. North is 360°, which is the same as 0°. East is wind coming from 90°, south is from 180°, west is from 270° and calm is no wind at all. Directions are further subdivided; for example, we have a southwest wind, which is wind coming about halfway between south and west. We can further sub-divide into directions such as south-southwest, which is between south and southwest.

In the Northern Hemisphere, the wind is said to _veer_ when it shifts in a clockwise fashion. Look again at figure 21-3 above and observe the following:

a. if the wind is blowing from the north and then shifts to come from the east, then the wind has veered to the east;

b. if the wind is blowing from the west-southwest and then shifts to come from the northwest, then the wind has veered to the northwest.

The term "veering" is also used for the forward motion of large storms such as hurricanes and extra-tropical (nontropical) low pressure systems. If a hurricane is coming up the east coast of the U.S., or a typhoon is heading north towards Japan, and then the hurricane or typhoon which was heading northward then heads towards the northeast (in these cases, heading out to sea), then the storm is said to have veered away from the coastline.

In the Northern Hemisphere, the wind is said to **back** when it shifts in a counterclockwise fashion. Look again at figure 21-3 above and observe the following:

a. if the wind is blowing from the west and then shifts to come from the southwest, then the wind has backed to the southwest;

b. if the wind is blowing from the east-northeast and then shifts to come from the northwest, then the wind has backed to the northwest.

Wind direction or wind speed alone are each a scalar; the total wind, which is the direction and the speed, is a vector. Thus, the total wind report would say something such as "the wind is from the northeast at 25 miles per hour with gusts to 45 miles per hour". Another way of saying this is: "The wind speed is not the same as the wind velocity. The speed gives the distance per unit time, but the velocity gives the direction and the speed per unit time." Therefore, for example, the wind speed might be 15 miles per hour, but the wind velocity might be from the west at 15 miles per hour. This is a distinction (speed vs. velocity) used in physics.

Wind speed is most commonly given is any of these dimensions:
- miles per hour (mph)
- feet per second (ft/sec)
- knots (kt)
- meters per second (m/sec)
- kilometers per hour (km/hr or kph)

One knot is approximately 1.15 mph. One km/hr is about 0.61 mph. One mph is about 1.61 km/hr. One m/sec is just under 2 kts, being about 2.2 mph.

WIND VELOCITY PLOTTED ON WEATHER MAPS

Some weather graphics give a printout of the wind direction to the nearest 10 degrees of direction, and the average speed. Other weather charts that give wind information use the plotting routine which is described fully in chapter 37.

INSTRUMENTS USED TO MEASURE THE WIND

A wind vane is a device that indicates the wind direction. (At one time the wind vane was also called a weather vane, since the wind direction is often an indicator of the type of weather to occur.) (The word "wind" comes from "wind", an Old English, then Middle English word.)

The wind vane consists of a piece of wood, metal or heavy plastic that is shaped like an arrow on one side and a rectangular tail on the other, which is attached to a rod in such a way that it moves freely when blown by the wind. The tail has a larger surface area compared to the arrow end, and the tail end is heavier, so that when the wind blows, it pushes the tail in the direction that it is blowing, and consequently the arrow points in the direction from which the wind is coming. Recall that the wind direction is the direction FROM WHICH the air is coming. (See figure 21-4.)

An anemometer is an instrument that measures the air speed. The "anemo" part of the word comes from the Greek "anemos", for "wind". The anemometer is a miniature generator that is calibrated to read in miles per hour, knots, kilometers per hour or meters per second, rather than in amperes. The typical anemometer contains three cups that are moved by the wind. These moving cups cause a shaft, which is located between two magnets, to move. This motion results in an electric current, which moves a dial inside a meter that is typically located indoors. The faster the cups move, the more electricity is produced, and the higher the reading.

Power plant generators work similarly except that the motion may be provided not just by wind, but by falling water or by steam produced by the burning of fossil fuel such as coal, or by nuclear energy.

The wind vane and anemometer are nowadays typically combined as one instrument package.

Windmills that generate electricity are similar to anemometers but are much larger and therefore generate larger amounts of electricity.

A wind vane indicates wind direction by pointing into the wind—the direction from which the wind blows.

Figure 21-4. A wind vane. (source: DOA)

Horizontal wind speed is measured by the rate of rotation of a cup anemometer.

Figure 21-5. An anemometer. (source: DOA)

Figure 21-6. An aerovane, which is a combination of a wind vane and an anemometer. (courtesy of Robert E. White Instruments, Inc.; Boston, MA)

Figure 21-7. Wind displays typically have one dial or display for the wind direction, and another for the wind speed. This dial, at right, shows both direction and speed. (courtesy: Robert E. White Instruments, Inc.; Boston, MA)

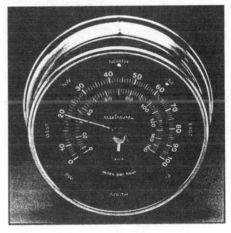

You can also estimate wind speed over land by using the **BEAUFORT WIND SCALE.** This scale was created by Sir Francis Beaufort (1774-1857), a British admiral. The only modification done to this scale since its creation is to change the threshold value for hurricane force winds to start at 74 mph rather than the 75 mph in the original scale. The scale ranges from a zero for calm winds to a 12 for hurricanes strength winds. The next page shows the Beaufort Wind Scale for estimating the wind speeds over land.

The wind speed is typically a one-minute average for the sustained wind; the wind report would also include any peak gust within that minute. Thus, the strongest wind gust for the day is not the same as the average wind speed for the day. The highest wind speeds ever reported on earth as of this writing have been:

231 miles per hour (372 kilometers per hour) at Mount Washington, New Hampshire on April 12th, 1934.

230 miles per hour (370 kilometers per hour) in Typhoon Angela on November 2nd, 1995 shortly before she slammed into the central Philippines.

Figure 21-8 on the next page is the Beaufort Wind Scale, and figure 21-9 on the page after that gives an estimation scale for over the ocean or over a large lake.   PAGE 145

Figure 21-8. The BEAUFORT WIND SCALE for estimating the wind speed over land.

Beaufort Number	Speed MPH	General Description	Specifications
0			
1	Less than 1	Calm	Smoke rises vertically
2	1 to 3	Light air	Wind direction shown by drift of smoke.
3	4 to 7	Slight breeze	Wind felt on face; leaves rustle.
4	8 to 12	Gentle breeze	Leaves and twigs in constant motion. Wind extends light flags.
5	13 to 18	Moderate breeze	Dust, loose paper, and small branches are moved.
6	19 to 24	Fresh breeze	Small trees begin to sway.
7	25 to 31	Strong breeze	Large branches in motion; whistling in telegraph wires.
8	32 to 38	Moderate gale	Whole trees in motion.
9	39 to 46	Fresh gale	Twigs break off trees; walking is impeded.
10	47 to 54	Strong gale	Slight damage to houses; chimney pots blown off.
11	55 to 63	Whole gale	Trees uprooted; considerable damage to houses.
12	64 to 73	Storm	Widespread damage.
	74 and above	Hurricane	Excessive damage.

Figure 21-9. A wind scale for estimating the wind speed over the ocean (away form the shore) and over a huge lake (away from the shore) such as one of the Great Lakes, Hudson's Bay, the Caspian Sea, Lake Tanganyika, etc.)

TERMS USED IN WEATHER FORECASTS	MILES PER HOUR	WIND EFFECTS OBSERVED OVER WATER
Light	0	Sea like a mirror
	1 - 3	Ripples with the appearance of scales formed, but without foam crests.
	4 - 7	Small wavelets, short but pronounced; crests appear glassy. They do not break.
Gentle	8 - 12	Large wavelets with crests beginning to break; foam appears glassy. Perhaps scattered white horses (white foam crests).
Moderate	13 - 18	Small waves, becoming longer; fairly frequent white horses.
Fresh	19 - 24	Moderate waves of a pronounced long form; many white horses. Possibly spray waves.
Strong	25 - 31	Large waves begin to form; white foam crests more extensive everywhere; possibly some spray.
	32 - 38	Sea heaps up; some white foam from breaking waves blows in streaks along the direction of the wind.
Gale	39 - 46	Moderately high waves. Edges of crests begin to break into spindrift. Well-marked streaks of foam blow along direction of wind.
	47 - 54	High waves. Dense streaks of foam along direction of wind. Spray may affect visibility.
Whole Gale	55 - 63	Very high waves with long overhanging crests; great patches of foam blown in dense white streaks along direction of wind. Sea surface takes on a white appearance. Visibility affected.
	64 - 73	Exceptionally high waves; sea completely covered with long white patches of foam lying along direction of wind; edges of wave crests everywhere blown into froth. Visibility affected.
Hurricane	74 and above	Air filled with foam and spray; sea completely white with driving spray. Visibility very seriously affected.

A _wind rose_ is a graphic representation of wind directions over a long time period, such as a month, season or a year, at a specific weather station. Monthly wind roses for over a ten year or longer period are made to show statistical wind direction averages.

Figure 21-10. Wind roses for Bismarck, North Dakota, at left, and for Midland, Texas, at right, for the month of July, based on the latest 10-year period of record. Each wind rose shows the percentage of time that the wind blew from each of the 16 compass points or was calm; the calm percentage is given inside the circle.

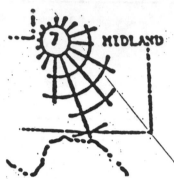

Note that for Bismarck during July, the wind is most likely to come from the west, west-northwest, northwest, north-northwest, north, east-northeast, east, east-southeast, southeast and south-southeast. Actually, the wind direction is fairly well divided around all points of the compass. However, in Midland in July, the most predominating wind directions are from the east-southeast, southeast, south-southeast and south. The occurrence of a wind from the northwest is greater in Bismarck in July than it is in Midland in July. Thus, climatological wind roses give a quick graphic display of the distribution of wind direction reports for a specific time period for a specific site, based on a reasonably long period of record. For the United States, wind roses for your general area are available from the National Climatic Data Center in Asheville, North Carolina.

DEMONSTRATION: MAKING A WIND ROSE FROM WIND DIRECTION DATA

The table below is the data set for a specific weather station, showing the frequency in percent during the month of January that the wind blew from a particular direction or was calm for thirty years of records.

MONTH	N	NE	E	SE	S	SW	W	NW	CALM
January	18	6	5	4	10	13	11	28	5

There are a few ways to do this, but we shall demonstrate one way. For this you will need a metric ruler and the instrument used to draw circles (called a compass).

1. Hold a blank 8½" by 11" (about 22 cm by 28 cm) piece of blank paper so that the long edge runs from left to right.

2. Choose a suitable scale, such as 0.5 cm equals 1 percent.

3. Using a pencil, draw diagonal lines that you can barely see, from corner of the paper to each adjacent corner, to determine the center of the paper.

4. Now draw a very faint vertical line and a very faint horizontal line, each through the center of the paper. These lines and the lines from step 3 will now represent the eight major directions.

(continued)

5. In the center of the paper, draw a circle that has a radius of one centimeter. Inside the circle write in the percentage of "days" that were calm. According to our table, this number is 5. (Since these climatological statistics are based on weather observations taken every hour of the month for 30 years, one calm "day" means that out of the average for 30 years worth of hourly observations in January at this location, there were about 24 calm hours; one calm "day" would be about 3%.)

6. Using the scale of 0.5 centimeter equals 1 percent, draw in the other wind directions, having them radiate from the outside of the circle. (For reference, figure 21-3 shows the eight major wind directions, plus the intermediate directions.)

7. Label the tip of each line that you have drawn, with the correct wind direction (N, NE, E, SE, S, SW, W and NW).

Figure 21-11. Your wind rose should look like this, but on an 8½" x 11" piece of paper. This figure is greatly reduced to fit on the page.

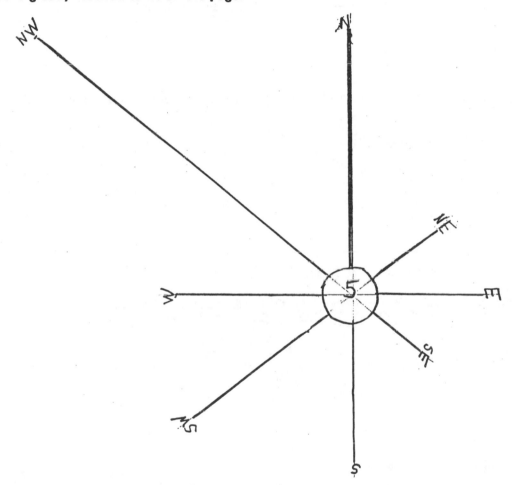

<u>Warnings and advisories for dangerous winds</u>

When winds are forecast to be sufficiently strong to cause damage or other problems, the National Weather Service issues alerts such as high wind warnings, small craft advisories, lake wind advisories, tropical storm or hurricane warnings, tornado warnings, etc. Along coastal areas, marine warnings may be accompanied by warning flags and lights on towers such as U.S. Coast Guard towers,. although nowadays, mariners generally get their warnings via radio and other communications media.

Figure 21-12. Flags and lights used in marine coastal wind warnings along the United States coastline. (source: NWS)

Small craft warning (winds under 39 mph; usually, the winds are from 21 up to 38 mph for a small craft warning, although the wind just offshore may be lighter and seas there may still be rough due to, e.g., a major storm farther out a sea churning up the sea, so a small craft warning would be issued even though the winds there could even be about calm.):

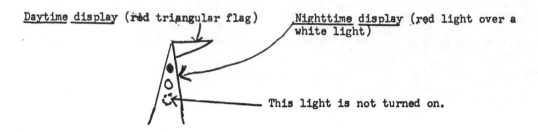

Daytime display (red triangular flag)   Nighttime display (red light over a white light)

This light is not turned on.

Gale warnings (winds 39 through 54 mph):

Daytime display (two red triangular flags)   Nighttime display (white light over a red light)

This light is not turned on.

Storm or whole gale warnings (winds 55 through 73 mph):

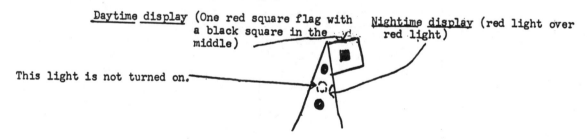

Daytime display (One red square flag with a black square in the middle)   Nightime display (red light over red light)

This light is not turned on.

Hurricane warnings (winds 74 mph or higher):

Daytime display (Two red square flags with a black square in the middle)   Nighttime display (a red light on top; a white light in the middle ; and a red light on the bottom)

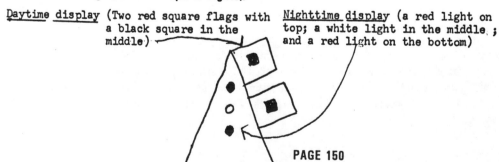

Figure 21-13. A Coast Guard station tower with daytime flag display and nighttime lights display, for marine wind warnings. This location is Chatham, Massachusetts.
(photo by Joseph Balsama)

Below depicts the daytime and nighttime marine signals. (source: USN)

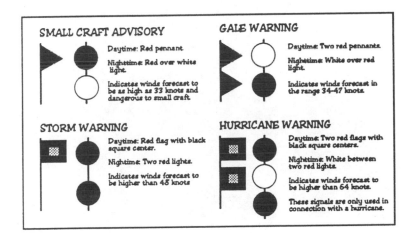

SMALL CRAFT ADVISORY
Daytime: Red pennant
Nighttime: Red over white light.
Indicates winds forecast to be as high as 33 knots and dangerous to small craft.

GALE WARNING
Daytime: Two red pennants.
Nighttime: White over red light.
Indicates winds forecast in the range 34-47 knots.

STORM WARNING
Daytime: Red flag with black square center.
Nighttime: Two red lights.
Indicates winds forecast to be higher than 48 knots

HURRICANE WARNING
Daytime: Two red flags with black square centers.
Nighttime: White between two red lights.
Indicates winds forecast to be higher than 64 knots.
These signals are only used in connection with a hurricane.

Waves caused by the wind:

Wind waves are waves that are caused by the wind. The height of these waves are determined by the wind speed, the length of time that the wind blows over the same fetch and the length of that fetch.

Wind speed example: a 40 mph wind blowing over an ocean, bay or lake area will produce higher waves than a 20 mph wind since there is obviously more force to lift the water up higher with the stronger 40 mph wind.

Length of time that the wind blows over the same fetch (stretch of water) example: the same 40 mph wind blowing for six hours across the same water area will produce higher waves than if the same 40 mph wind were blowing for only 2 hours.

Length of the fetch example: The same 40 mph wind blowing over a harbor will produce higher waves than if if blows over a small pond. Another example of this: consider Lake Erie. If a strong west-southwest wind blows across only the eastern half of this Great Lake, then the waves on the eastern end of the lake will not be as high as when the same strong wind blows across the entire fetch (stretch) of the lake.

Types of wind waves:

Storm waves are called seas. This is an unfortunate choice of word since the term, sea, also refers to a large body of water which is part of an ocean. Seas occur during a storm of high winds. Waves of 10 feet high mean the "seas are

10 feet". If you are by the ocean during a storm that is causing "seas", with the water surface appearing disorganized with storm waves rolling in to the coast from several directions, then these waves will be crashing into each other and into the coast and any sea-walls. Foam and spray would be visible for as far as the eye can see.

Figure 21-14. Seas (storm waves). Photo by Joseph Balsama.

After the storm, the ocean appears more organized. The larger waves have absorbed some of the smaller ones. The waves seem to come from one direction at definite intervals, and they appear to be approximately the same height. We call these waves <u>swells</u>. Figure 21-15 on the next page shows swells moving onshore.

As waves move from deeper to shallower water, they <u>crest</u> and then <u>break</u>. Before a wave crests, you cannot readily distinguish it from the rest of the ocean; after it crests, you can recognize it as a wave, since it has a <u>crest</u> (top) and a <u>trough</u> (bottom). A wave crests when the depth of water beneath it is equal to one-half the <u>wavelength</u>. The wave length is the distance from a point in one wave to the same corresponding point in another; e.g., from the crest of one wave to the crest of the next wave. For example, a wave with a 400-foot wavelength will crest in 200 feet of water. You can see that waves with a larger wavelength crest farther from the shore. During a day that the ocean is calm, you will notice the waves cresting only a few feet from the shore; during wind storms, they can crest as far as the eye can see.

As crested waves approach shallower water, they break, because the bottoms of the waves begin to drag along the bottom of the rising shoreline. The result is that the top of the waves move faster than their bottoms, which makes the waves unstable. The waves then topple over and break up.

Waves break when the ratio of the wave height to the depth of the water beneath them is 3 to 4. Thus, for example, a six-foot wave will break in 8 feet of water. A wave that is 3 inches high will break in 4 inches of water. The taller (higher) the wave, the farther from shore will it break. During storms, waves crest and then break at a greater distance from the shore, whereas when the water is relatively calm, they crest and then break only a short distance from the shore.

Figure 21-15. Swells. Swells are approximately the same height and are beautiful to watch, especially when the sky is blue, helping to give the ocean a more bluish color. Swells can occur from a storm such as a hurricane that is far out at sea. Thus, it is possible to have swells without having a storm or storm waves in the local area. (photo by Joseph Balsama)

Waves also break in deeper water when the slope of the wave, that is, the ratio of the wave height to the wave length, is 1 to 7. At this slope the wave becomes unstable, resulting in the crest toppling over. When this happens to smaller waves, whitecaps (waves with crests of foam) form. Short unstable waves are destroyed and the energy is transferred to waves which have a longer wave length and are therefore more stable. This enables the seas to continue to increase in height. The process repeats itself until the wind dies down or suddenly changes direction. As seas continue to build, the wave period, which is the time it takes a single wave to pass by a given point, increases with time.

A sea is "fully developed" when the waves cannot absorb any more energy from the wind. This occurs when the waves reach the same speed as the wind. Most open-sea waves are under 12 feet high. However, one of the largest wind waves ever observed occurred in the Pacific Ocean in 1933 by crew members on the USS Ramapo. By using geometry, a wave was measured at 112 feet high!

When waves break, they are called surf or breakers. There are two kinds of breakers: plunging breakers and spilling breakers. Plunging breakers occur whenever the wind is blowing in the same direction as the wave is moving; that is, a plunging surf occurs when the wind and waves are moving from the ocean to the land. Thus, winds blowing onshore cause plunging breakers. Surfers like plunging breakers because the water rolls over as the waves break. When there is very little to no wind blowing, the breaking waves also tend to be plunging breakers.

An offshore wind, that is, wind blowing from land to the ocean, therefore in the opposite direction towards which the waves are moving, if sufficiently strong, causes the waves to fall flat as they try to break. Waves that "fall on their face" are called spilling breakers.

Figure 21-16. A plunging breaker. This surf occurs when the wind is blowing in the same direction that the waves are moving, that is, towards the shore. The water rolls over as the waves break; thus, surfers like plunging breakers. (photo by Joseph Balsama)

Figure 21-17. A spilling breaker. This surf occurs when the wind is strong enough and blowing opposite to the incoming waves. The waves fall flat as they attempt to break. (photo by Joseph Balsama)

Besides wind waves, there are seismically-induced waves called tsunamis, which are so important that they are covered in a separate chapter devoted to that topic.

Some other related wind topics found in other chapters are the wind chill, discussed in chapter 11, the storm surge, discussed in chapter 33, and the tsunami, discussed in chapter 47.

Chapter 22. THE GENERAL CIRCULATION OF THE ATMOSPHERE

The average LARGE-SCALE air flow around the planet is driven first by the differential (unequal) heating of the earth by the sun, which helps form air masses and pressure differences, and by the fact that the earth is rotating. Let us start by first looking at how the sun heats the earth.

For the most part, the sun does not directly heat the lowest part of the atmosphere. The troposphere is essentially transparent to most of the incoming solar radiation. This radiation heats and ground, and the ground heats the air above it through heat emitted through infrared radiation (heat). The tropospheric heating occurs because water vapor and carbon dioxide have absorption bands for this returning long-wave radiation from the earth.

There is unequal heating of the earth's lower atmosphere (differential heating). On an annual average, there is a net excess of incoming radiation to outgoing terrestrial radiation from the earth) in the lowest latitudes, and a net loss of radiation by the earth in polar regions.

Thus, temperature differences are established across the planet. Temperature differences result in pressure differences. Therefore, pressure gradients are established which drive the wind. Wind normally blows from high pressure to lower pressure, driven by the pressure gradient force, and is deflected to the right in the Northern Hemisphere and left in the Southern Hemisphere because of the earth rotating. This is called the Coriolis effect, caused by the earth rotating from west to east. In the lowest 50 millibars [roughly 1500 to 2000 feet], which is called the planetary boundary layer, friction prevents this deflection from being 90 degrees. Over ocean areas, the total deflection may exceed 70 degrees with relatively smooth seas, but over land the effect of friction in the planetary boundary layer is to reduce the deflection to typically between 50 and 70 degrees.

Figure 22-1. How the winds would probably blow at the earth's surface and aloft if the earth did not rotate. The greatest heating by the sun would occur in equatorial zones, even on the side of the earth that would not be facing the sun, since the warm air would overspread the entire equatorial region. Since warm air weighs less than cold air, it would rise and move towards the polar regions. With the earth losing more heat to space in the polar regions than it receives from the sun, there would be cold air in these regions. Moreover, the air moving up from the equatorial region would be cooling and descending. Cold air weighs more than warm air, and therefore sinks. As a result, in the Northern Hemisphere the upper winds would blow from the south and the surface winds would blow from the north, and in the Southern Hemisphere the upper winds would blow from the north and the surface winds would blow from the south. (source: USAF)

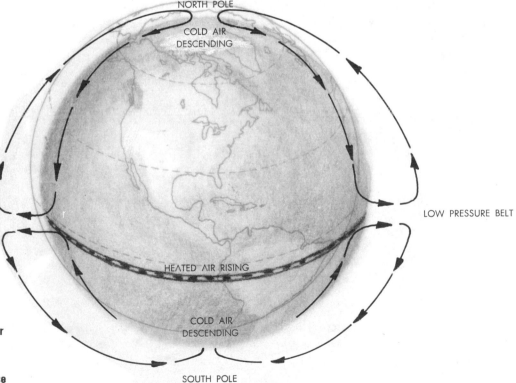

However, the earth does rotate, making one complete rotation in about 24 hours. Looking down at the earth from above the North Pole, the rotation is counterclockwise. What this rotation does is to deflect the wind as explained above (the Coriolis effect). The actual wind is the resultant of all the forces that cause the wind, and the contribution of the Coriolis force is to deflect the direction of the wind.

DEMONSTRATION: THE CORIOLIS EFFECT

Use a globe and a piece of soft colored chalk.

1. Without rotating the globe, draw a chalk line from the North Pole towards the equator. This represents a north wind.

2. Have someone rotate the globe from west to east, which is how the earth does rotate (which is why the sun "rises" in the east and "sets" in the west). While the other person is rotating the globe, draw a line from the North Pole towards the equator. Stop the globe and look at the chalk line. You will notice that the chalk mark shows that the wind is coming from the northeast, even though you had intended it to come from the north. The different portions of the globe, like the earth, do not all rotate at the same speed. At the equator, the earth (and globe) moves fastest, and as we travel from equator towards the poles, the earth (and globe) slows down.

When wind blows from a polar region towards the equator, it comes from an area where the earth is rotating relatively slowly, and as the air keeps moving equatorward, the earth's rate of rotation gets progressively faster. The wind's speed has not changed, but its direction has. The air has moved southward, but the earth has rotated eastward.

3. Without rotating the globe, draw a chalk line from the equator towards the North Pole. This represents a south wind.

4. Have someone rotate the globe from west to east as in step 2, as you draw a chalk line from the equator towards the North Pole. Stop the globe and look at the chalk line. You will notice that the chalk mark indicates that the wind is coming from the southwest. When the wind originates at the equator, it is rotating at the same speed as the earth at the equator, but as it moves north, the earth's rotational speed is progressively decreasing. The wind's speed has not changed, but its direction has. The air has moved northward, but the earth has rotated eastward.

Now, if you want to have more fun, repeat steps 1 through 4 for the Southern Hemisphere and compare your results!:

5. Without rotating the globe, draw a chalk line from the South Pole towards the equator. This represents a south wind.

6. Have someone rotate the globe from west to east, which is how the earth does rotate. While the other person is rotating the globe, draw a line from the South Pole towards the equator. Stop the globe and look at the chalk line. You will notice that the chalk mark shows that the wind is coming from the southeast, even though you had intended it to come from the south.

7. Without rotating the globe, draw a chalk line from the equator towards the South Pole. This represents a north wind.

8. Having someone rotating the globe from west to east as in step 6, now draw a chalk line from the equator towards the South Pole. Stop the globe and look at the chalk line. You will notice that the chalk mark indicates that the wind is coming from the northwest.

You can use chalk on an old 33 1/3 rpm phonograph record rotating on a record turntable, trying to draw a straight line from the edge, where the rate of rotation is the fastest, to the middle, where it is the slowest. The chalk line will not turn out to be straight, but will be deflected. This is another analogy demonstration of the Coriolis effect.

Yet another way to illustrate the Coriolis effect is to imagine that two people are sitting opposite each other on a merry-go-round that is not moving, and the two people are playing catch with a tennis ball. Now imagine the merry-go-round rotating. As the ball is thrown, the merry-go-round rotates under it. The person to whom the ball is thrown misses catching it. To a person standing aside the merry-go-round and observing this, this seems logical; however, to the receiver who is riding on the merry-go-round, it looks as if he/she has been thrown a curve ball.

In summary, the initial major driving factors in the general circulation of the earth's air are the unequal heating of the earth's surface by the sun (more heat received in lower latitudes than in higher latitudes) and the Coriolis effect due to the earth having rotation.

Pressure differences that blow air from high to lower pressure are induced initially by the thermal factor, so the pressure-gradient force as described in chapter 21 is a derivative of the differential heating of the earth by the sun. The effect of surface friction on the wind direction and speed is a variable, dependent upon the ruggedness of each local surface area of the planet.

The vertical temperature regime of the atmosphere is available in any basic meteorology textbook. The temperature generally cools as we ascend through the troposphere to the tropopause, and generally warms through the stratosphere to the stratopause.

Cooling again occurs through the mesosphere with warming in the thermosphere.

The stratospheric warming is caused by ultraviolet solar radiation causing some of the atmosphere's oxygen molecules to divide into oxygen atoms, and then these oxygen atoms combine with other oxygen molecules to form ozone:

$$O_2 \xrightarrow{\text{ULTRAVIOLET}} O + O$$

$$O_2 + O \longrightarrow O_3$$

Ozone has absorption wavelengths for incoming ultraviolet radiation and thus warms up. The greatest concentration of ozone in the stratosphere is at approximately 15 to 18 miles (about 25 to 30 kilometers) up.

As we rise higher in the atmosphere, the lighter gases in the atmosphere comprise a greater ratio to the heavier components. In the thermosphere, which is above about 50 miles (about 80 km), monatomic oxygen is found. This also absorbs short-wave solar radiation and warms up, which is why the thermosphere is a warm layer.

The top of the earth's atmosphere ranges to about 600 to 1000 miles (about 1000 to 1600 kilometers), depending on where the last atoms of hydrogen, the lightest gas, are found.

HISTORICAL DEVELOPMENT: EARLY CONTRIBUTIONS TO THE THEORY OF THE GENERAL ATMOSPHERIC CIRCULATION

In 1735, HADLEY postulated that solar heating would lead to a general rising motion in lower latitudes, and that cooling in very high latitudes would result in a sinking motion there, with the circuit being completed by equatorward motion at low levels and poleward motion aloft. But he rejected the idea that motion toward the sun would lead to any average westward or eastward air movement. He then noted that in the absolute sense, the earth's surface moves most rapidly eastward at the lowest latitudes, and he maintained that if the air were initially moving equatorward without any movement also to the west or east, it would arrive at lower latitudes then moving westward, because of a mathematical/physical concept called "conservation of absolute velocity". He found, in fact, that air travelling considerable distances would acquire a much greater westward velocity than any ever observed, and assumed that the frictional drag of the earth's surface would, in the course of a few days, reduce the velocities to those actually found, thus giving us our tropical "trade winds" (the easterly winds named after the old trading ships from Europe in the 1500's through 1700's).   PAGE 157

Figure 22-2:
GENERAL CIRCULATION MODELS:
These figures depict the average air circulation cells over the earth, and the average low-level wind directions [the arrows], as postulated by these early researchers.

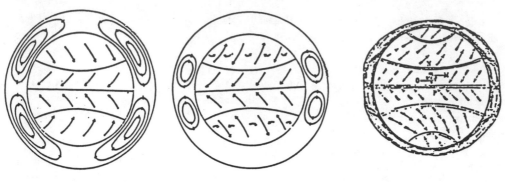

HADLEY's model (1735)   DOVE's model (1837)   FERREL's model (1856)

Hadley next noted that the required counter-drag of the air upon the earth would continually slow down the earth's rotation unless opposed by an opposite drag in other regions; this he assumed to occur in the belt of prevailing westerlies in middle latitudes. To account for the westerlies, he maintained that the air initially moving directly poleward at high levels would soon acquire an eastward relative velocity, and upon reaching higher latitudes and being cooled would sink and become the prevailing westerlies.

HADLEY'S BIG ERROR: In 1857, Thompson showed that in the absence of eastward or westward forces, air moving equatorward or poleward conserves its absolute angular momentum rather than its absolute velocity. Momentum is the product of the mass and the speed of individual parcels of air. Angular momentum is momentum plus the fact that the air parcels turn, primarily because the earth rotates. Thus, this is a somewhat difficult concept, but if you do some studying of this area in mathematics and physics, the subject of angular momentum is straightforward.

HADLEY'S CONTRIBUTION: Because there is continuity of mass (the air is not created or destroyed), the general equatorward motion at one level requires general poleward motion at some other level; because of conservation of total angular momentum, the general westward motion dragging upon the earth's surface at one latitude requires a general eastward motion at some other latitude.

Hadley's major contribution is the development of the concept of a global circulation, no one of whose major branches can be explained independently of the other branches. Also, he recognized that the prime forcing mechanism of the atmospheric circulation is the pole-to-equator density gradient caused by differential solar heating.

In 1837, DOVE (pronounced "Dove-ay") accepted Hadley's ideas for low latitudes, but he postulated that the predominating southwesterly winds in the middle latitudes are a continuation of the southwesterlies above the trade winds because , he believed, their warmth and humidity demanded an equatorial origin. He argued that at higher latitudes, alternating wind currents transported various properties. Unlike other atmospheric scientists at that time, Dove did not treat the general circulation as being completely symmetrical with respect to the earth's axis.

DOVE'S CONTRIBUTION: Dove introduced the concept of eddies within the generalized flow. It was not until well into the 20th century before it was shown that in the mid-latitudes, eddies (circulations such as low pressure systems) feed the westerlies aloft and the westerlies aloft also feed the eddies.

In 1856, FERREL postulated that there must be three general circulation cells in each hemisphere. He stated that these were demanded by virtue of the known observations.

FERREL'S ERROR: The way he drew his model, there should be easterlies aloft in mid-latitudes.   PAGE 158

FERREL'S CONTRIBUTION:
1. His 3-cell model shows, an indirect cell in the mid-latitudes which is forced, at least in part, by the direct tropical and polar cells;

2. Ferrel gave a correct account of the north-south component of the Coriolis Force;

3. He gave a quantitative description of the geostrophic wind and explained how it came about (a geostrophic wind is wind that blows parallel to the contours of height or isobars of pressure; thus it is above the planetary frictional layer, i.e., more than about 1500 to 2000 feet above the surface, and is a balance between the pressure-gradient force and the Coriolis force);

4. Ferrel showed that it is possible for the pressure field to adjust itself to fit the wind (a point overlooked by many contemporary meteorologists), besides the wind adjusting to the pressure field.

Hadley explained the trade winds and prevailing mid-latitude westerlies by noting that heating should produce a direct meridional cell in each hemisphere. The equatorward current at low levels should be deflected by the earth's rotation to become the trade winds. The returning poleward current aloft should be deflected to become the upper-level westerlies, which upon sinking should become the surface westerlies.

However, Hadley's circulation, and any other zonally-symmetric circulations, are not observed, because they are unstable with respect to small-amplitude wavelike disturbances of the large scale.

The observed circulation must therefore possess eddies. The transport of angular momentum by these eddies largely determines the distribution of surface easterlies and westerlies.

A DIRECT CELL is a circulation cell in which warm air rises and cold air descends; examples are the tropical and polar Hadley Cells; an INDIRECT CELL is a circulation in which warm air sinks and cold air rises; an example is the mid-latitude Ferrel Cell.

In 1855, MAURY postulated that instead of the single meridional cell in either hemisphere, or opposing currents side by side, there are two cells --a direct cell like Hadley's within the tropics, and an indirect cell in higher latitudes. The surface flow above the northeast trades is from the southwest, and the upper-level flow at higher latitudes is apparently supposed to be from the northeast. Maury could not offer an explanation for the indirect cell in higher latitudes.

In 1857, THOMPSON noted Hadley's error concerning the conservation of absolute velocity. (An example of relative vs. absolute is: if you are an observer on the earth watching the motion of a very small parcel of air, you are observing its relative motion; if, however, you are above the earth at a fixed point watching the motion of the same parcel, you are observing its absolute motion. The absolute motion is its actual relative motion plus the motion caused by the rotation of the earth in this sense.)

In 1888, OBERBECK represented the effects of friction by a simple coefficient of viscosity. He was the first person to represent the global circulation by solutions of the dynamic equations, rather than using the equations simply to deduce general properties.

EXCEPT FOR DOVE, THE GENERAL CIRCULATION WAS TREATED AS BEING COMPLETELY SYMMETRIC WITH RESPECT TO THE EARTH'S AXIS, BY THESE RESEARCHERS THROUGH 1888.

Also in 1888, HELMHOLTZ introduced the concept of turbulent viscosity. The principal deterrent to stronger winds aloft than what is actually observed is not surface friction but is the mixing of layers of different velocities by means of vortices forming on surfaces of discontinuity.

In 1926, JEFFREYS stated that in the long-run, angular momentum need not be conserved, because its net transport is proportional to the net mass (air) transport.   PAGE 159

The net angular momentum transport is proportional to the product of the eastward and northward wind components.

Jeffreys was the first to state the need for a horizontal angular momentum transport and also for correctly identifying the mechanism through which it is accomplished. The angular momentum transport across middle latitudes is accomplished mainly by the eddies.

Through the 1930s and '40s, ROSSBY promoted the concept of 3 atmospheric general circulation cells in each hemisphere. In 1939 he showed that the large scale horizontal mixing, i.e., wave motion, could explain the high altitude westerlies.

Later in the 20th century, some interesting work by KUO, ELIASSEN, LORENZ, D. JOHNSON and others show, mathematically, how the westerlies are produced and maintained against the effects of friction by employing the transport relations for mass and absolute angular momentum. (Thus, we can see how mathematically complex the explanation is of the earth's general atmospheric circulation!)

The following is a point in advanced meteorology: the frictional stresses in tropical latitudes in the region of surface easterlies transfer angular momentum from the earth to the atmosphere; the frictional stresses in the region of surface westerlies at higher latitudes transfer angular momentum back to the earth from the atmosphere. There must therefore be a transport of angular momentum from the source at low latitudes to the sink in mid-latitudes.

From the large scale circulation pattern we then come down in size to the high and low pressure systems and to the waves of air that move and flow aloft. We call these waves "long waves" and "short waves". Please see chapter 38 on "upper-level weather maps" to see how these waves look on a weather map. There are from 3 to 7 "long waves" across the hemisphere, and numerous smaller "short waves" forming, dying and moving through the long wave pattern. The largest and most vigorous short-wave troughs are associated with our surface low pressure systems (storms).

Thus, we can see how weather is four-dimensional: the three directions plus time.

Returning to our discussion on the large-scale general atmospheric circulation, the "bottom line" is this:

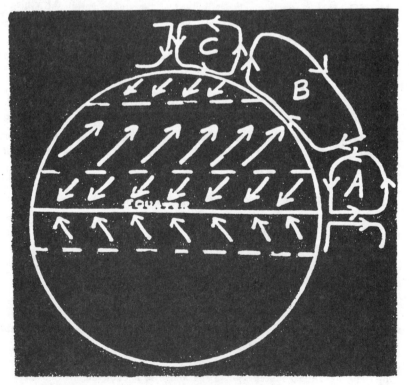

Figure 22-3a. Looking at the Northern Hemisphere first, there are three main general circulation cells. Cells A and C are direct circulation cells (warm air rising and cold air sinking and B is an indirect circulation cell forced in part by cells A and C. (Indirect is cold air being forced to rise and warm air forced to sink.) A is called the Tropical Hadley Cell, C is the Polar Hadley Cell and B is the Mid-Latitude Ferrel Cell. The most common surface wind directions are shown by the arrows. A more comprehensive global view is shown in figure 22-3b on the following page.

Figure 22-3b. Here is what we believe is the AVERAGE general LARGE-SCALE circulation of the general atmosphere over the earth, and the low-level or surface wind direction most of the time (arrows) in the zones shown on the diagram:

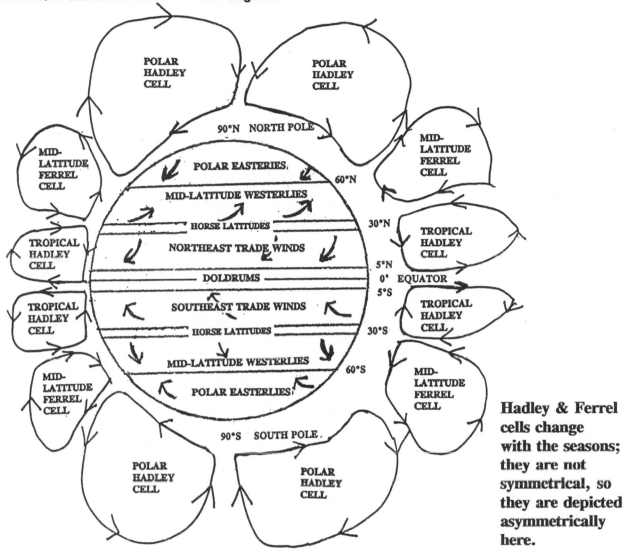

Hadley & Ferrel cells change with the seasons; they are not symmetrical, so they are depicted asymmetrically here.

Notice that the direct cell tropical and polar cells are named in honor of Hadley, and the mid-latitude indirect cells that are forced in part by the Hadley cells are named in honor of Ferrel.

The concept of first analyzing the large-scale weather pattern and then coming down to the "synoptic scale" (the highs, lows and fronts) and then to the mesoscale (more local scale) is one approach to determining what the weather is doing and is likely to do in the short-term. The smaller the scale, the more likely that many weather features are changing in the horizontal and vertical (waves of air, fronts, moisture and temperature profiles, for example).

Now let us explore some of the larger-scale weather features, some of which are continual or quasi-continual, and some of which are seasonal or vary in intensity throughout the year.

As air is heated at the equator, it rises and heads towards the poles. The region of rising air in the lowest latitudes is referred to as the <u>equatorial doldrums</u>. This region is characterized by being quite warm and humid. Tropical showers and thunderstorms are frequent. Most tropical cyclones (hurricanes, typhoons) originate here. Many locations, especially on windward sides of tropical land masses, receive heavy precipitation totals.

As the rising air moves north and south from the equatorial region, it tends to pile up at about 30°N and 30°S latitudes, producing subtropical high pressure areas. Over the western North Atlantic Ocean, this is the Bermuda High, which in the summer often extends eastward into the eastern North Atlantic, so that sometimes this feature is referred to as the Bermuda-Azores High.

A similar system in the eastern Pacific Ocean, where it is more prevalent during the warmer months, is called the Pacific High.

The weather under these highs is usually relatively tranquil. In the olden days of ships using big sails, many ships were stranded in these regions due to prolonged periods of nearly calm winds. To conserve what food and water they had, the people on these ships either ate the horses they were bringing to the New World (the Americas) or even threw them overboard. This led to calling these regions the horse latitudes.

Because the air pressure is higher in the horse latitudes than over the equator, the winds tend to blow from about 30°N and from about 30°S to the equator. In the Northern Hemisphere, this would be a north wind if the earth did not rotate, but due to the Coriolis effect of the earth's rotation, the surface wind in the Northern Hemisphere tropics is primarily from the northeast. It would be from the east, since the Coriolis force deflects the wind direction 90° to the right in the Northern Hemisphere, but friction of the surface with the wind prevents the deflection from being fully 90 degrees. The result is that the wind comes primarily from the east-northeast to northeast. When hurricanes, fronts and other organized weather systems move through the area, the wind direction is of course dependent more on the circulations of air in these systems and where you are in relation to these systems, but on the whole, this is the region of tropical northeasterlies. This region is also known from American colonial days as the region of the trade winds, since many trading vessels travelled through this region. The region is therefore also known as the northeast trade wind zone.

Similarly, in the Southern Hemisphere, the result of the south wind and the Coriolis effect is to create the southeast trade wind zone in the region from about 30°S to the equator. (Recall that the wind direction is the direction FROM WHICH the air is blowing; thus, a "southeast wind" blows from the southeast towards the northwest.)

Nearer the equator, the winds tend to be light; this region is known as the doldrums region (for "dull").

Where the northeast and southeast trade winds converge, we find the intertropical convergence zone (ITCZ). Clusters of showers and thunderstorms are common here as the ITCZ shifts like a wobbling snake across the globe in the lower Northern Hemisphere. Many tropical cyclones originate from organized thunderstorm systems forming in the ITCZ.

Not all of the air that converges at around 30 degrees North and South latitudes moves equatorward; some of it moves towards higher latitudes. In the Northern Hemisphere, the surface winds from about 30°N to about 60°N would be from the south if the earth did not rotate, but since the earth does rotate, the Coriolis force plus friction result in these winds being predominantly southwesterly. Of course, circulations around features such as highs, lows and fronts produce their own wind flows, but for the average, the most common surface wind direction in this region is from the southwest. This region is called the zone of the prevailing westerlies. In the Southern Hemisphere, similarly, the region is the zone of prevailing westerlies with the most common surface wind direction being from the northwest. Here, the wind would blow from the north between about 30 and 60 degrees South latitudes, but the effect of the Coriolis force and frictional force causes the wind direction to blow from the northwest.

The United States, except for the southern tip of Florida, Hawaii and Alaska, are in the prevailing westerlies. Most of the planet's population lives in this westerlies wind zone. This is the region whose climate has four distinct seasons. The zone of the prevailing westerlies is the "battleground for the air masses" because cold, dry air masses from the polar regions usually collide with warm, humid air masses from the low latitudes. The collision zones are the "fronts", named after battlefronts of the first world war, when fronts were discovered. The large-scale storms, the "extratropical low pressure systems", form on these fronts and pull warm air poleward up and over cold air that is lunging towards lower latitudes. Thus, the mid-latitudes are meteorologically very active, quite dynamic, and most interesting.

One example of much storminess is the Straights of Magellan at the southern tip of South America. Because of the often stormy weather there, mariners have long called this region the "roaring forties", named after these Southern Hemisphere latitudes.

Some areas of the world experience a seasonal switch in the wind, which changes the weather from dry to wet during this period; this wind switch, which may persist for months, is called a monsoon (refer to chapter 24 on local winds). Some examples of monsoon regions are India, southeast Asia and the desert southwest United States.

In the polar regions (but starting just outside them, from about 60°N and about 60°S, and extending to each respective pole), the prevailing winds are form the northeast in the Arctic and from the southeast in the Antarctic. In the Arctic, the build-up of cold air results in a southward flow down the globe thanks to heavy cold air moving towards lower pressure warmer, moister air, and the force of gravity helping the denser cold air slide down the globe. The north wind becomes northeast because of the Coriolis and frictional forces on it. Similarly, in the Southern Hemisphere, the northward flowing air (south wind) becomes a southeast wind. Thus, the prevailing or most prevalent surface wind direction in the Arctic is from the northeast, and in the Antarctic, is from the southeast.

Certain other surface features are permanent or quasi-permanent in our current climatic regime. For example, the Icelandic Low, a large low-pressure system centered most of the time near Iceland, and the Aleutian Low, a large low-pressure system centered most of the time around Alaska's Aleutian Islands, are around for most or all of the year, and are stronger during the colder half of the year when horizontal thermal differences between high and low latitudes are the largest.

Oceans and ocean currents:

The oceans cover a little over 70% of the earth's surface. Because of their great expanse, they are a major factor in the earth's climate. Most of the moisture that falls as precipitation has its origins in moist air due to the oceans. An entire science has emerged in the study of the oceans, called oceanography. Unfortunately, we know very little about what we could know about the ocean-atmosphere relationship for weather and climate; therefore, there is ample opportunity for new discoveries through research in oceanography, and in the combined interdisciplinary meteorology and oceanography.

Let us look at the major surface ocean currents. There are also deep ocean currents, such as an Antarctic bottom-water current.

Figure 22-4 on the following page shows some of the major ocean currents. In the Northern Hemisphere, the currents create a loop that moves clockwise across the Pacific Ocean, and another loop across the Atlantic Ocean; in the Southern Hemisphere, the circulation loops are counterclockwise. In the Northern Hemisphere, the more northward-moving currents are warm, while the more southward moving currents are cold. As you would expect for the Southern Hemisphere, the more southward-moving (away from the warmer, low latitudes) currents are warm, and the more northward-moving (away from the cold, high latitudes) currents are cold.

In the Northern Hemisphere, the Kuroshio Current of the western Pacific is analogous to the Gulf Stream of the western Atlantic: both are fast-moving, relatively narrow warm currents of water, somewhat analogous to the jet-streams of the atmosphere, which are relatively-narrow, fast-moving currents of air.

Positions, intensities and temperatures of these currents have shifted with climatic changes over the centuries. Thus, we know that the atmosphere-ocean-land system is one dynamic interrelated system that, with heating from the sun, determines our weather and climate.

Figure 22-4. Some of the major surface ocean currents. (There are also deep-water currents well below the top layers of the ocean.)

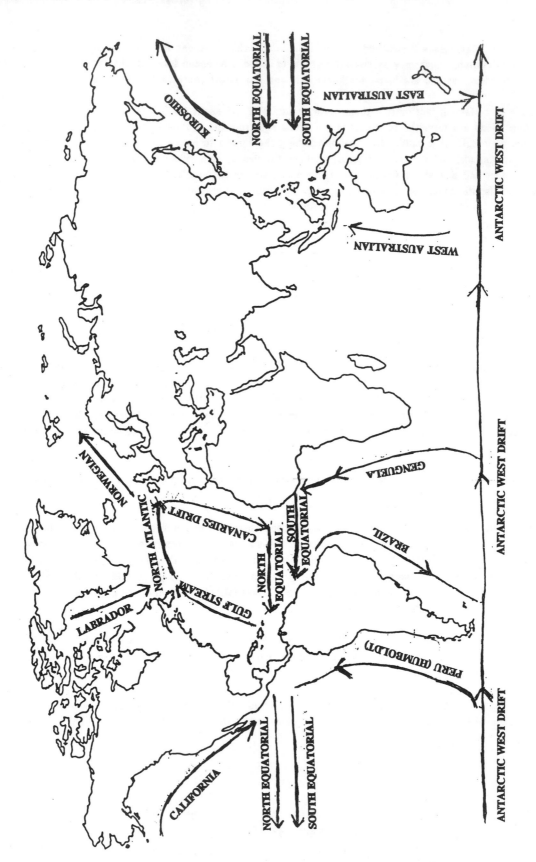

Chapter 23. THE JET-STREAM AND ITS JET-STREAKS

The jet-stream is a narrow and meandering belt of strong winds found at the tropopause. The jet-stream is not one continuous band of high winds, but is comprised of discrete segments called JET-STREAKS or JETLETS. The threshold value for the beginning speed of a jet-streak is 50 knots (about 58 miles per hour or 93 kilometers per hour).

Figure 23-1. The polar jet-stream (also called the northern stream), and south of it, the sub-tropical jet-stream (also called the southern stream).

The polar jet separates colder, polar air from the milder mid-latitude air to its south. The sub-tropical jet separates the mid-latitude air from tropical air.

Each jet-stream, composed of individual jet-streaks, can be visualized as a narrow "snake" of air, which can be 10,000 or more feet deep, and moves horizontally and vertically.

NORTHERN HEMISPHERE

Sometimes there is a third jet-stream, called the Arctic jet, which is north of the polar jet, and separates extremely cold Arctic air from the polar air. The Arctic jet can form only when extremely cold air develops in the far north during winter.

The polar jet-stream is caused by temperature differences between the polar region and lower latitudes. The greater this temperature GRADIENT, the stronger the jet-stream.

Temperature differences cause pressure differences which cause air to move: the wind. Wind is air in motion. Since the thermal gradient is larger in the colder half of the year, the polar jet is stronger during that time.

When a cold polar or Arctic outbreak advances down the globe towards lower latitudes, that part of the jet-stream on the south edge of the cold air also advances towards lower latitudes. Thus, the cold front is at lower levels below the polar jet. Where the warmer mid-latitude air is advancing poleward, that portion of the polar jet is also moving poleward.

For mid-latitudes, especially in the wintertime, the polar jet predominates in terms of having major weather effects on the mid-latitudes. When the jet-stream pattern is more-or-less from west to east, its air flow is called a ZONAL FLOW. There is a distinct separation between the cold, dry air to its north and the warm, moister air to its south. Along the polar front, there may be small ripples, so only minor and fast quasi-west-to-east moving low pressure systems occur.

Similarly, the Southern Hemisphere has its polar and subtropical jets.

Commercial and military aircraft flying at 32,000 feet or 35,000 feet may have to cross the jet-stream or may be flying right into it or, if they are fortunate, may have it as a tail wind to help them get to their destinations. The Japanese discovered the jet-stream during World War II, and tried to take advantage of it by launching big weather balloons with bombs attached, to fly across the Pacific to strike the United States and Canada. Only a very small percentage of these balloon-bombs made it to North America, and most fell in rural areas of British Columbia, Washington, Oregon and California, but at least one made it as far east as Michigan. Apparently, there were very few casualties. The first jet aircraft flying at jet-stream levels discovered the jet-streams, and we have since learned much about these high-level ribbons of fast-moving air.

Figure 23-2. A zonal flow of the polar jet-stream.

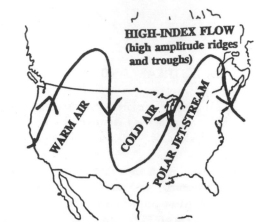

Figure 23-3. A high index flow of the polar jet-stream.

When a jet-stream has a big dip or dips, with ridges and troughs, then the wind change from west to east across it is abrupt, and this is called a HIGH INDEX wind flow of the jet-stream.

The basic upper-level (mid and upper tropospheric) air flow (direction of the air flow) is essentially the same for hundreds of miles on each side of the jet-stream; thus, the upper-air flow pattern can also be termed as "zonal" when it is more-or-less west to east, or "high index" when the flow has big ridges and troughs.

Well-developed low pressure systems occur when there is an interaction of cold, dry air and warm, humid air, with the warm air rising up over the colder air that is also displacing the warm air upward. Thus, e.g., when the polar jet-stream plunges to the Gulf of Mexico region, where warm, moist air is abundant, the interaction of the advancing polar air with the warm and moist air readily develops a cyclone.

CYCLOGENESIS, the development of low pressure systems (cyclones), occurs along the polar front when some warm air tries to move northward and the cold air is moving southward to the west of the warm air advection. Thus, a kink or wave will develop along a portion of the polar front. This wave may be initiated by a short-wave trough aloft, with its areas of positive vorticity advection, but if the wave, the incipient cyclone, is to develop into a major low pressure system, the temperature advections must then begin and intensify. Strong cyclogenesis is more likely during the colder half of the year, when the temperature difference between the polar air and the lower latitude air is significantly greater than in the warmer half of the year. In fact, the polar jet is driven by pressure differences caused by thermal gradients (temperature differences over a distance); therefore, with greater temperature differences in the colder months, the polar jet-stream is stronger then than in the warmer months.

A polar jet plunging into the southeastern United States may also lead to tornado outbreaks.

During the summertime, the polar jet is typically far north, in Canada, and significant extratropical cyclogenesis in the contiguous 48 states and vicinity is at a minimum.

The polar jet exists so that the low pressure systems that develop on it can transport heat and other properties poleward, and bring cold air southward. Otherwise, the equatorial areas would keep getting hotter and hotter and the polar areas would keep getting colder and colder, and our global climate would be much different from what we have now.

There is more solar radiation coming into the tropics to heat it than there is terrestrial (the earth's) radiation going out into space to cool the air there. In the polar regions, for an annual average, there is a net loss of heat since more radiation is emitted into space in high latitudes than is received from the sun.

Thus, in the summertime, as was stated before, when the polar jet is weaker, we find much fewer of these EXTRATROPICAL CYCLONES (what we call the non-tropical storm low-pressure systems) to transport the excess energy poleward. Then, Nature must create something else to do this transporting, so it develops HURRICANES, which are

TROPICAL CYCLONES. Thus, if we humans devised a way to destroy hurricanes, then Nature would have to create some other meteorological feature to move much of the excess energy poleward, or else the tropics would become even hotter and the poles even colder.

The transport of heat by polar-front extratropical cyclones and by tropical cyclones poleward and by their associated short-wave troughs aloft, is about the same total required to offset the radiative imbalance between low and high latitudes. Simply put, WE MUST HAVE STORMS!

The Arctic jet is similar to the polar jet, and it happens relatively infrequently. We always have a polar and a sub-tropical jet.

The role of the sub-tropical jet includes thermal transports but also the transport of a quantity known as angular momentum. Angular momentum involves the wind and its transport of mass on a rotating earth. This momentum is generated in low latitudes, and from this source region it is transported poleward to the "sink" region. The thermal gradients across the sub-tropical jet are not as great as across the polar jet; therefore, major cyclogenesis is not as common at the surface beneath the sub-tropical jet.

The jet-streams are lower in elevation in the winter and higher in summer. The 300 millibar chart (average mid-latitude height of about 29,000 feet) will catch most of the detail of jet-streaks in the winter, and the 200 millibar chart (average mid-latitude height is about 39,000 feet) is used in summer. The 250 millibar chart is a good compromise because it will likely catch the jet-stream winds. Keep in mind that each jet-stream jet-streak undulates and moves forward as it changes its size, including its depth. Thus, we can visualize each jet-streak as a "snake of air" containing very strong winds.

Jet-streaks start at 50 knots, and the core of the maximum winds can easily exceed 100 knots. Sometimes jet-streak maxima even exceed 170 knots, and have been observed to exceed 200 knots (over 230 miles per hour).

Now let us look at the specifics of the jet-stream jet-streaks and the roles they play in our weather. The following discussion is descriptive, yet technical. You can skip it without losing any of the basics of jet-streams. However, if you want a detailed explanation of jet-stream dynamics and how it is related to vertical motions in the troposphere, then read the following discussion.

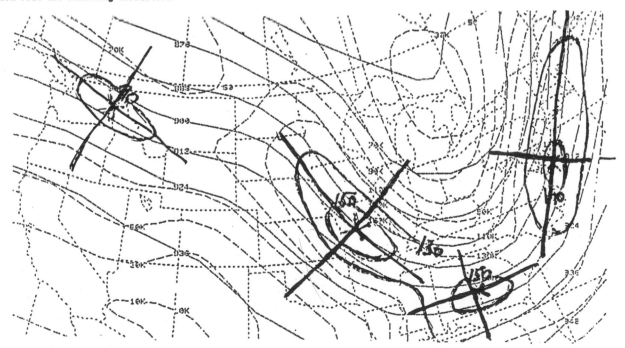

Figure 23-4. Jet-Streaks within the Polar Jet-Stream.

Figure 23-4 shows a 300 mb chart which was hand-analyzed to highlight the jet-streaks within the polar jet. Here, the jet cores or maximum winds were highlighted. Note that when the jet-streaks are fairly straight, you can divide each one into four quadrants. The left-front quadrant and right-rear quadrant are regions of upward moving air from the surface through the jet-stream level, and the other quadrants have descending air. The reason why is explained shortly. Thus, in using a jet-stream analysis for forecasting, see if the left-front or right-rear quadrants are headed your way, because if they are, then upward motion will be enhanced. When one of these quadrants passes over a developing low pressure system, we can have rapid cyclogenesis. In the convective time of year, one of these quadrants could condition the environment for thunderstorms that may become severe, even tornadic, especially in the Spring and early Autumn.

The jet-streaks themselves are moving through the flow, typically at 30 to 50 knots, but the air parcels blowing THROUGH the jet-streak are entering it, accelerating to the jet-max speed (e.g., 150 knots), and then exiting the jet-streak. The left-front and right-rear quadrants are named in reference to the jet-streak's movement. In our example in figure 23-4, a jet-max or jet core is over Missouri, with the jet-streak heading southeast parallel to the 300 mb height contours. The left-front quadrant is over Illinois, Indiana and essentially western parts of Kentucky and Tennessee; the right-rear quadrant is over essentially Kansas and Nebraska. These are the regions where the jet is inducing air to rise. If there is adequate moisture in the air in these regions, then clouds and subsequent precipitation would occur.

The left-front quadrant is usually more active than the right-rear quadrant, because the thermal gradient, especially aloft, may be greater there.

Now let us analyze an individual jet-streak to see why we have rising air in the left-front and right-rear quadrants of an essentially straight jet-streak.

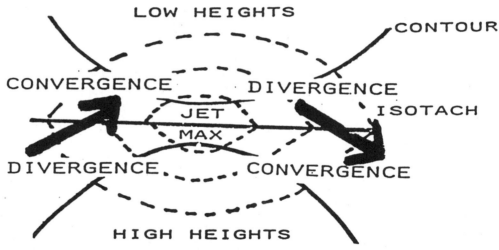

Figure 23-5. A straight jet-streak, showing the upper-level divergence regions in the left-front (upper right in this diagram) and right-rear (lower left in this diagram) quadrants, where upward vertical motion is occurring from the surface up through the jet-streak level. An isotach is a line of equal wind speed.

What happens is that the forces that cause the wind are out of balance in the vicinity of jet-streaks, and this leads to compensating vertical motions.

Normally, the air blows roughly parallel to the upper-level height contours, The pressure-gradient force blows the air from high to low heights, and the Coriolis force turns it to the right in the Northern Hemisphere, if there is no friction to prevent it from turning all the way to the right. The wind is then called GEOSTROPHIC, which is the balance of the pressure-gradient and Coriolis forces. Near the ground, there is friction, so that the wind is not turned 90 degrees to the right by the Coriolis force due to the earth's rotating, but is turned at an angle somewhat less than 90 degrees. Over the oceans, the frictional component of the wind is less than over the rougher land, so the wind is closer to geostrophic over the oceans than over the land. However, aloft, above the "FRICTION LAYER" (also called the PLANETARY BOUNDARY LAYER), the wind is geostrophic, blowing parallel to the height contours. (The planetary boundary layer is most commonly some 1500 to 2500 feet deep up from the ground, but can get shallower on some nights after the sun sets.)

When air parcels approach the jet-streak, they are in geostrophic balance: the pressure-gradient and Coriolis forces balance each other: the wind blows from the high heights to the low heights (the same as from high pressure to low pressure) and the Coriolis force turns it to the right. However, the pressure-gradient force is increasing very rapidly over a relatively short distance as the parcels enter the jet-streak and accelerate towards the jet maximum. The Coriolis force cannot increase fast enough to keep in balance with the pressure-gradient force. Therefore, the parcels are not turned the complete 90 degrees to the right but only partially to the right because the pressure-gradient force in that region is temporarily greater than the Coriolis force.

The air diverges from the entrance region and piles up or converges on the other side. Thus, the right-rear quadrant is a region of upper-level divergence, and the left-rear quadrant is one of convergence. Where the air is diverging..being depleted..aloft, it is being replaced by air from below), because air cannot be created or destroyed. In the convergence area, air is piling up and sinking (some may be forced upward above that level). We actually set up a circulation across the jet-streak and down to the ground in the rear of the jet-streak.

The forces do become in balance at the jet max, but then as the parcels of air leave the jet max, the wind gets progressively lighter in the jet-streak, meaning that the pressure-gradient force that causes the wind is decreasing very rapidly over a relatively short distance. However, the Coriolis force cannot decrease fast enough to stay in balance with the pressure-gradient force. Consequently, the air blows away from the left-front quadrant (divergence aloft) and toward the right-front quadrant (convergence aloft). Air rises in the left-front quadrant to replace the depleted air, and mostly sinks in the right-front quadrant. A three-dimensional circulation is established here also, from the surface up through the jet-streak.

Although this jet-streak discussion is complicated, especially to someone studying it for the first time, if you take the time to study what is going on with the air parcels entering, blowing through and exiting a jet-streak, a clear picture emerges about the jet-streak dynamics.

The reason there is not a continuous polar jet-stream and sub-tropical jet-stream across the hemisphere is because the vertical circulations would not be easily possible without the breaks between jet-stream segments.

The sub-tropical jet-stream is higher than the polar jet-stream because the tropopause, which separates the troposphere from the stratosphere, is higher as we move equatorward, and the jet-streams occur between overlapping tropopauses. On very infrequent occasions, the left-front quadrant of a sub-tropical jet-streak overlaps the right-rear quadrant of a polar jet-streak. Since these quadrants are regions of upper-level divergence and upward vertical motion, they combine their forcings of air upward, resulting in major air rises.

These are extreme events, and when they do happen, the resulting weather can be disastrous. For example, when these two jet-streaks overlapped over the eastern U.S. in March 1993 over a developing low pressure system, the storm "exploded". It intensified (DEEPENED [pressure kept getting lower]) very rapidly, resulting in a "snow hurricane".

Winds exceeded 100 mph and parts of the Northeast received over four feet of snow, accompanied by thunder and lightning. Snowfall rates exceeded five inches per hour during the height of the storm. In the late Spring, such overlapping jet-streaks can lead to major tornado outbreaks, with families of tornadoes sweeping across many states.

All of this jet dynamics is true when the air parcels blowing through the jet are moving faster than is the jet-streak itself. Otherwise, the convergence/divergence areas are reversed. This situation would be rare.

A jet-steak is not always fairly straight. When it is curved like a big "U", then the upper divergence area spreads out over most of the northern half of the U and the upper convergence region is over much of the southern half. Then, the upward vertical motion in essentially to the north of the jet-streak axis. The reverse is true when the jet-streak is shaped like an "inverted U" (the upward moving air being south of the jet-streak axis).

Jet-streaks within the general jet-steam flow may be from several hundred to over 2000 miles long and are typically from 100 to 400 miles wide and one to two miles deep.

There are long-term, large-scale general circulation cells in the tropics, mid-latitudes and polar regions. As we ascend to the top of the troposphere, known as the TROPOPAUSE, we find that the temperature stops falling with height. We then enter the stratosphere. The tropopause is higher in the tropical cell than in the mid-latitude cell, and is higher in the mid-latitude cell than in the polar cell.

Where the higher tropical tropopause overlaps the mid-latitude tropopause, we find the sub-tropical jet-stream, and where the mid-latitude tropopause overlaps the lower polar tropopause, we find the polar jet-stream.

Since the jet-streaks move through the upper level flow pattern, and since they have favorable areas for upward motion, the locations and predicted locations of the jet-streaks are useful in forecasting. When the upper-level dynamics associated with a jet-streak enhances upward vertical motion that is already occurring in low and middle levels of the troposphere, then we can have upward motion throughout the depth of the troposphere in a region, and as we know, the generation of precipitation requires upward-moving air and enough moisture to first create clouds and subsequently precipitation.

<u>Measuring the upper winds:</u>

At hundreds of weather stations around the world, at just before 00Z and 12Z daily, helium-filled weather balloons are launched which carry an instrument package known as a <u>radiosonde</u>. The balloon expands as it rises to higher and higher heights with progressively lower external atmospheric pressures, until it bursts, which is typically at about 100,000 feet elevation. A parachute carries the radiosonde (sounding information transmitted to earth via a battery-powered radio transmitter on the radiosonde package) gently downward where it lands somewhere on earth.

Figure 23-6. The weather balloon being inflated with helium. The radiosonde is then attached to the balloon and to a parachute so that when the balloon bursts at about 100,000 feet up, the radiosonde gently descends to earth, where, if recovered, it can often be reconditioned for reuse. If you find a radiosonde, you can keep it as a souvenir, or return it to the nearest post office (in the U.S.) who will return it to the National Weather Service. (source: NWS)

Inside the radiosonde box is a thermistor to measure temperature, a moisture sensor to measure the dewpoint, and an aneroid barometer to measure the air pressure. The radar on the ground monitors not only the vertical rise of the radiosonde but also the horizontal motion, so that the wind direction and speed at various levels can be determined.

Figure 23-7. The weather balloon, parachute and radiosonde being released. (source: NWS)

Figure 23-7. The radiosonde. At the top is a cord, which attaches to the parachute and weather balloon. At the bottom is the battery pack, which radios back to the weather office on the ground the vital weather observations taken by the instruments inside the radiosonde box. Inside, the thermistor is ceramic or ceramic coated, and looks like a short wire. Ceramic expands and contracts rapidly; thus it responds quickly to rapid temperature changes, which is what we find as the balloon rises. These changes are related to the current or electrical resistance. The moisture sensor is a small rectangular piece of metal or other material that is coated with lithium chloride, which is hygroscopic (absorbs moisture). The amount of electrical resistance of the sensor is proportional to the moisture content. The vacated (a vacuum inside of it) cylinder of the aneroid barometer expands as the air pressure lowers (or compresses if it rises), and this cylinder is attached to a dial whose other end flows across a plate that radioes back a signal proportional to the pressure value. The wind direction and speed at the various levels are determined by the radar dish simply following the path of the radiosonde. (source: NWS)

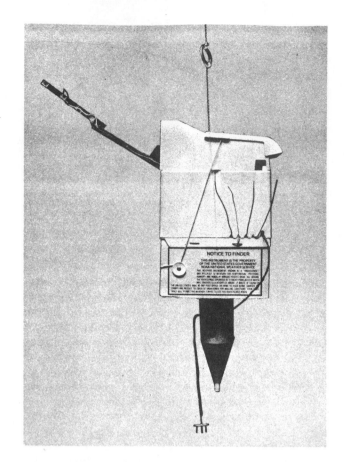

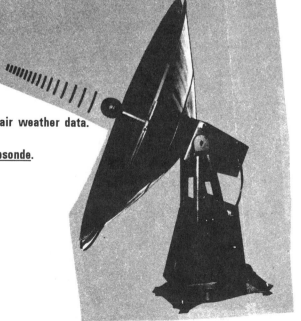

Figure 23-8. The radar is tracking the radiosonde, receiving data from the weather sensors in it. (source: NWS) Sometimes the term <u>rawinsonde</u> is used, when referring to a radiosonde whose path is used to also determine the wind.

Most of the information on upper-level weather charts comes from radiosondes. Sounders on weather satellites, Doppler radar soundings from the surface and up, and some data from aircraft also contribute to the upper-air weather data.

When a radiosonde is dropped from an aircraft, it is called a <u>dropsonde</u>. This is done chiefly when hurricane reconnaissance aircraft are flying through a hurricane to collect additional data.

Radiosondes have been sent aloft via rockets, and are each then called a <u>rocketsonde</u>.

In the early days of soundings, maximum and minimum thermometers were sent aloft, attached to kites.

Our computer forecast models could not be run without the data from radiosondes.

Chapter 24. LOCAL WINDS

There are hundreds of names given by local residents to their local winds. There are some types of local winds that are similar but have different local names because they occur in various parts of the world.

Geographical features play an important role in the development of winds that affect a localized area. All across the globe this phenomenon occurs, so we are describing here some typical examples.

<u>The sea breeze and the land breeze:</u>

Figure 24-1. A sea breeze during the late morning into late afternoon. (source: DOA)

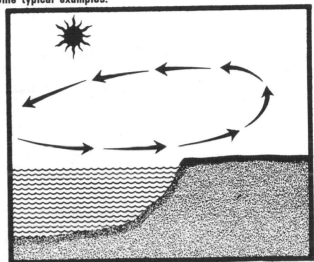

Water has a greater heat capacity than land; that is, it retains heat longer. This also means that water warms up and cools off more slowly than does land. During the daytime on a sunny or mostly sunny day, especially during the warmer half of the year, the ground heats up much faster and more than does the sea surface. Thus, the air over the land is warmer than the air over the ocean (or over the Great Lakes or other very large body of water). This causes the air over the land to rise, while the cooler air over the ocean starts moving inland. Since cooler air weighs more than warmer air, localized higher pressure develops over the water, and since air moves from relatively high to lower pressure, the air flow is from the water to over the land. The land is warming up from the sun, causing air to rise. The overall result, as depicted in the figure, is the establishment of a circulation. The sea breeze may extend inland for up to a couple of miles, sometimes more.

The temperature consequence of a sea breeze is that the area experiencing it is cooler than the region farther inland. For example, on a sunny and hot sunny summer day in New Jersey, the temperature may reach 95°F, but right along the shore the temperature may remain no higher than the upper 70s. Bathers at the sea shore may be in 78-degree air, but persons two miles inland would be sweltering in 95-degree temperatures.

For a sea-breeze to become established, the prevailing wind must be light, otherwise it would overpower any sea breeze effect. Since the daytime must be sunny or nearly so, this means that the region is most-often under the influence of a high pressure system. The sun needs some time to rise above the horizon to begin heating the ground along the shore; consequently, the onset of the sea-breeze is typically about two or so hours before solar noon, and it lasts until late afternoon or evening.

The depth of the cooler marine air is relatively shallow...the cooler air coming in from the ocean or large lake (lake breeze) may be from 800 to 1200 feet. If there any higher clouds, they are above this layer and are observed most often to be moving in a direction different from the wind direction within the sea-breeze.

However, a fairly strong sea breeze can be generated when the land gets very hot compared to the sea-surface. Recall that the greater the temperature difference between the land surface and water surface, the greater is the pressure difference, and the greater the pressure difference, the stronger the sea breeze. Then the wind speed within the sea-breeze over land may exceed 25 miles per hour (40 kilometers per hour) and may extend inland for even more than a couple of miles (more than a few kilometers). In fact, since the sea breeze is essentially a warm-season phenomenon, it often becomes pronounced over the southern part of the Florida peninsula, and sometimes a sea breeze from the east, from off the Atlantic Ocean, interacts with a sea-breeze from the west, from off the Gulf of Mexico, resulting in a convergence of air which is forced up and often produces thunderstorms at the intersections of these boundaries, which act as mini-fronts.

Figure 24-2. When the main wind flow is blowing towards the sea and is strong enough, it may block the sea breeze. (source: DOA)

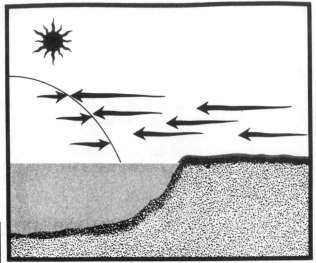

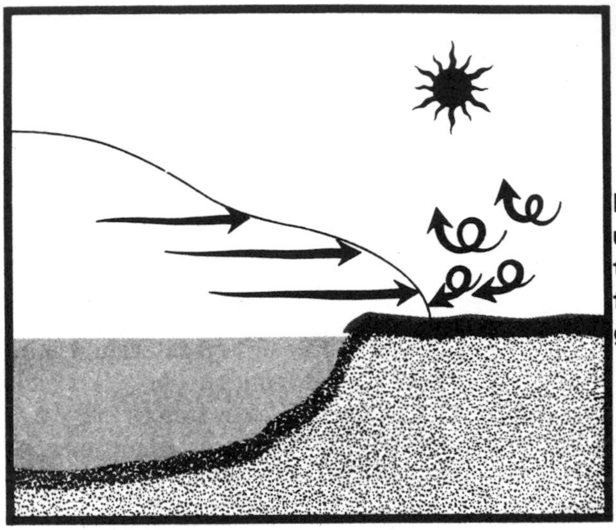

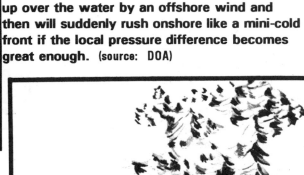

Figure 24-3. Sometimes the marine air can pile up over the water by an offshore wind and then will suddenly rush onshore like a mini-cold front if the local pressure difference becomes great enough. (source: DOA)

Figure 24-4. Sometimes large rivers and other deep passes that cut through coastal ranges provide a sea breeze flow route. source: DOA)

Land breezes are really the opposite of sea breezes. They typically occur on a calm or nearly calm night, especially during the warmer part of the year, when the air over the land is cooler (due to radiational cooling) than the air over the ocean or other large water body. (Recall that water takes a longer time to cool off than does the land, which cools off relatively rapidly.) The result is localized higher pressure over the land surface and relatively lower pressure over the water. Since wind blows from high to low pressure, the result is air flowing from the land to over the water. The difference in air temperature over the water and over the land is less at night than during the day (the land heats up considerably on a sunny day), so the pressure difference is less; the result is that any nocturnal land breezes are typically weaker than the daytime sea or lake breezes. The circulation in a land breeze is shallower than that of a sea breeze, and the land breeze may extend out to a couple or more miles out over the water. When the center of a high pressure system is over the region at night during the warmer part of the year, a land breeze is likely to form since the center of a high is normally calm or nearly calm, with clear or nearly clear skies.

Figure 24-5. The land breeze. (source: NOAA)

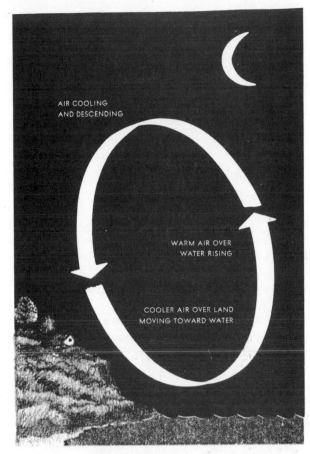

On a clear or mostly clear and calm or mostly calm nights during the warmer part of the year, the opposite of a sea breeze may happen. Since the land cools off faster and more than does the ocean, the air over the land will eventually be cooler than the air over the coastal ocean or large lake, and the cooler air pushes out over the water, establishing an offshore flow and a circulation. This is called the land breeze.

Monsoons:

The term, "monsoon" (from the Arabic, "mawsim" for "season", since this phenomenon is seasonal), refers to a wind that switches to a certain direction for a prolonged time and brings with it the same type of weather for a prolonged time. It is commonly used when it brings the rainy season to those climates that have distinct dry and wet seasons. Pronounced monsoons occur over India and vicinity, and in southeast Asia. A smaller-scale monsoon occurs in the southwest United States later in the summer, when tropical winds bring in Pacific Ocean moisture and cause thunderstorm activity which can lead to flash floods.

Since monsoonal winds are seasonal, we speak of a "summer monsoon" and a "winter monsoon".

A <u>summer monsoon</u> resembles a sea-breeze but occurring over a large area and persisting through much of the summer.

Figure 24-6. A summer monsoon. During the day, the wind speed is stronger since the greatest temperature difference occurs then between the air over the land and the air over the sea. This is the "wet season", since warm, moist air from over the ocean rise over the mountains and is cooled. Condensation produces clouds and subsequent precipitation. Some parts of the world receive their heaviest precipitation amounts during the summer monsoon season. An example is the climate of India. When the winds switch to a southerly direction and stay like that for many weeks, they bring in moisture from the warm, moist air over the Indian Ocean, producing torrential rainfalls. As the saturated air rises up the slopes of the Himalaya Mountains, the orographic lifting condense even more moisture out of the clouds and the rain just teems. Cherrapunji, India, in that area, received over one thousand inches of rain one year, thanks in large part to the summer monsoon.

A <u>winter monsoon</u> resembles a land breeze but occurring over a large area and persisting through much of the winter.

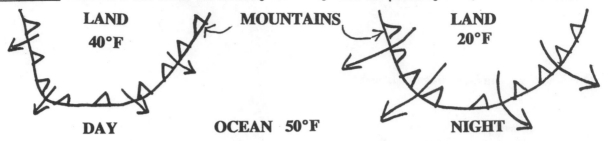

Figure 24-7. A winter monsoon. The wind speed is stronger during the night, since then there is a greater temperature difference between the air over the ocean and the air over the land. This is the "dry season" since cool dry air is descending from the land to the sea.

<u>Upslope and downslope winds:</u>

Figure 24-8. At right we depict upslope winds, which occur during the daytime as a result of surface heating. (source: DOA)

Upslope and downslope winds are local diurnal winds that can occur on sloping surfaces. <u>Valley breezes</u> are examples of upslope winds. They move up a mountain during the day. The slopes are heated by sunlight; the air that is heated becomes lighter and moves up from the valley. Valley breezes, like sea breezes, can occur only when the sun is shining and no other wind of significance is blowing.

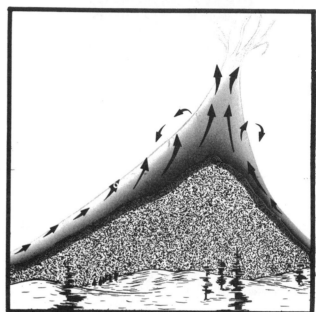

At night, we may have downslope winds because of surface cooling. Upslope and downslope winds are caused by a local pressure gradient (local pressure difference between locations) being generated by the local temperature difference between the air around the slope and the air at the same elevation away from the slope. Daytime upslope winds are shallow near the base of the slope, and increase in depth and speed as more heated air is funnelled along the slope.

Figure 24-9. Downslope winds at night are shallow, with the airflow tending to be straight (laminar). It is possible for some or all of the cold air to be temporarily dammed by obstructions such as dense forests or dense brush. The principle force here is gravity, which causes the denser cold air to flow downslope. (source: DOA)
<u>Mountain breezes</u> are examples of downslope winds. They move down a mountain at night. The air along the slopes is cooled by radiational cooling and becomes denser and sinks. Mountain breezes, like land breezes, can occur on clear, calm nights, which allow radiational cooling.

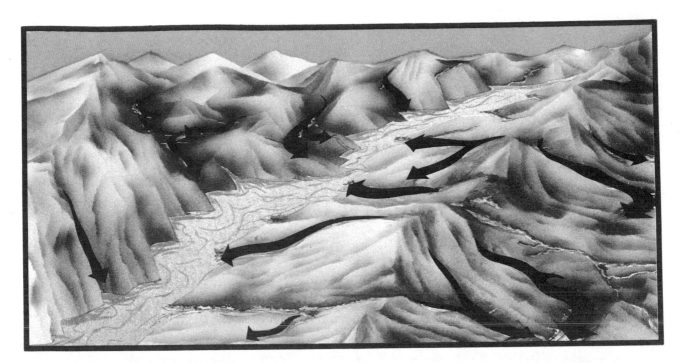

Figure 24-10. At night, the cooler and denser air near the surface of slopes flows downward, thanks to the force of gravity, flowing downward much like water would. The air flow follows the natural drainage paths in the topography. (source: DOA)

Chinook or foehn winds:

These are strong downsloping winds from mountains. Since the air is warming as it descends, these winds are relatively warm as they move into communities along the base of and just downstream from the mountain range. "Chinook" is an American Indian name. The same wind in Europe is called a "foehn" wind, and is used in the Alp Mountains, especially for winds descending the northern Alps.

They differ from mountain breezes in that they can occur either during the day or a night, as well as during clear or cloudy skies. Their cause is a significant difference in atmospheric pressure on opposite sides of a mountain chain. For example, when the pressure is high on the windward side and significantly lower on the leeward side of part of a mountain chain, the air is forced to ride up over the chain. As the air rises, it cools, and if it contains sufficient moisture, clouds and subsequent precipitation occur. As the air descends on the leeward side, it warms by being compressed, which causes a sharp temperature rise as this warm air advances away from the mountains. In the United States, chinook winds are common, warm and dry winds coming down the eastern slopes of the Rocky Mountains.

The chinook is also called a "snow-eater" wind, since the rise in temperature as the strong chinook moves in can be dramatic. For example, a chinook descending from the mountain range known as the Black Hills to the west of town caused the temperature in Rapid City, South Dakota to rise from 17 below zero Fahrenheit to 47 degrees above zero in about two minutes on a January night!

Santa Ana winds:

A Santa Ana wind is a foehn-type wind named for a community southeast of Los Angeles in southern California. When a strong high pressure system settles to the northeast of southern California, with low pressure to the southwest, the low-level winds moving into southern California will be from an easterly direction, from over the desert. These winds also blow over and down mountains, reaching southern California with very hot temperatures, typically over 100 degrees F, and typically in September. The Santa Ana is a hot, dry wind, and often fans brush fires in southern California. Even coastal communities in that region, which typically have daytime readings in the 70s and 80s, can heat into the 90s and 100s.

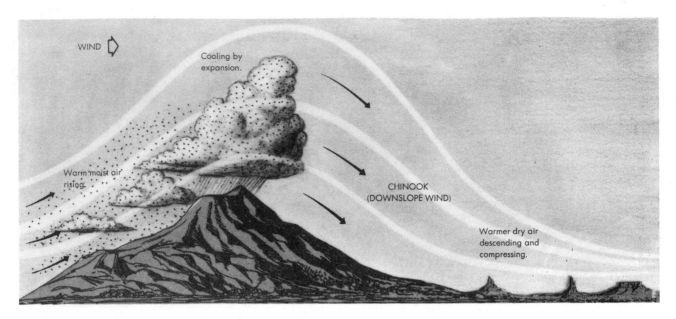

WIND ➩

Cooling by expansion.

Warm moist air rising.

CHINOOK (DOWNSLOPE WIND)

Warmer dry air descending and compressing.

Figure 24-11. A chinook wind. Warming of the air at 5½F° per one thousand feet of vertical descent makes this wind a very warm wind by the time it reaches the lower elevations of the mountains. (source: USAF)

<u>Katabatic winds</u>: Katabatic winds (sometimes called fall or gravity winds) occur when strong radiational cooling along the mountains causes the denser cold air to flow down the mountains. Even though there is warming of the air as it descends, the air is still cold when it reaches the bottom because it starts out quite cold, plus radiational cooling is occurring all down the slopes. Thus, katabatic winds are usually cold. An example is along the northern coast of the Adriatic Sea in a plateau region which rises at the rear of a narrow coastal plain. In the winter, air over this plateau sometimes becomes quite cold due to radiational cooling. The air then flows down the slopes as a cold, northeast wind known as a <u>bora</u>. The bora is most frequent and strongest in the latter part of the night, although it can occur even after sunrise if the air has not started descending by late at night. A similar cold wind coming from the higher and often snow-covered land to the north occurs during the winter on the Mediterranean Sea coast of France, and is called a <u>mistral</u>.

<u>Sirocco</u>: A sirocco is a hot, dry wind blowing northward from the Sahara-Libyan Desert. It sometimes works its way into extreme southern Europe, causing a heat wave. If it picks up enough moisture by passing over the Mediterranean Sea, it can cause hot and humid conditions in southern Europe. Similar hot, dry winds occur over the Great Plains of the United States in the summer.

<u>Whirlwinds and dust devils</u>: Little whirlwinds, which look like little tornadoes but occur in clear or mostly clear air, need local unstable conditions in a superheated layer of air hugging the ground, and require the environmental winds to be light. The energy is released by some triggering mechanism, and can even be released due to some obstruction to the air flow, such as a sharp ridge. When they form in very hot deserts, they fill with desert sand and dust and are called dust devils. Whirlwinds can grow to be several hundred feet tall, and in some cases even exceed 1000 feet in height. The winds are typically under 50 mph, but speeds in excess of 60 mph sometimes occur.

Children of all ages have had great fun in desert areas such as southern Nevada and southeast California by running into a dust devil. One of your authors drove his vehicle off the road and into the desert north of Las Vegas, Nevada, and got out, trying to chase a dust devil. Sometimes dust devils occur in families. These whirlwinds do not last long. If you see a dust devil or whirlwind, it means that intense local heating has been occurring.

<u>Dust storms and sandstorms</u>: These occur in dry conditions when strong winds pick up dust or sand and partially or totally obscure the sky. The topic is covered in chapter 35.

Figure 24-12. A whirlwind is a dust devil in the desert. A whirlwind forms during intense local heating, sunny or mostly sunny skies and light winds. (source: DOA)

Other winds:

There are hundreds of local winds, each with its own local name. In this chapter we gave the examples of the kinds of local winds that occur.

Moreover, sometimes synoptic or large-scale winds are given local names. For example, when a strong blast of arctic air plunges about due south into Texas, the residents of Texas, especially northern Texas, sometimes refer to this very cold, numbing wind as a "blue norther".

One type of synoptic-scale wind deserves description: the LAKE EFFECT WIND AND ITS SNOWS.

Lake Effect:

When very cold arctic air passes over the relatively warm Great Lakes of the United States, especially from late autumn into early winter when the lakes are free of widespread icing over, clouds form over the warmer lakes and these clouds tend to produce copious amounts of snow. When the dewpoint of the cold air is at least about 18 degrees colder than the surface temperature of the Great Lake it is passing over, the evaporation of moisture from the lake condenses into clouds, and these clouds have vertical growth because of the unstable conditions (warm at the bottom and much colder as we rise up for several thousand feet). This situation is analogous to what you see when you fill a bath tub to the top with hot water. There is evaporation, and the moist air condenses in the cooler air over the tub to form a fog (a cloud).

When the low-level winds steer the lake effect snowclouds inland, the heavy lake effect snows dump their snow not just over the lake but also onshore. The heaviest lake effect snowfall typically occurs about 10 to 20 miles inland from the coast. The land is higher in elevation than the lake's surface, so since the air is moving onshore already saturated, it must rise up and over the land and its hills, etc. Any additional lift to the saturated air squeezes out (condenses out) even more moisture to increase the snowfall rate. This phenomenon is known as <u>frictional convergence</u>. With frictional convergence, air parcels pile up and ascend higher terrain, condensing out more snow Thus, the heaviest lake effect snows (which can be three or four FEET and sometimes more, within several hours!) typically occur not along the shoreline but some 10 to 20 miles inland.

Lake effect snowstorms are discussed in chapter 30.

SECTION VIII: KEY WEATHER FEATURES

Chapter 25. AIR MASSES

An air mass is a large mass of air that often covers hundreds of thousands of square miles, in which the temperature and moisture content are much the same in a horizontal direction. For example, if your community is experiencing a cold, dry air mass and you take observations of temperature and dewpoint (moisture content of the air) over a grassy field at six feet off the ground, you might get 20 degrees Fahrenheit for the temperature and 2 degrees Fahrenheit for the dewpoint. Some five miles away in the same air mass, the temperature and dewpoint should be similar. If this is a very cold air mass with origins in the Arctic, then perhaps one hundred miles north of you, the temperature is 10 degrees F. with a dewpoint of minus 5 degrees F. Thus, the whole region is under the same cold and dry air mass.

An air mass forms over a large and nearly-uniform area of land, or forms over a large water surface. These are called <u>source regions</u>.

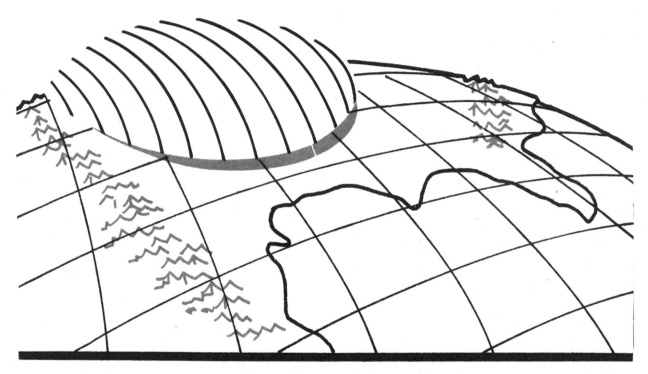

Figure 25-1. A cold polar air mass is forming in winter over the far northern latitudes, its source region. Because this air is dense due to its being very cold and getting colder almost daily, at some point in time it will be so dense that a part of the it or all of it will begin sliding down the side of the globe towards lower latitudes. You can analogize this to a blob of jello resting on the top of a large ball. Gravity will help cause the blob or chunks of it to slide down the globe. Note that the air mass has vertical extent also; thus, it is three-dimensional. (source: DOA)

Consider such a cold, dry air mass moving from the polar region southeastward into New England. Let's pick Boston, Massachusetts for our example. This air mass will bring with it to Boston the type of weather similar to what it had while in north-central Canada.

If the air mass settles over the northeast U. S. for several days, it is modified by the environment of that region. Thus, the characteristics of the Boston area will eventually modify the polar air mass over a period of days, changing its characteristics. The air mass will warm up by being over warmer terrain, and will also pick up pollutants and, near the coast, some salty odors. Thus, as an air mass moves away from its source region, it is modified by the characteristics of the new region over which it is passing.

Five main air masses affect the contiguous United States:

● CONTINENTAL POLAR

● CONTINENTAL ARCTIC

● MARITIME POLAR

● MARITIME TROPICAL

● CONTINENTAL TROPICAL.

Not all of the air masses routinely affect all the parts of the country. For example, if you live in the nation's heartland, then by the time a maritime air mass (an air mass whose source region is over the ocean) reaches you, it will be considerably modified. For example, it may not be quite as moist as initially since some of its moisture may have been spent as precipitation. The same is true for central Asia and for other areas of the world that are far removed from oceans.

In the United States, the Florida Keys infrequently experience a continental polar air mass, and when they do, the cold, dry air has been considerably modified by the time it reaches that far south. Similarly, Fairbanks and Barrow in Alaska, and northern Scandinavia and southern parts of Argentina and Chile do not usually experience maritime tropical air masses.

An air mass holds on to its characteristics better and longer when it arrives as one giant "blob", rather than a piece of it breaking off and moving, and when it passes through an environment that helps to preserve its characteristics. For example, when a bitterly cold continental Arctic air mass plunges en masse into the central plains of the United States, and it is passing over heavy snow cover all the way from the Arctic to northern Texas, it will retain most of its brutal coldness for up to several days. If this same air mass were leaving the snow fields of the Arctic and passing over a snowless central U. S., then it would be gradually warmed from below by passing over much warmer terrain.

Here is a description of each of these air masses.

CONTINENTAL POLAR: A continental polar air mass typically provides fair and cold (in winter) or cool (in summer) weather. In the Northern Hemisphere, as the continental polar air mass moves in, the surface wind is usually from the northwest to north, and sometimes west. The weather map symbol for this type of air mass is cP, the capital P showing that the air mass is of polar origin, and the c showing that it formed all or mostly over land ("continental"), rather than over the ocean.

Sometimes a small k or w will follow the cP (cPk and cPw). If this is used, the k means that at that time the air mass is colder than the ground it is over (from the German word, "kalt", for "cold"), and the w means that it is warmer than the ground it is over.

When a continental polar air mass is centered to the northeast of portions of Colorado and Wyoming, fair weather does not usually occur. In that case, the low-level winds are from the northeast to east, which rise up the gradually rising terrain and form clouds and often precipitation. It is an example of an "orographic or "topographical" effect.

In general, continental polar air masses that form in winter are colder than the ground that they cover, because their source region is quite cold due to up to 24 hours of polar nighttime. Thus, the air mass is not warmed by the sun (which actually warms the ground first which then warms the air). In fact, the air mass is losing more heat to space that it is receiving, which is how it forms as a cold air mass.

In the summertime, these air masses may be warmer than the ground they cover, because the land they cover in their source region is heated considerably by the sun, which may be out for up to 24 hours in the polar latitudes, and the land in turn heats the air above it.   PAGE 181

Contemporary meteorologists do not use air mass analysis anymore, except to note that the air mass is of polar or tropical origin, and that it is of continental or maritime origin. In this book, we are including generalized descriptions of air masses because their characteristics are important as we study about fronts and high and low pressure systems, and because it helps us to predict what kind of weather we will have.

If the surface weather map analysis does show the "k" symbol in describing any air mass, then the air mass is probably unstable: that is, since the ground is warmer than the air, bubbles of air will rise. Some cold air from above may also sink. This is called MIXING. Mixing causes bumpy rides in airplanes, but it also distributes and disperses pollutants, which results in the air quality tending to be good.

If the surface weather map analysis does show the "w" symbol in describing any air mass, then the air mass is probably stable: that is, with warmer and lighter air above the surface-based heavy cold or cool air, no or little mixing will occur. As a result, the air quality may become poor as pollutants are trapped in the cooler layer along and just above the surface. Now if you are in an airplane flying through such a stable air mass, the ride will be smooth.

When the air gets warmer as we go aloft, even though this layer may be only a few hundred to a few thousand feet thick, it is a layer which has a temperature inversion. This term is used because normally the temperature gets cooler as we rise in elevation, up to several miles up. So when this regime is reversed, that is, when it gets warmer for some depth in the lower atmosphere, we call that an inversion of the normal temperature profile, or a temperature inversion.

During surface-based temperature inversions, sound waves originating at the surface are likely to be reflected back to earth. Thus, late at night and early in the morning, when most temperature inversions occur, you may hear cars and trucks from a distant highway, that you would not hear during the middle of the day when the inversion is typically gone. Distant trains can also be heard.

CONTINENTAL ARCTIC: In the far north (or far south in the Southern Hemisphere), in the winter, it is dark for up to 24 hours per day. The earth and the air just above it are losing more heat out into space that it receives. Thus, is it easily to visualize an air mass forming that keeps getting colder and colder, until at some point it is so dense and heavy that it moves down the globe towards the warmer latitudes. These are our "Arctic outbreaks", the major cold waves. Temperatures in North America under such Arctic outbreaks have plunged to 70 below zero Fahrenheit in Montana. In a continental Arctic air mass, the temperature plummeted to 81 degrees below zero Fahrenheit at a place called Snag in the Yukon of Canada. A continental Arctic air mass plunged the temperature to 87 below zero F. at Northice, Greenland, and to 90°F. below zero at Oymykon, Russia.

Similarly, in the Southern Hemisphere, a continental Antarctic air mass over Antarctica sent the temperature plummeting to 127° below zero F. at Vostok station in Antarctica, and another invasion by a continental Antarctic air mass sent the thermometer falling to 27°F below zero at Sarmiento, Argentina.

A continental Arctic (sometimes labelled cA on some surface weather maps) air mass plunged all the way into northern Africa, and sent the temperature down to minus 11 degrees F. at Ifrane, Morocco. Another cA air mass, though considerably warmed by passing over the Pacific Ocean, did manage to advance rapidly southward to the Hawaiian Islands, and sent the temperature down to 14 degrees F. at Haleakala Summit on Maui, Hawaii. However, this is a mountain observation site at 9,750 feet elevation. Still, it is Hawaii.

A continental Antarctic air mass sent the temperature plunging to 8 below zero F. at Charlotte Pass in New South Wales, Australia.

The temperature and dewpoint temperature (moisture content) of cA air masses are so low, that when one invades your area, the air inside your house is very, very dry. If, for example, zero-degree Fahrenheit air comes into your house and is warmed to 72°F, the relative humidity would be below 10%. If you turn out the lights and rapidly rub your hand across a woolen blanket, you will see the sparks of static electricity, which would not occur if the humidity were higher. Obviously, people who live in climates wherein cA air masses reach from time to time, would need a humidifier in the house to keep the moisture level at the comfortable 40 to 50%.

Figure 25-2. Continental Arctic air masses cause the record coldest temperatures in the world. (source: DOE)

MARITIME POLAR: A maritime polar (mP) air mass forms over the high latitude ocean. It produces cold, damp, "raw" weather, often accompanied by clouds and fog. In North America, mP air masses from the northern Pacific Ocean often affect the weather from the south coast of Alaska through the Pacific northwest states of the U. S. For New England and the rest of the U. S. northeastern states, the mP air mass comes from over the northwest Atlantic Ocean.

Along the Pacific northwest, the air mass often arrives on northwest to west winds, while in the northeastern states, it comes in typically on northeast to east winds.

In New England, for example, an mP air mass arriving in the summer will bring relief from a heat wave, even though it may be accompanied by clouds, fog and drizzle. Since the air mass is invading New England from the northeast, its leading edge is called a backdoor cold front, since it is "sneaking" in from an easterly direction, whereas most weather systems travel the opposite way, heading from west to east (actually towards the northeast, east or southeast).

During the summer, mP air masses are usually cooler than the warm ground over which they are passing (this would be mPk), and are often somewhat unstable. The ocean in summer is cooler than the land, and these air masses form over the ocean.

During the winter, mP air masses are usually warmer than the cold ground over which they are passing (this would be mPw), and are therefore often stable. The ocean in winter is warmer than the land, and these air masses form over the ocean.

MARITIME TROPICAL: A maritime tropical (mT) air mass is warm and humid since its source regions are over warm oceanic waters such as the Sargasso Sea, the Caribbean Sea, the Gulf of Mexico, the southern parts of the North Atlantic and North Pacific Oceans, the northern parts of the South Atlantic and South Pacific Oceans and the Indian Ocean.

During the summertime, an mT air mass often gives us an uncomfortable combination of high humidity with very warm temperatures. Indoors, air conditioning is helpful not so much to cool the temperature alone, but more so to remove some of the moisture from the air.

Even on good pool and beach days, the maritime tropical air mass provides hazy skies with reduced visibility. When routine summertime thunderstorms form in this type of air mass, they and are referred to as "air mass thunderstorms". However, thunderstorms can form in any air mass provided that the necessary lift, instability and moisture exist simultaneously, without some weather feature to inhibit their development (such as being too warm aloft at about 10,000 feet up, for example).

Because of its high moisture content, an mT air mass often produces nocturnal fog as the air temperature cools to its high dewpoint temperature.

During the wintertime, having maritime tropical air working its way into higher latitudes where the ground is cold or snow-covered often results in the warmer air of the mT air mass cooling to its dewpoint and creating fog and low stratus clouds, often with drizzle or freezing drizzle. This inclement weather causes delays and closures at airports.

Because wintertime mT air masses are typically warmer than the ground or surface they are passing over, they are often stable. They may be labelled mTw; recall that the ocean is warmer than the land in winter, and these air masses form over the ocean.

Because summertime mT air masses are typically cooler than the ground or surface they are passing over, they are often unstable. They may be labelled mTk; recall that the ocean is cooler than the land in summer, and these air masses form over the ocean.

Most low pressure systems as well as many thunderstorms are the result of the interaction of continental polar and maritime tropical air masses.

CONTINENTAL TROPICAL: The continental tropical (cT) air mass forms over continents in the tropical regions of the world. They produce hot and dry weather. If you consider North America, examine a map to see just how thin it gets in the tropics. As a result, not much cT air can form in this continent year-round, but only in the summertime over northern Mexico and the southwest United States. Moreover, development of a cT air mass over northern Mexico and the southwest United States is prohibited by the occasional intrusion of a cP, and once in a while a cA, air mass that far south in the wintertime. The best developed continental tropical air masses form over the expansive Sahara-Libyan Desert of north Africa. Let's look at some of the temperatures around the world that have been produced by continental tropical air masses:

- in Azizia, Tripoli, Libya, the temperature shot up to 136°F. IN THE SHADE (and there wasn't any)!;
- in Death Valley, California, a summertime temperature reached 134°F. in the shade;
- in Tirat Tsvi, Israel, the thermometer sizzled at 129°F.;
- in Cloncurry, Australia, the temperature soared to 128°F.;
- in Seville, Spain, the thermometer surged to 122°F.;
- in Rivadavia, Argentina, the temperature sizzled at 120°F.

By contrast, in a maritime tropical air mass, the hottest ever reported thus far was 108°F. at Tuguegarao, Philippines, and in Antarctica, where there is never any intrusion of cT air, the temperature rose to 58°F. at Esperanza on the Palmer Peninsula.

Because a continental tropical air mass is typically hotter than the land it passes over, it is typically a cTw air mass and is often stable. (Keep in mind that stable air will not produce showers and thunderstorms, but unstable air may. In unstable air, the temperature decreases rapidly with increasing height in the troposphere [lower atmosphere]).

Because of their dryness, they tend to form only few clouds, and at night the temperature will drop lower than in a maritime tropical air mass because their dewpoints are lower. On a sunny day, the air will heat up more in a dry air mass than in a moist air mass, because in a moist air mass the water vapor in the air does prevent a good amount of the heat from the ground from heating the air as well as some of the sunlight from reaching the ground to warm it. The sun does not directly heat most of the air; the sun heats the ground which in turn heats the air in contact with it.

If you ever come across the term SUPERIOR air mass, this is a term that was used briefly in the mid-twentieth century for a hot and dry air mass that forms aloft, typically from about 5,000 feet to 20,000 feet above the surface. For example, the desert southwest of the United States may experience this in the summertime. Its heat and dryness aloft prevent showers and thunderstorms from forming. In contemporary meteorology, the superior air mass is considered to be an "aloft" portion of a continental tropical air mass.

Characteristics of Winter Air Masses

Air mass	Lapse rate	Temper-ature	Surface RH	Visibility	Clouds	Precipitation
cP at source region	Stable	Cold	High	Excellent	None	None
cP over mid-continent, South-eastern Canada and Eastern United States	Variable	do.	Low	Good, except in industrial areas and in snow flurries	Stratocumulus in hilly regions, stratocumulus or cumulus along lee shores of Great Lakes	Snow flurries in hilly areas and along lee shores of Great Lakes
mP at source region	Unstable	Moderately cool	High	Good	Cumulus	Showers
mP over west coast	do.	Cool	do.	do.	do.	do.
mP over Rockies	do.	do.	do.	Good, except in mountains and during precipitation	do.	Showers or snow
mP over midcontinent, South-eastern Canada, and Eastern United States	Stable	Mild	Low	Good, except near industrial areas	None, except in mountains	None
mT at source region	Unstable	Warm	High	Good	Cumulus	Showers
mT over Southern United States	Stable in lower layers	do.	do.	Fair in afternoon, poor with fog in early morning	Stratus and strato-cumulus	Rain or drizzle

Characteristics of Summer Air Masses

Air mass	Lapse rate	Temper-ature	Surface RH	Visibility	Clouds	Precipitation
cP at source region	Unstable	Cool	Low	Good	None or few cumulus	None
cP over midcon-tinent, South-eastern Canada, and Eastern United States	do.	Moderately cool	do.	Excellent	Variable cumulus	None
mP at source region	Stable	Cool	High	Fair	Stratus, if any	None
mP over west coast	do.	do.	do.	Good, except poor in areas of fog	Fog or stratus	None
mP over Rockies	Unstable	Moderately cool	Moderate	Good	Cumulus	Showers at high elevations
mP over midcon-tinent, South-eastern Canada, and Eastern United States	do.	Warm	Low	do.	Few cumulus	Showers wind-ward side of Appalachians
mT at source region	do.	Warm	High	do.	Cumulus, if any	Showers
mT central and eastern continent	do.	Hot	Moderate	Good during day except in showers; poor with fog in early morning	Fog in morning, cumulus or cumulo-nimbus in afternoon	Showers or thunderstorms
cT	Unstable	Hot	Low	Good except in dust storms	None	None

Figure 25-3. Characteristics of the main air masses that affect the contiguous United States. ("do" means "ditto".) On surface weather maps you may see a suffix "k" or "w" after the identifying name of the air mass. The "k" as part of the air mass symbol means that the air mass is colder than the ground/surface over which it is passing, and the "w" means that it is warmer than the ground/surface over which it is passing. A "k" air mass tends to be unstable, which can lead to showers and thunderstorms, whereas a "w" air mass tends to be stable, which, if dry, may lead to stagnant, polluted and low-visibility air, and if moist can lead to steady precipitation and/or fog. Not all parts of the world experience all the types of air masses. Think about what air masses probably affect the area where you live. (source: DOA)   PAGE 185

Figure 25-4 (right). Air mass source regions
for North America. (source: DOA)

Figure 25-5 (below). Characteristics of a stable air
mass and of an unstable air mass, assuming
enough moisture is available. (source: USAF)

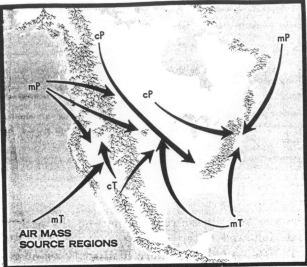

Stable Air Mass	Unstable Air Mass
Stratiform clouds and fog	Cumuliform clouds
Continuous precipitation	Showery precipitation
Smooth air	Rough air (turbulence)
Fair to poor visibility	Good visibility (except in precipitation, blowing sand or snow)

In stable air masses, sound waves reflect back to the surface and bounce ahead, similar to what weather radar signals do in a strong inversion. Thus, during stable conditions, such as in the early and mid-morning after a clear, calm night, you can hear sounds farther away than you otherwise would, such sounds including vehicles on highways, trains and tractors.

DEMONSTRATION: THE DIFFERENCE BETWEEN A STABLE AND AN UNSTABLE AIR MASS

Instead of air, the fluid used in this experiment is water. You need the following items:
● two identical glass or plastic jars;
● two index cards (but have a few spare ones too);
● blue food coloring;
● a deep tray to catch water that might spill.
● ice cubes

Procedure:

1. Fill one jar with lukewarm water, and the other with cold water to which the blue food coloring has been added. Initially, you can make the water cold by putting ice-cubes in a pitcher of water and then pouring that cold water into the jar, making sure that no ice cubes enter with it.
2. Place the jar with the lukewarm water inside a deep tray.
3. Cover the jar with the cold colored water with an index card and invert it over the jar with the clear lukewarm water, without removing the index card.
4. Carefully pull away the index card that separates the two jars.
5. You should see the cold colored water sinking into the clear lukewarm water, and the lukewarm water rising into the cold colored water. This represents an unstable air mass.
6. Now fill a jar with clear lukewarm water, and another jar with cold water, as before in step 1.
7. Place the jar with the cold colored water inside a deep tray.
8. Cover the jar with the clear lukewarm water with an index card and invert it over the jar with the cold colored blue water, without removing the index card.
9. Carefully pull away the index card that separates the two jars.
10. You should see no movement between the clear lukewarm water and the cold colored water. This represents a stable air mass.

For a variety on this experiment, you can color the cold water blue with blue food coloring, and color the warm water red with red food coloring. The initial movements of the red and blue water are analogous to stable and unstable behavior of air masses.

Chapter 26. FRONTS: cold front, warm front, stationary front, occluded front

During World War I, Norwegian meteorologists discovered that when the leading edge of colder air would pass through, the temperature would drop. When the warm air returned, its leading edge at the surface was the same boundary moving northward. It was like a battlefront, separating the different types of air masses. Thus, since there was a world war underway at the time, these meteorologists called this new discovery a battlefront, or front for short. The name "FRONT" has been used ever since.

A front is a boundary that separates different air masses. The "frontal boundary" zone may be only 50 miles wide, but can extend to a few hundred miles wide. In this zone there are atypically converging air parcels, which, because of the "piling up" (convergence) are forced to rise. With adequate moisture present, clouds and subsequent precipitation often forms in the frontal zone.

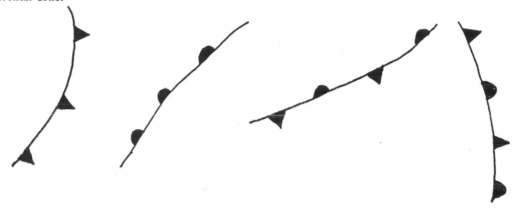

COLD FRONT WARM FRONT STATIONARY FRONT OCCLUDED FRONT

Figure 26-1. Above are the symbols on a surface weather map for the four types of fronts.

A front is the strongest when the temperature changes rapidly behind its passage if it is a cold front, and ahead of its passage if it is a warm front. Thus, the front is called a cold front if the cold air is advancing. Where the warm air is advancing, the front is called a warm front. Since the greatest temperature differences are found in the middle latitudes (which is where most people live) the fronts are strongest and most active in these latitudes.

Fronts therefore separate air masses. The properties of an air mass, such as its temperatures and moisture content, are the result of the source region -the environment- over which it forms. Thus, the air mass behind a wintertime cold front coming out of northern Canada would be a "continental polar" or "continental Arctic" air mass, which is cold are dry, except along the front. Low pressure systems, which can produce widespread rain and snow, form on the front.

The leading edge of air coming into the west coast of North America would likely be a "maritime Pacific" cold front, which would be fairly moist, since the source region was over the Pacific Ocean.

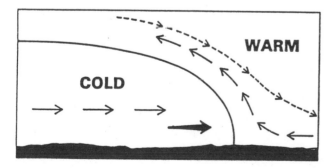 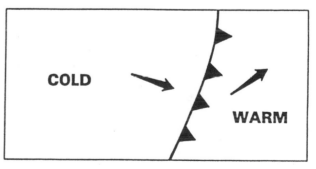

Figure 26-2. A cold front, illustrating denser, colder air advancing and lifting the warmer air ahead of it, and, at right, how a cold front is depicted on a surface weather map.

<u>Some characteristics of cold fronts</u>:

●Cold fronts are steeper than warm fronts because the cold air is denser and heavier than the warm air and can readily displace the warmer air ahead of it.
●When cloudiness and precipitation occur along an advancing cold front, it is typically convective (showers and thunderstorms), unless a low pressure system is forming somewhere along the front, which then can cause widespread and all or mostly more-steady (stratiform) precipitation.
●In the warmer half of the year in mid-latitudes, some of the most violent thunderstorms and tornadoes occur along a cold front, and sometimes in a <u>squall-line</u> that may develop some 100 miles ahead of the cold front (this happens when some of the cooler air advances aloft, say at about 6,000 to 12,000 feet above the surface, which destabilizes the atmosphere ahead of the front, enhancing thunderstorm development). A <u>pre-frontal squall-line</u> means that the some of the cooler air has advanced aloft and farther ahead of the surface front.
●After the cold front passes, as long as it keeps moving, skies tend to clear and the air is cooler and drier. A major exception is for eastern Colorado and eastern Wyoming in the cold season, when a cold front approaches from the north-northeast. Then, after the frontal passage, the low-level winds are coming from the northeast around the high pressure center which is usually to the northeast of that area in this scenario. What then happens is particularly interesting. The northeast winds are forced to rise up the sloping land which rises in elevation from the Kansas and Nebraska westward. This phenomenon is called "upsloping". When upslope conditions occur, the rising air is cooled to its dewpoint so that clouds form, and if the air then rises further and farther, snowfall (if cold enough) or rainfall occurs. Ironically, although high pressure systems are associated with fair weather most of the time, when upsloping occurs, some of the heaviest winter snowfalls occur in eastern Colorado and eastern Wyoming. Another major snow event after the passage of a strong winter cold front is lake-effect snow, which is discussed in chapter 30.

<u>The following typically occurs after the passage of a cold front</u>:
●The temperature drops, the dewpoint drops, the wind shifts to a westerly or northerly component in the Northern Hemisphere and to a westerly or southerly component in the Southern Hemisphere, and the skies usually clear as long as the front keeps moving equatorward.
●Sometimes in the winter, a large Arctic (or, in the Southern Hemisphere, Antarctic) brutally cold air mass is advancing away from the frigid polar regions, but the leading edge of it slides down the globe rapidly, maybe over 40 miles per hour (over 65 kilometers per hour), but the truly cold air is moving a little more slowly. Then, the first front passes through followed maybe a day later by the secondary cold front, which is the leading edge of the dangerously cold air. The temperature drops after the first cold front passes, and then plunges further following the secondary cold front.

Figure 26-3, below. Here is an actual National Weather Service forecast for the state of Minnesota during a brutally cold outbreak following the passage of a secondary cold front.

MINNESOTA STATE FORECAST:

...WIND CHILL WARNING STATEWIDE TONIGHT...

TONIGHT: EXTREME COLD. LOWS FROM 40 BELOW TO NEAR 60 BELOW ZERO NORTH, AND FROM NEAR 30 BELOW TO 50 BELOW SOUTH. MOSTLY CLEAR SKIES.
FRIDAY: PARTLY SUNNY BUT CONTINUED VERY COLD. HIGHS FROM 25 BELOW TO 10 BELOW ZERO.

(Note: wind chills would be in the extremely dangerous category, with any wind at all.)

•Although cold fronts move generally southward and eastward in the Northern Hemisphere, and northward and eastward in the Southern Hemisphere, sometimes the cold air spreads out a little to the west as the front moves away from higher latitudes. For example, if you are in New England and a cold front passes by from the northeast, heading southwestward, this is referred to as a "backdoor cold front". In these cases, you get some of the cold air, but the cold air usually retreats in about a day as that part of the front then moves back in the other direction as a warm front.

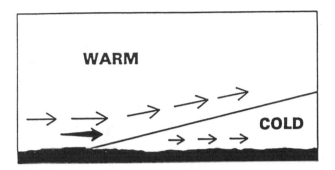 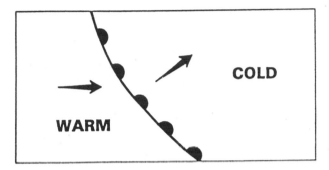

Figure 26-4. A warm front, showing the less dense warmer air first advancing aloft over the colder air, and eventually reaching the surface (where the front is placed on the surface weather map), and, at right, how a warm front is depicted on a weather map.

Some characteristics of warm fronts:

•Figure 26-5 at right illustrates that the warmer air, which is lighter than the cold air, rises above the cold air as it advances. Since clouds form when air is cooled to its dewpoint (usually by the air rising), warm fronts are typically accompanied by cloudiness and a more steady-type precipitation (this is called stratiform precipitation). Some showery-type precipitation, such as thunderstorms, can be imbedded in the steady rain or snow (showers and thunderstorms are called convective precipitation).

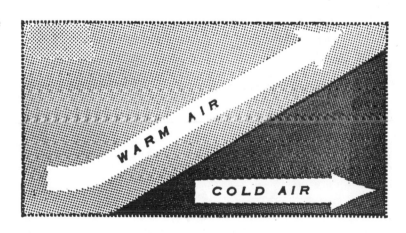

•As a warm front approaches, the high cirrus and cirrostratus clouds occur in your area first, following by gradually lowering and thickening cloudiness. The altostratus and altocumulus clouds occur, followed by stratocumulus and nimbostratus with their steady precipitation, which may include imbedded cumulonimbus clouds and their thunderstorms. The upslope is gradual, and the initial cirriform high cloudiness appears typically hundreds of miles ahead of where the warm front is on the earth's surface.
•After the warm frontal passage, the temperature and dewpoint are higher than before, the skies are clear to partly cloudy and you are in a warmer air mass. Since warm air holds more moisture than colder air, the dewpoint is higher and the relative humidity may be higher.

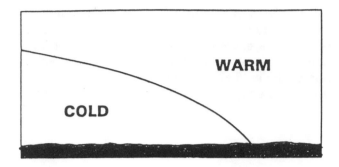
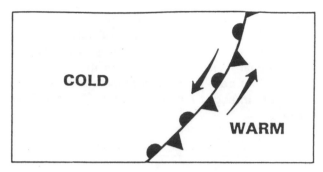

Figure 26-6. A stationary front, showing neither the cold air nor the warm air advancing, and, at right, how a stationary front is depicted on a surface weather map

Some characteristics of stationary fronts:

• Figure 26-7 at right depicts a stationary front on a surface weather map. Neither the cold air not the warm air is advancing. The temperatures and dewpoints are lower on the cold air side of the front than they are on the warm air side.

• Since the warm air rides up and over the colder air, it cools as it rises and forms clouds. Thus, on the cold air side of a stationary front is where we are more likely to find cloudy weather and maybe precipitation.

(The weather station symbol plot is described in chapter 37.)

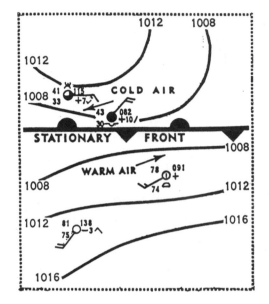

• If the front starts to develop a kink as shown in figure 26-8 at right, then some of the cold air is advancing, with that part of the front no longer stationary but now moving as a cold front (which is the leading edge of the colder air), and part of the once-stationary front may now be advancing as a warm front. This is how a low pressure system starts to form, along a frontal boundary, as the cold air sinks under the warmer air, causing the warm air to rise, (this is called **cold air advection**) and, also, with the warm front moving, that warm air is rising over the cooler air as the warm air advances (this is called **warm air advection**).

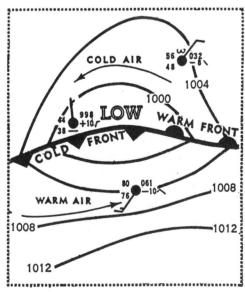

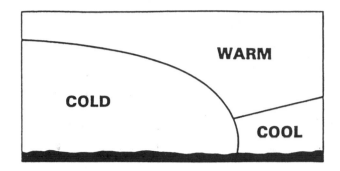

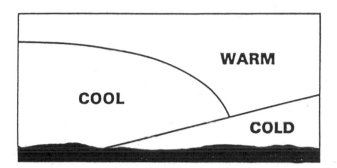

After a cold-type occlusion, the air eventually is all mixed, and the front in that region disappears

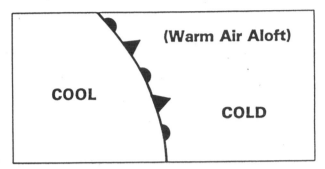

Figure 26-9. The two types of occluded fronts, where a cold front overtakes a warm front: on top is a cold-type occlusion an on bottom is a warm-type occlusion, and, at right, how an occluded front is depicted on a surface weather map. In both types of occlusion, the warmest air is forced aloft. Because this air is raised in the occlusion process, clouds form, and if there is sufficient moisture and lift, there will also be precipitation.

<u>Some characteristics of occluded fronts</u>:

● The point-of-occlusion is where, on the surface weather map, a cold front has caught up with the warm front and is overtaking it. Where the cold front has already overtaken the warm front is called the occluded front. There are two types of occluded fronts: a <u>cold- type occlusion</u> and a <u>warm-type occlusion</u>.

● Figure 26-10 at right shows an occluded front, where the cold front has caught up with the warm front, and also shows the rest of the fronts. The shaded area is where precipitation is occurring. Colder air is denser and heavier than the warm air, so it usually moves faster. This is one key reason why a cold front associated with a low pressure system ultimately overtakes the warm front. Eventually, the air mixes up and the low pressure system dies.

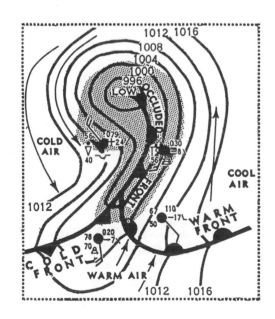

The figures on these next 3 pages summarize the typical weather we experience with fronts.
KEY TO SYMBOLS ON THESE NEXT 3 PAGES FOR CLOUD TYPES:

CU = cumulus (puffy), TCU = towering cumulus, CB = cumulonimbus (thunderstorm), STFR = fracto-stratus (low, scud clouds), NS = nimbostratus, SC = stratocumulus, AS = altostratus, AC = altocumulus, ASAC = combined altostratus and altocumulus, CI = cirrus (high clouds comprised of ice crystals), CS = cirrostratus, CC = cirrocumulus (very high-based cumulus clouds). (source for these figures: NOAA)

Figure 26-11. A cold front with slightly unstable cold air underrunning warm, moist, unstable air. Abrupt lifting at the front creates thunderstorms and showers. Behind the cold front are some fair weather puffy cumulus clouds since the cold air is slightly unstable. Cumuloform clouds may also develop ahead of the front in the warm, moist, unstable air. (source: NWS)

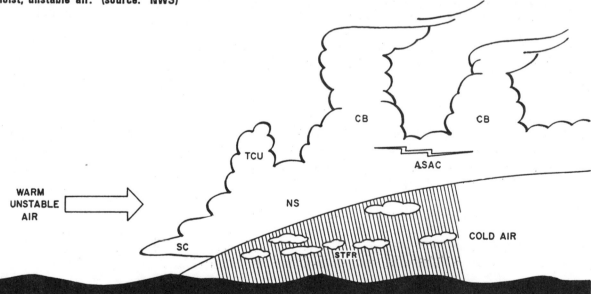

Figure 26-12. A warm front followed by warm, moist, unstable air, overriding cold stable air. The lifting of air along the warm front is more gradual than along the cold front in the previous figure. Rain, showers and thunderstorms are more spread out than in the preceding case. Thunderstorms may be imbedded within a general precipitation area. The scuddy strato-fractus clouds form in the precipitation because some of the water from the warm raindrops evaporate and subsequently condense into clouds in the cold air. (source: NWS)   PAGE 192

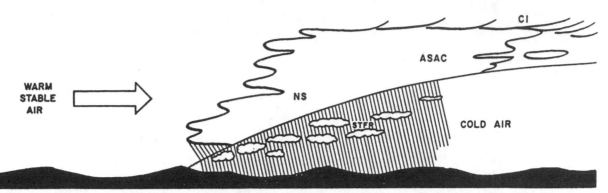

Figure 26-13. A warm front with overriding warm, moist, stable air. This case is similar to the previous figure, except that the warm air is stable, and imbedded thunderstorms do not develop in the extensive precipitation area. Note the extensive cloud area ahead of the surface front, as the lift and front move in aloft first, with the cloudiness gradually lowering as the front at the surface gets closer. (source: NWS)

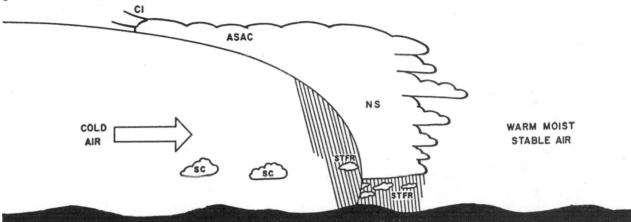

Figure 26-14. A cold front advancing into warm, moist, stable air, forcing the air along the front upwards. Stable stratified clouds form along the front, similar to the case with the warm front in the previous figure, except that the slope of the front is steeper and the clouds are not as widespread. The cold air is stable but may have a shallow convective layer. The typical clouds that form behind this cold front are stratocumulus. There is considerable middle and high cloudiness aloft for some distance after passage of the front. (source: NWS)

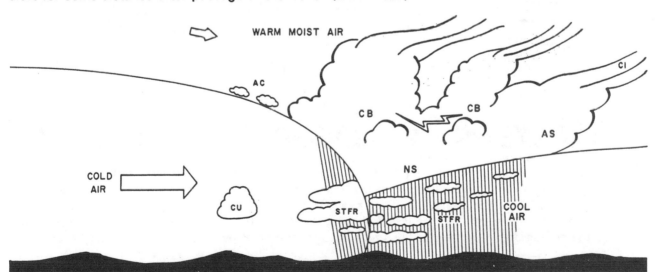

Figure 26-15. A cold-type occlusion. The cold air replaces cool air at the surface, forcing the warm front aloft. The cold air is moderately stable, the cool air is stable, and the warm air is unstable. Notice the combination of clouds. (source: NWS)

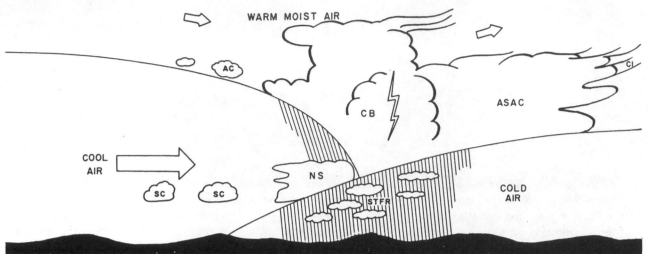

Figure 26-16. A warm-type occlusion. The cool air is overriding the cold air, forcing the cold front aloft. The cool air is stable, the cold air is stable, and the warm air is unstable. Notice the distribution of cloudiness typical of a warm-type occlusion. The greatest convective (for thunderstorms) cloudiness is along the cold front aloft; there is stratiform (for more steady precipitation) cloudiness with possible imbedded thunderstorms above the warm front. Stratocumulus clouds usually form in the stable cool air, and fracto-stratus (also called strato-fractus) clouds, which are low clouds also referred to as scud clouds, form in the cold air because of warm rain falling through the cold air. (source: NWS)

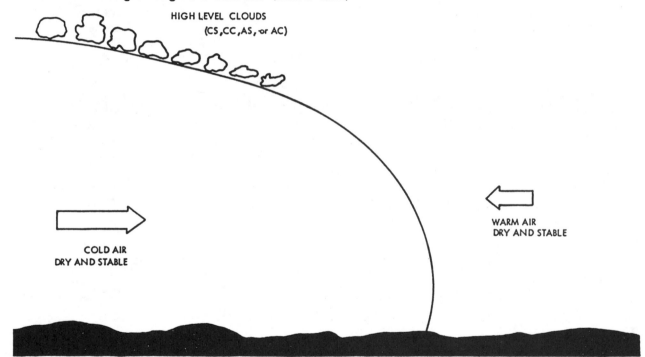

Figure 26-17. A dry cold front. This is when both cold and warm air are dry and stable. In this case, the warm air must rise or be raised to a considerable height before condensation of its water vapor occurs to form clouds. Clouds, if any, will be a considerable distance from the surface position of the front, and at high levels. The cloud heights depend upon how much water vapor is in the relatively dry warm air: the less moisture, the higher the cloud base heights. With a dry cold front, the clouds do not appear until some time after the passage of the front. (source: NWS)

A warm front can also be relatively dry, which would produce high-level clouds a great distance ahead of the surface front. These high clouds would be the feathery cirrus clouds at 20,000 to 40,000 feet of elevation in mid-latitudes, and would also include cirrostratus clouds. These high-level clouds clear sometimes several hours before the frontal passage at the surface.

The dry-line:

A front is a boundary. A boundary separates two sets of properties. When we speak about a cold, warm, occluded or stationary front, we are talking about a boundary that separates warm air from colder air. In fact, some meteorologists sometimes refer to a front as a "frontal boundary".

There are other, smaller-scale boundaries that are also important in meteorology. For example, a large thunderstorm or a thunderstorm complex will produce a leading edge of colder "outflow" air, which is called a thunderstorm outflow boundary.

On a sunny day, the land is heated more than the ocean is, so the cooler air from the ocean may move inland during the day. Its leading edge is called the sea-breeze front.

Such "mesoscale boundaries" are important because they provide a lift to the air as they advance. In the convective season, this could cause showers and thunderstorms along the boundary.

A significant type of boundary that can grow to have a length of several hundred miles is the dry-line. This phenomenon occurs mostly from spring through summer and into early fall, in the Southern and Central Plains of the United States. Similar dry-line phenomena occur in other parts of the world, e.g., in Africa and Australia.

What is needed for the dry-line phenomenon is a desert or semi-arid region on one side of the dry-line, and a large source of water on the other side. For example, in eastern New Mexico and in west Texas, the climate is much drier than in eastern Texas near the Gulf of Mexico. In west Texas, therefore, in the summer, the dry air is heated to the 90s or over 100°F (to over 38°C) and its dewpoint is quite low...lower than 40 degrees Fahrenheit, and often in the 20s or even lower. On the other hand, the warm, moist Gulf of Mexico helps raise the dewpoint of the air over eastern Texas into the 70s F. and sometimes around 80°F. The actual air temperature may be in the 90s. In the spring and especially in the summer, a boundary develops between the dry air to the west and the moist air; this boundary is called the dry-line and acts like a front, moving towards the coast or back to the west. At night, since the air is drier in the west, the air there cools to a lower temperature than it does in the east with the higher dewpoints. This changing from hotter out west during the day to cooler out west during the night results in the dry-line moving back-and-forth across Texas and Oklahoma. The dry-line "scoops up" air as it moves, often resulting in thunderstorms along this boundary. Sometimes these storms are severe, producing large hail and tornadoes. Even worse is when a dry-line boundary intersects a cold frontal boundary, which enhances the lift and can result in tornadic thunderstorms.

The dry-line separates continental tropical air to its west from maritime tropical air to its east.

The dry-line typically extends from Texas through Oklahoma into Kansas, and moves back and forth through this region, mostly during the warmer months. Sometimes the dry-line will extend as far north as Nebraska into South Dakota.

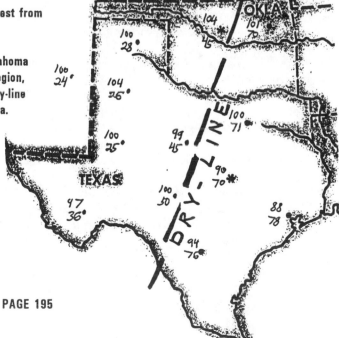

Figure 26-18. A surface weather data plot showing the temperatures (upper left) and dewpoints (lower left) and the dry-line, which is a boundary acting like a front. Note how dry (much lower dewpoints) the air is to the west of the dry-line, and how moist (high dewpoints) the air is to the east of the dry-line.

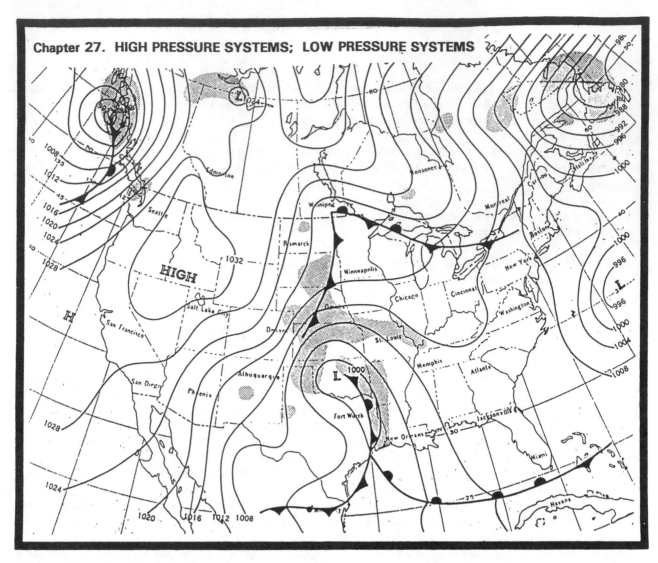

Figure 27-1. A surface weather map showing the high pressure systems, the low pressure systems and the fronts. The centers of highest air pressure are labelled "HIGH" or "H", and the centers of lowest pressure are labelled "LOW" or "L". The lines of equal pressure plotted on the map are the isobars, and are in intervals of 4 millibars and are labelled in millibars. (source: NWS)

In chapter 25, we already discussed air masses, and in chapter 26 we discussed fronts. Now we can integrate those chapters with this for a discussion on the high and low pressure systems.

In chapter 26 we discussed how air masses form. High pressure systems that form with these air mass characteristics of temperature and moisture content move across the globe, and gradually lose their original characteristics as they move across land and water and into either warmer or colder climatic areas. For example, a continental polar high pressure system is very cold and dry since it forms essentially over land in northern North America.

But as it moves southeastward towards the Gulf of Mexico, it warms up gradually, because it is passing over warmer land farther south. Moreover, by passing over the Great Lakes and more moist vegetative areas, moisture evaporates into the lower levels of the high pressure system; which changes it from a dry system into a more moist one, at least in lower levels initially.

Similarly, changes occur in warm, moist maritime tropical high pressure systems that work their way polewards.

Air circulations in and around high and low pressure systems:

Since air flows from where it is piled up (high pressure) to where there is less of it (low pressure), the air flow is downward and outward from the high and upward and inward to the low. The earth's rotation affects this flow, by turning it towards the right in the Northern Hemisphere and towards the left in the Southern Hemisphere. Moreover, within about a couple of thousand feet from the ground up, the objects on the earth's surface impart a frictional drag, which slows down the flow somewhat and prevents the turn to the right (in the Northern Hemisphere) or to the left (Southern Hemisphere) from being a full 90-degree turn. Over land, the turn might be closer to 60 degrees, but over the open ocean where there is less obstruction, therefore less friction, to the air flow, the turn due to the earth's rotating is closest to a full 90 degrees.

The net result is this: In the Northern Hemisphere, air blows clockwise around a high pressure system and counterclockwise around a low pressure system; in the Southern Hemisphere the air flow is reversed: counterclockwise around highs and clockwise around lows.

Figure 27-2. In the Northern Hemisphere, the circulation around a high is clockwise and spiralling outward. This divergent flow and downward motion means most highs are generally fair weather systems. The air flow around a low in the Northern Hemisphere is counterclockwise and spiralling inward. This converging flow and upward motion means most lows are generally weather systems with clouds and precipitation, provided sufficient moisture is available. (source: DOA)

In fact, you can tell where a low pressure system is by just standing with your back to the wind:

Figure 27-3. In the Northern Hemisphere, if you stand with your back to the wind and stretch out your left arm, the low pressure center will be in the direction in which your left arm is pointing!
(source: DOA)

Recall from chapter 21 what causes the air to move (what causes the wind): the pressure-gradient force (the difference in air pressure from one location to the next), the Coriolis force (the deflection of the wind's direction due to the fact that the earth is rotating) and, near the surface, the effect of friction on the moving air (which slows it down and prevents the Coriolis force from changing its direction a full 90 degrees). Above the first 1500 to 2000 feet or so of atmosphere (which is called the <u>planetary boundary layer</u>), the effect of friction is essentially negligible.

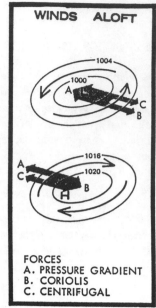
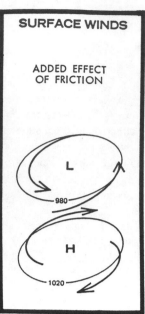

Figure 27-4. When the wind is a balance between only the pressure-gradient force and the Coriolis force, the wind is called the <u>geostrophic wind</u>. Thus, upper-level winds are geostrophic, whereas boundary layer winds, including the surface winds, are <u>nongeostrophic</u>. Curved flow adds a centrifugal force which is also included in the balance of forces causing the wind. (source: DOA)

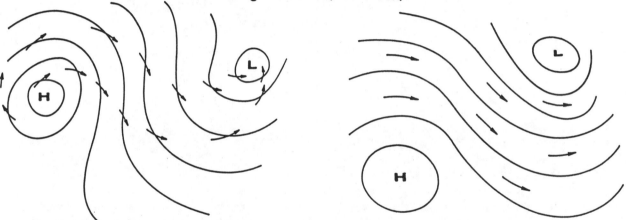

Figure 27-5. Northern Hemisphere wind flow around surface high and low, where the effect of friction prevents the Coriolis force from turning the wind completely 90 degrees (left), and the wind flow around upper-level (generally higher than about 2000 feet off the ground) highs and lows (right), where the effect of friction is negligible for changing the large-scale direction of the wind flow. (source: NOAA)

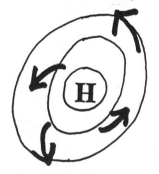

IN SOUTHERN HEMISPHERE

Figure 27-6. In the SOUTHERN HEMISPHERE, the Coriolis force acts in the opposite direction to what it is north of the equator; thus, in the Southern Hemisphere, the circulation around high pressure systems is counterclockwise, and around low pressure systems is clockwise. PAGE 198

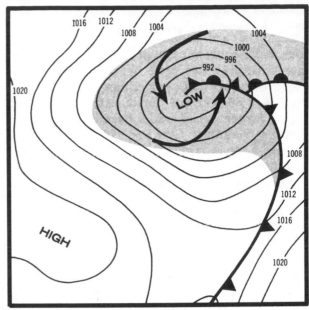

Figure 27-7. The circulation around a low pressure center is accompanied by horizontal convergence of air at low levels, which causes the air parcels to "pile up" and rise. With sufficient moisture in the air, the result is that low pressure systems are typically areas of cloudiness and precipitation. Frontal lifting adds to the lifting of air parcels. (source: DOA)

Now let us compare summer and winter, concerning pressure systems.

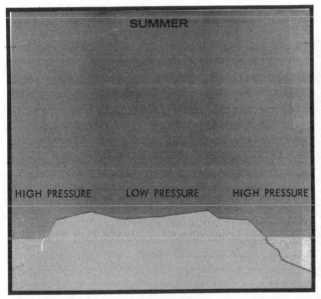
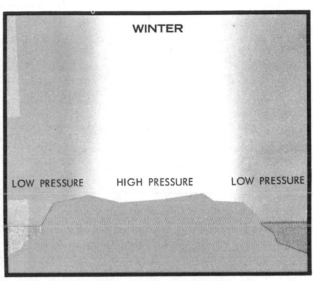

Figure 27-8. In the summertime, the continents are warmer than the oceans, resulting in a tendency for lower pressure over the continents and relatively higher pressure over the adjacent oceans. The significant exception is hurricanes, which are an extreme form of low pressure, that occur typically in summer and the first half of autumn. In contrast, in the wintertime, the continents are colder than the oceans, resulting in a tendency for cooling and therefore denser air to form high pressure systems over the continents, while lower pressure occurs over the adjacent oceans. (source: DOA)

Some of the high pressure and low pressure systems are so huge that they become well-established for months at a time. For example, during the warmer-half of the year, there is a high pressure system that stretches from around Bermuda in the western Atlantic Ocean to around the Azores Islands in the eastern Atlantic Ocean. This is called the Bermuda-Azores High. This is an example of a large-scale weather feature that is critical in determining whether many Atlantic hurricanes will smash into the eastern United States. When the Bermuda-Azores High is weak, the hurricanes tend to recurve out to sea, most of the time missing the mainland. However, when the Bermuda-Azores High is strong, its circulation extends westward over the east coast of the United States, causing hurricanes that move westward around its southern periphery to not recurve as soon as they otherwise would, thus causing them to smash into the United States. For example, in 1995 a weak Bermuda-Azores High spared the United States from being smashed by a conveyor-belt like supply of hurricane after hurricane in a year that saw an unusually large amount of tropical cyclones in the Atlantic basin.

Other quasi-permanent large-scale highs and lows exist around the world, such as the Siberian High, the Aleutian Low, The Arctic High, the Icelandic Low and the Pacific High. In January, for example, the Aleutian and Icelandic Lows are well-developed, causing increased storminess in those regions as well as helping to steer other highs and lows around them.

The quasi-permanent highs and lows sometimes move somewhat away from their typical or preferred locations, which then creates interesting weather changes in the areas they are temporarily affecting.

Besides these quasi-permanent features, the other highs and lows develop and die as they move across parts of the globe. This set of weather systems represents most of the highs and lows, which are migratory. First, let us look at the quasi-permanent large systems.

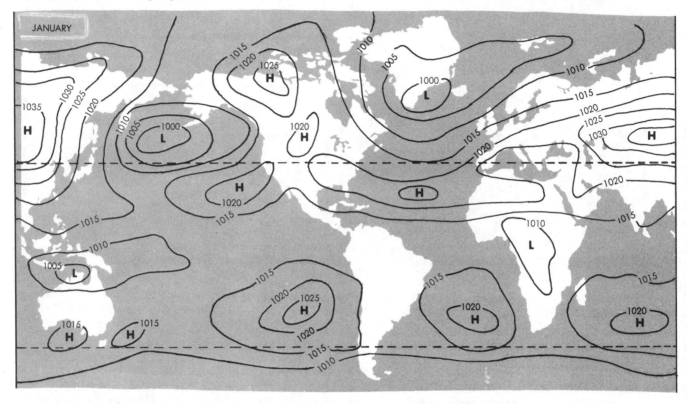

Figure 27-9. Here are the average locations of the quasi-permanent highs and lows in the Northern Hemisphere winter. Examples are the Icelandic Low, the Siberian High and the Aleutian Low. The thermal gradient between the arctic and the equatorial zone is greater in the winter than in the summer; this results in stronger pressure gradients and stronger weather systems in winter than in summer. (source: USAF)

Figure 27-10. The greater the pressure difference between two points, the closer the isobars of pressure (the stronger the pressure gradient or pressure difference). The result is stronger winds when the isobars on the surface weather map are packed closer together.

WEAK PRESSURE GRADIENT
(light winds)

STRONG PRESSURE GRADIENT
(strong winds)

Figure 27-11. Note the weaker quasi-permanent weather systems in the Northern Hemisphere summer, compared with winter. (source: USAF)

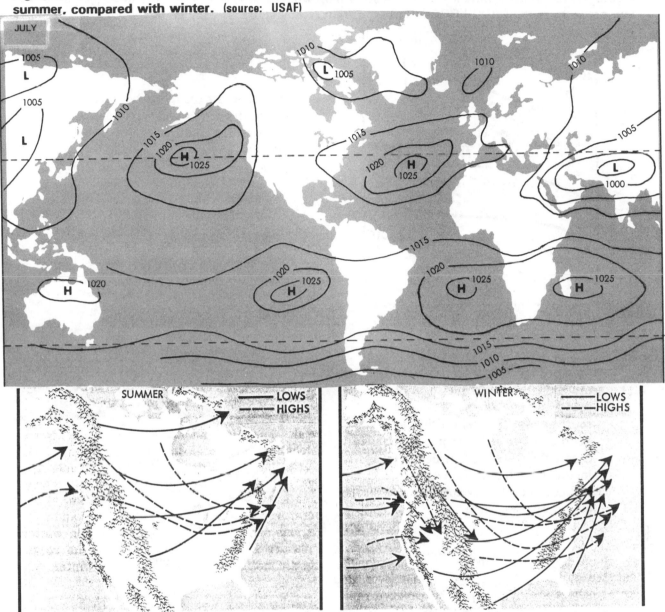

Figure 27-12. In summertime, the typical tracks of migratory highs and lows are far north, whereas in the wintertime, these storms are farther south. This does not show all the tracks, just the most common ones. (source: DOA)

The life-cycle of an extratropical low-pressure system:

A hurricane is called a tropical cyclone; all other low pressure systems are called extratropical cyclones or extratropical low-pressure systems. All extratropical lows form on a front, with the exception of a thermal low. A thermal low is a temporary area of low pressure caused by intense heating of desert areas. Examples are over the Death Valley area in the southwestern United States and over the Sahara-Libyan Desert in north Africa.

The next two pages expand upon the topic of a low developing on a front, discussed in the previous chapter. What follows is the complete life-cycle of an extratropical low pressure system. The example given is for the Northern Hemisphere. The winds blow in the opposite direction around the low, in the Southern Hemisphere.   PAGE 201

Figure 27-13. Here is how a surface weather map would show, over time, the development of a low pressure system (CYCLOGENESIS) on a front, followed by its occlusion and death.

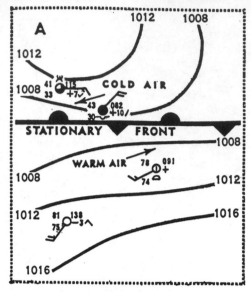

A stationary front, showing cold air to the north and warm air to the south. The arrows depict the wind flow.

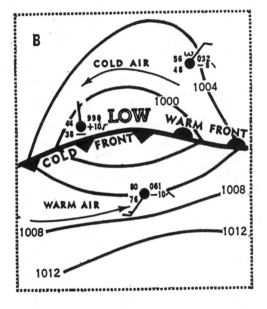

Some of the warm air tries to move northward while some of the colder air tries to move southward. This establishes a bend or kink in the front, which is called a "WAVE", which is an incipient cyclone. Some waves will continue to develop into a low pressure system.

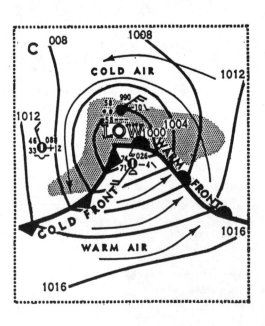

Now the warm air is advancing and rising northeastward while the cold air is sinking under the warm air as it advances southeastward. Thus, the stationary front is no longer quasi-stationary, but part of it is now advancing as a warm front and part of it is advancing as a cold front.

(cyclogenesis cycle continued on next page)

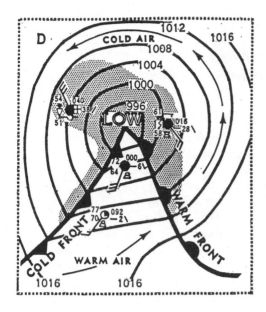

Now, just south of the low center, the cold front is catching up to the warm front, because the colder air is denser than the warm air and, being heavier, advances faster than the warm air. This is the beginning of the "OCCLUSION" process, and is when the storm is at its maximum intensity and lowest pressure.

The occluded front, which is the cold front overtaking the warm front, continues developing, which gradually ends the lifting required for precipitation, and also slowly terminates the cyclonic (counterclockwise in the Northern Hemisphere) circulation about the center of the low pressure. The storm is dying. The air is mixing.

The storm ends, and we wait for another wave on the front to intensify into a low pressure system.

Now we have a well-developed counter-clockwise circulation with warm air being lifted over cold air, and cold air pushing under the warm air. This is our intensifying low pressure system, also called an "EXTRATROPICAL LOW". If sufficient moisture is present in at least the first 10,000 feet of the troposphere, then the region with the rising air experiences precipitation.

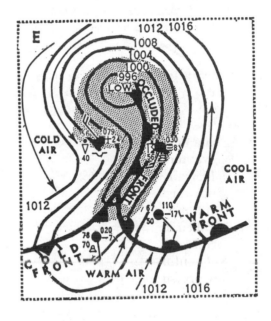

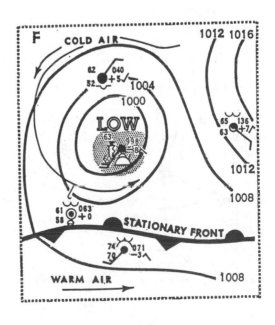

Chapter 28. CONVERGENCE, DIVERGENCE AND VERTICAL MOTION

Two of the most important aspects of weather are VERTICAL MOTION and MOISTURE DISTRIBUTION. To have clouds and subsequent precipitation, there must be sufficient moisture and rising air. As air rises and cools to its dewpoint, clouds form. Continued lifting causes cloud droplets to coalesce and accrete into precipitation which then falls from the clouds.

How strong is the vertical motion? Several thousand feet off the surface, a strong upward vertical motion in a well-organized low pressure system is on the order of 5 to 15 centimeters per second, which is not even one-fifth of a mile per hour! However, if such a lift is occurring for hundreds miles around and is persistent, and ample moisture is available, then clouds and precipitation will likely form. This type or scale of motion is known as SYNOPTIC SCALE vertical motion. The word "synoptic" is derived from the Greek "sunopsis" meaning "general view", that is, from observations taken at the same time to give a general view of conditions, but its meaning in meteorology has been somewhat changed to refer to a larger scale than just a local area, but smaller than a global scale. Thus, a major low pressure system that may cover over one thousand miles is considered a "synoptic scale" weather system. On the other hand, an individual thunderstorm is considered a MESOSCALE weather system, which is a smaller scale. At the extreme ends of the earth's weather scales, cloud droplets would be called a MICROSCALE weather event, whereas the general earth's average temperature and precipitation, that is, the average climate of our planet, would be a GLOBAL SCALE weather aspect.

On the mesoscale, the rapidly rising air in an updraft of an average thunderstorm, or the rapidly sinking air of a downdraft in a typical thunderstorm, has a speed of about 30 meters per second, which is about 60 knots or nearly 70 miles per hour. In a thunderstorm that produces softball-size hail, the updraft speed required to suspend such heavy hailstones is on the order of 75 meters per second, or 150 knots (about 170 miles per hour)! This is an extreme example of upward vertical motion in the lower atmosphere.

Thus, two important scales of vertical motion in the lower atmosphere are the synoptic scale and the mesoscale. Compare both. A very strong synoptic scale lift is about one-fifth mph, whereas a very strong mesoscale lift in a thunderstorm is about 125 mph. However, the thunderstorm lift is localized, within a few miles diameter, whereas the synoptic scale lift may extend for over one thousand miles in diameter in very large low pressure systems.

Moreover, a thunderstorm with mesoscale lifting may form in a region in which synoptic scale lifting is already underway.

10 cm/sec X 1 inch/2.54 cm X 1 foot/12 inches X 1 mile/5280 feet X 60 secs/1 minute X 60 minutes/1 hour = 0.22 mph

Figure 26-1. A simple mathematical exercise, converting a synoptic scale lift of 10 centimeters per second into the English units of miles per hour.

Convergence and Divergence of Air:

Because air is not being created or destroyed in any large extent, it is conserved. Thus, as the air flows, it is mostly converging or "piling up" in different locations around the globe, or is diverging of "spreading out" in other locations. A region experiencing converging air today may have diverging air, or no converging or diverging air, tomorrow. Thus, these changing conditions are part of the weather we experience.

Convergence is not the only lifting mechanism in Nature. For example, solar heating of the ground, especially on a hot, sunny day, heats the ground which in turn heats the air above it, causing it to rise. The spin (vorticity) of parcels of air is also related to vertical motion; this is discussed in the next chapter. Mechanical effects also give a vertical component to the motion of air, such as air flowing up and over and then down a mountain chain. However, because of the great importance of the role of converging and diverging air, they are given special consideration in understanding more about the physics of weather.

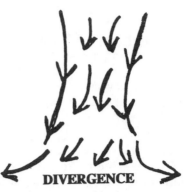

CONVERGENCE

DIVERGENCE

Figure 26-2. In the left figure, as air parcels converge or "pile up" at the surface, they must go somewhere, due to the conservation of air (air is not created or destroyed). Since they cannot go down because the ground is there, they are forced up. Thus, low-level convergence of air results in upward vertical motion. In the right figure, as air parcels diverge or "spread out" at the surface, they are coming from somewhere else...they are coming from above. Thus, low-level divergence of air is associated with downward vertical motion. There is not convergence of air all the way up to the top of the atmosphere, just as there is not sinking and divergence over an area all the way from the top of the atmosphere down; thus, at some point above the low-level converging or diverging air, the opposite must occur: that is, where there is convergence in the low levels, there is divergence aloft, and where there is divergence in the low levels, there is convergence aloft.

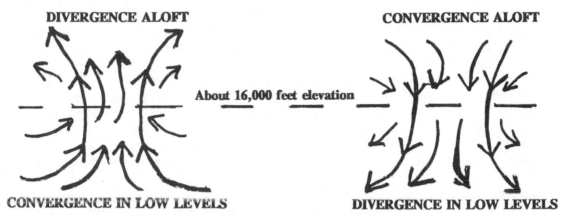

Figure 26-3. Converging air at the surface rises and diverges to spread out aloft, and converging air aloft typically sinks and spreads out below.

Actually, air that is converging aloft can go either up or down, but since its concentration makes it heavier than the surrounding air, it mostly sinks. Keep in mind that air also is moving laterally, that is, to the side, in the main flow.

Meteorological research has determined that the sign of the convergence/divergence changes at about the 550 mb level...or roughly about 16,000 feet above mean sea-level. That is, if there is convergence from the surface up to 16,000 feet, then there is divergence above 16,000 feet and up to some higher level, and if there is divergence from the surface up to 16,000 feet, then there is convergence above it to some higher level. This average level of 550 mb (hPa) or some 16,000 feet is referred to as the LEVEL OF NON-DIVERGENCE. There is neither convergence nor divergence at that level, because that is the level at which convergence changes to divergence or vice versa.

Thus, this concept, which may at first impression seem somewhat complicated, is actually rather simple and straightforward. This is how our atmosphere must behave. Thus, for example, we can't have air converging in broad columns all the way to the top of the atmosphere; the air must spread out and diverge aloft. Areas of convergence of air accompany the low pressure systems. Since the air is rising in much of the low, the pressure falls. Areas of divergence of air accompany much of the area of high pressure systems. Where the air is sinking in a high, the pressure is increased (recall that with surface divergence, air "piles up" or converges aloft, and then sinks and diverges).

Various patterns of the air flow create convergence and divergence aloft in low and higher levels of the atmosphere. When the air flow pattern causes strong winds to blow into an area of lighter winds, it is analogous to cars on a toll turnpike moving at 80 mph, then having to slow down to pay the toll. As the cars approach the tollbooth, they pile up or converge, then as they speed away accelerating, they diverge. When we are talking about air parcels, the convergence forces air parcels to rise. See the figure below.

Denver   Wichita   Kansas City   Los Angeles San Bernardino Las Vegas

Figure 26-4. The wind pattern at left is one of convergence and rising air through that region, since 30 knot winds are blowing into 20 then 10 knot areas. The wind pattern at right is one of divergence, since air parcels are speeding up as they move along (they are spreading apart), leading to replacement by some of the air from aloft. (The 3 side lines represent 30 knots, 2 are 20 knots and 1 is 10 knots).

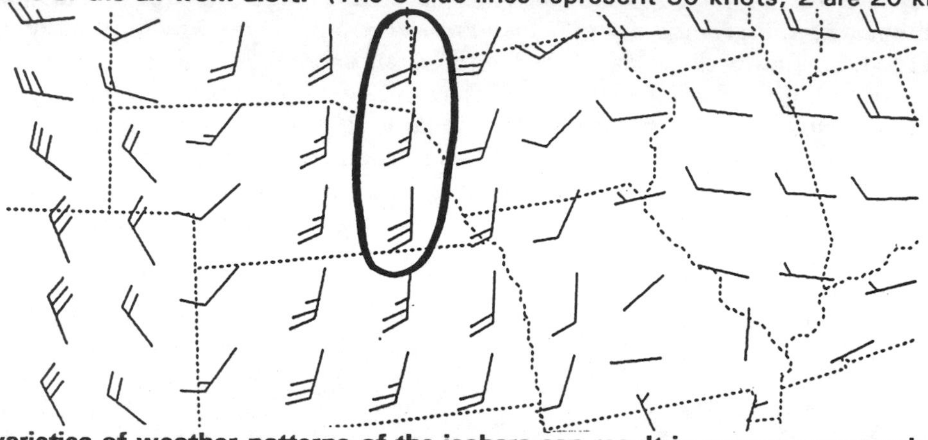

Figure 26-5. Many varieties of weather patterns of the isobars can result in convergence and divergence. At left, the outlined area from eastern Nebraska northward is an area of convergence, which eventually led to nocturnal thunderstorms forming. Strong 30-knot southerly winds were blowing into an area of 25-knot and then 20-knot winds, causing the air parcels to slow down and "pile up", which is convergence, causing the air to rise. (A full side-line is for every 10 knots of wind speed, and a half side-line is for 5 knots of wind speed. The wind barb is pointing towards the direction from which the wind is coming.)

Exercise: in the figure to the right, is the zone starting in western Nebraska, with southwesterly winds of 10 knots, and going northward from there into South Dakota, a region of low-level convergence and rising air, or one of low-level divergence and sinking air, and why?

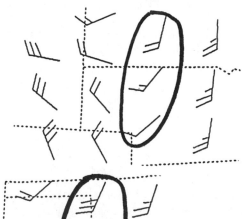

Answer: **Figure 26-6. Note that 10 knot winds in the indicated area of Nebraska are moving into 15 knot winds and then 20 knot winds. That means that the air parcels are moving out of a zone of light 10 knots winds and accelerating and spreading out as they move faster farther north. This is divergence, so that air sinks from above to replace some of the spreading-apart parcels of air near the surface.**

Figure 26-7. Here is an example of strong divergence over part of Texas and part of Oklahoma. The greater that the average wind speed changes in the flow over the same distance, the stronger is the convergence or divergence, which implies that the vertical velocities related to the convergence and divergence are greater than when the changes of wind speed are less.

Chapter 29. VORTICITY

An important concept in meteorology is that of VORTICITY, because it is one dynamic feature that is related to the vertical motion of air. Since rising air that has sufficient moisture will produce clouds and subsequent precipitation, weather forecasters like to identify all the features that cause air to rise. The two most important dynamic features are warm air moving in (called "warm air advection"), since warm air rises up over cooler air, and a type of spin in the air related to vorticity, called "positive vorticity advection".

First, we need to better define this concept of vorticity.

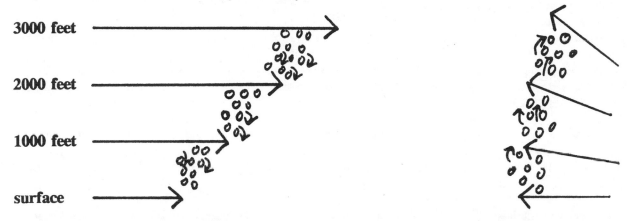

Figure 29-1. As the wind speed increases (or decreases) with height (left), or when the wind direction changes with height (right), a slight spin will be imparted on parcels of air. These parcels now have vorticity due to the speed shear or directional shear of the wind.

Figure 29-2. When air parcels move through a curved-flow pattern, they acquire some spin or vorticity.

Thus, vorticity of a parcel of air is caused by wind shear or by curvature of the flow of air. These parcels are thought to be about one cubic meter in volume.

Figure 29-3. The vorticity of air parcels can be divided into the vorticity about a vertical axis (left), which is called the horizontal vorticity, and the vorticity about a horizontal axis (right), which is called the vertical vorticity.

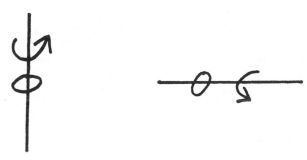

The rate of spin can be calculated from observations and forecasts of the wind field at various heights. In weather forecasting, the horizontal vorticity about a vertical axis turns out to be important for large-scale (called "synoptic scale") weather features, such as high and low pressure systems and the vertical motions associated with them.

Figure 29-4. When the horizontal vorticity spins from left to right (counterclockwise) in the Northern Hemisphere, it is called POSITIVE VORTICITY; when it spins clockwise, from right to left, it is called NEGATIVE VORTICITY.

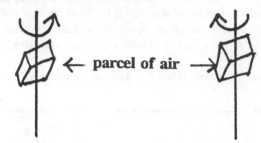

When increasing values of positive vorticity are moving into your area, you are experiencing POSITIVE VORTICITY ADVECTION, and when increasing values of negative vorticity are moving into your area, you are undergoing NEGATIVE VORTICITY ADVECTION.

The positive vorticity advection, known as PVA, is generally related to upward vertical motion and possible cloudiness and precipitation, whereas the NVA, or negative vorticity advection, is generally related to downward vertical motion and clearing or fair skies. Of course other causes of vertical motion must be combined with this cause to determine the resultant vertical motion field.

It can be shown mathematically, from fluid dynamics physics, that increasing values of PVA with increasing height causes the fluid (in this case, air) to spin up (to rise). The way positive vorticity advection is related to upward vertical motion is when we have increasing values of positive horizontal vorticity advection with increasing height, since the air parcels will then be forced to spin up. Air spins down when vorticity values decrease with increasing height.

This subject at first seems complicated, but in fact is rather basic...essentially, an aspect of very slowly spinning air parcels causes air in a column to rise or sink.

DEMONSTRATION: A FUN WAY TO ILLUSTRATE LOW PRESSURE SYSTEMS DEVELOPING ON A FRONT

1. In a long hallway or corridor, have a person holding each end of a large spring or slinky on the floor in such a way that they divide the length of the hallway in half.
2. A group of other persons makes a single line along the wall of the corridor, making sure that they face the spring.
3. Using an index card or piece of paper, label the floor, where the people are lined up, "maritime tropical air mass." Label the floor on the opposite side of the spring, "continental polar air mass."
4. Explain that the spring represents a front, and that the group is standing in the maritime tropical air mass, with the floor on the opposite side of the spring being the continental polar air mass.
5. When the two people who are holding the ends of the spring move it towards the group of people, this represents a cold front. When they move the spring away from the group of people, this represents a warm front. If they do not move the spring at all, this represents a stationary front.
6. Have one of the persons who is holding a spring-end, vibrate it to produce waves. You will note that the waves travel from one end of the spring (or slinky) to the other. In order for the waves to form, the spring must vibrate in such a way that it moves into the continental polar air mass as well as into the maritime tropical air mass. These waves represent low pressure areas that form on and travel along the front
7. Think about how vorticity is related to low pressure systems.

SECTION IX: STORMS

Chapter 30. WINTER STORMS

Winter storms can be broad areas of inclement weather, mostly snow, or can be localized storms of wintry weather, such as lake effect snow, or can be combinations of large-scale (called synoptic) weather systems and local effects.

In well-developed winter storms, the precipitation is typically accompanied by strong winds. The combination of heavy snowfall, strong winds and cold temperatures create beautiful snowstorms, but they are dangerous, which means that proper precautions must be undertaken by us when we have these storms, in order to cope with them.

In fact, although furious storms such as tornadoes and hurricanes receive the usual sensationalistic coverage in the news, it is the **winter weather that kills more people than any other weather phenomenon.**

Across most of the United States, winter is the most active weather season. Along the west coast, the Pacific high weakens and no longer serves as a blocking mechanism to prevent storms from the Pacific Ocean from making landfall. As a result, many storms enter the west coast, and when they pass over higher inland or mountainous terrain, they produce heavy snows. Many times these storms move across the lower 48 states to produce snow or rain storms all the way to the east coast.

Another reason for the active winter weather is that the polar jet stream dips farther south, with the very cold and dry air to its north interacting with warm and humid air, producing winter storms. These winter storms can form over the southern states, and move north, affecting the mid-west and/or the east coast of the United States. If they pass over the relatively warm Gulf Stream water of the North Atlantic Ocean, then they can "feed on" the moisture and can therefore develop into powerful storms as they move up or just off the east coast. (The Gulf Stream is a relatively narrow fast-flowing stream of warm water which moves generally northeastward from the western Caribbean Sea to off the mid-Atlantic coast, where it then heads more east-northeastward.) When the center of this intense low pressure system remains some 100 to 200 miles offshore, the left side, which is the cold side, of the storm has winds from the northeast which gradually shift to the northwest as the storm passes by as it heads generally north-northeastward. This type of storm is referred to as a "nor'easter" for northeaster. In the strongest of nor'easters, winds can reach hurricane force (74 mph or higher), and on rare occasion these storms even develop a central eye, leading some observers to refer to this variety of nor'easter as a "snow hurricane". An intense nor'easter pulls warm, moist air above the cold air and can also create imbedded thunderstorms within the general precipitation shield; this convection is known as thundersnow, and is quite significant since thunderstorms that produce snow can easily drop two, three, four, five or even more inches of snow per hour, greatly enhancing the snowfall from the overall snowshield itself. One thundersnowsquall from Lake Ontario once dropped eleven inches of snow in ONE HOUR!

Another example of a large-scale ("synoptic scale") weather system with a name is the Alberta Clipper, which forms on an arctic front as frigid air is moving in behind the developing storm and the front. This system is usually in a northwesterly, or in a developing northwesterly, air flow aloft over Alberta, Canada or vicinity, and plunges rapidly southeastward into the Central Plains of the United States, and then curves towards the east and then northeast towards the New England area. Most of the snow is to the north of the storm center, so its precise track is crucial in determining what areas will receive its snowfall.

By the time an Alberta Clipper reaches the east coast of the U.S., it has typically weakened, and therefore produces typically lighter precipitation. However, if it moves out to sea farther south, between North Carolina and Massachusetts, then it may reintensify over the relatively warm ocean waters, and turn into a nor'easter.

In chapter 27 we discussed the typical tracks of many of the migratory low pressure and high pressure systems that affect the contiguous United States. It is useful to review that information now. The next figure shows the winter tracks of these migratory systems (next page).

Figure 30-1. The typical tracks of the migratory low and high pressure systems that affect the contiguous United States during the wintertime. (source: DOA)

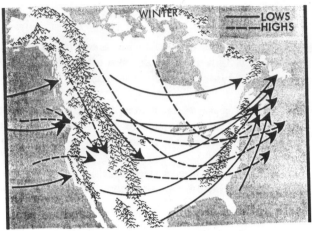

The preferred tracks of these systems are farther south in the winter than in the summer. Besides these tracks, there are occasional examples not shown here, such as the occasional cold high pressure system moving southward from the Hudson Bay region in Canada or moving southward from northwest Canada. Pacific highs move eastward across the continent, but stay put for a while in the Great Basin region in the west. Sometimes the quasi-permanent lows and high (see chapter 27) grow and/or move enough to also cause major weather changes.

Figures 30-2 (left) and 30-3 (right) show some of the results of snowstorms, as all of us who have lived through many of them, know so well: at left, digging out, and at right, driving problems. Some of the heaviest snowfalls in the United States occur over coastal Alaska, the western U.S. mountains, the Northern Plains, around the Great Lakes and in the middle-Atlantic states and in the northeastern states. When the ground is snow-covered, the temperature will not rise much, even on a sunny day, since most of the sunlight is reflected back towards space. When the snow melts or sublimes, it uses some heat from the atmosphere, which also prevents the temperature from rising as much as it would otherwise, during the daytime. Chapter 19 discusses the "latent heats of fusion and vaporization". (source: NOAA)

Figure 30-4. If you study weather maps, you will notice that to have a heavy snowstorm, the low pressure system is typically well-developed and its center passes about 100 miles (about 160 kilometers) to the SOUTH and/or EAST of you (in the Northern Hemisphere), so that you stay in the cold air. If the low passes to your north and west, then you will be in the storm's "warm sector", and will consequently receive all or mostly rain. (source: USN)

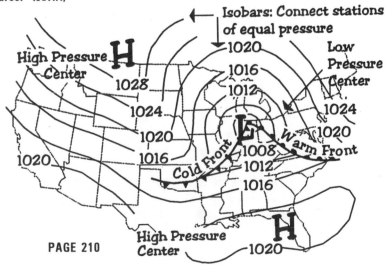

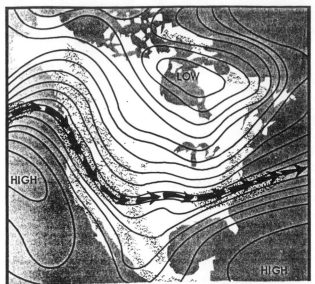

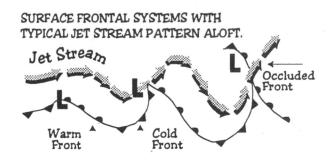

SURFACE FRONTAL SYSTEMS WITH
TYPICAL JET STREAM PATTERN ALOFT.

Figure 30-5 (left). The polar jet-stream (arrows) separates cold air to its north from milder mid-latitude air to its south. Extratropical low pressure systems form on kinks of the front that lies underneath and just to the south of the location of this jet stream. (source: DOA) **Figure 30-6 (right).** Notice how when a low is forming on the polar front, the jet stream is just to the north (about 100 miles to the north) of the front, and as the low becomes mature, the jet passes over the storm's center which by then is where the cold front is starting to catch up with and overtake the warm front, since the denser, colder air moves faster than does the less dense warm air, and then as the storm becomes occluded, that is, when the cold front catches up with and overtakes the warm front, the jet stream passes over the point of occlusion as the air around the low all mixes together as the low gradually dies. (source: USN)

Figure 30-7. Snowfall reports and other data from a major east coast winter low pressure system. This one storm system produced over 50 tornadoes in Florida, 9- to 12-foot storm surges along the northeast Gulf of Mexico coast, coastal flooding from the Carolinas through Cape Cod, New England, and winds gusting to over hurricane fury, 81 mph at Boston and 144 mph at Mt. Washington, New Hampshire. Blizzard conditions covered a wide swath of territory, and snow-depth reports at the end of the storm are shown at right. Record low barometric pressures were also set. (source: NOAA)

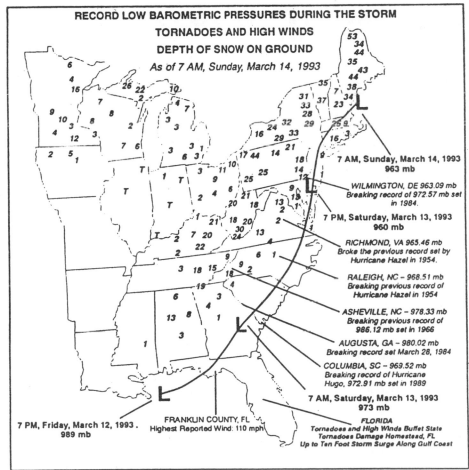

Another type of winter event is lake effect snow. First, let us review its description which was given in chapter 24 on local winds:

When very cold arctic air passes over the relatively warm Great Lakes of the United States, especially from late autumn into early winter when the lakes are free of widespread icing over, clouds form over the warmer lakes and these clouds tend to produce copious amounts of snow. When the dewpoint of the cold air is at least about 18 degrees colder than the surface temperature of the Great Lake it is passing over, the evaporation of moisture from the lake condenses into clouds, and these clouds have vertical growth because of the unstable conditions (warm at the bottom and much colder as we rise up for several thousand feet). This situation is analogous to what you see when you fill a bath tub to the top with hot water. There is evaporation, and the moist air condenses in the cooler air over the tub to form a fog (a cloud).

When the low-level winds steer the lake effect snowclouds inland, the heavy lake effect snows dump their snow not just over the lake but also onshore. The heaviest lake effect snowfall typically occurs about 10 to 20 miles inland from the coast. The land is higher in elevation than the lake's surface, so since the air is moving onshore already saturated, it must rise up and over the land and its hills, etc. Any additional lift to the saturated air squeezes out (condenses out) even more moisture to increase the snowfall rate. This phenomenon is known as frictional convergence. With frictional convergence, air parcels pile up and ascend higher terrain, condensing out more snow. Thus, the heaviest lake effect snows (which can be three or four FEET and sometimes more, within several hours!) typically occur not along the shoreline but some 10 to 20 miles inland.

Ironically, some of the heaviest snows in the lake-effect belt of the Great Lakes occur on the back of the low pressure system as the storm is pulling away, since behind it is the influx of very cold air from a very cold high pressure system moving in behind the low.

In fact, very cold air passing over any large and significantly warmer water body can produce lake-enhanced or ocean-enhanced snows. For example, when the upper-air pattern causes a winter blast of arctic air to spill over the western mountains and make all the way over to Puget Sound in Washington state, then ocean-enhanced snowfalls can occur, similar to the lake effect snows of the Great Lakes. Actually, any substantial water body is such a situation can produce or enhance snowfall.

For example, on occasion lake effect snowstorms will be generated by very cold air passing over the Great Salt Lake in Utah. The low-level wind direction determines where on land the heavy snow falls.

Some extremes of lake effect snowfall include over 100 inches during one episode on the Tug Hill Plateau southeast of the eastern end of Lake Ontario, in New York State, nearly six feet at Chardon, Ohio from a November 1996 Lake Erie lake effect storm, and the famous Buffalo, New York lake effect blizzard, accompanied by high winds, in January 1977, in which snow drifts covered telephone poles and even entire houses. After the storm, people had to dig tunnels through the snow from their front doors to the streets, which were eventually plowed, just to get out of their houses! The upper peninsula of Michigan is a prime snow-lover's area, due to frequent lake effect snows from Lake Superior; it is common there to have snow seasons with over 200 inches of snow for the season. Thus, lake effect snows can be quite impressive.

Besides lake effect snowstorms, there are some other conditions which generate snowstorms without needing the action of a low pressure system: examples are orographic lifting and upslope.

Orographic (topographical) lifting is the rising of air up mountains, with the air containing sufficient moisture to cool to its condensation point (dewpoint temperature), producing clouds and subsequent precipitation. The windward sides of mountains, especially high mountain ranges, receive orographic snows. Notable examples are the Himalaya Mountains of Asia, the Andes of South America, the Sierra Nevada and Cascade ranges of North America and the Alps in Europe. The mountain weather station at Paradise, Washington received over one thousand inches of snow in one season, due in great part to orographic lifting of moist Pacific air that keeps having its moisture squeezed out of it as the air ascended the mountains!

Upslope is air moving along a steadily rising terrain. If the air contains sufficient moisture to produce clouds as it cools while rising, and then to produce precipitation due to continued rise, then upslope precipitation occurs. Following is an example.

When a cold high pressure system is centered in the vicinity of northern Wyoming, then the air circulation outward from and around the high's center gives low-level winds over southeast Wyoming, over Nebraska, over eastern Colorado and over Kansas from an easterly direction, such as from the northeast. Since the elevation of the land gradually rises as we go from eastern Nebraska westward into eastern Wyoming, and from eastern Kansas westward into eastern Colorado, then the air as it travels "upslope" to the west is gradually rising. If the air contains sufficient moisture, and since the air is cooling as it is mechanically rising, then it may cool to its dewpoint. This causes clouds, and if the rising continues, then subsequent snowfall develops. Thus, western Nebraska, southeast Wyoming, western Kansas and eastern Colorado receive "upslope snow" from a high pressure system! In most other places, the high would cause clear skies!

Chapter 11 tells about wind chill, and chapter 18 tells about freezing rain (an ice storm) and sleet. It is worth recalling the wind chill here, since strong winds and very cold temperatures in a raging blizzard will, by themselves, be life-threatening.

Wind-Chill Equivalent Temperatures (°F)

Calm air	At 15 mph	At 30 mph	At 40 mph and over
30	9	- 2	- 6
20	- 5	-18	-22
10	-18	-33	-38
0	-31	-49	-54
-10	-45	-64	-70
-20	-58	-78	-87
-30	-72	-93	-101
-40	-85	-109	-116

To determine how much protection you really need, refer to the wind-chill table. Remember, at wind-chill equivalent temperatures below –25° F, exposed skin can freeze within one minute.

Figure 30-8. Wearing layers of warm clothing and making sure exposed flesh is covered are vital to do for very cold wind chills. The head should always be covered when in such conditions, as well as making sure no body part is exposed to the brutal combination of very cold temperatures and high wind speeds. The human body loses about half...even somewhat more...of its heat loss through the head. If you are stuck in a house without heat and it is very cold, have your head covered, besides wearing layers of warm clothing, warm sox and mittens. (source: DOE)

When a brutally cold arctic high pressure system rapidly plunges about due south into Texas, the blast of arctic air is called a "blue Norther", since its cold can "turn your flesh blue"!

Blizzard conditions can be caused by any of the storms we have been discussing in this chapter. A blizzard is a continued period of time with winds over 35 mph with falling snow and/or blowing snow reducing the visibility to near zero. Until recently, the definition for blizzard also included a temperature factor (being below, say, about 20 degrees Fahrenheit). But if it is cold enough to snow, and the wind is over 35 miles per hour, the wind chills are dangerously cold anyway. Deep drifts of snow occur in a blizzard. The blinding, swirling snow causes white-out conditions (all you see is white all around you). It is easy to get disoriented if caught outside in a raging blizzard.

The following preparedness information for winter storms is from the National Weather Service publication, "Winter Storms...the Deceptive Killers":

At home and at work...

Primary concerns are the potential loss of heat, power, telephone service, and a shortage of supplies if storm conditions continue for more than a day.
Have available:
• Flashlight and extra batteries.
• Battery-powered NOAA Weather Radio and portable radio to receive emergency information. *These may be your only links to the outside.*
• Extra food and water. High energy food, such as dried fruit or candy, and food requiring no cooking or refrigeration is best.
• Extra medicine and baby items.
• First-aid supplies.
• Heating fuel. Fuel carriers may not reach you for days after a severe winter storm.
• Emergency heating source, such as a fireplace, wood stove, space heater, etc.
  - Learn to use properly to prevent a fire.
  - Have proper ventilation.
• Fire extinguisher and smoke detector.
  - Test units regularly to ensure they are working properly.

In cars and trucks...

Plan your travel and check the latest weather reports to avoid the storm!
• Fully check and winterize your vehicle before the winter season begins.
• Carry a WINTER STORM SURVIVAL KIT:
  blankets/sleeping bags; flashlight with extra batteries; first-aid kit; knife; high-calorie, non-perishable food; extra clothing to keep dry; a large empty can and plastic cover with tissues and paper towels for sanitary purposes; a smaller can and water-proof matches to melt snow for drinking water; sack of sand (or cat litter); shovel; windshield scraper and brush; tool kit; tow rope; booster cables; water container; compass and road maps.
• Keep your gas tank near full to avoid ice in the tank and fuel lines.
• Try not to travel alone.
• Let someone know your timetable and primary and alternate routes.

On the farm...

• Move animals to sheltered areas. Shelter belts, properly laid out and oriented, are better protection for cattle than confining shelters, such as sheds.
• Haul extra feed to nearby feeding areas.
• Have a water supply available. Most animal deaths in winter storms are from dehydration.

DRESS TO FIT THE SEASON. Wear loose-fitting, light-weight, warm clothing in several layers. Trapped air insulates. Layers can be removed to avoid perspiration and subsequent chill. Outer garments should be tightly woven, water repellent, and hooded. Wear a hat. Half your body heat loss can be from the head. Cover your mouth to protect your lungs from extreme cold. Mittens, snug at the wrist, are better than gloves. Try to stay dry.

NOAA Weather Radio is an excellent means for receiving vital weather information, especially for weather watches and warnings. The following is from the National Weather Service publication, "Winter Storms...the Deceptive Killers":

WINTER STORM WATCH: Severe winter conditions, such as heavy snow and/or ice, are possible within the next day or two. Prepare now!

WINTER STORM WARNING: Severe winter conditions have begun or are about to begin in your area. Stay indoors!

BLIZZARD WARNING: Snow and strong winds will combine to produce a blinding snow (near zero visibility), deep drifts, and life-threatening wind chill. Seek refuge immediately!

WINTER WEATHER ADVISORY: Winter weather conditions are expected to cause significant inconveniences and may be hazardous. If caution is exercised, these situations should not become life-threatening. The greatest hazard is often to motorists.

FROST/FREEZE WARNING: Below freezing temperatures are expected and may cause significant damage to plants, crops, or fruit trees. In areas unaccustomed to freezing temperatures, people who have homes without heat need to take added precautions.

A DISASTER SUPPLIES KIT SHOULD INCLUDE:
A 3-day supply of water (one gallon per person per day) and food that won't spoil • one change of clothing and footwear per person • one blanket or sleeping bag per person • a first-aid kit, including prescription medicines • emergency tools, including a battery-powered NOAA Weather Radio and a portable radio, flashlight, and plenty of extra batteries • an extra set of car keys and cash • special items for infant, elderly, or disabled family member.

Figure 30-9. After a coastal New England blizzard on February 6th & 7th, 1978, this photograph shows how everyone in Swampscott, Massachusetts was forced to walk. The police car and officer stopped people from driving in and out of town. (photo by Joseph Balsama)

Figure 30-10. An example of wind damage, snowdrifts and debris from the ocean that had to be plowed from one of the main coastal roads in Swampscott, Massachusetts after the Feb. 6-7, 1978 blizzard. (photo by Joseph Balsama)

Figure 30-11. The day after the same storm, waves are breaking and the spray was going over the roof this motel in the same coastal town. Many rooms were destroyed. The motel was torn down after the storm. These past four photos illustrate that along ocean coasts, not only will snow and wind be major problems in a well-developed storm system, but coastal flooding and battering action will compound the damages. (photo by Christopher Ratley)

Chapter 31. THUNDERSTORMS; LIGHTNING; MESOSCALE CONVECTIVE SYSTEMS (MCSes)

About 2000 thunderstorms are underway as you are reading this.

Figure 31-1. A thunderstorm is a storm containing thunder and lightning. It forms when air rises or is forced to rise. These rising air parcels carry their warmth with them, although they cool as they rise: this process is known as convection. (source: NOAA)

Introduction:

We define a thunderstorm as any storm in which thunder is heard. Other storms, e.g., snowstorms and hurricanes, can also have thunderstorms imbedded in them; in fact, since hurricanes are convective, they originate as areas of thunderstorms and typically have thunder in them.

Thunderstorms used to be called "electrical storms", and perhaps more appropriately should be called lightning storms rather than thunderstorms. The term "thundershower" is obsolete; it used to refer to a relatively mild thunderstorm with little rain and wind; now, however, all electrical storms are referred to as "thunderstorms", since even a weak one produces lightning, and all lightning is potentially lethal.

All thunderstorms are accompanied by lightning. In fact, if it were not for the lightning, there would be no thunder. Thunder is caused by the rapid expansion of air once it is heated by lightning.

If you have seen a Van de Graaff generator (a device used to study static electricity), the crackling sound that you hear is really thunder, which is caused by the sparks (lightning) heating the air and the air subsequently expanding rapidly.

Thunderstorms are often accompanied by heavy rainfall and gusty winds. Sometimes they produce hail and occasionally they generate tornadoes.

A "severe thunderstorm" is a thunderstorm which produces either winds of 58 mph or more, or hail of 3/4 inch diameter or more, or both. Thus, severe thunderstorms are damaging.

Most of us think of thunderstorms as local storms that do not last too long, forming from large, swelling cumulonimbus clouds that look like giant cauliflowers. The diameter of most individual thunderstorms is about 5 to 6 miles. The vertical extent of these storms can grow to be over 50,000 feet high (about 10 miles), and even higher. In general, the taller the cloud, the more severe the thunderstorm is likely to be. During the daytime, the sky becomes noticeably darker as a thunderstorm moves in. This is because the storm's clouds are so thick (up to 10 miles or even more), that up to about 92% of the sunshine hitting its top is reflected back to space. Thus, not much of the sun's rays is making it through the thunderstorm, although there is also some scattered and reflected ambient light making it to the earth from the storm. The result, however, is that the sky turns much darker as a well-developed thunderstorm moves in.

In the warmer half of the year in mid-latitudes, showers become thunderstorms when the cloud tops exceed about 25,000 feet above the surface. The height of the thunderstorm cloud tops is impressive: they can grow to be over 40,000 feet high, with many of the most severe thunderstorm tops exceeding 55,000 feet. Tops are higher in the tropics than in the mid-latitudes, and higher in the mid-latitudes than in the polar regions; this is because the tropopause is highest in tropics, and becomes progressively lower as we move poleward. The rising air parcels no longer accelerate upward when they move into a stable region, such as the stratosphere which lies above the tropopause. When these rising parcels become cooler than the environment they are passing through, they slow down their ascent and eventually sink. Thus, thunderstorm cloud tops can grow only to a certain height. Moreover, eventually the moisture would be used up, which would mark the end of the cloud growth.

When a thunderstorm occurs during the daytime, we often do not see all the lightning until the cloud that produced it is very close to being overhead. This is because it is light outside. At night, however, we see the lightning before we hear its thunder. If someone shines a flashlight in your window on a bright sunny day, then you probably would not notice it unless you were looking out of the window; if this happens at night, then you would certainly notice it even if you were not facing the window. If we see lightning at night but do not hear its thunder, then we are observing what is called "distant lightning". Some people refer to this as "heat lightning", but this is a misnomer: there is no such thing as "heat lightning", or lightning produced by heat with no clouds; it is lightning observed at night from a distant thunderstorm. Typically, you do not hear thunder from a thunderstorm that is more than about 18 miles (29 kilometers) away. You may see only lightning if the storm is beyond about 18 miles or passes your area at this distance. As the storm gets closer, you may see the lightning and hear the thunder.

What comes first, the lightning or the thunder?: The lightning comes first, followed almost instantaneously by the thunder as the heated air rapidly expands in all directions from the lightning.

The reason we see the lightning before hearing the thunder is that the light from the lightning moves at the speed of light, about 186,000 miles per second, so that it is essentially instantaneous for us to see the lightning as it happens; however, the thunder moves at the speed of sound, which is about one-fifth of a mile per second. Therefore, it takes the thunder five seconds to travel one mile.   PAGE 218

<u>DEMONSTRATION</u>: DETERMINING HOW FAR AWAY AN INDIVIDUAL THUNDERSTORM IS FROM YOU

The next time a thunderstorm is forming and approaching you, do the following:

1. Count the number of seconds between when you see the lightning and hear the thunder.
2. Divide the number of seconds by five. Each multiple of five means the storm is one mile away.
3. Keep doing this as the storm approaches and then leaves. When the interval of time between when you see the lightning and hear the thunder decreases, the storm is getting closer; when this time interval increases, the storm is moving away.

Thus, if it takes 15 seconds between seeing the lightning and hearing the thunder, then the storm is 3 miles away. This works for individual thunderstorms. When there are clusters of thunderstorms, you may be seeing lightning and hearing thunder from more than one storm, so that you may not be able to do this demonstration. Moreover, storms sometimes form right over your location, and storms grow and die. When you see lightning and hear thunder about simultaneously from an individual thunderstorm cell, then the storm is directly overhead.

THE NECESSARY CONDITIONS FOR THUNDERSTORMS:

All four conditions must occur simultaneously:
1. **LIFT**
2. **INSTABILITY**
3. **MOISTURE**
4. **LACK OF A MID-LEVEL CAP AROUND 10,000 FEET (it cannot be too warm aloft)**

Let us look at each of these four conditions.

LIFT:

To form the cumulus clouds that will grow into towering cumulus and ultimately the cumulonimbus clouds that give us thunderstorms, the air must rise or be forced to rise. This is because clouds form when moist air rises and cools to its dewpoint. Air parcels expend energy in the form of heat as they rise, so they cool at a certain rate. When these parcels are not yet saturated, they cool as what is called the DRY ADIABATIC LAPSE RATE. The word "adiabatic" means that no heat is being added to or taken away from the parcel; thus, the parcel is expending its own heat as it rises. This rate is about 5½ Fahrenheit degrees per 1000 feet of ascent (about 9.8 Celsius degrees per 1000 meters of ascent). However, once the air parcel has cooled to its dewpoint (is saturated; i.e., the relative humidity is now 100%), it continues to cool as it rises, but now at less of a cooling rate as before. This cooling rate when saturated is known as the MOIST ADIABATIC LAPSE RATE, which varies with height, but is about 60% of the dry adiabatic lapse rate. The moist adiabatic lapse rate in the low and middle troposphere is about 3F° per 1000 feet of ascent (about 6C° per 1000 meters of ascent).

The reason the air parcels cool at a slower rate once saturated is that since they are already saturated, any additional cooling releases the heat of condensation (see chapters 13 and 14). By adding some heat to the parcel, the parcel does not then cool at its original rate.

This convective lifting is not the same as the synoptic lifting for widespread rainstorms and snowstorms caused by winter-type low pressure systems. The gradual lifting in these low pressure systems is over hundreds and hundreds of miles and is on the order of a few centimeters per second (less than one-fifth of a mile per hour). Compare this to the convective lifting in localized showers and thunderstorms, in which the rising air currents (updrafts) are on the order of 30 to 50 miles per hour, and are much greater in severe and hail-producing storms. Indeed, to generate softball-sized hailstones, the updrafts in a thunderstorm need to be about 150 mph!

The lifting mechanisms for thunderstorm development are characterized as dynamic lifting mechanisms and mechanical lifting mechanisms. The following are examples of some common types of lift for convection.

Some dynamic lifting mechanisms for convection:

●Heating of the day. The sun heats the ground, which in turn heats the air above it, which rises as parcels of warm air.

●An advancing cold front. The leading edge of the colder air at the surface scoops up the warmer air just ahead of it. Sometimes the cold front slows down at the surface but some of the colder air advances aloft, say at about 5,000 to 10,000 feet up. This destabilizes the mid-levels of the troposphere, which enhances convective lift.

●On the cool air side of an advancing warm front, especially if the warm air is moist and unstable. Steady precipitation with imbedded showers and thunderstorms often occur ahead of and along the warm front.

●Intersection of low-level boundaries. Intersections of any two boundaries can create lift. Such boundaries include the outflow of air from the leading edge of a thunderstorm (or dying thunderstorm) intersecting the outflow of air from another thunderstorm. These outflows are termed "outflow boundaries". Another example is a sea-breeze front (or lake-breeze front) intersecting another boundary. On a peninsula, for example, two sea-breeze fronts from two different directions may bang into each other, resulting in cumuloform clouds forming there, which may grow into thunderstorms if the other necessary conditions for thunderstorms are present.

Some mechanical lifting mechanisms for convection:

●Upslope. This occurs when the low-level air is forced to rise up over gradually rising terrain. An example is an easterly flow of air (air moving westward) from central Kansas to eastern Colorado. If sufficient moisture is present in the air, it will cool to its dewpoint as it rises, and if the environment is unstable, the clouds will grow.

●Orographic lifting. Clouds may form when air is forced to ascend mountains. Upslope is one type of orographic lifting.

In each of these lifting episodes, the air that is rising or being lifted must have ample moisture to generate clouds once the air is cooled to its dewpoint temperature. Keep in mind that the dewpoint is in reality a measure of the amount of moisture in the air. The higher the dewpoint, the more grams of moisture per kilogram of air. Thus, many of the heaviest rainfalls in thunderstorms occur from storms (especially slow-moving ones) that form in air with dewpoints of 70 degrees F. or higher.

Figure 31-2. Examples of some of the lifting mechanisms that would produce thunderstorms if they occur in moist and unstable air, without a cap (too warm) aloft existing about 10,000 feet off the ground. (source: DOA)

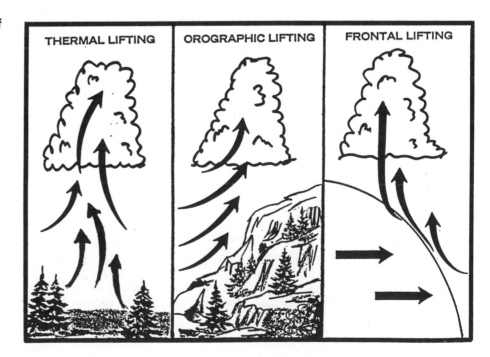

Figure 31-3. As a cold front moves through, it scoops up the warmer air ahead of it. If the warmer air is also moist and unstable without a cap aloft, thunderstorms are likely just ahead of and along the front. Sometimes a cold front slows down as it tries to dislodge hot air, but some of the cooler air advances aloft at some 5,000 to 10,000 feet above the ground. This destabilizes the mid-troposphere and can lead to a line of thunderstorms some 100 miles ahead of the front (a pre-frontal squall-line), while along the cold front there is another line of thunderstorms. (source: DOA)

Figure 31-4. An advancing warm front first has the warmer air coming in aloft over the cool or cold air, since the warmer air is lighter than the cool or cold air. Where the warm air is at the surface is where the warm front is located on the surface weather map. If the warm air is also moist and unstable, imbedded showers and thunderstorms are likely within the general precipitation area on the cold air side of the warm front. (source: DOA)

INSTABILITY:

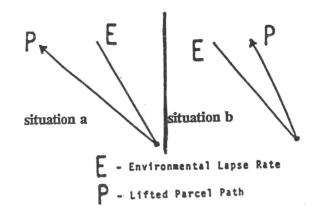

Figure 31-5. Stability vs. instability. E represents the environmental temperature lapse rate; i.e., E shows the actual temperature of the air (a falling temperature) as we ascend. P shows how an air parcel that is rising or is being lifted, cools as it ascends. The parcel cools at a specific rate, as explained earlier. In situation a, the parcel would be cooler than the environment, so it would sink and not form thunderstorms. The environment in situation a is said to be stable. In situation b, the parcel, although cooling as it ascends, remains warmer than the environment so it keeps rising. With moisture and no mid-level cap, showers and/or thunderstorms may form.

PAGE 221

In an unstable environment, the air keeps accelerating upwards until it reaches a stable region aloft (this could be as high as the stratosphere if the whole troposphere were unstable!). Once the parcels have risen into a stable region aloft, they decelerate and eventually stop rising, which visibly would be seen as the tops of the convective clouds.

Meteorologists routinely examine plotted vertical "soundings" taken by weather balloon instrument packages known as radiosondes, to predict the likelihood of thunderstorms. These plots of temperature, dewpoint and wind and various altitudes allow the forecaster to determine if the air is stable and unstable, and to what magnitude. The more unstable the air, the more likely thunderstorms are. Very unstable air often results in severe thunderstorms that produce downpours, frequent lightning, strong to damaging winds, hail and sometimes tornadoes and downbursts or microbursts of descending air at high speeds.

MOISTURE:

If any of the four conditions for thunderstorms does not exist, the storms will not occur. All four requirements of lift, instability, moisture and lack of a mid-level cap must exist simultaneously for thunderstorms to form.

Thunderstorms can occur at any time of the year, but they are more likely during the warmer half of the year. The dewpoints are higher then. Relative humidities in the lower levels of the troposphere should be as high as possible...at least 50%, so that rising air can carry with it an abundance of moisture to be subsequently released as clouds and precipitation. Spring dewpoints in mid-latitudes should be in the 40s and 50s or higher, and late spring through summer dewpoints should be in the 50s and 60s or higher, and preferably about 70 degrees Fahrenheit or higher to provide ample moisture for thunderstorms.

Sometimes it is relatively dry above the surface but moist somewhat above the surface, typically a few thousand feet up, and sometimes it is stable near the surface but unstable several thousand feet aloft. In such cases, thunderstorms can form above the stable layer. This sometimes occurs in the western high plains, resulting in "mid-based thunderstorms", so-called because their cloud bases are in the range of "mid-level clouds", several thousand feet up. Some of the precipitation from mid-based thunderstorms evaporates before reaching the ground. Precipitation falling from the clouds but evaporating before reaching the ground is called virga. The occurrence of virga under a thunderstorm may indicate an environment favorable for microbursts of very high winds (discussed later). When thunderstorm bases are high (say 8,000 to 12,000 feet above the ground) and are above a dry, stable layer, then as impulses of air rise buoyantly through the unstable air aloft, some air bubbles may receive a push downward from that level and would be colder than the environment, so would accelerate downward, reaching the ground as a microburst.

LACK OF A MID-LEVEL CAP AROUND 10,000 FEET:

All three main "ingredients" of a thunderstorm may co-exist in an area (lift, instability and moisture), so that the convection commences. However, if the clouds grow and then stop growing at say 8,000 or 10,000 or 12,000 feet up, then the rising air parcels have moved into a stable area and stopped rising. If the environment through which the parcels are passing is warmer than the temperature of the parcels, then the rising parcels are CAPPED out at that level. A cap or lid on any further growth exists. The "bottom line" is this: if it is too warm aloft, then thunderstorm development will be inhibited. A good forecast rule-of-thumb based on decades of empirical use is this (for mid-latitudes during the warmer half of the year): if the 700 millibar temperature is 12°Celsius (54° Fahrenheit) or higher, then this is a cap which will prevent thunderstorm growth most of the time, and a 14°C (57°F) temperature at 700 mb virtually assures a strong enough cap to stop thunderstorm development. A "cap inversion" occurs in a high pressure system. Highs have slowly sinking, diverging air from their centers to generally eastward (in the Northern Hemisphere), but sometimes a section of the sinking air aloft sinks more persistently than the rest, and since these air parcels warm up as they subside, the environment is gradually warmed. This phenomenon typically occurs anywhere between about the 600 and 800 millibar levels, typically around 700 mb. (The 700 millibar level is the height [about 10,000 feet elevation] to which we must rise to have the atmospheric pressure be 700 millibars, or about 21" on the barometer. The average sea-level pressure is 1013.25 millibars.)

HOWEVER, if the instability is so intense below the cap that bubbles of rising air are struggling to force themselves up, then eventually after a couple or a few hours of convective streams surging into the cap, the capped air will mix with the rising air to cool down the cap. If it cools sufficiently, then the rising air parcels will shoot through the cap --the cap is broken-- and thunderstorm development will be explosive.

Often a shallow cap aloft that is about 50 mb thick and only about 2 Celsius degrees warmer than instability, will set the stage for severe thunderstorms that form as the cap is suddenly broken.

Reviewing, then, this critical aspect of thunderstorm formation: we need four conditions co-existing in the same region for thunderstorms to develop: we need LIFT, INSTABILITY, MOISTURE and LACK OF A CAP AROUND 10,000 FEET UP.

Stages of development of a thunderstorm:

The cumulus stage (the initial building-up stage) is characterized by updrafts. Cumulus clouds grow into towering cumulus. This is not typically a dangerous stage. You may see a few bolts of lightning and hear some rumbles of thunder and rain may begin to fall as the towering cumulus continue to grow.

The mature stage is characterized by continued updrafts and growing into cumulonimbus, and also by downdrafts caused by the drag of air by precipitation as it falls. In severe thunderstorms, flash flooding rains, hail and downbursts of air (as well as concentrated downbursts called microbursts) may occur, and on occasion, tornadoes form. You can tell whether the damage caused by thunderstorm winds is from a microburst or tornado, since microbursts (and downbursts) blow objects over in one direction, whereas the tornado damage is more circular.

The dissipating stage is characterized by downdrafts, as the function of the thunderstorm (which is to overturn the atmosphere in the local environment) becomes completed and the air stabilizes. The rain slackens, the winds diminish and clouds gradually evaporate In the sinking air.

THE THREE STAGES OF A THUNDERSTORM:

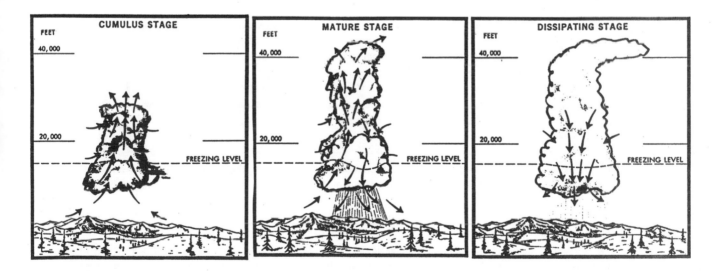

Figure 31-6. The cumulus (left), mature (middle) and dissipating (right) stages of a thunderstorm. In the incipient or cumulus stage, air is converging into the developing cloud from all around, resulting in updrafts. The cloud grows into the mature stage, which is the most active part of the thunderstorm life-cycle. The first rain typically occurs when the first lightning and thunder are observed. The rain and/or other precipitation that would now be falling, drag down colder air as they fall, initiating downdrafts. In the mature stage of a thunderstorm, we find warm updrafts and cold downdrafts. In the dissipating stage of a thunderstorm. Downdrafts characterize this stage as the thunderstorm dies. The precipitation becomes progressively lighter, finally ending, and the cloud matter that remains is debris cloudiness, which eventually dissipates. (source: DOA)   PAGE 223

Sample problem:

A thunderstorm is moving from west to east through these cities: Leavenworth (in northeast Kansas), Kearney and Excelsior Springs (both in northwest Missouri). Leavenworth has growing puffy clouds and starts to receive raindrops and some lightning and rumbles of thunder. Thirty minutes later, Kearney is getting hail of 2-inches diameter, very heavy rain, wind gusts over 60 miles per hour and nearly continuous lightning and thunder. Twenty minutes later, Excelsior Springs is receiving light rain, some lightning and thunder, and the tops of the puffy clouds are diminishing in height. What thunderstorm stage is occurring at each city?

Solution:

at Leavenworth: the cumulus stage;
at Kearney: the mature stage;
at Excelsior Springs: the dissipating stage.

Life-span of a thunderstorm:

The life-cycle of a typical thunderstorm cell is from 20 to 60 minutes, with most cells averaging about 45 minutes of life from cumulus through mature stages into dissipation.

However, supercell thunderstorms, the kind that produces most of the tornadoes, especially the most powerful tornadoes, can persist for hours.

If you are experiencing thunderstorms for say all night, it is because you are experiencing many thunderstorm cells. As cells are dying, new ones are forming. Cells also merge to form thunderstorm complexes, and within these complexes cells grow and die along side of each other.

Types of thunderstorms:

Thunderstorms are actually very easy to predict. As we have been discussing throughout this chapter, when we have LIFT, INSTABILITY, MOISTURE and LACK OF A CAP AT ABOUT 10,000 FEET UP co-existing in the same region, we WILL have thunderstorms. Lifting mechanisms are commonly intersecting boundaries as discussed earlier, but also just heating of the day. Although some meteorologists may not use the term "air mass thunderstorms", there really is such a type. When the air mass you are in is warm or hot and is also moist and unstable without the mid-level cap, then the thunderstorms that form from solar heating in this soupy air mass are called AIR MASS THUNDERSTORMS. The thunderstorms that occur within a hurricane are also air mass thunderstorms, since they are occurring within a contained mass of tropical air.

When a cold or warm front is entering your area, the storms would be frontal thunderstorms or both air-mass and frontal. Thus, if only solar heating in a soupy air mass is the lifting mechanism for the convection, then these storms are air mass thunderstorms.

The supercells discussed above typically form at the intersection of boundaries, such as at the intersection of a cold front and an outflow boundary from another thunderstorm, or at the intersection of a dry-line (which separates dry air from moist air) and a cold front, or when a sea-breeze front intersects another boundary. These are just some common examples of intersecting boundaries that may cause supercells when the air is extremely unstable.

Geographic distribution of thunderstorms in the United States:

A thunderstorm day is a calendar day in which at least one thunderstorm occurs at a specific location.

In parts of the tropics, there are some 200 thunderstorm days per year. In the United States, thunderstorm days range from near zero along the West Coast of the lower 48 states as well as much of Alaska and Hawaii, to over 50 thunderstorm days in the Central Plains, to over 100 thunderstorm days over south Florida.

Local conditions such as topography and moisture supply help determine the number of thunderstorms and number of thunderstorm days. Some other factors are the types of air masses, the frequency of frontal passages, the frequency of intersecting boundaries (such as dry-lines, fronts, sea and lake breezes) and any other factors that lead to lift, instability, moisture and no cap aloft.

Interior Alaska around Fairbanks does get some thunderstorm activity during the warm season, although the tops of those thunderstorm clouds are much less (often under 30,000 or even under 25,000 feet high) than in mid-latitudes (where tops can easily exceed 40,000 feet) and in the tropics (where tops can exceed 55,000 feet in many cases). The main reason for this tops variation is that the tropopause is lowest in the polar regions, higher in mid-latitudes and highest in the tropics.

The figure below shows the number of thunderstorm days in the United States annually.

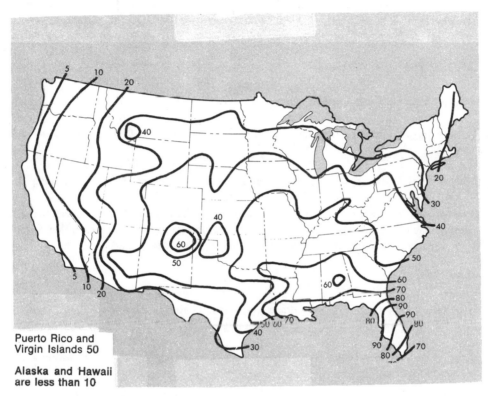

Figure 31-7. The number of thunderstorm days per year in the contiguous 48 states of the United States. Parts of Florida experience the most thunderstorm days while the west coast (and Alaska and Hawaii) experience the fewest. (source: NOAA)

<u>Lightning</u>:

Lightning is a form of electricity that can not be seen by the human eye; what happens is that the electricity, which is comprised of particles, "bangs" into air atoms, causing them to give off visible light (to glow); thus, this is how we see lightning. This reason is also why we see the aurora: particles from the sun "bang" into the earth's atmosphere, causing the particles to glow. The earth's magnetic field causes the concentration of the particles to be greater in the vicinity of the magnetic poles.

According to contemporary climatological statistics, the earth averages having about 44,000 thunderstorms each day! That is a lot of energy. In your hemisphere, more occur during the warmer half of the year, when convective processes are more active. There are some 9 million bolts of lightning ripping though the air each day, which is a rate of about 6,000 per minute or about 100 every second. A routine thunderstorm produces about 10,000 lightning strikes, and the supercell thunderstorm, which lasts three or more times longer, produces much more.   PAGE 225

Some United States Lightning Statistics

- On the average, there are some 26 million lightning strikes annually.
- In the 1940s, when the population was much less than around the year 2000, there typically were more than 2000 lightning deaths each year; however, as we approached the year 2000, the annual lightning death was around 100, thanks to weather education about lightning safety. Flash floods kill more people than does lightning, and most flash floods also come from thunderstorms. Thus, flash flood safety education is also a priority. One chief way people die in flash floods is by driving a vehicle into water that is overflowing from a stream, which can overturn the vehicle.
- Thousands of fires are started every year by lightning strikes. Especially vulnerable are forests in the American west where summertime precipitation is mostly light and infrequent.

A single bolt of lightning can have up to 100,000 volts of electrical potential and up to 20,000 amperes of electric current. It takes only about one-tenth of an ampere (amp) to kill a human being! Lightning also momentarily heats the air it is passing through to as high as about 10,000 degrees Fahrenheit, which is the temperature of the surface of the sun (the interior of the sun is much, much hotter).

Two common misconceptions about lightning:

1. Lightning does not strike the same place twice.

This is false, because tall objects (e.g., the Empire State Building in New York City) may be struck several times during a single thunderstorm.

2. It is the rubber tires of a vehicle, or the rubber soles on shoes, that protect people from being struck by lightning.

This is also false, because lightning can travel many miles through the air, which is an insulator, so it can readily travel through several inches of rubber found on a tire and through less than an inch of rubber found on shoes. It is the metal of the car that safely carries the electricity that strikes it, to the ground.

Types of lightning:

Lightning is categorized by the following descriptions: intercloud lightning, cloud-to-cloud lightning, cloud-to-air lightning, cloud-to-ground lightning, ball lightning and lightning into space from the tops of thunderstorms.

Intercloud lightning, which includes intracloud lightning, is when the lightning bolt occurs within a cloud or clouds, so that the cloud or clouds light up.

When the bolt is visible as it streaks from cloud to cloud, it is categorized as cloud-to-cloud lightning.

When the bolt darts from the cloud outward but does not strike a target, it is cloud-to-air lightning.

When the lightning bolt extends from the cumulonimbus cloud to a target on the ground, it is cloud-to-ground lightning.

When the rare case of lightning occurs in which it is a ball of sparks descending from the storm and rolling along the ground, it is ball lightning. This rare type of lightning, averaging about the size of a basketball, is attracted to (it chases!) anything that is animate. It chases after people and animals and has been documented entering aircraft and even squeezing through keyholes and under doors to enter rooms and resumes its ball shape, then proceeding to chase a person, dog or cat, for example. Ball lightning persists for from seconds to usually no more than about one minute.

Lightning can also shoot upward into space (lightning-to-space form of lightning).

The term "sheet lightning" is sometimes used to describe the condition of part of the thunderstorm cloud lighting up because the lightning bolt is within the cloud. When the bolt is visible, its appearance is also sometimes characterized by terms such as forked, zigzag, streak and chain lightning.

It is possible for a lightning bolt to come out of the thunderstorm sideways and then dart down, striking a target such as a person a few miles away from the thunderstorm, who may be under sunny blue skies! This phenomenon is called "a bolt out of the blue".

St. Elmo's Fire consists of short streamers of light appearing at the ends of pointed objects, especially on mountains, the tops of observation towers, the wings of aircraft and the tips of spars and masts of sailing vessels. It is created by electrical charges building up on the earth and leaking into the air. St. Elmo's Fire often precedes a thunderstorm. It gets its name from St. Elmo who is the patron saint of sailors.

The most likely candidates for a lightning strike from regular lightning are the tallest objects, such as skyscrapers and towers. In more open areas, trees are potential targets. If you are the tallest object around in a thunderstorm, then you are in danger of being struck.

Besides hearing thunder and looking for lightning visually, another way you can tell if lightning is around or near you is that it creates static on AM radio stations.

How lightning forms:

The current thinking about the electrical charge considerations of the ground and the thunderstorm is as follows. Lightning forms when the difference in electrical charge is great between the ground and the thunderstorm cloud. The two types of electrical charge are positive and negative. The ground is normally negatively charged. When a thunderstorm passes overhead, the negative charge in the bottom of the cloud induces a positive charge in the ground below the storm. In the cloud vicinity the air ionizes, i.e., either gains or loses electrons, causing a conductive channel over which the lightning flows.

After the path for the lightning has been determined by a developing electrical potential differential between the cloud and the ground, then the lightning starts to follow that path to the target. The initial electricity, before we see the visible lightning, moves very swiftly in increments or steps, as depicted in figure 31-8 below.

The first darting of electricity from the cloud is called the step leader. It is invisible to a human observer. The step leader moves rapidly, at about 450,000 mph, but in spurts...that is, in steps, not continuously. Each step is probably on the order of from 150 feet to 400 feet. The very brief hesitations between the surge steps might be caused by the recharging of the tip of the surge with charged particles from the cloud base.

The step leader typically takes the path of least resistance and can branch out up to several times.

When the main stem of the step leader gets to within about 150 to 200 feet of the ground, an upward streamer of positive ions is triggered. This is called the return stroke. This is able to happen because the electrical potential difference between the negatively-charged step leader and the positively-charged ground target is sufficiently strong to trigger the electrical discharge. Then, when this streamer hits the step leader, the circuit is complete.

Figure 31-8. At left, a step leader moving down in steps from the cloud base; and at right, the first electrical streamer connects with the step leader.

Time-lapse videos of lightning indicate that the brightly luminous return stroke races up the pathway at over 100,000,000 mph. The temperature of a strong electrical discharge can exceed 50,000°F, although commonly, the temperature is about 10,000°F.

Immediately following this upward discharge is a charge shooting downward to the ground as a lightning strike.

All of this is happening so fast that to us as observers it appears as one bolt of electrical discharge.

Sometimes multiple strokes occur from about one-fiftieth to about one-fifth of a second between each return stroke. This is usually long enough for the naked eye to sense flickering.

On the average, about 4 sequences of step leaders and return strokes comprise a single lightning bolt. The typical lightning flash averages 3 to 5 strokes. Some flashes have been observed to have up to 26 separate strokes.

Over 95% of cloud-to-ground lightning strikes are negatively charged. The positively-charged strikes are significantly more powerful and last longer than the negative strokes.

Most deaths from lightning occur in the open, with most fatalities during the afternoon. Most air mass thunderstorms develop during the afternoons and that time is also when the largest number of people are outside. Some people are killed by lightning during the evening and night, with the fewest deaths around daybreak.

Figure 31-9. Zigzag, forked lightning over Swampscott, Massachusetts Harbor. (photo by Mark Garfinkel)

<u>Some lightning safety information:</u>

●If you are outside during thunderstorm activity and your skin starts to tingle with your hair standing straight out, this means that lightning has picked you for a target. You may have typically only about one to two seconds to put your hands on your knees and drop to the ground, making yourself as small a target as possible, so that the lightning would strike something near you that is a little taller.   PAGE 228

Figure 31-10. A bolt of lightning at the right, and ball lightning on the horizon in the center of the photograph. Note the standard eight-inch rain gauge at the left, and to its right is an instrument shelter where maximum and minimum thermometers and a psychrometer are kept. (photo by Joseph Balsama)

●Get out of any lake, pond and swimming pool! Water conducts electricity, and a lightning bolt hitting the water could electrify you.

●Finish your shower and bath immediately and get out of the water. If lightning makes a direct strike on the house and comes through the plumbing, it can electrify you while you are taking a shower or bath!

●Believe it or not, and this is rare: lightning can zap you when you are on the toilet.

●Definitely get to shelter if you hear thunder or see lightning when you are on a field, including being on such fields as baseball/softball and soccer fields. These areas are wide open, so that people would be the tallest objects that would attract lightning. Parents: take your children off the field immediately when there is thunder or lightning. Even if the lightning is a few miles away, it has been known to dart out of the cloud sideways and then move down to strike a target. Also, get off a golf course (holding a golf iron and playing golf during a thunderstorm is double jeopardy).

●Get off the telephone. In Kansas City, Missouri two teenage girls in the same neighborhood were killed when lightning hit the phone lines and came through the telephones that they were using.

●Even with one or two surge protectors on appliances such as televisions and computers, a direct lightning strike on or near a house can send the powerful electric surge through the appliance, causing an explosion and possible fire. Therefore, you should unplug appliances such as computers and television sets, especially during storms with excessive lightning.

●Never use an umbrella with a metal handle that is not covered with wood, rubber or some other protective material. Metal conducts electricity.

●You are usually safe in a car. The lightning goes along the car body into the ground. (continued)   PAGE 229

•During a thunderstorm, never take shelter under a tree. If lightning hits the tree, you could also be struck by the bolt. In some cases, with the most intense bolts, the heat from the lightning may cause tree sap to instantly boil, causing the tree to explode!

When lightning strikes a person, much of the lightning goes around the perimeter of the body, and can stop the heart. If cardio-pulmonary resuscitation (CPR) is applied right away, the person can usually be revived.

Lightning can enter your body through your feet after striking the ground hundreds of feet away.

Some people seem to attract lightning. Every now and then you may read about a person who has been struck by lightning several times. There was even such a man who had been blind, and a lightning strike restored his sight (he claimed).

Lightning detection:

1. Some weather enthusiasts and hobbyists have purchased lightning detection sensors. Otherwise, you can detect lightning by observing increasing amounts of static on AM radio (NOT on FM).

2. Lightning detection systems use a device to detect cloud-to-ground (called CG) lightning strikes. It detects radio waves produced by lightning. These waves are called sferics (derived from the word, "atmospherics"). A network of these devices across the United States and Canada allows scientists to study lightning activity from a storm as it travels. We have learned from this that the most intense part, including the most intense rainfall, from a thunderstorm occurs where the greatest frequency and concentration of CG lightning strikes occurs. The computer monitor displays from lightning detection systems typically show colored dots for each CG strike. The fiercest strikes are the 5% of CGs that are positively charged (about 95% are negatively charged).

Some beneficial aspects of lightning:

1. Lightning helps to balance the electrical charges of the atmosphere with those of the earth. Recall that before the lightning strike, the bottom of the cloud is usually negatively charged and the ground is positively charged. A lightning bolt tends to return electrons from the cloud to the ground, thus making both the bottom of the cloud and the ground neutral in relation to each other.
2. Lightning combines dust, smoke and other solid particles in the air into larger particulate matter that fall or are washed to the ground by the falling rain. Have you ever noticed how clear the air is after a healthy thunderstorm? Without rain and lightning, the lower atmosphere would become so polluted that life would be threatened.
3. Lightning is the world's largest manufacturer of natural fertilizer. It produces some 100 million tons of nitrogen compounds annually! This is done by the lightning causing nitrogen and oxygen in the air to combine to form nitrates. Nitrates are solids that dissolve rapidly in rainwater, which causes them to fall to the ground. They penetrate the top layer of the soil and are absorbed by plants. Plants use the nitrates to produce plant protein, without which they would die.

SEVERE THUNDERSTORM:

A severe thunderstorm is a thunderstorm producing either or both of the following:
•wind gusts of at least 50 knots (58 miles per hour);
•hailstones of 3/4 inch diameter or larger.

A thunderstorm producing a tornado is also obviously classified as a severe thunderstorm because the tornado's winds would almost always be 58 mph or greater.

In the United States, the National Weather Service issues a severe thunderstorm or tornado watch when conditions are favorable for the development of severe thunderstorms or tornadoes, respectively, and issues a severe thunderstorm or tornado warning when a severe thunderstorm or tornado, respectively, is developing, moving in or underway.

Figure 31-11. A squall-line (line of thunderstorms) as viewed from above, looking northeast to southwest. (source: FAA)

Downwind from mountains:

Figure 31-12. The downdraft and outflow from a high-level-based thunderstorm may reach the lower elevations even though the precipitation evaporates before reaching the ground. The air may be quite gusty coming through narrow canyons. (source: DOA)

MESOSCALE CONVECTIVE SYSTEMS (MCSes):

When thunderstorms merge into clusters and then these clusters merge into a thunderstorm complex, we have a mesoscale convective system or MCS. These areas of heavy rain and thunderstorms are important because they average about the size of the state of Iowa and can persist for 12 hours or longer. When they are passing over an area, it typically takes several hours, which means that the significant rainfall continues for hours. Thus, MCSes are responsible for most of the flash flood episodes. In the United States, for example, most MCSes occur between the Rocky Mountains and the Appalachian Mountains. These blobs of organized convection plus the routine convection account for about one-half of the annual rainfall in this region, the nation's breadbasket.

MCSes form in areas of concentrated warmth and moisture. (For a detailed discussion on this topic, you are referred to the book, "WEATHER MAPS - How to Read and Interpret all the Basic Weather Charts", available from Chaston Scientific, Inc. at P.O. Box 758 in Kearney, MO 64060. Its cost is $29. Specifically, the chapter on "Theta-E" details how mesoscale convective systems form, propagate and die.) When there also exists a plume of moisture in mid- and upper-levels of the troposphere, coming out of the tropics, then the MCS is being constantly fed additional moisture to turn into precipitation. This tropical moisture plume is known as a TROPICAL CONNECTION.

Thus, if the conditions for thunderstorms exist in an area of concentrated heat and moisture, the thunderstorms that form there are prone to merge and eventually become a mesoscale convective system. Moreover, if a tropical connection exists, feeding into the developing MCS, then the MCS will become an even greater rainfall producer and a greater flash flood threat.

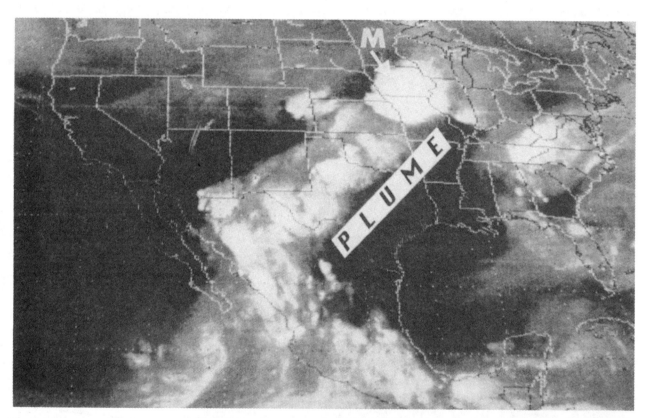

Figure 31-13. A mesoscale convective system, labelled M, forming in a plume of tropical moisture, as observed on a visible image from a weather satellite. (source: NOAA)

MCSes are typically oval-shaped. Sometimes, with weak winds aloft, an MCS will become more circular, in which case it is called an MCC: a mesoscale convective complex. Because they move more slowly than the oval-shaped MCS, an MCC type of MCS is even more dangerous for being a flash flood producer.

DERECHO:

A derecho is a fast-moving thunderstorm or thunderstorm cluster, usually moving northwest-to-southeast, bringing damaging straight-line winds that can exceed 100 miles per hour (over 160 kilometers per hour). They form in areas that have exceedingly high dewpoints, along with the other necessary conditions for thunderstorm development.

Northern Wisconsin, for example, is battered on the average of once every few years by a derecho. Dewpoints need to be in the upper 70s to around 80 (Fahrenheit) for a favorable derecho environment. You might ask how could dewpoints get so high, even into the low 80s, in a location as far north as northern Wisconsin, far removed from the moisture-laden air that can come off the Gulf of Mexico? The answer is EVAPO-TRANSPIRATION, the evaporation and transpiration (plants giving off water directly to the atmosphere) that goes on in the densely forested region of northern Wisconsin. In the mid-latitudes, a mature oak, maple or pine tree will evapotranspirate from about 50 to 100 gallons of moisture into the lowest layer of the atmosphere on a sunny summer day. Consider how much moisture is being emitted therefore from a dense and large forest! Thus, dewpoints can from time to time pool as high as the low 80s. There is a tremendous amount of energy to be released by hot and exceedingly moist air during thunderstorms, and derechos develop. One such derecho carved a path up to a mile wide and over 100 miles long that passed over Rhinelander, Wisconsin, knocking pine trees over in one direction, carving out a quite noticeable path.
A derecho can have a path as wide as about 100 miles and as long as several hundred miles. Derechos have occurred in Indiana, Oklahoma, Texas and southern Canada, for example.

Incidentally, all else being equal, the first cumulus clouds of convection are typically visible over wooded areas first, because of the extra moisture that the trees supply to the lowest layer (called "[planetary] boundary layer) of the atmosphere.

NOCTURNAL HEAT BURSTS:

This strange weather phenomenon tends to occur in the Plains states, essentially between the Rocky Mountains and the Appalachian Mountains.

With the exception of some rolling hills and local low-elevation mountains such as the Ozarks in southern Missouri and northern Arkansas, this area is relatively flat. In the western portion, the land slopes upward as we approach the foothills of the Rocky Mountains.

Often, during the warmer half of the year, because of the flatness, what is called a "low-level jet" develops and lowers at night towards the surface. A low-level jet is a band of strong winds typically some 5000 feet above the surface. At night, the sun's effect of stirring the air up and mixing it is ended, and the "mixing layer", which is up to 2000 feet deep from the surface up, during the day, shrinks to being only a few hundred feet up. If a low-level jet is underway, then at night it will lower closer to the ground. The effect is to bring the stronger winds lower. If these winds are coming in from a southerly component, they will bring in warm, moist air which may include moisture evaporated into it from the Gulf of Mexico. The effect is to "destabilize" the area, which meteorologically means, in this case, the additional low-level heat and moisture primes the atmosphere for increased thunderstorm potential. How the atmosphere does this is explained later in the book. The "bottom line" is this: this destabilization process creates nighttime thunderstorms in the Plains states.

Thunderstorms develop in the afternoon and evening, but it is not unusual to have thunderstorms occasionally develop at night, especially in the Plains. What is unusual is the rare event that occurs in this nocturnal storms: a nocturnal heat burst.

Seemingly all of a sudden, in the midst of a raging thunderstorm with heavy rain, strong and gusty winds and possibly some hail, the precipitation stops and the temperature surges to well over 100 degrees. This is typically around 2 to 3 o'clock in the morning!

It may be 65 or 70 degrees during the rain, yet suddenly the temperature shoots up to 105 or 110 or even higher, stays there for perhaps 10 minutes, and then gradually falls back to where it should be.

the worst of these nocturnal heat bursts, the temperature has soared to over 130°F, scorching crops and threatening the lives of livestock.

(For a rather interesting documentation of events such as nocturnal heat bursts and ball lightning, you are referred to the book, "Terror From the Skies!", available from Chaston Scientific, Inc.; its cost is $29.)

The National Weather Service is responsible for issuing watches and warnings for severe weather, including for short-fused situations such as severe thunderstorms, tornadoes and flash floods.

DEMONSTRATION: USING A VAN DE GRAAFF GENERATOR TO PRODUCE LIGHTNING

This demonstration should be performed by a teacher or other person who is experienced in using a Van de Graaff generator.

Material/equipment needed:
●Van de Graaff generator
●brass ball mounted in a metal rod (This comes from a ball and ring set that is used to test for thermal expansion. You do not need the ring.) Tape the brass ball and metal rod with masking, fiber or duct tape securely to a three-foot wooden dowel or other piece of wood such as a wooden yard stick.
●a pith ball electroscope
●a fluorescent bulb which has been taped to another three-foot wooden dowel or other piece of wood

Procedure:

1. Place the pith ball electroscope on a wooden stool or wooden chair within two feet of the Van de Graaff generator, making sure that it is at about the same level as is the dome.

2. Cover the dome of the generator with the woolen cloth.

3. To prevent a slight shock, which is quite uncomfortable, use the wooden dowel when you turn the Van de Graaff generator on and off.

4. Turn the generator on, leaving it on until you turn it off in step 9.

5. What happens to the woolen piece of cloth and the pith ball electroscope? What causes this to happen? Recall that an electrical field is an area in space in which an electrical force has an effect on an object. Would you say that the woolen piece of cloth and the pith ball electroscope are in the electrical field produced by the Van de Graaff generator?

6. Use the wooden dowel to dim or turn off any overhead lights so that you can better observe what happens next.

7. Slowly approach the dome of the generator with the brass ball and rod, which you are holding with the wooden dowel, until you observe an electrical discharge in the form of a spark. The electric spark is analogous to lightning, and the crackling sound to thunder since it is caused by the rapid expansion of air as it is heated by the electric spark.

8. Approach the generator with the fluorescent bulb which you are holding by the wooden dowel. What happens to the bulb once it is within the generator's electrical field?

9. Use the wooden dowel to turn off the generator.

10. Get rid of all the charge so that no one will get a slight electrical charge, by placing the dome of the Van de Graaff generator on a metal pipe or faucet. You will hear a crackling sound as it is discharging.

Figure 32-1. The tornado is a rapidly rotating vortex of air, having a diameter from a few hundred feet to sometimes over a mile; the air within the tornado is also rising into the cumulonimbus cloud from which the tornado forms. (source: NOAA)

Although the tornado is one of the smallest storms in Nature, it is the most violent. Winds vary from about 50 to 60 mph in the weakest "twisters" to over 300 mph in the most extreme.

They have occurred on every continent except Antarctica. The United States experiences more tornadoes than any other country, with about 1000 tornadoes reported annually. Every state of the U.S. has reported tornadoes. They occur in China and India with some frequency also, and on occasion have occurred in Europe.

Characteristics of tornadoes:

Most tornadoes come from a type of thunderstorm known as the supercell. Whereas a typical or routine thunderstorm cell has a life cycle of from 20 to 60 minutes , a supercell may persist for 3 hours or more. Most tornadoes typically emerge from the southwest part of the storm from wall clouds that are attached to a rain-free area called the rain-free base, which often follows large hail (one-inch or larger in diameter), which, in turn, follows heavy rain. This sequence of events occurs as the one looks to the southwest (first comes the rain, then the large hail, then the tornado).

PAGE 235

When the speed of the wind increases with height, and when the wind direction profile is favorable, tornadoes are possible. A favorable wind direction profile is as follows. Suppose the surface wind is from the south, but about 1000 feet off the ground the wind is from the south-southwest, and then another 1000 feet higher the wind is from the southwest, and 1000 feet above that the wind is from the west-southwest. You can see that the wind is veering with height in the lowest part of the atmosphere. Since air is rising into the thunderstorm and is accelerating upward (an updraft), this veering wind profile also causes the air to begin rotating or swirling as it rises. The result is sometimes a mesocyclone, or a small counterclockwise rotation within the thunderstorm. (On rare occasion, the rotation can be the opposite, clockwise.) This is the incipient stage of a potential tornado.

Typically, what follows is a sudden lowering of part of the base of the cloud, which is called a wall cloud, and if this wall cloud is rotating (the mesocyclone), then the tornado formation is trying to get underway. Out of the wall cloud descends the tornado.

Sometimes more than one funnel protrudes from the thunderstorm. If a funnel stays aloft (not making contact with the ground), it is termed a funnel cloud.

Tornadic thunderstorms often produce a cloudform in another part of the storm, called mammato-cumulus (also referred to as cumulonimbus mammatus). These are pouches or cloud sections that look like huge grapes hanging from the sky. The bases of these clouds are fairly high and they do not produce tornadoes; however, they indicate that severe turbulence with powerful updrafts and downdrafts are occurring with this thunderstorm.

The word TORNADO comes from the Spanish "tornar", which means "to turn" and from the Spanish "tronada", which means "thunderstorm". A tornado is also called a twister. The appearance of the tornado ranges from slim and rope-like to elephant-trunk-like. The thinner, snake-like appearance occurs usually as the tornado is dying. In the United States, the largest tornadoes tend to occur between the Rocky Mountains and the Appalachians. For example, tornadoes in Denver are usually thinner than tornadoes in Kansas City. Tornadoes generate the best in the flatter plains areas.

Figure 32-2. A rotating wall cloud. When a part of the thunderstorm cloud base, typically in the southwest part of the storm, lowers, then that lowered cloud part is called a wall cloud. If the wall cloud starts to rotate, usually counterclockwise in the Northern Hemisphere, then a tornado may develop as an outgrowth of that rotation. (source: NOAA)

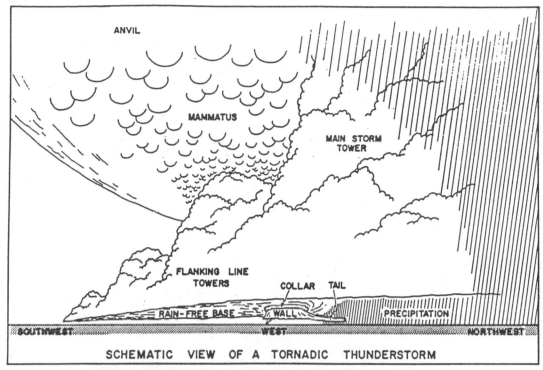

ANVIL

MAMMATUS

MAIN STORM
TOWER

FLANKING LINE
TOWERS

COLLAR TAIL

RAIN-FREE BASE   WALL   PRECIPITATION

SOUTHWEST   WEST   NORTHWEST

SCHEMATIC VIEW OF A TORNADIC THUNDERSTORM

Side view of a supercell storm. View is to the northwest.
Prominent features of the storm are indicated.

Figure 32-3. A depiction of what most tornado-producing thunderstorms look like. This shows how the tornadic thunderstorm would look if you were looking at it when located east of the storm, looking westward. The main updraft of warm air is entering the storm at the cloud base below the main storm tower. Strong winds aloft are blowing from the southwest to the northeast. Air in the upper portion of the updraft eventually becomes colder than the surrounding air. At this level, the cloud spreads out rapidly, forming an anvil. The term "wall" stands for wall cloud, "collar" is for collar cloud, which is a circular ring of cloud surrounding the upper portion of the wall cloud, and "tail" is for tail cloud, which is a low tail-shaped cloud extending outward from the northern quadrant of a wall cloud. "Flanking line towers " refers to a line of cumulus/towering cumulus clouds connected to and extending outward from the most active portion of the parent cumulonimbus. (source: NWS)

Tornadoes do fill in with cloud matter, but also take on the color of the debris they are carrying. For example, when a tornado passes over a field of plowed topsoil, it will lift some of the topsoil to appear black. A tornado in Nebraska passed over heavy snow cover and became a white tornado, filled with snow, which is unusual.

Sometimes the tornado vortex is initially invisible, but the observer will recognize that a tornado is occurring because debris will begin swirling around at the tornado's base and will eventually be lifted into the funnel, making the funnel visible. Moreover, the funnel soon fills will cloud material, making it visible.

Sometimes the tornado cannot be seen because of poor visibility due to flying debris, heavy rain and low clouds. At night, illumination by lightning should show the vortex. Although there is typically no precipitation occurring where the tornado is located, some tornadoes in the southeastern United States are enshrouded in heavy rain, making their visible detection difficult, especially at night.

Hurricanes making landfall can also spawn tornadoes. When a hurricane moves inland, the frictional action of the land surfaces, plus the hurricane losing contact with its chief source of energy, the warm moist oceanic air, weaken the wind at the surface. But the wind a little higher, at about 2000 to 4000 feet off the ground, remains at full fury for a hours longer, before it is eventually lowered. So what is happening is that the wind shear dramatically increases in the first few thousand feet, creating a favorable environment in the warm,moist unstable air, for tornadoes. Hurricane tornadoes tend to occur in bunches and are usually smaller and shorter-lived than supercell thunderstorm tornadoes.

Even if you cannot see the tornado, you should be able to hear it. The strongest tornadoes, with their furious wind speeds, sound somewhat like an approaching freight train. Their wind speeds range from about 40 to 50 mph (about 65 to 80 km/hr) in the weakest or minimal tornadoes, to over 300 mph (over 480 km/hr) in the most powerful. Tornado intensity is rated on a Tornado Force Scale developed by Ted Fujita, wherein F0 (F-zero) is a minimal tornado, F1 is stronger, etc., until F5 for is reached for the strongest tornadoes. Most tornadoes are F0s through F3s.

Tornadoes range from a few hundred feet diameter to over one-half mile. Sometimes tornadoes over a mile in diameter occur. The biggest tornadoes typically last the longest. Tornadoes may last for from a few minutes to over a half hour. Supertornadoes can persist for up to several hours. Most tornadoes move at about 30 to 45 miles per hour (about 48 to 72 kilometers per hour), although some have been observed to remain stationary for a while, and some have been clocked to move at around 70 mph.

Figure 32-4. Most tornadoes last from several minutes to about a half-hour. Huge tornadoes can persist for over a hour. They typically move at from 20 to over 50 mph with winds inside the funnel of from around 50 mph to as extreme as over 300 mph! Their widths range from a few hundred feet to sometimes over a mile. The monster ones can pick up people and automobiles and fling them through the air. (source: NOAA)

Since the winds are so powerful in such a small storm, and since wind is caused by air blowing from high pressure to low pressure, we can therefore estimate what the pressure gradient must be from the outside edge of a tornado to its center. If we know the radius of the tornado, we can estimate the central pressure. In the F2 through F5 tornadoes, the air pressure in most of them is probably in the range of 15" to 22" on the barometer. Recall that average sea-level pressure is near 30", and the height of half the atmosphere would be where the barometer reads 15", the 500 millibar level, which is about 18,000 feet up. Thus, in the bigger twisters, the pressure is what you would expect to find at from about the 730 millibar level to about the 500 millibar level.

Figure 32-5. **The life-cycle of a typical tornado.** (source: Environment Canada)

0   0.5   1.0 km

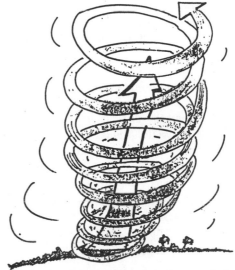

Figure 32-6. **The air is swirling as well as rising around the center of the tornado.** Tornado-genesis requires the right proportion of buoyancy of the local environment and wind shear, especially shear in wind direction. Here is the explanation of these conditions. Buoyancy of the local environment means that air parcels are warmer than the environment, so they become buoyant and rise. The wind shear is the change of wind direction or speed with height. For tornadoes, we are looking at the wind shear in the first few thousand feet from the ground up. Let us say, e.g., that the wind at the surface is from the south at 15 mph, and at 1000 feet up the wind is south-southwest at 20 mph, and at 2000 feet up it is southwest at 25 mph, and at 4000 feet up it is west-southwest at 35 mph. You can see that rising air parcels, called updrafts, would be twisting as they rise. If they accelerate, they could form a localized rotation in the thunderstorm cloud, leading to tornado development. If the air is too buoyant, then whole layers of air rise, which is too difficult for the local wind shear to start rotating to form a tornado. Thus, the ratio of buoyancy to shear must lie within a specific range to permit the development of tornadoes. (source: NOAA)

<u>Destructive agents</u>:

A major tornado destroys a house by the combined action of intense winds and suddenly much lower pressure. By relating the intense wind speed to the size of the funnel, we can estimate the pressure-gradient force in the tornado. This force implies that the barometric reading inside a major tornado is under 20 inches, perhaps in extreme cases under 15". This is typical of air pressures found at some 10,000 to 20,000 feet high. Such drastic pressure changes that are almost instantaneous can cause enclosed structures to explode as the inside air pushes outward. The extremely low pressure is caused by the rapid outflow of air from the top of the storm, and is intensified by the failure of the incoming air to make up this loss.

When a tornado passes over a home, the roof usually comes off first and then the destructive winds continue to do more damage. The reason the roof usually comes off initially is because most homes have roofs that overlap the sides of the house, and since the air in a tornado is not only swirling around but is also rising, this rising air lifts the roof off. Thus, a house's roof becomes like an airplane wing. Having many heavy-duty leather or metal straps to fasten the roof to the house would be helpful in tornado-prone areas; this could be done during the initial home construction so that these <u>tornado fasteners</u> are inserted on the inside of the house and would be hidden by the halls and ceilings. These strips are also called <u>hurricane strips</u> since they serve a similar function in areas prone to being struck by hurricanes.

As the winds of the tornado pick up debris and fling it through the air at high speeds, the debris become missiles; many of the tornado deaths result from fast-moving debris striking people. A classic example of the effect of tornado winds is that of a straw driven into a telephone pole.

To help prevent flying objects from crashing through glass windows, some public and private buildings in tornado-prone areas use laminated glass, which is similar to the glass used in automobile windshields. This type of glass is comprised of at least two pieces of glass with a tough plastic liner placed between them. The result upon impact is that the glass typically will not shatter when it breaks.

When a meteorologist investigates storm damage from a suspected tornado, how the damage is distributed is a key to identifying whether the storm that produced the damage was a tornado. Tornado damage is typically flung around in a circular/oval fashion, whereas straight-line wind damage is typically blown over in one direction.

How far up into the cumulonimbus thunderstorm cloud does a tornado extend? Based on research from Doppler weather radars, which show the wind profile in the clouds, the answer is that the vertical extent of the tornado in the thunderstorm varies. Small tornadoes may extend upward for thousands of feet, and the strongest and largest tornadoes may extend upward past the middle of the thunderstorm. For example, if a particular thunderstorm has clouds that grow to 50,000 feet above the ground, then the largest of tornadoes may extend from the ground to some 35,000 feet up.

Places and times of occurrence:

Because of the geography and climate of the United States east of the Rocky Mountains, this region is the most tornado-prone in the world. Tornadoes have occurred in all 50 of the United States, but the most vulnerable regions are the area between the Rocky Mountains and the Appalachian Mountains, and the Florida peninsula. Oklahoma is at the strongest risk for having tornadoes, especially the central part of that state. From the figure below, you can see that the region extending from northern Texas through Oklahoma into Kansas and Nebraska is the main "TORNADO ALLEY". The peak tornado season starts early in the year in the southeastern states and gradually moves northward during the spring, peaking in May in the central plains, and then moves northward into the northern plains during the summer when it peaks there. Most tornadoes occur during the afternoon and evening.

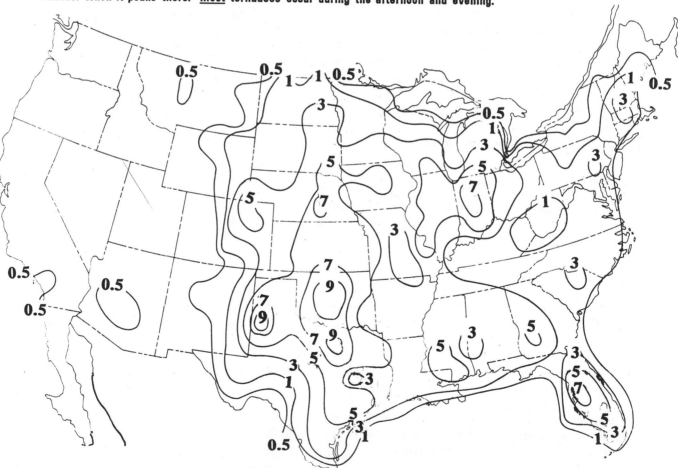

Figure 32-7. The number of tornadoes annually per area of 100 miles long by 100 miles wide. Note that the highest figures are in north Texas, central Oklahoma, south-central Kansas, eastern Nebraska, central Indiana and the Florida peninsula. (source: NOAA)

Figure 32-8. The Tornado Force Scale, developed by T. Fujita.

F0	Gale Tornado	weak	40-72 mph
F1	Moderate Tornado	weak	73–112 mph
F2	Significant Tornado	strong	113–157 mph
F3	Severe Tornado	strong	158–206 mph
F4	Devastating Tornado	violent	207–260 mph
F5	Incredible Tornado	violent	261–318 mph

Estimate of F-scale Wind from Structure Type and Damage Category

Structure Types		DAMAGE CATEGORIES						
		No Damage	Minor Damage	Roofing Blown off	Whole Roof Blown off	Some Walls Standing	Flattened to Ground	Blown off Foundation
Outbuilding Mobile Home	▫	F 0	F 0	F 0	F 1	F 1	F 1	F 2+
Weak Frame House	▨	F 0	F 0	F 1	F 1	F 2	F 2	F 3+
Strong Frame House	▯	F 0	F 0	F 1	F 2	F 3	F 4	F 5+
Brick Building	▨	F 0	F 1	F 2	F 3	F 4	F 5+	F 5++
Concrete Building	▬	F 1	F 2	F 3	F 4	F 5+	F 5++	F 5+++

MINIMUM WINDSPEEDS: F 0(40mph)   F 1(73)   F 2(113)   F 3(158)   F 4(207)   F5(261mph)

Waterspouts:

Figure 32-9. A waterspout.
Tornadoes can move across rivers, ponds and small lakes. They are still tornadoes. Sometimes, funnels form over large lakes or over the ocean and look like thin tornadoes but are much weaker than most tornadoes (they would be an F0 or F1 on the Tornado Force Scale); such funnels are called waterspouts. When they do move onshore, they may cause minimal damage. (source: NOAA)

Cold-air funnels:

During cool weather in northern states, such as around Lake Ontario in the autumn, funnels may form which look like thin tornadoes. These are cold air funnels and are not particularly dangerous.   PAGE 241

Although tornado season is primarily spring and early summer, tornadoes do occur in the winter, primarily in the southeastern United States. These winter tornadoes, unlike the typical tornado, can be enshrouded in rain, yet still be major tornadoes.

Watches and warnings:

When the atmospheric conditions are prime for tornado development, or are expected to become ideal, then the National Weather Service issues a <u>tornado watch</u>. When a tornado is developing, or when imminent development is suspected, or when a tornado is already in progress, then the National Weather Service office that has forecast and warning responsibility for that area issues a <u>tornado warning</u>.

Local radio and television broadcast severe weather warnings, as does the <u>weather radio</u>. Since the warnings are issued by the National Weather Service, they will be immediately disseminated on the weather radio. Weather radios have a tone alert feature, so that as the warning goes out, even if it is the middle of the night, a loud tone at the 1050 Hertz frequency will alert you to the potential danger. Many stores that sell electronics also market weather radios.

Shelter from a tornado:

If caught in an open area outdoors, try to determine which way the tornado is moving. In the Northern Hemisphere, tornadoes move <u>most often</u> towards the northeast. Run at right angles to its path. If the tornado is going to pass over or very near you, or when its debris is being hurled your way, jump into a ditch. If on a highway, get under the girders of an overpass. A strong tornado can pick up and hurl an automobile with people inside through the air.

In a building, go the basement and take shelter under a heavy piece of furniture. If there is no basement, get away from windows and move to the interior of the house. A door opening of a closet is also recommended. Cover your head first and try to cover your entire body to protect it from flying missiles and other debris. If time permits, you can pull a mattress over yourself.

Trained weather spotters:

In the United States, the National Weather Service has the responsibility for issuing tornado watches and tornado warnings. A <u>tornado watch</u> means that the weather conditions are favorable for tornado development; a <u>tornado warning</u> means a tornado is developing or is already underway. Persons in the path of the tornado must take immediate shelter to save themselves from injury or death. As part of its mission, the National Weather Service trains volunteers who watch the skies for tornado development. These persons are called **weather spotters (Figure 32-10, at right)**. Their reports along with data from the velocity display of

Doppler weather radar are responsible for information that leads to tornado warnings that routinely save large numbers of lives. Local law enforcement personnel and others are also often trained in weather spotting for severe weather. (source: NOAA)

The following safety and preparedness information are from the National Weather Service:

Spotter Aids

ESTIMATING HAIL SIZE:
pea size ¼ inch; marble size ½ inch; dime size ¾ inch; quarter size **1 inch**; golfball size **1.75 inch**; baseball size **2.75 inch.**

ESTIMATING WIND SPEEDS (miles per hour)

25-31 . . . . . Large branches in motion; whistling heard in telephone wires

32-38 . . . . . Whole trees in motion; inconvenience felt walking against wind

39-54 . . . . . Twigs break off trees; wind generally impedes

55-72 . . . . . Damage to chimneys and TV antenna; pushes over shallow rooted trees

73-112 . . . . Peels surface off roofs; windows broken; light trailer houses pushed or overturned; moving automobiles pushed off roads

113-157 . . . Roofs torn off houses; weak buildings and trailer houses destroyed; large trees snapped and uprooted

158 & up . . Severe damage; cars lifted off ground

Follow these basic steps to develop a family disaster plan...

I. **Gather information about hazards.** Contact your local National Weather Service office, emergency management or civil defense office, and American Red Cross chapter. Find out what type of disasters could occur and how you should respond. Learn your community's warning signals and evacuation plans.

II. **Meet with your family to create a plan.** Discuss the information you have gathered. Pick two places to meet: a spot outside your home for an emergency, such as fire, and a place away from your neighborhood in case you can't return home. Choose an out-of-state friend as your "family check-in contact" for everyone to call if the family gets separated. Discuss what you would do if advised to evacuate.

III. **Implement your plan.** (1) Post emergency telephone numbers by phones; (2) Install safety features in your house, such as smoke detectors and fire extinguishers; (3) Inspect your home for potential hazards (such as items that can move, fall, break, or catch fire) and correct them; (4) Have your family learn basic safety measures, such as CPR and first aid; how to use a fire extinguisher; and how and when to turn off water, gas, and electricity in your home; (5) Teach children how and when to call 911 or your local Emergency Medical Services number; (6) Keep enough supplies in your home to meet your needs for at least three days. Assemble a disaster supplies kit with items you may need in case of an evacuation. Store these supplies in sturdy, easy-to-carry containers, such as backpacks or duffle bags. Keep important family documents in a waterproof container. Keep a smaller disaster supplies kit in the trunk of your car.

> **A DISASTER SUPPLIES KIT SHOULD INCLUDE:**
> A 3-day supply of water (one gallon per person per day) and food that won't spoil • one change of clothing and footwear per person • one blanket or sleeping bag per person • a first-aid kit, including prescription medicines • emergency tools, including a battery-powered NOAA Weather Radio and a portable radio, flashlight, and plenty of extra batteries • an extra set of car keys and a credit card or cash • special items for infant, elderly, or disabled family members.

IV. **Practice and maintain your plan.** Ask questions to make sure your family remembers meeting places, phone numbers, and safety rules. Conduct drills. Test your smoke detectors monthly and change the batteries at least once a year. Test and recharge your fire extinguisher(s) according to manufacturer's instructions. Replace stored water and food every six months.

Before the Storm:

- Develop a plan for you and your family for home, work, school, and when outdoors.
- Have frequent drills.
- Know the county/parish in which you live, and keep a highway map nearby to follow storm movement from weather bulletins.

- Have a NOAA Weather Radio with a warning alarm tone and battery back-up to receive warnings.
- Listen to radio and television for information.
- If planning a trip outdoors, listen to the latest forecasts and take necessary action if threatening weather is possible.

Who's Most At Risk?

- People in automobiles
- The elderly, very young, and the physically or mentally impaired

- People in mobile homes
- People who may not understand the warning due to a language barrier

EVERY School Should Have A Plan!

- Develop a severe weather action plan and have frequent drills,
- Each school should be inspected and tornado shelter areas designated by a registered engineer or architect. Basements offer the best protection. Schools without basements should use interior rooms and hallways on the lowest floor and away from windows.
- Those responsible for activating the plan should monitor weather information from NOAA Weather Radio and local radio/television.
- If the school's alarm system relies on electricity, have a compressed air horn or megaphone to activate the alarm in case of power failure.
- Make special provisions for disabled students and those in portable classrooms.
- Make sure someone knows how to turn off electricity and gas in the event the school is damaged.
- Keep children at school beyond regular hours if threatening weather is expected. Children are safer at school than in a bus or car. Students should not be sent home early if severe weather is approaching.
- Lunches or assemblies in large rooms should be delayed if severe weather is anticipated. Gymnasiums, cafeterias, and auditoriums offer no protection from tornado-strength winds.
- Move students quickly into interior rooms or hallways on the lowest floor. Have them assume the tornado protection position (shown at right).

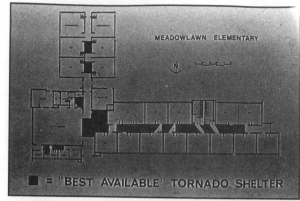

MEADOWLAWN ELEMENTARY

■ = "BEST AVAILABLE" TORNADO SHELTER

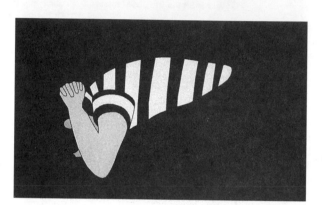

Occasionally, tornadoes develop so rapidly that advance warning is not possible. Remain alert for signs of an approaching tornado. Flying debris from tornadoes causes most deaths and injuries.

If a Warning is issued or if threatening weather approaches:

- In a home or building, move to a pre-designated shelter, such as a basement.
- If an underground shelter is not available, move to an interior room or hallway on the lowest floor and get under a sturdy piece of furniture.
- Stay away from windows.
- Get out of automobiles.
- Do not try to outrun a tornado in your car; instead, leave it immediately.
- If caught outside or in a vehicle, lie flat in a nearby ditch or depression.
- Mobile homes, even if tied down, offer little protection from tornadoes and should be abandoned.

Some tornado extremes: The widest tornadoes are over a mile in diameter. The fastest moving have been known to race forward at up to about 70 mph (near 115 km/hr), and the longest lasting tornadoes have stayed on the ground for over 100 miles, even for more than 200 miles, but this is quite rare. On April 3rd-4th, 1974, a major tornado outbreak resulted in about 150 tornadoes touching down in eleven U.S. states and in Ontario Province, Canada. And in June 1995 at Lazbuddie, Texas, SIX tornadoes were on the ground at the same time from the same thunderstorm!

DEMONSTRATION: MAKING A TORNADO MODEL

Introduction:

We will attempt to make a model that will imitate some of the conditions necessary to form a tornado. We will need an unstable air mass; that is, we need one in which the air is very warm at the bottom and relatively cool at top. This is achieved by heating the air from below with the resulting convection increased by having the heated air rise through a chimney. The rising air must have a rotating motion. This is done by allowing the cool air that enters the model to force the hot air up the chimney. Steam is condensed into water droplets to make the rotating warm air visible as a cloud-funnel does in nature.

Materials needed:

(for non-U.S. readers, use 1 inch = 2.54 centimeters, or 1 cm = 0.394")
4 sheets of masonite, 7½" x 8"
1 sheet of masonite, 8" x 8"
1 metal baking pan, 8" x 8" x 2"
2 sheets of clear plastic, 6" x 6½"
1 stove pipe, 30" to 36" long, with a 3" diameter
4 pieces of stiff wire, each 2½" long (you can use wire from opened up paper clips)
4 strips of wood (molding), each about ¾" x ¾" x 6"
flat black paint
waterproof glue
short screws
masking tape
a light source, such as a slide projector
a heat source, such as a stove or hot plate

Procedure for constructing the model:

1. Cut out a square of about 6" x 6½" from two pieces of 7½" x 8" sheets of masonite. Leave the other two pieces alone for now. These will make up the sides of the box, which will fit into the baking pan later on. See the sketches at right.

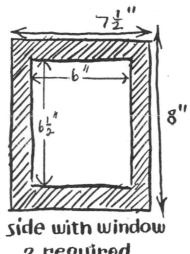

side with window
2 required

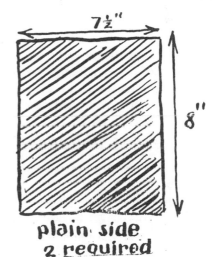

plain side
2 required

2. Carve a circle with a diameter of 2¾" out of the center of the fifth sheet of masonite, which is 8" x 8", and will be the top of the box. See the diagram at right.

3. Screw four strips of wood molding of about ¾" x ¾" x 6" to the underside of the top sheet. This is where the sides of the box will be attached to the top.

4. Paint the surfaces that will be the inside of the box with flat black paint.
(continued on next page)

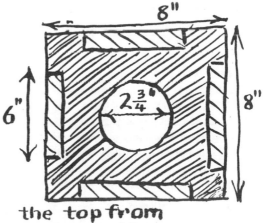

the top from
underneath

5. When the surfaces are dry, fasten the sides of the box with small screws to the top piece so that the two windows are next to each other and there is a half-inch slot on the right-hand side of each of the four sides as shown in figure 32-11 which appears at the end of this demonstration instructions.

6. About (3/8)" above the bottom edge of each side, punch or drill a small hole about 1" from the left end and another hole about (3/8)" from the right end. See the diagram after step 7.

7. Cut four pieces of stiff wire, each about 2½" long, from the opened paper clips or other source, and pull them through the holes across each corner. See the diagram below.

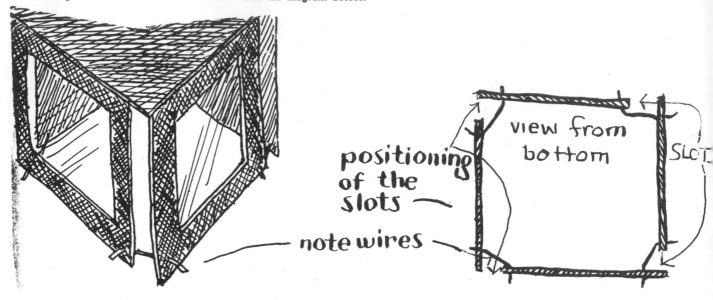

positioning of the slots —

— note wires —

view from bottom

SLOT

8. Set the box on the pan so that the rim of the pan is inside the box, and the wires rest on the pan's corners. Press the wire ends tightly against the box sides and pull them while bending, so that the box sits fast on the pan.

9. Glue or tape the plastic sheets over the cut-out area of the two window frames.

10. Fasten the stove pipe to the top of the box with masking tape. The diameter of the circle cut out of the top of the box is slightly smaller than the diameter of the stove pipe, in order to assure a tight fit.

11. Make sure that there are no air leaks between the chimney and the box, between the sides and top of the box, and between the box and pan. Air should enter the box only through the slots.

12. Feel free to make any improving modifications to this model.

<u>Using the model to simulate a tornado:</u>

1. Fill the pan through a slot with hot water to within one-half inch from the rim.

2. Place the entire model on a stove or hot plate.

3. The water should be heated until steam rises and condenses to tiny droplets of water above the pan. The water should approach the boiling point but not boil vigorously.

4. Shine a bright light source, such as from a slide projector, through one of the windows and observe through the other. Wait a few minutes. What do you see?

5. The motion of the water can be made better visible by blowing a small amount of chalk dust into the water.

6. The funnel cloud can be made more visible by blowing smoke into the box.

7. What would happen if the half-inch slots were on the left-hand side instead of being on the right-hand side?

This demonstration is a modification of the one described on pages 104 to 107 of the <u>Manual of Lecture Demonstrations, Laboratory Experiments, and Observational Equipment for Teaching Elementary Meteorology in Schools and Colleges</u> by Hans Neuberger and George Nicholas of The Pennsylvania State University. **Figure 32-11 at right shows this device.**

PAGE 246

DEMONSTRATION: A SIMPLER VERSION OF A TORNADO MODEL

Materials needed:
2 transparent two-liter soda containers from which the labels have been removed
3 inches of plastic tubing that will fit over the opening of each container. Usually, tubing with an internal diameter of 1 inch will fit over most containers; however, if you want to be sure, take your two empty containers to a local hardware store and select the tubing that best fits your containers.
blue food coloring

Procedure:
1. Place about 3 inches of plastic tubing over the opening of one of the 2-liter containers. The tubing should fit snugly. Now fill the container with water.
2. Invert the other, empty, container and attach its opening to the other end of the plastic tubing.
3. Invert the container that is filled with water over the empty container. What happens?
4. Now place the bottom container so that it is on top of the empty container, spinning it in a clockwise direction as you do so. What happens?
5. Repeat step 4 while spinning the top container in a counterclockwise direction.
6. If you want the water to appear more prominently in the containers, then add several drops of blue food coloring to the water.

DEMONSTRATION: CREATING A TORNADO IN A ROOM, FROM FLOOR TO CEILING

You can do this demonstration if you have access to a room that has an exhaust ceiling fan. You would need to also suspend about 3 room fans from the ceiling around the ceiling fan so that you can create rotation of the air as it rises. If you can do this, then get some "dry ice" (solid, i.e., frozen, carbon dioxide) and place it on a piece of cardboard directly under the ceiling fan. Never touch the extremely cold "dry ice" with your bare flesh!!! Start all the fans. Have long black sheets taped on the wall as a background so that you can see the funnel better when you look at it with the black background behind it. The dry ice will cause water vapor in the room to condense, forming a white cloud, which rotates as a vortex, stretching from the floor to the ceiling. It is quite impressive! You can even put miniature figurines of people, animals and cars into your tornado.

Downbursts and microbursts:

The early stages of a thunderstorm are characterized by updrafts. As precipitation develops and gravity causes it to fall through the cloud, this precipitation drags some air down with it, initiating <u>downdrafts</u>. Sometimes some downdrafts become concentrated and more intense, and are then called <u>downbursts</u>. Sometimes, a downburst can become even more concentrated (smaller in area) and even more intense than a downburst; this is called a <u>microburst</u>. According to the National Weather Service, if the path of destruction is under 2 1/2 miles, the downburst is a microburst.

Figure 32-12. The wind in a downburst or microburst. The plunging air hits the ground and spreads out. Where the air is rising on the edges of the downburst or microburst, it can lift the roof off a house similarly to how a tornado with its rising air does. Many people think that when they have experienced a powerful downburst or microburst, that it was a tornado. **Most damage from downbursts and microbursts is in one direction...items such as trees are blown over in one direction as the burst progresses. Tornado damage is more strewn about, usually more circularly or ovally.**

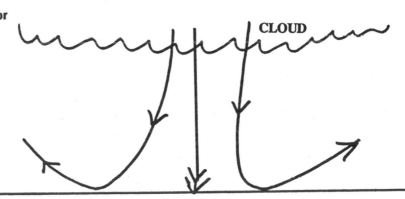

CLOUD

In regions that also have from time to time thunderstorms whose cloud bases are fairly high (say 10,000 to 14,000 feet above the surface), such as western Kansas, eastern Colorado and the U.S. desert southwest, the precipitation from the clouds often falls into drier air below and would take a while to moisten that layer. Thus, it is evaporating since the falling moisture-laden air warms and dries as it descends. Precipitation that evaporates before reaching the ground is known as virga. When it is coming from a thunderstorm, it may indicate a downburst or microburst with it. Just as unstable air keeps rising and accelerating (speeding up) when buoyant, it will also accelerate as it sinks when falling into dry air below; even though these sinking air parcels are warming as they descend, if they remain cooler than the environment through which they are falling, they will fall faster and faster (keep accelerating). Thus, when you see virga from a high-based thunderstorm and you find yourself under this virga, beware of the potential of being blasted by a downburst or microburst, whose winds can readily exceed 50 mph and can exceed 100 miles per hour!

Dust devils (sometimes also called whirlwinds and dust whirls):

Dust devils are swirls or vortices of air that look like little tornadoes, but whose winds are typically from 35 to 60 miles per hour, rarely somewhat higher. They are caused by very localized intense heating of the surface, so they occur during the greatest heat of the daytime. If you drive in Nevada from Las Vegas to Reno on a sunny and very hot summer day, you often see dust devils in the desert. If you run into one, you will be sandblasted by winds of about 50 miles per hour or somewhat more. They can also form on a sunny cool day when intense local heating of the surface creates an unstable column of air and creates dust devils that can rotate either counterclockwise or clockwise, filling with dust, leaves and small pieces of debris such as paper.

It is unusual for this type of whirlwind to cause serious trouble, although some cases have been investigated and documented that were more serious. Consider, for example, these cases from New England, which were investigated by Robert E. Lautzenheiser who was the State Climatologist in Massachusetts at that time.

In Dudley, Mass., a 3-year old child was picked up and tossed about ten feet, giving her a cut and some bruises.

In Ipswich, Mass., a 9-year-old girl and her bicycle were picked up by an unusually strong dust devil, and were flung about 40 feet across the road. The girl's shoes were carried about 100 feet. She, too, was cut and bruised, but not seriously. She described the sound as "awful, like the roar of a lion".

Near Northboro, Mass., eight turkey feeders, some weighing about 300 pounds, were toppled, and their covers, which were 3 x 10 feet, were sent spinning through the air. The dust devil also lifted a hood from a truck, pushed a calf into a fence and broke a large tree branch before disappearing. A witness described the sound as that of a baritone siren of a freight train.

In Methuen, Mass., a dust devil damaged a roof of a home and picked up some lawn furniture.

In Belfast, Maine, a dust devil picked up a garage, spun it and carried it nearly 100 feet, demolishing it. The dust devil moved southeastward about one-half mile until it reached the bay. Then over water it picked up a column of spray to a height of 12 to 14 feet, looking like a little waterspout, and then continued about another half-mile before dissipating.

Thus, although dust devils are usually relatively harmless, there are rare events of their being stronger than usual.

The topic of dust devils is also covered in chapter 24 on local winds.

The Coriolis force due to the earth's rotating is negligible in such vortices, since the rotation is occurring over a very small area. The wind in a tornado, around the eye of a hurricane and in a dust devil is a balance between the pressure-gradient force and the centrifugal force; such wind is called a cyclostrophic wind.

Figure 33-1. A hurricane moving in on a coastal community. The devastating winds and flash flooding rains are accompanied by the surge of sea-water known as the "storm surge", upon which powerful waves occur.

A <u>hurricane</u> is a large storm that forms in the tropics and sometimes just outside the tropics, having sustained winds of at least 74 miles per hour (about 120 kilometers per hour). The general name for these storms is <u>tropical cyclone</u>. The name, "hurricane", is used in the Atlantic and eastern and central Pacific (coming from the Carib Indian word "huracan"), whereas in the western Pacific basin, the term used is typhoon is used. Around Australia the term used is "tropical cyclone", and in the Indian Ocean area the terms "cyclone' and "tropical cyclone" are used.

The hurricane is a normal aspect of the earth's climate. If we were able to destroy hurricanes before they made landfall, Nature would have to generate another means to transport the net build-up of tropical energy towards cooler latitudes. Thus, the function of the hurricane is to contribute to the moderating and regulating of the earth's climate. Because these storms are so significant, hurricanes are given names for historical reference.

Hurricanes can grow to be as large as several hundred miles across, but the winds get stronger as wo approach tho center of the storm. In the center itself, the wind is nearly calm.

The air pressure in and around the center is quite low; only the relatively tiny tornado can have lower central pressures. Pressures have fallen below 26.00" on the barometer, close to 850 millibars (hectoPascals) in the most powerful tropical cyclones. For example, in October 1979, Typhoon Tip in the western Pacific had a pressure of 25.69".

Around North America, most hurricanes occur between June 1st and November 30th, with the peak of the hurricane season being between August 15th and October 15th. September is the month with the most hurricanes. In the eastern Pacific, the season typically starts about a month earlier. In the western Pacific, typhoons can develop during any month. In the Southern Hemisphere, tropical cyclones are most likely from January through March.

The naming of tropical cyclones:
Human names were first given to hurricanes in 1953, and were female names. In 1979, all Atlantic basin storm names started alternating between male and female names. When a hurricane causes widespread major damage and/or loss of life, the name is retired for the near future, rather than being recycled several years later. At present, in the North Atlantic basin, the letters Q, U, X, Y and Z are not used due to the scarcity of names beginning with these letters.

Hurricane development:
Areas of thunderstorms in the tropics (and sometimes just outside the tropics) often organize into a complex of convection. This is a region of converging air, which rises through most of the tropopause. These blobs can form initially over land, such as over equatorial Africa, and move into the Atlantic Ocean, or they can form over the ocean. About one-fourth of all tropical storms form in the Intertropical Convergence Zone (ITCZ), which is an area of converging winds in the tropics.

During the hurricane season, there are about 100 seedlings that have the potential to become tropical storms. An average of 10 to 12 of them make it every year. When the highest sustained winds in the system reach 39 mph, the storm is then called a tropical storm. If the storm's highest sustained winds reach the threshold value of 74 mph, it is then termed a hurricane. Out of the 10 to 12 tropical storms, about 6 to 8 of them grow into hurricanes.

Most seedlings are called easterly waves since they initially typically move westward through the tropics. Such systems are initially called tropical depressions. Tropical depressions also form out of squall lines that move into the ocean from Africa, and from remnants of other weather systems that have some vertically rising air to them and have been lingering for several days (such as the remnants of an old cold front that made it into or near the tropics).

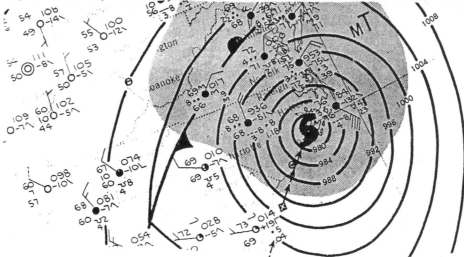

Figure 33-2. How a hurricane is depicted on a surface weather map. Notice how tightly wound-up the isobars, or lines of equal pressure, are, especially as we get closer to the center of the storm, which is called the eye. The shaded area is where rain is falling. (source: NWS)

Now, let us take a detailed look at the structure of a hurricane.

a. outer-hurricane squall-line

Figure 33-3 on the next page shows a radar composite of the many hurricanes, illustrating a composite average of many hurricanes. No one hurricane necessarily looks exactly like this, but most hurricanes appear like this composite, so that we can use it to conceptualize what the structure of most hurricanes looks like.

When a hurricane is moving towards you, the first weather element you will likely observe is the appearance of high-level clouds on the storm's periphery. These are the cirrus and cirrostratus clouds, which subsequently lower and thicken into the middle-level clouds and then low-level clouds as the storm approaches.

Then, there often exists an outer-hurricane squall line at the leading edge of the storm relative to how the storm is moving. This is a gusty line of showers and thunderstorms and may be a broken line rather than a solid one. The wave heights should also begin increasing. The outer-hurricane squall line is typically fairly straight. It does not have the spiral pattern which is to follow when the outer convective bands move in. The outer-hurricane squall line is as much as 50 or more miles out ahead of the first ragged rainfall areas of the hurricane's outer bands. The line is typically about 100 to 200 miles ahead of the eye, but in very large hurricanes, has been observed on radar to occur as much as some 500 miles ahead of the hurricane's eye. Bursts of showery rain and some gusty winds occur when the line passes through, but winds are not particularly strong.

The first significant wind and rain from the hurricane is next, as the first of the outer convective spiral bands moves in.

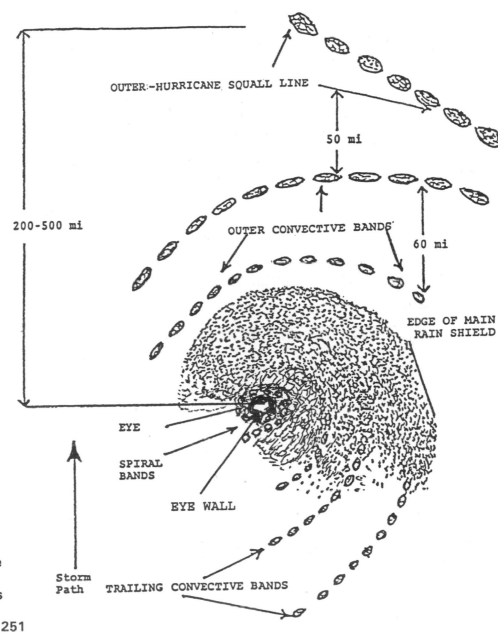

Figure 33-3. At right is a composite average of many hurricanes, based on many years of looking at radar images of hurricanes. The shaded-in sections are areas of rainfall. There may be more outer convective spiral bands than indicated in the diagram.   PAGE 251

b. outer convective bands

A hurricane typically has two to five outer convective bands, which are comprised of thunderstorm and shower cells. These bands are before the main rain shield moves in. Each successive convective band closer to the eye may contain progressively stronger wind gusts, especially if the hurricane contains more than two of these spiral bands. The term convective means relating to convection, that is, to cumuloform clouds that grow into showers and thunderstorms.
The outer convective bands are typically from 40 to 80 miles...65 to 130 kilometers...apart, and in large hurricanes the outermost one can be as much as some 300 miles...480 kilometers...out from the eye.

c. rain shield

After the passage of the last outer convective band, the next part of the hurricane to arrive is the solid or nearly-solid rain shield. The rain typically become progressively heavier and the wind steadily increases as the eye approaches. When the sustained winds reach 39 mph, the tropical-storm-force wind threshold has been reached. When the sustained winds reach 74 mph, the hurricane-force threshold has been reached. There are gusts that are higher than the sustained wind. When hurricane conditions are occurring, the gust can be 30 mph or somewhat higher than the sustained windspeed. For example, it is common for a category four hurricane with sustained winds 150 mph to be producing gusts of 175 to 180 mph or even somewhat more.

Because of the intense winds, the rainfall is difficult to measure. Since much of the precipitation occurring with the rain shield is blowing horizontally, some estimates indicate that perhaps a considerable amount of the rain may not be caught by every rain gauge in the affected area. Even so, radar and satellite estimates of rainfall in hurricanes easily justify five to ten inch rainfalls in even a minor hurricane, and considerably more in a powerful and large system. Exacerbating the excessive rainfall threat is a hurricane with a slow movement...one advancing at no more than ten miles per hour. Rainfalls of over fifteen inches from a hurricane are not unusual. In an extreme example, Hurricane Easy deluged Yankeetown, Florida on September 5th, 1950 with a torrential rainfall of about forty inches in a 24-hour period. Thus, most of the hurricane's rainfall occurs in the usually-solid rain shield.

The rain shield typically surrounds the eye in a well-developed hurricane, and as its outer edge moves in over your area, you observe that the leading edge is usually well-defined.

d. eye-wall

The region of intense convection that surrounds the hurricane's eye is called the eye-wall. It may be vertical or slanted around the eye. Within the eye-wall is where the most intense windspeeds are observed...the hurricane's maximum sustained winds. The eye-wall also usually produces the most intense rainfall. It often appears to contain straight-line segments along its inner-edge, forming a changing polygon as parts of the segments grow and others die, to be replaced by new ones. This is why hurricanes sometimes appear on radar to be wobbling rather than taking a smooth straight or curved path, i.e., the ever-changing line segments of the inner-edge of the eye-wall "relocates" the eye perhaps a mile or more to the left or right of its average path from hour to hour.

Within the rain shield and eye-wall, an observer can often find either spiral-shaped rain and wind patterns, if a hurricane is asymmetrical (a weak or minimal hurricane), or the observer can often find ringlike regions of very active convective heat release surrounding the eye, if a hurricane is symmetrical, which would be in a strong hurricane.

The spiral bands curve counterclockwisely in the Northern Hemisphere, and clockwisely in the Southern Hemisphere, inward toward the center of the storm and seemingly merge to form the eye-wall that surrounds the eye. These bands can be fairly wide, but become narrow near the eye. A more-steady stratiform rain occurs between convective spiral bands.

When the storm is moving inland, hurricane tornadoes, when they are spawned, seem to occur chiefly in these convective rings or bands that feed into the hurricane.

e. eye of the hurricane

The cyclonic circulation around the center of the hurricane is comprised of the air spiraling in towards the center but also rising. At the center of low pressure the eye does not appear until the winds reach about hurricane strength. A study by two researchers, L. Shapiro and H. Willoughby, found that in most cases, the eye of the hurricane first appears when the maximum sustained tangential wind speed exceeds about 78 mph.

The eye of a hurricane is typically quasi-circular or quasi-oval, tending to be more circular in the more intense storms. The winds are light and the skies are clear to partly cloudy, and typically free of rain. The sun shines in the daytime as the eye passes over. Sometimes entire flocks of birds that got trapped in the storm will fly with the eye for sanctuary.

Once you are in the rain shield as the hurricane moves in, the wind and rain gradually intensify as the eye approaches. You are experiencing the greatest fury of the wind when suddenly the eye-wall passes and the wind drops to nearly nothing. The sun usually comes out, or if the hurricane is passing over at night, you usually see the stars. Then, after the eye passes, the full fury of the winds strike suddenly as the eye-wall on the other side passes over. Subsequently, with the hurricane's center moving away, the wind and rain gradually subside, in opposite progression to what occurred as the eye approached. Although the air rises to condense and form the clouds and subsequent precipitation as it spirals within the hurricane around the eye, the air sinks and warms as it does so, inside the eye.

Figure 33-4. Here is a weather satellite picture of a major hurricane (Hurricane Gilbert) west-northwest of Jamaica. Notice the eye, cyclonic circulation, feeder bands and anticyclonic outflow aloft. (source: NHC)   PAGE 253

The average diameter of the eye of a hurricane is from 20 to 30 miles. However, eyes have been observed to be as large as 50 miles across, with the extreme example being about 100 miles. When Hurricane Donna was passing New York City on Sept. 12th, 1960 with 100+ mph winds, the western edge of the eye was just off the Staten Island shore and the eastern edge was south of eastern Long Island. Donna may have been one of those hurricanes with a double-eye, one off Staten Island and the other eye south of Suffolk County, Long Island. However, it is arguable whether it is physically possible for a hurricane to have more than one eye, since it is expected to have one center of circulation. The smallest eyes have been from 5 to 10 miles across, with an eye as small as 5 to 7 miles being unusual. Hurricane eyes typically like to stay in the range of about 20 to 30 miles in diameter.

As a hurricane "spins-up" or intensifies, the swirl of air circulating around the eye causes the eye to shrink. Therefore, one sign that a hurricane is undergoing intensification is the shrinking in size of its eye.

Hurricanes require sea-surface temperatures of at least 79°F (26°C) to flourish. If another weather system has strong winds aloft in such a direction as to shear off the tops of the tropical cyclone, then the tropical system will fall apart.

TABLE 1. PRINCIPAL AREAS OF TROPICAL CYCLONE FORMATION IN THE TROPICAL NORTH ATLANTIC

SEASON	AREA
JUNE - NOVEMBER	GULF OF MEXICO
JUNE & LATE SEPTEMBER - EARLY NOVEMBER	WESTERN CARIBBEAN SEA
JUNE - OCTOBER	NORTH OF THE WEST INDIES
JULY - EARLY OCTOBER	CARIBBEAN SEA EAST OF 70 W
JULY - EARLY OCTOBER	EAST OF LESSER ANTILLES

TABLE 2. AREAS OF TROPICAL CYCLONE FORMATION IN THE EASTERN NORTH PACIFIC

SEASON	AREA
JUNE - OCTOBER	OFF THE WEST COAST OF CENTRAL AMERICA

IMPORTANT TERMS: The following is from the National Weather Service:

TROPICAL WAVE: A trough of low pressure in the trade-wind easterlies.

TROPICAL DISTURBANCE: A moving area of thunderstorms in the Tropics that maintains its identity for 24 hours or more. A common phenomenon in the tropics.

TROPICAL DEPRESSION: A tropical cyclone in which the maximum sustained surface wind is 38 mph (33 knots) or less.

TROPICAL STORM: A tropical cyclone in which the maximum sustained surface wind ranges from 39-73 mph (34-63 knots) inclusive.

HURRICANE: A tropical cyclone in which maximum sustained surface wind is 74 mph (64 knots) or greater.

TROPICAL STORM WATCH: Is issued for a coastal area when there is the threat of tropical storm conditions within 36 hours.

TROPICAL STORM WARNING: A warning for tropical storm conditions, including sustained winds within the range of 39 to 73 mph (34 to 63 knots) which are expected in a specified coastal area within 24 hours or less.

HURRICANE WATCH: An announcement that hurricane conditions pose a possible threat to a specified coastal area within 36 hours.

HURRICANE WARNING: A warning that sustained winds of 74 mph (64 knots) or higher are expected in a specified coastal area within 24 hours or less.

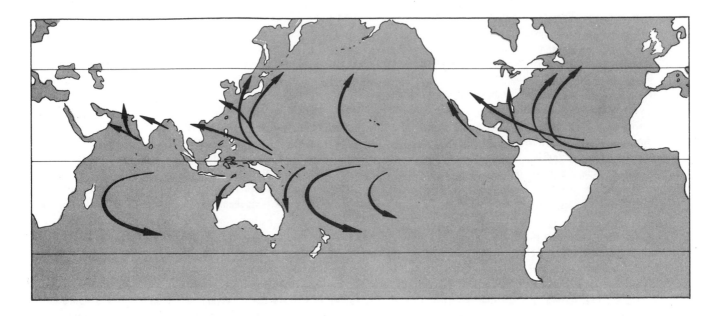

Figure 33-5. The MAIN (not all) areas of tropical cyclone formation and favored storm tracks. In the North Atlantic Basin, most tropical cyclones occur in August, September and October. (source: USAF)

THE HURRICANE INTENSITY SCALE

CATEGORY	CENTRAL PRESSURE		WINDS	STORM SURGE	DAMAGE
	INCHES	MILLIBARS (HectoPascals)	OR	OR	
1	≥28.94"	≥980 mb	74 to 95 mph	4 to 5 feet	minimal
2	28.50" to 28.91"	965 to 979 mb	96 to 110 mph	6 to 8 feet	moderate
3	27.91" to 28.47"	945 to 964 mb	111 to 130 mph	9 to 12 feet	extensive
4	27.17" to 27.88"	920 to 944 mb	131 to 155 mph	13 to 18 feet	extreme
5	<27.17"	<920 mb	>155 mph	>18 feet	catastrophic

Figure 33-6. The Hurricane Intensity Scale. (source: National Hurricane Center)

These groupings typically complement each other. For example, in a category 3 hurricane, the pressure is usually between 27.91" and 28.47" with a sustained wind of 111 to 130 mph producing a storm surge upon landfall of 9 to 12 feet. However, there can be situations e.g. in which a hurricane with a category 3 speed has a category 2 pressure; in such cases the worse category number is assigned to that hurricane at that time, since the categorization is based on the worst of EITHER the pressure OR the winds OR the storm surge. Keep in mind that if the sea-floor going out from the shore drops rapidly, the storm surge is not as great as when the continental shelf has a gradual slope.

The Hurricane Intensity Scale was developed by Herbert Saffir and Robert Simpson. Saffir was a consulting engineer in Coral Gables, Florida and Simpson was then the Director of the National Hurricane Center. Saffir and Simpson developed the Hurricane Intensity Scale in the early 1970s, based on observations of numerous North Atlantic Basin hurricanes.

DESCRIPTIVE DAMAGE FOR THE HURRICANE INTENSITY SCALE

Category 1 Hurricane: Damage is primarily to shrubbery, trees, foliage and unanchored mobile homes. There is no substantial damage to other structures. Some damage occurs to poorly constructed signs. Low-lying coastal roads are inundated. There is minor damage to piers. Some small craft in exposed anchorages are torn from their moorings.

Category 2 Hurricane: There is considerable damage to shrubbery and to tree foliage, with some trees blown down. Major damage occurs to exposed mobile homes. There is extensive damage to poorly constructed signs and some damage to roofing materials of buildings, and to windows and doors. No major destruction occurs to buildings. Coastal roads and low-lying escape routes inland are cut off by rising water about 2 to 4 hours before the arrival of the hurricane center. There is considerable damage to piers, and marinas are flooded. Small craft in unprotected anchorages are torn from their moorings. Evacuation of some shoreline residences and of low-lying areas is required.

Category 3 Hurricane: Foliage is torn from trees and large trees are blown down. Nearly all the poorly constructed signs are blown down. There is some damage to roofing materials of buildings, and to windows and doors. Some structural damage occurs to small buildings. Mobile homes are destroyed. Serious flooding occurs at the coast and many smaller structures near the coast are destroyed; larger structures near the coast are damaged by battering waves and floating debris. Low-lying escape routes inland are cut by rising water about 3 to 5 hours before the hurricane center arrives. Flat terrain 5 feet or less above sea-level is flooded up to 8 or more miles inland. Evacuation of low-lying residences within several blocks of the shoreline may be required.

Category 4 Hurricane: Shrubs, trees and all signs are blown down. There is extensive damage to roofing materials and to windows and doors, with complete failure of roofs on many small residences. Mobile homes are demolished. Flat terrain which is 10 feet or less above sea-level is flooded inland for as far as 6 miles. The flooding and the battering by waves and floating debris cause major damage to the lower floors of structures near the shore. Low-lying escape routes inland are cut by rising water about 3 to 5 hours before the arrival of the hurricane center. There is major erosion of beaches. Massive evacuation of all residences within 500 yards of the shore may be required, as well as of single-story residences in low ground within 2 miles of the shore.

Category 5 Hurricane: Trees, shrubs and all signs are blown down. There is considerable damage to roofs of buildings, with very severe and extensive damage to windows and doors. Indeed, complete failure of roofs occurs on many residences and industrial buildings. There is extensive shattering of glass in windows and doors. Some complete buildings are destroyed. Small buildings are overturned or blown away, and mobile homes are demolished. There is major damage to lower floors of all structures which are less than 15 feet above sea-level within 1500 feet of the shore. Low-lying escape routes inland are cut by rising water about 3 to 5 hours before the arrival of the hurricane center. Massive evacuation of residential areas on low ground within 5 to 10 miles of the shore may be required.

Note on the maintenance of the hurricane:
Evaporation of some very warm surface water provides the warm, moist air which contains much of the energy potential for hurricane development. As this air rises into the storm, it cools to its dewpoint, forming clouds, and as it keeps rising, cloud droplets coalesce and accrete to form the raindrops. In this condensation process, the "heat of condensation" is released. This is a form of energy. The hurricane uses this energy to maintain itself and to grow.

When the temperature and dewpoint are high, as over the tropical waters, the energy available is enormous. One study concluded that the amount of energy expended by a typical hurricane would, if it could be harnessed, supply the entire energy needs for the United States for half a year!

The air circulation in a hurricane:
Air spirals into the hurricane, rising as it does so, encircling the relatively calm eye. In the eye, the air is sinking, warming adiabatically as it descends. Although the perfect model of the circulation and energy evolutions of a tropical cyclone has not been formulated, we do have sufficient observations and data to suggest some circulation models of the storm. Much of the air is also recycled within the storm. There is vertical exchange of energy, moisture and momentum. There are smaller-scale, called mesoscale, features within the hurricane. For example, not all hurricanes

should be expected to have vertical eye-walls. Indeed, one study of five hurricanes found that their eye-walls leaned outward, which would suggest a sloping updraft.

Some of the details that a comprehensive hurricane circulation model should account for are:
- the maintenance of the hurricane's convection;
- the lifting of evaporated water out of the planetary boundary layer;
- the greater tapping of the ocean energy source through downdraft drying and cooling of the boundary layer; and
- the balancing of the hurricane's circulation against radiational cooling.

Note about the anticyclonic outflow aloft:
The air does not just keep spiralling in counterclockwise in the Northern Hemisphere and clockwise in the Southern Hemisphere, and disappearing. Due to conservation of mass, the air has to go somewhere to maintain a circulation. Aloft in the hurricane, towards and at and over its top, the air comes out in an anticyclonic (clockwise in the Northern Hemisphere and counterclockwise in the Southern Hemisphere) fashion. Thus, a hurricane moving across the Atlantic towards the United States, and a typhoon heading across the western Pacific towards Japan, and a tropical cyclone heading across the Indian Ocean towards India, all have, since they are Northern Hemisphere tropical cyclones, a counterclockwise cyclonic circulation with an anticyclonic outflow aloft. This outflow is hard to distinguish on individual weather satellite pictures, but on time-lapse video-loops of these pictures you can detect a surge of high cirroform clouds spiralling clockwise aloft out of the storm.

Violent winds and flash flooding rains are not the only onslaught from a hurricane. The storm surge is the greatest killer in a hurricane. A storm surge killed at least 6,000 people...perhaps as many as 12,000...in Galveston, Texas in September 1900, and killed upwards of some 500,000 people in Bangladesh in November 1970.

THE HURRICANE'S STORM SURGE:

Definition of a storm surge:
The storm surge is a rapid increase in the height of a dome of water as the hurricane's eye approaches the shoreline. At sea, the much lower pressure in and immediately around the eye causes the sea surface to be raised up by several feet. As this dome approaches the coast with its much shallower water, the dome becomes higher. In superhurricanes, storm surges have exceeded 20 feet. In category 5 Hurricane Camille, for example, the storm surge at Pass Christian, Mississippi was 27 feet, with waves of some 15 feet high on top of the water dome. The three-story Richelieu Garden Apartment complex was swept into the Gulf of Mexico by that storm surge. A 30-foot storm surge from the Great 1938 Hurricane on the Rhode Island shore put downtown Providence under water up to 14 feet deep.

Some of the highest storm surges from hurricanes and typhoons are on the order of 30 to 40 feet. Moreover, at sea, waves in excess of 50 feet, which are wind driven and are not the storm surge, occur in the most powerful, large tropical cyclones. The extreme wave heights have reached 100 feet in powerful typhoons.

The causes of the hurricane's storm surge are:
- the much lower atmospheric pressure in and immediately around the eye causes the sea surface to rise in a dome
- the fetch of the intense winds will force water in advance of the storm's eye to rise
- the dome of water rises rapidly...which can be several feet in minutes...as the surge approaches the shallower shore; where sea-floor level drops off rapidly from the shoreline, the storm surge is not as great as where the continental shelf is a gradual slope; the water swoops up as the dome moves over the shallower waters to the shore
- the best attack angle of the hurricane on the shoreline optimizes the height of the storm surge. For example, a superhurricane moving in just to the west of New Orleans would handily bury the city under 20 or more feet of water, whereas if the same storm makes landfall just to the east of the city, the storm surge may be only several feet.

People take shelter from dangerous winds, but if this shelter is along the coast, then even it may not save their lives from a huge storm surge upon which are battering waves.

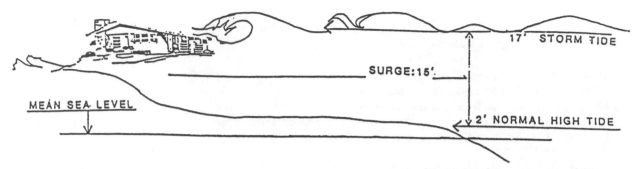

Figure 33-6. An example of a hurricane's storm surge. A normal 2-foot tide has a 15-foot storm surge, which produces a net storm tide of 17 feet.

Figure 33-7. A storm surge inundating a coastal area. (source: NOAA)

The effects of a hurricane storm surge:

The storm surge is not a wall of water, such as a tsunami which can be generated by an earthquake or volcanic eruption on land or under sea; rather, the storm surge is a rapidly rising water level as the hurricane's eye approaches land. For example, in the Sept. 1900 Galveston hurricane storm surge, the water rose four feet in four seconds, with a 20-foot storm tide.

As witnessed in the Galveston disaster and in the August 1969 Camille superhurricane, and especially in the November 1970 Bangladesh holocaust, people within several blocks of the coast can be swept out to sea. Entire buildings are destroyed or swept away. What the storm surge does not destroy, the fierce winds may finish off. And then there is the flash flooding to exacerbate the misery.

The storm surge is not confined to a small area. It may be from five to over 50 miles long up and down the coastline. Some parts of the coast will be harder hit than others.

To determine the height of the storm surge, one needs to obtain from the tide tables the height of the normal astronomical tide and compare this with the observed storm tide. The storm tide minus the astronomical tide is the height of the storm surge.

Typically, the stronger and larger the hurricane, the greater is its storm surge if it makes landfall. Over the ocean, the storm surge is created by the significant pressure drop associated with the moving hurricane and by the persistent intense winds blowing for several hours over fetches of at least several miles.

Since the storm surge is increasing as it approaches the shallower water at the beaches, and the moving water contains essentially the same amount of energy as it moves to the shore, the result is an increase in the surge height.

One study in 1982 found that the waves on top of the storm surge will batter structures along the coast and dampen out at some 300 to 700 feet inland.

Observations of hurricane storm surges show that the surge is worse if the hurricane is moving more perpendicular to the coast, rather than moving more parallel to the coast, upon landfall. The greatest storm surge tends to occur to the right of the landfall position in a slowly moving storm making landfall at an attack angle perpendicular to the coast. The height of the storm surge may increase by twofold or more when the track of a major hurricane causes the surge to funnel into a bay.

The hurricane storm surge and astronomical tides
The worst possible scenario for a hurricane's landfall is for the storm surge to coincide with astronomical high tide. SPRING TIDE is the astronomical highest tide, occurring when the moon is in the full or new phase. NEAP TIDE is the astronomical lowest tide, occurring when the moon is in the first quarter or last quarter phase.

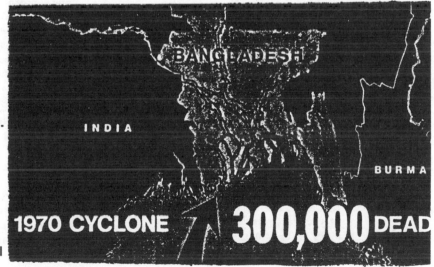

Figure 33-8. The storm surge from a tropical cyclone in November 1970 swept out into the Indian Ocean or otherwise drowned at least 300,000 people in coastal Bangladesh. A more recent estimate places the death toll at about 500,000. Many perished by being on islands just off the coast, that are only several feet above sea-level. A storm surge of 20 to 30 feet caused the greatest death toll in the 20th century from a hurricane. According to R. Anthes (1982), the 1970 Bay of Bengal Bangladesh storm surge was up to 30 feet, and occurred at the time of high tide. The storm surge occurring at high tide vs. low tide obviously makes a difference in its height, but when it occurs during the time of spring tide, then the worst possible scenario is underway. (source: NOAA)

Figure 33-9. Folly Beach, South Carolina before a hurricane storm surge struck (top photo), and after the storm surge bottom photo). (source: NOAA)

The following preparedness and safety information is from the National Weather Service.

Be Prepared **BEFORE** the Hurricane Season:

✓ Know the storm surge history and elevation of your area.
✓ Learn safe routes inland.
✓ Learn location of official shelters.
✓ Review needs and working condition of emergency equipment, such as flashlights, battery-powered radios, etc.
✓ Ensure that enough non-perishable food and water supplies are on hand to last for *at least* 2 weeks.
✓ Obtain and store materials, such as plywood and plastic, necessary to properly secure your home.
✓ Check home for loose and clogged rain gutters and downspouts.
✓ Keep trees and shrubbery trimmed. Cut weak branches and trees that could fall or bump against the house. When trimming, try to create a channel through the foliage to the center of the tree to allow for air flow.
✓ Determine where to move your boat in an emergency.
✓ Review your insurance policy to ensure it provides adequate coverage.
✓ Individuals with special needs should contact their local office of emergency management.
✓ For information and assistance with any of the above, contact your local National Weather Service office, emergency management office, or American Red Cross chapter.

When a "**Hurricane WATCH**" is issued:

✓ Frequently monitor radio, TV, NOAA Weather Radio, or hurricane hotline telephone numbers for official bulletins of the storm's progress.
✓ Fuel and service family vehicles.
✓ Inspect and secure mobile home tie downs.
✓ Prepare to cover all window and door openings with shutters or other shielding materials.

✓ Check food and water supplies.
  — Have clean, air-tight containers on hand to store at least 2 weeks of drinking water (14 gallons per person).
  — Stock up on canned provisions.
  — Get a camping stove with fuel.
  — Keep a small cooler with frozen gel packs handy for packing refrigerated items.
✓ Check prescription medicines—obtain at least 10 days to 2 weeks supply.
✓ Stock up on extra batteries for radios, flashlights, and lanterns.
✓ Prepare to store and secure outdoor lawn furniture and other loose, lightweight objects, such as garbage cans, garden tools, potted plants, etc.
✓ Check and replenish first-aid supplies.
✓ Have on hand an extra supply of cash.

When a "**Hurricane WARNING**" is issued:

✓ Closely monitor radio, TV, NOAA Weather Radio, or hurricane hotline telephone numbers for official bulletins.
✓ Follow instructions issued by local officials. *Leave immediately if ordered to do so.*
✓ Complete preparation activities, such as putting up storm shutters, storing loose objects, etc.
✓ Evacuate areas that might be affected by storm surge flooding.
✓ If evacuating, leave early (if possible, in daylight).
✓ Leave mobile homes in any case.
✓ Notify neighbors and a family member outside of the warned area of your evacuation plans.

If Evacuating:

Plan to evacuate if you...
- live in a mobile home. Do not stay in a mobile home under any circumstances. They are unsafe in high wind and/or hurricane conditions, no matter how well fastened to the ground.
- live on the coastline or on an offshore island, or live near a river or in a flood plain.
- live in a high-rise. Hurricane winds are stronger at higher elevations. Glass doors and windows may be blown out of their casings and weaken the structure.

✓ Stay with friends or relatives or at a low-rise inland hotel or motel outside of flood zones. Leave early to avoid heavy traffic, roads blocked by early flood waters, and bridges impassable due to high winds.

✓ Put food and water out for pet if you cannot take it with you. *Public shelters do not allow pets nor do most motels/hotels.*

✓ Hurricane shelters will be available for people who have no other place to go. Shelters may be crowded and uncomfortable, with no privacy and no electricity. Do not leave your home for a shelter until government officials announce on radio and/or television that a particular shelter is open.

What to bring to a shelter: first-aid kit; medicine; baby food and diapers; cards, games, books; toiletries; battery-powered radio; flashlight (per person); extra batteries; blankets or sleeping bags; identification, valuable papers (insurance), and cash.

If Staying in a Home:

Reminder! Only stay in a home if you have not been ordered to leave. If you *ARE* told to leave, do so immediately.

✓ Store water:
- Fill sterilized jugs and bottles with water for a 2-week supply of drinking water.
- Fill bathtub and large containers with water for sanitary purposes.

✓ Turn refrigerator to maximum cold and open only when necessary.

✓ Turn off utilities if told to do so by authorities.

✓ Turn off propane tanks.

✓ Unplug small appliances.

Stay inside a well constructed building. In structures, such as a home, examine the building and plan in advance what you will do if winds become strong. Strong winds can produce deadly missiles and structural failure. If winds become strong:

- Stay away from windows and doors even if they are covered. Take refuge in small interior room, closet, or hallway. Take a battery-powered radio, a NOAA Weather Radio, and a flashlight with you to your place of refuge.

- Close all interior doors. Secure and brace external doors, particularly double inward opening doors and garage doors.
- If you are in a two-story house, go to an interior first-floor room or basement, such as a bathroom, closet, or under the stairs.
- If you are in a multiple-story building and away from the water, go to the first or second floors and take refuge in the halls or other interior rooms away from windows. Interior stairwells and the areas around elevator shafts are generally the strongest part of a building.
- Lie on the floor under tables or other sturdy objects.

Be alert for tornadoes which often are spawned by hurricanes.

If the "EYE" of the hurricane should pass over your area, be aware that the improved weather conditions are <u>temporary</u> and that the storm conditions will return with winds coming from the <u>opposite direction</u> sometimes in a period of <u>just a few minutes</u>.

AFTER the storm passes:

✓ Stay in your protected area until announcements are made on the radio or television that the dangerous winds have passed.

✓ If you have evacuated, do not return home until officials announce your area is ready. Remember, proof of residency may be required in order to re-enter evacuation areas.

✓ If your home or building has structural damage, do not enter until it is checked by officials.

✓ Avoid using candles and other open flames indoors.

✓ Beware of outdoor hazards:
- Avoid downed power lines and any water in which they may be lying.
- Be alert for poisonous snakes, often driven from their dens by high water.
- Beware of weakened bridges and washed out roads.
- Watch for weakened limbs on trees and/or damaged overhanging structures.

✓ Do not use the telephone unless absolutely necessary. The system usually is jammed with calls during and after a hurricane.

✓ Guard against spoiled food. Use dry or canned food. Do not drink or prepare food with tap water until you are certain it is not contaminated.

✓ When cutting up fallen trees, use caution, especially if you use a chain saw. Serious injuries can occur when these powerful machines snap back or when the chain breaks.

Chapter 34. FLOODS AND FLASH FLOODS

Here are factors that play roles in the various types of flooding.

HEAVY AND EXCESSIVE RAINFALL
The most obvious cause of flooding is heavy rainfall continuing for many hours, or excessive rainfall (an inch or more [about 25 millimeters or more] per hour). The heavier the rainfall rate, then obviously the greater is the flooding or potential for flooding.

Heavy rains from thunderstorms and tropical systems (tropical depressions, tropical storms and hurricanes) often induce flooding.

Here are two examples of conditions that produced worst-case scenario flooding from heavy rains:

In August of 1955, Hurricane Connie saturated the soils of southeast New York state and southern New England. Just a few days later, Hurricane Diane moved into the same region, dumping up to 20 inches (over 500 millimeters) of rain from August 17th through 19th, resulting in widespread flooding and damage. Diane weakened to a tropical depression but stalled between Long Island and Cape Cod.

During the spring and summer of 1993, a strong and enduring El Nino episode (see chapter 45 on El Nino) contributed to frequent Mesoscale Convective Systems (large areas of organized thunderstorm activity) dumping excessive rainfalls over the central plains of the United States, causing rivers and streams to flood to record levels.

RAPIDLY MELTING HEAVY SNOWCOVER
When there is a very heavy accumulation of snow (especially from many storms, since the snow becomes more compact and the water content of the snow builds up with each storm) , and especially in the mountains, and rapid thawing and/or warmer heavy rainfalls occur there, then the runoff is fast and can lead to flooding. Runoff is the amount of rainfall and/or water from melting snowcover that is not absorbed by soil and vegetation, and flows over the ground into streams, rivers and other bodies of water.

Some examples include the rapid melting of heavy snowcover, exacerbated by heavy spring rains, over eastern North Dakota in 1997, which resulted in the worst flooding in history in Grand Forks, North Dakota. Too rapid a snowmelt leads to flooding in the mountains of the western United States, especially when the snow season had much above average (excessive) snowfall.

SATURATED SOIL
The soil moisture content is crucial in determining how much of the rainfall and/or melting snowfall becomes runoff to cause flooding. When the soil is fairly dry, it typically initially absorbs much of the runoff, but when the soil becomes saturated, then all the rainfall and/or melting snow is runoff.

SOIL TYPE
The rainfall to runoff conversion (how much runoff occurs from rainfall and/or melting snowcover) also depends upon soil type. Heavy clay soil holds more water than does sandy or loamy soil. This is why deserts are more prone to flooding from the same amount of rain that would otherwise not be such a flood-threat in areas with clay-type soils. Scientists who study what happens to water on the ground, hydrologists, have a name for this property of soil: tension water storage. Tension water storage is a measurement of the ability of the soil to hold onto moisture before releasing it as runoff.

VEGETATION
The more vegetation, including trees, an area has, the more runoff is absorbed by them, potentially lessening the flooding.

(continued)   PAGE 262

EVAPOTRANSPIRATION

Runoff is less when rates and amounts of evaporation (such as inbetween thunderstorm events) and transpiration increase. For example, on a typical sunny day in summer in mid-latitudes, a mature oak, maple or pine tree emits from about 50 to 100 gallons of moisture into the planetary boundary layer of the atmosphere! Imagine how much water vapor patches of trees and forests emit, which helps to explain why trees are so important to enhancing precipitation, since they provide additional moisture for the local atmosphere to work with in producing convective precipitation. Evaporation comes from all surfaces, and transpiration is the process by which vegetation gives off moisture directly into the atmosphere, chiefly through the leaves. Both processes are often referred to as evapotranspiration.

TOPOGRAPHY

All else being equal, the runoff varies as the terrain varies. Runoff is faster in hilly and mountainous terrain than in flatter terrain. The hydrologic rule-of-thumb is that a rainfall rate of one inch or more per hour, or two inches or more per two hours, is enough to cause flash flooding in mountains.

STATE OF THE GROUND

Rainfall over a frozen ground yields more runoff than rainfall on a non-frozen ground. When frozen, the surface acts much like a slate or paved area. This would be the case with no snowcover. However, when the ground is covered with a heavy snowcover (well over a foot deep), then when it rains heavily on top of the snow, the snow at first will absorb some of the rain, but eventually the rain and melting snow will be released as runoff.

URBANIZATION AND OTHER MAN-MADE EFFECTS

When a rural or natural area is paved over, then the runoff is not all flowing over soil where it can be partially absorbed at first, but all or most of the rainfall becomes runoff.

The same rule-of-thumb applies to major cities that applies to mountains: a rainfall rate of one inch or more per hour, or two inches or more per two hours, is normally sufficient to induce flash flooding.

Dams, levees and man-made reservoirs are other modifiers of the runoff, and typically prevent flooding unless they break or overflow.

INTERCEPTION BY PONDS, LAKES, ETC.

Some runoff may empty into ponds, lakes or an ocean. Thus, the level of a pond or lake may rise, but that runoff is no longer in a water channel such as a stream (creek).

The above factors that we just discussed are actually factors that affect the amount of runoff that we get from rainfall and/or melting snowcover. The water that flows over the ground from rainfall (the runoff) that is not absorbed by vegetation, makes its way into the streams (also called creeks) and rivers. Too much water leads to the streams and rivers overflowing, giving us flooding.

PONDING FLOODING

This type of flooding occurs when water collects in low areas.

ICE JAM FLOODING

Ice jams form in rivers and streams when thawing causes chunks of ice to break away from the frozen water channel and then flow downstream. As the river or stream winds and bends, these ice pieces get stuck and soon pile up, creating a jam of downstream flowing water. Ice jam flooding occurs upstream once the jam forms, and a sudden flash flood downstream from the jam can occur if the jam breaks apart rapidly.

STRONG ONSHORE WINDS FLOODING

People who live along large lakes and oceans are subject to flooding when strong winds, persisting from the same direction for many hours, push water onshore. For example, residents at the west end of Lake Erie can experience water flooding onshore when strong winds from the east-northeast last for many hours, since these winds are blowing across the fetch of the entire Great lake. Another example is along the coasts of Washington, Oregon and northern and central California, during episodes of powerful winds blowing from over the ocean to the shore (onshore winds) push the water onshore; this is most likely during the winter and spring. Any coastal storm with powerful winds, including a hurricane/typhoon, can blow ocean water onshore. Moreover, the hurricane storm surge is a special case of coastal flooding (see chapter 33 on hurricanes and typhoons).

STORM SURGE FLOODING
The previous chapter on hurricanes discusses this topic in depth. Not only hurricanes and typhoons, but powerful coastal storms with winds around hurricane force can also generate storm surge flooding of coastal areas. Even without a "storm surge", coastal flooding from any cause of persisting high winds from the same direction over a period of time can lead to coastal flooding.

TSUNAMI FLOODING
When the huge wave of a tsunami, caused by an earthquake and/or volcanic eruption typically under the ocean, moves ashore, its power can create much damage. (See chapter 47 on tsunamis.)

A note about tides: along ocean beaches and the beaches of large lakes, any onshore flooding is enhanced when it occurs during the time of high tide. The astronomical high tides known as spring tides (during full and new moons) would be the worst-case scenario for an onshore flooding episode to coincide with. (Chapter 46 discusses tides.)

Flood stage is when the river or stream overflows its banks. The crest is the highest stage reached.

Here are the definitions of flooding and flash flooding.

FLOOD: A flood is an inundation of a normally dry area caused by an increased water level in an established watercourse, such as a river, stream or drainage ditch, or ponding of water at or near the point where it fell.

FLASH FLOOD: A flash flood is an inundation by rapid rising, flowing water, caused by heavy or excessive rainfall and/or rapid snowmelt, in a short period of time, and may also be caused by factors such as a dam break, a levee failure, and a volcanic eruption diverting waterways and rapidly melting any heavy snowcover. The National Weather Service Operations Manual defines a flash flood as generally occurring in less than 6 hours from the start of the causative event.

If the flooding occurs in under six hours from the start of the rain or other causative event, then it is a flash flood, and if it takes 6 hours or more, then it is a flood. This typically results in flash floods occurring mostly on streams and creeks (streams and creeks are synonymous terms), and floods occurring on rivers, since they are wider, deeper water channels which have streams emptying into them, and hold much more water than streams.

The National Weather Service has also identified a separate type of flooding, which is more nuisance flooding than dangerous, called URBAN AND SMALL STREAM FLOODING. This is flooding of small streams, streets and low-lying areas, such as railroad underpasses and urban storm drains.

Annually, flash floods usually kill more people in the United States than does any other severe weather phenomenon, although severe winter cold and winter storms kill more people than any of the weather killers.

Most flood deaths are from flash floods, since there is sufficient time to get out of the way of a flood from a large river. Many of the deaths from flash flooding occur when persons drive their vehicles on a road covered by swiftly moving water that is overflowing from a stream. Even a large vehicle such as a large sport utility vehicle can be overturned by rapidly flowing water that is only half way up the hub-caps or wheelcovers! Consider this: water is very heavy. If you carry a bucket of water in each hand for several hundred yards, you will know how heavy it is! Imagine water flowing at about 30 to 35 miles per hour (which is typical of flash floods). This moving, heavy water has a large amount of momentum (mass times speed). The power of such moving water is awesome. A person driving a car through such a flow, risks having the vehicle overturned. Even if the person manages to escape from the vehicle, he/she still has to try to swim against the raging torrent and get out of it. Some people die this way.

Figure 34-1. Billions of dollars of property damage can occur within one year in the United States from flooding and flash flooding. (source: NOAA)

	FLASH FLOODS	**FLOODS**
CAUSES	Heavy convective rainfall; ice jam breakup; levee/dam break	Prolonged heavy rainfall and/or snowmelt; upstream from ice jam
TIME UNTIL CREST	From 0 to less than 6 hours after start of causative event	Generally 6 hours or more after start of causative event
WATER CHANNELS	Streams, flashy -usually mountainous- rivers, urban areas, low-lying areas, sewers, culverts	Rivers and major streams
DANGER	Warnings can save lives and reduce some property damage*	Warnings can save some lives and reduce property damage*

* Because flash floods happen with rapidity, they are more life threatening than general floods or river floods, which take longer to happen. Thus, more lives are potentially saved by people heeding accurate flash flood warnings than are saved by flood warnings. However, more property can be saved in a gradual flood than in a flash flood.

HOW PEOPLE DIE IN FLASH FLOOD AND FLOODS:

Almost all the deaths are in the flash floods rather than the floods.

According to statistics published by the National Weather Service:
- 60% of flood deaths occur in urban areas
- 75% of flood deaths occur at night

    Most flash floods are caused by slow-moving heavy thunderstorms, most of which start during the afternoon and continue into the night.
- Specifically, how the flood deaths (almost all caused by flash floods) occur:

  49% die in their cars, mostly from driving into rapidly flowing water from a stream or river overflowing onto a street. The force of water moving at about 30 to 35 mph on a vehicle can overturn the car and sweep it downstream.

  25% die while walking, playing or swimming

  19% die in their homes

  6% are killed while camping

  2% die during rescue attempts

(total just exceeds 100% due to rounding off)

Figure 34-2. A raging flash flood on the James River at Richmond, Virginia, caused by some 30 inches of rain within a few hours, from the remnants of Hurricane Camille. (source: Virginia Department of Highways)

Figure 34-3. Coastal flooding caused by strong onshore winds. (source: NWS)

<u>Other consequences of flooding</u>: mudslides.....sinkholes.....avalanches

<u>AUTOMATIC FLASH FLOOD & FLOOD WARNING SYSTEMS</u>
There are various types of automatic alarm systems to notify officials that the stream or river is rising and approaching flood stage. The simplest system has sensors set at some level (say a foot or two) just below flood stage, so that when the water hits the sensors, it sets off an alarm that is relayed to an appropriate office such as a firehouse, preparedness office, weather office, etc. The elaborate systems include automatic recording rain gauges and even hydrologic computer models to predict how high the water will rise based on the rainfall intensity (amount + time of rainfall).

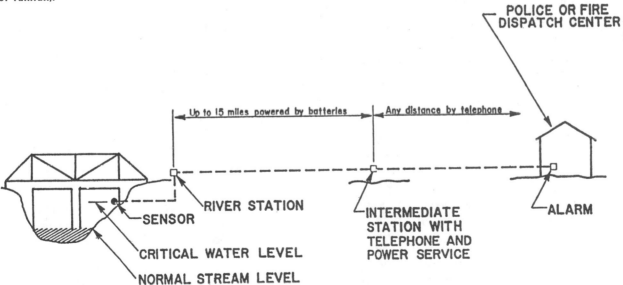

Figure 34-4. A schematic of a simple flash flood & flood warning system on a river or stream.
(source: NOAA)

The following information about preparedness and safety are from the National Weather Service:

FLASH-FLOOD WATCH:

Heavy rains may result in flash flooding in the specified area. Be alert and prepared for the possibility of a flood emergency which will require immediate action.

FLASH-FLOOD WARNING:

Flash flooding is occurring or is imminent in the specified areas. Move to safe ground immediately.

Before the flood, know the elevation of your property in relation to nearby streams and other waterways, and make advance plans of what you will do and where you will go in a flash-flood emergency.

When a flash-flood watch is issued for your area:

- Listen to area radio and television stations for possible flash-flood warnings and reports of flooding in progress from the National Weather Service and public-safety agencies.
- Be prepared to move out of danger's way at a moment's notice.
- If you are on a road, watch for flooding at highway dips, bridges, low areas.
- Watch for signs (thunder, lightning) of distant heavy rainfall.

When a flash-flood warning is issued for your area:

- Act quickly to save yourself and those who depend on you. You may have only seconds.
- Do not attempt to cross a flowing stream on foot where water is above your knees.
- If you are driving, don't try to ford dips of unknown depth. If your vehicle stalls, abandon it immediately and seek higher ground; rapidly rising water may sweep the vehicle and its occupants away. Many deaths have been caused by attempts to move stalled vehicles.

- Be especially cautious at night, when it is harder to recognize flood dangers.
- When you are out of immediate danger, tune in area radio or television stations for additional information as conditions change and new reports are received.

Heavy rainfall, even for short periods, may be followed by flash flooding in mountain or hilly areas. When you go into remote areas:

- **Stay away from natural streambeds,** arroyos, and other drainage channels during and after rainstorms. Water runs off the higher elevations very rapidly.
- **Never camp on low ground.** A flash flood can catch you while you sleep.
- **Use your maps.** Know where you are and whether you are on locally low ground.
- **Remember:** you don't have to be at the bottom of a hill to be a target for flash flood dangers.
- **Know where the high ground is and how to get there.**
- **Stay out of flooded areas.**
- **Keep alert to signs of wet weather,** either rain where you are or signs of rain—thunder and lightning—nearby.
- **Keep as informed as you can.** If you are out of range of broadcast information, be sure to watch for these indicators of flash flooding: increase in the speed of river flow, rapid rise in river level. BE PREPARED TO MOVE TO SAFETY.

After the flash-flood watch or warning is cancelled, stay tuned to radio or television for follow-up information. Flash flooding may have ended, but general flooding may come later in headwater streams and major rivers. REMEMBER: ANY HEAVY RAIN CAN CAUSE LOCALLY DESTRUCTIVE FLASH FLOODING.

FLOOD SAFETY RULES

Before the flood:

- Keep materials on hand such as sandbags, plywood, plastic sheeting, and lumber.
- Install check valves in building sewer traps to prevent flood water from backing up in sewer drains.
- Arrange for auxiliary electrical supplies for hospitals and other operations which are critically affected by power failure.
- Keep first aid supplies at hand.
- Keep your automobile fueled; if electric power is cut off, filling stations may not be able to operate pumps for several days.
- Keep a stock of food that requires little cooking and no refrigeration; electric power may be interrupted.
- Keep a portable radio, emergency cooking equipment, lights and flashlights in working order.
- Know your elevation above flood stage.
- Know your evacuation route.

When you receive a flood warning:

- Store drinking water in clean bathtubs and in various containers. Water service may be interrupted.
- If forced to leave your home, and time permits, move essential items to safe ground; fill fuel tanks to keep them from floating away; grease immovable machinery.
- Move to a safe area before access is cut off by flood water.

FLOOD MITIGATION

Houses, businesses and other structures should not be built too close to water channels; they should not be built in a flood plain. A flood plain is an area that has a history of being flooded from time to time. Even though walls, levees and dams may help, if they do not break, we must give each river and stream its space; each river and stream has its natural flood plain, and it is normal and expected for rivers and streams to flood from time to time.

Comment on flood insurance:
Homeowners' insurance policies generally cover water damage if from leaking or burst plumbing, but not from flooding by Nature. A separate flood insurance rider needs to be purchased to insure for damage from natural flooding.

Chapter 35. DUST STORMS AND SANDSTORMS

Figure 35-1. Top photo is an aerial photo of a dust storm moving in to a community in the southwest United States (source: NOAA), **and bottom photo is blowing sand (a sandstorm)** (source: USAF).

In desert or in semi-arid regions, when it is dry and very windy, the wind can pick up the dust carry it along, lowering visibility and even obscuring the sun on a bright, sunny day. This is a <u>dust storm</u>. When the wind also picks up considerable sand, we have a <u>sandstorm</u>. The dust and sand can be carried hundreds to even thousands of feet high. It is irritating when blown into your face and eyes, and can choke the carburetors of vehicles.

When the wind direction is blowing the dust and sand directly at doors and other openings of houses, the dust and sand will come through spaces and enter the homes.

If a rain shower should commence during a dust storm, then it is possible for a while to receive blowing mud!

<u>Devastating Dust storms</u>

In the 1920s and 1930s, not much concern was given to conservation of natural resources, including soil. Thus, as new settlers cleared and plowed the land to plant crops in parts of Texas, and in Oklahoma, Kansas and Nebraska, they were essentially unaware that by removing most of the trees without planting new ones, they were putting themselves in a position of potential crop disaster should a few years of dry springs and summers occur. This was life during that period which has since become known as the "dust bowl era".

Farmers in the United States learned about dust storms the hard way. In the winter of 1921, much of the topsoil in the "dust bowl" was blown away. In fact, during one event, the soil was blown into a snowstorm which moved over Washington, D.C., depositing black snow over the area! The black snow was the result of the top soil being mixed with snow. When the snow melted, the streets of the U.S. capital city had two inches (5 centimeters) of new top soil, courtesy of the dust bowl farmers and ranchers.

Thus, when the droughts did occur in the early and mid 1930s, the crops dried up and the rich topsoil was replaced by sand. When windstorms developed, the sand was blown into drifts. Some of the dust storms and sandstorms approached as a wall of dust and/or sand as they blocked out the sun and blew sand into houses, clogged carburetors of vehicles and sandblasted people caught outside who were also trying to breathe as the sand and dust blew all around them. One account from April 14th, 1935 in Stratford, Texas said that these dust storms "were like rolling black smoke. We had to keep the lights on all day. We went to school with the headlights on and with dust masks on.". Despite these dust masks, many people suffocated.

Nowadays, to attempt to prevent dust bowls from reoccurring, most farmers plant grass in the fall after they harvest their crops. Even though the grasses die as a result of the first killing frost, they serve two purposes: the roots of the grasses hold the soil in place so that the wind cannot blow it around, and they also are a source of food for cattle.

We give due attention now to the need for trees. Not only do the tree and shrub roots hold the soil together, but they help retain moisture in the top level of the soil, and they keep the humidity higher near the surface because of the release of moisture by them into the lower atmosphere.

In middle-latitudes on a sunny summer day, a mature oak, maple or pine tree can release into the atmosphere approximately 50 to 100 gallons of moisture. Consider, therefore, how much moisture can be released by stands of trees. The trees also absorb carbon dioxide as they generate oxygen. Moreover, they serve as windbreaks.

Thus, it is easy to justify advocacy of reforestation of some of our land. It helps agriculture and ranching and the trees help to cleanse our atmosphere.

Sand and dust storms did not suddenly materialize in the 1930s. During prolonged droughts they naturally occur in areas where trees do not normally grow. An ad in the Junction City, Kansas newspaper in 1873 read, "Real estate for sale at this office, by the acre or bushel".

A drought is a extended period of time with drier than normal weather. Droughts occur whenever a given area does not receive any precipitation, or its precipitation is below normal for several months. Droughts can occur just about anywhere. Besides making a land area prone to dust storms, they yield conditions making the area vulnerable to brush and forest fires as the vegetation dries out. Thousands and even tens of thousands of acres can burn, which can also destroy homes and other structures in their fiery paths.

Sometimes, fierce sandstorms over the Sahara Desert lift massive quantities of sand sufficiently high into the atmosphere to be transported by the winds aloft and by weather systems for thousands of miles. When the finer of these particles act as condensation nuclei for cloud particles and precipitation, episodes of "dirty rain" and differently-colored snow occur. Volcanic ash also is involved in such incidents. Over parts of Asia, "red rains" and "red snows" have occurred, with the condensation nuclei being desert sand and dust.

In December of 1859, a large part of Germany received a snowstorm of red snow.

Back in the United States, the 1930s saw hundreds of millions of tons of central plains topsoil blown all over the globe, but mostly over the eastern half of the United States. In the worst of the dust storms, even places such as New York City and Washington, D.C. had their skies turned black during sunny days because of all the dust in the air.

Droughts cannot be stopped, but mitigation techniques, including reforestation, may, at least in some episodes, prevent a serious situation from becoming extreme.

Another aspect of dust and ash, that comes from volcanic ash eruptions and possibly from desert sand and dust storms, is the phenomenon of clouds of dust about 50 miles up which glitter in spectacular colors when the rising or setting sun reflects its light off these particles. These wispy dust clouds, which resemble the feathery cirrus or the cirrostratus clouds, are called **noctilucent clouds**. Some noctilucent clouds may also contain meteoritic dust. The name refers to the visible-best-about-twilight (quasi-nocturnal) nature of the clouds visibility to the human observer on earth, and to their translucent appearance. After major volcanic ash ejections into the stratosphere and higher, spectacularly-colored sunrises and sunsets occur as these particles divide the visible light of the sun into the separate colors of the rainbow.

SECTION X: WEATHER MAPS AND DATA

Chapter 36. WEATHER SYMBOLS

Symbols are used on weather maps to display features such as high and low pressure centers, cold fronts, warm fronts, stationary fronts and occluded fronts; symbols are also used to display the individual weather elements such as precipitation type and obscuring phenomena (fog, dust, smoke, blowing snow, etc.). The symbols are a short-hand easily identifiable method to tell what the weather is doing, which would be lengthy to display in words.

Depending on where you obtain your weather data, you will see some slight variations in displays of the information, but the basic symbols are used worldwide. For example, look at this simplified weather map below.

Figure 36-1. A simplified surface weather map, without isobars, as it may appear on a TV weather program. The locations of the centers of high and low pressure systems are signified by an H and L, respectively. The depictions for cold, warm, stationary and occluded fronts are as given in chapter 26. In color presentations, cold fronts are blue, warm fronts are red, occluded fronts are purple and stationary fronts are red with the bumps and blue with the pips. Areas where precipitation are occurring are shaded in the above map, and in a color presentation would be shaded green. The dots and asterisks are being generically used to show areas of rain and snow, respectively. Arrows can be used to show how each weather system (high, lows, fronts) is moving.Exercise: refer to the chart of symbols on the next page to tell in general what types of precipitation are occurring in the indicated areas.

Figure 36-2. If the low pressure system is a tropical storm (sustained winds of 39 mph through 73 mph), the left symbol is used, and when the storm has strengthened to hurricane intensity, 74 mph or greater, the right symbol is used.

Details for the plot of weather data for an individual weather station are included in the next chapter, which is the chapter on the "surface weather map". For a full detailed explanation of every common weather map, you are referred to the book, "WEATHER MAPS - How to Read and Interpret all the Basic Weather Charts". The book costs $29 from Chaston Scientific, Inc.; P.O. Box 758; Kearney, MO 64060. With the profusion of weather data via the internet and other sources, this book on weather maps is your ready reference on how to read and use each weather map.

PAGE 272

Figure 36-3. The symbols for the present weather, as authorized by the World Meteorological Organization (WMO).

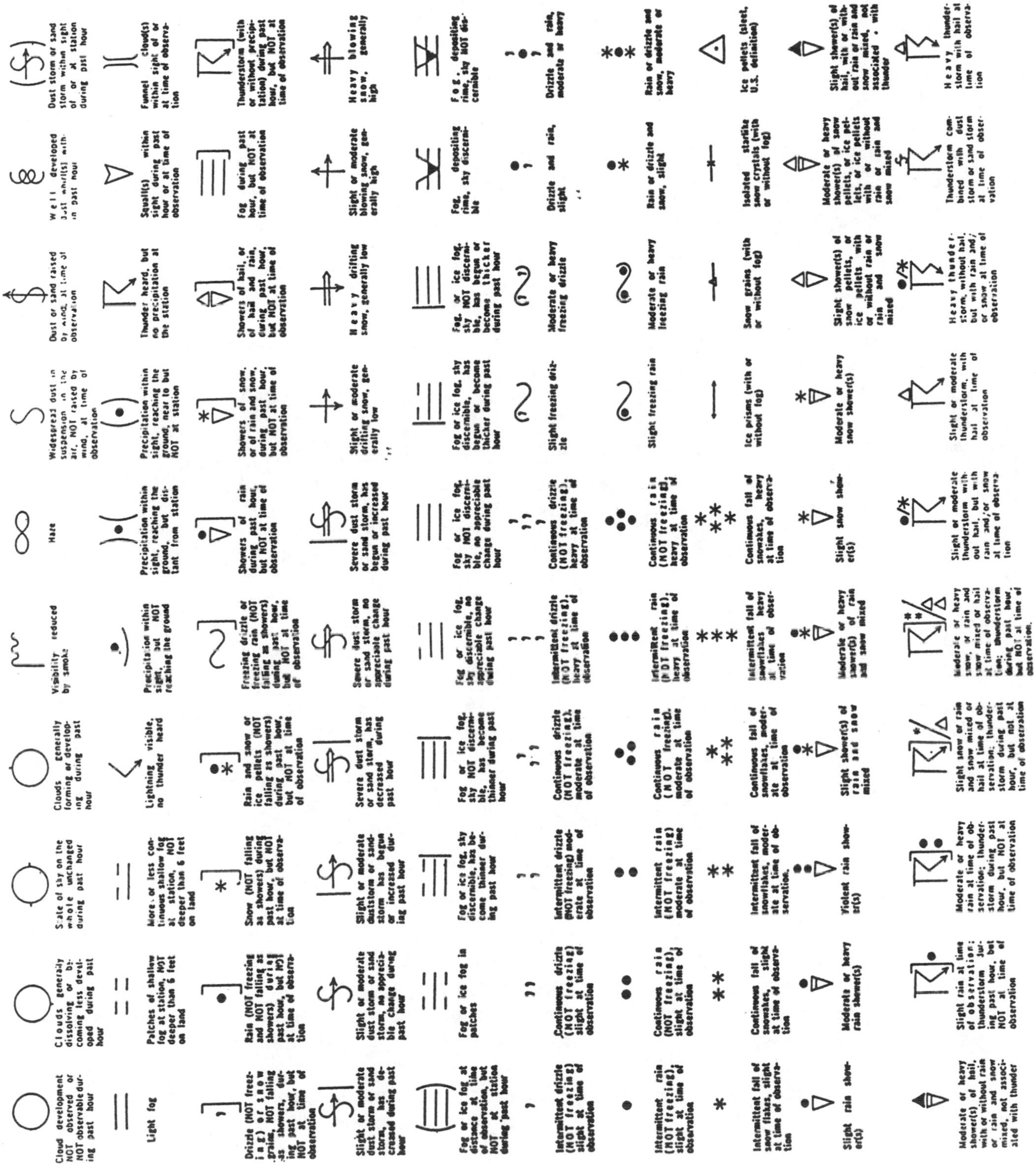

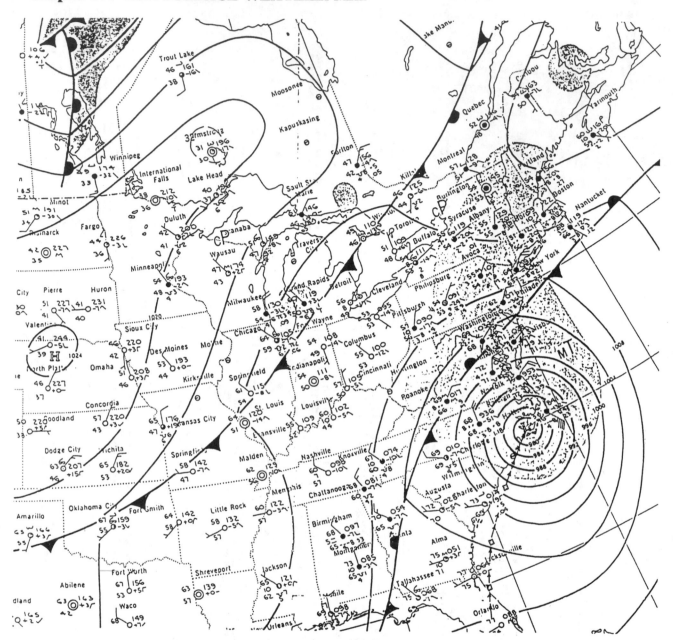

Figure 37-1. A Surface Weather Map. Here is a section of a U.S. surface weather map. Each weather station has a circle and some characters around the circle that describe the weather at that location. Lines of equal air pressure, called <u>isobars</u>, are drawn and the centers of highest and lowest air pressure are located. Boundaries that separate warm and colder masses of air are drawn; these boundaries are called <u>fronts</u>. (source: NWS)

In the following pages; the weather reporting stations' plotting symbols are explained, as are the isobars, high and low pressure systems, fronts, etc. First, we need to start with an explanation of weather observations and how to read them.

READING PLOTTED WEATHER OBSERVATIONS:

Most weather observing stations across the country are located at airports, because the pilots need to know vital weather conditions for safety consideration. Most weather observations are taken just before each hour, with special observations (which are called just that -- special observations) at any time when the weather changes importantly.

WEATHER OBSERVATION
STATION MODEL

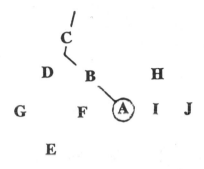

EXAMPLE OF A PLOTTED
WEATHER OBSERVATION

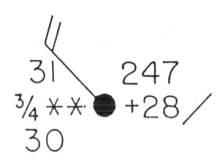

Figure 37-2. How to Read a Plotted Weather Observation. Listed below is the most common style for plotting weather observations on a surface weather map. On the following few pages are the detailed explanations of the various coded weather elements.

A = Total Cloud Cover. A clear sky has an open circle, with the circle filled in as more clouds occur. In the sample, the sky is overcast.

B = Wind Direction. The arrow points into where the wind is coming from. In the example, the wind is coming from the northwest.

C = Wind Speed. A half-barb is five knots; a full barb is 10 knots; a flag is 50 knots. This is explained later. In the example, the wind is 20 knots (2 barbs). A knot is approximately 1.15 miles per hour, so 20 knots is about 23 mph.

D = Temperature. In the example, the temperature is 31°F. Some maps use Celsius, °C.

E = Dewpoint. In the example, the dewpoint temperature is 30°F.

F = Current Weather. These weather symbols are given in the "present weather symbols" table in the previous chapter. In the example, the two asterisks mean a continuous fall of steady light snow.

G = Visibility. This is the average distance the observer can see, horizontally. In the example, the visibility is three-quarters of a mile.

H = Sea-level Pressure. This is given in a unit called millibars, also called hectoPascals. In the example, the pressure is 1024.7 millibars (the first digit or digits is/are a 9 or a 10, and are left out). At sea-level, 1024.7 millibars would be about 30.15" on the barometer.

I = Pressure Change, usually within past 3 hours. Example shows 3-hour change of plus 2.8 millibars.

J = Pressure Tendency, usually within past 3 hours. Example shows steady 3-hour rise.

DETAILED EXPLANATIONS OF EACH CODED WEATHER ELEMENT

A. TOTAL CLOUD COVER

Circle over station location	Amount of cloud cover:

Figure 37-3. Total Cloud Cover Plotted on a Surface Weather Map for Each Weather Observation Site. If the sky is clear, then the station circle is clear. As each one-eighth of cloud cover occurs, the station circle is gradually filled in.

For example, if about a quarter (two-eighths) of the sky) is covered by clouds, then the station circle is filled in (shaded-in) a fourth. If the sky condition is partly cloudy with four-eighths cloud cover, then half the station circle is filled in. An overcast sky has the circle completely filled in. If the sky or clouds cannot be discerned at all because of an obscuration (e.g., dense fog), then the sky report is "obscured" and an X is drawn into the station circle.

The sky cover total is cumulative from the surface up. That is, the lowest cloud deck is then added to by the next higher cloud deck, and then the next higher, and so forth. For example, if the first cloud deck has its base at 2000 feet high and covers 2/8ths of the sky, and the next deck is 8000 feet high and covers 2 eights more, then the total sky cover is 4/8ths which is partly cloudy. When the clouds cover 1 to 2 eighths of the sky, the sky condition is reported as "few clouds", 3 through 4 eighths sky cover is called "scattered", 5 through 7 eighths is "broken", 8/8ths "overcast". If the sky is partially obscured due to a surface-based phenomenon such as fog, haze or smoke, or partially obscured due to heavy precipitation, then the sky condition is called just that: a "partial obscuration", and it may also be partly cloudy or overcast, for example, since the sky cover is cumulative from the surface up. If the sky cannot be seen at all due to one or more obscuring phenomena (even cloud decks cannot be seen), then the sky is called "obscured".

B. WIND DIRECTION
C. WIND SPEED

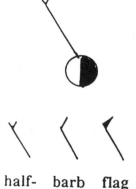

Figure 37-4. The Plot of the Wind Direction and Wind Speed. In meteorology, the convention is to report the wind in the direction from which it comes. Thus, a northwest wind means that the air is coming from the northwest. The top of the station circle is north, the right is east, the bottom is south and the left is west. In the example given, the wind is coming from the northwest. The speed is in knots (nautical miles per hour), a knot being approximately 1.15 mph. A half barb is 5 knots, a full barb is 10 knots and a flag is 50 knots. The example shows a northwest wind at 20 knots (23 mph). Thus, the wind is plotted to the nearest 5 knots. The sky is partly cloudy.

half-barb   barb   flag

Calm

At left is a report of an obscured sky with the wind coming from the southeast at 75 knots (86 mph). This may be a report from a location in a hurricane. The 86 mph wind is the average wind typically for over a minute or two at observation time, and there may be higher gusts. For example, the weather report may say the wind is southeast at 75 knots with gusts to 100 knots. (In a hurricane the sky would probably be obscured with blinding rain with these winds.)

Sometimes, the gust report is plotted at the end of the wind barb on a weather map. An example is given below:

The wind is coming from the northeast at 35 knots with gusts to 55 knots.

D. TEMPERATURE
E. DEWPOINT

Figure 37-5. The Temperature is Plotted in the Upper Left of the Station Plot and the Dewpoint Temperature in the Lower Left. On a surface weather map in the United States, the temperature and dewpoint temperature are plotted in degrees Fahrenheit.

In our example, the temperature is 31°F and the dewpoint is 30°F. These temperatures may be in Celsius, so check carefully.

The daily minimum temperature may fall as low as the dewpoint if the atmosphere were allowed to locally cool off to the coldest it could get. For example, if the early evening temperature is 60 degrees and the dewpoint is 40 degrees with light winds and clear skies expected overnight, then the atmosphere can radiate heat (infra-red radiation) out into space at night until it cools off to its dewpoint. Dew would then form on grass and other surface objects. If the dewpoint is 32 degrees F or lower, frost would form.

The dewpoints over hundreds of areal miles define the type of air mass we are in. If the dewpoints are high in the summer, e.g., 70° or higher, then we are in a soppy, moist warm air mass; if dewpoints are low, such as well below zero degrees F in the winter, then we are in a cold polar or arctic air mass. When dewpoints are rapidly increasing or decreasing, e.g., changing by two or more degrees per hour for several hours, then either moister or drier air is moving in.

The closer the temperature and dewpoint are to each other, the more moist is the air (the higher is the relative humidity). When the temperature and the dewpoint are the same, then the relative humidity is 100%; that is, when both temperature and dewpoint temperature are identical, the air at that pressure is holding 100% of the moisture that it can hold.   PAGE 277

F. CURRENT WEATHER

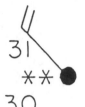

Figure 37-6. The Symbol for the Current Weather is Plotted to the Left of the Station Circle, Beneath the Temperature and Above the Dewpoint.

In our example, the two asterisks represent steady light snow. Page 273 gives all the present weather symbols used. On some surface weather maps, simplified symbols are used, especially for precipitation. For example, just one asterisk might be plotted, which would stand for snow. The snow could be light, moderate or heavy. One dot would represent rain; a comma stands for drizzle. All the standard symbols are in the table on page 273.

There are precise definitions for precipitation intensities. For snow, the rate of fall will lower the visibility. This gets confusing if something else, such as fog, is also contributing to a lower visibility. (Visibility is the average distance you can see in the horizontal.)

When snow is occurring alone (no other precipitation mixed in and no other visibility-limiting parameter such as fog, haze or smoke), then light snow is snow that does not reduce the average visibility to less than 5/8ths of a mile. The next lower reportable visibility value is 1/2 mile. When the visibility in snow is one half mile or less but not lower than 5/16ths of a mile, then the snowfall is reported as moderate snow. When the visibility in snow is below 5/16ths of a mile (i.e., 1/4 mile or lower), then the snow is reported as heavy snow. We are referring here to the rate of snowfall, not the total accumulation. For accumulation purposes, a heavy snowstorm is generally one which dumps greater than 6 inches of snow in 12 hours or less, although regions of the country that infrequently receive significant snows typically set lower threshold values for defining a heavy snowfall.

For weather observation purposes, when the visibility is reduced by moderate snow (under 1/2 mile down to 5/16ths of a mile), the snow is falling at a rate of typically an inch an hour. At visibilities of 1/4 mile or less, the rate is in excess of an inch an hour.

Light rain is not drizzle. Drizzle is very fine drops of water and occurs in fog. Fog is a stratus cloud whose cloud base is resting on the ground. Thus, when you are in fog, you are inside a stratus cloud. When enough cloud particles combine to form a drizzle drop, the drizzle precipitates out. Raindrops are larger than drizzle, and fall out of clouds such as stratocumulus, cumulonimbus and nimbostratus.

Drizzle drops are generally not larger than 0.02" in diameter (about 0.5 mm maximum diameter). Raindrops are larger.

All the symbols for the present weather, as agreed to by the World Meteorological Organization (WMO) in Geneva, Switzerland, are found in figure 36-3 on page 273. Please refer to that page of symbols for this element of the station weather plot.

G. VISIBILITY

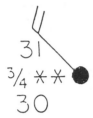

Figure 37-7. The Visibility is Reported in Whole Miles or Fractions and is Plotted to the Left of the Symbol for the Current Weather. In our example at the left, the visibility, or the average distance for how far one can see in all directions, is 3/4ths of a mile. The visibility in this case is reduced due to snow, which the symbol for the current weather shows is occurring at this reporting station at observation time. Fog, haze or smoke are not reported unless it or they by themselves reduce the visibility to under 7 miles.

H. SEA-LEVEL PRESSURE

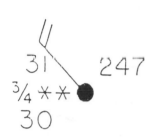

Figure 37-8. The Sea-Level Pressure is Reported to the Nearest Tenth of a Millibar and is Plotted in the Upper-Right of the Station Plot. Most sea-level pressures will lie between 930 and 1050 millibars, or from over 28.00" to over 31.00", with the pressure most of the time between 29.20" and 30.80". The average sea-level atmospheric pressure around the world is about 29.92" which corresponds to 1013 millibars. In our station model plot at the left, the 9 or 10 is left off. Therefore, the plotted 247 stands for either 924.7 millibars or 1024.7 millibars. Since pressure generally lie between 930 and 1050 millibars except for rare events, our 247 is very likely 1024.7 millibars. This term for pressure, millibars, is abbreviated mb in data reports and on weather charts. HectoPascals (hPa), which equals millibars, is also used as a term for pressure.

I. PRESSURE CHANGE

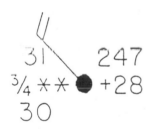

Figure 37-9. The Pressure Change is Plotted to the Right of the Total Cloud Cover (Sky Condition) Symbol and is Given to the Nearest Tenth of a Millibar. Thus, in our example, the +28 means that the pressure has risen 2.8 millibars since the last pressure change report, which typically is three hours ago. Thus, pressure changes on most weather maps are for three-hours. A zero pressure change is plotted as just 00.

J. PRESSURE TENDENCY

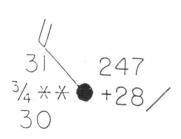

Figure 37-10. The Pressure Tendency is Plotted to the Right of the Pressure Change. The pressure tendency is for the same time period as the pressure change, usually for the past three hours. This plot tells how the pressure has been changing. For example, has it been a steady rise, or a rise then a fall, or a steady fall, or a fall then a rise?

Exercise: return to the weather map at the beginning of this chapter and practice decoding some of the observations, especially where precipitation is occurring along the east coast. Note: some plotted observations may add additional elements, e.g., cloud types, but what is given here is the basic weather plot universally used.

Z-TIME or UTC TIME:

Usually, the time put on a weather map to designate the time of the observation or the time of the forecast conditions, is given in Greenwich (for Greenwich, England) mean time; that is, the time at the 0° longitude meridian. This is because except for local-use regional maps, weather maps are distributed throughout the country and the world, especially maps that cover up to an entire continent or hemisphere. Therefore, the whole world's weather community refers to the same time zone when recording and archiving some of its weather data.

Z-time is commonly referred to in weather circles as "ZULU TIME", from an older version of the phonetic alphabet. (Alpha bravo charlie delta means A B C D in old-style radio reports, in order to make sure the listener was being given a C and not a B, for example, in a radio transmission that involved giving letters.) Zulu time or Z-time is also called UTC for Universal Temps Coordinee, or French for Universal Coordinated Time. This time is the time if you were on the 0° meridian in England.

For example, if a weather observation for JFK Airport in New York City says it is the 1500Z observation, then it is 1500 o'clock (3:00 p.m.) at 0 degrees longitude in England, but it is the 10 a.m. observation in New York City, because New York City is five hours earlier than England (in daylight savings time it would be four hours earlier). Thus, all weather observation sites such as airports that take an observation at that hour all around the globe, would report that observation as the 15Z observation (1500Z or 1500 UTC). If an observing site were to take a special observation a half-hour later, then that report would have the time 1530Z.

WHAT ARE ISOBARS?:

After all the data from the data sites are plotted on a map, the meteorologist then starts to draw the analysis so that a snapshot or picture of the weather at that observation time is drawn. This is why the weather observatories record and transmit their observations every hour around the world, and reference their observations to Z-time (UTC time).

The surface weather map is drawn from these observations which give the weather parameters at the earth's surface. The temperature is read from thermometers in an instrument shelter that allows the air to flow through it, but protects the sensors from sunlight and precipitation. The thermometers are typically six feet above the ground. Lines of equal temperatures can be drawn (these are called isotherms), but usually these lines are drawn on the so-called upper-air charts. Upper-air charts are weather maps showing conditions, including air flow, well into the atmosphere above the surface. The lines connecting points of equal atmospheric pressure are called isobars. Isobars are critical to analyzing the weather because from them we can determine where are the highest air pressure regions and the lowest air pressure regions. The air flows from high to low pressure, being turned some due to the fact that the earth is rotating. Typically, a region of high pressure is one of sinking "diverging" air and dry, fair conditions, whereas a region of low pressure is one of rising "converging" air and usually storminess.

Figure 37-11. Isobars and Fronts on a Surface Weather Map. (source: NWS)

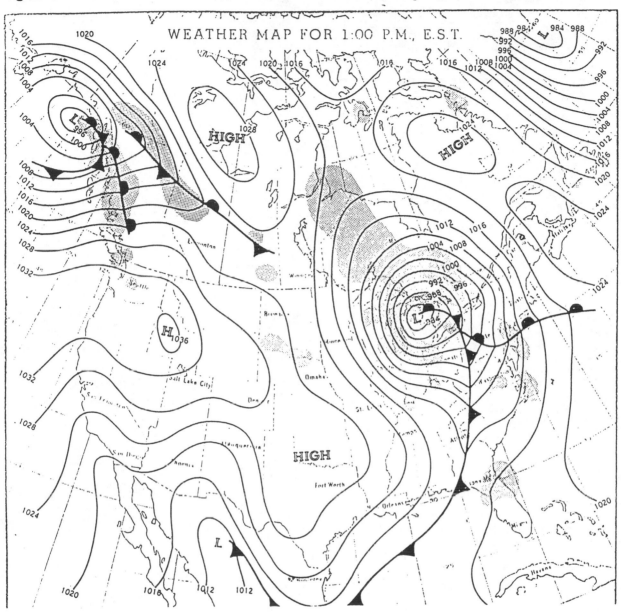

On this weather map, the isobars are lines of equal air pressure. An H identifies the center of the high pressure system (the highest pressure) and an L is the center of lowest pressure. A region of highest pressure is called a high pressure system, and of lowest pressure, a low pressure system. Highs and lows evolve, move and die, because the air is in motion and unequally warming and cooling in different regions. Thus, weather maps are excitingly active, because weather never stands still. The weather map depicts the state of the atmosphere for that level or environment at a specific time. On some surface weather maps, areas receiving precipitation are shaded in, as in the example above. Time-lapse animation of surface weather maps show the movements and evolutions of the highs, lows and fronts.

Refer to chapters in this book on high and low pressure systems (chapter 27) and on fronts (chapter 26) for more detailed information on these weather features.

<u>Ridges and troughs</u>:

Portions of a high pressure system may poke out in one or more directions, which creates a ridge of high pressure. Ridges are usually areas of fair weather.

Portions of a low pressure system may poke out in one or more directions, which creates a trough of low pressure. Troughs are usually areas of inclement weather, especially to the east of the trough axis (in the Northern Hemisphere).

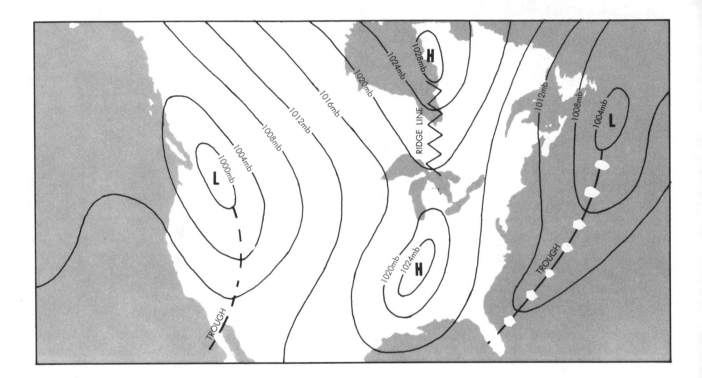

Figure 37-12. A surface weather map showing a ridges and two troughs. The squiggly lines represent ridges and the dashed lines represent troughs. We refer to a "ridge of high pressure" and a "trough of low pressure". When a ridge is passing through your area, the weather is typically fair, but when a trough of low pressure moves through, it may produce precipitation since air typically rises to the east of a trough axis, and if there is sufficient moisture, then cloudiness and subsequent precipitation, which may be in the form of showers, can occur. Ridges and troughs may not always be analyzed on the surface weather map, but they are easy for you to find. (source: USAF)

Chapter 38. UPPER-LEVEL WEATHER MAPS

Weather is four-dimensional: it occurs in both horizontal dimensions, in the vertical and changes with time. Therefore, not only must meteorologists analyze weather features at the surface, but they must look at weather maps aloft in the troposphere, since upper-level features are connected to those that we experience at the surface of the earth.

Surface low pressure systems are part of the upper-level low or trough, and surface high pressure systems are part of the upper-level high or ridge.

Although the surface map shows <u>isobars</u>, or lines of equal atmospheric pressure, the upper-air charts show <u>contours</u>, which are lines of equal height. That is, an 850 millibar (also called 850 hectoPascal) chart has lines that show how high you have to go to reach the 850 millibar (mb) pressure level. The wind blows more-or-less parallel to these lines.

Here are some examples of upper-level charts and what they are used for. For a thorough description of each chart, we refer you to the book, "WEATHER MAPS - How to Read and Interpret all the Basic Weather Charts", available from this book publisher for $29.

First, let's review the average height for the various pressure levels in the lower atmosphere. The lines on the upper-air charts show the heights in meters. These lines of equal height are called contours.

200 mb	39,000 feet
300 mb	29,000 feet
500 mb	18,000 feet
700 mb	10,000 feet
850 mb	5,000 feet
1000 mb	near sea-level

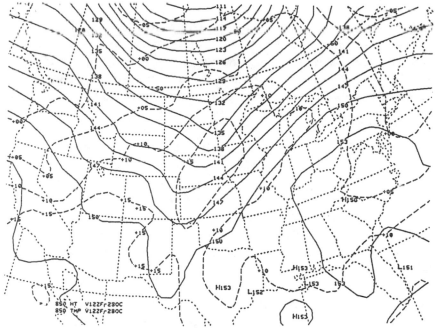

Figure 38-1. An 850-millibar chart. The solid lines are the contours and the dashed lines are lines of equal temperature called <u>isotherms</u>. The flow shows warmer air moving into the upper mid-west. A 700 mb chart is also produced.

<u>Deciphering the labelling on these charts</u>:
At the bottom of these charts is the chart identification. For example, "850" means 850 millibars. The valid time and date of the chart is given, in Greenwich Mean Time (UTC).

"HT" means the height contours of that pressure level. For example, on the 850 millibar chart on the previous page, the solid lines are called the <u>contours</u> of height. Notice the solid line cutting over Kansas. It is labelled "147", which stands for 1470 meters of height (the zero is left off). Thus, over central Kansas, you would have to go up 1470 meters (over 4800 feet) to reach the level at which the atmospheric pressure is 850 millibars (about 25½" on the barometer). But notice north of there, over northern Nebraska, there's a 141 contour, that is, 1410 meters. Thus, over northern Nebraska you have to go up only 1410 meters to hit 850 mb. You don't have to go up as high over northern Nebraska as you do over central Kansas. Thus, the 850 mb surface slopes downward from Kansas to Nebraska. Low heights on an upper-level weather chart are analogous to low pressure on a surface weather map. A low pressure system at the surface has an upper low or trough with lower heights associated with it, aloft at 850 mb and up through 700 mb, 500 mb and sometimes up to 300 or so mb.

On an upper-level chart such as the 850 millibar map on the previous page, the labelling "TMP" means the temperature lines are on the map; these are the isotherms, or lines of equal temperature. The dashed lines on this map are the isotherms, which are labelled in degrees Celsius for 5-degree intervals. Notice the warm air at 850 mb with +15°C in the middle of the country, and cooler air with +5°C over Montana at 850 mb. Since the air blows from a general west-to-east direction, the winds aloft are parallel to the contours of height. From this you can see the southwest to northeast airflow from Kansas to the Great Lakes bringing in or transporting the warmer air. Thus, that entire region is undergoing "warm air advection". The winds are bringing cooler air in a northwest flow from Montana towards Nebraska. The winds also transport moisture.

Notice the wave pattern of the upper-air flow. The bigger waves are called long-waves and the shorter ones are called short-waves. The short-waves move through the long-wave pattern, and the long-waves move, change, form and dissipate more slowly than do the short-waves. The short-wave troughs are the storms and cyclones, since they typically have upward motion ahead of the trough axis, and downward motion behind the trough axis.

Look at the 500 mb chart on the next page. The contour over southern Utah is labelled "582" which stands for 5820 meters (about 19,000 feet) for the height of the 500 mb level there. The label "VOT" stands for vorticity. A parameter called absolute vorticity, which is a measure of a component of spin of air parcels, is plotted with the dashed lines. An "X" is a vorticity maximum and an "N" is a minimum. In general, as higher values of vorticity move in, air is likely to be rising because of it, and vice versa for lowering vorticity. Thus, meteorologists use this analysis to see if vorticity advections will contribute to the vertical motion field.

On the subsequent page is a 300 mb chart on which the dashed lines are wind-speeds in knots, and are so labelled. The label "ITAC" on the chart bottom stands for isotach, which is a line of equal wind speed. Over western New Mexico, the 960 contour stands for 9600 meters (about 31,500 feet) for the height of 300 millibars over western New Mexico.

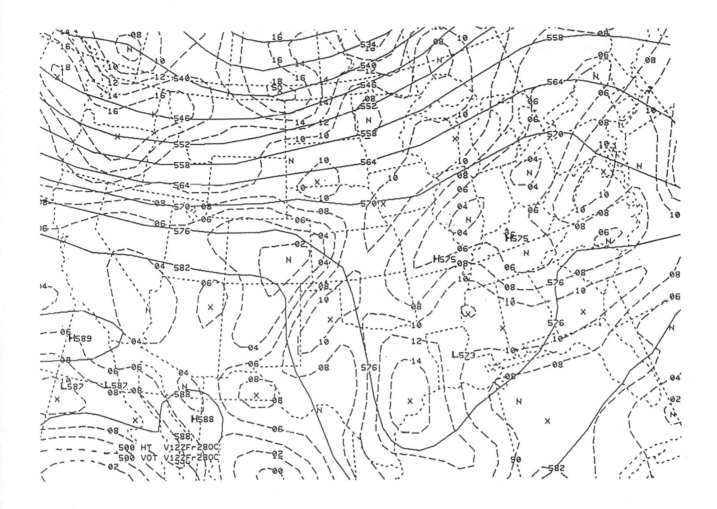

Figure 38-2. A 500 mb chart. This chart shows the contours of height of the 500 millibar atmospheric pressure level in solid lines, and shows what is called absolute horizontal vorticity in dashed lines. Vorticity is a measure of spin of air parcels, and spin is one parameter related to vertical motion of air. An X is a center of highest vorticity and an N of lowest. Please refer to chapter 29 for an explanation of vorticity. This chart shows how the vorticity pattern is moving with the wind.

Note: the legends (labels) in the lower left of each weather map in this chapter tell the type of map, define each set of lines and give the valid time of the map in Z-time. The map may be a current analysis or a forecast map (prognostication) from a computer forecast model. For example, on the map on this page, "500" means this is a 500 millibar map, "HT" means one set of lines is height lines (contours), "VOT" means the next set is vorticity lines. "V12ZFr28OC" means the analysis of the data is valid at 12Z Friday, October 28th. On this map, the solid lines are the height contours of the 500 mb level, labelled in decameters (e.g., a label of "564" means the height of the 500-millibar pressure level along that line is 5,640 meters above sea-level), and the dashed lines are units of a component of vorticity (spin) of the air parcels (see chapter 29 on vorticity). Higher values of vorticity moving in at 500 mb generally imply increasing upward vertical motion of air from the ground up through the 500 mb level.

The jet-streaks of a jet- stream are pockets of very strong wind, and are best found on the 300 mb chart in winter, 250 mb chart in spring and fall, and on the 200 mb chart in summer.

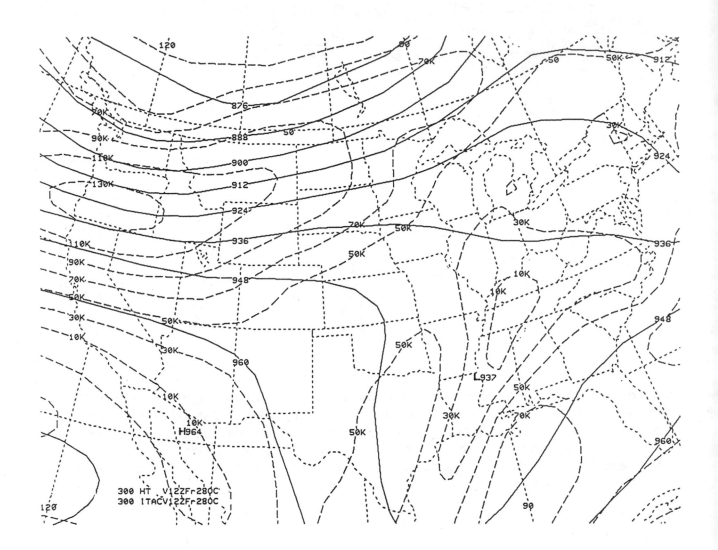

Figure 38-3. A 300 mb chart. The solid lines are the height contours and the dashed lines are ISOTACHS, lines of equal wind speed, given in knots. The areas of winds, known as jet-streaks, evolve as they move through the flow pattern. Please see chapter 23 for an explanation of jet-streams and their jet-streaks

Chapter 39. COMPUTER FORECAST MODELS

(NOTE: For a comprehensive and rigorous explanation of computer weather forecast models, refer to the book, "WEATHER MAPS - How to Read and Interpret all the Basic Weather Charts", available from Chaston Scientific, Inc. at the address on the back cover; its cost is $29.)

Around the year 1900, weather researcher Vilhelm Bjerknes in Europe stated that the future weather could be predicted by the following procedure:
1. take the mathematical equations of motions that define atmospheric behavior;
2. insert this data into the equations, as the initial conditions that describe the state of the atmosphere; and
3. solve the equations out in time to generate weather maps showing forecasted conditions at the surface and aloft that could be used as guidance in weather forecasting.

We know much about atmospheric processes. Meteorologists know the equations of motion for the atmosphere and relevant related equations dealing with (defining, known as the "parameterization" of) such things as the effects of friction, radiation and moisture transport. Thus, if we have the means to collect a plethora of data at the surface and aloft and insert it as the initial conditions into these equations and then calculate the results, we can generate forecast weather maps (prognostications or "progs").

In Bjerknes time, there were no computers to grind out solutions for these integrated equations, so the concept remained a wish item.

Then, during the World War I period of 1914-1918, a British researcher, Lewis F. Richardson, while on duty in France as a medical corpsman, wrote a manuscript describing a scheme for using current weather observations of surface and upper-air parameters, with the basic (called "primitive") equations of motion of the atmosphere, to forecast "by the numbers" (called "NUMERICAL FORECASTING").

Richardson's manuscript on numerical modeling was later lost in a coal bin. It was recovered several months later, refined, and published in 1922 as "Weather Prediction by Numerical Process". Richardson determined that with the use of mechanical hand calculators, it would require some 6000 persons, all working at the same time, to do the necessary computations to generate a 12- to 24-hour set of forecast maps! Computers were not even a viable concept at that time.

Eventually, in 1948, John von Neumann, a Hungarian mathematician, working at Princeton University, used one of the very first computers to successfully generate a numerical forecast. The first computer forecast model was born.

The first model took up to a few hours to create an analysis, and 12-, 24- and 36-hour forecasts of conditions at the 500 millibar level. Eventually, more sophisticated models were developed, including global models forecasting conditions for the surface and aloft. Thus, there are now computer forecasts, from several weather forecasting models, of the maps of surface and upper-air conditions, including forecast maps showing the distribution of moisture and predicting derived fields such as the vertical velocity field.

This is a complex topic, but anyone who enjoys meteorology would likely find it fascinating how these forecast models are set up and how they work, which is why we recommend obtaining the "WEATHER MAPS" book referenced at the top of the page. What follows here is an overview of the four steps of the prediction process by weather forecasting computer model programs.

The Four Steps of Numerical Weather Prediction by Computer Models:

1. ANALYSIS - objectively analyze the data

2. INITIALIZATION - adjust the analysis so that the model can be run with it

3. PREDICTION - run the computer model

4. POST-PROCESS - generate products such as forecasted weather maps, from the computer-model output, and clean up any erroneous lines or data

STEP 1. ANALYSIS

The technique called "objective analysis" of the data puts these observations into the computer. The computer program then reads these numbers at data points called grid points. Thus, an analysis grid can to be created. This can be the same grid as the final result in the forecast grid. "Grid" or data points (locations) can be as small as under 20 miles apart.

STEP 2. INITIALIZATION

A computer forecast model is set up using equations to solve for the state of the atmosphere at future times. The analysis done in step 1 is therefore then rewritten, redescribed, so that it is compatible with being input to these equations used by the forecast model.

STEP 3. PREDICTION

There are many equations used to describe the atmosphere and atmospheric processes. These equations account for such things as air movements horizontally and vertically, moisture distribution, the transport of atmospheric properties, atmospheric thermodynamics, radiation, and other aspects of atmospheric dynamics including the forces that are related to pressure differences and wind. All of these equations are tied together, as they must be to present as comprehensive as possible a mathematical/physical description of what the entire atmosphere is doing. We are analyzing for the surface up to the top of the troposphere, either for a huge part of the world, or, better yet, for the entire globe. The next step is to run the model, that is, to forecast the future conditions for say 3, 6, 9 and 12 hours, and out to 72 hours and even beyond. Predicted weather maps, called prognostications, or "progs", are generated and printed out by the program. Meteorologists use these as a possible "guidance" overview to start their forecasting thought process.

These computer models actually forecast the conditions in small time-steps of only a few minutes, but generate data and maps for designated forecast times, starting with the original conditions and then for say every three hours.

STEP 4. POST-PROCESS

After the model makes its set of forecasts, the output is interpolated from the model coordinates to the display coordinates. The data and maps are also "cleaned up", i.e., filtered, for cosmetic purposes. The results are the model forecast weather maps and numerical data from the models. Grid-point data from the models are also used by contemporary software to generate weather graphics. Thus, you can create your own weather maps from the output of various forecast models.

The models keep evolving over the decades. For detailed explanations of the various forecast models in use in the U.S., contact the National Centers for Environmental Prediction, currently at the World Weather Building; 5200 Auth Road; Camp Springs, MD 20746.

Chapter 40. WEATHER RADAR

The word "RADAR" started out as an acronym for "RAdio Detection And Ranging".

During World War II, bursts of electromagnetic energy were transmitted through an antenna. The energy went out in the form of waves. The length of the wave (called the "wavelength") could be fixed so that the radar waves would bounce off (reflect off) targets of a certain size-range. Thus, for example, an energy wavelength of 23 centimeters could detect aircraft.

It was discovered by accident that precipitation, especially heavy rain and hail, often also showed up on the radar scope. Thus, radar wavelengths were experimented with to find the optimum wavelength range for detecting precipitation. Weather radars use either 10 or 5 centimeter wavelengths.

Figure 40-1a (left). The radar antenna within a near-parabolic dish, and figure 40-1b (right), illustrating how the electromagnetic energy comes out of the <u>feedhorn</u> and is directed to the dish which then bounces it outward.

<u>Radar classification</u>: The two types of radar are PULSED and NONPULSED. A pulsed radar emits bursts (pulses) of electromagnetic energy for very short time periods (short bursts), and uses the time intervals between these emitted bursts to listen for (to detect) any returned energy. When the transmitted energy hits precipitation, it is scattered, but the part that is scattered directly back to the radar is called <u>reflection</u>. A nonpulsed radar emits a continuous flow of electromagnetic energy and requires a second antenna next to it to detect any returned energy. Thus, it is cheaper to have a pulsed radar since only one antenna is required, but the antenna takes turns transmitting pulses of energy and listening. Most of the time, the radar is in the listening mode (between the pulses). The transmitting and receiving modes of the pulsed radar are alternated by a piece of equipment called the <u>duplexer</u>.

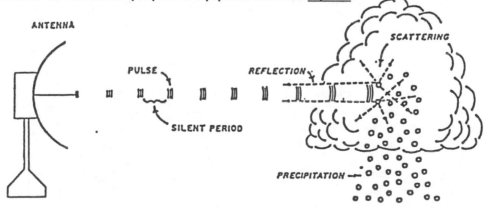

Figure 40-2. A schematic showing radar pulses scattered and reflected from precipitation occurring within a convective (cumulo-form) cloud.

Figure 40-3. The radar antenna is enclosed within a fibreglass dome called a <u>radome</u>. Inside the radome, the antenna is rotating as it sends out signals and listens for any returns. Returns are displayed on a radarscope or computer monitor and are called radar <u>ECHOES</u>. (source: NOAA)

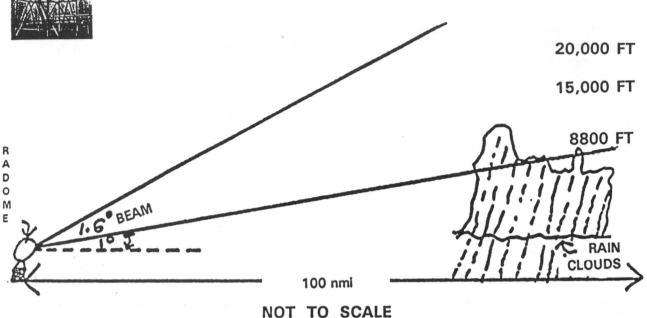

20,000 FT

15,000 FT

8800 FT

RADOME

1.6° BEAM

1°

100 nmi

RAIN CLOUDS

NOT TO SCALE

Figure 40-4. The radar beam goes out at a slight elevation above the horizon. The above example shows the radar signal being transmitted at a one degree elevation angle. The beamwidth itself starts out as a 1.6° beam in this example. With this radar, the beam at 100 nautical miles out extends from 8800 feet to 25,800 feet high. It is easy to see that if most echo tops are below 10,000 feet at about 100 nmi. out, then the beam is not completely filled with precipitation at that range. Thus, we have a problem of representativeness. (One nautical mile = 1.15 regular [statute] miles, so that 100 nmi. equals about 115 regular miles.)

Figure 40-5. This figure illustrates the problem of beamwidth resolution. The figure is exaggerated to illustrate this problem. As the beam gets farther out, it gets wider. If two separate showers are within the beam width, then they will appear on the radar display as one elongated shower. At location A, as the radar antenna and beam rotate, the beam will first pick up one shower and then the other, but at B and C, if the radar beam detects both showers along or within the beamwidth, then they will appear as one rain area. Thus, it is easy to make the mistake of interpreting such radar displays as having more widespread rain than is really occurring, and then concluding that the rain area is decreasing as it approaches the radar, and then increasing again as it leaves the area! Of course, some times that will really be the case. The key in interpreting weather data sets is to look at radar, satellite and observed data to determine what is actually occurring.

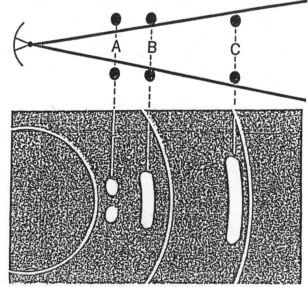

A   B   C

Refraction is the amount of bending or curving of the radar beam as it gets farther from the source.

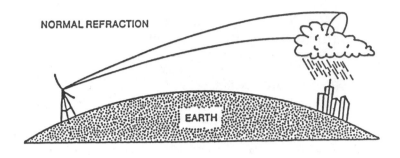

NORMAL REFRACTION

EARTH

Figure 40-6. Normal refraction of the radar beam occurs under standard atmospheric conditions. In normal refraction, the radar beam bends slightly upward from the curve of the earth. (source: NWS)

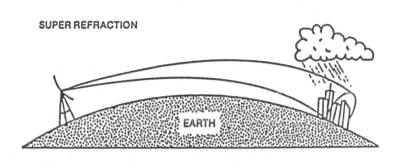

SUPER REFRACTION

EARTH

Figure 40-7. Superrefraction of the radar beam occurs when the beam bends back to the earth. The most common cause is a surface-based temperature inversion, i.e., when a layer of warmer air rests above cooler, surface-based air. This happens often on clear, nearly calm nights when the surface temperature cools off due to radiational cooling (discussed in chapter 5). After the sun comes up, the air is warmed and mixed which usually ends the inversion. (source: NWS)

Superrefraction can also exist near the earth's surface near thunderstorms, especially in their latter stage. The cold-air outflow from the thunderstorm, running along the surface of the earth, is much colder than the air it is displacing and forcing upward, resulting in a temporary temperature inversion. Another cause of superrefraction is during episodes of moisture content decreasing sharply with increasing altitude.

Thus, superrefration occurs when the radar beam bends towards the earth, compared to normal refraction when the beam bends slightly away from the earth as it goes out from the radar antenna. When the ground targets are showing up on the radar display during superrefraction episodes, such echoes are called ANOMALOUS PROPAGATION.

Figure 40-8. An extreme case of superrefraction known as ducting. Ducting is the radar beam superrefracting towards the earth, bouncing off the earth's surface and then refracting upwards. This can occur in extreme low-level temperature inversions, where the air near the surface is much colder than a layer of warmer air just above it. This is called a very stable condition, and permits the radar to detect targets much farther

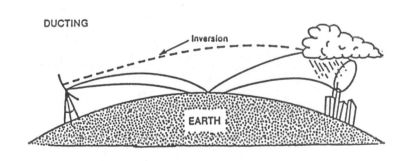

DUCTING

Inversion

EARTH

than its normal range! Most radars have a "short-range" display, which is out to 125 nautical miles, and a "long-range" display, which is out to 250 nautical miles. When no precipitation is occurring within the short range, the long range is used. The representativeness is better in the short range. (source: NWS)

Ducting occurs with television and radio signals too. When ducting occurs, it is sometimes possible to pick up broadcast stations far beyond what you normally receive. One of your authors, who lived and worked for awhile in the Rochester, New York area, turned on TV in the morning to watch the news and picked up a TV station from Casper, Wyoming, and listened to THEIR weather report!

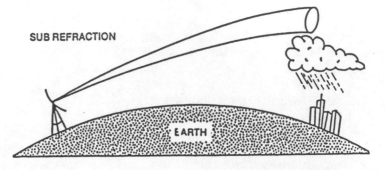

SUB REFRACTION

Figure 40-9. <u>Subrefraction</u> occurs when the radar beam bends upward greater than during normal refraction. This typically occurs in hot arid regions during the hottest, driest daylight hours. It occurs where the temperature lapse rate with height is steeper than normal --an unstable atmosphere. It can also occur where moisture increases with height. Subrefraction is less common than superrefraction, and its effect is to shorten the range of the radar beam, since the beam can overshoot weather targets at shorter ranges than is normal. (source: NWS)

The intensity of the radar echo return is measured in a unit called <u>decibels</u>. The number of decibels is proportional to the rainfall rate. Thus, rainfall rates can be estimated by weather radar! Rainfall estimations based on radar data are used only for out to 75 nautical miles from the radar site; this range is called the <u>HYDROLOGIC RANGE</u> of the radar. Beyond about 75 nmi., some of the beam may be overshooting too much of any rain, which makes any rainfall rate estimates unreliable. Thus, **the hydrologic range of the weather radar is the maximum range out from the radar within which the rainfall estimates from radar data are reasonably reliable.**

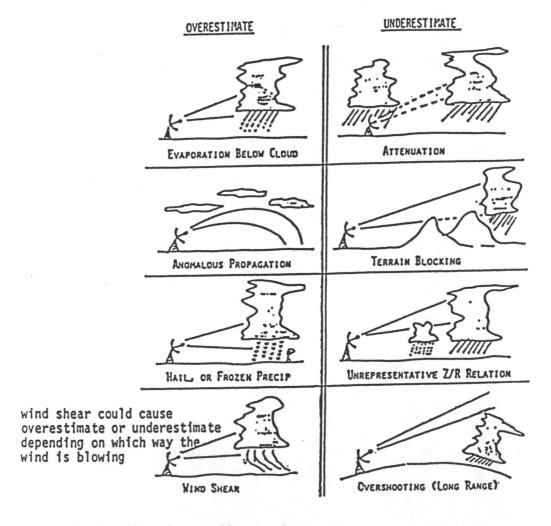

Figure 40-10. Conditions that would cause the weather radar to overestimate or underestimate the rainfall rate. (source: NWS)

Figure 40-11. The electromagnetic radiation spectrum, showing where the weather radar bands ("C" and "S") lie in relation to other forms of electromagnetic radiation.

WAVELENGTH (cm)

10^{-12} cosmic rays

10^{-11}

10^{-10}

10^{-9} gamma rays

10^{-8}

10^{-7}

10^{-6} ultraviolet

10^{-5}

10^{-4}

10^{-3}

10^{-2} infrared

10^{-1}

10^{0} EHF

10^{1} SHF

10^{2} UHF   TV

10^{3} VHF   TV FM

10^{4} HF (short wave)

10^{5} AM radio

10^{6} LF

10^{7} VLF

10^{8}

10^{9}

FREQUENCY (Hertz)

10^{23}

10^{22}

10^{21}

10^{20}

10^{19}

10^{18}

10^{17}

10^{16}

10^{15} visible light

10^{14}

10^{13}

10^{12}

10^{11}

10^{10}

10^{9}

10^{8}

10^{7}

10^{6}

10^{5}

10^{4}

10^{3}

10^{2}

10^{1}

x-rays

K
X
S < C   radar bands
L
P

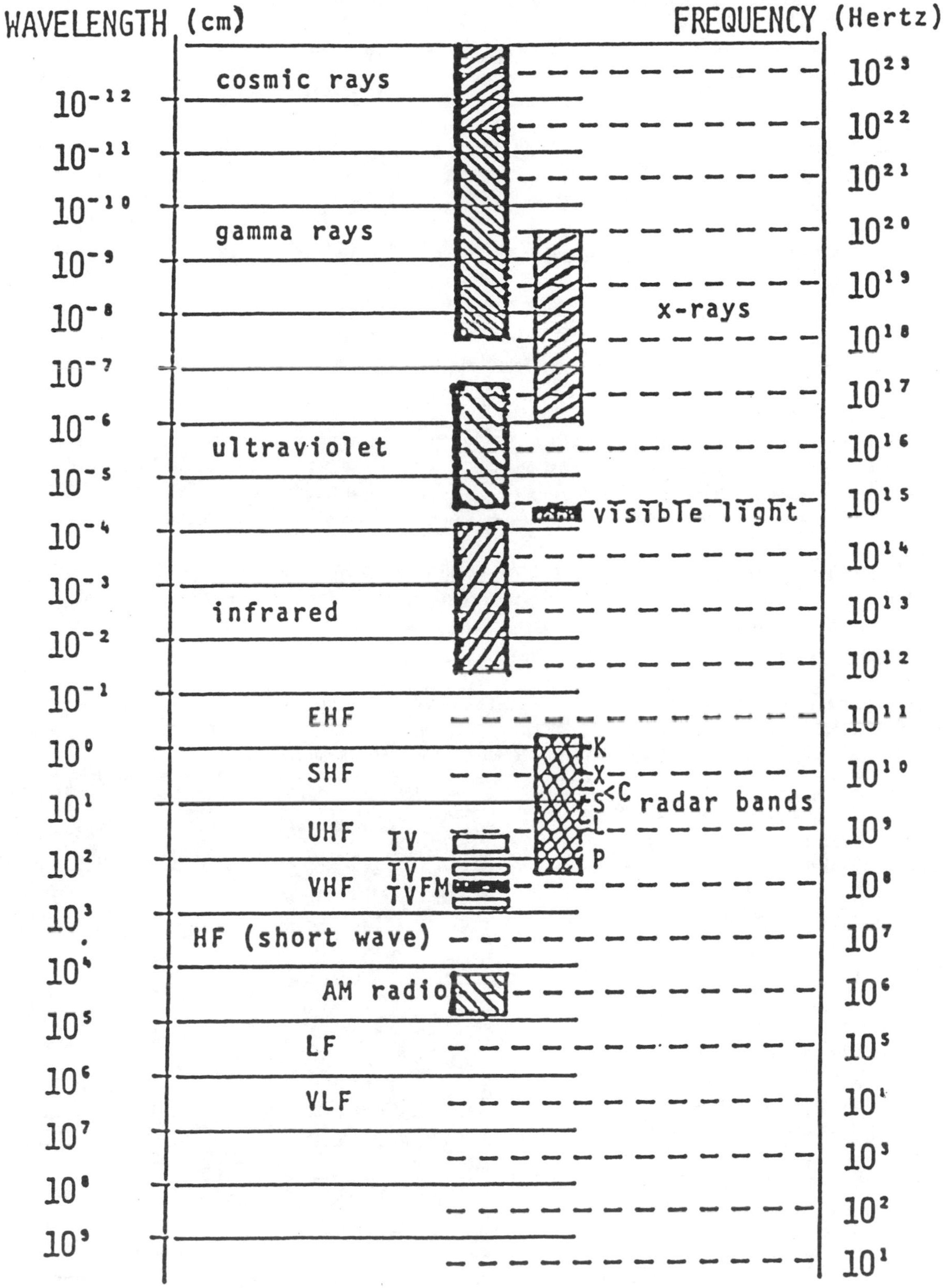

dBZ	RAINFALL CATEGORY	CONVECTIVE AMOUNT (inches per hour)
under 30	LIGHT RAIN	under 0.20" per hour
30	MODERATE RAIN	0.2" to 1.0" per hour
40	HEAVY RAIN	1.1" to 2.0" per hour
45	VERY HEAVY RAIN	2.1" to 3.0" per hour
50	INTENSE RAIN	3.1" to 4.0" per hour
55	EXTREME RAIN	greater than 4.0" per hour

Figure 40-12. Convective rainfall rates as estimated by weather radar, using the decibels (dBZ) value to empirically relate to the rate of rainfall. The distance out to which the reflectivity/rainfall-rate relationships are reasonably reliable is the hydrologic range of the radar, namely, about 75 nautical miles (about 85 regular miles).

The radar operator can also stop a radar antenna from rotating when he/she notices a powerful weather target, such as a strong thunderstorm, forming or already underway, and can then make the antenna tilt to scan up and down through the thunderstorm. The meteorologist would be looking for very high decibel levels within the clouds, especially aloft, since these may be signatures of flash flooding rain, hail or, when they descend, of a microburst.

Hail reflects and scatters the radar energy that hits it best of all precipitation types. Its echoes show up very brightly on the radar scope, i.e., these echoes have a very high decibel value. Snow does not reflect as well as rain or hail, because the shapes, forms and textures of the snowflakes (with air pockets in them) scatter the radar energy in many directions, with less of it returning to the radar antenna.

Radar images can appear as various brightnesses of white, or can be color-enhanced so that the lightest rain can show as green, heavier as yellow, then orange, and up to red for very heavy and purple for the most intense. Various shades of these colors can be used to further subdivide the intensities, which are the decibel levels.

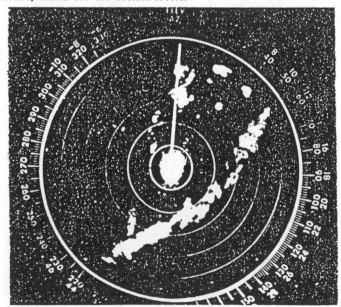

Figure 40-13. A radar scope showing a line of thunderstorms. In the middle of the scope is the radar site. Each concentric ring is 25 nautical miles distance from the next ring. Notice the blob of echoes in the middle where the radar site is. This is called **GROUND CLUTTER**, and is always there. It is the radar beam hitting buildings, hills, trees, etc. within several miles of the radar. In the early days of weather radar (late 1950s and 1960s), many radar sets were installed right in big cities, which resulted in lots of ground clutter where most people in the region lived, so they could not see on radar where any precipitation was right around the radar site! Learning from this experience, most of today's weather radars are located in the country, in order to minimize the ground clutter. Besides ground clutter, other "false precipitation echoes" occur when the radar shows precipitation where there is none occurring. This is anomalous propagation, which has been discussed earlier in this chapter. (source: NWS)

Let us look at some radar signatures of severe or potentially severe weather.

Dry-Air Intrusion

Figure 40-14. Here is a "V-notch", which often indicates large hail at the notch, and sometimes also a tornado. (source: NWS)

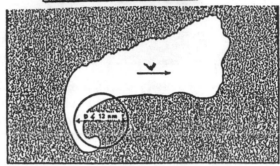

Figure 40-15. Here is a <u>HOOK ECHO</u>, which is the classic echo signature of a tornado on the reflectivity display. (source: NWS)

Figure 40-16. A time-series of radar images showing the development and movement of a hook echo (tornado) going just north of the radar site. (source: NWS)

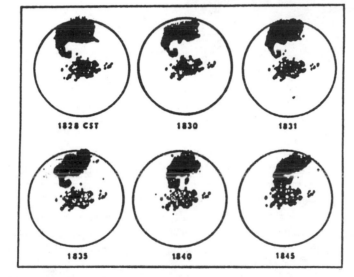

1828 CST   1830   1831

1835   1840   1845

Figure 40-17. A <u>line-echo wave-pattern (LEWP)</u>, which is a wavy squall-line of thunderstorms, and a <u>BOW ECHO</u>. A LEWP is typically associated with severe thunderstorms. As parts of the line merge, new and severe storms rapidly form at the merging. Where the line bows in, we have rapidly descending air (no echoes) and a possible microburst of winds downward from the clouds, often in excess of 100 miles per hour. On the back side of where the radar echo shows a "bowing out" may imply the rapid descent of air behind the rain echo, indicating a possible downburst of air, or a more concentrated downburst known as a microburst. The "H" refers to relatively higher air pressure (a mini-high caused by sinking air) and the "L" to a mini-low (relatively lower pressure due to rising air).

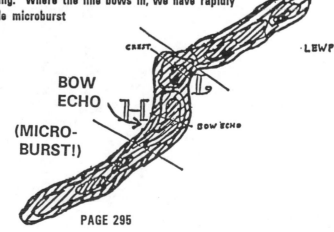

CREST

·LEWP

BOW ECHO

(MICRO-BURST!)

BOW ECHO

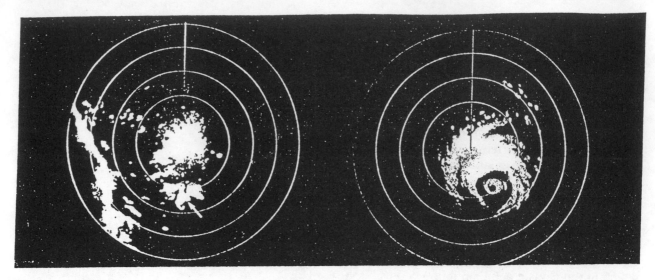

Figure 40-18. Radar reflectivity showing at left a hook echo (at the arrow), which is a tornado, and at right a hurricane with a double eye (no precipitation in the eye). The bright (white) areas on both displays are rainfall, and we also find the continuous ground clutter in the middle of each picture right around the location of each radar set. (source: NWS)

Figure 40-19. A schematic showing the radar dish with its feedhorn (the dish and feedhorn are the antenna) inside the radome, on a pedestal, and some electronic equipment inside the weather station.

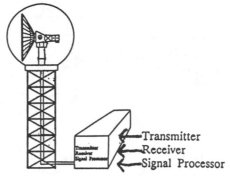

Transmitter
Receiver
Signal Processor

Range-Height Indicator:

The radar antenna can keep rotating, sending out signals that look for precipitation to reflect off and try to return to the radar site. The radar antenna rotation can also be stopped so that the radar can aim in one direction at a precipitation area that may be worthy of detailed examination. For example, if a severe thunderstorm is rapidly growing, the radar can do a tilt-sequence, scanning up and down to see how high and how intense the echoes are. When high decibel levels are occurring in mid-levels of a developing thunderstorm, this heavy precipitation must plunge to the surface, meaning that such a signature may be indicative of a downburst of strong and damaging winds. Moreover, high decibel levels through a deep vertical range indicate that torrential rainfall may be occurring with that storm.

Figure 40-20. A display on the range-height indicator (RHI). The radar antenna has stopped rotating and is scanning up and down, looking for the vertical extent and intensities of precipitation echoes. The vertical scale of the RHI display at right is labelled in tens of thousands of feet, and the bright areas are precipitation. One cell, for example, has precipitation tops to nearly 50,000 feet. The bright areas here are convective (shower, thunderstorm) cells. (source: NWS)

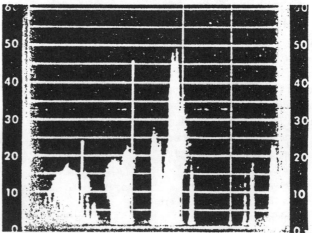

Doppler radar:

The Doppler effect is named for Christian Johann Doppler of Austria, who revealed his principle in 1842. The Doppler effect is the apparent change in the frequency of waves, such as sound waves and light waves, which occurs when the source of the waves and the observer of the waves are moving, relative to each other. The frequency increases when the source and the observer approach each other, and decreases when they move away from each other.

The Doppler part of radar uses this Doppler effect to measure the radial component of air, i.e., the component of the wind moving towards the radar site or away from the radar site. Thus, a weather radar detects precipitation echoes, and the Doppler component of the radar detects air motion.

Before discussing Doppler radar a little more, let us discuss the Doppler principle some in a little more detail.

The frequency of waves is the number of waves that pass a given point in a given period of time, such as per second. Thus, frequency is measured in cycles (number of waves) per second. The correct terminology is Hertz/second, kiloHertz/second, megaHertz/second, etc. One thousand cycles per second is one kiloHertz/second; one million cycles per second is one megaHertz/second.

The Doppler effect can occur with all phenomena that emit waves. Thus, electromagnetic waves, including radar waves, are included. When a source emitting energy in the form of waves is approaching a second object, more waves pass by the second object, thus increasing the frequency. In like manner, when the source and second object are moving away from each other, fewer waves pass by the second object, thus decreasing the frequency.

DEMONSTRATION: DETERMINING THE FREQUENCY OF WAVES THAT PASS YOU WHILE IN THE WATER AT THE BEACH

This demonstration works best when the ocean is calm with perhaps gentle swells. It will work with large bodies of water such as the Great Lakes, but is more difficult to do in smaller bodies of water such as ponds. It does not work with rivers and streams.

1. Walk out into the water until it is about knee-deep.

2. Stand still and count the number of waves that pass by in a minute. You may want to repeat this several times to determine the average frequency. Frequency in this case refers to the number of waves that pass by you in a minute.

3. Very slowly and at a constant gait (speed), walk towards the deeper water and determine the number of waves that pass by. Since you are moving towards the source, this wave number should be greater than when you were standing still. You may want to repeat walking from knee-deep water into deeper water several times in order to determine the average frequency.

4. From your deep position, walk towards the shore, counting the number of waves that pass you in a minute. This number should be lower, since you are moving away from the source of the waves. Again, you may want to repeat doing this several times in order to determine the average frequency.

Most of us probably notice the Doppler effect when an approaching and then departing train goes by. For example, as the train approaches you, more sound waves are entering your ear per second, producing a higher frequency and therefore a higher pitch. As the train moves away from you, fewer sound waves reach your ear per second, producing a lower frequency and therefore a lower pitch. The same thing happens at an automobile race track. As the cars pass the observers and move away, the pitch drops.

Astronomers can tell the relative motion of stars in relation to the earth; that is, are the stars approaching or moving away from the earth, or is the earth moving towards or away form the stars, or are both the earth and the stars in question all moving towards or away from each other? Recall that visible white light is comprised of the following colors: red, orange, yellow, green, blue, indigo and violet, with red having the lowest frequency and violet the highest.

When a star is approaching the earth, the color shifts towards the violet end of the spectrum, because more light waves are entering the eye per second, therefore producing a higher frequency wave. For example, a star that normally appears as a red star may appear to become reddish-orange or orange as it approaches the earth. On the

other hand, as a star moves away from the earth, the color shifts towards the red end of the spectrum, because fewer light waves enter the eye per second, therefore producing a lower frequency wave. For example, a star that normally appears yellow may appear to become yellow-orange or orange as it moves away from the earth.

Now let us move on to discuss Doppler weather radar.

Doppler radar: the movement of air parcels (the wind) creates density changes in the air, which can also be detected by weather radar and converted into a wind display. The Doppler aspect of radar allows us to have displays of the wind component coming at the radar and moving away from the radar. This is known as the radial component of the wind. This principle allows a tornado, including a developing tornado, to be detected in the clouds before it descends to the ground. Thus, the circulation is detected. The way this is done is to assign a set of colors...typically the "warm" colors of shades of red, orange and yellow, to air moving away from the radar, and the "cool" colors of shades of green, blue and violet, to air coming towards the radar. If red and green are the highest speeds, with red indicating air moving away from the radar and green indicating air moving towards the radar, and the radar display shows a small area of red next to a small area of green, then a rotation is occurring there. This could be a tornado or developing tornado, and a tornado warning will be issued, perhaps even before the twister has touched down. It may not touch down, but the warning allows people to take shelter from the potential tornado.

Sophisticated versions of Doppler weather radars also have computer software that includes algorithms (problem-solving techniques) which search for and alert the forecaster about locations of possible hail, tornadoes, wind shear, heavy rain, etc.

Thus, weather radar is a valuable took to the meteorologist. And via the internet, you can call up weather radar displays and follow the progress of storms yourself.

Surface and upper-air observations, weather maps, weather radar data and weather satellite imagery and data are used together to give us a three-dimensional and a four-dimensional (the 3 directions plus time) description of our always changing weather!

Chapter 41. WEATHER SATELLITES

a. weather satellite systems

There are two types of meteorological satellites: geosynchronous and polar-orbiting. The geosynchronous satellites are placed in an orbit 22,300 miles from earth, over the equator, so that they can move from west to east, the same as the earth, at the same rotational speed of the earth at the equator, about 1000 mph. Since the circumference of the earth is about 25,000 miles, the earth, rotating at a little over 1000 mph at the equator, makes its complete rotation in 24 hours, with the geosynchronous satellites moving at the same speed, and therefore staying over the same location.

The current family of geosynchronous satellites is called GOES, which stands for "Geostationary Operational Environmental Satellite". Five GOES systems circle the globe, all over the equator. One is off the east coast of the Americas and one is off the west coast of the Americas. The others are at about the longitude of Japan (south of Japan), over the Indian Ocean and over Africa. Thus, the world is covered.

The other family of meteorological satellites is the polar orbiter series. These satellites are at a much lower altitude, about 1000 miles out, and are placed in an orbit that roughly goes from pole to pole, taking images in a swath averaging some 1500 miles across.

The main weather satellite images are visible, infrared, enhanced infrared and water vapor imagery. Images are returned to ground stations on earth, processed and enhanced to depict the weather features.

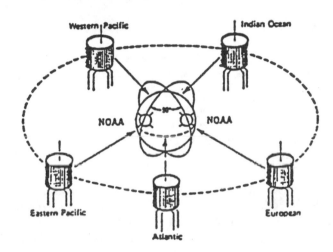

Figure 41-1. A schematic depicting the geosynchronous GOES weather satellites in orbits 22,300 miles out, and the polar orbiter weather satellites, currently known as NOAA satellites, in quasi-pole-to-pole orbits several hundred miles out. The GOES satellites stay over the same locations over the equator, sending images of the same part of the globe from North to South polar regions. In very high latitudes, cloud tops are displaced farther poleward by GOES satellites, which is why the polar orbiters are more useful in polar regions.

Types of weather satellite imagery:

Weather satellites have sensors that give us visible, infra-red, water vapor and other imagery of the tops of clouds and, where there are no clouds, the surface of the planet. Visible pictures are useable obviously only during the daytime. Infra-red (heat) imagery senses the temperature of the tops of the clouds or the ground, water or ice surface. The Stefan-Boltzmann Law of physics relates the emitted energy of the surface of an object to the fourth power of its absolute temperature. The more radiation emitted by each square centimeter surface area of an object, the higher the object's surface temperature.

Infra-red satellite sensors use this principle to obtain the temperatures of cloud tops. The colder the cloud-top temperature, the higher the cloud tops are. For example, for convective clouds, this enables weather forecasters to assess the severity of thunderstorms, since cooling cumulonimbus tops imply that updrafts are building the storm's clouds higher, intensifying the thunderstorm.

Infra-red imagery can be used at day and during the night, since the infra-red sensors on the weather satellites are detecting radiation emitted from the cloud tops, and this information is then converted to the temperatures of these cloud tops. Computer enhancement allows for coloring or shading the imagery based on its temperature.

Water vapor imagery is particularly clever. At the 6.7 micrometer wavelength, the water vapor in the atmosphere absorbs outgoing infra-red radiation (heat) from the earth, and then reradiates it. Sensors on the satellites set to detect this reradiated energy will show where water vapor is present between about 10,000 feet and 30,000 feet up, whether it is in cloud form or not.

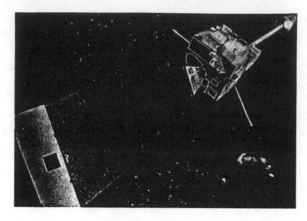

Figure 41-2. Weather satellites have been operational since 1960. Each new generation of satellites has improved quality of their imagery.
(source: NOAA)

A fine resolution of imagery is desired. Resolution is the smallest object that can be shown by itself. For example, a satellite image having a half-mile resolution means that the smallest object it can show in its images, say its visible pictures, is one-half mile across. Thus, if there were a lone thunderstorm that was one-half mile in diameter, it would be the smallest object that the image would show.

b. visible weather satellite imagery

Visible pictures are just like pictures taken by an ordinary camera, but are looking down from space. Since they need reflected light to show a picture of any target, the visible satellite pictures are available only during the daytime.

How well a cloud-top or snow-covered field or the ground or ocean show up depend on how much of the sun's rays they reflect back towards space. This reflectivity is called <u>albedo</u>. For example, the tops of a large thunderstorm will reflect back about 92% of the sunlight; thus its albedo is .92. This means that it will appear very bright on a visible satellite picture.

Fresh new snow reflects back about 88% of the sunshine impinging on it, but old snow (say 3 to 7 days old) does not reflect back as much (only 59%). A forest of pine trees or other coniferous forest hardly reflects any sunlight at all (only 12%); therefore, forested areas that are not covered by clouds show up dark on a visible picture from space. Oceans appear even darker, since their albedo is about .09 (9%).

1.	Large thunderstorm	92%	7.	Thin stratus	42%
2.	Fresh new snow	88%	8.	Thin cirrostratus	32%
3.	Thick cirrostratus	74%	9.	Sand, no foliage	27%
4.	Thick stratocumulus	68%	10.	Sand and brushwood	17%
5.	White Sands NM USA	60%	11.	Coniferous forest	12%
6.	Snow, 3-7 days old	59%	12.	Water surfaces	9%

Figure 41-3. The amount of sunlight reflected back towards space by various targets. The more that is reflected, the better the target will show up on the visible satellite picture.

SUBPOINT   .5N   75.5W

Figure 41-4. A Western Hemispheric full-disk visible picture view from a GOES weather satellite, showing the cloud cover and areas of clear weather. (source: NOAA)

Figure 41-5. A visible satellite image. The state and Canadian province borders are superimposed on the photo. Note the puffy clouds along the Kansas/Colorado border: these are the tops of thunderstorms, cumulonimbus clouds. (source: NOAA)

In the top-right of the image:

HURRICANE EMILY
AUGUST 31, 1993
8:51 AM EDT
NOAA 12 HRPT 2KM VIS

Labels on map: KNOTTS ISLAND, CAPE HATTERAS, WILMINGTON

Figure 41-6. A visible image of a small, compact hurricane, showing its clouds and clear eye in the middle. (source: NOAA)

c. enhanced infra-red weather satellite imagery

At night, visible pictures are not possible; therefore, infrared technology is used. Infrared images are also taken during the daytime.

Infrared radiation is a means to transmit heat. The earth and clouds emit infrared radiation. Therefore, sensors have been developed for the weather satellites to detect the amount of radiation being emitted by the cloud tops and, if no clouds are present, by the targets below (the ground, ocean surface or snow- or ice-covered surfaces).

On an infrared black-and-white image, colder objects appear white and warmer objects appear black. Thus, if we were comparing a weather satellite picture in the visible with an image in the infrared, with both showing part of the earth and its clouds and also past the curve of the earth to show outer space, then cold outer space would appear black in the visible picture and white in the infrared image.

In meteorology, we have developed what are called "enhancement curves" which cause the infrared image to depict temperature ranges in shades of gray, white and black. Thus, we can start the enhancement at some desired temperature that would give some idea of the height of the cloud tops, and use a medium gray for say -32°C to -41°C, then a light gray for -42 to -52 degrees, etc., followed by a dark gray, then black , then white. We can set black to represent cloud tops colder than -62°C, which would mean very impressive thunderstorms if these clouds are the tops of thunderstorms. If they are, then the white, set at -80°C or colder, would represent very cold tops, i.e., very high-topped thunderstorms, likely 50,000 to 60,000 feet high and even higher (in mid-latitudes), and would be associated with the heaviest rainfall, maybe flash-flood producing, and/or the most severe weather, since these "overshooting tops", which are overshooting the rest of the thunderstorm or thunderstorm complex, represent the area(s) likely having the strongest convective updrafts. We can also colorize these different enhancement levels, making them easy to interpret plus visually more stunning, as we observe them on computer monitors or in a color image picture.

Infrared imagery has limitations. Ground targets such as fog and snow-cover do not show up well. Thus, professional and amateur meteorologists look at both visible and infrared images during the daytime, and infrared images at night, to identify features. The infrared imagery most commonly used is enhanced infrared imagery. Moreover, another type of infrared depiction called the "water vapor imagery" is used to detect moisture in the troposphere, whether in cloud form or not, between approximately 10,000 and 30,000 feet up, which is essentially between about 700 and 300 mb. Water vapor imagery will be discussed later.

Figure 41-7. An enhanced infra-red satellite image. Shades of gray, and white and black are used to identify cloud top temperatures. For example, in the thunderstorm over Arkansas, the "black" area represents cloud tops colder than -62°C but not colder than -80°C. These tops may be between 40,000 and 50,000 feet high, indicating a strong thunderstorm. In the unenhanced infra-red depiction areas, colder objects, such as outer space, appear white, and warmer objects, such as the ground or tropical ocean, appear dark. (source: NOAA)

Figure 41-8. Compare the visible picture of Hurricane Frederic of 1979 (top) with an enhanced infrared image of the same storm (bottom) (the infrared image is enlarged somewhat to show the detail). In the infrared image, gray areas on the outer part of Frederic are clouds at cirrus-level, and the black area of the hurricane is the rain shield, within which a large white area represents the coldest cloud tops and most intense convective rainfall.
(source: NOAA)

Thus, the most intense rainfall of the storm, which tends to correlate with the fiercest winds in the storm, can be followed in the enhanced infrared weather satellite imagery. Video-loops easily identify development, movement and diminution of storm systems.

d. water vapor satellite imagery

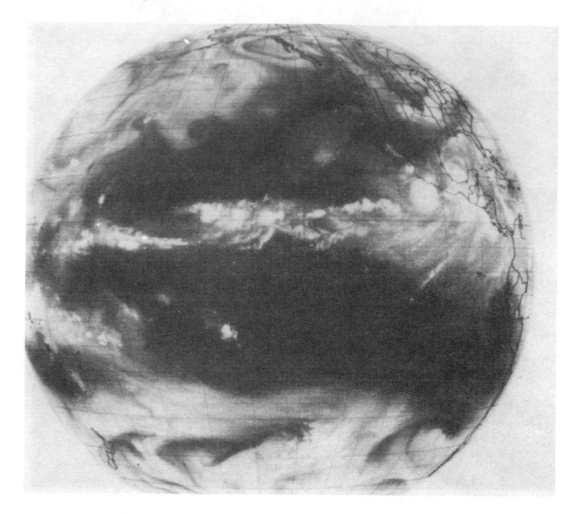

Figure 41-9. A water vapor image from a GOES weather satellite. The milky white areas are moisture in the air, not in cloud form, and the bright white areas are moisture which has condensed into clouds, most of the data being detected between approximately 10,000 and 30,000 feet up, thus the water vapor image depicts MID- AND UPPER-LEVEL MOISTURE, WHETHER IN CLOUD FORM OR NOT. ("Mid- and upper-level" refers to the middle and upper portions of the troposphere, respectively.) Note the clouds and moisture in the intertropical convergence zone just north of the equator. There is a developing tropical cyclone off the west coast of Mexico. (source: NOAA)

Here is the physical basis for water vapor satellite images. The earth receives radiation from the sun in many frequencies, short-wave and long-wave, converting that radiation to energy forms which include heat, which is a form of long-wave radiation. The earth, and clouds, emit this heat, which is the infrared radiation sensed by the weather satellites. At the 6.7 micrometer wavelength, which is a part of the infrared band, water vapor in the air has the property of absorbing this infrared radiation. It then reemits it. Thus, a sensor on a satellite can be designed to measure the flux of radiation from targets emitting radiation at 6.7 micrometers. The amount of radiation received is proportional to the temperature of the emitter, which is the basis for enhancement of infrared images. Moreover, the more moisture in the depth of atmosphere being sensed, the brighter the area will appear on the water vapor image. Therefore, moisture that is not or not yet condensed into cloud form appears a fuzzy or a milky light white, whereas clouds appear bright white. Areas that are relatively dry and/or are drying due to subsiding air, show up dark. Recall that water vapor imagery sensing works essentially for the 10,000- to 30,000-foot range depth of atmosphere, essentially sensing moisture between about 700 and 300 millibars (hectoPascals). Looking at a water vapor image is analogous to looking at a fog from the top down. The more of it there is, and/or the greater its vertical extent, the thicker it will appear.

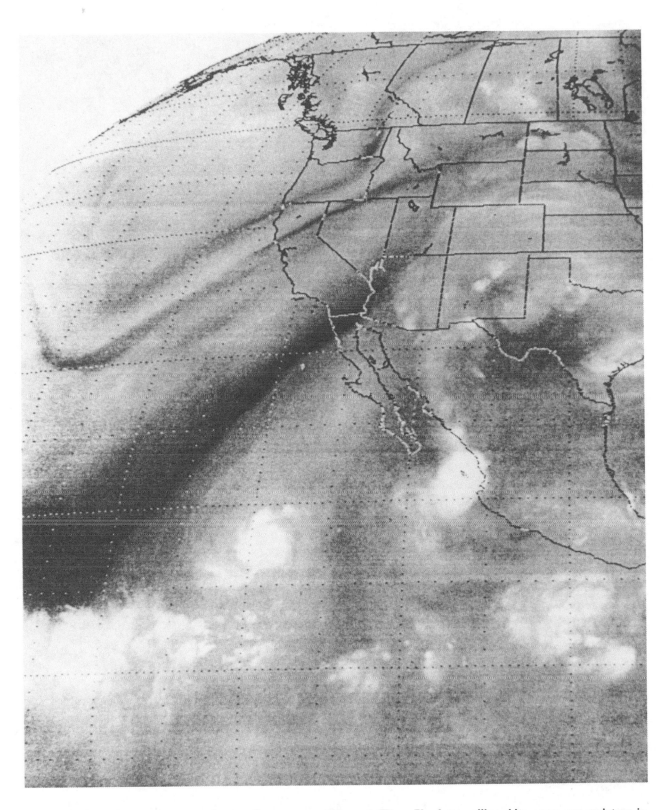

Figure 41-10. A water vapor image from a weather satellite. The fuzzy milky-white areas are moisture in the middle and upper troposphere, about 10,000 through 30,000 feet up, and the bright white areas are where moist air has been lifted and cooled sufficiently to form visible clouds. Dark regions show relatively dry, and often sinking, air.

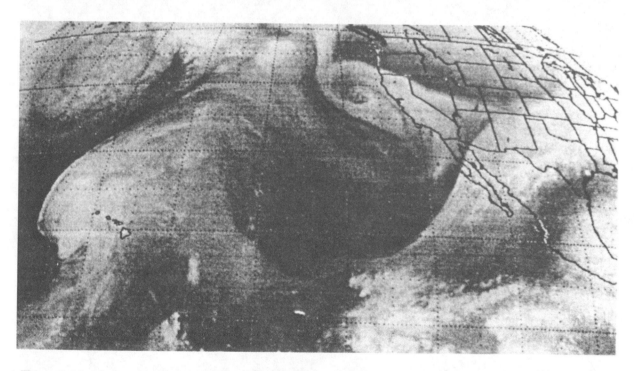

Figures 41-11, top, and 41-12, bottom. Visible satellite picture, top, and water vapor image, bottom, of Hurricane Iwa approaching the Hawaiian Islands on November 23rd, 1982. (source: NOAA)

The infrared image shows the greater extent of the mid- and upper-level moisture associated with Iwa. The water vapor image also helps to identify the location of the upper-level anticyclonic cirroform outflow aloft, located to the north and northeast of the storm center.

SECTION XI: CLIMATOLOGY

Chapter 42. WORLD CLIMATE

Climate is the average weather conditions for an area over a period of time (at least decades) plus the records of the extremes.

Whereas weather is a day-to-day (and hour-to-hour) description of local atmospheric conditions, the climate is the average of continuous decades of weather, plus a listing of the extremes of conditions. For example, suppose for the past forty years ending at the end of the last decade, that the average monthly temperature for July for your area is 70.0 degrees Fahrenheit, with the average daily low of 59.5°F and the average daily high of 80.5°F. This is your climatic average. However, to complete the temperature aspect of climate, the extremes are also included. Thus, let us say that in our example for July, even though the average daily high temperature for that month is 80.5° with the average daily low being 59.5°, the all-time daily high is 112°F and the all-time daily low is 36°F. By including the extremes, we fully describe the temperature aspect of the local climate for that area, since we are giving the averages and the extremes. By giving the extremes, we define the greatest range of temperature for the month of July in that area.

Over the decades, the climate may change...possibly slightly or possibly significantly. Thus, after some more decades pass, a new set of climatic regions will be developed.

Our example is for temperatures, but the total climate description of course includes all the other reported weather elements also, such as precipitation, including snowfall.

Currently, for the United States, the repository for climatic records is the National Climatic Data Center which is currently located in Asheville, North Carolina. The World Meteorological Organization, currently headquartered in Geneva, Switzerland, also publishes climatic atlases, including for the entire world.

Since geography affects the weather, geography influences the climate for regions of the planet. When you study charts of climate around the world, it is easy to see the effects of geography; for example, the windward side of a large mountain range typically receives more precipitation than does the leeward side, and the low-elevation non-mountainous interior of a continent has a greater temperature range than does an island in the ocean, because land heats up and cools off faster than does water.

If you are interested in reading the climate records from around the world, they are available in tabular and graphic forms from the National Climatic Data Center and from the World Meteorological Organization. The information is also on computer disk.

Here are examples of questions that can be answered by exploring some of the statistics on a region's climate. Imagine that you were considering moving to a certain area. Some of these questions are those you would probably ask, and hopefully the information would be available from the climatic data of (in the U.S.) the National Climatic Center.

1. **Temperature**: What is the monthly, seasonal and yearly average temperature? Which month is the warmest, and which the coldest? (You can get that information from the monthly average temperature.) What is the highest temperature ever recorded, and what is the lowest temperature ever recorded?

2. **Sunshine**: What is the average percent of possible sunshine for each month, as well as for each season and for the entire year?

3. **Cloudiness**: What is the average number of clear, partly cloudy and cloudy days for each month?

(continued)

4. **Precipitation**: What season(s) and months are the wettest, driest? What is the total annual precipitation? What type of precipitation might you expect (during the winter months, e.g.)? How many days in the year are there with thunderstorms? What is the most snowfall to occur in a season?

5. **Humidity (relative humidity and/or dewpoint)**: Is the air usually fairly dry or fairly humid? Which month(s) and season(s) are the most humid and the driest?

6. **Visibility**: Is visibility often reduced due to fog, haze, smog (pollution), etc.?

7. **Winds**: Is it windy enough each month to give me a bad hair day? Is it windy enough to make the generation of electricity by wind practical? What is the prevailing wind direction for each month? If near a large body of water, does the prevailing wind blow off land or off water? What is the average monthly wind speed? What is the strongest wind gust ever reported?

8. **Pressure**: Are there relatively large fluctuations in barometric pressure between fair weather and stormy weather as well as between seasons?

Regional climatology is the study of climatic conditions throughout the regions of the world. The varying climates are caused by a combination of conditions called climatic controls. Following is an overview of the major climatic controls.

MAJOR CLIMATIC CONTROLS:

1. **LATITUDE**: In general, the closer an area is to the equator, the warmer the overall climate, and the closer to a pole, the colder the overall climate.

2. **ALTITUDE**: The higher in elevation a region is, the colder the climate. For example, some of the highest mountain peaks in the Hawaiian Islands, in the tropics, receive snow. If you climbed from sea-level in the South American tropics to the summit of a very high mountain, you would ascend through a number of climatic regimes.

3. **LAND AND WATER MASSES**: In general, if your region is surrounded by a large expanse of land, then your climate has a greater diurnal, monthly and yearly variation in temperature than if you lived on an island surrounded by a great expanse of water. Recall that land masses heat up and cool off more rapidly than do bodies of water.

4. **MOUNTAIN BARRIERS**: When a mountain chain is essentially perpendicular to the prevailing wind direction, then areas on the side that faces the direction of the wind, called the , windward side, experience a wetter climate than areas on the opposite side of the mountain chain, called the leeward side. The reason for this is that the air is forced up and over the mountains, and in so doing it is cooled, condensing its water vapor into clouds and subsequent precipitation. Then after the air crosses the tops of the mountains it descends on the leeward side, warming and drying during the descent, which dissolves much of the clouds through evaporation. Thus, the leeward sides of mountain chains have drier climates than do the windward sides. An example is Glacier National Park in northwest Montana, where the western slopes of the Rocky Mountains, which is the windward side, receive much more rain and snow during the year than the eastern slopes, which is the leeward side. Of course, occasional storms do come in from the south, even on the eastern side, and a powerful succession of strong storms and convection can still produce precipitation on the leeward side, but in general, when there exists a discernable windward side of a mountain range, the climate is wetter on the windward side than on the leeward side.

Most major deserts are on the leeward side of mountain ranges. For example, Death Valley, California, which is in a desert basin of about 1500 square miles on the leeward side of the Amargosa Mountain Range and contains the lowest point in the Western Hemisphere at 280 feet below sea-level, has had temperatures as high as 134°F (56°C) in the shade! If all mountains and mountain chains were eliminated, there would probably be very few deserts.

There are two major reasons why the temperature drops as we ascend and rises as we descend:

a. When we ascend, the air becomes thinner because there is less of it the higher we go.

This is because gravity forces most of the air to accumulate near the surface of the earth. The heavier gases of the atmosphere, such as nitrogen, oxygen and argon, are more concentrated at the bottom of the atmosphere, near the earth.

Because the air becomes thinner with height, the number of collisions between and among air molecules becomes fewer, and the fewer the number of collisions, the less heat is generated by friction; the result is cooler air. A body, such as a molecule, has a temperature above absolute zero when there is motion within or of the body. This motion can be translational (moving), rotational and vibrational.

As you descend, the air becomes thicker; therefore, the greater is the number of molecular collisions and hence the warmer the air becomes.

DEMONSTRATION: FRICTION

1. Slowly rub your hands together.

2. Gradually increase the rate of rubbing. What do you observe?

In general, the rate that dry air cools as it ascends is approximately 5½ Fahrenheit degrees per thousand feet of elevation rise. In like manner, a parcel of dry air warms at the same rate as it descends, that is, it warms at about 5½ Fahrenheit degrees per thousand feet of elevation descent. This rate is known as the dry adiabatic lapse rate. The term, lapse rate, is the rate of change of a parameter with height. The term adiabatic means no heat is added to or taken away from the air parcel during the ascent or descent; any heat given off or taken on is strictly internally induced as the parcel expands while rising and compresses while sinking. As an air parcel is rising, work is expended as the parcel expands, so it releases heat and cools off; as an air parcel is sinking, its molecules are compressed, increasing the number of collisions of particles and warming the parcel. Notice that the environment itself neither takes away heat or gives heat to the parcel. Strictly speaking, however, there is a slight mixing of the environmental air with the parcel's air, which is called entrainment of environmental air into the rising or sinking parcels. However, except for rapidly rising or sinking parcels that are found in deep convection (large thunderstorms), the entrainment of outside air into the parcels is minimal and is ignored for this discussion.

Now let us consider moist air. The air in low levels may start out being saturated, or if it rises enough, it will cool to its dewpoint temperature and become saturated. Then we are dealing with the lapse rate of moist parcels. Ascending moist air cools at a lower rate than that of dry air. This is because the water vapor it contains condenses as it cools, which releases heat at the rate of about 600 gram (small) calories per gram. That is, about 600 calories of heat energy are released by each gram of water vapor that condenses to form visible cloud matter. This heat energy is latent in the moist air; that is, it is potential energy that will not be released or used unless condensation occurs. That is why we call this potential energy the latent heat of condensation. Thus, because of the release of the latent heat of condensation as a moist parcel rises, the rate of cooling for a moist parcel is less than that of a dry parcel. In like manner, as moist air descends, evaporation of the water vapor absorbs heat at the same rate, about 600 calories per gram; that is, about 600 calories of heat energy are needed to evaporate one gram of water. Thus, we now refer to the moist adiabatic lapse rate, which is roughly 3 Fahrenheit degrees per every 1000 feet elevation change. This discussion is true in the lower troposphere. The higher we go, into the colder height of the troposphere, the more variable is the moist adiabatic lapse rate.

Note: for a"rule-of-thumb", we think of rising air as conserving its moisture content (keeping its dewpoint value) as it rises, but because the air pressure is lower as we rise and as the parcel expands, there actually is a slight dewpoint lapse rate with height, but we may consider the moisture content to be unchanged as the unsaturated parcel rises.

clauds and rain

windward side

34°F at 12,000 feet

MOUNTAIN

leeward side

89°F at 2000 feet

sea-level 70°F

OCEAN

Figure 42-1. Initially saturated air parcels (air flow) moving up the windward side of a mountain and then drying out as they move down the leeward side. As the saturated air rises up the windward side, it cools at the moist adiabatic lapse rate for the lower troposphere, about 3 F° per thousand feet of ascent. (This could be air coming from a storm moving inland from the ocean, affecting a mountain or mountain range just inland, as in the American and Canadian west coast.) As the air rises, it produces clouds and precipitation. At the mountain's base, the air parcels are at the same temperature as the environment, because they are the environment. As they rise up the mountain, they are replaced by air coming in from upstream. For our example, use the sea-level air temperature of the parcels as 70°F; so the parcels initially are at 70°F. By the time the air reaches the summit of the mountain, say 12,000 feet, they have cooled to 34°F. They have cooled at about 3 F degrees per 1000 feet in their ascent. The total travelled distance of the parcels up the slope is greater than 12,000 feet, depending on the angle of the slope, but the VERTICAL component of the distance travelled is 12,000 feet. If the air expends all its moisture by the time it reaches the summit, it will descend on the leeward side of the mountain and warm at the dry adiabatic lapse rate, which is about 5.5 Fahrenheit degrees per thousand feet. In our example, the elevation of the terrain on the other side of the mountain is 2000 feet above sea-level. So the temperature of the air parcels when they reach that terrain will be about 89°F! The air parcels started out on the summit at 34° F and warmed approximately 5.5 Fahrenheit degrees per 1000 feet of descent from 12,000 feet elevation to 2000 feet elevation, therefore warming 55 F. degrees. The result is a temperature of 89°F. Thus, even though the air started out at sea-level with a temperature of 70 degrees, it winds up on the other side of the mountain, and at a higher elevation, at 89 degrees.

Problem: In the same scenario given above, now suppose the elevation of the other side of the mountain is also sea-level. What would be the temperature of the air parcels when they reach the terrain at the mountain's base on the leeward side?

Answer: The air on the summit, 12 thousand feet above sea-level, is 34°F. It descends dry adiabatically through 12,000 feet of vertical drop. Thus, by warming at the dry adiabatic lapse rate of 5.5 F° per thousand feet, the parcels will warm by 66 degrees, resulting in their temperature being 100°F! This, for example, is typical of air found east of San Diego, California, on the other side of the mountains in Death Valley, California. The air may not start out saturated when it ascends the mountains, but after some rise it will cool to its dewpoint, which means the parcels are then saturated, and will then cool at the moist adiabatic lapse rate. When the air is not saturated initially, the parcels cool at the dry adiabatic lapse rate until they become saturated, and then cool at the moist adiabatic lapse rate.

More rigorously, the dry adiabatic lapse rate is about 5.5°F per 1000 feet, which is about 9.8°C per 1000 meters, and the average value for the moist adiabatic lapse rate in the low and middle troposphere is about 3.3°F per thousand feet, which is about 6°C per 1000 meters. The average lapse rate is closer to the moist abiabatic lapse rate, since, more often than not, air contains sufficient moisture as opposed to being completely or nearly dry.

The air would not cool or warm ADIABATICALLY when the environment is adding heat to or taking heat away from the parcels. The Latin prefix, "a", means "not". So when we have DIABATIC heating or cooling also occurring to the parcels, the heating or cooling needs to be included in calculating the temperatures of the parcels as the move with a vertical component. Examples of diabatic heating and cooling are solar heating and radiational cooling, respectively.

Thus, geographic features play a crucial role in affecting the weather and climate; we used the mountain and mountain range example to illustrate this point.

b. The second major reason why the air cools as it rises and warms as it sinks is that the surface of the earth absorbs sunlight and changes it into heat. In a sense, therefore, the earth's surface acts like a stove. The farther above the surface of the earth you go, you would be receiving less heat from the earth. This is analogous to moving away from a stove or roaring fireplace. Similarly, as you get closer to the stove or roaring fireplace, you observe the air to be warmer.

5. <u>PREVAILING WINDS</u>: Coastal areas receive sea-breezes often, especially during the warmer half of the year. Right along the coast, springs and summer are cooler than they are just a few miles or kilometers inland. You can get just as sunburnt in San Diego as in Death Valley on a sunny summer afternoon, but the air temperature in San Diego may be in the 70s (F) while in Death Valley it may be in the 120s.

Areas just east of deserts, where the prevailing winds are from the west, are hotter and drier in late spring, summer and early fall than other inland areas that have prevailing westerly winds but do not have deserts just to their west.

Thus, we can see how the prevailing winds, combined with the geography, affect the weather and climate.

6. <u>AIR MASSES</u>: Most places in the middle latitudes (between the tropics and the polar regions) are visited by both cold, dry and warm, humid air masses. Those areas closer to the tropics are dominated by the warm, more humid air masses, while those areas closer to the polar regions are frequented by the colder, drier air masses.

Coastal areas are affected by maritime masses of air, causing these regions to have cooler springs and summers and warmer falls and winters than they otherwise would. Consider, for example, the climate of Seattle, Washington, near the northwest coast of the contiguous Untied States. Seattle's climate is strongly influenced by maritime polar air masses, which usually keeps it cooler in spring and summer, and warmer in the fall and winter, than in inland areas of the same latitude. This is the average condition. Of course occasionally an arctic air mass will invade from the northeast, or and easterly downslope flow from the mountains will occur. In the first case, Seattle may then briefly experience bitter cold and snow, and in the latter case, the area will briefly experience hot weather. But most of the time, the oceanic influence is predominant.

7. <u>STORMS AND PRESSURE CENTERS</u>: During the summertime, the east coast of the United States has periods of warm and humid weather, because of the air circulation around the Bermuda (or Bermuda-Azores) High. This large high pressure system is usually centered around the Bermuda area. When it is unusually strong and centered farther west, then a strong southwesterly flow over the eastern U.S. occurs with heat-wave conditions. When this high pressure system is centered farther east than usual, then any cool air masses from higher latitudes can more easily move into the eastern U.S.

During the wintertime, low pressure systems often develop or move into the east coast area and then move more-or-less up the coast. Some of these storms become powerful, producing widespread winter storminess with heavy snow and high wind causing blizzards. These storms are called "nor'easters" because the winds along the coast and somewhat inland ahead of their centers come from the northeast, and because these low pressure systems themselves typically move north-northeastward.

Another United States example is the Florida peninsula, which receives the most thunderstorm days of any place in the United States. Collisions of boundaries produce much of these storms, such as the intersecting of a sea-breeze from the east cost with one from the west-coast, or the intersection of a front with a sea-breeze. Intersecting thunderstorm outflow boundaries from thunderstorms caused by the heating of the day of the humid air, also generate new storms where they intersect.

Around the globe, in all countries and areas, we can observe germane conditions.

8. <u>**OCEANS AND OCEAN CURRENTS**</u>: Figure 22-4 in chapter 22 shows the main ocean surface currents. We repeat here an overview:

The oceans cover a little over 70% of the earth's surface. Because of their great expanse, they are a major factor in the earth's climate. Most of the moisture that falls as precipitation has its origins in moist air due to the oceans. An entire science has emerged in the study of the oceans, called <u>oceanography</u>. Unfortunately, we know very little about what we could know about the ocean-atmosphere relationship for weather and climate; therefore, there is ample opportunity for new discoveries through research in oceanography, and in the combined interdisciplinary meteorology and oceanography.

Again, refer to figure 22-4 in chapter 22, which shows some of the major ocean currents. There are also deep ocean currents, such as an Antarctic bottom-water current. In the Northern Hemisphere, the currents create a loop that moves clockwise across the Pacific Ocean, and another loop across the Atlantic Ocean. In the Southern Hemisphere, the loops are counterclockwise. In the Northern Hemisphere, the more northward-moving currents are warm, while the more southward moving currents are cold. As you would expect for the Southern Hemisphere, the more southward-moving (away from the warmer, low latitudes) currents are warm, and the more northward-moving (away from the cold, high latitudes) currents are cold.

In the Northern Hemisphere, the Kuroshio Current of the western Pacific is analogous to the Gulf Stream of the western Atlantic: both are fast-moving, relatively narrow warm currents of water, somewhat analogous to the jet-streams of the atmosphere, which are relatively-narrow, fast-moving currents of air. Positions, intensities and temperatures of these currents have shifted with climatic changes over the centuries. Thus, we know that the atmosphere-ocean-land system is one dynamic interrelated system that, with heating from the sun, determines our weather and climate.

9. <u>**LOCAL RELIEF**</u>: Above 23½° N latitude, in the Northern Hemisphere, the south slopes of hills and mountains have a warmer climate than do the north slopes, since the south-facing slopes face the sun. So, if someone wants to attach a greenhouse to a home, it would be built on the south side of the house, in the Northern Hemisphere, and on the north side in the Southern Hemisphere. In the Northern Hemisphere, the north-facing slopes are the last to melt snowcover.

Low-lying areas get colder on clear nights that are calm or nearly calm, since the cold air settles in the lowest areas since colder air is denser than warm air, and air, a fluid, flows with the denser fluid moving into areas where it the fluid is less dense, lifting the lighter fluid. An excellent example of this is Fairbanks, Alaska. On a clear, nearly calm night in the dead of winter, the temperature may fall to sixty below zero Fahrenheit, but on the hills overlooking Fairbanks, the temperature at that time may be 20 below zero. Hill tops are windier than lower elevations. There are fewer obstacles, such as trees, to block some of the air-flow on the summits. These are examples of local geographic influences on weather and climate.

<u>CLIMATE CLASSIFICATIONS</u>:

Over the decades, from the study of weather statistics, attempts have been made to classify the different types of regional climates. Over land and ocean, the climates vary based on the interaction of the climatic controls we just discussed. The next chapter is about causes of climatic change. We can argue that climatic "normals" are really just statistical averages for a region or location over the past few decades, and when we look at the weather statistics 50 years from now for the previous 30 or so years up to that time, we will have new "normals". The new normals may or may not be significantly different from what we have now. The point is: we know that the climate changes over time. There are areas of the world with wet climates and areas with dry climates. There are hot and cold climates. There are hot, dry climates and hot, wet climates; there are cold, dry climates and cold, wet climates. From the following three figures, you can identify the climates of the world.

Figure 42-2. Average January temperature. (source: DOC)

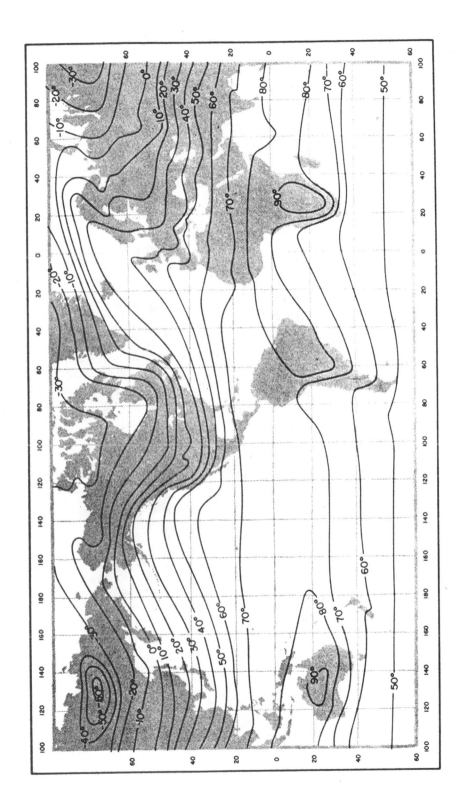

Above are the world-wide average surface temperatures in January, when the Northern Hemisphere is in its cold season and the Southern Hemisphere is in its warm season. Note how in the Northern Hemisphere the continents are colder than the oceanic areas at corresponding latitudes, and in the Southern Hemisphere the continents are warmer than the oceans.

Figure 42-3. Average July temperature. (source: DOC)

Above are the world-wide average surface temperatures in July, when the Northern Hemisphere is in its warm season and the Southern Hemisphere is in its cold season. Note how in the Northern Hemisphere the continents generally are warmer than the oceanic areas at corresponding latitudes, and in the Southern Hemisphere the reverse is true, but the contrast is not as great because there are more oceanic areas and sparcer land surfaces in the Southern Hemisphere.

Figure 42-4. Average precipitation around the world. (source: DOC)

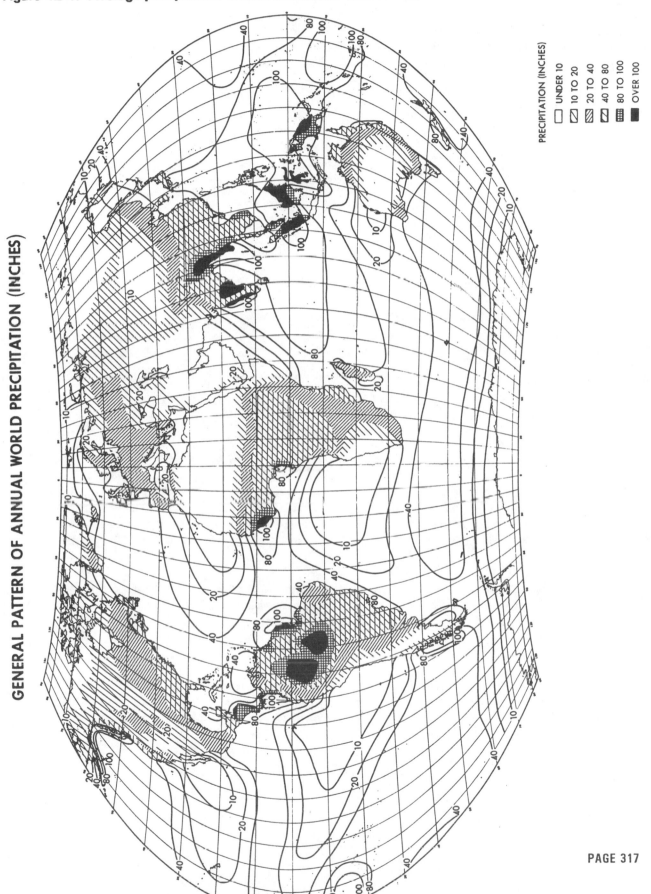

GENERAL PATTERN OF ANNUAL WORLD PRECIPITATION (INCHES)

PRECIPITATION (INCHES)

UNDER 10
10 TO 20
20 TO 40
40 TO 80
80 TO 100
OVER 100

Chapter 43. CAUSES OF CLIMATIC CHANGE

Several major factors can cause the Earth's climate to change. The following is not an exclusive list, but meteorologists do know enough about these factors to address them inquisitively:

a. solar variability
b. orbital variability and earth's axis variability
c. collisions with other astronomical bodies
d. volcanic eruptions
e. the runaway greenhouse effect; carbon dioxide
f. plate tectonics and mountain building
g. changes in the stratospheric ozone layer

We shall now address each of these major factors that could change the Earth's climate.

a. solar variability

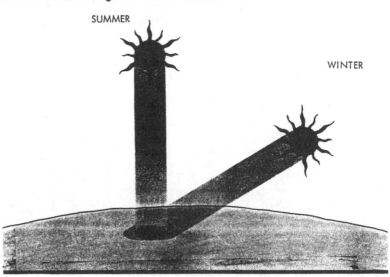

SUMMER

WINTER

Figure 43-1. Although the amount of sunlight we receive at the surface varies, the amount received from the sun at the top of the atmosphere is essentially a constant. The sun is a thermonuclear furnace that emits the same amount of energy at a constant rate. This energy emission is known as the <u>solar constant</u>. Its value is 1372 watts of power per square meter of area at the top of the earth's atmosphere. Thus, 1372 watts, which is 1372 joules of energy per second, are impinging on every square meter of the top of our atmosphere. The solar constant is also given as 1.97 calories per square centimeter per minute, or roughly 2 cal/cm^2/min. Actually, even though the amount of energy from the sun is steady, what the earth receives does vary based on our distance from the sun. At perihelion (when we are closest to the sun), we receive about 1421 watts/meter^2, and at aphelion (when we are farthest from the sun), we receive about 1330 watts/meter^2. (source: DOA)

Even a slight change in the amount of radiation we get from the sun would drastically affect our weather and climate. An ice age would be initiated by a sudden slight cooling of the planet, and a more tropical climate would be initiated by a sudden slight warming of the planet. Indeed, in various computer simulations, it appears that if the earth's temperature were to cool by about 15C° (27F°) from the current global average temperature of about 15°C (59°F), an ice age would commence.

An ice age is not a big blob of ice advancing equatorward from the poles. What happens is that as the climate gradually cools, the winter snows start earlier and earlier each year and end later and later each year, so that eventually it snows every month of the year, with the snow area also spreading farther into lower latitudes. Snow cover piles up and compacts into a glacier.

b. orbital variability and earth's axis variability

The shape of the earth's orbit varies from elliptical to nearly circular. Astronomers currently believe that the cycle from nearly circular to elliptical to nearly circular takes about 100,000 years.

The more elliptical the earth's orbit, the greater is the variation in the solar energy the earth receives during perihelion and aphelion. In the 21st century A.D., the earth is in a period of low eccentricity; i.e., the earth's orbit is nearly circular. Perihelion is about January 3rd, during the Northern Hemisphere's winter, and aphelion is about July 3rd, during the Southern Hemisphere's winter. The difference is distance of the earth from the sun from aphelion (94,500,000 miles) to perihelion (91,500,000 miles) is about 3 million miles, which varies the solar energy received by the earth, as explained on the previous page. However, when the earth's orbit is more elliptical, the change of energy received is more significant, and would affect the climate with likely greater temperature variability. Thus, if there is indeed variability of the earth's orbit around the sun, our climate would gradually change.

There is also the possibility of the earth's axis having variability; i.e., our 23½° tilt may not be fixed.

As the earth rotates, it may wobble somewhat (like a spinning top). This wobbling is called the earth's <u>precession</u>. Astronomers currently think that it takes about 23,000 years for the earth to complete a precession cycle. In about half of this cycle (11,500 years), instead of the Northern Hemisphere being closer to the sun in winter and farther in summer, it will be closer in summer and farther in winter, and instead of the Southern Hemisphere being closer to the sun in their summer and farther in their winter, it will be closer in their winter and farther in their summer.

Astronomers currently think that the tilt of the earth's axis varies from about 22° to about 24½°, and they think that it takes about 41,000 years for the tilt to vary from 22° to 24½° to back to 22°. In the 21st century A.D., the earth's axis tilt is 23½°. The greater the tilt, the more season variation we have between summer and winter in the middle and high latitudes.

When the tilt is greatest, we should experience hotter summers and colder winters, and when the tilt is least, we should have cooler summers and milder winters.

It can be argued that during the times of lesser tilt, more snow will fall in the winters since the relatively warmer air (though still cold enough for snow lots of times) can hold more water vapor; thus, more snowfall is likely. The corresponding cooler summers might prevent all of the snows from the winters from melting. The implication is that during periods of minimum tilt, glacier formation and expansion is likely in higher latitudes.

c. collisions with other astronomical bodies

Figure 43-2. Representation of a comet about to collide with the earth. Collisions with comets and possibly asteroids are a part of the earth's history.

<u>Comets</u> are objects made up of ice and/or rock and/or frozen gasses, that revolve around our sun in an elliptical orbit; their orbits occasionally intersect with the earth's orbit. <u>Asteroids</u> are believed to be solid objects that are mostly in orbit between Mars and Jupiter, but some of which leave their original orbits. Comets have smashed into the earth, and it is possible that the earth may have also been impacted by asteroids. Although many comets are no more than several miles across, the asteroids can be as large as over 1000 miles (over 1600 kilometers) in diameter, and for that reason these celestial bodies, the asteroids, are sometimes referred to as <u>planetoids</u>.

Some scientists believe that a large comet or asteroid about 6 miles (10 kilometers) in diameter smashed into the earth on Mexico's Yucatan Peninsula, producing the Chicxulub Crater which is about 160 miles (about 260 kilometers) across, and that this impact might have led to the extinction of the dinosaurs and about 70 percent of all species living at that time. The collision stirred up an enormous amount of dust and ash into the atmosphere and effectively blocked enough of the sun's rays to cool the climate for a while. Thus, it is possible for an impact from a large comet or asteroid to at least temporarily (for a year or two, perhaps) affect the climate in a major way. It may even be possible for a major collision to change the tilt of the earth's axis and possibly affect the orbit of the earth around the sun. Either of these could result in significant climate changes.

There are many evidences of the earth being struck by celestial objects; some of these are:
- Barringer Crater in Arizona, which is about 4000 feet across, is believed to have formed when the area was hit by a comet or meteorite only 150 feet across, about 50,000 B.C.;
- The biggest impact from an extraterrestrial object in the 20th century occurred in 1908 in the Tunguska Site in Siberia, Russia, where a large object from space, probably a comet, exploded in the atmosphere, leaving no crater; the blast flattened trees over a 50-mile-wide area;
- About 100 craters have been discovered on land masses throughout the world, with about 50 on North America.

Since the earth is about 70% covered by ocean, it is logical to assume that most comets, meteors and any asteroids that reach the earth would smash into the oceans. (A meteorite is what a meteor is called after it hits the earth's surface.)

Friction with the increasing density of the earth's atmosphere as extraterrestrial objects head to the earth's surface will cause these objects to become very hot. Small meteors therefore burn up before making impact with the surface, and even the larger objects, depending upon the toughness of their compositions, may partially burn up around their extremities before striking the earth.

Further evidence of objects from space entering earth's environs is to look at our moon. The moon has no atmosphere to burn up even small meteors and comets, and therefore it is pock marked from many collisions.

Some scientists are fearful that the earth could be struck by a comet or asteroid, or a series of them, so large that life would be exterminated. What could we do if we observed, for example, a large asteroid heading for earth? In May of 1996 and asteroid about one-third mile across (about 5% to 10% of the size of the asteroid that might have killed off the dinosaurs) came to within only 279,000 miles of the earth! That is an astronomical "near-miss". Had the asteroid been somewhat larger, then the gravitational force of the earth might have pulled it tangentially in towards the earth to smash into our planet. If it struck on a land mass, the crater it might have produced would be many miles wide, and the devastation would likely have extended outward for hundreds of miles in all directions from the impact site.

In 1997, the Hale-Bopp Comet put on an interesting show for observers, but was only discovered months before it passed by the earth. Thus, we may not have more than a few months or perhaps weeks before we even know that a large comet or large asteroid is on a collision course with the earth. If the object strikes on land, there is mass devastation. If is smashes into the ocean, it would likely generate monster tsunamis that would race outward in all directions from the impact location.

What could humanity do to avert such a disaster? Some discussion has been focused on sending out missiles, perhaps with nuclear explosives, to meet the comet or asteroid in space and explode it into many small pieces, and/or to attempt to divert its path. Some day we will have this challenge, but at present there is no definitive emergency preparedness plan of action for a collision with a large comet or large asteroid.

d. volcanic eruptions

1816: The Year Without a Summer

The scenario for the year without a summer began about a year earlier. In the East Indies in 1815 a huge volcano known as Tambora literally exploded. The sound of this upheaval was heard thousands of miles away in the Hawaiian Islands.

Tambora ejected massive amounts of volcanic ash well into the atmosphere, to heights in excess of 10 miles high. During the following months, the winds in the high atmosphere spread the ash vertically (to over 20 miles high) and horizontally so that the earth was encircled by a noticeable deep layer of volcanic ash. The chief reason most of the ash particles stayed in the air at those heights for over a year was because they were violently thrust into the stratosphere. The stratosphere is a layer of the atmosphere encircling the globe, starting at from 6 to 8 miles up and ending at about 25 to 30 miles out.

Figure 43-3. Certain volcanoes can affect the weather. Volcanoes can spew out lava, which is molten rock, or ash, or both. When volcanoes eject massive volumes of ash over 50,000 feet high, the ash typically spreads out aloft and blocks some of the sun's rays from heating the earth and its atmosphere.

As the ash spread out to encircle the planet, extraordinary phenomena started to occur. Sunrises and sunsets became profusions of beauty as the oblique angle of the sun's rays at these times resulted in red, orange, yellow and purple skies, with the colors changing in only minutes as the sun's angle changed.

The very small ash particles, when hit by the sun's light, separated the visible light into the colors of the spectrum. Usually, the longer wavelengths (the reds and oranges) were separated out the most so that the sky took on these hues. On a clear or mostly clear twilight time in the morning or evening, the effect was spectacular just before sunrise and just after sunset when the sun was barely below the horizon. However, despite the beauty of the skies, the eruption of Mount Tambora, which more succinctly could be described as the **explosion** of Mount Tambora, caused a drastic change in the planet's weather.   PAGE 321

By the spring of 1816, Tambora's ash had completely spread out in the stratosphere around the globe. In the United States, which was primarily agricultural at that point in our history, farmers were clearing, plowing, tilling and planting, in anticipation of a season of abundant yield. Their joy soon turned into surprise and then shock as the weather turned colder during May.

Diaries and weather records from New England, Pennsylvania, the Great Lakes region and the settled areas of the Ohio Valley show that snowfalls were occurring in June. Temperatures fell below freezing at night, and it was well past the normal date of the last killing frost. Then, as summer arrived, the weather got even worse.

For example, three diaries exist from the Rochester, New York area from 1816: one from a farmer, one from a teacher and one from a minister. All told the same chilling tale. It snowed every month of the year in 1816. Snowfalls occurred in June, July and August, wiping out the growing season in northern states. Ice formed on the Finger Lakes of Upstate New York during the summer months. Residents of New England and other northern areas had to import food from Virginia, the Carolinas and farther south in order to survive. Temperatures were colder in the southern states also, but there the weather was at least mild enough to allow for a shortened growing season.

Similar reports came from Europe and Asia, for the phenomenon was worldwide.

By the end of 1816, much of the volcanic ash in the atmosphere became disbursed, settling to earth, and the world's climate returned to "normal".

The lesson from this dramatic experience is that one major volcanic eruption can disrupt the normal climate so drastically that it can have a profound impact on civilization. Historians can research for possible food riots and even wars as a result of the inability to grow food across a large part of the world that year, and meteorologists such as this writer, and geologists and other natural scientists can create computer models to simulate the effect on the climate if several Tambora-type volcanoes were to erupt in the same year. Social scientists could study the effects on the worldwide societies of 1816, but what would we speculate for the effects of such an eruption now, with a much larger population to feed? Moreover, consider a worst-case scenario: a series of such volcanic eruptions occurring over a period of years or decades. Weather history has a record of occasional perturbations from the mean, which have significant implications for how we survive on this planet.

After Tambora, another East Indies volcano threatened to cause a repeat of the 1815-16 experience. The Krakatoa Volcano on Krakatoa Island between Sumatra and Java exploded in 1883 with a roar heard some 3,000 miles away. It is estimated that some four cubic miles of earth were belched into the atmosphere, where some of it remained for about two years. However, as massive as this volcano was, its eruption was not as great as Tambora's, so its effect was to temporarily (for about two years) lower the earth's temperature by up to a degree or two, although some areas had a greater cooling. Again, as with Tambora, once the volcanic ash disbursed from the stratosphere, the climate resumed its normal state.

In May of 1980, Mount St. Helens erupted in Washington state. This was not a lava eruption but an ash eruption. This time, weather satellites existed to record the event. Although this eruption was relatively "puny" compared with Krakatoa and Tambora, it did eject volcanic ash particles into the stratosphere where much of them then resided for about two years. The temperature drop in the earth's climate was small, but the eruption did signal perhaps the beginning of activity in western North America of some of the volcanoes that had been inactive for centuries and longer.

The largest volcanic belt on the planet is the Circumpacific Ring of Fire that extends from the southwest Pacific up the east coast of Asia to the Alaskan coast and down to the southwest tip of South America. This region, around the periphery of the Pacific Ocean, contains the greatest volcanic zone on Earth. It is also geologically active in earthquakes. The Eurasiatic land mass was connected to the Americas land mass, but floated apart as the plates on which they rest shifted away from each other.

On the following page is a weather satellite photograph of an ash volcano during eruption.

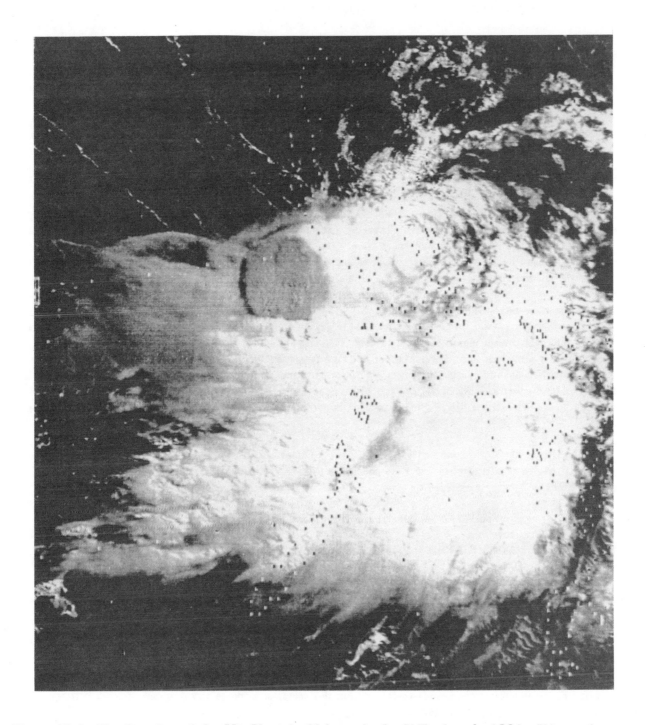

Figure 43-4. The Eruption of the Mt. Pinatubo Volcano in the Philippines in 1991. This eruption was captured in an image from a weather satellite. The dark gray oval is the ash shooting out of the volcano. The white areas are the tops of clouds and the black areas are land or sea not covered by clouds and/or ash. Notice that some of the ash is blown by the winds to the left (to the west) of the volcano. This eruption was far less significant than those of Krakatoa in 1883 and Tambora in 1815 which noticeably cooled the earth's climate temporarily. (source: NOAA)

e. the runaway greenhouse effect; carbon dioxide

Because of waste output from some industrial activity, and from automotive emissions and the burning of fossil fuels, there has been some increase in atmospheric carbon dioxide and other 'greenhouse gasses". These gasses absorb some of the outgoing heat (infrared radiation) from the earth and thus warm the climate. Thus, if there is too much of a build-up of these gasses, then the lower atmosphere acts somewhat like a greenhouse to trap some of the heat that otherwise would be released to space, and the climate warms. Although the main greenhouse gas is carbon dioxide, there are other gasses that also contribute to the potential warm-up, such as water vapor, methane, nitrous oxide and the chlorofluorocarbons (CFCs). The other side of the argument is that the oceans are a massive "sink" for excess carbon dioxide in the atmosphere; that is, as we generate additional carbon dioxide, the oceans absorb it, thus keeping the climate in check.

Ironically, a warming of the climate could lead to an ice age. This is known as a <u>negative feedback mechanism</u>. Thus, the increase in greenhouse gasses which should warm the climate in the relatively short-term, could have the long-term effect of being a negative feedback for the climate by doing just the opposite and cooling the climate. This is because by warming the air, the air can then hold much more water vapor to generate cloudiness, and ultimately the planet would be enshrouded by cloudcover which would reflect to space much of the sun's incoming radiation; the result is a cooling of the climate which, if sufficient, could initiate an ice age.

It should be pointed out that, technically, the warming of the lower atmosphere by a build-up of greenhouse gasses is not how a greenhouse works. In the atmosphere, these gasses are acting as radiative filters, being transparent to incoming solar radiation but more opaque to outgoing terrestrial radiation. The glass or plastic-like materials used in a greenhouse cause greenhouses to warm to about a steady temperature. Thus, the term "greenhouse effect" when applied to potential climatic change has caught on since the mental image of the purpose of a greenhouse is easy to relate to any global warming due to the build-up of these gasses. Thus, for climatic discussion, we should properly be discussing the "radiative filter effect", but generically in our vernacular, the term "greenhouse effect" is in common use.

We need this atmospheric greenhouse effect to produce our current world climate, so what we are concerned about is actually a **"runway greenhouse effect"** in which there is excessive build-up of these greenhouse-effect gasses, leading to excessive global warming.

Following is a demonstration illustrating how water absorbs carbon dioxide:

<u>DEMONSTRATION</u>: MAKING YOUR OWN SODA WATER (CARBONIC ACID):

Items needed: two glass containers, such as two 100 milliliter beakers; a straw; and litmus solution (local high school chemistry teachers might have this).

1. Fill a glass container about three-fourths full with room-temperature water.

2. Add enough litmus solution to give the water a deep purple color.

3. Put half of the liquid into the second container. Put this container aside so that you can compare it to the solution in the first container at the end of the demonstration.

4. Blow your breath into the first container until you see a definite color change. The solution turns from purple to reddish, indicating the presence of an acid which, in this case, is carbonic acid (soda water!).

5. Compare this color with the color of the original solution in the second container.

f. plate tectonics and mountain building

The land masses of the earth sit on plates which move very slowly, either separating or colliding; these plates are called tectonic plates. For example, southern California rests on a tectonic plate which is slowly trying to move in a different direction from the rest of much of North America. Pressures and stresses lead to earthquake faults, especially where plate edges interact.

Consider the Indian subcontinent. As the plate on which India rests tries to move poleward into the underbelly of Asia on the Eurasian continent, it pushes the Himalayan Mountains even higher. The Himalayas are the highest mountains on earth, if we start measuring elevation at sea-level. However, some mountains in the Hawaiian Island chain are in reality the tallest, since their bases are as deep in the ocean as 18,000 feet below sea-level, and extend over 10,000 feet above sea-level, so some of these mountains have a vertical extend of over 30,000 feet.

All the main land masses originally were probably one large land mass (now given the name Pangea). Look at the globe or a world map. Notice, for example, how the west coast of Africa nicely fits into the east coast of South America.

When plates are separating, lava flows from undersea fissures in the earth's top layers and from undersea volcanoes, forming new islands when the magma eventually builds to above sea-level. For example, this is how the Hawaiian Islands and the Icelandic Islands continue to be formed. Lava volcanoes that are already above the surface, such as on the island of Hawaii in that island chain, also add new land mass as the lava flows into the sea and cools into new rock, some of which eventually breaks down into soil.

Geologically new mountains such as those found in western North America, are slowly building up, whereas geologically old mountains such the Appalachians in the eastern United States, are slowly eroding.

Geography is a major factor in the earth's climate. For example, the windward side of tall mountains receive much more precipitation than the leeward side, since air that must rise up over the mountains cools to its dewpoint forming clouds and subsequent precipitation, whereas this air warms and dries out as it descends the mountains. The main tornado belt in the world is in the central plains of the United States because of the geography of North America (mountains to the west and a moisture source, the Gulf of Mexico to the south-southeast). Local weather affects abound everywhere due to geography. Examples include lake-effect snows, sea-breezes, valley pockets of overnight cold air and dust-devils in southwest U.S. deserts. Thus, **as the geography of the earth changes, the climate changes from that cause alone.**

g. changes in the stratospheric ozone layer

An entire book has been written on this subject, entitled, "TERROR FROM THE SKIES!" by Peter R. Chaston, and is available from the address on the back of this book (its cost is $29). Essentially, if sufficient stratospheric ozone is destroyed, then much of the ultraviolet radiation would not be filtered, resulting in harmful effects on living organisms (as stated in chapter 4). Moreover, since fewer ultraviolet rays would be absorbed by ozone in the stratosphere, the area now known as the stratosphere would become colder or cease to exist, which would make it unstable. The likely result would be the earth's weather and climate becoming extremely severe, with thunderstorm cloud tops growing to well over 100,000 feet before they ran out of moisture, for example, leading to gigantic-sized hail (hailstones bigger than watermelons!), deluges of rain, cascades of lightning, and very high thunderstorm downbursts of wind. This is only one set of weather changes that would affect the climate. An ultimate ice-age is possible as the initial warming of the climate leads to more cloudiness which reflects much incoming solar radiation and ultimately cools the global climate.

Concluding remarks:

The climatic-change factors discussed in this chapter are not an inclusive list. Other factors (nuclear war, for example) may also change the climate. We know that the earth goes through ice-ages, and this is a normal aspect of our climatic system through the millennia. Thus, we can state that the climate we have been experiencing through the 20th century and into the 21st century has been relatively favorable, on the whole, for human survival.

SECTION XII: EFFECTS OF OCEANS AND OTHER LARGE WATER BODIES

Chapter 44. HOW OCEANS AND LARGE LAKES AFFECT WEATHER AND CLIMATE

Land surfaces heat up and cool off more rapidly than do water surfaces. Water takes longer to both warm and cool. Walk along a beach on a hot summer day. The beach sand may burn your feet. Then step into a water for a refreshing cool-off. Yet both the beach sand and the shore water have been receiving the same amount of sunshine, also called <u>insolation</u>, which stands for "incoming solar radiation".

<u>Why land heats (and cools) faster than water:</u>
1. Water usually moves, and the solar heat is distributed because of this movement. When sunlight hits the land, its heat is more or less confined to the top layers.

Figure 44-1. The sun's rays go deeper into the water than they do into the land. The solar heat is more distributed in large bodies of water. (source: DOA)

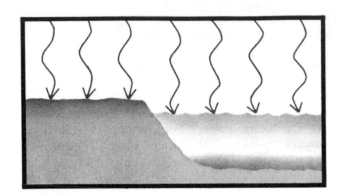

2. Because water is transparent, the sun's rays can penetrate deeper than they can when they impinge upon land, which is opaque. The sun's rays can penetrate only up to a few inches on land.

3. The <u>heat capacity</u> (<u>specific heat</u>) of water is higher than that of land. It therefore takes more heat to raise the temperature of say one kilogram of water one Celsius degree than it does to do the same for land. In fact, water has the highest specific heat of all common substances. If you place an empty aluminum container, and another one filled with water, on the stove, it will take only a few minutes to heat the empty one to say 200°F, but the one filled with water will take much longer to reach 200°F. Then after turning off the stove, if we feel the empty container about a half-hour later, it will be at room temperature, but the one with the water will feel noticeably warmer.

Figure 44-2. People who live near a large body of water usually have cooler summer days compared with communities well-removed from this ocean or large lake. On the other hand, at night the areas adjacent to the ocean or large lakes will typically be warmer than the farther inland areas. Thus, large bodies of water temper the diurnal temperature range for their adjacent land areas. (source: DOA)

Figure 44-3. At left: Oceans are the main source of moisture for the lower atmosphere. In middle: Vegetation over land is another important source of moisture. If we deforest a large area, we decrease our annual rainfall amount. If we reforestate, we increase our precipitation. At right: arid areas (deserts) add little moisture to the lower atmosphere. (source: DOA)

Figure 44-4. Wind enhances evaporation by blowing away stagnated layers of moist air over a large water body, and mixing this moist air with the drier air aloft. The wind also transports moisture. An excellent example is when moist air from over the Gulf of Mexico is transported by the winds into the United States. (source: DOA)

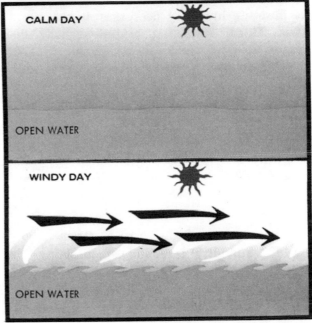

In Swampscott, Massachusetts, a coastal community north of Boston, the warmest the ocean gets is about 70°F, around the end of August and early September. If you go swimming on a hot 90-degree day in May, your feet will feel like they want to fall off, because the water temperature may be only in the upper 40's. The coldest water temperatures usually occur around the end of the winter, about late February. In most years, they may be slightly below 32°F. The salt dissolved in the ocean acts somewhat as an antifreeze, allowing the temperature to go slightly below 32°F without freezing. If the air temperature is in the teens, single numbers or below zero (Fahrenheit) for several days, then the water will freeze, first near the shore and eventually farther out.

Because ice is less dense than water, it floats on top of the water. During extremely cold winters, the Coast Guard ice-choppers cut paths in the ice so that fishing vessels can maneuver in and out of port. It is not uncommon to see a fleet of fishing boats following a Coast Guard ice-cutter.

When you touch a piece of <u>sea ice</u>, it feels rough, like sandpaper. The roughness is because some of the salt comes out of the solution when cooled, and crystallizes on the surface of the ice. Just the opposite occurs when we heat water: for example, if you want to dissolve more salt or sugar, then heat the water.

Icebergs are not the same categorization as sea ice. An <u>iceberg</u> is a massive body of ice that has broken away from a glacier, and is therefore frozen freshwater. Only about 10% of an iceberg's mass is above the surface of the water.

In the mid 1980s, a group of scientists was heading for Antarctica via ship when they ran out of freshwater some two days before reaching Antarctica. They gathered some sea ice, scraped off the loose salt, melted the ice, and ended up with water no saltier than what was in the canned soups they had been eating.

<u>Some additional interesting aspects about earth's water:</u>
The oceans cover 71% of the earth's surface; land covers just 29%. Between 35° South latitude and 65° South latitude, the ocean covers 97.5% of the earth's surface! The Northern Hemisphere has much more land than does the Southern Hemisphere. Of the world's total water supply, about 97.2% is stored in the oceans, 2.2% in glaciers and snow cover and the remaining under 1% available for every living organism on the earth. Nearly all the earth's water is billions of years old and is continually recycled!

Figure 44-5. The two types of icebergs. At bottom is a flat or tubular iceberg, which is typical of chunks of ice breaking off a large ice shelf such as an Antarctic ice shelf, and at top is a rugged or pinnacled iceberg, whichis typical of chunks of ice slicing off a glacier and dropping into the sea. (source: USN)

Figure 44-6. United States military personnel looking at sea ice from their ice-cutter ship. (source: USN)

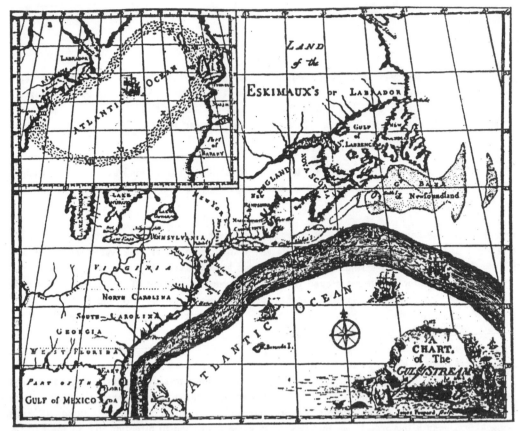

Figure 44-7. Here is Benjamin Franklin's map of the Gulf Stream, which is a relatively narrow current of very warm water off the U.S. east coast. Franklin published this map in 1777, which is what you are seeing here (Franklin's original print). Notice the somewhat fuzzy drawings of two figures in the lower right hand part of Franklin's map. Here, Franklin put a drawing of himself having a conversation with Neptune, the Roman god of the sea. When Franklin was an assistant postmaster general for the American colonies, he noted that ships coming to America from Great Britain often took longer than ships heading to Britain. The oceanic observations of the currents showed that there was a narrow but strong current of warm water, which Franklin thenceforth depicted as the Gulf Stream when he published this chart.

Before leaving this topic, <u>here is an overview of the economic significance of the oceans</u>:
1. Oceans are a source of most of the moisture for the earth's precipitation.
2. The oceans are a source of food with their fish, shellfish, etc.
3. The oceans are navigated for commercial, recreational and military uses. Many old cities developed along the oceans and rivers. Shipping is still an economical way of transporting goods. Many important military battles have been fought at sea.
4. Swimming, boating, fishing and other recreational uses of oceans, lakes and rivers are commonplace around the world. Over half of the population of the United States is within a reasonable driving distance of the ocean. This is a result of the original population demographics from the early days of settlement in the United States.
5. Oceans are a source of many minerals, including gold, magnesium and table salt (sodium chloride).
6. Oceans are a major source of oxygen and a major sink of carbon dioxide. (A sink means the oceans absorb excess carbon dioxide produced in the atmosphere by natural and human causes; this nicely takes care of one of the potential agents for a runaway greenhouse effect that would initially warm the earth's climate.) Also, about 90% of all photosynthesis occurs in the ocean by one-celled organisms called <u>diatoms</u>. <u>Photosynthesis</u> is the process in which green plants and other organisms with chlorophyll go about combining carbon dioxide and water, with the help of sunlight, to produce glucose, which is a simple sugar that is a plant food. Diatoms are part of a larger group of organisms called <u>phytoplankton</u>, which also make their own food by the process of photosynthesis.

The sun, land, oceans, <u>cryosphere</u> (snow and ice-covered surface) and atmosphere interact to produce our weather. The science of <u>oceanography</u>, which studies the oceans in depth (no pun intended) is therefore related to the science of meteorology.

Chapter 45. EL NINO

El Nino is a sudden warming of a vast area of equatorial Pacific Ocean surface (and for at least some depth below the surface) water, typically starting off Peru and working up the coast to western Mexico and even California, as well as extending to the south-central North Pacific. El Nino gets its name for the Christ Child, since it typically starts about November and peaks in December through March. Sometimes it is referred to as ENSO, for El Nino Southern Oscillation.

The term, El Nino, means little baby boy, and refers to the Christ Child; it was coined by fishermen along the coasts of Ecuador and Peru to refer to a warm ocean area that usually appears a little before Christmas and persists for at least several weeks.

Because certain fish are less abundant in water that is too warm, many fishermen usually took some vacation time to be with their families and repair their gear. During some years, this warm water area, which begins to develop in November or December, persists until spring and sometimes even longer. When this occurs, not only is the local marine life affected, but so are weather conditions around the world. Nowadays the term El Nino also refers to these longer time periods of accompanying changes in weather conditions brought about by the warming of part of the Pacific Ocean. **The ocean waters that suddenly warm to form El Nino are in the equatorial Pacific Ocean.**

First, let us look at conditions when El Nino is not occurring:
1. The atmospheric pressure is higher in the equatorial regions of the eastern Pacific than in the equatorial regions of the western Pacific. As a result, the trade winds strengthen as they blow from an easterly component, that is, from the eastern to the western Pacific. In the tropics north of the equator, the prevailing wind direction is from the northeast, and in the tropics south of the equator, the prevailing wind direction is from the southeast. Recall that winds blow from high pressure towards lower pressure, with some deflection in direction due to the earth's rotating. The result in the tropics is that surface water is transported from the eastern tropical Pacific to the western tropical Pacific, causing the sea-level to be higher in the western Pacific than in the eastern Pacific. Some return of water is done just outside the tropics and by currents under the surface.

2. Since warm water weighs less than colder water, it floats on top of colder water. The winds that blow from the eastern to the western Pacific push the warm surface water off the coast of equatorial South America out to sea; this warm water is replaced by colder water from below; this process is known as upwelling. The region in which the temperature lowers as we descend below the surface is known as the thermocline. The thermocline is closer to the surface in the eastern Pacific and deeper beneath the surface in the western Pacific where upwelling is not occurring.

3. Gasses dissolve better in cold water than in warm water. Therefore, the gasses needed to sustain life (oxygen for animals and carbon dioxide for plants and small plant-like organisms such as phytoplankton which make their own food through the process of photosynthesis) are more abundant in the colder waters. Along the west coast of South America, where the combination of the cold Peru Current and upwelling occurs, the cold waters, which are rich in life-sustaining gasses and nutrients, give rise to large fish populations, especially anchovies and sardines, which support a large population of marine birds, whose droppings, called guano, produce a large amount of fertilizer rich in phosphates. A large fertilizer industry depends on this.

4. The colder surface water in the eastern Pacific prevents the air along the surface of the water from heating up, making the air more stable (i.e., colder air near the surface with the air being warmer just above it). One weather result is fewer chances of storminess, since the colder heavier air tends to remain closer to the surface rather than being lifted to form cloudiness and subsequent precipitation.

Now let us look at conditions when El Nino is occurring:
1. The atmospheric pressure becomes higher in the equatorial regions of the western Pacific than in the equatorial regions of the eastern Pacific. As a result, the tropical easterly winds (the trade winds) weaken, allowing winds to blow from a westerly direction, that is, from the western Pacific to the eastern Pacific. This results in the surface water being transported from the western Pacific to the eastern Pacific, causing the sea-level to be higher in the eastern than in the western Pacific.

2. Warm surface water piles up along the west coast of equatorial South America, resulting in a deep layer of warm, nutrient-poor water. Upwelling along the east coasts of land masses in the western Pacific causes the thermocline to be closer to the surface. In the eastern Pacific, the thermocline is deeper beneath the surface. Pressure reversal occurs at opposite ends of the Pacific Ocean, along with the warming of the ocean in the east Pacific tropics, with the warming then extending into the central Pacific tropics. The term EL NINO refers to this warming of this ocean water. The oscillation of warm and cold conditions is also called the Southern Oscillation, so sometimes the term ENSO is used, which stands for "El Nino/Southern Oscillation".

3. Because of the shortage of life-sustaining gasses (oxygen and carbon dioxide) in the eastern Pacific, the fishing industry along the west coast of South America suffers.

4. The warm surface water in the eastern and central equatorial Pacific Ocean heats the air along the surface of the water. The warm air rises, its moisture condenses, and clouds and subsequent precipitation are produced. Therefore, the weather in the central and eastern Pacific becomes more stormy as a result of the warmer ocean temperatures there.

DEMONSTRATION: GASSES DISSOLVE BETTER IN COLD WATER THAN THEY DO IN WARM WATER

Materials needed: two transparent containers of soda pop; one of the containers needs to be refrigerated overnight, with the other container at room temperature.

Procedure:
1. Place the two containers next to each other.
2. Remove the excess pressure from these containers by removing their caps.
3. Once this is done, you will see the gas, which in this case is carbon dioxide, come out of solution, forming bubbles.
4. The room-temperature container should produce a louder popping noise when you remove the cap, and it should form more bubbles; this is because the gas is coming out of the solution more rapidly than when the liquid is cold. By analogy, the gasses also dissolve faster into the water when the water is cold.

After an El Nino episode, the water returns to the colder temperatures in the tropical east Pacific, and the warm water with its accompanying stormy weather is confined to the western tropical Pacific. After some El Nino episodes, the trade winds become especially strong, which causes increased upwelling off the South American coast. The ocean waters there then become even colder; this condition is called LA NINA, which means girl child. During prolonged and strong El Nino and La Nina episodes, significant large-scale weather effects usually result. For example, the major drought in the spring and summer of 1988 in North America may have been related to a strong La Nina, and the great mid-west United States floods of 1993 may have been related to an usually strong and prolonged El Nino. Keep in mind that during a strong El Nino, plenty of warm moist air is rising from over the ocean surface, and some of this moisture flows as a steady stream into North America, carried in part by the subtropical jet-stream once the moisture reaches higher levels. These tropical connections, or plumes of tropical moisture, actually extend down to lower levels of the troposphere, and feed growing thunderstorm complexes with additional moisture for precipitation production.

Some past El Nino episodes have been documented through records of sea-surface temperature, pressure, rainfall and fisheries records along the Peruvian and Equadorian coast and from Darwin, Australia, for example, as well as from the logs of merchant ships. An early El Nino has been documented from records from 1567-68. The more significant El Ninos occur every few years and are a normal aspect of the earth's climate. Each El Nino event is unique; no two are exactly alike and so no two El Ninos produce exactly the same weather results. The most significant El Nino episodes last for up to a year, and even somewhat longer, and cause a relatively large warming of sea-surface temperatures, e.g., 10 Fahrenheit degrees or more, over a large expanse of ocean surface water, which of course has a major impact on weather. The incredible 1992-93 El Nino caused the greatest, most widespread floods in the history of the United States up to that time, during the spring and summer of 1993. The weather over the entire globe is affected by very strong and prolonged El Ninos.

The weather satellite image on the next page shows a tropical connection of moisture caused by El Nino, enhancing rainfall from organized thunderstorm activity over part of the United States during the 1993 great floods.

Figure 45-1. A weather satellite image known as a water vapor image", showing moisture and clouds feeding into an organized area of thunderstorms known as a mesoscale convective system (MCS), labelled M, producing flash flooding rain. This picture was taken at 9 p.m., Central Daylight Time, on June 30th, 1993, from a weather satellite 22,300 miles over the equator. Since water vapor in the atmosphere absorbs some infrared radiation (heat) from the ground and then reradiates it at a wavelength of 6.7 micrometers, scientists have designed sensors on the satellite that detect radiation at 6.7 micrometers coming out of the moisture. Thus, we can "see" the moisture, whether it is in cloud form or not. This moisture shows up best at from about 5000 feet elevation to about 30,000 feet. The duller white is moisture in the air, which is not in cloud form, and the bright white is moisture that has been lifted and condensed into clouds. Note the plume of moisture coming out of the tropics across Mexico into the developing areas of thunderstorms; this plume is known as the <u>tropical connection</u>. This steady influx of moisture greatly enhances the rainfall that would otherwise occur from organized areas of convection. Under the blob of thunderstorms labelled M over northeast Kansas, northern Missouri and over Iowa, a deluge causing flash flooding was underway. This was just a long string of MCSes that caused flash flooding from the Plains through the mid-west that spring and summer. (source: NOAA)

It is possible for one or more regions of the world to be receiving numerous flash flooding episodes while one or more other regions would be experiencing drought, during a strong prolonged El Nino.

Here is an example of weather conditions that occurred during one of the strongest, prolonged El Nino episodes of the 20th century, the El Nino of 1982-83:

1. By October 1982, sea-level rises of up to a foot (nearly one-third of a meter) occurred along Ecuador.
2. In the western Pacific, the sea-level dropped, exposing and destroying the upper layers of the fragile coral reefs which surrounded many tropical islands.
3. Sea-surface temperatures at the Galapagos Islands and along the coast of Ecuador rose about 15 F. (8C.) degrees. Because of the warm and nutrient-poor waters, sea birds abandoned their young and travelled for many miles in search of food. Most fish relocated to colder waters.
4. Along the coast of Peru, about 25% of the year's fur seal and sea-lion adults and all of their pups perished.
5. In Ecuador and northern Peru, up to 100 inches (about 250 centimeters) of rain fell during a 6-month period, which temporarily changed coastal deserts into grasslands dotted with lakes and ponds. The new lush vegetation attracted grasshoppers, which helped increase the toad and bird populations that do some of their feeding on the grasshoppers. The temporary new lakes became the temporary habitat for fish that had migrated up streams. In some of the flooded coastal estuaries, shrimp production set new records. Anopheles mosquitoes increased, resulting in a major malaria outbreak.
6. The fishing industries of Peru and Ecuador suffered heavily because of greatly reduced anchovies and sardines.
(continued)   PAGE 332

7. The temporary change in wind pattern helped to steer tropical cyclones more to Hawaii in the equatorial North Pacific and Tahiti in the equatorial South Pacific. For example, in Hawaii, high property damage was caused by Hurricane Iwa which passed just south of Oahu island and just west of Kauai island on November 23rd and 24th, respectively, 1982. Honolulu was buffeted by high winds and drenching rains, and mountainous regions had mudslides. There was flash flooding. Winds on land were 65 mph with gusts to 117 mph. Warmer ocean temperatures in the central Pacific sustained the intensities of tropical cyclones.

8. Monsoonal rains fell over the central Pacific rather than along the western Pacific. The lack of rain in the western Pacific produced drought and major forest and brush fires in Indonesia and Australia.

9. Southern California was hit by major winter storms, causing widespread coastal flooding, erosion and mud slides. As these storms moved inland, the southern United States received widespread flooding rains but northern ski resorts had a shortage of snow and mild weather. El Nino pushed the polar jet-stream, which separates cold polar air from milder mid-latitude air, farther north into Canada.

10. The world economy suffered by billions and billions of dollars.

The cause of El Nino is unknown. Some type of dynamic heating process, perhaps related to a change in prevailing tropical winds, is suspected. Thus, El Nino remains a fascinating mystery of oceanography.

When such a vast ocean surface warms up...sometimes by more than 5 Fahrenheit degrees, it warms the air above it. Warmer air can hold more moisture than when it was cooler; consequently, this warm air absorbs more water vapor from the ocean. Much of this moisture works its way up to mid-levels of the troposphere (700 to 500 mb), and some of the moisture is transported to the upper-troposphere (above 500 mb, up to 300 to 200 mb).

Next, we would want to know how the moisture gets transported across the Pacific into North America in tropical plumes. We know that tropical connections occur throughout the year around the globe, but when El Nino occurs, we have intense and persistent tropical connections, with major, continuous infusions of moisture from the tropical North Pacific into North America in the mid- and upper-troposphere.

Figure 45-2. The tropical Pacific Ocean and the overlying atmosphere influence and react to each other. If the easterly surface winds along the equator change, they will induce changes in surface ocean currents and in upwelling. This induces changes in sea-surface temperatures which then contributes to building weather systems, which alter the distribution of rainfall. Then the strength of the tropical easterlies can be altered, and on it goes. Thus, global weather is significantly affected by strong El Ninos. (source: NOAA)

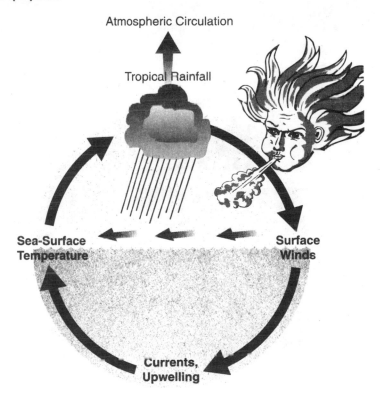

There are two chief sources of this transport: the sub-tropical jet-stream and anticyclonic outflow aloft from organized convection in the tropics.

Jet-streaks of the sub-tropical jet readily carry the air and its moisture from the source region of this tropical moisture east-northeastward across the central and eastern Pacific and over the North American continent.

The other major source of this moisture plume is in the Intertropical Convergence Zone (ITCZ). There are typically large high pressure systems over the North Atlantic and North Pacific Oceans, and there are also large highs over the South Atlantic and South Pacific Oceans. The low pressure systems move through and around these highs. The circulation around a high is clockwise in the Northern Hemisphere and counterclockwise in the Southern Hemisphere. This results in air coming together or converging near the equator, with climatological statistics showing us that the greatest convergence is a few degrees latitude north of the equator. This is the axis of the Intertropical Convergence Zone. The ITCZ axis migrates some to the north and south, but stays north of the equator. Most hurricanes form in the ITCZ since it is a zone of converging, rising and very warm tropical air. Hurricanes form out of organizing convection which is an MCS, mesoscale convective system. Since air is converging and rising into the MCS in low and middle levels of the troposphere, the air must come out of the system and diverge aloft. It does so as anticyclonically-curved plumes of air, which also contain the moisture.

Thus, each of these MCSes in the tropics, including those that become hurricanes, generate their own tropical moisture plumes.

Thus, **when El Nino occurs, the tropical connections are more intense and prolonged, and if they stream into MCSes over North America forming in areas of concentrated warm, moist air, then the heavy rain/flash flood potential from these MCSes is enhanced.**

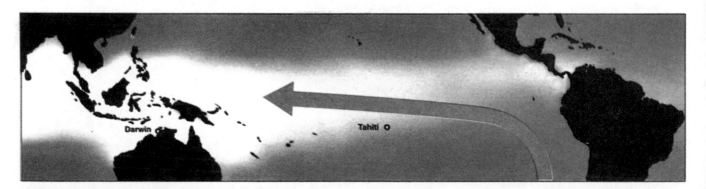

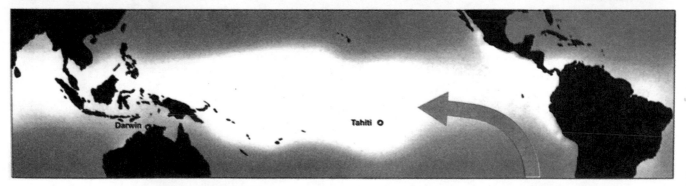

Figure 45-3. El Nino and the Southern Oscillation. (source: NOAA)
The Southern Oscillation: top figure has higher air pressure east of Tahiti and lower towards Darwin, Australia, and bottom figure has higher pressure west of Tahiti to Darwin. Notice how the surface tropical easterly winds (arrow) compare in each case. The lower case is usually accompanied by El Nino.

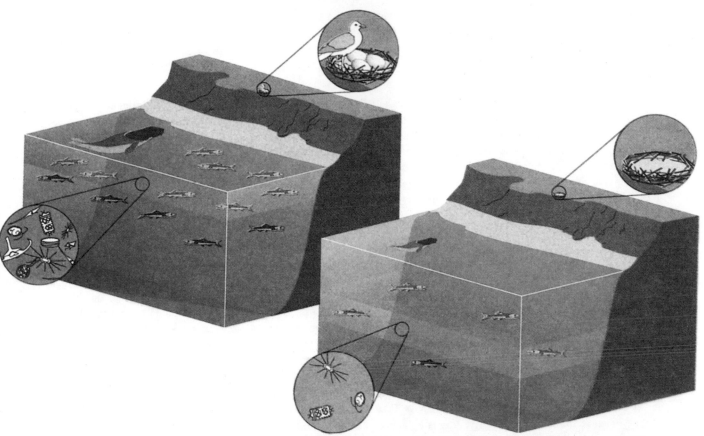

Figure 45-4. At left is the marine ecosystem along the Ecuador and Peru coasts during non El Nino times (that is, most of the time), and at right shows how this marine ecosystem changes during El Nino. The warm surface waters caused by El Nino are poor in nutrients, so there is not much phytoplankton, which are the tiny creatures that are the base of the marine food chain. Therefore, fish, and sea animals such as sea lions, must dive deeper to find food. Sea birds scatter across the ocean, often abandoning their young. When El Nino disappears, the upwelling that brings up the colder nutrient-rich waters returns, and fishermen can resume their normal living catching plenty of fish off Ecuador and Peru. (source: NOAA)

El Nino monitoring and prediction:

Observations of the following are monitored for changes: air and ocean surface temperatures, the thermal profile of the thermocline in many tropical Pacific locations, the wind in the equatorial Pacific, sea-levels, weather satellite data of moisture plumes, and other relevant ocean surface water information such as the water's density, salinity, dissolved oxygen content, color and clarity. Thus, as all the changes occur, an episode of El Nino getting underway is readily identified.

Besides the weather observations taken by land stations, much of the data from over oceans are obtained through the following sources: sensors on weather satellites that detect moisture in the air over the ocean, as well as inferring air motion; tidal gauge stations; moored buoys, which monitor air temperature and winds, and water temperatures at several levels below the ocean surface; drifting buoys which measure parameters such as water temperature and movement of surface ocean currents; and many ships, including merchant ships, whose staff voluntarily takes weather and ocean observations, so that from the ocean data are produced on temperature, salinity, density, dissolved oxygen content, color and clarity at various depths.

The air and ocean data are used in numerical computer models which keep track of and attempt to predict El Nino behavior and its affect on global and regional weather.

El Nino affects the weather in the tropics and mid-latitudes, especially in the tropics. Therefore, weather interests in countries in the tropical regions are aware that their economies, especially their agricultural businesses, are sensitive to weather changes induced by strong El Nino episodes.

Chapter 46. TIDES AND TIDAL CURRENTS

Tides are the up and down (vertical) movement of the ocean waters caused by the combined gravitational pull of the moon and the sun. In certain areas, the tides are quite noticeable, because there is a significant difference in height between high and low tides; in other places, the difference is so small that it is almost impossible to tell whether the tide is high or low. Tides also occur on larger bodies of water such as the Great Lakes, but the differences in height between high and low tides may be just a few inches. An exciting time to visit a beach with a significant tidal range is during low tide, because you will be able to see how low the water has fallen. Areas that are submerged during high tides are now exposed. If you visit the shore during high tide, every beach in the area will look the same, because the water will be close to the sea-wall (if there is one).

Basic terms concerning tides:
1. High tide (high water) is the highest that the water rises in a period of 12 hours and 25 minutes.
2. Low tide (low water) is the lowest that the water falls in a period of 12 hours and 25 minutes.
3. A flooding tide is a rising tide (a tide that is coming in); the term flood tide is another name for high tide.
4. An ebbing tide is a lowering tide (a tide that is going out); the term ebb tide is another name for a low tide.
5. Mean low tide is the average low tide level in a given area and is the zero mark on a tide-measuring scale.
6. Tidal range is the difference in height between a high tide and its corresponding low tide. Here is an example. The height of high tide is 10.2 feet, which means it is 10.2 feet above the mean low tide level which is zero feet, and the height of low tide is 1.5 feet, which means it is 1.5 feet above the mean low tide level; in this scenario, the tidal range would be 8.7 feet. Here is another example. Let us say that the height of the high tide is 12.4 feet and the height of low tide is -2.1 feet. The tidal range is 14.5 feet. Note the following:
   a. Whenever the height of the low tide is a positive number, you subtract it from the height of the high tide to obtain the tidal range;
   b. Whenever the height of the low tide is a negative number, you add it to the height of the high tide to get the tidal range;
   c. Whenever the height of the low tide is below zero (which is the mean low tide level), and thus has a minus sign in front of it, the low tide is ideal for clamming and tidepooling, because areas that are usually submerged during an average low tide are uncovered; and
   d. Let us assume that two adjacent beaches have the same tidal range but not the same slope. For the beach with the steeper slope, the water does not go out as far (in a horizontal direction) at low tide. For the beach with the lesser slope, the water goes out much farther during low tide. The following demonstration illustrates this.

DEMONSTRATION: DETERMINING THE POSITION OF LOW TIDE. All that you need for this demonstration is a ruler and a piece of paper (8½: x 11"). Figure 46-1. Beach A and adjacent beach B each has the same tidal range, but the water goes out farther during low tide for the beach with the more shallow slope. For example, suppose that the tidal range on a particular day is 2 feet. Using a scale of one inch equalling one foot on the diagram below, we can find the drop in water level at each beach during low tide by placing a ruler at the high tide level and moving it to the right until you read 2 inches along the slope. This 2 inches represents the drop in water level of 2 feet. Note that you have to walk a greater horizontal distance to the water's edge at low tide at beach B than at beach A. Some beaches have such a gentle slope that it is not uncommon to walk a quarter of a mile or more to the water's edge if there is a large tidal range. For example, the beach just east of Anchorage, Alaska sees the water go out more than one-quarter mile at low tide, and some people have died by walking or driving out onto the mud and then getting stuck, even sinking to past their knees in the mud, only to be drowned as the high tide then came in.

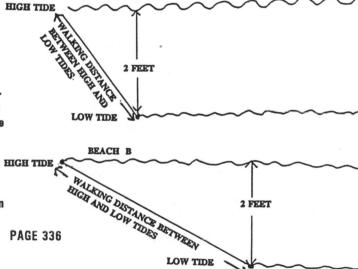

7. <u>Mean sea-level (MSL)</u> is the average distance between high and low tides over a long period of time (usually 18.6 years).

<u>Why there are two high tides and two low tides in most places every day:</u>
An easy way to explain this is to assume for a few moments that the earth is entirely covered by water (in reality, the earth is about 70% covered by water).

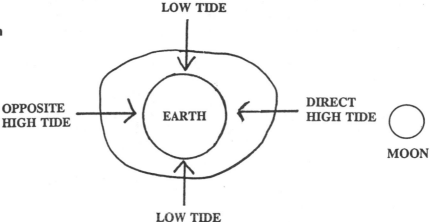

Figure 46-2. The earth, the moon and the tides. Note the following:
1. The high tide underneath the moon is called the direct high tide.
2. The high tide on the opposite side of the earth from where the moon is located is called the opposite high tide.
3. In between, we have the low tides. The water is low at these places because there is only so much water in the ocean and it has to come from somewhere to produce the high tides.

On the side of the earth that is closer to the moon, the moon's gravitational pull is stronger, resulting in the water being pulled by the moon's gravity, creating a bulge of water underneath where the moon is. This is the direct high tide.

It is more complicated explaining the opposite high tide. As you probably know, the moon's revolution around the earth takes about 29½ days, which is called a <u>lunar month</u>. What you may not be aware of is that the earth also revolves around the moon; however, its path is much smaller than that of the moon's because the earth is more massive. Whenever two objects revolve around each other, they are revolving around a center-of-mass. The center-of-mass of the earth-moon system is called the <u>barycenter</u>, and is located at a point 1,068 miles beneath the earth's surface, on the side towards the moon and along a line connecting the individual centers-of-mass of the earth and the moon.

Whenever objects revolve around each other, a <u>centrifugal force</u> is created. If you tie a rubber ball to the end of a piece of string and twirl it around, you can feel the ball trying to move away from your hand. This force is the centrifugal ("center-fleeing") force. The string is exerting a force on the ball which prevents it from breaking away. This force is analogous to the gravitational force. Note that the centrifugal force is always in the opposite direction to the gravitational force. (The centrifugal force is trying to pull the ball away from your hand whereas the force exerted by the string is pulling the ball towards your hand.) Now, please study the next figure in order to explain the opposite high tide. **Figure 46-3. The tide-producing forces.**
(source: NOS) Note the following from the figure:
1. We have a diagram showing the earth completely covered by ocean.
2. The bulge on the side of the earth facing the moon is the direct high tide.
3. The bulge on the opposite side of the earth is the opposite high tide.

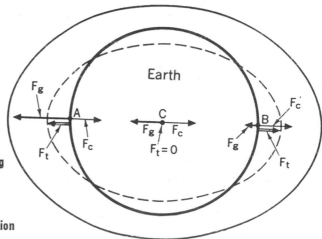

4. F_c is the centrifugal force due to the earth and moon revolving around each other. This is represented by a thin arrow.
5. F_g is the gravitational force due to the moon. This is represented by a thicker arrow.
6. F_t is the total tide-producing force as a result of the combination of the moon's gravitational force, F_g, and the centrifugal force, F_c. This is represented by the double-shafted arrow. (continued)

7. On the side of the earth that faces the moon, the gravitational force due to the moon is greater than the centrifugal force, and the difference between these two forces is the total tide-producing force, which is towards the moon, and it causes a bulge which is the direct high tide.

8. On the side of the earth that is opposite the moon, the centrifugal force is greater than the gravitational force due to the moon. The total tide-producing force (the resultant force) is in the opposite direction and therefore causes the second bulge which is the opposite high tide.

9. Note that the moon's gravitational force is less on the opposite side of the earth that the moon is on, because that side of the earth is farther from the moon.

10. The centrifugal force on each side of the earth is equal to each other and opposite in direction from the gravitational force due to the moon.

11. In the center of the earth, the gravitational force due to the moon equals the centrifugal force, and the net force equals zero.

Before we explain the sun's effect on the tides, we should point out that a similar complex of forces exists between the earth and the sun (the earth-sun system), because the earth revolves around the sun. The sun's gravitational force is in the opposite direction as the centrifugal force that results due to their rotating around a center of mass, which is located below the surface of the sun. Because the moon's average distance from the earth is so much closer (some 239,000 miles) than the sun's average distance from the earth (some 93,000,000 miles), even though the sun is much more massive, the tide-producing force of the moon is approximately 2½ times that of the sun. If the sun and the moon were the same distance from the earth, then the sun's tide-producing forces would be much greater than those of the moon. In general, the more massive an object, the greater is its gravitational force. Also, the farther two objects are from each other, the less is their gravitational attraction.

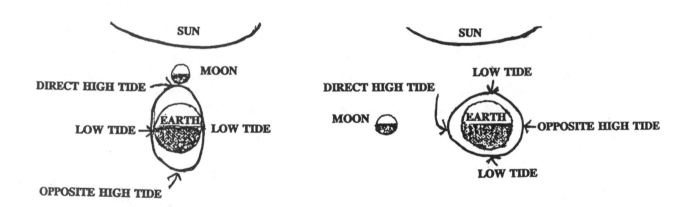

Figure 46-4 (LEFT) (not drawn to scale). 1. The phase of the moon here is called the new moon. We cannot see the moon from the earth because the half that faces the earth is not receiving any sunlight, so none is reflected back to earth. 2. The moon and sun are pulling on the ocean waters at the same time and in the same direction, resulting in the tide rising very high and falling very low; i.e., there is a large tidal range. This is called a spring tide (which has nothing to do with the spring season). The term simply means "welling up" of the water. 3. After the time of the new moon, the tidal ranges gradually decrease until they are noticeably less one week later during the moon's first quarter phase. Figure 46-5 (RIGHT) (not drawn to scale). 1. The phase of the moon is first quarter. Only half of the surface of the moon that faces the earth receives sunlight, so only a quarter of the moon is receiving sunlight (half of a half). 2. The moon is pulling the ocean waters in one direction while the sun is pulling them in another direction, resulting in the tide not rising very high or falling very low; thus, the tidal range is small. This is called a neap tide. ("Neap" is from a Greek word meaning "scanty".) After the first quarter, the tidal ranges gradually increase until once again they are quite large at the time of full moon, which occurs about one week later.

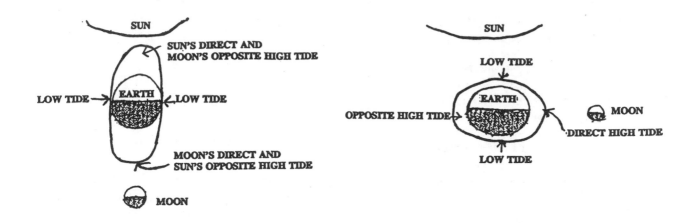

Figure 46-6 (LEFT) (not drawn to scale). 1. The phase of the moon is full; the entire half of the moon that faces the sun receives sunlight. 2. The direct high tide of the moon merges with the opposite high tide of the sun to make a large high tide. The opposite high tide of the moon merges with the direct high tide of the sun to make another large high tide. The result is that the tide rises very high and falls very low. In other words, there is a large tidal range. We have a spring tide just as we did around the time of new moon. After the time of full moon, the tidal ranges gradually decrease each day until they are quite small one week later during the time of the last quarter.

Figure 46-7 (RIGHT) (not drawn to scale). 1. The phase of the moon is last quarter; only half of the surface of the moon that faces the earth receives sunlight, and half of a half is a quarter. 2. As in the case of first quarter, the moon is pulling on the ocean waters in one direction while the sun is pulling in another. The result is that the tide does not rise very high or fall very low. In other words, there is a small tidal range. We have a neap tide as we did during the time of first quarter. After the time of last quarter, the tidal ranges gradually increase each day until the time of new moon, which occurs about a week later.

In summary: at the times of new and full moon , spring tides occur; these tides have a larger than average tidal range; during the times of first and last quarter, neap tides occur; these tides have a smaller than average tidal range.

Because the moon revolves around the earth at the same time and in the same direction as the earth rotates on its axis, the first high tide of Tuesday is approximately 24 hours and 50 minutes later than the first high tide of Monday. When the earth is in the same position as it was 24 hours ago, it must rotate an additional 50 minutes to catch up with the moon. Consider the figure below.

Figure 46-8. Points X and Y are having high tides. In order to be in the same position relative to the moon as they were on Monday, they have to wait until the earth has rotated for 50 extra minutes to catch up with the moon, which has revolved while the earth was rotating.

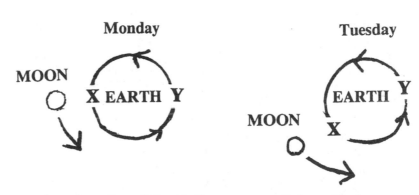

The 24 hours and 50 minutes is referred to as a <u>lunar day</u>. If we divide this by two, we get 12 hours 25 minutes, which is referred to as a <u>tidal period</u>. Thus, a tidal period is the interval of time between two corresponding high tides or between two corresponding low tides. If we divide the tidal period by 2, we get 6 hours and 12½ minutes, which is the time between a high tide and its corresponding low tide.

Figure 46-9. Let us calculate the times of high tides and low tides for a given day, using the interval of 6 hours 12½ minutes. Let us assume that the first high tide of day 1 is at 1:00 a.m., and include the times of the tides along with their heights in the table at right. From the table, we can make the following conclusions: 1. There is approximately a 6 hour 12½ minute interval between a high tide and its corresponding low tide.

		DAY 1
High Tide	1:00 A.M.	Height 13.2 feet
Low Tide	7:12½ A.M.	Height -0.3 feet
High Tide	1:25 P.M.	Height 12.4 feet
Low Tide	7:37½ P.M.	Height 0.2 feet
		DAY 2
High Tide	1:50 A.M.	Height 11.9 feet

2. The interval between one high tide and the next high tide, or between one low tide and the next low tide, is approximately 12 hours 25 minutes, which is the tidal period (sometimes called the <u>tidal cycle</u>). 3. The interval between the first high tide of day 1 and the first high tide of day 2 is 24 hours 50 minutes, which is the <u>tidal day</u>.

Figure 46-10, at right. A table comparing tidal ranges at different places along the United States shoreline, and some extremely high tidal ranges around the world.
Note that *most* places do not have a large tidal range. (Later on in our discussion of tides, we will explain some of the reasons for different tidal ranges in different places.)

Place	Average Tidal Range, In Feet
Boston, MA	9.5
Marblehead, MA	9.1
Siconset (Nantucket Island), MA	1.2
Portland, ME	9.0
Bar Harbor, ME	10.5
Calais, Me	20.0
Portsmouth, NH	7.8
Newport, RI	3.5
Providence, IR	4.6
Bridgeport, CT	1.9
New London, CT	2.6
New York, NY	4.5
Atlantic City, NJ	4.4
Sandy Hook, NJ	4.6
Philadelphia, PA	5.9
Wilmington, DE	5.7
Baltimore, MD	1.1
Ocean City, MD	3.4
Washington, D.C.	2.9
Norfolk, VA	2.8
Virginia Beach, VA	3.0
Cape Hatteras, NC	3.6
Charleston, SC	5.2
Savannah, GA	7.4
Jacksonville, FL	1.2
Miami Beach, FL	2.5
Naples, FL	2.3
Tampa Bay, FL	1.4
Bay of Fundy, Canada	44.0
West Coast of England	33.0
North Coast of France	28.0
Cook Inlet, Alaska	30.0

Moon at perigee, 221,463 miles from earth
Perigean tides occur at this time.

Moon at apogee, 252,790 miles from the earth
Apogean tides occur at this time.

Figure 46-11, above. Perigean and apogean tides.
Since the path (orbit) of the moon around the earth is that of an ellipse during the course of a lunar month (about 29½ days), there will be a day during which the moon will be closest to the earth, which is called the moon's <u>perigee</u>. At that time, it will have a greater gravitational effect on the tides. The tides at this time are called <u>perigean tides</u> and have a larger tidal range, similar to those during spring tides. In like manner, there will be a day during which the moon is farthest from the earth, which is called the moon's <u>apogee</u>. The tides at this time are called <u>apogean tides</u> and have a smaller tidal range, similar to those during neap tides.

About three times a year, the day that the moon is closest to the earth (the moon's perigee), occurs around the time of new or full moon. This results in extremely high tides and extremely low tides, i.e., a very large tidal range. These tides are referred to as <u>perigean spring tides</u>. In like manner, about three times a year, the day that the moon is farthest from the earth (the moon's apogee), occurs around the time of first and last quarter phases of the moon. This results in very small tidal ranges. These tides are referred to as <u>apogean neap tides</u>.

Figure 46-12. The earth's path around the sun is elliptical, rather than circular. This means that during a certain time of the year, the earth is closest to the sun, and at another time, it is farthest from the sun. On or around January 3rd, the earth is closest to the sun, which condition is called perihelion (incorporates the Greek word root "helios" for "sun"). In the Northern

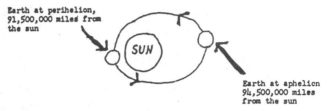

Earth at perihelion, 91,500,000 miles from the sun

Earth at aphelion 94,500,000 miles from the sun

Hemisphere, perihelion occurs in winter; in the Southern Hemisphere, in summer. On or around July 3rd, the earth is farthest from the sun, which condition is called aphelion. In the Northern Hemisphere, aphelion occurs in summer; in the Southern Hemisphere, in winter. Thus, people who live in the Southern Hemisphere have their winter when the earth is farthest from the sun, and summer when the earth is closest to the sun. Thus, you would think that the Southern Hemisphere would be colder in winter and hotter in summer than the Northern Hemisphere, but because the Southern Hemisphere is mostly ocean covered, the temperatures over the land masses are modified. However, even so, the South Polar region does get colder in winter than its counterpart, the North Polar region, during its respective winter.

On occasion, an extremely large tidal range occurs around January 3rd, if that date is also when the moon is closest to the earth as well as being the day of a new or full moon. This set of conditions occurring simultaneously is known as syzygy. Thus, syzygy is a condition in which the gravitational forces of both the moon and the sun combine to produce a maximum gravitational pull for the tides.

When syzygy occurs during a major coastal storm, widespread destruction can occur. For example, a great "nor'easter" coastal low pressure system came up the East Coast of the United States on January 2nd and 3rd, 1987. A barrier island that had protected Chatham Harbor in Massachusetts from large storm waves was broken through during this storm which was occurring at the time of syzygy. Several houses surrounding the harbor fell into the ocean, due to the extremely high tides and storm waves.

In like manner, an extremely small tidal range occurs around July 3rd, if that date is also when the moon is farthest from the earth as well as being the day of the first or last quarter phase of the moon. This set of conditions occurring simultaneously is asyzygy, having the opposite effect of syzygy.

During the course of a lunar month, which lasts about 29½ days, the moon travels approximately as far north and south of the equator as the sun appears to travel during the course of the year. Because the moon's orbit is inclined to only about 5 degrees to the plane of the earth's orbit, then during the course of a lunar month the moon travels to within 5 degrees of the Tropic of Cancer (23½° N) and then moves south, crossing the equator and travelling to within 5 degrees of the Tropic of Capricorn (23½° S), subsequently crossing the equator again.

Figure 46-13. A tide table for Boston, Massachusetts, showing that on the two days during the lunar month when the moon is directly over the equator, the tidal ranges at any given location are the same for the two tidal cycles.

High Tide	1:00 A.M.	Height	10.2 feet
Low Tide	7:12½ A.M.	Height	-2.0 feet
High Tide	1:25 P.M.	Height	10.2 feet
Low Tide	7:37½ P.M.	Height	-2.0 feet

Figure 46-14. On the two days during the lunar month when the moon is directly over the equator, the tidal ranges at any given location are the same for the two tidal cycles. The reason for this is that as the earth rotates, the tidal bulge is the same for each place for the two tidal cycles. (source: NOS)

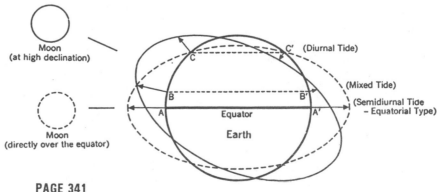

Moon (at high declination)

Moon (directly over the equator)

(Diurnal Tide)

(Mixed Tide)

(Semidiurnal Tide – Equatorial Type)

Equator

Earth

Figure 46-14 shows that when the moon is over the equator (dashed line), the tidal ranges for both tidal cycles are the same; and when the moon is at its farthest distance from the equator (solid line), the tidal ranges are quite unequal.

As the moon moves north or south of the equator, the tidal bulge becomes different for each of the two tidal cycles. On the day that the moon is approximately as far north as the Tropic of Cancer or about as far south as the Tropic of Capricorn, the tidal range of the two tidal cycles becomes quite different. This is especially true the closer you get to the poles and less so nearest the equator (refer again to figure 46-14). When the moon is nearly above the Tropic of Cancer or the Tropic of Capricorn, we refer to these tides with the uneven tidal range as tropic tides. When the moon is above the equator and thus producing two equal tidal ranges, we refer to these tides as equatorial tides.

Figure 46-15. Using Boston, Massachusetts again for our example, here is the tide table during a tropic tide. (The table on the previous page is for the equatorial tide.)

High Tide	1:00 A.M.	Height	12.4 feet
Low Tide	7:12½ A.M.	Height	-2.4 feet
High Tide	1:25 P.M.	Height	10.1 feet
Low Tide	7:37½ P.M.	Height	-1.0 feet

We classify tides according to how they behave on the days that the moon is farthest from the equator:

1. Semi-diurnal or semi-daily-type- tides occur in areas that have nearly the same tidal range during a lunar day in spite of the fact that the moon is at one of its farthest points from the equator. These types of tides are found, e.g., along the east coast of the United States.

2. Mixed tides occur when the two high tides and the two low tides during a lunar day differ greatly in height. The higher tide is referred to as higher high water; the lower of the two high tides is referred to as lower high water. The higher of the low tides is called higher low water; and the lower of the two low tides is called lower low water. Mixed tides are common on the west coast of the continental United States, and at coastal Alaska and Hawaii.

3. Diurnal or daily-type tides occur when a lower high water is about the same depth as the higher low water. This is sometimes referred to as a vanishing tide. The result is that there is only one high tide and one low tide in a lunar day. Diurnal tides are found in the along the northern Gulf of Mexico and in southeast Asia.

Figure 46-16. A graphic representation of the three types of tides discussed above: semidiurnal tide, mixed tide and diurnal tide. (source: NOS) A graphic representation of the rise and fall of tides is called a marigram. In the marigrams shown at the right, the term, datum, is the mean low tide, which is where the zero mark is fixed on a tide-measuring scale.

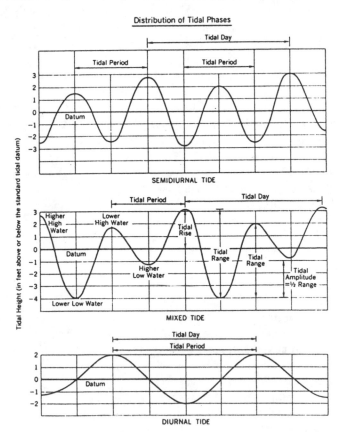

<u>Non-astronomical factors on tides:</u>

Channel narrows   Channel widens

Figure 46-17. If the harbor, bay , channel, etc. narrows as one moves away from the open ocean, then the tidal range will increase the farther up one goes. An example of this is the Bay of Fundy, an inlet of the Atlantic Ocean in southeastern Canada between New Brunswick and Nova Scotia. Conversely, if the harbor, bay, channel, etc. widens as one moves away from the open ocean and into it, then the tidal range will decrease. The Gulf of Mexico is an example of this.

The oceans of the world are broken up into smaller basins by the geological structures (i.e., mountain ranges, seamounts, volcanoes, guyots {table mounts} rising up from the ocean floor. These basins <u>oscillate</u> (vibrate) at a constant rate. The following demonstration illustrates this.

<u>DEMONSTRATION</u>: DETERMINING THE PERIOD OF OSCILLATION OF AN OCEAN BASIN
<u>Equipment/supplies needed</u>: a table; one large and one small glass casserole dish or pans; a timing device such as a stop watch or timer; one metric ruler; two people.

Procedure:
1. Fill each container about halfway with water.
2. While one person lifts and lowers one end of the larger container about 3 centimeters above the table, the other person turns on the timing device and turns it off when the wave which began at the end of the container that was lifted and lowered, returns to the same place from whence it began. The period of oscillation should be recorded to the nearest tenth of a second.
3. Repeat this procedure for the smaller container. You should find that the period is longer for the larger container. The same thing happens in ocean basins except that, because the oceans are much larger than our experimental basins, the periods are much longer. The closer the period of vibration is to the period between two consecutive high tides, or between two consecutive low tides (i.e., 12 hours 25 minutes), the greater will be the tidal range.

<u>DEMONSTRATION</u>: SIMULATING THE PERIOD OF OSCILLATION OF AN OCEAN BASIN
<u>Equipment/supplies needed</u>: this time, you will need only one of the glass casserole dishes that you used in the previous demonstration.

Procedure:
1. Fill a glass casserole dish about halfway with water.

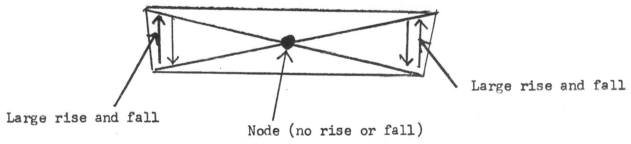

Large rise and fall

Large rise and fall

Node (no rise or fall)

Figure 48-18. A diagram showing the direction of the water motion in this demonstration.

2. Hold it at eye-level and slowly lift one end and then slowly lower it, in a manner similar to what you would do if you were imitating a slow motion video. You would likely notice that the water rises and falls more near the ends of the container and does not rise or fall very much near the center.
3. Now pretend that you live along the coast near the end of an oscillating basin. You should expect a rather large tidal range. If you have a summer place on an island in the vicinity of the node (center of basin), you should expect a small tidal range.

As you may know, the Bay of Fundy in southeast Canada has the largest tidal range in the world, with its average being some 44 feet (about 13½ meters)! The tidal range is greater during the times of full and new moon and when the moon is closest to the earth, and is less during the times of first and last quarters of the moon and when the moon is farthest from the earth.

Based upon what we have discussed, we can now list <u>three reasons why the Bay of Fundy has such a large tidal range</u>:
1. it gets narrower as one moves away from the ocean and into the bay;
2. the bay's period of oscillation is 12 hours 17 minutes, which is very close to the 12 hours 25 minutes half lunar day (a half-lunar day is the period of time between 2 high tides or 2 low tides); and
3. the bay is at the end of an oscillating ocean basin.

Onshore winds (winds blowing from over the water to over the land) cause the tide to rise higher than normal, which can be a problem during the time of high tides if these winds are strong. The low tide would not fall as low as usual. On the other hand, offshore winds (winds blowing from the land out towards over the ocean), cause the tide to fall lower at low tide but not rise as much as usual during the time of high tide. Moreover, low barometric pressure causes water to rise. During major storms, the combination of onshore winds and low pressure causes water to pile up along shores. When you consider that wind waves are on top of this dome of water, we have a storm surge with battering waves on top of it. This happens during a landfalling hurricane/typhoon and with a powerful yet non-tropical coastal storm.

Strong high pressure areas can depress the water level. You can show this by doing the demonstration described below:

<u>DEMONSTRATION</u>: DEPRESSION OF WATER LEVEL BY A HIGH PRESSURE AREA
You will need the following: a casserole dish; a large piece of plastic tubing or a large straw; a tall glass or a 1000 ml beaker.
<u>Procedure</u>:
1. Place the tall glass upside down into the casserole dish in which the water level is less than the height of the glass.
2. Place the large piece of plastic tubing into the glass and increase the pressure by blowing air into it. You will notice that there is a drop in the water level.

A Review of the Factors that Affect the Tides at One Given Location:
1. The gravitational pull of the moon.
2. The gravitational pull of the sun.
3. The distance of the moon from the earth.
4. The distance of the sun from the earth.
5. The phase of the moon.
6. Where the moon is located with respect to the earth's equator.
7. Where the beach, harbor or port is located with respect to an oscillating ocean basin.
8. The period of oscillation of the ocean basin in which the beach, harbor or port is located.
9. The surface configuration of the beach, harbor or port.
10. The wind direction and wind speed.
11. The barometric pressure.

Items 1 through 6 are astronomical factors, and items 7 through 11 are non-astronomical factors. Items 1 through 9 can be predicted well in advance, but items 10 and 11 depend on the weather conditions and are as accurate as the weather forecasts.

Figure 46-19. High tide at Swampscott Harbor (Swampscott is a coastal community along the northeast shore of Massachusetts). (photo by Joseph Balsama)

Figure 46-20. Low tide at Swampscott Harbor, Massachusetts. (photo by Joseph Balsama)

Prediction of tides:

In order to predict tides for a given location, actual observations of the tide must be made for at least 18.6 years. Within this period, just about all possible positions of the moon and earth in relation to each other will have occurred. This period of time is referred to as a full 18.6-year tidal cycle. During this period, we are able to study the effects of items 7, 8 and 9 on the previous page, at a given location as well as all of the factors previously listed.

The arrival times of high and low tides as well as the tidal range at a given location all result from all the eleven factors, plus several additional ones of lesser significance. All the factors are computer-processed, giving us analyses and printouts. Before the age of the computer, these variables were represented by a series of weights and pulleys in an old-fashioned tide-predicting device. At the time of printing of this book, the National Ocean Survey (NOS) maintains a continuous network of some 140 tidal gauges, which are located along coasts, bays, harbors, ports, etc. of the United States and its territories and possessions. NOS also prepares tables giving the times and heights of high and low tides for a large number of locations, including for some other countries. These predictions are published annually for approximately one year or more in advance.

Tidal currents:

In order for water to rise and fall at a specific harbor, port, bay, etc., the water must move in a horizontal direction to and from the open ocean. This horizontal movement is called the tidal current.

As the tide is rising, the water moves from the open ocean towards the harbor; as the tide falls, it moves from the harbor to the ocean. As you can see, the water flows in one direction for approximately 6 hours and flows in the opposite direction for about another 6 hour period.

At the mouth of the harbor, bay, river or port during the times of high and low tides, there is practically no horizontal movement of the water. This is called slack water. Technically, slack water is defined as a period of time in which the speed of the tidal current is less than one-tenth of a knot. (One knot is approx. 1.15 miles per hour.) The farther one moves upstream, the more the time of slack water will vary from the times of high and low tides. This time difference can be from just a few minutes to several hours. In places that have two high tides and two low tides each day, there are four periods of slack water. The length of time of slack water is a function of the speed of the tidal current. What this means is that a river with a very strong tidal current has its periods of slack water lasting for only a short period of time, such as 10 to 15 minutes, whereas a river with a weak tidal current has much longer periods of slack water. During the rest of the day, the tidal current is moving either towards the open ocean or upstream towards the harbor. The speed of the tidal current usually reaches its maximum half-way between high tide and low tide, and half-way between low tide and high tide. Because the gravitational pulls of the moon and sun have very little effect on rivers (since they are so relatively small compared with the sizes of oceans), most river tides are produced when tidal currents from the open ocean move upstream and downstream. The same factors that affect the tides affect tidal currents. For example, during the times of full moon and new moon, when we are experiencing spring tides, the tidal currents increase in speed. During the times of first and last quarter phases of the moon, when we are experiencing neap tides, the tidal currents decrease in speed.

Special types of tidal currents:

1. Tidal rips (also called whirlpools or maelstroms) are caused by very strong tidal currents flowing over very uneven surfaces. This creates turbulence which produces eddies that resemble large whirlpools. Tidal rips can also be produced when two strong tidal currents, each coming form one side of a peninsula, collide while moving toward the open ocean, or rapidly separate while moving toward land. Tidal rips usually disappear during the time of slack water.

Figure 46-21. Tidal rips. The right side of the figure is a drawing of how the ocean might look in the vicinity of the tidal rip, the dots on the left side of the diagram.

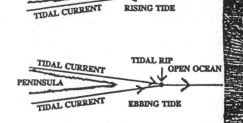

2. <u>Reversing falls rapids</u> (<u>reversible tidal waterfalls</u>) occur when a river with a swift current has its channel narrowed considerably by a narrow gorge that does not permit the passage of large volumes of water. When the tide is going out, water piles up where the channel narrows, forming waterfalls that flow toward the open ocean. In like manner, when the tide is coming in, the water piles up, forming waterfalls that flow upstream. Perhaps one of the best places to observe reversing falls rapids is at the mouth of the 450-mile long St. John River as it attempts to empty into the Bay of Fundy at St. John, New Brunswick, Canada. At low tide, the level of the Bay of Fundy is much lower than the river. As the water rushes downstream, its flow is restricted by a narrow gorge so that the water on the upstream side of the gorge cannot fall as rapidly as on the ocean side; consequently, a higher level now results on the upstream side of the gorge, with a waterfall in the downstream direction.

When the tide of the Bay of Fundy rises so that the level of the water on both sides of the gorge is equal, slack water occurs. This is sometimes referred to as <u>low slack</u>. At St. John, this lasts for about twenty minutes. It is the only time that you will see boats moving about. During slack water, the speed of the current is less than one-tenth of a knot. As the tide of the Bay of Fundy continues to rise, the narrow gorge does not permit the passage of the large volume of water upstream; consequently, the water rises higher on the ocean side of the gorge and a waterfall is formed in the upstream direction. The water depth in the gorge at high tide ranges from 150 to 175 feet (45 to 55 meters).

As the tide of the Bay of Fundy goes out to the point where the level of the water on either side of the gorge is equal, another slack water period occurs. This is referred to as <u>high slack</u>.

The most spectacular phase is low tide at which time the river thunders in whirling rapids and whirlpools water out to sea. In order to appreciate the reversing falls rapids, you should see them three times: at low tide, low slack and high tide (or at high tide, high slack, and low tide).

Date	A.M.				P.M.			
	Low Tide	Low Slack	High Tide	High Slack	Low Tide	Low Slack	High Tide	High Slack
1 Sunday	1:05	4:55	7:25	9:50	1:35	5:25	7:50	10:15
2 Monday	2:15	6:05	8:30	10:55	2:40	6:30	8:55	11:20

Figure 46-22. The interval of time between low tide, low slack water, high tide and high slack water for an October 1st and 2nd at St. John Harbor in New Brunswick, Canada.

Figure 46-23. High tide at Reversing Falls Rapids at St. John, New Brunswick, Canada. (photo by Joseph Balsama)

Figure 46-24. Low tide at Reversing Falls Rapids at St. John, New Brunswick, Canada. (photo by Joseph Balsama)

Figure 46-25. Low slack water at Reversing Falls Rapids at St. John, New Brunswick, Canada. (photo by Joseph Balsama)

<u>Tidal bores:</u>

Tidal bores occur in a river with a broad mouth. The river needs to have a strong enough current to prevent the ocean tide from backing up the river. After a "struggle", the incoming tide overwhelms the river current, which always moves towards the ocean, and forms several large waves, which travel upstream. These waves are referred to as <u>the bore</u>. The bore occurring on the Petitcodiac River in Moncton, New Brunswick, Canada is an example of this.

The height of the bore at Moncton varies with the seasons and the phases of the moon, from a few inches to several feet. It is usually highest in spring, because the addition of melting snow increases the speed of the river current. In summer, it may be only a ripple, but there are times when, driven by strong winds in the Bay of Fundy, it reaches over 6 feet in height. After the bore passes, the tide comes in rapidly for about two hours. In Moncton, after the bore passes, the broad river basin of the Petitcodiac River is filled with about 30 feet (9 meters) of water. After this, both the water forced up by the ocean and the normal fresh water head toward the Bay of Fundy and manage to keep flowing in this direction until approximately three hours after the tide has begun to come in. At this time, the cycle described above is repeated.

At Moncton, the bore travels up the Petitcodiac River for a distance of about 20 miles (32 kilometers). In the Amazon River, bores travel upstream for a distance of approximately 200 miles (320 kilometers); consequently, as many as five bores may actually be moving up the river at one time!

Figure 46-26. The tidal bore moving upstream along the Petitcodiac River at Moncton, New Brunswick, Canada. The water rises rapidly as soon as the tidal bore passes. (photo by Joseph Balsama)

If you travel to St. John, New Brunswick to see the reversing falls rapids, you should travel to Moncton to see the tidal bore. Moncton is not too far from St. John.

On the Tsientang River, which empties into the China Sea, all shipping is controlled by the bore, which is the largest and most dangerous in the world. During most of the month, the bore advances up the river in a wave 8 to 11 feet high, moving at a speed of 12 to 13 knots. During spring tides (at the times of new and full moon), the crest of the advancing wave rises over 25 feet above the surface of the river!

<u>Other local currents:</u>

1. <u>Rip currents</u> form when waves break on a shallow bar (sandbar), causing the water level to rise on the bar. The excess water flows rapidly towards the ocean through narrow channels on the sandbar. This return flow of water is the rip current.

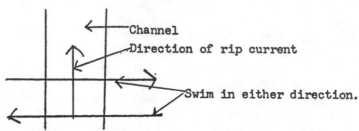

Figure 46-27. If you should get caught in a rip current, do not try to swim against it, but swim at right angles to it. For example, if you are on a beach and a rip current is carrying you out away from the beach, swim parallel to the shore, not towards the shore. Rip currents are usually narrow, and if you swim at right angles to the direction that they are carrying you, you will be out of their influence by just swimming a short distance.

You can observe rip currents from the shore quite easily on clear, calm days. The rip currents appear as grayish areas that are quite distinct from the blue color of the ocean. The gray color is due to the rapidly moving current in the narrow channels churning up sediments such as clay, silt, sand, pebbles, etc., from below.

2. <u>Swash</u> is the movement of water towards the shore when a wave breaks.

3. <u>Backwash</u> is the movement of water towards the ocean to meet the next oncoming wave. If the waves are large and the beach has a steep slope, then backwash becomes an <u>undertow</u>, which can be very dangerous to swimmers.

4. <u>Beach drift</u> is the combination of swash and backwash.

5. <u>Longshore currents</u> occur whenever waves hit a beach at an angle, which they do most of the time because it is highly unlikely that the entire length of a beach will be perpendicular to the body of water adjacent to it. In the vicinity of the <u>surf zone</u> (where the waves break), the water moves parallel to the shore and carries sediment along with it. (Near the shore, it can be fun to float near the surf zone just offshore. You might find yourself having to walk several hundred feet to the right or left because the longshore current would carry you parallel to the shore.)

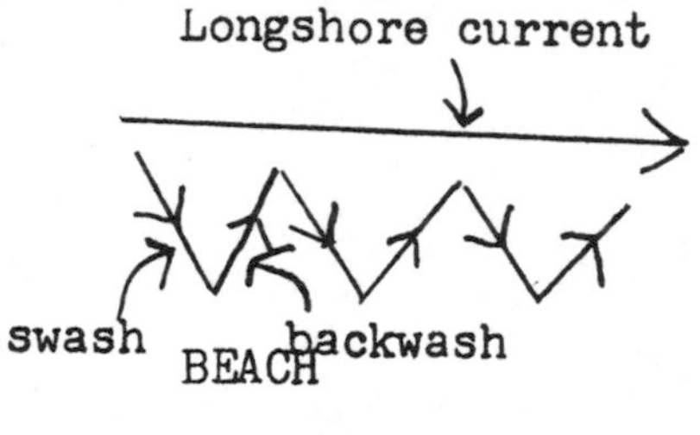

Figure 46-28. The swash and backwash (beach drift) and longshore current at a beach.

6. <u>Longshore transport</u> is the combination of beach drift and the longshore current; this is also sometimes referred to as <u>shore drift</u>.

Figure 46-29. Rip currents (right). The grayish areas are the rip currents. (photo by Joseph Balsama)

DEMONSTRATION: HOURLY CHANGE IN WATER LEVEL BETWEEN HIGH AND LOW TIDE

You will need a camera and film, and a local tide table to determine the times and heights of high and low tides. This demonstration can be done for readers who are near an ocean or visiting by the ocean.

1. Go to a local beach that is on the ocean and photograph it at the water's edge from the same spot as follows:

a. at high tide
b. one hour after high tide
c. two hours after high tide
d. three hours after high tide
e. four hours after high tide
f. five hours after high tide
g. six hours after high tide, which is then low tide.

2. Place the photographs in the correct sequence on a table or on a piece of poster paper. Between what hours was there the greatest change in water level? Can you think of at least one reason for this?

Note the following:
1. Start early enough in the day to assure that it will still be daylight at the end of the six-hour period.
2. You may also begin this demonstration at low tide and work your way towards high tide. If so, make sure that your reference point (i.e., the place from where you photograph) is a short distance in front of the high tide level. If you are not sure where this is, then look for deposits of seaweed and other debris or areas where the sand might be damp in the vicinity of the upper beach or sea-wall.

DEMONSTRATION: PHOTOGRAPHING TIDAL RANGES AT SEVERAL LOCAL BEACHES

You will need a camera and film, and a local tide table to determine the times and heights of high and low tides. This demonstration can be done for readers who are near an ocean or visiting by the ocean.

1. Go to several beaches on the ocean at high tide and photograph the water level.

2. Return to these beaches at low tide and photograph the water level from the same reference point.

3. Place the photographs showing each beach at high tide and low tide next to each other on a table or piece of poster paper. On which beach or beaches did the water level seem to drop the most between high and low tide? What might be a reason for this?

Note the following:
1. If you are in an area where there are fewer than six hours of sunlight at the time of the year when you want to take photographs of high and low tides, then take a photograph at high tide and wait for about a week and the low tide will occur about the same time of day as that high tide. Consult a local tide table for the exact times of high and low tides. Of course in both this demonstration and in the one above, do not do them if a major storm with high winds in underway, since coastal flooding would not permit you to do these demonstrations.
2. You may reverse the procedure by taking photographs of the beaches at low tide and then returning to do the same during the time of high tide. If so, then make sure your reference point is a short distance in front of the high tide level.

Chapter 47. TSUNAMIS

The word TSUNAMI is a Japanese word, from the roots TSU for port, and NAMI for wave.

Tsunamis, which can be also called seismic sea waves, are large waves caused by earthquakes (seaquakes) and by underseas volcanic activity. Although they used to be called tidal waves ("they produced their own tides"), they have nothing to do with the tides, and the term is no longer used.

If you were at sea and a seismic wave passed you, you would not notice it because its <u>wavelength</u> (the distance from the point on one wave to the corresponding point on the next) is so long that you do not realize that you are going from <u>trough</u> (bottom of the wave) to <u>crest</u> (top of the wave), since this is done so gradually. It is only when they approach shallow water or the shore that they build up to their terrifying heights. They are much more dangerous on flat shores than on steep ones.

Figure 47-1. A terrifying tsunami approaching a beach at Hilo, Hawaii. As a tsunami approaches the shore, it can rapidly grow to heights exceeding 100 feet (over 30 meters)! (source: NOAA)

In the open ocean, tsunamis, or seismic sea waves, do not appear as a single wave but as a series of waves. The waves are separated by intervals of several minutes to over an hour. Another way of stating this is that the <u>period</u> (the time it takes one complete wave to pass a given point) is between several minutes to over an hour. The third to the eighth wave in the series is typically the largest. When an undersea earthquake is the cause of the tsunami, the steepest waves appear to occur on shores facing the direction of the seaquake.

An ordinary wind wave is rarely more than a few hundred feet long from crest to crest; i.e., wind waves typically do not have a wave length over a few hundred feet. In fact, an Atlantic Ocean wind wave is usually no longer than about 320 feet, whereas in the Pacific Ocean, a typical wind wave is no longer than about 1000 feet. The Pacific Ocean's larger and deeper expanse provides more water for the waves to develop.

Figure 47-2. A killer tsunami strikes at Hilo, Hawaii, moving onshore and causing widespread destruction. In the United States, coastal sections of Alaska and Hawaii are particularly vulnerable to being struck by tsunamis since an earthquake and volcano zone surrounds the rim of the Pacific Ocean. This zone is called the Circum-Pacific Ring of Fire.

Wind wave forward speeds are from several miles per hour up to about 60 mph. Compare this with tsunamis, whose wave lengths are usually from about 100 to 600 miles, and whose speeds can reach to about 600 mph, nearly the speed of sound!

Wind waves in the ocean can reach heights over 50 feet in major storms such as a very intense "Nor'easter" coming up the East Coast of the U.S. in winter, or in a similar storm striking the British Isles in winter, or in a major and large hurricane. Tsunami waves, on the other hand, are only a few feet high from trough to crest in the open sea, but can grow rapidly to one hundred feet high or more as they approach the shore line. Imagine sitting on the beach and suddenly seeing a rapidly growing monster wave charging at high speed towards you! If you do not get away fast enough, the tsunami will cover you with perhaps over 100 feet of water as it crashes onshore.

When the tsunami is racing towards the coast, the water along the coast retreats to meet the incoming wave. Thus, at least you would have the warning of the water suddenly racing out a great distance.

Tsunamis are translational (shallow-water) waves because the depth of water beneath their troughs is less than one-half their wave length. This makes it crest; that is, the tsunami looks like a wave with a definite crest and trough. A tsunami with a wave length of 500 miles has to be a shallow-water wave because it is not possible to have the depth of water beneath it trough to be 250 miles, since the deepest trench, the Mariana Trench, in the vicinity of the Philippine Sea, is approximately 7 miles deep.

An example of an open-ocean wave would be a wind wave with a wave length of 200 feet, having a depth of water beneath its trough greater than 100 feet. Open-ocean waves are not detected by the human eye, except when they crest (become shallow-water waves) after which time we can distinguish the crests and troughs and their forward movement.

Therefore, we can say that **a tsunami is a translational or shallow-water wave with a long wavelength, a long period and a high speed.**

An example of a serious tsunami event is from the Good Friday (March 27th) Alaska earthquake of 1964, when parts of Anchorage were turned upside down. The quake measured 8.6 on the Richter Scale. Its tsunami that hit around Anchorage and hit especially hard at Valdez, Alaska, was moving at 510 miles per hour (815 km/hr). Its wavelength was about 130 miles. Since the ocean is not 65 miles deep, the water under the trough was less than one-half the wave length; therefore, these were shallow-water or translational waves.

Figure 47-3. An amazing photograph which was taken just as a tsunami was moving into the harbor of Hilo, Hawaii back in 1946. Notice the man in the lower-left of this picture, watching the tsunami move in. Needless to say, this man was killed moments after this picture was taken. (source: NOAA)

Tsunamis potentially could occur in any ocean. Significant earthquake or volcanic activity in or just around the ocean could trigger tsunamis.

Figure 47-4. The result of a tsunami crashing ashore on Scotch Cap, Unimak Island, in the Aleutian island chain of Alaska. An earthquake in the Aleutian Trench produced a tsunami which minutes after the quake, reached over 100 feet (over 30 meters) high when it hit this location. The left photo shows the Scotch Cap lighthouse before the tsunami, and the right photo shows what was left after the tsunami struck. Some five hours later, a tsunami from the same earthquake struck Hawaii. Thus, tsunamis can travel for great distances and fast speeds. (source: NOAA)

Figure 47-5. The Circum-Pacific Ring-of-Fire, from the tip of South America, up along the Pacific coast of the Americas and around down the east coast of Asia. Many earthquakes and volcanic eruptions occur along the rim and some occur in the Pacific. Thus, all coasts along the rim and in the ocean are vulnerable to tsunamis generated by major earthquake and volcanic activity. (source: NOAA)

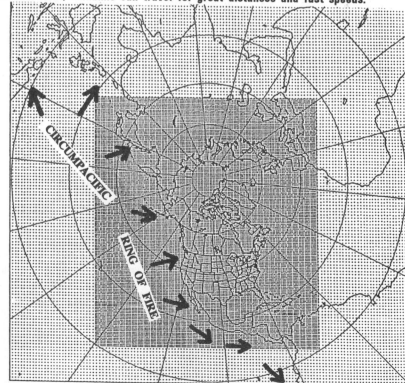

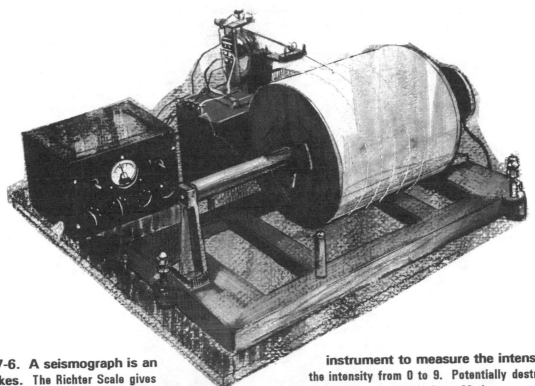

Figure 47-6. A seismograph is an earthquakes. The Richter Scale gives earthquakes are 6.0 or higher, and in the worldwide. The scale is not linear. That is, a 7 is not twice as powerful as a 6. A 6.1 is TEN TIMES more powerful than a 6.0. A 7.0 earthquake is ONE HUNDRED TIMES more powerful than a 6.0 earthquake. Thus, there is much more energy released in a 7.3 earthquake compared with a 7.2, than in a 3.4 earthquake compared with a 3.3.

instrument to measure the intensity of the intensity from 0 to 9. Potentially destructive 20th century, occurred about 40 times a year

Another way of looking at it, a magnitude 7.0 earthquake releases ONE THOUSAND TIMES more energy than does a 5.0 earthquake, on the Richter Scale. Thus, the scale increase is progressive in terms of how it defines the energy released by an earthquake.

Before seismographs were invented, people assessed damage by comparing it with damage from previous earthquakes. In the 19th century, a man named Mercalli developed an earthquake measuring scale based on his personal observations. The scale has since been revised, as is now the <u>Modified Mercalli Scale</u> for earthquake intensity. It runs from I to XII, from weakest to strongest. Thus, we have the Richter Scale (the preferred) and the Modified Mercalli Scale to assess earthquake intensity.

Keep in mind that the tsunami generated by an earthquake or a volcanic eruption is a SERIES of travelling ocean waves of extremely long length and period. When a volcanic eruption generates a tsunami, it does so by causing earthquakes itself as well as causing vibrations in the earth.

The Pacific Tsunami Warning System of the National Weather Service, based in Honolulu, Hawaii, issues Tsunami Watches and Warnings.

The Tsunami Warning System, whose center is at Honolulu, Hawaii, was established after 1946. The members of this system use a device consisting of a series of pipes and a pressure-measuring chamber which records the rise and fall of the water surface. Ordinary water movements, such as wind waves and tides, are disregarded. But when waves with a period of about 10 to 40 minutes begin to roll over the ocean, they set in motion a corresponding oscillation in a column of mercury which closes an electric circuit. This, in turn, sets off an alarm, notifying the observers at the station that a seismic wave (tsunami) is in progress.

The National Weather Service in cooperation with the U.S. Coast and Geodetic Survey issues a **TSUNAMI WATCH** when an earthquake occurs which has a magnitude great enough to cause a tsunami.

Figure 47-7. Comparing the values of the Richter Scale (right) with the Modified Mercalli Scale (left), and the characteristic effects of earthquakes with their corresponding values on both scales. The Richter Scale is the preferred scale for earthquake and seaquake classification. (source: Massachusetts Emergency Management Agency)

MODIFIED MERCALLI INTENSITY		CHARACTERISTIC EFFECTS	RICHTER MAGNITUDE
I	INSTRUMENTAL	DETECTED ONLY BY SENSITIVE INSTRUMENTS	LESS THAN 3.0
II	FEEBLE	FELT ONLY BY FEW AT REST	3.0
III	SLIGHT	FELT INDOORS, LIKE THE VIBRATIONS OF A TRUCK	3.0
IV	NOTICEABLE	PEOPLE AWAKENED, OBJECTS ROCK, WINDOWS RATTLED	3.7
V	MODERATE	PLASTER FALLS, WINDOWS BROKEN, TALL OBJECTS SWAY	4.3
VI	RATHER STRONG	FELT BY ALL, CHIMNEYS DAMAGED, OBJECTS FALL	5.0
VII	STRONG	WALLS CRACKED, PLASTER FALLS, WAVES ON PONDS	5.6
VIII	VERY STRONG	BUILDINGS DAMAGED, CHIMNEYS FALL, GENERAL ALARM	6.3
IX	DESTRUCTIVE	MANY BUILDINGS DESTROYED, UDERGROUND PIPES FAIL	7.0
X	DISASTROUS	ONLY BEST BUILDINGS AND STRUCTURES UNDAMAGED	7.7
XI	RUINOUS	FEW MASONRY STRUCTURES SURVIVE, BRIDGES FALL	8.4
XII	CATASTROPHIC	TOTAL DESTRUCTION, OBJECTS THROWN INTO THE AIR	9.0

If you are in an area which is under a tsunami watch, you must make the same preparations as you would for a major flood watch, provided there is ample time to do so.

When a tsunami is detected, a **TSUNAMI WARNING** is issued for the threatened coastal areas. If you are in such a situation, then the amount of time that you would have for action, including evacuation, is dependent upon:
● the location of the epicenter of the earthquake; and
● the estimated time of arrival (E.T.A.) of the tsunami.

Definition of epicenter: the area on the surface of the earth (in this case, most likely the ocean floor) directly above where the earthquake actually occurred. (On the other hand, , the focus of the quake is the distance beneath the earth's surface [beneath the ocean floor] where the quake actually occurred.)

The E.T.A. of the tsunami is determined by the distance to the location of the epicenter, and the speed of the tsunami.

You can expect the same type of damage that you would get from a hurricane storm surge, or even worse. Local civil defense and preparedness agencies, as well as other relevant authorities (police, fire and rescue, etc.) would know what homes, businesses and other structures are on a low-enough coastal area to be prone to a tsunami attack as well as being prone to a hurricane/typhoon storm surge.

Through the 19th and 20th centuries, hundreds of tsunamis have blasted coastal regions along the Circum-Pacific Ring of Fire. Tsunami attacks have been documented along the coasts of Japan, southeast Asia, Alaska and South America.

For example, when the Krakatoa volcano literally blew up in the western Pacific Ocean in 1883, the resultant earthquakes created tsunamis that were over 100 feet (over 30 meters) high, which swept over adjacent islands, drowning tens of thousands of people.

In recent times, most tsunami watches and warnings that involve the United States have been issued for Hawaii and Alaska, although the National Weather Service is prepared to issue them also for any coastal location (e.g., for Washington, Oregon, California, New England).

The east coast of the United States is not immune from tsunamis, although in recent centuries tsunamis striking the east coast are quite rare. However, there have been east coast earthquakes that produced tsunamis. For example, on November 18th, 1755, an earthquake which has been estimated to be about 6.2 on the Richter Scale, was epicentered in the ocean east of Cape Ann, Massachusetts. In Boston, twelve brick buildings fell, and some 100 chimneys fell from Cape Ann, which is on the north shore of Massachusetts, to Boston. Over 1000 others were damaged. Much worse was the 1886 earthquake at Charleston, South Carolina, estimated to be a 6.6 quake, which left most of the city destroyed...in rubble...and was felt over 2 million square miles. The extent of tsunamis generated by these east coast earthquakes has not been fully documented.

Thus, the relationship between earthquakes and tsunamis has been established and a watch and warning system is operational to try to save lives and as much property as feasible.

SECTION XIII: OTHER INTERESTING PHENOMENA

Chapter 48. Optical Phenomena

In this chapter we will discuss some of the more common types of optical phenomena; but in order to do so we must review some basic concepts and simple demonstrations in <u>optics</u>, the study of light. Let us begin by explaining the difference between the two types of images.

1. <u>Real images</u> are made by the actual rays of light. They can be projected on a screen and photographed. They are upside-down and can be smaller, the same size or larger than the object.
2. <u>Virtual images</u> cannot be projected on a screen but can be photographed. They are usually inside a mirror or lens in a place where you cannot get at them. They are right-side up and can be smaller, the same size or larger than the object.

Although light travels in a straight line, it can be bent by reflection, diffusion (scattering), refraction, dispersion and diffraction. As we discuss the various types of optical phenomena, we will be using at least one of these in our explanation; therefore, let us discuss each one separately.

<u>Reflection</u> - the bouncing of light off a shiny surface, usually producing an image.

1. The instruments used to demonstrate reflection are mirrors. There are three types of mirrors.
a. <u>Plane mirrors</u> - produce a virtual image that is the same size as the object. The image appears to be as far into the mirror as the object is in front of it.

DEMONSTRATION: PLANE MIRRORS
You will need a plane mirror to do this demonstration. Use a large one if possible. In fact, you might want to stand in front of the mirror of your bathroom cabinet.
1. Look at yourself at different distances from a plane mirror. What do you observe? (Remember, you are the object and what you see in the mirror is the image.)
b. <u>Convex mirrors</u> - produce a virtual image that is smaller than the object.

DEMONSTRATION: CONVEX MIRRORS
You will need a large convex mirror (about 8 to 12 inches in diameter). You may already have one. Look around the house to see if you have a mirror that looks like it is set in a ship's wheel. If not, perhaps you can borrow one from a local high school or college physics teacher.

1. Figure 48-1. Look at yourself at different distances from a convex mirror. What do you observe? Look at the diagram

OBJECT (STUDENTS)   **VIRTUAL IMAGE**   **CONVEX MIRROR**

c. <u>Concave mirrors</u> - These are the most exciting of all mirrors, because they produce a real image that could be larger, smaller or the same size as the object, as well as a virtual image that is larger than the object. What you get depends upon where you place the objects. (See demonstration.) The real images will appear upside-down in front of the mirror. The virtual image will appear inside the mirror right-side up as it did in the plane and convex mirrors.

DEMONSTRATION: CONCAVE MIRRORS
Borrow a large concave mirror at least 12 to 15 inches in diameter from a high school or college physics teacher. Stand it up at the end of a long table. The table should be between 3½ to 4 feet long. You can use two bricks to hold it up. Place a 40-watt bulb into a socket and plug the lamp into an extension cord. Place this in front of the mirror at varying distances. In order for you to see anything, you must stand in front of the mirror at the opposite end of the table. Therefore, only one or two people can see this at one time.

(continued)

1. **Figure 48-2.** Place the light at the opposite
end of the table from the mirror. Keep moving
it towards the mirror until you see a real image
which is smaller than the object in front of the mirror. You may have to adjust the mirror if you do not see anything.

OBJECT   REAL IMAGE   CONCAVE MIRROR

REAL IMAGE

OBJECT   CONCAVE MIRROR

2. **Figure 48-3.** Now move the light until you
see a real image which is the same size as the
object right over the object (the real light bulb).
This is called Pepe's Ghost.

REAL IMAGE   OBJECT   CONCAVE MIRROR

3. **Figure 48-4.** Now move the light source
towards the mirror until you see real image
larger than the object.

4. **Figure 48-5.** Now move the light source
closer to the mirror until you see no object but
a beam of light shining in your eyes. This
occurs when the light source is at the focus of
the mirror. This is how headlights and search
lights work.

OBJECT AT FOCUS   CONCAVE MIRROR

5. **Figure 48-6.** Now move the light source
closer to the mirror until you see a large virtual
image inside the mirror.

OBJECT   CONCAVE MIRROR   VIRTUAL IMAGE

Diffusion (Scattering) is a form of reflection. It occurs when light is reflected off a rough surface or from small particles such as dust or smoke. Look at the drawing below that shows the difference between reflection and scattering.

INCOMING INCIDENT RAY   REFLECTED RAY   INCOMING RAY   REFLECTED RAY

REFLECTION   SCATTERING

Figure 48-7. Reflection vs. scattering. Note that in both reflection and scattering, the incoming rays are parallel. In reflection, the reflected rays are also parallel; in scattering, the reflected rays move in any direction, depending upon where they hit the rough surface.

Scattering makes surfaces look white. Snow is white because it scatters light. Flat white paint is white because it has a rough texture. If you place a coat of oil such as furniture polish over it, then some of the roughness is made smooth by the oil, resulting in your beginning to see an image.

DEMONSTRATION: DIFFUSION (SCATTERING)
You will need a strong light source (such as a slide projector), two chalkboard erasers that are dirty with chalk dust, a flashlight, one piece of clear glass about 2" by 2", one piece of frosted glass about 2" by 2", and a hard-cover book (not this book).
1. Darken a room and shine the slide projector or similar bright light source on a wall. Clap the chalkboard erasers together, in the path of the light. The beam of light becomes more visible because the chalk dust is scattering the light.
2. Shine a flashlight through a piece of frosted glass. You will see light but not the light source as you would if you shined the flashlight through a piece of clear glass. The rough surface of the frosted glass scatters the light. We say that the frosted glass is translucent. On the other hand, the clear piece of glass is called transparent, because it allows all or most of the light to pass through without being scattered. If you place a textbook in front of the flashlight, no light passes through. We say that the book is opaque.

Refraction is the bending of light as it passes from one medium into another. Examples: passing of light from air into water, from water into air, from air into glass, from glass into water, etc.

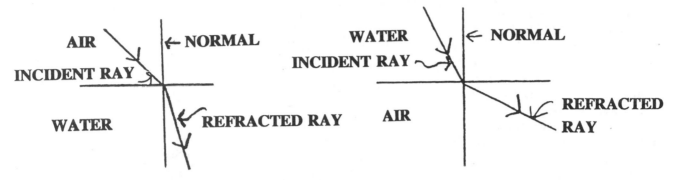

Figure 48-8. The bending of light as it travels from one medium into another. Whenever light travels from a medium in which it travels fast, e.g., air, into a medium in which it travels a little slower, e.g., water, glass, the light bends towards the "normal". The normal is an imaginary vertical line that is drawn perpendicular to the two media. Whenever light travels from a medium through which it travels more slowly to one through which it travels faster, it bends away from the normal.

DEMONSTRATION: REFRACTION
You will need a 1000 milliliter (one liter) beaker and a 12-inch ruler.
1. Place a 12-inch ruler in a 1000 ml beaker that is about half-filled with water. Do not hold on to the ruler. You will notice that the ruler looks magnified and distorted. This is because the light being reflected from the part of the ruler that is not submerged in water is reaching your eye slightly faster than is the light coming from the part that is submerged.

The instruments used in refraction are lenses. There are two types of lenses: convex and concave.
Convex lenses are like concave mirrors in that they produce a real image that can be smaller, the same size or larger than the object, depending upon where you place the object. They also produce a virtual image that is larger than the object.
DEMONSTRATION: CONVEX LENSES
You will need the following: a large magnifying glass with a diameter of at least three inches, with a handle; a ring stand with a clamp that fits on the handle; a 40-watt light bulb in a socket which has been plugged into an extension cord; and one sheet of paper with print or writing on it.
1. Hang the magnifying glass that is at least 3 to 4 inches in diameter on a ring stand. You may have to borrow a clamp that can be attached to a ring stand. Place this fairly close to a wall. Move the light source (the 40-watt bulb in a socket attached to an extension cord) and/or the ring stand different distances from the wall to get three different real images (smaller, the same size or larger than the object). The real images will be upside-down on the wall.
2. To show a virtual image larger than the object, place a piece of paper with print or writing on it behind the lens, using the lens as a magnifying glass. You could also place the light source behind the lens then look at it through the lens. The light source should appear very large.

Concave lenses are like convex mirrors in that they produce a virtual image that is smaller than the object.
DEMONSTRATION: CONCAVE LENSES
You will need a concave lens with a diameter of at least three inches, and a sheet of paper with printing or writing on it.
1. Look at the printed/written-on sheet through a concave lens. The print will appear smaller.

Dispersion is a special form of refraction in which a prism takes white light, which is comprised of the visible colors of the spectrum (red, orange, yellow, green, blue, indigo, violet) and bends each color by a different amount so that the colors separate out. The bending is caused by the rate by which the prism slows down the speed of light of each color. Because the violet light is slowed the most, it bends the most. Red is slowed down the least, so it bends less than the other colors.

DEMONSTRATION: DISPERSION
You will need a glass prism or plastic prism and a strong light source such as a slide projector.
1. Place the prism next to the lens of the projector or other good light source. Rotate the prism until you see a spectrum on the wall or ceiling, etc.

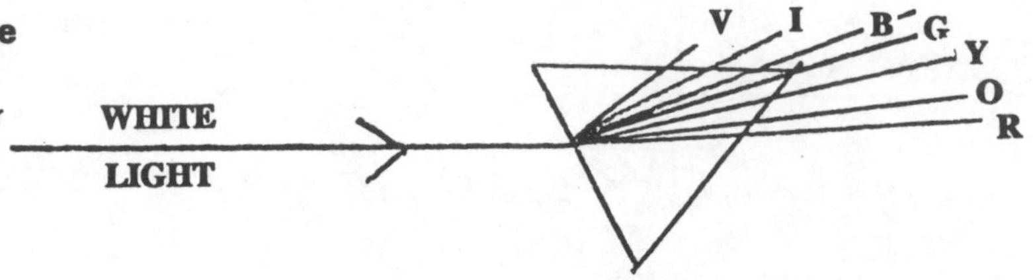

Figure 48-9. A prism separating white light into the visible colors that comprise it. (Note: to remember the order of the colors of the rainbow, remember the name, "Roy G. Biv", which stands for red, orange, yellow, green, blue, indigo, violet.)

Diffraction is the spreading out of light after it passes an obstruction.
DEMONSTRATION: DIFFRACTION
You will need the following items: a piece of blank paper, a pencil, a strong light source such as a slide projector, a movie screen or light-colored wall to serve as a screen, a small piece of window screen about 3" by 3", a show-case bulb screwed into a socket, 2 tongue depressors, 5 blank microscope slides, black paint or lampblack, a single-edged razor blade and a ruler.

1. **Figure 48-10.** Draw a diagram of either a solar or lunar eclipse on a piece of paper. Note how the shadow becomes smaller as you move away from the obstructing body. This is due to diffraction.

2. Turn on the slide projector and aim it at the movie screen or light-colored wall just as if you were going to show slides. Get a small piece of window screen about 3" by 3" and place it close to the movie screen or wall until it casts a sharp shadow. Now slowly walk away from the screen with the window screen in your hand. Make sure that you walk towards the projector and that the light of the projector passes through the window screen at all times. You will notice that the shadow gets less distinct until you get to a point where you cannot see it at all. When you arrive at the projector, place the window screen in front of the light source, then quickly remove it, then place it in front of the light source, then quickly remove it, etc. Do this several times. The only way you can tell that you have a window screen in front of the projector is that the light becomes brighter when this screen is removed.

3. Plug a show-case bulb into a socket and place it on a desk. (A show-case bulb is a long cylindrically-shaped light bulb with a thick filament.) You might be able to borrow one from a high school or college physics teacher. Look at the bulb while squinting your eyes. As the light passes through your eyelids (the obstruction), it spreads out into the colors of the spectrum (colors of the rainbow). You should see these colors. To make this even better, you can look at the light through the smallest opening that you can make while holding two tongue depressors together. You can even do this by looking at the light through the smallest opening you can make when holding your fingers together.

4. Paint four or five microscope slides with a black paint or lampblack. When the paint completely dries, make small slits on it by using a one-edged razor blade and a ruler. The smaller you make the slits, the better will be the effect. Now look at the show-case lamp through the different slits that you make. Make two or three slits close enough together so that you can look through them at the same time. Make one or two of them far enough apart so that you can only look through one slit at a time. What you have made is a simple diffraction grating. A diffraction grating is a piece of plastic with thousands of microscopic slits in it. When you hold it up to a light source, you see a spectrum. Diffraction gratings are used in making spectroscopes and have replaced the more expensive prisms.

Now let us discuss some of the most common optical phenomena, using the terminology we have just discussed, as well employing more illustrations through a series of demonstrations.

a. why the sky is blue

The daytime sky is blue because sunlight, which is comprised of the colors of the visible spectrum (red, orange, yellow, green, blue, indigo, violet), passes through the thicker layers of the atmosphere. Those colors that have a higher frequency and therefore a smaller wavelength, such as those found in the blue-end of the visible spectrum, are diffused (scattered) back toward outer space, thus giving the sky a bluish color.

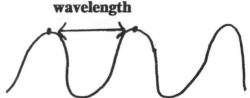

Figure 48-11. A wave, such as a wave of travelling light. Frequency is the number of light waves that pass a given point in a time-period (typically in a second), and wavelength is the distance from a point on one wave to the corresponding point on the next wave (from crest to crest, say).

As the frequency of a wave increases, its wavelength decreases, and vice versa. When referring to "electro-magnetic radiation" such as visible light, its frequency multiplied by its wavelength gives you the speed of light. Refer to figure 40-11 on page 293 which shows the **electro-magnetic radiation spectrum** , including wavelengths and frequencies of the known spectrum.

For the components of visible light, red light has the longest wavelength and lowest frequency, while violet light has the shortest wavelength and highest frequency. **Frequency is measured in units called Hertz, or kiloHertz (units of 1000 Hertz) or megaHertz (units of 1 million Hertz), where 1 Hertz is one cycle per second.**

Wavelength is measured in centimeters or meters or a unit called Angstrom units, where one Angstrom unit equals 10^{-8} centimeter which is also 10^{-10} meter (0.0000000001 of a meter).

The average wavelength for red light is 8000 Angstrom units, and its average frequency is 3.8×10^{14} Hertz (cycles or waves per second). The average wavelength for violet light is 4000 Angstrom units and its average frequency is 7.5×10^{14} Hertz. When we multiply the wavelength times the frequency, we will get the speed of light through space. For example, cycles (per second, frequency) times centimeters (wavelength) yields about 30,000,000,000 (3×10^{10}) centimeters per second. In the more commonly used units using meters, cycles per second times the wavelength in meters yields 300,000,000 (3×10^{8}) meters per second, the speed of light. When we convert to the standard English units used in the United States, the speed of light is about 186,000 miles per second.

An astronaut looking at the sky from a space vehicle will see black, because as we get hundreds or thousands of miles above the earth, there is little or no air at all (the top of the atmosphere is from about 600 to 1000 miles out, where the last hydrogen atoms are found), and therefore there is little of no scattering of light. (Above about 1000 miles out from the earth's surface, there is no more atmosphere, so there is no scattering of sunlight by atmospheric gasses.)

DEMONSTRATION: BLUENESS OF THE SKY

You will need the following materials: a transparent two-liter bottle, a small container with a very small amount of milk, an eye-dropper, one large stirring rod or ruler, a strong light source such as a slide projector, and a sheet of black paper.
1. Fill the two-liter bottle with water and place a sheet of black paper behind it.
2. Allow a beam of light from the slide projector or similar strong light source to shine from the left side to the right side of the 2-liter bottle.
3. While looking at the 2-liter container towards the black sheet of paper, use an eye-dropper to add a few drops of milk, and stir with the stirring rod or ruler. Do this until the mixture shows a distinct bluish-whitish color. The fine particles suspended in the milk scatter the smaller wavelengths of light.
4. Now look directly at the light source through the 2-liter bottle. What color is the light source?

In addition to the air molecules, which are very small, larger particles such as dust, ash, ice crystals, water droplets, etc. scatter some of the longer wavelengths such as red, orange, yellow and green. The more numerous and larger the particles are, the paler blue the sky becomes. You may have noticed that In humid air masses the sky is a much paler blue than during dry air masses.   PAGE 361

b. why the sun appears reddish-orange
   when it is on the horizon

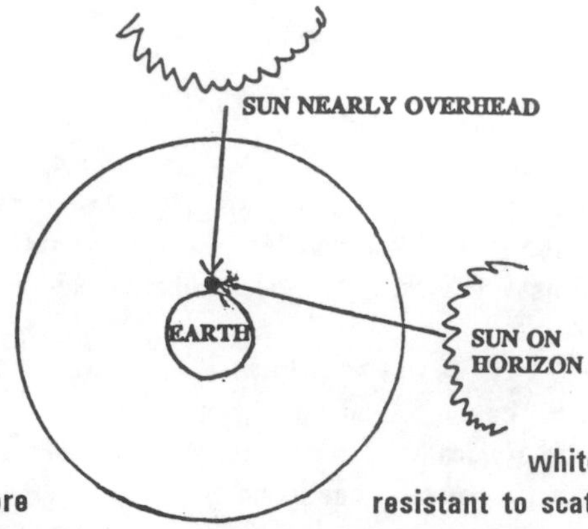

Figure 48-12. When the sun is on the horizon, its light has to travel through a thicker layer of air compared to when it is higher in the sky, before the light reaches the earth.

This thicker layer of air scatters more of the colors that make up the white light, leaving the longer wavelengths such as red and orange, which are more resistant to scattering. If there are thin clouds, especially cirrus-type clouds (which are comprised of ice crystals), dust and/or ash (including volcanic ash) on the horizon, then a beautiful sunset or sunrise occurs, with various shades of reds and oranges. Some of the most spectacular sunsets and sunrises occur during these circumstances.

When you see the sun through smoke particles coming form a chimney, or see the sun through a frosted glass window, it will appear reddish-orange even when it is well above the horizon.

DEMONSTRATION: LOOKING AT A STRONG LIGHT SOURCE THROUGH FROSTED GLASS
You will need a strong light source such as a slide projector, and several pieces of frosted glass about 2" by 2" each.
1. Look directly at the light source through one piece of frosted glass. What color does the light appear?
2. Now look directly at the light source through two, three or some more pieces of frosted glass. How many pieces of frosted glass does it take before you are unable to see any light at all? (The answer depends on the thickness of each piece of frosted glass.)

Now consider this: why does the sun or moon look larger when on the horizon? When the sun or moon is on the horizon, its rays are going through a thicker layer of air before arriving on the earth's surface, and they are coming in at an angle rather than being nearly vertical as when the sun or moon is overhead or nearly overhead. This causes the atmosphere to act as a convex lens, and through refraction magnifies the image of the sun or moon. The thicker a convex lens, the more greatly it can magnify. However, this explanation accounts for only a slight increase in the apparent size of the moon or sun. Carl Wenning of the Physics Department of Illinois State University suggests that the moon or sun looks larger when it is near the horizon also because of the different background of the sky. When we look at clouds that are overhead, we logically find that they are much nearer than those along the horizon (when the cloud bases are all the same). Over the years, however, we develop the perception that high (overhead) equals near, and that low (along the horizon) equals far. We use this same conception when we look at the moon or sun. When the moon is on the horizon against the more distant sky, it therefore appears large to us, and when it is viewed higher up against the nearer sky, it therefore appears smaller. Look at the figure below.

Figure 48-13. Assume that the left circle represents the moon when it is overhead, and the right circle the moon when it is near the horizon. Even though the circles are of IDENTICAL size, the one on the right appears larger to us because of its surroundings!

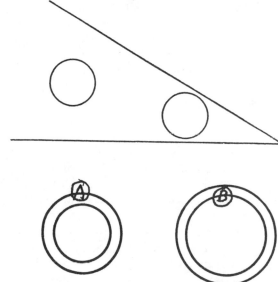

Figure 48-14. The two circles labelled A and B are of identical size. Notice, though, that they appear unequal because of the other circles that are in their vicinity.

PAGE 362

DEMONSTRATION: RECREATING THE EFFECT OF THE MOON APPEARING LARGER WHEN IT IS ON THE HORIZON

This demonstration should be done in a dark room or at night. You will need one showcase lamp in a socket, a table, and an 8½" x 11" sheet of white paper.

1. Place the showcase lamp and socket on a table and turn it on. Make sure that no other lights in the room are turned on.
2. Stare at the light bulb for about 30 seconds.
3. Turn off the light. You will see the after-image (negative image) of the bulb's filament.
4. Now look in such a way as to project the image of the bulb's filament on a piece of white paper held closer than an arm's length. What do you observe?
5. Now project the image onto a piece of white paper held at arm's length. Does the after-image appear larger?

DEMONSTRATION: PARTIALLY CANCELLING OUT THE EFFECT OF THE MOON APPEARING LARGER WHEN IT IS ON THE HORIZON

This demonstration makes the rising moon look smaller; however, it will not cancel out the effect of refraction which is caused by the light from the moon having to pass through a thicker layer of air before it reaches the surface of the earth. Thus, the moon will look smaller but not as small as it does when it is nearly overhead.

● You will need the following: a piece of t-shirt through which you can see a lighted bulb but not other objects around it. The transparency of the t-shirt can be increased by stretching the shirt.
● This demonstration must be done with a full or nearly-full moon. Look up (in your local newspaper, e.g.) the time of the local moonrise.
● Go to an area where you will have an unobstructed view of the moon rising. This demonstration works best from the time of moonrise to about 30 minutes later.
● To get the maximum effect, view the rising moon while standing under a streetlight.
● Make sure that as you begin, the moon looks much larger to you than it does when it is nearly overhead.
● **NEVER** attempt to do this demonstration with the sun, because sunlight can damage your eyes and cause blindness!

1. Observe the moon when it is as close to the horizon as possible. It should appear much larger than it does when it is close to being overhead.
2. Now look at the moon through the t-shirt. Adjust the t-shirt so that you can see the moon but not the surroundings. This adjustment can be made by stretching the t-shirt until you get the desired effect, which is that the moon no longer looks as large.

DEMONSTRATION: THE ANSWER TO AN AGE-OLD QUESTION

To do this demonstration, you will need a 1000 milliliter beaker and an evaporating dish that has a diameter of from 2 to 3 inches. These items you can borrow from a high school or college chemistry teacher. You will also need one coin and one large or small paper clip.

1. Carefully place a coin and a paper clip into an evaporating dish and place the dish into the 1000 millimeter beaker.
2. Look at the evaporating dish, coin and paper clip from both the top and the side of the beaker.
3. Now fill the beaker with water and look at the same objects from both the top and side of the beaker.
4. How does this compare with what you saw when you looked at the objects before filling the beaker with water?

c. rainbows

Rainbows occur when the sun is shining on one side of the sky, being lower than about 54 degrees above one horizon (thus, approaching sunset or just after sunrise), and it is raining in the vicinity of the other horizon.

Rainbows are most common in the tropics and during the warmer months in the temperate zones (mid-latitudes) in the rain clouds in the western sky in the morning, and in the rain clouds in the eastern sky in the evening. People living in high enough latitudes where the sun does not rise very high above the horizon, especially from late fall through early spring, can see a rainbow at any time during the day when it is raining on the opposite horizon to where the sun is shining. Most showers and thunderstorms are small enough to allow for sunshine on one side of the sky and rain falling on the other, as these rain cells move through. The key point is, **to have a rainbow, you need sunlight shining on raindrops.** The raindrops act as a prism and separate the white light of the sun into its constituent visible colors: red, orange, yellow, green, blue, indigo and violet. Snowflakes are less likely to cause colorbows because they do not act as a prism the way raindrops do.

Primary rainbows

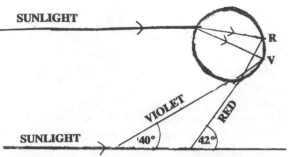

Figure 48-15. What happens to light in one of the many thousands of raindrops that form a primary rainbow. A primary rainbow is what we see most of the time when we witness a rainbow. As sunlight enters a raindrop, refraction occurs; once it is inside the raindrop, dispersion (the separating of white light into its constituent colors) occurs. These colors are reflected when they hit the opposite inner surface of the raindrop; refraction occurs again when the colors move from inside the raindrop to the air. The light that is not reflected internally is transmitted and comes out the other side of the raindrop.

In the diagram, each color emerges at a different angle relative to the parallel rays of the sun. For red light, the angle is about 42°; for violet light, it is about 40°. The light that is being reflected off the opposite inner surface of the raindrop is being reflected by what is known as <u>total internal reflection</u>.

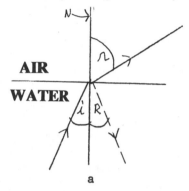

(Not drawn to scale.)

Figure 48-16 (a, b and c). What happens to light travelling from water (as from raindrops in a cloud or falling below the cloud), to air. When light travels from water to air, the emerging ray (refracted ray) bends away from

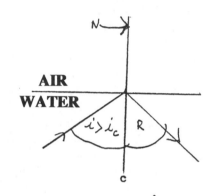

Key:
- N = normal (perpendicular - an imaginary line)
- i = angle of incidence (angle made by incoming ray with the normal)
- r = angle of refraction (angle made by the refracted ray (bent ray) with the normal)
- R = angle of reflection (angle made by the reflected ray with the normal)
- i_c = angle of incidence is equal to the critical angle, which for water is 48.5 degrees
- $i > i_c$ = angle of incidence is greater than the critical angle

the normal (an imaginary perpendicular line). When the incident (incoming) ray makes an angle of more than 48.5 degrees with the normal, no light leaves the water. The light rays hit the surface of the water and are reflected back into the water (total internal reflection). The 48.5 degrees is called the <u>critical angle</u> of water. If light were travelling from another substance (e.g., from oil) to air, the critical angle for that oil would be different from what it is for water. All transparent liquids and solids each have a specific critical angle, which in physics tables is normally listed with their other physical properties.

In figure 48-16a, with light travelling from water to air, the angle of incidence, i, is less than the critical angle for water, which is 48.5 degrees; therefore, the light beam leaves the water and bends away from the normal. The angle of refraction, r, is greater than the angle of incidence. Note that some light (represented by a dashed line) is reflected back into the water. The angle of incidence, i, is equal to the angle of reflection, R.

In figure 48-16b, the angle of incidence, i, is equal to the critical angle of water, i_c. The refracted beam of light skims the surface of the water. The makes r, the angle of refraction, equal to 90 degrees. Note that i for which r equals 90° is called the critical angle. Note also that some light, represented by a dashed line, is reflected back into the water. i_c, which in this case is equal to the critical angle, is also equal to the angle of reflection, R.

In figure 48-16c, the angle of incidence, i, is greater than the critical angle, i_c, which results in all of the light being reflected back into the water; we have total internal reflection, in which the angle of incidence, i, equals the angle of reflection, R.

DEMONSTRATION: TOTAL INTERNAL REFLECTION

You will need the following materials: a glass or plastic aquarium of at least 10 gallon capacity, a waterproof flashlight, two chalkboard erasers loaded with chalk dust, and green food coloring.

1. Fill the aquarium about three-quarters with water. 2. Add enough green food coloring to give the water a light green color. Do not add too much coloring because we want the water to remain transparent. We are adding the coloring so that the particles in the coloring scatter light, thus making a beam of light inside the water more visible. 3. Hold the waterproof flashlight with its front facing up, almost vertically and turn it on. You will see the light beam emerging from the water to the air. Have someone clap the two chalk-loaded chalkboard erasers above the aquarium. The chalk dust will scatter the light so that you can see the light beam bend away from the normal. 4. Now gradually lower the front of the flashlight until the beam skims the surface of the water. At this point, you have reached the critical angle of water, which is about 48.5 degrees from the normal (from the perpendicular). 5. Gradually lower the front end of the flashlight until all of the beam is reflected back into the aquarium water. At this point, you have exceeded the critical angle.

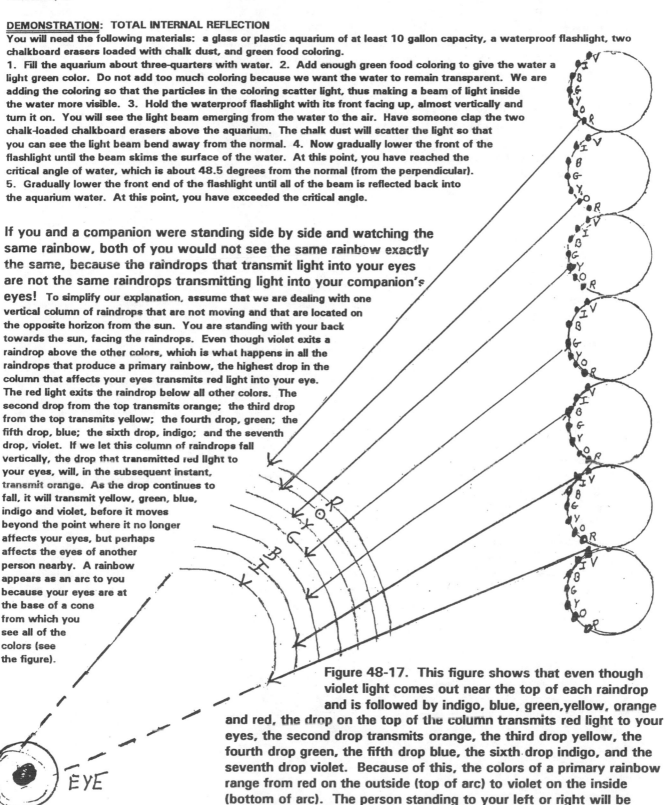

If you and a companion were standing side by side and watching the same rainbow, both of you would not see the same rainbow exactly the same, because the raindrops that transmit light into your eyes are not the same raindrops transmitting light into your companion's eyes! To simplify our explanation, assume that we are dealing with one vertical column of raindrops that are not moving and that are located on the opposite horizon from the sun. You are standing with your back towards the sun, facing the raindrops. Even though violet exits a raindrop above the other colors, which is what happens in all the raindrops that produce a primary rainbow, the highest drop in the column that affects your eyes transmits red light into your eye. The red light exits the raindrop below all other colors. The second drop from the top transmits orange; the third drop from the top transmits yellow; the fourth drop, green; the fifth drop, blue; the sixth drop, indigo; and the seventh drop, violet. If we let this column of raindrops fall vertically, the drop that transmitted red light to your eyes, will, in the subsequent instant, transmit orange. As the drop continues to fall, it will transmit yellow, green, blue, indigo and violet, before it moves beyond the point where it no longer affects your eyes, but perhaps affects the eyes of another person nearby. A rainbow appears as an arc to you because your eyes are at the base of a cone from which you see all of the colors (see the figure).

Figure 48-17. This figure shows that even though violet light comes out near the top of each raindrop and is followed by indigo, blue, green, yellow, orange and red, the drop on the top of the column transmits red light to your eyes, the second drop transmits orange, the third drop yellow, the fourth drop green, the fifth drop blue, the sixth drop indigo, and the seventh drop violet. Because of this, the colors of a primary rainbow range from red on the outside (top of arc) to violet on the inside (bottom of arc). The person standing to your left or right will be affected by a different column of drops. Thus, we all have our own personal rainbow!

Secondary rainbows

In a secondary rainbow the sunlight enters the raindrops at an angle that allows the light to be totally internally reflected twice instead of once as in the case of a primary rainbow. During the second internal reflection, more light is absorbed, resulting in a secondary rainbow which is fainter and larger than the primary rainbow. The colors are reversed , with the red exiting the raindrops on top of the other colors, and violet exiting at the bottom. In a secondary rainbow, the highest drop that affects your eye transmits violet light and the lowest drop red light; you therefore see the colors of the secondary rainbow from violet on the outside (top of arc) to red on the inside (bottom of arc). The secondary rainbow may appear above or to one side of the primary rainbow.

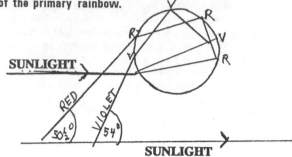

Figure 48-18. What happens to light in one of the many thousands of raindrops that form a secondary rainbow. The light is internally reflected twice. Each color emerges at a different angle relative to the parallel rays of the sun. For red light, the angle is about 50½°; for violet it is about 54°.

DEMONSTRATION: HOW TO CREATE A RAINBOW OUTDOORS
You must do this on a sunny day. You will need a garden hose with a nozzle that can produce a fine spray.
1. With your back to the sun, turn on the garden hose and adjust the nozzle to the finest spray possible. You should see a primary rainbow with the red on top and violet on the bottom of the arc.
2. Move the hose around. By trial and error, you might be able to produce a secondary rainbow as well, with violet on top and red on the bottom of the arc.

DEMONSTRATION: HOW TO CREATE A RAINBOW INDOORS
You will need a strong light source such as a slide projector, 4 pieces of white paper about 8½" x 11" and a 1000 milliliter beaker. The demonstration can be done on a card table or someplace similar. This demonstration works better at night or in a darkened room.
1. Tape the four sheets of 8½" x 11" white paper together in such a way to make a rectangle that is 22 inches long and 17 inches wide. Place the paper on the floor next to the table.
2. Fill the beaker until it is almost completely filled with water and place it at the edge of the table on the same side as the white paper.
3. Aim the light source so that the beam of light travels through the rim of the beaker on its way to the paper on the floor. You may have to lift the light source in order to do this.
4. What colors do you observe?

d. why we can see the sun and moon after they set and before they rise
Light coming from the sun, and reflected sunlight from the moon, when the sun or moon is on the horizon, travel through a thickness of air that is about 12 times thicker than when they are more-or-less overhead. This additional thickness produces more refraction (bending) of the light, resulting in the sun or moon appearing to be higher on the horizon than they actually are. Consequently, they rise about two minutes earlier and set about two minutes later than they would if the earth had no atmosphere.

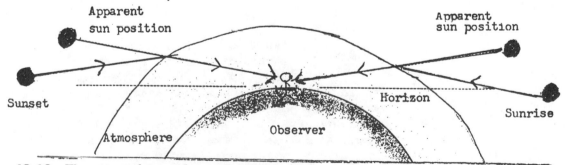

Figure 48-19. The atmosphere refracts (bends) sunlight so that we see the sun about two minutes before it rises and for about two minutes after it sets.

The sun and moon appear to be flatter on the horizon. This is because the light rays coming from the lower part of the sun or moon are bent more due to refraction , than those from the upper part, because they are travelling through a thicker layer of air.

e. what is meant by twilight

On clear days the sky is bright for some time after the sun sets and for some time before the sun rises. The thicker layers of the atmosphere near the surface refract and scatter sunlight back towards the earth's surface even though the sun is below the horizon. We call this period of time, twilight. The length of the twilight period depends upon the season and the latitude. It increases with distance from the equator, especially during the late spring and early summer. During this time in the middle latitudes, twilight adds from about 30 to 60 minutes of light to the morning and also to the evening. As one approaches the latitude of the Arctic and Antarctic Circles, during the late spring and early summer months, the evening twilight may merge with the morning twilight so that it never gets completely dark at that time of year. This is sometimes referred to as white night or nightlong twilight.

f. why stars twinkle

Stars appear to twinkle or flicker whenever their light passes through regions of our atmosphere with differing air densities which are due to differences in temperature and pressure, plus the fact that air parcels of varying densities are typically in motion. As the starlight passes through each region, its light is refracted by varying amounts, causing the apparent position of the star to keep changing. This condition is called scintillation. Because planets are much closer to us and appear larger than the stars (although the stars, which are suns, are much much larger than our planets), they (the planets) usually do not twinkle. Their apparent larger sizes do not allow us to observe refractive changes in their positions, unless they are on the horizon where the bending of light is greater because of increased refraction, at which time they may appear to twinkle. Thus, **stars twinkle, and planets do not, except when they are on the horizon.**

DEMONSTRATION: SCINTILLATION (WHY STARS TWINKLE)

You will need the following: a candle in a candle holder; a square grid made on a sheet of white paper, with a black crayon, on which six heavy straight parallel lines up and down are drawn one inch apart; a metal can about 3 inches long and 2 to 3 inches in diameter, with the top and bottom removed; matches; masking tape.
1. Tape the grid on a wall at the same level as your eyes.
2. Light a candle and hold it about a foot from your eye.
3. Cover the candle with the metal can: the upper rim of the can should be slightly above the flame.
4. Now look at the grid from a distance of about 2 to 3 feet so that you line-of-sight is about one or two inches above the tip of the flame.
5. The light passing through the heated gasses will be refracted, because the density of these hot gasses is lower than the air at room temperature and therefore the light travels through them at different (higher) speeds, causing the twinkling affect. In the summer, this phenomenon can be seen when looking at an object behind a car that is parked in the sun.

g. halos

Halos can be produced whenever cirroform clouds occur. These clouds (cirrus, cirrostratus and sometimes cirrocumulus) are comprised of ice crystals because of their high heights (20,000 to over 40,000 feet above the ground). The sunlight or moonlight is refracted as it passes through the ice crystals, yielding a halo. The most common type is a 22-degree halo; that is, the ring of light is 22 degrees from the sun or moon. If you extend your arm and spread your fingers apart, an angle of 22 degrees is about the distance from the tip of your thumb to the tip of your pinky.

Most halos appear as a bright, white ring ; however, under certain conditions you might see a ring of colors because of dispersion. The ice crystals in that case act like a prism, breaking the white light into the colors of the rainbow. This is more likely with the bright sun rather than with the moon. The red light would be on the inside of the halo, and the violet light on the outside.

Figure 48-20. A halo is a ring of light circling and extending outward from the sun or moon. This picture shows part of a halo in cirroform clouds. (source: NOAA)

DEMONSTRATION: HOW TO MAKE A HALO
You will need the following: a clean piece of glass about 2" by 2"; a point light source that you can make by taping a circular piece of black paper with a tiny hole in its center to the lens of a light source such as a slide projector, so that the entire lens is covered (you can make the tiny hole with a needle or pin); some vaseline (petroleum jelly); and a card table or similar stand.
1. Place the point light source on the table or stand.
2. At about 12 feet away, look at the light source through a clean piece of glass. Move up, down, kneel, etc. to get the maximum amount of light reaching your eye.
3. Place a small amount of petroleum jelly on your index finger and stroke the surface of the glass square all over in the same direction.
4. Look through the glass at the point light source. Make sure you are in the same position that you were in for step 2; that is, be in the position that allowed the maximum amount of light to reach your eye. What do you see?
5. Now turn the glass 90 degrees and look at the point light source. What do you see?
6. Stroke the other side of the glass plate with the petroleum jelly, at right angles to those on the previous side. Look at the point light source. What do you see?

h. sundogs
A <u>sundog</u>, also called a <u>mock sun</u> or a <u>parhelion</u>, is a special type of halo that forms when platelike six-sided ice crystals are falling slowly and are oriented so that the largest plate-like surfaces are facing up and down. This situation can happen as ice crystals fall from cirroform clouds, or when ice crystals form in clear and very cold air and the wind is calm or nearly calm. (When this happens, it is a type of precipitation called ice crystals, which is the only type that can form directly in clear air, although in reality it is a thin cirrus cloud of ice crystals. They can tingle gently to the ground all night and for a few hours after sunrise, for example, but leave only a trace of accumulation because they are so light. Temperatures are typically around or below zero Fahrenheit for ice crystals to form.)

If you take a piece of hexagonal bathroom floor tile and hold it so that the large surfaces face up and down, then you have an idea of how these ice crystals are oriented. However, each ice crystal, being very tiny (around 30 millimicrons in diameter) is much smaller than one of the bathroom tiles.

Figure 48-21. The bright spot on the left is the sun, and the bright spot on the right is a sundog. (photo by Joseph Balsama)

Not all the ice crystals will be falling or suspended in this orientation, but when there are enough of them so oriented, they do not form a ring halo but rather form what looks like another sun on either side of the sun. This is even more likely when the sun is near the horizon, such as at and shortly after sunrise, and the observer and ice crystals are all in the same horizontal plane. When the sun is well above the horizon, you typically see only one sundog. Under very favorable conditions, you might see the colors of the spectrum, because there is dispersion occurring. Most of the time you will not see these colors, but if and when you do, the red will face the sun and the violet will appear on the side opposite to the sun.

i. coronas

A corona is produced around the sun or moon when tiny water droplets or small particles diffract light. (You might want to quickly review the section on diffraction given early in this chapter.) The word, corona, means "crown". Do not get this term mixed up with the use of the same word for the sun's atmosphere, which is visible during a total solar eclipse. Because the sun is so bright, it is difficult to see a corona around the sun; it is most often observed around the moon. Coronas can be seen around street lights or the headlights of approaching cars, when looking through a dirty windshield. For most coronas in the sky, thin layers of altostratus and altocumulus clouds are responsible. Most coronas appear white, and some may have alternating bands of dark and light areas. Under very ideal conditions, the colors of the visible spectrum might be seen, with violet appearing on the inside of the ring and red on the outside. This is opposite to what occurs in dispersion, as in the case of halos, where red appears on the inside and violet on the outside. When light waves begin to move behind an obstruction, they interact (interfere) with each other in such a way that the colors of the spectrum can be seen in much the same way as through a diffraction grating, discussed earlier in this chapter.

DEMONSTRATION: OBSERVING A CORONA
You will need the following: a clean piece of glass, about 2" by 2"; a point light source which you can make by taping a circular piece of black paper with a tiny hole at its center (made by a needle or pin) to the lens of a light source such as a slide projector, so that the entire lens is covered; a fine powder such as lycopodium powder or talcum powder; and a card table or similar stand. 1. Place the point light source on the table or stand. 2. At about 12 feet away, look at the light source through a clean piece of glass. Move up, down, kneel, etc. to get the maximum amount of light reaching your eye. 3. Breathe on the clean piece of glass and quickly hold it close to your eye while looking at the point light source. Make sure that you are in the same position that you were in in step 2, allowing the maximum amount of light to reach your eye. What do you see? 4. Dust lycopodium powder or talcum powder on the glass and look at the point light source through the dusted glass. What do you see?   PAGE 369

j. sun pillars, and k. glitter path (see photo and description of items 2 and 3 below)

Figure 48-22. This is a beautiful photograph of a sunrise at King's Beach at Lynn, Massachusetts. **There are several optical phenomena occurring.** Study the photo carefully: the sky is reddish-orange because of scattering of light by a layer of cirrus-type clouds (the upper layer of clouds); the vertical shaft of light which is most noticeable above the sun, especially above the lower dark layer of clouds, is a <u>sun pillar</u>, which is produced by the reflection of sunlight off the ice crystals; and the reflection of sunlight off the water trapped on the ripple marks is producing a <u>glitter path</u>. (photo by Lawrence G. Power)

Figure 48-22a. A primary and secondary rainbow. Note that the secondary rainbow is on top of the primary rainbow. Here it is barely noticeable at the upper right. (photo, showing the Swampscott, Mass. Fish House, built in 1896, is by Mark Garfinkel)   PAGE 370

I. mirages

A mirage occurs when we see objects in places where we do not expect to see them. A mirage is an optical phenomenon that creates the illusion of water, often with inverted reflections of distant objects, and is caused by distortion of light by alternate layers of hot and cool air. Deserts, during the daylight, are excellent places for mirages. When you drive down a blacktop road on a sunny and very hot day, the sun has heated the blacktop which, in turn, is sending up parcels of hot air. As you look ahead of you, the road appears wavy and looks like water. This is a mirage. Since cold air is denser than hot air, the light travels faster in the warmer air. The denser the medium, the slower the light travels through it. So, when light travels from hot to cooler air, it bends towards the normal, just as it does when it travels from air to water. In like manner, when light travels from cool to hot air, it bends away from the normal, just as it does when it travels from water to air. Study the next four figures, concerning mirages.

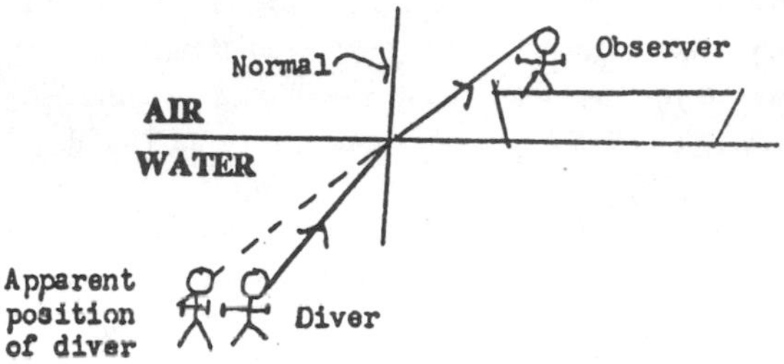

Figure 48-23. The light from the diver's body moves from water to air, bending away from the normal (imaginary perpendicular line). The human brain interprets light as travelling in a straight line, so the observed is "tricked" into believing that the diver is in a different position.

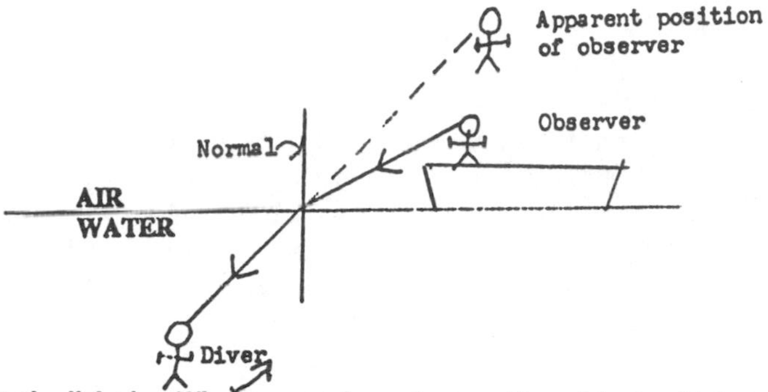

Figure 48-24. As the light from the observer's body moves from air to water, it bends towards the normal (perpendicular). The diver sees the observer on the boat in a different position.

In a mirage, our minds are not playing tricks but the light is. What we see is an image of an object, which can be photographed! There are two major types of mirage: an _inferior mirage_ and a _superior mirage_.

Inferior (lower) mirages occur when the air near the ground is much warmer than the air above. The objects appear below their true locations and may also appear inverted.

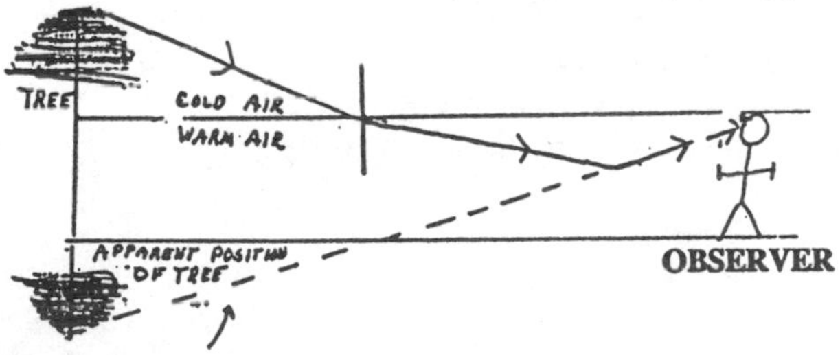

Figure 48-25. An inferior mirage. As light rays from the top of the tree travel down into the hot air near the surface, they gradually bend upward because of unequal temperatures near the surface, and reach the observer's eye from below. This is interpreted by the observer's brain as an upside-down tree. What appear to be wet areas on the road ahead of your vehicle, as stated earlier, is a mirage. Sometimes these apparent wet areas look like they are shimmering. This is similar to the conditions that cause stars to appear to twinkle. As light from above moves into the warmer air of different temperatures and densities, it is refracted several times, which causes the shimmering effect. Just as in desert mirages, these "wet areas" disappear as you approach them.

The second type of mirage, the superior mirage, is so-named because the image of the object you are seeing is above its true position and is right-side up. A common example of this is a phenomenon called _looming_. Assume that a ship or lighthouse is far enough out at sea that it cannot be seen by an individual on the beach because of the curvature of the earth. Then one day, the observer on the beach sees the ship or light house above the horizon! Looming can sometimes be observed during sharp temperature inversions in which the air next to the ground is much colder than the air above it. This can occur when a very cold land surface or a cold ocean surface cools the air next to it so that that air is much colder than the air above it. As the light from the distant object moves from the warmer to the colder air and bends towards the normal (perpendicular), the observer sees the image of the object suspended above the horizon.

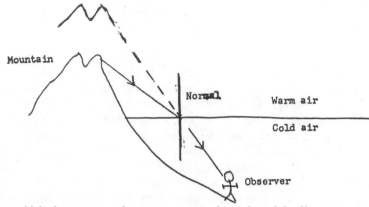

Figure 48-26. Looming, an example of a superior mirage. The observer sees the mountain above the horizon, because his/her brain interprets light as travelling in a straight line. If there are several layers of air with different densities and temperatures between the mountain and the observer, then the mountain will also appear to shimmer.

On January 3rd, 1977, a beautiful clear day during which there was a sharp temperature inversion, John Howe, an observatory staff engineer on the summit of Mount Washington, New Hampshire, saw Cadillac Mountain in Maine, 155 miles away, in the sky, well above the horizon! It remained visible for about an hour. He also saw Cape Ann, Massachusetts and the five-flash sequence of the Thatcher Island Lighthouse, which is off Rockport, Massachusetts.

DEMONSTRATION: MIRAGES
You will need an electric hot plate that has a smooth, solid top, and a table or stand.
1. Place the hot plate on the table or stand, allowing it to heat to its highest possible temperature.
2. Move about 3 to 4 feet away from the hot plate and place your eye at almost the same level as the solid top. What do you observe? What type of a mirage do you see?

m. the green flash
If you happen to be at the right place at the right time and with a lot of luck, you might observe a flash of green light just before the disk of the sun goes below the horizon. This phenomenon is called the green flash. When the sun is on the horizon, its light travels through a thick layer of air before reaching the earth, refracting the violet end of the spectrum more than the red end. More of the violet end should appear along the top of the sun; however, since some of the violet, indigo and blue lights are scattered more than the other colors, green light appears instead. This is the green flash.

The green flash can also appear at sunrise just as the disk of the sun appears to emerge above the horizon. The green flash typically lasts only about one second, but can last longer in polar regions where the elevation of the sun changes slowly, allowing the green flash to persist for up to several minutes. One episode in the South Polar region was recorded lasting about 35 minutes. (This was around Sept. 21st during an Admiral Byrd expedition.)

n. crepuscular rays
Crepuscular rays are bright beams of sunlight that occur when the sun's light shines through breaks in the clouds, or when haze or other particles scatter light from the rising or setting sun.

o. blue haze
Some mountains and hills may appear blue at times, especially when viewed from a distance. Examples are the Blue Ridge Mountains of Virginia and the Blue Hills of Massachusetts. The blue haze is caused by the scattering of blue light by air molecules and other tiny particles in the air. The air particles typically contain moisture that was evaporated by the vegetation on the hills and mountains. The particles are smaller than the wavelength of visible light.

p. why some clouds appear white and others appear dark
Clouds that appear white do so because the cloud droplets comprising them scatter the white light from the sun in all directions, with some of this light reaching our eyes. Snow appears white for the same reason, but it is the ice crystals of snow scattering the white light in all directions. (Refer to the sections on reflection and scattering found early in this chapter.)

Dark clouds appear dark because they contain so much moisture through a considerable depth that they prevent much of the sunlight from passing through them to reach the earth. The thicker the clouds, the less sunlight reaches the surface, and thus the darker the clouds appear.

Chapter 49. SOME WEATHER-RELATED PHENOMENA

a. why leaves turn color (leaf coloration)

The leaves of most <u>deciduous</u> trees (trees that lose their leaves in the fall) turn beautiful shades of color before they fall. The colors are caused by different pigments. Most pigments are present in the leaves during the spring and summer, but are masked by <u>chlorophyll</u>, which is the green pigment that is necessary for the leaves to make food for the tree through the process of photosynthesis. <u>Photosynthesis</u> is the process by which plants and other organisms that contain chlorophyll make their own food, with the help of chlorophyll and sunlight, by combining carbon dioxide and water to produce glucose, which is a basic carbohydrate, and giving off oxygen as a by-product. Once glucose is produced, plants can use it to make compound sugars, starches, fats, oils and proteins. Now let us briefly discuss what pigments produce the colors we observe.

Green is produced by chlorophyll, which is present in the leaf from spring through fall. Yellow is produced by a pigment called <u>xanthophyll</u>, and orange is produced by the pigment, <u>carotene</u>. Xanthophyll and carotene are present during the entire life of the leaf, but appear when the leaf stops manufacturing chlorophyll, typically during the autumn. In late summer and early autumn, some leaves use some of their surplus sugar and make a red pigment called <u>anthocyanin</u>, which turns leaves red or purple.

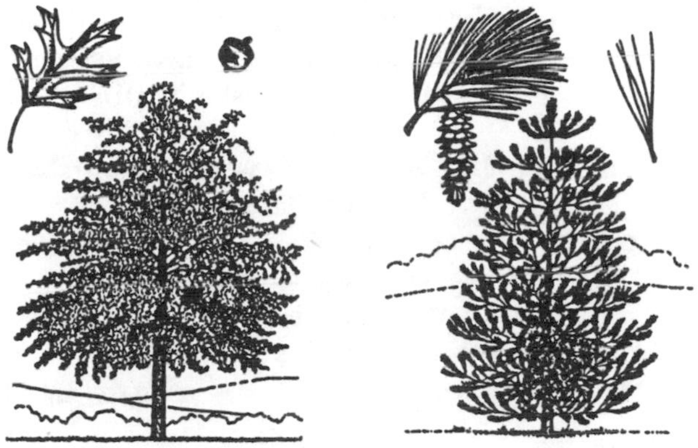

Figure 49-1. The leaves of deciduous trees such as the pin oak at left, turn beautiful colors in the fall, while the conifers, such as the white pine at right, stay green throughout the year, except for some old thistles that turn brown and fall off. (source: Missouri Dep't. of Conservation)

Combinations of bright sunny days and clear, cool nights with temperatures dropping below about 45°F (7°C) but remaining above freezing, are believed to enhance the brightness of the colors. Combinations of the leaf pigments produce other colors. Leaf coloration is typically observed in regions of the world that have four distinct seasons. In warmer climatic regions, leaf coloration can be observed on mountains at heights where temperatures are comparable to those in temperate latitudes. The brown color that we see is formed by <u>tannic acid</u>, which forms when leaf tissue dies. Thus, we may see leaves on the ground that have turned brown when leaves of other colors fell from the trees and subsequently died. We might also see brown leaves clinging to a tree that has died. The tannic acid that forms when leaf tissue dies is also found in tea.

The falling of leaves off trees during the fall is a normal function of healthy trees. A layer of cells called the <u>abscission layer</u> forms between the leaf petiole (leaf stem) and the twig, which causes the leaf to fall off. You might have observed leaves falling from a tree on a day when there has been little or no wind.

Not all species of trees produce an abscission layer; therefore, the leaves from those trees might fall during the spring when the new leaves that grow will physically push them off the branches and twigs. Some species of oak trees and the ornamental Bradford pear are examples of this tree type.

In some tree species, the abscission layer does not grow when the tree is very young. It may take one or two growing seasons for it to form.

If a tree dies before the fall season, then it does not produce an abscission layer, resulting in the leaves turning brown and clinging to the branches until they eventually disintegrate.

Most trees in places with warm climates, that keep their leaves throughout the year do not form an abscission layer, so they lose their leaves only when new ones grow to replace the older ones. In some areas, the raking of leaves occurs in the spring, due to new leaves causing the older ones to fall.

b. pollen count, hay fever, mold spores, pain indices, etc.

A substance that causes allergic reactions in susceptible people is known as an <u>allergen</u>. Allergens enter our body through the nose, mouth and skin. Those that enter via the nose include pollen, mold spores, and house dust (which includes mite particles and cat and dog danders). The most common diseases caused by allergens are: 1. <u>Allergic rhinitis (hay fever)</u>. This causes nasal stuffiness, sneezing, nasal itching, clear nasal discharge, and itching of the roof of the mouth and/or the ears. 2. <u>Allergic asthma</u>. This produces symptoms of wheezing, coughing and shortness of breath. 3. <u>Allergic conjunctivitis (eye allergy)</u>. This produces redness and itching of the eyes and chronic mucus-related eye discharge. 4. <u>Allergic eczema</u>. This is an allergic skin rash. 5. <u>Allergic contact dermatitis</u>. This is the itchy rash and oozing rash that occurs when the skin comes in contact with poison ivy, poison oak or poison sumac. Some allergens can be ingested by mouth. Many people are allergic to certain foods. Other allergens can be injected into the body, such as, for example, an allergic reaction to penicillin or another drug, or a sting from an insect injecting venom (a bee or spider, e.g.).

The following table gives the color of the leaves of some deciduous trees in the autumn in places that have four seasons:

TREE	AUTUMN LEAF COLOR
Beech	Yellow
Silver Maple	Pale Yellow
Mountain Maple	Brilliant Red
Striped Maple	Yellow
Red Maple	Red
Aspen	Yellow
Birch	Yellow
Hickory	Yellow
High Bush Blueberry	Deep Red
Mountain Holly	Yellow
Dwarf Sumac	Purple to Red
Smooth Sumac	Red
Black Chokeberry	Bright Red
Scarlet Oak	Red
Black Oak	Yellow
White Oak	Reddish to Violet
Pin Oak	Rust
Black Gum	Scarlet

<u>Pollen</u> is formed in seed-bearing plants. It develops into sperms which, in turn, fertilize plant eggs (ova) to produce <u>seeds</u>. Some seed-bearing plants produce flowers while others do not (e.g., pine trees). Plants including weeds, trees and grasses are the chief offenders, because at certain times of the year they discharge billions of pollen particles.

In most areas that have four distinct seasons, there are certain times during the growing season where pollen from various plants are more prevalent. For example, in New England, from March through May, tree pollen becomes a serious problem for allergy sufferers. In early spring, pollen from the cottonwood, willow, maple, elm and ash prevail. Later in the spring, oak, beech and birch pollen become a problem. June through July is referred to as the grass season, and includes pollen from timothy, bluegrass and meadow fescue. From mid-August through early October is the ragweed season, which often includes pollen from mugwart (sage) cocklebar and lamb's quarters. About three out of four people are affected in various degrees by ragweed pollen!

Local weather reports often include the pollen count during the allergy season. The <u>pollen count</u> is the number of pollen grains per cubic meter of air. For example, if the pollen count is 395, this means that there are 395 pollen grains per cubic meter volume of air. The pollen count varies from zero to over 2,000. To simplify the matter, some meteorologists and others may use the terminology, "low", "moderate" or "high" to describe the pollen count. Some use a scale of 0 to 10 in which 0 to 3 is low, 4 to 6 is moderate and 7 to 10 is high. or severe. During the pollen season, the pollen count that you may see in today's newspaper would be yesterday's pollen count.

Weather conditions have a significant effect on the pollen count, and are a key to forecasting what the pollen count might be: 1. On sunny days, the pollen count is usually high. Most pollen is released shortly after sunrise, between about 6 and 9 a.m. On the other hand, birch and oak pollinate between about noon and 2 p.m. 2. Because rain literally washes pollen out of the air, the pollen count is low on rainy days. Dry spells allow much pollen to be airborne. 3. On humid days, the pollen count is also low, because plants tend to release less pollen when the air is humid. 4. The wind affects pollen on sunny days: a. Studies show that wind speeds of 15 to 17 mph are ideal for pollen transport. b. Slower winds do not seem to spread too much pollen. c. Winds over 17 mph tend to scatter the pollen higher over a greater area, thus reducing its concentration. 5. Cool weather (temperatures in the 40s F.) in the spring and fall can prevent the release of pollen at the expected time. If after a long cold spring the weather suddenly warms up, much pollen is released in a short period of time, causing much suffering. 6. Weather conditions that have occurred already can help predict future pollen counts. For example, if the spring and summer have been warmer and wetter than normal, we can expect a high pollen count in the fall.

Most pollen is typically out of the air before the first freeze, unless the first freeze is unusually early. Most mid to late fall allergies might be due to mold spores and dust. In areas of the country that have winters with below freezing temperatures, there are about four months of completely pollen-free days.

There are several ways to reduce exposure when the pollen count is high. Among them are the following:
1. Stay indoors as much as feasible. Use air conditioners, since they not only cool the air but also remove excess moisture and filter the air. 2. In a car, make sure that the windows are closed and the air conditioner is on. 3. If you live near the ocean or a large lake, the pollen count will be low near the shore when the sea-breeze or lake-breeze occurs during the daytime.

Although people with allergies and asthma know how important it is to avoid exposure to airborne allergens, especially pollen, many may not realize that mold and mildew found both outdoors and indoors produce one of the most powerful airborne allergens of all: <u>mold spores</u>. Molds and mildews are examples of fungi, as are yeasts, mushrooms, puffballs, athlete's foot (ringworm) fungus and plant diseases such as wheat rust, corn smut and Dutch elm disease.

One of the most common ways for fungi to reproduce asexually is by producing spores. Most mold spores are smaller than pollen grain, although some are larger. They can range from being light to dark in color, resembling dust or fine dirt particles. In most parts of the United States, mold spores are a problem during the spring, summer and fall due to wet leaves, damp dirt and rotting wood. Local weather reports may include the outdoor mold spore count. Sometimes these reports say that the mold spore count is low, moderate or high. Just as with reporting the pollen count, a scale of 1 to 10 is sometimes used, with 0 to 3 being low or mild, 4 to 6 being moderate and 7 to 10 being high or severe. Prolonged periods of rain, dampness and cloudy weather enhance the mold spore count.

Indoor mold spores can also be a problem, especially during warm, humid and damp weather when basements become damp and bathrooms are moist due to people taking showers. Even in the winter, they can be found on firewood, Christmas trees, indoor plant soil and dried arrangements.

Some good ways to try to control indoor mold spores include the following:
1. Use a dehumidifier to keep the relative humidity between 25% and 50%. Empty and clean the dehumidifier regularly to keep mold growth out of the machine itself.
2. If you have had a problem with mold growth in the past, you should dry-clean rather than steam clean your carpets. Steam cleaning leaves carpets and carpet pads damp for hours and sometimes days.
3. Never lay carpeting on concrete floors or in damp areas such as bathrooms or unfinished basements. It is virtually impossible to keep carpets dry in these areas.
4. Clean all surfaces where molds can grow, at least weekly. Such areas include refrigerator drip pans, shower stalls and their doors or curtains, and damp areas underneath sinks and around toilets. Molds also grow inside air conditioners and humidifiers. You should follow the manufacturer's cleaning instructions.
5. Check your entire home for leaks. Pay special attention to your bathrooms, closets and walls.
6. If you can smell mold or mildew, then obviously you have a mold and mildew problem!

People who suffer pain because of weather or weather changes have some form of rheumatoid arthritis, or have had broken bones, or have recently had an operation. Cold, moist and stormy weather affects them more adversely than does weather that is warm, dry and storm-free .

Most respiratory diseases are spread from person to person through fine droplets ejected by coughing and sneezing. Microorganisms are carried in these droplets which move through the air as a fine mist. In air with low relative humidity, these droplets evaporate, causing the microorganisms to perish. High humidities slow down the rate of evaporation, thus allowing these microorganisms to live longer and infect more people as they are carried along by the moving air currents.

Ultraviolet radiation from the sun, an overexposure of which can be harmful to our skin, is lethal to these microorganisms. In higher latitudes during late spring and early summer, the longer days provide more sunlight and therefore more ultraviolet radiation which is part of the solar radiation, which kills these pathogens. From late autumn through winter, when there is less sun and there is also more cloudiness since major winter storms are common at that time of year, the germ-carrying droplets have a better chance for survival. This is probably one of the reasons why there is more illness during the late autumn and winter months. Cold and damp winters, such as those that occur in northwest Europe, are ideal for germ survival, resulting in high incidences of colds, bronchitis and influenza (the flu). However, very cold temperatures are hostile to these droplets carrying the microorganisms, because the droplets freeze at about 5°F (-15°C).

c. acid rain

Acid rain is rain that is somewhat acidic. It occurs when certain pollutants, such as sulfur dioxide and some oxides of nitrogen, combine with water vapor in the air to form acids. These acid pollutants wash out of the air by precipitation; hence, a better (an accurate) name for acid rain is actually acid precipitation. The major sources of these pollutants are human-made sources such as power plants, industrial processes, and gasoline-fueled automotive vehicles. All these pollutants become part of the air masses that move across the globe.

Acid precipitation is part of a more general process called atmospheric deposition, during which other pollutants, such as heavy metals and toxic organic compounds, fall to the earth, in both wet and dry weather. High concentrations of acid precipitation are especially harmful to plants and water resources. Freshwater ecosystems are quite sensitive to changes in acidity. Many lakes and ponds have or had become so acidic that entire fish populations were killed. Fortunately, the problem was identified and many industries and individuals have been taking actions to alleviate the problem. For example, one way to reduce acidity in small lakes is to add some lime as a neutralizing agent. Some forests and smaller stands of trees have also been adversely affected by acid depositon. Many trees have died and many others have been weakened, making them more susceptible to wind and storm damage and to plant and insect parasites. Many outdoor statues, monuments and old historical structures, especially those made of stone, including marble, and of metal, have been damaged by acidic deposition from acid precipitation.

The acidity or alkalinity of precipitation is measured in terms of pH, which stands for "potential of hydrogen". The pH values range form 0 to 14, with 7 being neutral. The lower the value below 7, the higher the acidity, and the higher the number above 7, the higher the alkalinity. (Technically, pH is the logarithm of the reciprocal of the hydrogen ion concentration in water at 25°C.) Because the pH scale is logarithmic, a small difference in pH is a large difference in acidity or basicness (alkalinity). (Acid vs. base is acid vs. alkaline, although the terms "basic" and "base" seem to be less used now than the terms "alkalinity" and "alkaline".) Thus, a pH of 4.9 is twice as acidic as a pH of 5.0, and a pH of 4.0 is ten times more acidic than a pH of 5.0.

The following table gives the acid precipitation classification:

Description	pH Range
Unpolluted rain water	5.6
Slightly acidic	4.7 to 5.6
Moderately acidic	4.3 to 4.7
Very acidic	3.6 to 4.3
Highly acidic	lower than 3.6

Normally, precipitation is somewhat acidic with a pH of 5.6. The table at right shows this pH as "unpolluted rain water". The reason for this is that carbon dioxide, being one of the components of the atmosphere, dissolves in precipitation, which creates diluted carbonic acid (diluted soda water). The table at right compares the pH of common substances with "pure unpolluted rain water". Compare it with the acidities of the acid rains in the table above.

Beside acid precipitation, acid fog can occur. Some of the worst acid fogs in Los Angeles have had pHes as low as 1.7, which is more acidic than lemon juice (pH of 2.3)! This could irritate eyes and corrode paint on vehicles. PAGE 376

SUBSTANCES	pH	
0.1 molar solution of hydrochloric acid (This concentration of acid is commonly used in many high school chemistry lab experiments.)	1.0	
Lemon Juice	2.3	
Vinegar	2.8	
Carbonated water (Soft Drinks)	3.0	MORE ACIDIC
Oranges	3.5	
Tomato Juice	4.1	
"Pure Rain"	5.6	
Urine	6.6	
Distilled Water	7.0	NEUTRAL
Blood	7.4	
Eggs	7.8	
Sea Water	8.3	MORE BASIC
Milk of Magnesia	10.5	
Household Ammonia	11.0	
0.1 molar solution of sodium hydroxide (This concentration of base is commonly used in many high school chemistry lab experiments)	13.0	

DEMONSTRATION: DETERMINING THE pH OF RAINFALL

You will need the following: any reasonable sized metal can; a roll of pH paper (usually available from aquarium supply or swimming pool supply stores and from chemistry teachers); a small container such as a 25 millimeter beaker or a small metal can. 1. When it is raining, place the larger metal can in the rain to collect some rainfall. 2. Bring the can inside and put some of the water into the smaller container. 3. Place an approximately 2-inch (5 cm) strip of pH paper into the rainwater for about 5 seconds, and then place the paper next to the color scale that is found in the container that houses the pH paper. 4. To determine the pH of your sample, match the color that your pH paper became, with the closet shade on the color scale. 5. Repeat this demonstration as often as you like, but perform it at least once for each season of the year. If you are determining the pH of a snowstorm, let the snow you collected melt before placing the pH paper into the container. 6. You can determine which season has the most acidic precipitation, and which the least. Try to determine a reason for this.

DEMONSTRATION: DETERMINING THE BUFFERING CAPACITY OF SOIL

You will need a small plastic trash bag for each soil sample you collect; a scale (a balance); pH paper; vinegar; a large container or pail; an empty gallon plastic bleach container; paper towels; a small (1 pint) container; a metric measuring cup or a graduated cylinder with a 500 milliliter capacity. Because acid rain can destroy life in lakes, ponds and streams, we can test the soil to determine if there are sufficient alkaline salts to neutralize or partially neutralize acidic precipitation. You will test the soil from 2 or 3 places in the same yard, to determine if it can neutralize an acid solution that you will pour into the soil samples. 1. Make a funnel by cutting away the bottom of the plastic bleach container. 2. Place paper towels to cover the bottom of that funnel. 3. Put a paper towel on a scale and weigh about one pound of soil from the yard. Place the soil in the funnel. 4. Into the smaller (pint) container, pour 150 milliliters of water and then add 50 milliliters of vinegar. This should make a solution having a pH of 4. Check this with your pH paper (place a piece of the pH paper into the solution for about five seconds and then compare the paper's color with the color scale on the pH scale found with the container of pH paper). 5. Now take the pH of this liquid once it has percolated through the soil and has accumulated into the larger container. Do this by placing the pH paper into the liquid in the larger container for about five seconds and once again comparing the color it turns to the closest shade on the pH scale, to get your pH reading. 6. If the pH of the liquid in the large container is higher than the pH of the vinegar solution, then your soil has buffering chemicals in it. The higher the pH, the better buffer your soil is. 7. Repeat steps 2 through 6 with soil samples from other parts of the yard. You can use the same funnel and large container as long as you wash them thoroughly before use. Replace the dirty paper towels in the funnel with clean ones.

d. the names of the different full moons

As you look at almanac data, you often see names for the full moons of each month. Most of the names come from American Indians and folklore sources. Most months have more than one name for their full moon, and the publisher of the almanac or calendar may pick one of them. In some cases, the full moons of two months may have the same name. Some publishers choose to refer to the Harvest Moon as the full moon that occurs in September. Others prefer to name the Harvest Moon as the first full moon that occurs on or after the autumnal equinox, which occurs on or about September 22nd. If the September full moon occurred before the autumnal equinox, then the next full moon would most likely be in October and would be called the Harvest Moon. The lunar month (the time it takes the moon to revolve around the earth) is approximately 29½ days. Thus, once in a while there will be two full moons in one month, one full moon at the very beginning of the month, and the other at the very end. This second full moon would be given one of the other names for that month, but typically WHEN A SECOND FULL MOON OCCURS AT THE END OF A MONTH, IT IS REFERRED TO AS A "BLUE MOON". Think of the 1961 song, "Blue Moon", by The Marcels. The expression, "once in a blue moon" means an event happens infrequently.

MONTH	NAMES OF THE FULL MOONS
January	Wolf Moon, Moon After Yule, Old Moon
February	Snow Moon, Hunger Moon, Wolf Moon
March	Sap Moon, Crow Moon, Lenten Moon
April	Pink Moon, Grass Moon, Egg Moon
May	Flower Moon, Planting Moon, Milk Moon
June	Strawbery Moon, Rose Moon, Flower Moon
July	Buck Moon, Thunder Moon, Hay Moon
August	Sturgeon Moon, Green Corn Moon, Grain Moon
September	Harvest Moon, Fruit Moon
October	Harvest Moon, Hunter's Moon
November	Beaver Moon, Frosty Moon
December	Cold Moon, Moon Before Yule, Long Night Moon

SECTION IX: WEATHER SERVICES

Chapter 50. WEATHER SERVICES AND WEATHER FORECASTING

The science of meteorology is so important to our lives. Weather and climate help to determine whether we can exist on this planet. Our primitive ancestors had to learn how to read the weather signs and make their own weather projections. So, now, weather services such as forecasts and warnings are an established part of our human culture.

Countries have established government-run weather agencies to provide weather forecasts and weather warnings to their populaces. Where free enterprise flourishes, there are also private weather companies and individuals who provide specialized weather services for a fee to their clients. In the United States, the cost for one full year's worth of weather services from the National Weather Service has over the last few decades cost each tax payer no more than the cost of a quarter-pound hamburger, large fries and a large soda...yes, for a full year's service, 24 hours a day! It is easily arguable that the National Weather Service of the United States is one of the most efficient government agencies.

Weather bureaus or agencies were first formed in Europe in the middle 1800s. The United States Weather Bureau began in 1870, and one hundred years later had its name changed to the National Weather Service.

Public and private forecasters serve their users with precious weather information.

Historically, 1873 saw the establishment of the International Meteorological Association, comprised of directors of meteorological services from various nations. In 1951, this association became the World Meteorological Organization (WMO), under the United Nations umbrella. The WMO is headquartered in Geneva, Switzerland and attempts to coordinate and standardize such aspects of weather as weather codes, procedures and cooperation among national weather services.

Who needs weather forecasts, warnings, data, climatological statistics and weather education? Where are you on the following list (you will likely find yourself in at least one category)?: the general public who need weather forecasts and warnings; agricultural interests; the aviation community; marine interests; the news media (radio, television, newspapers); fire weather interests; researchers; resorts (such as ski resorts) and tourism, and business and commerce.

Weather forecast offices are typically located in or near major metropolitan areas. Most weather observing locations that take the full complement of observed weather parameters, and are therefore called "first order weather observation stations", are located at airports, to also serve the weather observing need of the aviation community. Networks of "second order stations" are located elsewhere, including in rural areas. and report data that can also be useful for climatological purposes, adding to the climat data provided by the first order stations. Many of these are part time stations. There are also networks of cooperative weather observers...essentially volunteers...who enjoy recording and reporting their weather data. Moreover, automated weather observing sites, which may include many first order stations, report continuous weather information 24 hours a day. Add to this the data from weather balloon soundings, weather radars and weather satellites, and you can see how expansive the collection of weather data such as temperatures, humidity, atmospheric pressure, wind direction, wind speed, ceiling, visibility, precipitation and other weather parameters has become. The real-time (current) data is used as the initial conditions describing the state of the atmosphere in computer programs that forecast future weather conditions (the computer forecast models). Output and derived information from these models are used as forecast guidance by weather forecasters. On the INTERNET you also have access to this weather information, and with training you can make your own weather forecasts! Many people enjoy keeping their own weather observations as well.

The philosophy of weather forecasting:

The contemporary methodology of weather forecasting starts with looking at the continuity of the evolution of weather affecting your area. Thus, how have the weather patterns been evolving over the past 24 to 48 hours to give us our current conditions? Then the meteorologist uses his/her knowledge of the science to forecast the continued evolution for the next few days, especially for the next 48 hours. Current surface and upper-air data, and radar and weather satellite data are combined to develop this picture of weather development. Then, guidance from weather forecasting computer models is studied to determine if the guidances are in line with the meteorologist's analysis and perspective.

It is wrong to base a forecast entirely on guidance from the models, since that would be adopting "METEOROLOGICAL AIDS', i.e., the "Artificial Intelligence Dependency Syndrome". However, we hasten to add that it would also be a mistake to not consider the computer guidance, since these models now have a record of providing quite useful prognosticated weather charts, forecasting the weather for out to a few days with reasonable accuracy.

Therefore, the contemporary weather forecaster combines his/her knowledge of meteorology with output from the computer-generated weather forecast prognostications to make the best possible forecast. When a forecast is wrong, the meteorologist must analyze what happened and learn from it, thereby growing in skill and expertise.

Space weather:

Weather forecasting has expanded to extraterrestrial forecasting. As we explore other planets and their moons, we need to learn more about their weather so that we can forecast for our own space missions to these bodies. Space forecasting also includes forecasts and warnings for solar flares, which are emissions of huge amounts of particles from the sun. These are electromagnetic storms, the worst of which can disrupt electromagnetic communications, such as to and from satellites in orbit around planets, and can adversely affect electric power distribution systems.. Therefore, in 1995 the United States established the National Space Weather Program.

Thus, meteorology is a fascinating science, and, for those of us interested, we can also each learn to take our own observations and make our own forecasts, which should result in our enjoying meteorology even more!

Figure 50-1. Just one of the many facets of weather that meteorologists need to learn about: the jet-streams. Hopefully, this book will be helpful in describing meteorology. We have learned much in the past century, and will learn more as we progress through the 21st century. (source: USAF)

The beauty of this science is that all you need to do is to step outside, and the sky and atmosphere are your laboratory...and it is all free! Thus, everyone can enjoy meteorology!

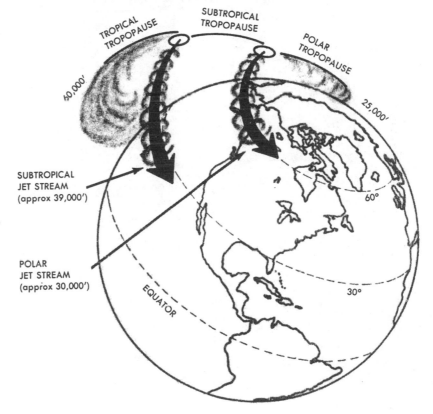

APPENDIX A: LIST OF WEATHER DEMONSTRATIONS INCLUDED IN THIS BOOK

INDEX: